T0332770

Research Anthology on Artificial Neural Network Applications

Information Resources Management Association
USA

Volume III

Published in the United States of America by
IGI Global
Engineering Science Reference (an imprint of IGI Global)
701 E. Chocolate Avenue
Hershey PA, USA 17033
Tel: 717-533-8845
Fax: 717-533-8661
E-mail: cust@igi-global.com
Web site: http://www.igi-global.com

Library of Congress Cataloging-in-Publication Data

Names: Information Resources Management Association, editor.
Title: Research anthology on artificial neural network applications /
  Information Resources Management Association, editor.
Description: Hershey, PA : Engineering Science Reference an imprint of IGI
  Global, [2022] | Includes bibliographical references and index. |
  Summary: "This book covers critical topics related to artificial neural
  networks and their multitude of applications in a number of diverse
  areas including medicine, finance, operations research, business, social
  media, security, and more, covering everything from the applications and
  uses of artificial neural networks to deep learning and non-linear
  problems,"-- Provided by publisher.
Identifiers: LCCN 2021034008 (print) | LCCN 2021034009 (ebook) | ISBN
  9781668424087 (hardcover) | ISBN 9781668424094 (ebook)
Subjects: LCSH: Neural networks (Computer science)
Classification: LCC QA76.87 .R47 2022 (print) | LCC QA76.87 (ebook) | DDC
  006.3/2--dc23
LC record available at https://lccn.loc.gov/2021034008
LC ebook record available at https://lccn.loc.gov/2021034009

British Cataloguing in Publication Data
A Cataloguing in Publication record for this book is available from the British Library.

The views expressed in this book are those of the authors, but not necessarily of the publisher.

For electronic access to this publication, please contact: eresources@igi-global.com.

List of Contributors

Table of Contents

Section 2
Development and Design Methodologies

Section 3
Tools and Technologies

Section 4
Utilization and Applications

Section 5
Organizational and Social Implications

Section 6
Emerging Trends

Preface

Intelligent technologies such as artificial neural networks have played an incredible role in their ability to predict, analyze, and navigate different circumstances in a variety of industries ranging from medicine to education, banking, and engineering. Artificial neural networks are a growing phenomenon as research continues to develop about the applications, benefits, challenges, and impacts they have. These statistical modeling tools are capable of processing nonlinear data with strong accuracy and are an effective and efficient problem-solving method. Helping to solve real-world issues, the advantages of artificial neural networks are difficult to ignore, as more and more businesses begin to implement them into their strategies.

Staying informed of the most up-to-date research trends and findings is of the utmost importance. That is why IGI Global is pleased to offer this three-volume reference collection of reprinted IGI Global book chapters and journal articles that have been handpicked by senior editorial staff. This collection will shed light on critical issues related to the trends, techniques, and uses of various applications by providing both broad and detailed perspectives on cutting-edge theories and developments. This collection is designed to act as a single reference source on conceptual, methodological, technical, and managerial issues, as well as provide insight into emerging trends and future opportunities within the field.

The *Research Anthology on Artificial Neural Network Applications* is organized into six distinct sections that provide comprehensive coverage of important topics. The sections are:

1. Fundamental Concepts and Theories;
2. Development and Design Methodologies;
3. Tools and Technologies;
4. Utilization and Applications;
5. Organizational and Social Implications; and
6. Emerging Trends.

The following paragraphs provide a summary of what to expect from this invaluable reference tool.

Section 1, "Fundamental Concepts and Theories," serves as a foundation for this extensive reference tool by addressing crucial theories essential to understanding the concepts and uses of artificial neural network applications. Opening this reference book is the chapter "Fundamental Categories of Artificial Neural Networks" by Profs. Arunaben Prahladbhai Gurjar and Shitalben Bhagubhai Patel of Ganpat University, India, which provides an overview on the various types of neural networks like feed forward, recurrent, feedback, classification-predication. This first section ends with the chapter "A Journey From Neural Networks to Deep Networks: Comprehensive Understanding for Deep Learning" by Profs. Priyanka P. Patel and Amit R. Thakkar of Chandubhai S. Patel Institute of Technology, CHARUSAT University,

India, which discusses deep learning fundamentals and the recent trends and mentions many advanced applications, deep learning models, and networks to easily solve those applications in a very smart way.

Section 2, "Development and Design Methodologies," presents in-depth coverage of the design and development of artificial neural networks for their use in different applications. This section starts with "Artificial Neural Network Models for Large-Scale Data" by Prof. Vo Ngoc Phu of Duy Tan University, Vietnam and Prof. Vo Thi Ngoc Tran from Ho Chi Minh City University of Technology, Vietnam, which proposes algorthims to process and store big data sets succesfully. The section ends with "Artificial Neural Network (ANN) Modeling of Odor Threshold Property of Diverse Chemical Constituents of Black Tea and Coffee" by Prof. Jillella Gopala Krishna of NIPER Kolkata, India and Prof. Probir Kumar Ojha from Jadavpur University, India, which develops an artificial neural network model using odor threshold (OT) property data for diverse odorant components present in black tea (76 components) and coffee (46 components).

Section 3, "Tools and Technologies," explores the various tools and technologies used in the implementation of artificial neural networks for various uses. The section starts with "Tool Condition Monitoring Using Artificial Neural Network Models" by Prof. Srinivasa P. Pai of NMAM Institute of Technology, India and Prof. Nagabhushana T. N. from S. J. College of Engineering, India, which deals with the application of artificial neural network (ANN) models for tool condition monitoring (TCM) in milling operations in order to develop an optimal ANN model, in terms of compact architecture, least training time, and its ability to generalize well on unseen (test) data. The section ends with "A Novel Prediction Perspective to the Bending Over Sheave Fatigue Lifetime of Steel Wire Ropes by Means of Artificial Neural Networks" by Profs. Tuğba Özge Onur and Yusuf Aytaç Onur of Zonguldak Bulent Ecevit University, Turkey, which focuses on a novel prediction perspective to the bending over sheave fatigue lifetime of steel wire ropes by means of artificial neural networks.

Section 4, "Utilization and Applications," describes how artificial neural networks are used and applied in diverse industries for various technologies and applications. The section begins with "Literature Survey for Applications of Artificial Neural Networks" by Profs. Pooja Deepakbhai Pancholi and Sonal Jayantilal Patel of Ganpat University, India, which discusses the major applications of artificial neural networks and the importance of the e-learning application and presents an investigation into the explosive developments of many artificial neural network related applications. It ends with "Forecasting and Technical Comparison of Inflation in Turkey With Box-Jenkins (ARIMA) Models and the Artificial Neural Network" by Prof. Erkan Işığıçok of Bursa Uludağ University, Turkey and Profs. Ramazan Öz and Savaş Tarkun from Uludağ University, Turkey, which predicts inflation in the next period based on the consumer price index (CPI) data with two alternative techniques and examines the predictive performance of these two techniques comparatively.

Section 5, "Organizational and Social Implications," includes chapters discussing the impact of artificial neural networks on society and shows the ways in which artificial neural networks are used in different industries and how this impacts business. The section opens with "Comparative Analysis of Proposed Artificial Neural Network (ANN) Algorithm With Other Techniques" by Profs. Deepak Chatha, Alankrita Aggarwal, and Prof. Rajender Kumar of Panipat Institute of Engineering and Technology, India, which develops robust edge detection techniques that work optimally on mammogram images to segment tumor area and presents output results of proposed techniques on different mammogram images of MIAS database. It ends with "Forecasting Automobile Sales in Turkey with Artificial Neural Networks" by Profs. Aycan Kaya, Gizem Kaya, and Ferhan Çebi of Istanbul Technical University, Turkey, which aims to reveal significant factors which affect automobile sales and estimates the automobile sales in Turkey by using artificial neural network (ANN), ARIMA, and time series decomposition techniques.

Section 6, "Emerging Trends," highlights areas for future research within this field. The final section opens with "Artificial Neural Networks in Medicine: Recent Advances" by Prof. Steven Walczak of the University of South Florida, USA, which examines recent trends and advances in ANNs and provides references to a large portion of recent research, as well as looks at the future direction of research for ANN in medicine. The last section ends with the chapter "Convolutional Neural Network" by Prof. Mário Pereira Véstias of INESC-ID, Instituto Superior de Engenharia de Lisboa, Instituto Politécnico de Lisboa, Portugal, which focuses on convolutional neural networks with a description of the model, the training and inference processes, and its applicability and provides an overview of the most used CNN models and what to expect from the next generation of CNN models.

Although the primary organization of the contents in this multi-volume work is based on its six sections, offering a progression of coverage of the important concepts, methodologies, technologies, applications, social issues, and emerging trends, the reader can also identify specific contents by utilizing the extensive indexing system listed at the end of each volume. As a comprehensive collection of research on the latest findings related to artificial neural networks, the *Research Anthology on Artificial Neural Network Applications* provides researchers, computer scientists, engineers, practitioners, educators, strategists, policymakers, scientists, academicians, and students with a complete understanding of the applications and impacts of artificial neural networks. Given the vast number of issues concerning usage, failure, success, strategies, and applications of artificial neural networks in modern technologies and processes, the *Research Anthology on Artificial Neural Network Applications* encompasses the most pertinent research on the applications, impacts, uses, and development of artificial neural networks.

Chapter 48
Using Artificial Neural Networks (ANNs) to Improve Agricultural Knowledge Management System (KMS)

Mriganka Mohan Chanda

National Institute of Technology, Durgapur, India

Neelotpaul Banerjee

National Institute of Technology, Durgapur, India

Gautam Bandyopadhyay

National Institute of Technology, Durgapur, India

ABSTRACT

Agriculture is an important sector of the Indian economy. In the present paper an attempt has been made to theoretically explore the development of an agricultural knowledge management system (KMS) in respect of various micro irrigation techniques for agriculture, as well as relevant crop-/region-specific agricultural practices in different regions of the country, as the same has been observed to be very much necessary for the overall benefits of wider cross section of farmers, agricultural scientists, economists, and other stakeholders in the domain. It is further observed that artificial neural networks (ANNs), which are a part of soft computing techniques, can be used as a KMS tool for effective management of various sub sectors of agriculture. In this context, it has been shown that use of ANNs as a KMS tool can improve the effectiveness of applications of the above mentioned agricultural KMS by accurately forecasting the year-wise estimated yield of food grains of India with the help of past data of various relevant parameters.

DOI: 10.4018/978-1-6684-2408-7.ch048

INTRODUCTION

As per the study paper of Jennex (2005), Knowledge Management (KM) may be defined as the practice of selectively using knowledge from previous experiences of making decisions to current and future decision making process with the main objective of improving the organization's effectiveness. In this context, it has viewed a Knowledge Management System (KMS), as that system which is created to facilitate or improve the capture, storage, retrieval, transfer, and reuse of knowledge. The perception of KM and KMS is that they holistically combine organizational and technical solutions to achieve the goals of knowledge retention and reuse to ultimately improve the effectiveness of organizational and individual decision making.

Thus an Agricultural Knowledge Management System (KMS) is a KMS which can be developed in certain specific area(s) or domain(s) or sub-area(s) of agriculture sector for facilitating capture, storage, retrieval, transfer, and reuse of knowledge in the specific domain(s).

Agriculture is a vital sector of Indian economy, which contributes about 17% of its total GDP (Gross Domestic Product) and generates employment for around 60% of the population (Arjun, 2013). As per the Annual Report 2016-17 of Department of Agriculture & Cooperation (DAC), Ministry of Agriculture, Government of India, the food grains in India consist of Rice, Wheat, Coarse Cereals (such as, Jowar, Bajra, etc.), and Pulses. The other major agricultural products/ crops are Oilseeds, Sugarcane, Cotton, Maize, Jute and Mesta. Every year, DAC makes estimates of production of each of the individual items of food grains as well as other major crops in million tonnes and total area sown in lakhs or million hectares (Ha) [1 million = 10 lakhs]. From these two estimates year wise Yield of Food Grains in Kg per Hectare (Kg/ Ha) can be obtained by dividing former by the latter. The year wise yield of food grains is very important parameter in the overall agriculture sector in India and all out efforts are generally made by the Central and all State Governments as well as concerned stakeholders to increase the same.

From time to time various researchers in their studies (discussed subsequently in this paper) have observed that the quantum of effective irrigation, especially minor or micro irrigation at farm level is a vital input for improving/ increasing the overall productivity in agriculture sector including yield of food grains of India in a particular year besides other factors. In this context, micro irrigation may be defined as the frequent application of small quantities of water directly above and below the soil surface; usually as discrete drops, continuous drops or tiny streams through emitters placed along a water delivery line (Lamm et.al, 2007).

In view of above, it is observed that development of a related Agricultural Knowledge Management System (KMS) in respect of various micro irrigation techniques for agriculture, as well as relevant crop/ region specific agricultural practices in different regions of India is very much necessary and can be explored, for the overall benefits of wider cross section of farmers, agricultural scientists, economists and other stakeholders in the domain.

There are various tools for properly managing and making decisions in a KMS such as, Soft Computing (SC), Artificial Intelligence (AI) based techniques, Machine Learning (ML) or combinations of all these. Out of the above, Soft Computing based techniques can be used for effective and proper management of different sectors of national economic planning including agriculture. These techniques are built on several sub fields namely, Artificial Neural Networks (*hence forth designated as ANNs*), Fuzzy Logic (FL), Genetic Algorithm (GA), etc., and/ or their combinations. In fact, some of the major practical problems, which can be effectively handled by using soft computing techniques, involve aspects of uncertainty, imprecision, vagueness, sub-optimality, to name a few, where classical mathematical methods cannot be used as such due to very large amount of data involvement and/ or absence of having sufficient theoretical knowledge on the concerned problem.

Out of different constituent methodologies of soft computing techniques, ANN based technique is one of the major methods of making predictions on certain variables based on past trends of relevant parameters.

The present paper has been divided into two parts. In Part-I of this paper an attempt has been made to theoretically explore the possible development and applications of an Agricultural Knowledge Management System (KMS) in the area of various micro irrigation techniques for agriculture, as well as relevant crop/ region specific agricultural practices in different regions of the country. In Part-II of this paper it has been shown that how use of ANNs as a KMS tool can improve the effectiveness of applications of such Agricultural KMS by accurately forecasting the year wise estimated yield of food grains of India with the help of past data of various relevant parameters.

PART ONE

Exploring Possible Development and Applications of an Agricultural KMS on Micro Irrigation

This part of the paper is a theoretical research towards exploring possible development and applications of an Agricultural Knowledge Management System (KMS) in respect of various micro irrigation techniques for agriculture, as well as relevant crop/ region specific agricultural practices in different regions of the country.

Review of Literatures on Development of Agricultural KM

Chantarasombat, C., Srisa-ard, B., Kuofie, M.H.S., and Jennex, M.E. (2010), in their research paper showed that Knowledge Management (KM) based model could be successfully implemented in a low technology environment for helping traditional social structures in changing the way of transferring knowledge and achieving economic gains. In this regard, it was observed that in Thailand the youths were gradually migrating away from their rural villages to get better opportunities in various urban centers and as a result the remaining villagers were facing economic downfall as the traditional family structures were failing to pass knowledge to villagers outside of the family. This research showed that any social process mainly depending on a traditional, family based knowledge pass down approach (such as, father to son, mother to daughter and parent to child) could be successfully maintained by changing the knowledge transfer process to a more social basis. In this context, a pilot study was done in two selected villages of Thailand, wherein it was observed that the development of traditional knowledge base already possessed by experienced villagers in different agricultural societies' related domains could be successfully integrated into a KM based model, which in turn could assist those persons who still remained in the villages. It was finally observed that the two villages where the KM Process Model was implemented as a pilot study, achieved success in economic terms over the study period. Thus implementation of appropriate KM based models in different relevant areas of agriculture was able to create economically sustainable and self-reliant communities in rural villages of Thailand.

Alemu, D., Jennex, M.E., Assefa, T. (2018), in their research paper showed the practical ways and means of integrating Scientific Knowledge with Indigenous Knowledge (IK) possessed by different Communities of Practice (CoPs) towards development and applications of an effective Agricultural Knowledge Management System (KMS) in Ethiopia. Their research identified three different social groups in the agricultural KMS development namely, (i) agricultural researchers possessing scientific knowledge arising from their educational background; (ii) local farmers who were major source of possessing IK and also users of the scientific knowledge and technology emanating from research; and (iii) extension agents who could play an effective role in the process of transferring knowledge and technology from research to local communities and vice versa and thus act as a knowledge broker for integrating and sharing of knowledge towards development and application of agricultural KMS. The project was implemented in two districts of Ethiopia. The shared KMS was developed using Web 2.0 tools with knowledge brokering activities support. The overall result showed that the users of the above mentioned agricultural KMS from different groups used to very much communicate, interact and collaborate with each other towards their common interest and as a result knowledge sharing and integration improved substantially.

Exploring Need for Developing Agricultural KMS on Micro Irrigation

In order to explore and justify the need for developing an Agricultural KMS in respect of various micro irrigation techniques for agriculture and crop/ region specific agricultural practices in India, an extensive review of literatures has been made in the present paper which is briefly discussed below:

1. Amarsinghe and Stefanos (2009) in their study paper highlighted the urgent need for recharging groundwater for distributing benefits from irrigation to a wide cross section of people, by taking appropriate measures such as, setting up of watersheds, combining several micro-watersheds in the nearby area, recharging ground water through a number of dug wells, converting small tanks to percolation ponds, changing irrigation scheduling in canal commands to increase combined usage of water, etc.;

2. Gover et al. (2013) in their study report brought out the outcome of conducting a survey in respect of incorporating traditional methods of irrigation with water management in Mandi situated in the State of Himachal Pradesh in India. It was observed that the design of irrigation system mainly depended on certain important factors namely, topography of the area, available water sources, patterns of monsoon and types of crops being sowed with their respective water requirements. During the process of survey, the researchers' team had visited local farmers, district agricultural office and state irrigation and public health departments and gathered information on the above mentioned relevant aspects. It was learnt that in places like Mandi being situated at higher altitude, there would be a greater need for drinking water than irrigation water. So based on the above mentioned facts the researchers team came out with the design of a sustainable minor irrigation system model (using 'SolidWorks' software and SODIS (Solar Water Disinfection) system for water purification), which utilized water-harvesting techniques to gather rain water in a tank that could be used for irrigation or routed through a water-purification system for drinking purposes. The paper also evaluated the different sources for water that were available and came out with the design of a plan that farmers could use for their farms located on hilly terrains;

3. Bhamoriya and Mathew (2014) conducted an extensive survey to assess the experiences in adoption of a particular type of micro irrigation technique namely, drip irrigation and the impact of the

technology on the conservation of the water resources and benefits to the farmers and submitted a detailed report to Indian Institute of Management (IIM), Ahmedabad, in this regard. The above survey was conducted across a total of 4 states in India (namely, Andhra Pradesh, Gujarat, Maharashtra and Tamil Nadu) and 16 identified pockets and a total of 499 respondents were administered the survey instrument and their responses collected.

It was observed that drip irrigation technology (of micro irrigation) was having the potential capability of making economic benefits to the farmers in respect of both irrigation and agriculture at the farm level, subject to certain conditions such as, creation of better market linkages by the Government, ability of the farmers to master the technology and adopting the same effectively and greater benefits could be obtained with the availability of concentrated clusters of relatively high proportion of land adopting the same. Additionally, it was observed that there would be lot of scope for bringing new and more innovative techniques in the domain of drip irrigation technology and agricultural practices, for further improving the overall quantum of benefits or returns to the farmers.

4. Viswanathan and Bahinipati (2015) made a survey for making techno-economic analysis on the impact of a Micro Irrigation System (MIS) based on the installation of 122 tube wells with pressure-induced irrigation network in the nine talukas (sub-divisions) of Banaskantha district in the State of Gujarat in western India. The results showed substantial economic and social benefits to the farmers such as, increase in yields of crops during all sowing seasons; appreciable savings in energy consumption; reduction in the use of chemical fertilizers and pesticides; decrease in cost of weeding; fall in groundwater over-extraction; reduction in the migration of labours due to water scarcity, etc.;

5. The Strategy Paper titled: "Accelerating growth of Indian Agriculture: Micro irrigation an efficient solution" (prepared by Grant Thornton, Irrigation Association of India (IAI) and Federation of Indian Chamber of Commerce & Industry (FICCI) and brought out by Department of Agriculture & Cooperation (DAC), Ministry of Agriculture, Government of India, in February 2016), pointed out lot of benefits of adopting micro irrigation (MI) in India such as, increase in water efficiency (to the tune of 50 to 90%); savings in energy consumption (to the tune of 30.5%); savings in fertilizer consumption (to the tune of 28.5%); increase in productivity of fruit/ crops (to the tune of 42.4%) and Vegetables (to the tune of 52.7%); savings in cost of irrigation (to the tune of 31.9%); introduction of new crops by farmers (to the tune of 30.4%); increase in the income of farmers (to the tune of 42%); etc. Further, as an effective solution/ game changer to expedite the implementation of micro irrigation in India the suggested measures are as follows: (a) adopting a new type of fund flow model namely, Information Technology (IT) - enabled system, based on Direct Benefits Transfer (DBT) that allows a farmer with the choice of a service provider to go with for improving efficiency and transparency and also reduce delays in the release of funds/ subsidy; (b) introducing better process management, through a dedicated team, with high priority for promoting micro irrigation projects at the state level; (c) moderating subsidy levels in states where penetration of micro irrigation is already above the national average and re-routing that subsidy to states with very low penetration, where the technology still needs to be promoted; (d) granting the micro irrigation (MI) sector the infrastructure industry status, for making it entitled for priority sector lending, so as to ensure that banks are more comfortable in providing funding to this industry and this can reduce its dependence on subsidy over time; (e) devising region and crop-specific micro irrigation

packages for example, "Sugarcane in Maharashtra State package" or "Cotton in Punjab State package", etc., where the concerned developing agency would prescribe the equipment and guidelines for effective use of techniques and equipment for the specific region and crop in question; etc.;

6. Jha et al. (2016) conducted an experimental research to evaluate the effect of different types of irrigation methods namely, furrow irrigation vis-à-vis drip irrigation on the productivity of nutritious fodder tree species during off-monsoon dry periods in different elevation zones of central Nepal. It was observed that drip type irrigation led to 73% less usage of water as compared to that in furrow type irrigation, which resulted in increased yield of fodder crops and in turn higher milk productivity for livestock smallholders;

7. Department of Water Resources Development & Management of Indian Institute of Technology (IIT) Roorkee and Indian Water Resources Society (IWRS) jointly organized a national workshop on 'Challenges in Irrigation Management for Food Security' during November 26-27, 2016. The major recommendations of the above mentioned workshop were as follows: changing the existing mind-set of farmers from 'more water more yield' to 'precise irrigation more yield'; growing requirement for development of a 'Decision Support System (DSS)' for scientific decision making and canal automation aiming towards efficient irrigation and making such system available in mobile platform for easy access to farmers and other stakeholders; resorting from flood type to pressurized type of irrigation with judicious use of micro-irrigation technology coupled with scientific methods of delivering water and nutrients directly to plant root zone for cost saving and increased agricultural production with less water; strong requirement for improving the water use efficiency (WUE) by implementing a sustainable trade-off between productivity and water saving; encouraging participatory irrigation management (PIM) and use of solar energy and reuse of municipal waste water especially in hilly region; etc.;

8. National Water Academy (NWA) in its report titled 'Water – Its Conservation, Management and Governance' (2017), described about the ground water based irrigation in Patkhori village in Mewat region of Haryana State in India, located in a semi arid zone. The community in the above village developed a 25,000 litres capacity community water tank for storing water, which was having five outlets from where about 200 households of the village used to take turns to collect water, thereby reducing water scarcity in the area. Further, abandoned wells in the village were revived and converted into recharge wells, which were able to collect a vast amount of water flowing down the catchment area. The whole system was able to mitigate the scarcity of drinking as well as irrigation water in the area to a large extent;

9. Priyan and Panchal (2017) have observed that micro-irrigation is an efficient technology for India's sustainable agricultural growth with tremendous potential for increasing water and land productivity. It has been observed that micro irrigation technology offers lots of benefits in terms of irrigation efficiency (to the tune of 50 to 90%), fertilizer usage efficiency (around 28.5%) and energy utilization efficiency (about 30.5%) and hence this technology is very much useful for promoting sustainable and long term agriculture in the country;

10. Chand (2017) in his paper on 'Doubling Farmers Income – Rationale, Strategy, Prospects and Action Plan' (as submitted to NITI (National Institution for Transforming India) Aayog, Government of India, in March 2017) stressed the need of expanding 'Area under irrigation' by 1.78 million hectare and 'Area under double cropping' by 1.85 million hectare every year, for achieving the goal of doubling the Indian farmers' income by 2022 amongst other factors.

From the above mentioned review of literatures it is very much evident that there exists a strong need for developing a dedicated Agricultural KMS in respect of various micro irrigation techniques for agriculture and relevant crop/ region specific agricultural practices at various levels (such as, farm level or aggregate level), for the benefits of wider cross section of farmers, agricultural scientists, economists and other stakeholders in this domain.

Discussions on the Development of Agricultural KMS on Micro Irrigation

The major issue that comes up here is what type of Agricultural Knowledge Management System (KMS) in the field of micro irrigation (MI) system and relevant crop/ region specific agricultural practices at various levels is going to be most useful for all the concerned stakeholders in this sector and how to maximize its usages/ applications in various relevant areas, so as to reap the full benefits out of it.

In this context, we may refer to the research paper of Jennex, M. E. (2017) on 'Big Data, the Internet of Things (IoT) and the Revised Knowledge Pyramid', in which it has been pointed out that the earlier concept of conventional knowledge pyramid consisting of Data (D) – Information (I) – Knowledge (K) – Wisdom (W) or Actionable Intelligence approach has undergone substantial changes, due to the recent developments in the availability of enormous amount of data (i.e. big data) on various subjects/ sectors, as well as analytics and business/ customer intelligence and as a result the effective management of knowledge has really become a very much complex issue. In fact, it is shown in the paper that in case of proper knowledge management on any aspect now there may be a need for 'top to bottom approach' down the knowledge pyramid with strong filtering criteria for effectively separating the 'non-required knowledge/ data' from the 'required knowledge/ data', so as to make the resulting KMS capable of providing proper insight and guidance to create comprehensive decision support strategies in the relevant areas. Further, the revised knowledge pyramid model illustrated in the paper shows that decision making is now supported by many tools, technologies and processes and in fact all these need to work in an integrated manner, so as to improve the efficiency and effectiveness of decision making processes.

An effective application of the above mentioned concepts has been described in the paper of Whitney, J., Jennex, M.E., Elkins, A., Frost, E. (2018), in which the ways of using knowledge management principles and natural language processing (NLP) methods have been illustrated for developing an improved ontology of online sex trafficking advertisements based on a new type of indicator namely 'emoticons'.

From the foregoing discussions it is evident that micro irrigation (MI) system in India is having tremendous potential in increasing the overall yield of food grains and crops with lot of other benefits and there exists a strong need for developing a dedicated Agricultural KMS in respect of various micro irrigation techniques for agriculture and relevant crop/ region specific agricultural practices.

The above mentioned dedicated Agricultural KMS on micro irrigation (MI) needs to be developed in the form of an interactive portal/ website to be available in the web/ internet, which can be easily accessed by the various users from their computers as well as mobile phones. Such portal can also be made available in English, Hindi as well as different regional languages of India, so as to popularize its uses across all farmers' communities and other stake holders in the domain. The above Agricultural KMS may also be coupled with a GIS (Geographical Information System) based software platform.

Possible Framework of Agricultural KMS on Micro Irrigation

The proposed Agricultural KMS on micro irrigation (MI) system needs to contain relevant data/ information mainly on the following aspects:

1. Various types of micro irrigation (MI) techniques and/ or procedures being practiced in India and other countries;
2. The crop wise as well as location/ region/ zone wise suitability of different types of micro irrigation (MI) techniques and/ or procedures;
3. Soil type, crop and climate wise suitability of different types of micro irrigation (MI) methods/ techniques;
4. Details of the crop wise process and timing of actual irrigation;
5. Complete details of components/ equipment to be used/ required with approximate cost and availability for different types of micro irrigation (MI), as well as maintenance methods of such equipment;
6. Approximate average energy requirement for running micro irrigation (MI) equipment;
7. Different subsidies/ funding being made available by the Central and/ or State Governments or other agencies under their various schemes for procuring the MI equipment and the detail procedures for availing the same.

Besides the above mentioned aspects, more items/ aspects on micro irrigation (MI) and related issues can be included in such Agricultural KMS based on the different users' feedbacks/ comments to be obtained/ received from time to time.

The above mentioned web portal containing Agricultural KMS on micro irrigation (MI) needs to be developed and managed by an Inter Ministerial Group/ Committee consisting of experts from Ministry of Water Resources (MOWR), Ministry of Agriculture with Department of Agriculture & Cooperation (DAC) and Department of Agricultural Research & Education (DARE)/ Indian Council of Agricultural Research (ICAR) of Government of India, as well as experts/ representatives from the agricultural departments of different State Governments. Moreover, wide spread publicity of the above mentioned portal should be made by the Government through various media like newspaper, television channels and web, for promoting its maximum usage amongst all stakeholders especially farmers.

DSS of Agricultural KMS on Micro Irrigation

The proposed dedicated Agricultural KMS in the form of a web portal on various micro irrigation (MI) techniques for agriculture and relevant crop specific agricultural practices is required to be coupled with an IT based interactive Decision Support System (DSS) as recommended in the National Workshop jointly organized by Indian Institute of Technology (IIT), Roorkee and Indian Water Resources Society (IWRS) in November 2016 (as mentioned earlier in this paper).

The above mentioned DSS needs to be interactive with a user friendly interface, in which the various potential users can make different queries relating to specific aspects/ issues on micro irrigation for getting expert advices/ suggestions such as, crop/ location specific techniques, methods, processes, timings, usages, etc., which may be suitable for a particular crop in a particular location with different amounts of fertilizers and probable rainfall. Besides above, the users may pose some specific types of problems, which in turn can be referred to the expert group managing the above portal and/ or amongst other peer users/ members for getting effective advices/ suggestions/ solutions.

Further, in this regard, the different experts associated with/ managing the above Agricultural KMS portal as well as other researchers on micro irrigation may need to carry out/ conduct various research studies from time to time in the relevant fields, using different tools of decision making such as, ANN, AI, ML, or combination of all these, so as to ascertain the best possible/ available technology/ feasible solutions on different problem areas. The results of such types of research studies using different types of KMS tools may be periodically added in the database of the above mentioned DSS of the Agricultural KMS on micro irrigation, which in turn is expected to correctly and accurately guide the farmers and other stakeholders in the agriculture sector and increase its overall efficiency and usefulness.

For designing the minute details including the database of the proposed Agricultural KMS on various micro irrigation techniques for agriculture and relevant crop/ region specific agricultural practices *and the design of related DSS,* a pilot study may however be carried out by the Ministry of Water Resources (MOWR) in association with Department of Agricultural Research & Education (DARE) of Government of India and State Governments, in certain selected regions of the country.

Such Agricultural KMS in respect of various micro and/ or local irrigation methods for agriculture and crop/ region specific agricultural practices is expected to widely promote relevant knowledge sharing amongst farmers, agricultural scientists and other stake holders in the domain. This in turn is also expected to become very much instrumental in increasing the overall quantum of effective irrigation for agriculture at farm/ local/ regional level and consequent yield of food grains/ crops.

PART TWO

Development of an ANN Based Model as a KMS Tool for Forecasting the Year Wise Estimated Yield of Food Grains of India

In this part of the paper it has been shown that how use of Artificial Neural Networks (ANNs) as a KMS tool can improve the effectiveness of applications of the Agricultural KMS on micro irrigation methods and crop/ region specific agricultural practices (as discussed/ explored in Part-I of this paper), by accurately forecasting the year wise estimated yield of food grains of India with the help of past data of various relevant parameters.

Theoretical Background

A multilayer feed forward Artificial Neural Network (ANN) is having numbers of layers namely, an output layer and an input layer, as well as one or more intermediate layers called hidden layers (Haykin, 1994). Each layer of such network comprises of one or several processing or computational units called neurons.

Each of the input layer neurons is connected with the entire hidden layer neurons and each such connection is associated with a certain weight. The weights of these connections are known as input-hidden layer weights. Furthermore, each of the hidden layer neurons are connected to the entire output layer neurons and the corresponding weights are known as hidden-output layer weights.

A multilayer feed forward ANN with a configuration of '$l - m - n$', indicating an input layer consisting of 'l' number of neurons, a hidden layer having 'm' number of neurons, and an output layer consisting of 'n' number of neurons, with the assumption that there is only 1 hidden layer in this case, is presented in Figure 1 (Rajasekaran and Pai, 2003).

Figure 1. A multilayer feed forward neural network of (l-m-n) configuration

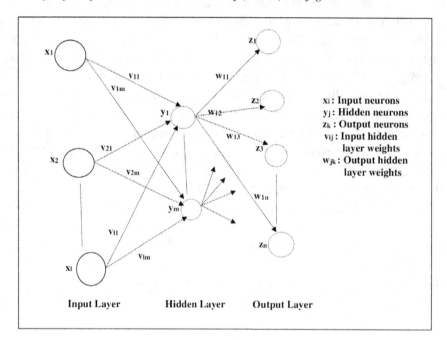

[*Source:* "Neural Networks, Fuzzy Logic and Genetic Algorithms Synthesis and Applications", by S. Rajasekaran and G. A. Vijaylakshmi Pai, published by Prentice Hall of India Private Limited, New Delhi – 110001, 2003, pp – 18.]

An ANN often learns by examples. Hence, with familiar examples of a specific problem, an ANN based system can be trained so as to gain knowledge regarding the same. When an ANN is properly trained, it can further be effectively used in fixing unfamiliar or untrained cases pertaining to the problem. Some of the major fields, in which the concept of ANNs has been successfully applied in solving various related problems, are forecasting, classification, optimization, pattern recognition, image processing, data compression, etc (Goswami, 2012).

Review of Literatures on Use of ANNs in Agriculture

Jha and Sinha (2013) observed that the recent innovation in ANN based methods could provide a reliable agricultural price forecasting technique.

The research paper of Bejo et al. (2014) presented a review on the use of ANN in predicting crop yield using various crop performance factors namely: (a) soil factors, such as pH, available nutrients, texture, organic matter content and soil-water relationships; (b) weather and climatic factors including temperature, rainfall and light intensity; (c) crop and cultivar factors; (d) post harvest handling and storage factors; (e) fertilizer applications factors; (f) cultural practices factors; etc. From the review, it was observed that ANN based method provided better interpretation of crop variability as compared to the other methods.

Dahikar, Rode and Deshmukh (2015) in their study paper demonstrated an ANN based methodology for predicting crop yield based on various soil parameters and use of particular types of fertilizers.

Ghadiyali and Lad (2016) attempted to predict agriculture commodity market price using ANN based methodology, which would be expected to help farmer community in their decision making, properly planning the cultivation period, and agribusiness commodity trading, thereby achieving the ultimate goal of profit making.

Francik et.al. (2016) have reviewed the present trends in research on applications of ANNs in agriculture and agricultural engineering and it has been observed that since 1991 the numbers of such research papers are constantly growing over the years covering various domain specific problems/ issues.

In the present research paper, an attempt has been made to estimate/ predict the yield of food grains of India based on various related economic and financial parameters, using back propagation type of ANNs based methodology of soft computing.

Research Methodology

Secondary data has been considered to fulfill the objectives of the study. Past data regarding Indian Agricultural Planning has been obtained from various published materials, journals, reports, plan documents, etc. Accordingly, the sources of data, used in the present study, are:

1. Twelfth Five Year Plan (2012-17) Documents (Volumes – I, II and III; Planning Commission, 2013) as available on the website of Planning Commission (now renamed as NITI Aayog i.e. www.niti. gov.in);
2. Data Books for use of Deputy Chairman, Planning Commission (Planning Commission, 2014);
3. Agricultural Statistics at a Glance, 2016, published by Directorate of Economics & Statistics, Department of Agriculture & Cooperation, Ministry of Agriculture, Government of India;
4. Expenditure Budgets 2015-16 and Economic Survey 2015-16 published by Ministry of Finance, Government of India (and also past years Expenditure Budgets);
5. Annual Reports of Department of Agriculture & Cooperation, Ministry of Agriculture and Ministry of Water Resources, Government of India.

Selection of Key Input Parameters

For estimating the year wise yield of food grains of India, the key input parameters which are found to be mostly relevant in this regard have been identified for using in the proposed ANN based model for estimating the year wise Yield of Food Grains. The reasons for choosing the relevant input parameters/ variables are discussed below:

1. Total expenditures in respect of all plan schemes of Department of Agriculture & Cooperation (DAC) of Ministry of Agriculture, Government of India, since the overall objectives of all the Plan Schemes of DAC are aimed towards promotion and growth of agriculture sector of India as a whole including agricultural productivity and/ or yield of food grains;

2. Total expenditures in respect of all plan schemes of Ministry of Water Resources (MOWR), Government of India, which is responsible for the promotion and growth of Irrigation and Water Resources Sector of India as a whole, and on which growth of agriculture sector including yield of food grains depends is also considered as an input parameter in the present study;

3. In addition, it has been observed that certain special plan schemes/ programs of Department of Agriculture & Cooperation (DAC), Ministry of Agriculture, Government of India, takes into account the issues raised in the above discussed research papers in a more focused manner. The details of such special plan schemes of DAC considered in this regard are mentioned below:

    a. Total year wise expenditures in respect of the plan scheme of 'Rashtriya Krishi Vikas Yojana (RKVY)' of DAC, where the major objective is to incentivize the states to come up with plans for their respective agriculture domain in a more comprehensive manner. While implementing the same, individual states need to take into consideration their agro-climatic conditions, natural resource issues and technology, along with integrating the animal husbandry part i.e. livestock, poultry and fisheries more fully (RKVY-Operational Guidelines for 12th Five Year Plan, 2014). The major areas of focus of the different programs/ sub schemes/ sub-sectors under RKVY are to use improved quality of seeds and fertilizers, Integrated Pest Management Testing laboratories, Horticulture, Farm Mechanization, Extension, Crops Marketing and Cooperatives, Animal Husbandry, etc.;

    b. Total year wise expenditures in respect of the plan scheme of 'National Food Security Mission (NFSM)' of DAC. The major objectives of the scheme are – (i) increasing production of food grains namely, rice, wheat, pulses and coarse cereals through area enlargement and productivity improvement in a sustainable manner in the identified districts of the country; (ii) reestablishing soil fertility and productivity at the individual farm level; and (iii) increasing farm level economy to restore confidence amongst the farmers (NFSM– Operational Guidelines for 12th Five Year Plan, 2012);

4. The parameter of effective irrigation in the agriculture sector has been observed as, 'Percentage or Ratio of Gross Irrigated Area over Gross Cropped Area', which indicates the ratio of the total irrigated area under various crops during the year to the total area sown once as well as more than once in a particular year. When the crop is sown on a piece of land for twice, the area is counted twice in Gross Cropped Area (GCA). On the other hand, Net Sown Area is the area sown with crops but is counted only once. This data is available in the Agricultural Statistics as collected, compiled and published by the Directorate of Economics & Statistics, DAC, Ministry of Agriculture, Government of India.

Further, the above-mentioned parameters have been clubbed together in the following manner:

1. Year wise total expenditure in respect of all plan schemes of DAC (DACE) to GDP (Gross Domestic Product) Ratio (DACEGDPR);

2. Year wise total expenditure in respect of special plan schemes of DAC (SSEDAC) (namely NFSM and RKVY) to total expenditure of DAC (DACE) Ratio (SSEDACER);

3. Year wise total expenditure in respect of all plan schemes of MOWR (MOWRE) to GDP Ratio (MOWREGDPR);

4. Year wise Ratio of Gross Irrigated Area over Gross Cropped Area (AREAIRR).

By clubbing together, the parameters considered in the present study in the form of ratios, the effects of inflation can be neutralized, since both the numerator and denominator in the ratios are subject to having equal influences of inflation in a particular year. In addition, the ratios have been further scaled down/ up suitably, so that their values lie within the range of 0 to 1, being suitable for analysis under ANN methodology of soft computing. These parameters from (1) to (4) as mentioned above are now designated as: DACEGDPR2, SSEDACER, MOWREGDPR3, AREAIRR respectively. In the present study, these parameters are considered as input parameters to the proposed economic modeling system for estimating year wise yield of food grains.

The only output parameter in the present case is Year Wise Yield of Food Grains (YRR) in Kg/Ha (with suitable scaling down to make the values lying within 0 to 1). Further, the output parameter YRR being a physical quantity, the issue of inflation does not arise at all.

Data Collection

For the purpose of training of the proposed neural network model, year wise data in respect of the parameters for the financial years ranging from 1997-98 to 2013-14 (i.e. data for 17 years or 17 training examples or data points or sets) have been considered in the study. For testing or predicting purpose, the relevant data for 3 years namely from 2014-15 to 2016-17 have been considered. The year wise data sets for training as well as testing purposes are shown in Table 1.

Table 1. Year wise data sets for training and testing

Year	DACEGDPR2	SSEDACER	MOWREGDPR3	AREAIRR	YRR	Data For
1997-98	0.0875	0.0000	0.0000	0.3980	0.1552	Training
1998-99	0.0568	0.0000	0.0000	0.4100	0.1627	Training
1999-00	0.0803	0.0000	0.0000	0.4200	0.1704	Training
2000-01	0.0846	0.0000	0.0000	0.4110	0.1626	Training
2001-02	0.0913	0.0000	0.0000	0.4170	0.1734	Training
2002-03	0.0720	0.0000	0.0000	0.4200	0.1535	Training
2003-04	0.0815	0.0000	0.0000	0.4110	0.1727	Training
2004-05	0.0998	0.0000	0.0000	0.4240	0.1652	Training
2005-06	0.1156	0.0000	0.0000	0.4370	0.1715	Training
2006-07	0.1239	0.0000	0.0000	0.4510	0.1756	Training
2007-08	0.1512	0.2021	0.0306	0.4510	0.1860	Training
2008-09	0.1848	0.3944	0.0729	0.4550	0.1909	Training
2009-10	0.1739	0.4495	0.0782	0.4500	0.1798	Training
2010-11	0.2341	0.4715	0.1104	0.4490	0.1921	Training
2011-12	0.1969	0.5495	0.1082	0.4690	0.2078	Training
2012-13	0.1880	0.5734	0.1078	0.4751	0.2129	Training
2013-14	0.1663	0.4858	0.0808	0.4767	0.2120	Training
2014-15	0.1523	0.5448	0.0830	0.4767	0.2028	Testing
2015-16	0.1119	0.3336	0.0373	0.4767	0.2056	Testing
2016-17	0.2612	0.1212	0.0317	0.4767	0.2217	Testing

Limitations in ANN Training

In this context, it may be mentioned that the total number of training data points considered here is not very high, as the basic aim of this paper is to show that by using ANN based soft computing technique it can be possible to develop an effective model for the estimation of the level of Yield of Food Grains of a country in a particular year. However, with more training data points (i.e. relevant data over larger number of years) the accuracy of the final results is expected to improve further and this issue can be suitably addressed and explored in future research in the area.

ANALYSIS AND FINDINGS

The input and output parameters of the present problem of estimating Year Wise Yield of Food Grains (YRR) of India are as shown in Table 2.

Table 2. Input and output parameters

Input Parameters	DACEGDPR2; SSEDACER; MOWREGDPR3; AREAIRR
Output Parameters	YRR

The degrees of correlation or Karl Pearson Correlation Coefficients between the output parameter YRR and each of the input parameters DACEGDPR2, SSEDACER, MOWREGDPR3, and AREAIRR have been calculated between 2 selected columns of parameters containing data in MS Excel Spreadsheet. These correlation coefficients between the output parameter and each of the input parameters are shown in Table 3.

From Table 3 it is observed that the degrees of correlation or Karl Pearson Correlation Coefficients between the output parameter YRR and each of the input parameters DACEGDPR2, SSEDACER, MOWREGDPR3, and AREAIRR are quite high and positively correlated.

Table 3. Correlation coefficients between input and output parameters

Karl Pearson Correlation Coefficient Between			
DACEGDPR2 and YRR	**SSEDACER and YRR**	**MOWREGDPR3 and YRR**	**AREAIRR and YRR**
0.81	0.77	0.74	0.93

Construction of Artificial Neural Networks (ANNs)

For the present problem, an ANN based model has been constructed, which comprises of following elements and layers:

1. Input Layer comprising of 4 Neurons representing 4 input parameters namely, DACEGDPR2, SSEDACER, MOWREGDPR3, and AREAIRR;
2. Output Layer comprising of 1 Neuron representing 1 output parameter namely, YRR.

In the present study, back propagation type of ANN has been used for computation, as it has the advantages of accuracy and versatile applications ability (Sivanandam and Deepa, 2007). For the purpose of training and testing of the ANN in the present study, 'EasyNN Plus' Software has been used.

Regarding choice of number of hidden layers and corresponding numbers of neurons in each of the hidden layers, trial and error method has been used. It has been observed that with 2 hidden layers having 4 neurons in the 1st hidden layer and 1 neuron in the 2nd hidden layer, the errors between the actual and calculated/ observed test data are least. So, in the present study the configuration of '4 – 4 – 1 – 1' in the architecture of ANN has been adopted. The final architecture of the ANN is shown in Figure 2.

Figure 2. Final architecture of ANN in the present study

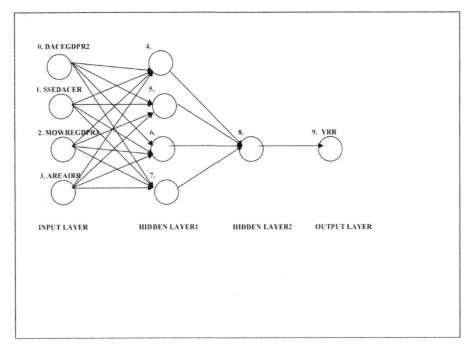

[*Source:* EasyNN Plus software]

Working of ANN Based Model

In the present study ANN has been trained by using back propagation methodology with 17 training data sets, as exhibited in Table 2, implementing 'EasyNN Plus' Software with a target error of 0.01 between the actual and calculated/ observed values of output parameter. The network has stopped learning/ training after 154 cycles on achieving an actual average training error of 0.00996277, as shown in Table 4.

Table 4. Results obtained during learning/ training of the ANN in the present study

Item	Results Obtained
Learning rate:	0.60000000
Momentum:	0.80000000
Accelerator:	0.00000000
Maximum Training Error:	0.03989944
Average Training Error:	0.00996277
Minimum Training Error:	0.00011362
Target Error:	0.01000000
Nos. of Training Examples:	17
Learning/ Training Stopped After:	154 Learning Cycles
Nos. of Nodes in Input Layer:	4
Nos. of Nodes in Hidden Layer-1:	4
Nos. of Nodes in Hidden Layer-2:	1
Nos. of Nodes in Output Layer:	1
Nos. of Weights between Input Layer & Hidden Layer-1:	16
Nos. of Weights between Hidden Layer-1 & Hidden Layer-2:	4
Nos. of Weights between Hidden Layer-2 & Output Layer:	1

Source: EasyNN Plus software

RESULTS

Based on the learning/ training of the ANN, the data sets for 3 consecutive financial years namely, 2014-15 to 2016-17 (as shown in Table 2) have been tested. The final results indicating the percentage Root Mean Square Error (RMSE) between the actual values of the output YRR and the corresponding observed/ calculated values of the same are represented in Table 5. It is observed in Table 5 that in case of 3 numbers of test data sets of output parameter YRR, the Overall Average Root Mean Square Error (RMSE) is 0.00011043 or 0.01% and the Overall Average Root Mean Square Relative Error (RMSRE) is 0.00227508 or 0.23%.

The sensitivity analysis of different input parameters on output parameter indicates as to what extent the output parameter changes with the change of input parameters, which has been carried out with the help of 'EasyNN Plus' software, the results of which are shown in Table 6/ Figure 3. It is observed from the same that the relative sensitivities of different input parameters on output parameter YRR are as follows (in descending order): AREAIRR, MOWREGDPR3, SSEDACER, and DACEGDPR2.

Table 5. Errors in output parameter 'YRR' in case of test data sets

Year	Output Parameter YRR (Actual)	Output Parameter YRR (Observed/ Calculated)	Error	Root Mean Square Error (RMSE)	Relative Error	Root Mean Square of Relative Error (RMSRE)
2014-15	0.2028	0.2074	0.0046	0.00011043	0.0227	0.00227508
2015-16	0.2056	0.2050	-0.0006		-0.0029	
2016-17	0.2217	0.2041	-0.0176		-0.0794	

Figure 3. Sensitivity analysis of different input parameters on output parameter

Input Layer Node No.	Input Name	Sensitivity
3	AREAIRR	0.699592226
2	MOWREGDPR3	0.107914378
1	SSEDACER	0.034122297
0	DACEGDPR2	0.005185450

Relative Sensitivity

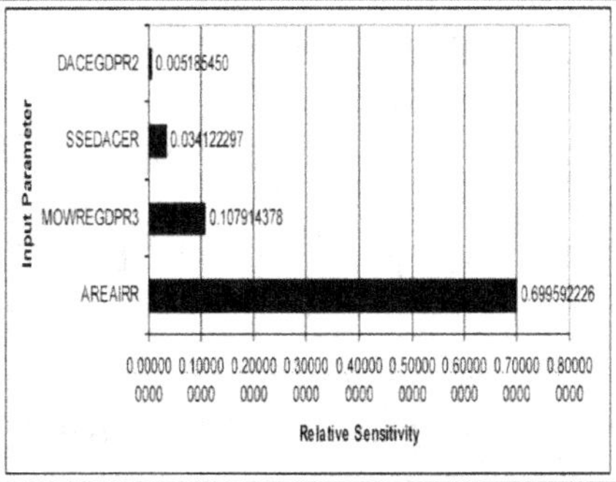

[*Source:* EasyNN Plus software]

Table 6. Sensitivity analysis of different input parameters on output parameter

Input Layer Node No.	Input Name	Sensitivity
3	AREAIRR	0.699592226
2	MOWREGDPR3	0.107914378
1	SSEDACER	0.034122297
0	DACEGDPR2	0.005185450

From the analysis of proposed ANN based model for estimating Year Wise Yield of Food Grains (YRR) of India, it has emerged that YRR of India is positively correlated (as shown in Table 3) and highly dependent on all the input parameters and hence these are extremely important in increasing the final value of the Yield of Food Grains. Further, it has also been observed above that the year wise quantum of 'Percentage or Ratio of Gross Irrigated Area over Gross Cropped Area' (i.e. input parameter 'AREAIRR') is having maximum influence on increasing the year wise yield of food grains (YRR), as its degree of positive correlation with the output parameter YRR is the highest amongst all input parameters (as shown in Table 3). Thus, we can conclude that the quantum of effective irrigation, especially minor or micro irrigation at farm level is a vital input for improving/ increasing the overall yield of food grains of India in a particular year.

Overall Conclusion

In PART-I of this paper it has been shown that there is strong need for developing a dedicated Agricultural Knowledge Management System (KMS) in respect of various micro irrigation techniques for agriculture and relevant crop/ region specific agricultural practices at various levels (such as, farm level or aggregate level) in different regions of the country, which may be made available in the form of an interactive portal/ website that can be easily accessed by the various users such as, farmers, agricultural scientists and other stake holders in the domain from their computers as well as mobile phones.

Such Agricultural KMS on micro irrigation may be coupled with a DSS (Decision Support System) and it needs to be so designed as to be able to advise/ help the farmers/ other stakeholders for taking proper decisions in respect of different micro irrigation techniques for agriculture and crop/ region specific agricultural practices.

The above mentioned Agricultural KMS on micro irrigation (MI) along with relevant DSS in the form of an interactive web portal needs to be developed and managed by an Inter Ministerial Group/ Committee consisting of experts from Ministry of Water Resources (MOWR), Ministry of Agriculture of Government of India, as well as agricultural departments of different State Governments.

In PART-II of this paper it has been shown that how an ANN based model can be effectively used as a tool for the Agricultural KMS on micro irrigation (as discussed/ explored in Part-I of this paper) for accurately estimating the year wise yield of food grains in India based on certain relevant parameters (namely, total expenditure in respect of all plan schemes of DAC, total expenditure in respect of certain special plan schemes of DAC, total expenditure in respect of all plan schemes of MOWR, percentage or ratio of gross irrigated area over gross cropped area, and GDP of India). It has also been shown that how such ANN based model/ tool can improve the overall efficiency and usefulness of the Agricultural KMS.

All the above mentioned measures taken together are expected to greatly improve the year wise overall productivity of entire agriculture sector including Yield of Food Grains (YRR) of India.

REFERENCES

Alemu, D., Jennex, M. E., & Assefa, T. (2018). Agricultural Knowledge Management System Development for Knowledge Integration. In *51st Hawaii International Conference on System Sciences*. IEEE Computer Society. 10.24251/HICSS.2018.544

Amarasinghe, U. A., & Xenarios, S. (2009). Strategic Issues in Indian Irrigation: overview of the proceedings. *IWMI Conference Proceedings 212440, International Water Management Institute (IWMI)*.

Arjun, K. M. (2013). Indian Agriculture - Status, Importance and Role in Indian Economy. *International Journal of Agriculture and Food Science Technology*, 4(4), 343–346.

Bejo, S. K., Mustaffha, S., & Ismail, W. I. W. (2014). Application of Artificial Neural Network in Predicting Crop Yield: A Review. *Journal of Food Science and Engineering*, (4), 1-9.

Chand, R. (2017). *Doubling Farmers Income – Rationale, Strategy, Prospects and Action Plan.* Working Paper, NITI Aayog.

Chantarasombat, C., Srisa-ard, B., Kuofie, M. H. S., & Jennex, M. E. (2010). Using Knowledge Management to Create Self-Reliant Communities in Thailand. *International Journal of Knowledge Management, 6*(1), 62–78. doi:10.4018/jkm.2010103004

Christa, S., Phuritshabam, R., & Suma, V. (2016). Impact of Soft Computing in Indian Agricultural Scenario. *International Journal of Computer Applications in Engineering Sciences, 6*(3).

Dahikar, S. S., Rode, S. V., & Deshmukh, P. (2015, January). An Artificial Neural Network Approach for Agricultural Crop Yield Prediction Based on Various Parameters. *International Journal of Advanced Research in Electronics and Communication Engineering, 4*(1), 94–98.

Department of Agriculture & Cooperation (DAC). Ministry of Agriculture, Government of India. (n.d.). *Annual Report 2016-17.* Author.

Department of Agriculture & Cooperation (DAC), Ministry of Agriculture, Government of India. (2014). *Rashtriya Krishi Vikas Yojana (RKVY) – Operational Guidelines for 12th Five Year Plan.* Author.

Directorate of Economics & Statistics, Department of Agriculture & Cooperation (DAC), Ministry of Agriculture, Government of India. (2016). *Agricultural Statistics at a Glance 2016.* Author.

Francik, S., Slipek, Z., Fracze, J., & Knapczyk, A. (2016). Present Trends in Research on Application of Artificial Neural Networks in Agricultural Engineering. *Agricultural Engineering, 20*(4), 15–25. doi:10.1515/agriceng-2016-0060

Ghadiyali, T., & Kalpesh, L. (2016). Risk Minimization in Agribusiness using Soft Computing Technique. *IOSR Journal of Computer Engineering, 18*(5), 20-25.

Goswami, G. (2012). *Introduction to Artificial Neural Networks.* New Delhi, India: S. K. Kataria & Sons.

Gover, A., Kant, S., Payret, A., Pyakuryal, B., Seneres, L., & Singal, D. (2013). Incorporating *Traditional Methods of Irrigation with Water Management in Mandi, India.* Joint Report prepared by Indian Institute of Technology (IIT), Mandi and Worcester Polytechnic Institute (WPI).

Grant Thornton India L. L. P. Irrigation Association of India (IAI), & Federation of Indian Chamber of Commerce & Industry (FICCI). (2016). Accelerating Growth of Indian Agriculture: Micro Irrigation an Efficient Solution. Strategy Paper. Author.

Haykin, S. (1994). *Neural Networks: A comprehensive foundation.* New York, NY: Macmillan Publishing Company.

Indian Council of Agricultural Research (ICAR). (1999). 2020 *Vision.* Author.

Jennex, M. E. (2005). What is knowledge management? *International Journal of Knowledge Management, 1*(4), i–iv.

Jennex, M. E. (2017). Big Data, the Internet of Things and the Revised Knowledge Pyramid. *The Data Base for Advances in Information Systems, 48*(4), 69–79. doi:10.1145/3158421.3158427

Jha, A. K., Malla, R., Sharma, M., Panthi, J., Lakhankar, T., Krakauer, N. Y., ... Shres, M. L. (2016). Impact of Irrigation Method on Water Use Efficiency and Productivity of Fodder Crops in Nepal. *Climate (Basel)*, *4*(4), 4. doi:10.3390/cli4010004

Jha, G. K., & Sinha, K. (2013). Agricultural Price Forecasting Using Neural Network Model: An Innovative Information Delivery System. *Agricultural Economics Research Review*, *26*(2), 220–239.

Karandikar, S. G. (2015). A Review of Soft Computing Based DSS in Fertilizer Management in India. *AADYA: National Journal of Management and Technology*, *5*, 118–122.

Kurtener, D., & Dragavtsev, V. (2017). Application of soft computing in plant breeding and crop production. *European Agrophysical Journal*, *4*(1), 10–24.

Lamm, F. R., Ayars, J. E., Nakayama, F. S., & Bucks, D. A. (2007). Micro irrigation for Crop Production: Design, Operation and Management. In *Development in Agricultural Engineering* (Vol. 13). Oxford, UK: Elsevier.

Liakos, K. G., Busato, P., Moshou, D., Pearson, S., & Bochtis, D. (2018). Machine Learning in Agriculture: A Review. *Sensors (Basel)*, *18*(2674). PMID:30110960

Ministry of Finance, Government of India. (n.d.http:///). *Economic Survey 2018-19*. www.finmin.nic.in

Ministry of Water Resources (MOWR), Government of India. (n.d.). *Annual Report 2016-17*. www.wrmin.nic.in

National Water Academy (NWA). (2017). Water – Its Conservation, Management and Governance. Report submitted to Central Water Commission (CWC), Government of India.

Planning Commission, Government of India. (2013). *Twelfth Five Year Plan (2012-17) Documents (Volumes – I, II and III)*. Sage Publications. Available at: http://planningcommission.gov.in/plans/planrel/12thplan/welcome.html

Planning Commission, Government of India. (2014). *Data Books for use of Deputy Chairman, Planning Commission*. Available at: http://planningcommission.nic.in/data/datatable/1203/databook_1203.pdf

Priyan, K., & Panchal, R. (2017). Micro-Irrigation: An Efficient Technology for India's Sustainable Agricultural Growth. *Kalpa Publications in Civil Engineering*, *1*, 398–402. doi:10.29007/gbzv

Rajasekaran, S., & Pai, G. A. V. (2003). *Neural Networks, Fuzzy Logic and Genetic Algorithms Synthesis and Applications*. New Delhi, India: Prentice Hall of India Private Limited.

Rao, V. B., & Rao, H. (1995). *C++ Neural Networks and Fuzzy Logic*. New Delhi, India: M & T Books.

Samborska, I. A., Alexandrov, V., Sieczko, L., Kornatowska, B., Goltsev, V., Cetner, M. D., & Kalaji, H. M. (2014). Artificial neural networks and their application in biological and agricultural research. Signpost Open Access Journal of NanoPhotoBioSciences, 2, 14-30.

Sivanandam, S. N., & Deepa, S. N. (2008). Principles of Soft Computing. Wiley India (P) Limited.

Viswanathan, P. K., & Bahinipati, C. S. (2015). Exploring the Socio-Economic Impacts of Micro-Irrigation System (MIS): A Study of Public Tubewells in Gujarat, Western India. *South Asia Water Studies (SAWAS) Journal, 1*(1).

Whitney, J., Jennex, M. E., Elkins, A., & Frost, E. (2018). Don't Want to Get Caught? Don't Say It: The Use of EMOJIS in Online Human Sex Trafficking Ads. In *51st Hawaii International Conference on System Sciences, HICSS51*. IEEE Computer Society. 10.24251/HICSS.2018.537

Yadav, V. K. G., & Yadav, S. M. (2015). An Introduction to Soft Computing Techniques in Water Resources System. *Journal of Emerging Technologies and Innovative Research, 2*(11), 120–123.

This research was previously published in the International Journal of Knowledge Management (IJKM), 16(2); pages 84-101, copyright year 2020 by IGI Publishing (an imprint of IGI Global).

Chapter 49
Mapping Ground Penetrating Radar Amplitudes Using Artificial Neural Network and Multiple Regression Analysis Methods

Eslam Mohammed Abdelkader

Building, Civil and Environmental Engineering, Concordia University, Montreal, Canada

Mohamed Marzouk

Structural Engineering Department, Faculty of Engineering, Cairo University, Giza, Egypt

Tarek Zayed

Department of Building and Real Estate, The Hong Kong Polytechnic University, Hong Kong

ABSTRACT

Bridges are aging and deteriorating. Thus, the development of Bridge Management Systems (BMSs) became imperative nowadays. Condition assessment is one of the most critical and vital components of BMSs. Ground Penetrating Radar (GPR) is one of the non-destructive techniques (NDTs) that are used to evaluate the condition of bridge decks which are subjected to the rebar corrosion. The objective of the proposed method is to develop standardized amplitude scale for bridge decks based on a hybrid optimization-decision making model. Shuffled frog leaping algorithm is employed to compute the optimum thresholds. Then, polynomial regression and artificial neural network models are designed to predict the prioritizing index based on a set of multi-criteria decision-making methods. The weibull distribution is utilized to capture the stochastic nature of deterioration of concrete bridge decks. Lastly, a case study is presented to demonstrate the capabilities of the proposed method.

DOI: 10.4018/978-1-6684-2408-7.ch049

INTRODUCTION

Infrastructure systems are systems that support the prevailing of the society. Infrastructure systems are divided into: bridges, highways, dams, waste water systems, sewer water systems, etc. Existing infrastructure systems are continuing to age and deteriorate and at the same time, demands for better services are growing in response to the higher standards of health. As per Canada Infrastructure Report Card, 40% of infrastructure systems are in a "Good" condition, 40% of infrastructure systems within 20 years will be in "Fair" condition, 40% of infrastructure systems within 40 years will be in "Poor" condition, 40% of infrastructure systems within 60 years will be in "Very Poor" condition (Felio, 2016). Moreover, there is a significant increase in the risk of service disruption where one-third of the municipal infrastructure systems are either: fair, poor or very poor.

American Society of Civil Engineers (2017) stated that $3.32 trillion are needed to maintain the infrastructure in a good condition which corresponds to grade "B" in the United Sates. There is a funding gap of $1.44 trillion for funding the infrastructure in the United States. Grade "A" is exceptional, grade "B" is good, grade "C" is mediocre", grade "D" is poor, and grade "E" is failing. The national grade of America's infrastructure is "D+". The grade of bridges is "C+." The grade of roads is "D" while the grade of waste water systems is "D+".

Bridges are one of the vital elements of the infrastructure systems that are subjected to aggressive influences such as overloading, chloride ingress, cycles of the freeze and thaw, earthquakes, etc. Thus, they are more likely to deteriorate significantly. Based on the Canadian infrastructure report card, 17% of the bridges are in a "Very Good" condition, 57% of the bridges are in a "Good" condition, 22% of the bridges are in a "Fair" condition, 3% of the bridges are in a "Poor" condition, and 1% of the bridges are in a "Very Poor" condition (Felio, 2016). This means that 26% of the bridges were given either "Fair", "Poor" or "Very Poor "ratings.

There are two main reasons for the significant deterioration of bridges which are: the decrease in the public investment, and the high age of bridges. The investment in bridges is below the required level to maintain the age of bridges constant, whereas the age of bridges increased by 3.2 years from 21.3 years in 1985 to 24.5 years in 2007. Quebec has about 9,600 bridges and overpasses where 4,300 bridges are a part of the municipal network while 5,300 bridges are a part of the provincial network. 70% of the bridges in Quebec were constructed between the 1960s and 1980s. Consequently, there is a major challenge in order to maintain the aging bridges efficiently and effectively (Farzam et al., 2016). In the United States, 9.1% of the bridges were structurally deficient and 13.6% of the bridges were functionally obsolete in the United States. Therefore, $20.8 billion should be invested annually to remove the bridge deficient backlog by 2028. However, $12.8 billion are currently invested annually (American Society of Civil Engineers, 2017).

BRIDGE MANAGEMENT SYSTEMS

AASHTO defined Bridge Management System as "a system designed to optimize the use of available resources for inspection, maintenance, rehabilitation and replacement of bridges" (Abd Elkhalek et al., 2016).

The development of comprehensive and efficient Bridge Management Systems has become a fundamental imperative nowadays for three main reasons:

1. Bridges are vulnerable to several deterioration agents, which amplify their aging and deterioration. These deterioration agents include: freeze-thaw cycles, excessive distress loads due to the traffic overload, chloride-induced corrosion of the steel reinforcement, sulphates, alkali-silica reaction (ASR), poor construction practices, poor workmanship, design errors, poor quality of materials, and deferred maintenance actions, etc.;

2. The presence of limited funds and resources for rehabilitation and maintenance action, which is demonstrated in the form of the huge variance between the need for maintenance actions, and the available funds to perform such actions;

3. The existence of large number of bridges in transportation networks;

4. Condition assessment is one of the key pillars of BMS.

Visual inspection is considered as one of the most common techniques in the condition assessment of bridge decks. However, there is a lot of vagueness and subjectivity associated with the visual inspection because it deals with defects visible on the surface. Moreover, it depends extensively on the experience of the user. Non-destructive techniques (NDTs) gain popularity due to their various advantages including; providing a high level of safety for the labor staff, time saving, providing high rates of production in comparison to traditional methods. Ground penetrating radar (GPR) is one of the NDTs that are used to evaluate corrosion of reinforcing rebars in concrete bridge decks based on the electromagnetic waves produced from the transmitting antenna. However, there is a major challenge associated with the GPR, which is the absence of standardized amplitude threshold values. The absence of such values does not provide an equal basis of comparison between the levels of corrosion present in bridges, which subsequently affects the prioritization of the maintenance actions.

LITERATURE REVIEW

The literature review is divided into two main sections: 1) condition assessment and maintenance prioritization, and 2) deterioration modeling.

Condition Assessment and Maintenance Prioritization

Previous efforts have been made in order to develop a condition index for the concrete bridge decks. The index can be used subsequently to prioritize the maintenance actions of bridge elements. Alsharqawi et al. (2016) utilized Quality Function Deployment (QFD) to develop a comprehensive bridge deck condition index. The QFD is divided into five main components, which are: house of quality (HOQ), customer demands (Whats), quality characteristics (Hows), relationship matrix, correlation matrix, and absolute weights of Whats. Wasserman's normalization technique was used in order to take into consideration the interdependency between the bridge defects. Srinivas et al. (2016) developed a decision-making system to calculate the condition rating of bridges by combining both fuzzy weighted average (FWA) and resolution identity technique. The main component of the decision-making system is the knowledge-based expert system (KBES), which aggregates forward and backward chaining inference strategy. Moreover, it can deal with large data.

Valença et al. (2017) presented an automatic concrete health monitoring (ACHM) method for the assessment of concrete surfaces. This method integrates photogrammetry, digital image processing and multi-spectral analysis in order to characterize crack pattern, displacement and strain fields, map damages and assess and define restoration tasks. Bukhsh et al. (2017) designed a multi-criteria decision-making based approach to prioritize the maintenance activities for maintenance in the network level. The maintenance activities were evaluated using the analytical hierarchy process (AHP) based on some performance indicators such as reliability, safety, availability, economic, social and environmental aspects.

Amiri et al. (2019) utilized a set of multi-criteria decision-making methods to rank the maintenance actions of bridges. The risks on bridges were analyzed using failure mode and effects analysis (FMEA) method. Then, AHP, analytical network process (ANP) and technique for order preference by similarity to ideal solution (TOPSIS) were applied to compute the ranking index. Gao et al. (2016) applied VIKOR (Vlse Kriterijumska Optimizacija I Resenje) method to rank the repair actions of bridges, which refers to multi-criteria optimization and compromise solution in Serbian. The bridges were evaluated based on the structural and functional status of a group of bridge elements such as deck, substructure, superstructure and culvert. Tajadod et al. (2016) conducted a comparison between a set of multi-criteria decision-making methods to prioritize the maintenance actions. The weights of the performance indicators were calculated based on Mikhailov's fuzzy preference programming (FPP) method. Finally, AHP, fuzzy AHP, ANP and fuzzy ANP were compared to select the most feasible maintenance plan.

Deterioration Modeling

Recently, several studies have been performed to model the deterioration of the concrete bridges. Zambon et al. (2017) compared a group of stochastic models which are: Markov chain with exponentially-distributed and weibull-distributed sojourn times, and gamma process. They concluded that the gamma process has better prediction capabilities when compared to the Markov chain models. Muñoz et al. (2016) presented a methodology to predict the deterioration of the bridges using both Markov chain and regression analysis in the case of small sample size. They illustrated that the proposed methodology provided conservative estimates for the future condition ratings as well as similar estimates to the traditional methods in calibrating the Markovian models and regression analysis. Shim and Lee (2016) modeled the deterioration of the bridge decks based on stochastic Markov decision process. They estimated the transition probabilities as a function of the median duration years.

Qiao et al. (2016) developed deterioration models for a group of bridge components using ordered binary probit (BP) method, whereas the BP method was used to compute the probability that the element will deteriorate from a certain condition state to the lower condition state within an interval of time. They highlighted that material type is only significant in the deterioration modeling of superstructure components. Contreras-Nieto et al. (2016) developed deterioration models to forecast the future performance of superstructure elements using some machine learning methods such as linear regression, neural network and decision tree. They highlighted that neural network provided the best deterioration prediction for the pre-stressed concrete bridges while decision tree provided the most accurate deterioration prediction for the steel bridges.

Hussein and Abu Tair (2019) applied feed forward neural network to predict the deterioration age of reinforced concrete bridges based on actual historical records. They highlighted that artificial neural network provided better performance than regression models. Moreover, they illustrated that Levenberg Marquardt algorithm provided a faster learning rate than Gradient descent algorithm. Lu et al. (2016) developed a group of regression models for the deterioration prediction of highway bridges. They stated that the multiple liner regression with data filtering provided the best prediction accuracy based on some performance metrics.

RESEARCH METHODOLOGY

The framework of the proposed research methodology is depicted in Figure 1. The condition assessment model heavily depends on the inspection type. The process of monitoring bridges should be cost-effective, efficient, and fit for the purpose (Alani et al., 2013). Thus, bridge inspectors should use techniques to assess accurately and effectively the corrosion of the bridge decks. Bridge inspection can be defined as "a process in which the defects on a bridge are identified, recorded to be used for assessing bridge condition". Inspection techniques are divided into two main categories which are: 1) destructive techniques (DT), and 2) non-destructive techniques (NDT). Destructive Techniques (DT) provide accurate and direct results, but they cause damage to the element under investigation, and they are expensive and time-consuming. Non-Destructive Techniques (NDT) are inexpensive and quick, but they do not provide direct information about the element under inspection. NDTs gain popularity due to their various advantages including; providing a high level of safety for the labor staff, time-saving, providing high rates of production in comparison to traditional methods.

Ground penetrating radar (GPR) is one of the NDTs that are used for field investigation in structural engineering. The proposed model utilizes GPR in order to evaluate the corrosion of the reinforcement rebars in the concrete bridge decks. The scanned profiles using GPR are imported into the GSSI RADAN7 software in order to extract the needed information. GSSI RADAN7 software is used to extract the amplitude values of the top reinforcing rebars. The numerical-amplitude method is used to interpret the corrosion of the bridge decks. Numerical amplitude method depends on the value of the amplitude of the reflected waves from the top layer of reinforcement. The higher the amplitude the better the condition of the bars will be. On the other hand, the lower the amplitude the higher the corrosion the reinforcement bars will be and consequently, the lower condition state the bridge deck will be. This major drawback of this method is its lack of an exact and clear value for the thresholds that define the different categories of corrosion. The absence of the standardized thresholds results in inaccurate comparison between the condition of different bridge decks.

The multi-objective optimization module considers a pre-specified number of bridge decks and it calculates the optimum thresholds based on four objective functions. The first three objective functions tend to find the optimum threshold based on a local search, i.e., dealing with each threshold individually. On the other hand, the fourth objective function tends to find the optimum threshold based on a global search. The proposed method utilizes shuffled frog leaping algorithm, genetic algorithm, fminsearch search algorithm, and fminunc search algorithm. The fminsearch method utilizes the Nelder-Mead simplex algorithm while the fminunc method utilizes the trust region algorithm to find the optimum solution of a given optimization problem (Mehta and Jain, 2015). Multi-criteria decision-making (MCDM) is applied to select the best solution among the set of the optimal solution. Six MCDM methods are investigated because each one of them depends on a certain calculation methodology. Thus, each one of them provides a distinct ranking from the other. The six MCDM methods are: weighted sum model (WSM), weighted product model (WPM), technique, Complex Proportional Assessment (COPRAS), Modified Technique for Order Preference by Similarity to Ideal Solution (M-TOPSIS), Operational Competitiveness Ratings Analysis (OCRA) and Multi-Objective Optimization on The Basis of Ratio Analysis (MOORA).

Group decision making is very important to aggregate the rankings obtained from the six MCDM methods. The proposed method utilizes the simple additive weight (SAW) method to obtain a consensus ranking for the optimal solutions and select the most feasible optimal solution. The corrosion index is computed as the weighted sum of the condition categories. The corrosion index can be used for maintenance prioritization of concrete bridge decks, whereas the bridge decks that should be repaired first, are the ones subjected to high levels of corrosion. Then, Spearman's rank correlation coefficient is utilized to measure the correlation between each pair of MCDM methods. Moreover, it is utilized to determine the best MCDM method, i.e., the MCDM method that provides the closest ranking to the final ranking of the optimal solutions. Multiple linear regression, multiple Poisson regression, multiple polynomial regression and feed forward artificial neural network models are designed to forecast the ranking index. The prediction model is useful to select the best performing clustering algorithm. Moreover, it can beneficial for the user to compare between different threshold amplitude threshold values based on their own calculation methodology.

The four prediction models are compared in terms of three performance indicators are: root-mean squared error (RMSE), mean absolute error (MAE) and determination coefficient (R^2). The best prediction model is the one which achieves the lowest *RMSE*, lowest *MAE* and highest R^2. Coefficient of variation metric is utilized to determine the best performing clustering algorithm. Finally, a probabilistic deterioration model is constructed to model the future condition rating of bridge decks. Anderson darling test is used to select the most feasible probability distribution functions. Three probability distributions are investigated, which are exponential distribution, lognormal distribution and Weibull distribution. The parameters of the probability distributions are computed using maximum likelihood estimation.

Figure 1. Flowchart of the proposed research methodology

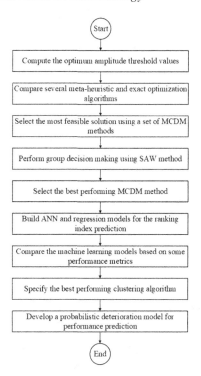

MULTI-OBJECTIVE OPTIMIZATION MODEL

Design of the Optimization Problem

The proposed model assumes that there are four categories for the condition of the bridge deck, i.e., three threshold values. The optimization module constitutes four objective functions. The first objective function is to minimize the root mean-squared error (RMSE), i.e., minimize the distance between the threshold obtained from the different clustering algorithms of some bridges, and threshold (1). The second objective function is to minimize the RMSE of threshold (2). The third objective function is to minimize the RMSE of threshold (3). The fourth objective is to evaluate the quality of evaluation clusters and it is calculated as the average of the Davies-Bouldin index and Dunn index:

$$F1 = \min RMSE_1 = \min\sqrt{\frac{\left(\sum_{j=1}^{m}\sum_{i=1}^{n}\left(X_{ij} - n \times m \times X^-\right)^2\right)}{n \times m}} \tag{1}$$

$$F2 = \min RMSE_2 = \min\sqrt{\frac{\left(\sum_{j=1}^{m}\sum_{i=1}^{n}\left(Y_{ij} - n \times m \times Y^-\right)^2\right)}{n \times m}} \tag{2}$$

$$F3 = \min RMSE_3 = \min\sqrt{\frac{\left(\sum_{j=1}^{m}\sum_{i=1}^{n}\left(Z_{ij} - n \times m \times Z^-\right)^2\right)}{n \times m}} \tag{3}$$

$$F4 = \min CLU = \frac{\sum_{i=1}^{n}\left(DBI - DUI\right)}{2 \times n} \tag{4}$$

where; m indicates number of clustering algorithms. Eight clustering algorithms are investigated which are: K-means, fast K-means, kernel K-means, K-medoids, expectation maximization, fuzzy C-means, X-means, and agglomerative clustering. n indicates number of bridges. X^-, Y^-, and Z^- depict threshold (1), threshold (2), and threshold (3), respectively. Threshold (1) represents the threshold that separates the "very severe" category form the "severe" category. Threshold (2) represents the threshold that separates the "severe" category form the "medium" category. Threshold (3) represents the threshold that separates the "medium" category form the "good" category. *CLU* represents the clustering index. *DBI* represents the Davies-Bouldin index.

Shuffled Frog Leaping Algorithm

Shuffled frog leaping (SFL) algorithm is a population-based meta-heuristic algorithm that simulates the social behaviour of the frogs in searching for the location that has the maximum amount of available food. The SFL algorithm was originally developed by Eusuff and Lansey in 2003. SFL algorithm contains both elements of local and global search. Consequently, it is capable of solving complex optimization problems such as non-linear, non-differentiable, and multi-modal problems (Venkatesan and Sanavullah, 2013). The SFL algorithm is characterized by its convergence speed, where it combines the advantages of both the genetic-based memetic algorithm (MA), and the social behaviour-based particle swarm optimization algorithm (Ebrahimi et al., 2011).

In the SFL algorithm, a population of possible solutions is defined as a set of virtual frogs. The virtual frogs are divided into subsets called "memeplexes". The different memeplexes represent the different cultures of the frogs, where each frog performs a local search within each memeplex. Within each memeplex, each frog holds ideas and the behavior of the frog is affected by the behavior of other frogs in the memeplex. After a predefined number of evolution steps, ideas are passed between memeplexes through a shuffling process, and the local search and the shuffling process continue until the predefined convergence criteria is satisfied (Ebrahimi et al., 2011).

The flowchart of the shuffled frog leaping algorithm is described in Figure 2. The first step of the SFL algorithm is to create an initial of "F" frogs that are randomly scattered in a S-dimensional search space. The dimension of the frog is equal to the number of the decision variables, where an objective function is calculated for each frog. Then, the frogs are arranged in a descending order based on their fitness. Subsequently, the frogs are divided into subsets using a partitioning strategy. A frog i is represented as $X_i = \{X_{i1}, X_{i2}, \ldots, X_{iS}\}$. The entire population is divided into "M" groups of "memeplexes", where each memeplex consists of "N" frogs i.e., $F = M \times N$. The strategy of partitioning can be performed as follows: the first frog goes to the first memeplex, the second frog goes to the second memeplex, the Mth frog goes to the Mth memeplex, and the $M+1$ frog goes to the first memeplex, and so on.

The positions with the best and the worst fitness functions are identified, which are: X_b, and X_w, respectively. The frog with the global best fitness function is denoted as X_g. Then, a process (frog leaping rule) is applied, which is similar to the PSO algorithm to improve the position of the frog of the lowest fitness function in each cycle (not all the frogs). The frog leaping rule is performed within each memeplex using Equations 5, and 6 such that the frog with the lowest fitness leaps towards the frog of the best position (Venkatesan and Sanavullah, 2013):

$$D_i = \text{Rand} \times (X_b - X_w) \tag{5}$$

$$X_{new} = X_w + D_i - D_{max} <= D_i <= D_{max} \tag{6}$$

where; Rand represents a random number between 0 and 1. D_i represents the change in the frog's position in one jump. D_{max} represents the maximum allowable change in the frog's position. X_w represents the current position of the frog. X_{new} denotes the new updated position of the frog.

If the frog leaping rule generates a better solution, therefore the better solution replaces the worst frog. Otherwise, Equations 5 and 6 are repeated to produce a better solution but the global best solution (X_g) replaces the best solution in the memeplex (X_b). If no improvement can be achieved, a new solution is generated randomly within the search space, and it replaces the worst solution. Therefore, SFL algorithm performs an independent local search within each memeplex using a process similar to the PSO algorithm. After a predefined number of memetic evolutionary steps, the solutions of the evolved memeplexes $\{X_{i1}, X_{i2}, \ldots, X_P\}$ are replaced into a new population. Global shuffling occurs, which allow the frogs among the memeplexes to exchange the information. The population is then ranked in a descending order, and the frog of the global best fitness is updated and the process continues until the convergence criteria are satisfied, i.e., until reaching maximum number of iterations.

Figure 2. Flowchart of shuffled frog leaping algorithm

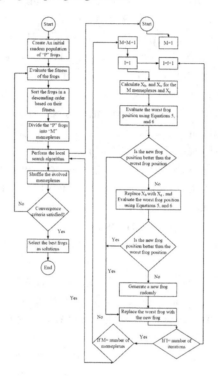

MULTI-CRITERIA DECISION MAKING

Multi-criteria decision making became one of the fastest growing areas in operation research during the second half of the twentieth century as many decision-making techniques were introduced in this period (Dragisa et al., 2013). The importance of multi-criteria decision-making methods has grown extensively in the last two decades. MCDM is concerned with theories and methodologies that have the ability to solve complex problems in management, business and construction fields. Multi-criteria decision-making methods are group of methods that allow aggregation and consideration different attributes in order to rank alternatives and choose the best alternative. There are three steps that most multi-criteria decision-making methods pursue which are: 1) define relevant alternatives and attributes, 2) link numerical measures to the relative importance of different attributes and to the impact of alternatives on these attributes and 3) apply numerical measures to sort and rank different alternatives (Mulliner et al., 2013).

MCDM methods are employed to select the most feasible solution among the set of optimal solutions. The optimal solutions are the solutions obtained from shuffled frog leaping algorithm, genetic algorithm and non-linear programming algorithms. The attributes of the MCDM method are the four objective functions of the multi-objective optimization problem. The weights of the attributes are computed using Shannon entropy method because this method doesn't require questionnaire surveys. It depends on the computation of the degree of dispersion of the measures of performance to compute the weights

(Akyene, 2012). Due to the paper size limitations, the WPM and OCRA methods are described only in the following lines.

WPM

The preference of each alternative based on the weighted product model can be calculated using Equation 7. The best alternative is the one with the highest preference in the maximization case. On the other, the best alternative has the lowest preference in the minimization case (Kolios et al., 2016):

$$P_i = \prod_{j=1}^{n} x_{ij}^{w_j} \left(1 \le i \le m, 1 \le j \le n \right) \tag{7}$$

where; P_i represents preference of each alternative. x_{ij} represents measure of performance in the normalized matrix. w_j represents weight of each criteria. m and n represent number of alternatives and number of criteria, respectively.

OCRA

OCRA method is divided into five procedures (Chakraborty et al., 2013).

The first procedure is to compute preference rating for non-beneficial attributes. This is done through Equation 8:

$$I_i = \sum_{j=1}^{m} W_j \frac{\max\left(X_{ij}\right) - X_{ij}}{\min\left(X_{ij}\right)} \tag{8}$$

where; I_i refers to a measure of relative importance of the i-th alternative for non-beneficial attribute. X_{ij} refers to performance score of the i-th alternative with respect to j-th attribute.

The second procedure is to calculate linear preference ratings for input criteria. The linear preference rating is performed in order assign a zero value for the least preferable alternative. This is done through Equation 9:

$$II_i = I_i - \min(I_i) \tag{9}$$

where; II_i refers to aggregate preference rating of the i-th alternative with respect to j-th input attribute.

The third procedure is to compute the preference rating for beneficial attributes. When the alternative's score is high, this indicates a higher preference for this alternative. Preference rating for beneficial attributes is calculated through Equation 10:

$$O_i = \sum_{n=1}^{h} W_j \frac{X_{ij} - \min\left(X_{ij}\right)}{\min\left(X_{ij}\right)} \tag{10}$$

where; h refers to number of beneficial attributes. O_i refers to a measure of relative importance of the i-th alternative for beneficial attribute.

The fourth procedure is to calculate linear preference ratings for output criteria. This is done through Equation 11:

$$OO_i = O_i - \min(O_i) \tag{11}$$

where; OO_i refers to aggregate preference rating of the i-th alternative with respect to j-th output attribute.

The fourth procedure is to calculate overall preference rating. The alternatives with high overall preference ratings constitute high rank. The overall preference rating is calculated by Equation 12:

$$PP_i = II_i + OO_i \tag{12}$$

where; PP_i refers to overall preference rating of the i-th alternative with respect to j-th output attribute.

GROUP DECISION MAKING

Each one of the MCDM methods provides a different ranking for the optimal solutions from the other. Thus, group decision making is applied in order to integrate and aggregate different rankings obtained from the different MCDM methods into one ranking. Group decision making is performed using SAW as shown in Equation 13:

$$RI = \sum_{DM=1}^{G} w_{DM} \times r_{DM} \tag{13}$$

where; RI indicates the ranking index utilized to prioritize the optimal solution, whereas the smaller the index, the better the solution. r_{DM} represents the ranking obtained for each optimal solution from the MCDM. w_{DM} represents the weight of the MCDM, whereas the MCDM method are assumed to be of equal weight.

SPEARMAN'S RANK CORRELATION COEFFICIENT

Spearman's rank correlation coefficient is used to determine the correlation between two rankings (including positive and negative relationships) obtained from two multi-criteria decision-making methods. The value of Spearman's rank correlation coefficient is between -1 and 1. Each range of correlation coefficient indicates the specific nature of correlation. If the range of correlation coefficient values ranges from 0.9 to 1, 0.7 to 0.9, 0.4 to 0.7, 0.2 to 0.4 and less than 0.2, then the corresponding nature of correlation is very high, high, moderate, low and slight, respectively. Spearman's rank correlation can be calculated using Equation 14 (Banerjee and Ghosh, 2013):

$$R = 1 - \frac{6 \times \sum_{i=1}^{m} D_i}{m\left(m^2 - 1\right)} \qquad (14)$$

where; D_i represents different in ranking for the same alternatives and m represents the number of alternatives and R represents spearman's rank correlation coefficient.

RANKING INDEX PREDICTION

Regression and back propagation artificial neural network models are developed in order to be able to forecast the final ranking index. The prediction model is utilized to compare between the clustering algorithms based on their proximity to the standardized amplitude thresholds. Moreover, they can be utilized by the users for the comparison of different amplitude scales based on their calculation methodology.

Regression Model

Regression analysis is a method utilized to build a functional relationship between a set of independent variables and dependent variables. The independent variable is sometimes called "response" while the dependent variable is sometimes called "predictor". The multiple linear regression model is shown in Equation 15 (Tosun et al., 2016):

$$y = \beta_0 + \beta_1 x_1 + \beta_2 x_2 + \beta_3 x_3 \dots \beta_n x_n \qquad (15)$$

where; y represents the dependent variable. $x_1, x_2, x_3, \dots, x_n$ represent the independent variables. β_0 is a constant. $\beta_1, \beta_2, \beta_3, \dots, \beta_n$ are the coefficients, which are computed based on the least square method.

The Poisson regression assumes that the response variable follows a Poisson distribution. The Poisson regression is described in Equation 16 (Nishiyama and Filion, 2013):

$$y = \exp\left(\beta_0 + \beta_1 x_1 + \beta_2 x_2 + \beta_3 x_3 \dots \beta_n x_n\right) \qquad (16)$$

The polynomial regression model can be defined using Equation 17 (Gupta et al., 2011):

$$y = \beta_0 + \beta_1 x_i + \beta_2 x_i^2 + \beta_3 x_i^3 \dots \beta_n x_i^n \qquad (17)$$

Artificial Neural Network

A neural network can be defined as a parallel distributing process between input layer, output layer, and one or more hidden layer that are connected by neurons. Each neuron receives one or more inputs and produces an output through an activation function. The architecture of the back propagation artificial neural network is described in Figure 3 (Nasr et al., 2012; Wang et al., 2015).

Each neuron in the hidden layer receives a signal from all the input layers which is equal to the weighted sum of all neurons entering the neuron and it can be calculated using Equation 18:

$$x_j = \sum_{i=1} I_i \times W_{ij} \tag{18}$$

where; I_i represents the input and W_{ij} represents the weight of the connection between input neurons and hidden layers.

There is a weight for each connection between neurons. The most common transfer or activation function is sigmoid function and it can be calculated using Equation 19:

$$h_j = F\left(x_j\right) = \frac{1}{1 + e^{-x_j}} \tag{19}$$

The neuron in the output layer receives an activation signal from the hidden layer which is presented in Equation 20:

$$y_k = \sum_{i=1} h_j \times W_{jk} \tag{20}$$

where; y_k represents the input of the neuron k in the output layer. W_{jk} represents the weight of the connection between j neuron in the hidden layer and k neuron in the output layer.

The input of the neurons in the output layer should be also transformed using the sigmoid activation function using Equation 21:

$$O_k = F\left(y_k\right) = \frac{1}{1 + e^{-y_k}} \tag{21}$$

The error function at the output neuron should be minimized and it can be calculated using Equation 22:

$$E\left(W\right) = \frac{1}{2} \sum_{k=1} \left(d_k - O_k\right)^2 \tag{22}$$

Based on the gradient descent algorithm, the weights are adjusted during each training epoch (k) based on Equation 23, whereas the error partial derivative is computed during each training epoch and subsequently, as per the error partial derivative and the learning rate, the weights are updated (Yu and Xu, 2014):

$$W_{ij}\left(k+1\right) = W_{ij}\left(k\right) + \Delta W_{ij}\left(k\right) = W_{ij}\left(k\right) - \eta \times \frac{\partial E\left(k\right)}{\partial W_{ij}} \tag{23}$$

where; $\Delta W_{ij}(k)$ represents the adjustment or increment in the weights (weight updates). $W_{ij}(k+1)$ and $W_{ij}(k)$ represent the new (updated) and current (old) weights, respectively. η depicts the learning rate. $\frac{\partial E\left(k\right)}{\partial W_{ij}}$ represents the error partial derivative with respect to the weights.

Figure 3. Architecture of the back propagation artificial neural network

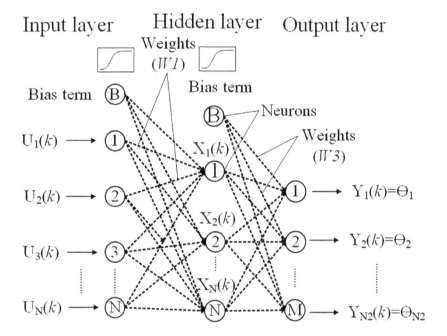

Performance Metrics

The proposed model utilizes three performance metrics to compare between the four prediction models. The three performance indicators are: root-mean squared error (*RMSE*), mean absolute error (*MAE*), and determination coefficient (*R²*). *RMSE*, *MAE*, and *R²* can be calculated using Equations 24, 25, and 26, respectively (Nazari et al., 2015; Ranjith et al., 2013; Maran and Priya, 2015):

$$RMSE = \sqrt{\frac{1}{K}\sum_{i=1}^{K}\left(O_i - P_i\right)^2} \tag{24}$$

$$MAE = \frac{1}{K} \sum_{i=1}^{K} \left| \left(O_i - P_i \right) \right| \tag{25}$$

$$R^2 = 1 - \frac{\sum_{i=1}^{K} \left(O_i - P_i \right)^2}{\sum_{i=1}^{K} \left(O_i - O^- \right)^2} \tag{26}$$

where; O_i indicates the actual ranking index of the amplitude scale. P_i indicates the predicted ranking index of the amplitude scale. K represents the number of observations (bridge decks). O^- represents the average of the actual values.

DETERIORATION MODELING

Deterioration model is one of the main pillars of the BMS because it enables the transportation authorities to predict the future bridge condition ratings. Planning of maintenance, repair and rehabilitation activities of bridges is based on calculating accurate future bridge condition ratings. A high-quality deterioration model enables infrastructure managers to optimize maintenance, repair, and rehabilitation (MR&R) activities and minimize un-planned maintenance activities. The deterioration model constructs a relationship between the facility condition rating and a group of explanatory variables such as age, traffic volume, weather conditions, percentage of commercial vehicles, etc.

The proposed method utilizes stochastic model to model the deterioration process in order to overcome the limitations of the stochastic model. Deterministic models such as artificial neural network and multiple regression, often fail to capture the uncertainty and randomness of the deterioration process, whereas there is no certainty associated with the condition state the bridge element will enter within the next period of time (M. Abdelkader et al. 2019).

Goodness of fit is a statistical measure that is used to determine the compatibility of fitting set of data to probability distributions. Goodness of fit is a means to evaluate different probability density functions and to determine discrepancies between observed values and expected values in a certain statistical model. There are several goodness o fit tests such as Kolmogorov-Smirnov test, Anderson Darling and chi-squared test. The proposed model utilizes Anderson Darling statistic.

Anderson Darling test (A^2) is used to determine the best-fit distribution by comparing the fit of an observed cumulative distribution function to an expected cumulative distribution function. Anderson darling provides more weight to the distributions' tail than the Kolmogorov-Smirnov test. Anderson Darling Statistic can be calculated as follows (Love et al., 2013):

$$A^2 = -n - \frac{1}{n} \sum_{i=1}^{n} \left(2i - 1 \right) \times \left(\ln F \left(x_i \right) + \ln \left(1 - F \left(X_{n-i+1} \right) \right) \right) \tag{27}$$

There are different methods for parameter estimation of probability density function such as maximum likelihood estimation and least squares, method of moments estimation (MME), and median rank regression (MRR). The proposed model utilizes maximum likelihood estimation (MLE) algorithm as a parameter estimation method. MLE is based on finding the parameters that maximizes the likelihood function where the observations are assumed to be independent. The MLE is characterized by being asymptotically efficient where larger the sample size the more likely the parameters converge to precise values.

MLE is based on finding the unknown parameter θ that maximizes the log $L(\theta/y)$ because it is often easier to maximize the log-likelihood function than the likelihood function itself (Nielsen, 2011):

$$\log L\left(\theta \,/\, y\right) = \sum_{i=1}^{n} \log\left(f\left(y_i \mid \theta\right)\right) \tag{28}$$

where; Y_i represents a set of independent variables. $f(y_i|\theta)$ denotes the probability density function of the random variable y_i

The proposed method adopts the weibull distribution in modeling the deterioration process. The shape and scale parameters of the stochastic distributions are computed based on the maximum likelihood estimation algorithm as mentioned before. The condition index at a certain time t is computed based on the derivation of cumulative distribution function (CDF) of the weibull distribution as follows:

$$C\left(t\right) = \left[1 - e^{-\left(\frac{t}{\beta}\right)^{\alpha}}\right] \times a \tag{29}$$

where; $C(t)$ represents the condition index of the bridge element at a certain time t. β and α represent the scale parameter and shape parameter of the weibull distribution, respectively. a represents the initial condition of the bridge deck, which is 100 in the present study.

MODEL IMPLEMENTATION

The proposed methodology is implemented for four bridge decks in North America: three of them are in Quebec, Canada, and one of them is in New Jersey, United States. The four bridges are denoted as bridge "A", bridge "B", bridge "C", and bridge "D". The signals were collected using a GSSI 1.5GHZ antenna. All the calculations and optimization algorithms took place on a 2.6 GHZ Intel laptop. As a result of the differences in the thresholds obtained from the clustering algorithms, the multi-objective optimization module is performed based on the four objective functions defined in the "Research Methodology" section. In order to provide a fair comparison between the optimization algorithms, the population size and number of iterations are assumed the same for all the optimization algorithms. For the shuffled frog leaping algorithm, the number of memeplexes is assumed 25, i.e., 10 frogs per each memeplex. For the genetic algorithm, tournament selection is the parent selection strategy. Two-point crossover is utilized, and the crossover rate is assumed 0.8. Mutation rate is assumed 0.1.

A sample of the optimal solutions obtained from the genetic algorithm is shown in Table 1. A comparison between shuffled frog-leaping algorithm, genetic algorithm, fminsearch search algorithm, and fminunc search algorithm is described in Table 2. Shuffled frog-leaping algorithm achieved the lowest objective function value regarding objective functions 1, 2 and 3 while the fminunc search algorithm had the lowest objective function value regarding objective function 4. The worst objective function values of shuffled frog-leaping algorithm are better than the genetic algorithm for objective functions 1, 2 and 3. On the other hand, genetic algorithm achieves the best worst objective function value for objective function 4. The optimization algorithms are compared in terms of the mean and standard deviation. A lower standard deviation indicates higher stability of the algorithm while a higher mean value indicates more accuracy of the optimization algorithm. The mean values of the SFL algorithm are better than the genetic algorithm regarding the first three objective functions while GA achieved the best mean value for the fourth objective function SFL achieves the lowest standard deviations for the four objective functions.

Table 1. Sample of the optimal solutions of the genetic algorithm

Optimal Solutions (Decibels)	Objective Function "1"	Objective Function "2"	Objective Function "3"	Objective Function "4"
[-29.279, -8.598, -3.522]	69.712	1.472	2.921	0.886
[-35.554, -8.861 -3.544]	104.65	0.004	3.044	0.344
[-29.145, -8.676, -5.536]	68.967	1.036	47.514	0.963
[-39.656, -9.819, -2.304]	127.489	5.330	3.859	0.132
[-39.474, -10.043, -2.75]	109.772	6.574	1.376	0.328
[-35.558, -9.872, -2.723]	126.539	5.623	1.528	0.141
[-28.522, -8.861, -3.536]	104.671	0.005	3	0.344
[-35.565, -9.093, 5.843]	65.499	1.288	49.226	1.13

GA has the lowest coefficient of variation for the first objective function while SFL algorithm has the lowest coefficient of variation for the remaining three objective functions. SFL algorithm has the largest hypervolume (84.87%) while genetic algorithm achieves the lowest hypervolume (50.58%). In terms of the inverted generational distance, the SFL algorithm has the least inverted generational distance (0.0034) while genetic algorithm achieves the highest inverted generational distance (0.011). Thus, the meta-heuristic algorithms significantly provides better performance when compared to the non-linear programming methods, which illustrates that exact optimization methods fail to find the global optimum solutions in case of complex and large search space problems. Moreover, the SFL algorithm outperformed the genetic algorithm as per the comparison conducted.

The MCDM methods are used to select the best solution among the optimal solutions. The four attributes are the objective functions of the multi-objective optimization model. The weights of the attributes are computed via Shannon entropy method (see Table 3). The weights of the four attributes are 28.159%, 23.192%, 44.907%, and 3.741%, respectively. A sample of the solution ranking obtained from the WPM method is described in Table 4. Each one of the decision-making methods provides a distinct ranking for the solutions. For instance, WPM method selects the solution [-16.711, - 8.727 -2.997] as the best solution. On the other hand, M-TOPSIS selects the solution [-16.761, -8.816, -2.974] as the best solution. Thus, group decision-making is performed to aggregate the rankings obtained from the several MCDM methods based on SAW method. The best solution based on the SAW method is [-16.761, -8.816, -2.974]. A corrosion map is developed for a bridge that is located on the Chemin Saint-Grégoire in municipality Les Cèdres that overpasses Autoroute 20, Quebec, Canada. As shown in Figure 4, the area percentages of the "good", "medium", "severe", and "very severe" categories are 45.78%, 34.26%, 12.98%, and 6.98%, respectively. The corrosion index is 77.6% which indicates that the bridge deck is in the "medium" category.

Table 2. Comparison between shuffled frog-leaping, genetic algorithm, fminsearch search algorithm, and fminunc search algorithm

Index	Objective Function	Shuffled Frog-Leaping	Genetic Algorithm	fminsearch Search Algorithm	fminunc Search Algorithm
Minimum	Objective function "1"	**0.0187**	65.4994	5.105	132.052
	Objective function "2"	**0.0282**	0.0044	45.253	76.521
	Objective function "3"	**0.0019**	1.3756	0.002	130.694
	Objective function "4"	1.5998	0.1321	1.698	**-0.052**
Maximum	Objective function "1"	**0.6957**	127.4886	....	....
	Objective function "2"	**0.7561**	10.9924	....	....
	Objective function "3"	**0.8545**	49.2263	....	....
	Objective function "4"	1.6018	**1.5843**	....	....
Mean	Objective function "1"	**0.2598**	89.1582	....	....
	Objective function "2"	**0.3177**	3.2343	....	....
	Objective function "3"	**0.3259**	12.3022	....	....
	Objective function "4"	1.6006	**0.6197**	....	....
Standard deviation	Objective function "1"	**0.196**	34.197	....	....
	Objective function "2"	**0.2312**	3.5267	....	....
	Objective function "3"	**0.2755**	18.1101	....	....
	Objective function "4"	**0.0008**	0.4647	....	....
Coefficient of variation	Objective function "1"	0.7546	**0.3836**	....	....
	Objective function "2"	**0.7280**	1.0904	....	....
	Objective function "3"	**0.8453**	1.4721	....	....
	Objective function "4"	**0.0005**	0.7498	....	....
Hypervolume indicator (HV)	....	**84.87%**	50.58%	....	....
Inverted generational distance (IGD)	....	**0.0034**	0.0037	....	....

A correlation matrix is constructed in order to measure the correlation between each two multi-criteria decision-making methods. The correlation matrix is obtained based upon Spearman's rank correlation coefficient. The Correlation matrix is depicted in Table 5. The maximum five spearman's rank correlation coefficients are between (M-TOPSIS, COPRAS), (M-TOPSIS, MOORA), (COPRAS, MOORA), (WSM, OCRA) and (WSM, WPM). The minimum five spearman's rank correlation coefficients are between (WPM, MOORA), (WPM, M-TOPSIS), (WPM, COPRAS), (WSM, COPRAS) and (WSM,

M-TOPSIS). WPM provides a very different raking from the other MCDM methods. On the other hand, M-TOPSIS provides the highest average correlation with other MCDM methods. The correlation coefficients of WSM, WPM, M-TOPSIS, COPRAS, OCRA and MOORA with the final ranking of alternatives are 91.7%, 85.672%, 95.158%, 94.565%, 94.071% and 93.577%. Therefore, M-TOPSIS is the MCDM method which provided the closest ranking to the final ranking of the optimal solution. Thus, M-TOPSIS is the best MCDM method.

Table 3. Entropy values, variation coefficients, and the weights of the attributes

Index	$RMSE_1$	$RMSE_2$	$RMSE_3$	CLU
Entropy value (e_j)	0.622	0.688	0.397	0.95
variation coefficient (d_j)	0.378	0.312	0.603	0.05
weights of the attribute (w_j)	28.159%	23.192%	44.907%	3.741%

Table 4. Sample of the solutions' ranking obtained from WPM method

Solution (Decibels)	Optimization Algorithm	P_i	Solution Ranking
[-16.711, - 8.727 -2.997]	SFL	0.4125	1
[-16.761, - 8.833, -2.974]	SFL	1.0468	2
[-16.81, - 8.726, -2.993]	SFL	1.3386	3
[-16.766, - 8.867, -2.844]	SFL	1.8411	4
[-16.663, - 8.767, -2.988]	SFL	2.0562	5
[-16.75, - 8.882, -2.877]	SFL	2.2865	6
[-16.729, - 8.816, -2.974]	SFL	2.8316	7
[-16.663, - 8.767, -2.988]	SFL	2.8428	8

Figure 4. Corrosion map for bridge deck "A"

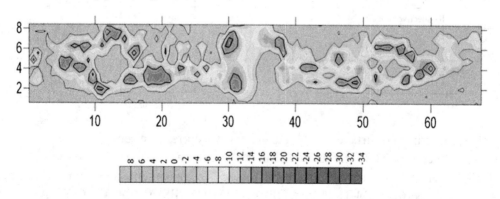

Good	Medium	Severe	Very severe
45.78%	34.26%	12.98%	6.98%

Table 5. Correlation matrix between each two MCDM methods

MCDM Method	WSM	WPM	M-TOPSIS	COPRAS	OCRA	MOORA
WSM	1	89.081%	80.534%	78.854%	89.723%	83.597%
WPM	89.081%	1	76.136%	77.322%	86.117%	73.073%
M-TOPSIS	80.534%	76.136%	1	99.11%	88.340%	95.455%
COPRAS	78.854%	77.322%	99.111%	1	88.043%	94.368%
OCRA	89.723%	86.117%	88.340%	88.043%	1	85.079%
MOORA	83.597%	73.073%	95.455%	94.368%	85.079%	1

Three regression models and feed forward back propagation artificial neural network models are developed to forecast the final ranking index. For the artificial neural network, the number of hidden layers, number of hidden neurons and momentum coefficient are assumed 1, 5 and 0.001, respectively. The topography of the developed neural network is depicted in Figure 5. A comparison between the linear regression model, Poisson regression, polynomial regression and artificial neural network model is shown in Table 6. The independent variables X_1, X_2 and X_3 represent the amplitude threshold (1), amplitude threshold (2) and amplitude threshold (3), respectively. As shown in Table 6, the artificial neural network model outperformed the regression models, whereas the *RMSE, MAE,* and R^2 are equal to 1.218, 1.483 and 96.279%, respectively. Poisson regression provides the least performance, whereas *RMSE, MAE,* and R^2 are equal to 3.295, 2.772 and 81.871%, respectively. Polynomial regression has the best performance among the regression models, whereas *RMSE, MAE,* and R^2 are equal to 2.17, 1.663 and 92.102%, respectively.

Figure 5. Topography of the developed artificial neural network model

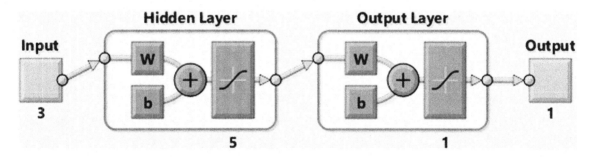

Table 6. Comparison between several ranking index prediction models

Model	Equation	RMSE	MAE	R²
Linear regression	$y = -34.4 - 0.4872X_1 - 4.31X_2 + 1.54X_3$	2.818	2.247	86.565%
Poisson regression	$y = \exp(1.114 - 0.0375X_1 - 0.31112X_2 + 0.09937X_3)$	3.295	2.772	81.871%
Polynomial regression	$y = 604 - 0.6087X_1 + 129.6X_2 + 1.495X_3 + 6.94X_2^2$	2.17	1.663	92.102%
Artificial neural network	.....	1.218	1.483	96.279%

The ranking index prediction model can be used as a comparison tool to select the best clustering algorithm. The best performing clustering algorithm is the one which has the smallest ranking index. The clustering algorithms are compared on the basis of the coefficient of variation because it considers both the quality and stability of the solutions. The smaller the coefficient of variation, the better is the clustering algorithm (compact and well-separated clusters). The best three clustering algorithms are fuzzy C-means clustering algorithm followed by kernel K-means clustering algorithm and finally the K-medoids clustering algorithm. The coefficients of variation of fuzzy C-means algorithm, kernel K-means algorithm and K-medoids are 89.93%, 95.344% and 98.702%, respectively. Based on the Anderson Darling test, weibull distribution is the best-fit distribution followed by the lognormal distribution, and finally the exponential distribution, whereas the Anderson Darling statistics of the previous distributions are: 2.308, 2.359, and 2.463, respectively. The parameters of the weibull distributions are obtained based on the maximum likelihood estimation, whereas the shape factor and scale factor are 1.68, and 62.73, respectively. The deterioration model based on the weibull distribution is shown in Figure 6.

Figure 6. Deterioration model based on Weibull distribution

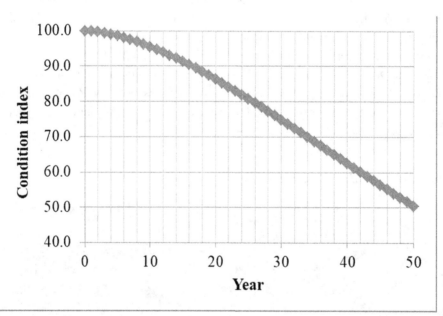

CONCLUSION

Ground penetrating radar is a non-destructive technique utilized to evaluate the corrosion in concrete structure. Nevertheless, the absence of standardized amplitude thresholds represents a major limitation. A multi-objective optimization model is designed to compute the optimal thresholds based on a combination of meta-heuristic and exact optimization algorithms. The proposed method employs shuffled frog leaping algorithm, genetic algorithm, fminsearch search algorithm, and fminunc search algorithm to search for the optimum thresholds. Six MCDM methods are utilized to compute the optimum solution, which are: WSM, WPM, COPRAS, M-TOPSIS, OCRA and MOORA. Then, group decision making is performed based on SAW to aggregate the results obtained from the MCDM methods.

A correlation matrix is constructed in order to measure the correlation between each two MCDM methods based upon Spearman's rank correlation coefficient. WPM provides the lowest average correlation with other MCDM methods while M-TOPSIS has the highest average correlation with other MCDM methods. A further analysis is conducted to measure the correlation of the six MCDM methods with the group decision making ranking. Based on this comparison, M-TOPSIS provides the most consensus ranking among the six MCDM methods. Three regression and feed forward back propagation neural network models are developed to build a relationship between the threshold values and the final ranking index. The artificial neural network provided the best performance whereas the *RMSE, MAE,* and R^2 are equal to 1.218, 1.483 and 96.279%, respectively. On the other hand, Poisson regression had the least performance, whereas *RMSE, MAE,* and R^2 are equal to 3.295, 2.772 and 81.871%, respectively. The prediction model is used to conduct a comparison between the clustering algorithms based on the coefficient of variation. Fuzzy C-means algorithm achieved the lowest coefficient of variation followed by kernel K-means algorithm, and finally K-medoids algorithm. Finally, a deterioration model is constructed based on the weibull distribution to model the deterioration process of the concrete bridge decks.

ACKNOWLEDGMENT

This project was funded by the Academy of Scientific Research and Technology (ASRT), Egypt, JESOR-Development Program - Project ID: 40.

REFERENCES

Abd Elkhalek, H., Hafez, S. M., & Elfahham, Y. M. (2016). Budget Optimization for Maintenance of Bridges in Egypt. *International Journal of Economics and Management Engineering, 10*(1), 339–347.

M. Abdelkader, E., Zayed, T., & Marzouk, M. (2019). Modelling the Deterioration of Bridge Decks Based on Semi-Markov Decision Process. International Journal of Strategic Decision Sciences, 10(1), 1-23. doi:10.4018/IJSDS.2019010103

Akyene, T. (2012). Cell Phone Evaluation Base on Entropy and TOPSIS. *Interdisciplinary Journal of Research In Business, 1*(12), 9–15.

Alani, A. M., Aboutalebi, M., & Kilic, G. (2013). Applications of Ground Penetrating Radar (GPR) in Bridge Deck Monitoring and Assessment. *Journal of Applied Geophysics, 97,* 45–54. doi:10.1016/j.jappgeo.2013.04.009

Alsharqawi, M., Dabous, S. A., & Zayed, T. (2016). Quality Function Deployment Based Method for Condition Assessment of Concrete Bridges. In *95th Annual Meeting of the Transportation Research Board,* Washington, DC, January 10-14.

American Society of Civil Engineers. (2017). *America's Infrastructure Report Card.* Retrieved from http://www.infrastructurereportcard.org/

Amiri, M. J. T., Abdollahzadeh, G., & Haghighi, F. (2019). Bridges Risk Analysis in View of Repair and Maintenance by Multi Criteria Decision Making Method (Case Study: Babolsar Bridges). *International Journal of Transportation Engineering*, 7(1).

Banerjee, R., & Ghosh, D. (2013). Faculty Recruitment in Engineering Organization Through Fuzzy Multi-Criteria Group Decision Making Methods. *International Journal of u-and -Service Science and Technology*, 6, 139–154.

Bukhsh, Z. A., Oslakovic, I. S., Klanker, G., Hoj, N. P., Imam, B., & Xenidis, Y. (2017). Multi-criteria decision making: AHP method applied for network bridge prioritization. In *Joint COST TU1402–COST TU1406–IABSE WC1 Workshop: The value of Structural Health Monitoring for the reliable Bridge Management.*

Chakraborty, R., Ray, A., & Dan, P. K. (2013). Multi criteria decision making methods for location selection of distribution centers. *International Journal of Industrial Engineering Computations*, 4(4), 491–504. doi:10.5267/j.ijiec.2013.06.006

Contreras-Nieto, C., Lewis, P., & Shan, Y. (2016). Developing Predictive Models of Superstructure Ratings for Steel and Prestressed Concrete Bridges. In *Construction Research Congress 2016*, San Juan, Puerto Rico, May 31-June 2. 10.1061/9780784479827.087

Dragisa, S., Bojan, D., & Mira, D. (2013). Comparative Analysis of Some Prominent MCDM Methods: A case of Ranking Serbian banks. *Serbian Journal of Management*, 8(2), 213–241. doi:10.5937jm8-3774

Farzam, A., Nollet, M.-J., & Khaled, A. (2016). Integration of site conditions information using geographic information system for the seismic evaluation of bridges. In *Canadian Society of Civil Engineering Annual Conference: Resilient Infrastructure*, London, Canada, June 1-4.

Felio, G. (2016). *"Canadian Infrastructure Report Card"*. Canadian Construction Association, Canadian Public Works Association, Canadian Society for Civil Engineering, and Federation of Canadian Municipalities, Canada. Retrieved from www.canadainfrastructure.ca/downloads/Canadian_Infrastructure_Report_2016.pdf

Gao, Z. K., Patnaik, A., & Liang, R. (2016). VIKOR method for ranking concrete bridge repair projects with target-based criteria. In *Corrosion Risk Management Conference*.

Gupta, B. B., Joshi, R. C., & Misra, M. (2011). Prediction of Number of Zombies in a DDoS Attack using Polynomial Regression Model. *Journal Of Advances In Information Technology*, 2(1), 57–62. doi:10.4304/jait.2.1.57-62

Hussein, A., & AbuTair, A. (2019). Estimating Bridge Deterioration Age Using Artificial Neural Networks. *IACSIT International Journal of Engineering and Technology*, 11(1), 29–32.

Kolios, A., Mytilinou, V., Lozano-minguez, E., & Salonitis, K. (2016). A Comparative Study of Multiple-Criteria Decision-Making Methods under Stochastic Inputs. *Energies*, 9(7), 566. doi:10.3390/en9070566

Love, P. E. D., Wang, X., Sing, C., & Tiong, R. L. K. (2013). Determining the Probability of Cost Overruns. *Journal of Construction Engineering and Management*, 139(3), 321–330. doi:10.1061/(ASCE)CO.1943-7862.0000575

Lu, P., Pei, S., & Tolliver, D. (2016). Regression Model Evaluation for Highway Bridge Component Deterioration Using National Bridge Inventory Data. *Journal of the Transportation Research Forum, 55*(1), 5–16.

Maran, J. P., & Priya, B. (2015). Ultrasonics Sonochemistry Comparison of response surface methodology and artificial neural network approach towards efficient ultrasound-assisted biodiesel production from muskmelon oil. *Ultrasonics Sonochemistry, 23,* 192–200. doi:10.1016/j.ultsonch.2014.10.019 PMID:25457517

Mehta, S., & Jain, M. (2015). Comparative Analysis of Different Fractional PID Tuning Methods for the First Order System. In *2015 International Conference on Futuristic Trends on Computational Analysis and Knowledge Management*, Greater Noida, India, February 25-27. 10.1109/ABLAZE.2015.7154942

Mulliner, E., Smallbone, K., & Maliene, V. (2013). An assessment of sustainable housing affordability using a multiple criteria decision making method. *Omega, 41*(2), 270–279. doi:10.1016/j.omega.2012.05.002

Muñoz, Y.F., Paz, A., Fuente-Mella, H.D. La, V., Fariña, J., and Sales, G. (2016). Estimating Bridge Deterioration for Small Data Sets using Regression and Markov Models. *International Journal of urban and Civil Engineering, 10*(5).

Nasr, M. S., Moustafa, M. A. E., Seif, H. A. E., & El Kobrosy, G. (2012). Application of Artificial Neural Network (ANN) for the prediction of EL-AGAMY wastewater treatment. *Alexandria Engineering Journal, 51*(1), 37–43. doi:10.1016/j.aej.2012.07.005

Nazari, A., Rajeev, P., & Sanjayan, J. G. (2015). Offshore pipeline performance evaluation by different artificial neural networks approaches. *Measurement, 76,* 117–128. doi:10.1016/j.measurement.2015.08.035

Nielsen, M. A. (2011). Parameter estimation for the two-parameter weibull distribution [M.Sc. thesis]. Brigham Young University, United States of America.

Nishiyama, M., & Filion, Y. (2013). Review of statistical water main break prediction models. *Canadian Journal of Civil Engineering, 40*(10), 972–979. doi:10.1139/cjce-2012-0424

Qiao, Y., Moomen, M., Zhang, Z., Agbelie, B., Labi, S., & Sinha, K. C. (2016). Modeling Deterioration of Bridge Components with Binary Probit Techniques with Random Effects. *Transportation Research Record: Journal of the Transportation Research Board, 2550*(1), 96–105. doi:10.3141/2550-13

Ranjith, S., Setunge, S., Gravina, R., & Venkatesan, S. (2013). Deterioration Prediction of Timber Bridge Elements Using the Markov Chain. *Journal of Performance of Constructed Facilities, 27*(3), 319–325. doi:10.1061/(ASCE)CF.1943-5509.0000311

Shim, H. S., & Lee, S. H. (2016). Balanced Allocation of Bridge Deck Maintenance Budget Through. *KSCE Journal of Civil Engineering*.

Srinivas, V., Sasmal, S., & Karusala, R. (2016). Fuzzy Based Decision Support System for Condition Assessment and Rating of Bridges. *Journal of The Institution of Engineers (India): Series A, 97*(3), 261-272,

Tajadod, M., Abedini, M., Rategari, A., & Mobin, M. (2016). A Comparison of Multi-Criteria Decision Making Approaches for Maintenance Strategy Selection. *International Journal of Strategic Decision Sciences, 7*(3), 51–69. doi:10.4018/IJSDS.2016070103

Tosun, E., Aydin, K., & Bilgili, M. (2016). Comparison of linear regression and artificial neural network model of a diesel engine fueled with biodiesel-alcohol mixtures. *Alexandria Engineering Journal*, *55*(4), 3081–3089. doi:10.1016/j.aej.2016.08.011

Valença, J., Puente, I., Júlio, E., González-Jorge, H., & Arias-sánchez, P. (2017). Assessment of cracks on concrete bridges using image processing supported by laser scanning survey. *Construction & Building Materials*, *146*, 668–678. doi:10.1016/j.conbuildmat.2017.04.096

Venkatesan, T., & Sanavullah, M. Y. (2013). Electrical Power and Energy Systems SFLA Approach to Solve PBUC problem with Emission Limitation. *Electrical Power and Energy Systems*, *46*, 1–9. doi:10.1016/j.ijepes.2012.09.006

Wang, L., Zeng, Y., & Chen, T. (2015). Back propagation neural network with adaptive differential evolution algorithm for time series forecasting. *Expert Systems with Applications*, *42*(2), 855–863. doi:10.1016/j.eswa.2014.08.018

Yu, F., & Xu, X. (2014). A Short-term Load Forecasting Model of Natural Gas Based on Optimized Genetic Algorithm and Improved BP Neural Network. *Applied Energy*, *134*, 102–113. doi:10.1016/j.apenergy.2014.07.104

Zambon, I., Vidovic, A., Strauss, A., Matos, J., & Amado, J. (2017). Comparison of stochastic prediction models based on visual inspections of bridge decks. *Journal of Civil Engineering and Management*, *23*(5), 553–561. doi:10.3846/13923730.2017.1323795

This research was previously published in the International Journal of Strategic Decision Sciences (IJSDS), 10(2); pages 84-106, copyright year 2019 by IGI Publishing (an imprint of IGI Global).

Chapter 50
Prediction of Water Level Using Time Series, Wavelet and Neural Network Approaches

Nguyen Quang Dat
https://orcid.org/0000-0001-5988-3651
Hanoi University of Science and Technology, Hanoi, Vietnam

Ngoc Anh Nguyen Thi
https://orcid.org/0000-0002-6555-9740
Hanoi University of Science and Technology, Hanoi, Vietnam

Vijender Kumar Solanki
https://orcid.org/0000-0001-5784-1052
CMR institute of Technology (Autonomous), Hyderabad, India

Ngo Le An
https://orcid.org/0000-0002-6527-4745
Thuyloi University, Hanoi, Vietnam

ABSTRACT

To control water resources in many domains such as agriculture, flood forecasting, and hydro-electrical dams, forecasting water level needs to predict. In this article, a new computational approach using a data driven model and time series is proposed to calculate the forecast water level in short time. Concretely, wavelet-artificial neural network (WAANN) and time series (TS) are combined together called WAANN-TS that encourages the advantage of each model. For this real time project work, Yen Bai station, Northwest Vietnam was chosen as an experimental case study to apply the proposed model. Input variables into the Wavelet-ANN structure is water level data. Time series and ANN models are built, and their performances are compared. The results indicate the greater accuracy of the proposed models at Hanoi station. The final proposal WAANN–TS for water level forecasting shows good performance with root mean square error (RMSE) from 10−10 to 10−11.

DOI: 10.4018/978-1-6684-2408-7.ch050

1. INTRODUCTION

Time series forecasting is the importance of prediction in various research projects such as individual, natural, social, technological, organizational, economical strategic decision under uncertainty environments. For example, forecasting financial data suggests investors to invest safely in the uncertainty financial market (Panigrahi & Behera, 2017); forecasting electricity load (Raza & Khosravi, 2015; Behera & Biswal, 2010), helps in better power system planning (Panigrahi & Behera, 2017); forecasting product price helps consumers having better choices; forecasting water level help decision maker better in control irrigation system; forecasting temperature helps planner predicting crop yields (Nury, Hasan, & Alam, 2017). Therefore, many researchers are interested in time series forecasting research because of various applications (Raza & Khosravi, 2015; Behera & Biswal, 2010; Panigrahi & Behera, 2017; Nury, Hasan, & Alam, 2017).

Time series forecasting techniques have been proposed in the literature in which past observations of the same variable are collected and analyzed to develop a model describing the underlying relationship (Zhang, 2003). The form a time series is represented by a vector $X_t = \left[x_{t-1}, x_{t-2}, \ldots, x_{t-n} \right]^T$ where the number of time $t - 1$, $t - 2$, …, $t - n$ series used in forecasting and x x may be multivariate or univariate. Time series forecasting techniques are classified into two types that are linear or nonlinear. Specifically, a type of linear models is often used moving average (MA), autoregressive moving average (ARMA), autoregressive integrated moving average (ARIMA) and a type of nonlinear model is often used the artificial neural network (ANN).

G.P. Zhang was the first author proposed hybrid ARIMA and ANN for time series forecasting (Zhang, 2003). His hybrid methodology took advantage of the unique strength of ARIMA and ANN models in linear and non-linear modeling. If $\{x_t\}_{t \geq 0}$ is a time series to be composed of linear and non-linear components that are represented by

$$x_t = Linear\ Component_t + NonLinearComponent_t \tag{1}$$

In the fact that ARIMA is used for the linear component and ANN is applied for nonlinear components. His experimental results showed that his hybrid methodology is more accuracy achieved than individual models. He suggested that by using dissimilar models or models that disagree like ARIMA and ANN make his hybrid methodology more strongly. However, his methodology has not shown the stationary property for non-linear component. Thus, this paper, the stationary of each component is then it is decided using ANN or WAANN.

S. Panigrahi and H. S. Behera proposed a hybrid model for time series forecasting by linear and nonlinear exponential smoothing (ETS) (Panigrahi & Behera, 2017). The time series is assumed that the sum of two components which are linear and nonlinear components.

Their hybrid algorithm is produced by 4 processes:

1. Computing ETS from original time series;
2. Subtracting ETS from original series to have the residual error sequence;
3. ANN is applied for the residual error sequence;
4. Combining ETS predictions with ANN predictions.

Their experimental results described their proposed model are effective than (Hyndman & Khandakar, 2008), (Babu & Reddy, 2014), and (Zhang, 2003) in some data sets. They also showed that no model was best for all cases. They concluded that hybrid models often have better performance than individual models in most of the cases (Table 1).

Concretely, methodologies are used in prediction problems are survey in (Table 1).

Table 1. Methods

Methods	Pros	Cons	Pubs
ANN	−Not require a priori knowledge of the process. − Effective with nonlinear data. − Able for long–term forecasting.	−Limitations with non–stationary data. − Results depend on the architect of the network. − Black box in solving.	(Adamowski & Chan, 2011)
ARIMA	− Accurately. − Quickly predicted. − Range of inputs.	− Requirement of a large number of input parameters, assume the data is linear and stationary. − Short–term forecasting.	(Adamowski & Chan, 2011)
Discrete wavelet transform	− Non–stationary signal analysis. − Capable of deconstructing complex signals into basis signals of finite band with, and then reconstructing them again with very little loss of information. − Not using a kernel is that you are not biasing the shape of your signal to be similar to an arbitrary, pre−selected shape.	− Greater complexity. The theory is more. − Difficult to understand. − The flexibility of DWTs is a two−edged sword – it is sometimes very difficult to choose which basis to use. − It is more difficult to interpret the results.	(Adamowski & Chan, 2011)

The ANN is one of the machine learning models, that is data–driven model. This model can combine time series to reduce error.

In "*A moving−average filter-based hybrid ARIMA–ANN model for forecasting time series data*", the model used an MA filter to decompose given data into a linear and nonlinear component. The Jarque-Bera normality test was performed and the kurtosis of the random variable was compared with 3. If the kurtosis value of the data was 3, which means the data was low – volatility, then ARIMA model was suitable. Sequences which did not have the kurtosis value of the data 3 were high volatility and is modeled by an ANN. The decomposition made more accuracy of individual models, respectively, the total model error will be small. The proposed model was applied for time series data of various kinds (sunspot, electricity, stock market). The comparison of prediction accuracy was the mean absolute error and mean squared error. The predictions were performed by both one– step– ahead and multistep ahead (Table 2).

In (Panigrahi & Behera, 2017), the ETS model captures linear and nonlinear components with input data (train 60%, validation 20%). Then the residual series (original series − the first prediction) were applied by the ANN model. The final prediction combined two ETS prediction and ANN prediction. To evaluate forecast the accuracy, root mean square error and symmetric mean absolute percentage error were considered. Five models compared with the proposed model were ETS, ARIMA, MLP, Zhang's hybrid ARIMA – ANN model (Zhang, 2003) and Babu and Reddy's hybrid ARIMA – ANN model (Babu & Reddy, 2014). The models were tested on one step ahead prediction for sixteen time series data. No model is the best for all data sets but the proposed model achieved the highest rank among all the models.

Table 2. The objective prediction, methodology, and case studies in water level prediction using artificial intelligent models.

Prediction	Objective problem	Methodology	Case studies	Pubs
Prediction of groundwater level	Comparative performances of SVM, ANN, and LRM	Linear regression model, support vector model, ANN	Prediction of groundwater level in India	(Mukherjee & Ramachandran, 2018)
Prediction of the change of the average temperature	Comparative study of Wavelet–ARIMA and Wavelet–ANN model	coupled wavelet and ANN, coupled wavelet and ARIMA	Temperature in northeastern Bangladesh	(Nury, Hasan, & Alam, 2017)
A hybrid error trend season ETS–ANN for time series forecasting	Comparative performances 5 models (2 single models and 3 hybrid model)	Proposed model by combing ETS and ANN	Testing 16 data sets in multi fields	(Panigrahi & Behera, 2017)
A moving average filter for forecasting time data before applying hybrid ARIMA–ANN model	Comparative performances 4 models (2 single models and 2 hybrid model)	Proposed model by combing ARIMA and ANN	Testing sunspot data, electricity data and stock market data	(Babu & Reddy, 2014)

The main objective of this paper is to develop models for forecasting the next 2, 6, 12, and 24 hours water level in Hanoi station. Concretely, (i) hybrid model using techniques of feed forward back propagation supervised learning of ANN, ARIMA and wavelet analysis are developed, and results are compared (Figure 1); (ii) compare the results and trends of actual and predicted values; (iii) To evaluate the performance of the models by calculating mean square error (MSE) and mean average deviation (MAD) and compare their values; (iv) To apply new hybrid into a case study and compare the results and trends between the traditional hybrid and new hybrid approach for forecasting water level in Vietnam.

Figure 1. The new hybrid model combining WAANN and time series

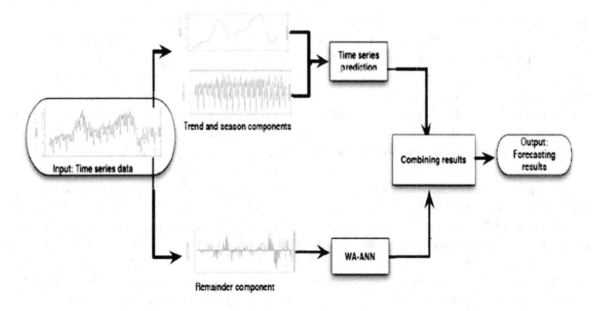

The paper is structured into four sections. The introduction and related work of water level forecasting Section 1. The methodology about the WA–ANN, time series and a proposed hybrid model is shown in Section 2. Section 3 presents the experiments and results are applied in Wavelet – Artificial Neural Network, Time series and our new proposed model. Finally, Section 4 concludes the paper, discusses the advantage and the disadvantage of our proposed model and proposes some future works.

2. METHODOLOGY

2.1. Wavelet Analysis (WA)

Wavelet analysis is a mathematical procedure that transforms the original signal (especially in the time domain) into a different domain for analysis and processing. Wavelet transforms divide into three classes: continuous wavelet transform, discrete wavelet transform, and multiresolution-based.

$$W_{(a,b)} = \int_{-\infty}^{+\infty} f(t) \frac{1}{\sqrt{|a|}} \Psi\left(\frac{t-b}{a}\right) dt = \int_{-\infty}^{+\infty} f(t) \Psi_{a,b}(t) dt \tag{2}$$

with

$$\Psi_{a,b}(t) = \frac{1}{\sqrt{|a|}} \Psi\left(\frac{t-b}{a}\right) \tag{3}$$

In this:

- The parameter 'a' – the scaling parameter. The parameter 'a' measures the degree of compression. While $|a|>1$, the wavelet is the version of extension from the original wavelet. While $0<|a|<1$, the wavelet is the version of compression.
- The parameter 'b' – the translation parameter. Parameter 'b' determines the time location of the wavelet.

It is computationally impossible to analyze a signal using all wavelet coefficients. It's so complex work. So that, can pick a discrete subset of the set from all parameter, to be able to reconstruct a signal from the corresponding wavelet coefficients. In this case, can choose the discrete subset of all the points $(a_m, b=na_m)$ with $m,n ∈ Z$.

The discrete wavelet transform (DWT) use a multiresolution pyramidal decomposition technique. The researcher uses a high-pass filter and a low-pass filter, divide the digitized time signal $S(n)$ into two parts: a detailed signal $D_1(n)$ and smoothed signal $A_1(n)$. Low frequency is viewed as representative for mean values and high frequency is viewed as representative for variation. This decomposition is repeated to further increase the frequency resolution and the approximation coefficients decomposed with high and low pass filters (like the binary tree). And that, can get a set of detailed signals $(D_1(n), D_2(n), ...)$ and $(A_1(n), A_2(n), ...)$.

The discrete wavelet transform is so easy to run and reduces the required computation time and resources. The decomposition can be run in the data set $\{Y_m\}$. In our discrete subset, the scale parameter '*a*' will be equal 2^m and the translation parameter *b* is equal to$n2^m$ $(m, n\hat{I}Z)$. The discrete wavelet function has the flowing form:

$$\Psi_{m,n}(t) = 2^{\frac{m}{2}} \Psi\left(\frac{t - n2^m}{2^m}\right) \qquad (4)$$

2.2. Artificial Neutral Network (ANN)

The predictive model is the most widely used model form for time series modeling and forecasting, in fact, it performs a nonlinear functional mapping from the past observations $(y_{t-1}, y_{t-2}, ..., y_{t-p})$ to the predictive value y_t:

$$y_t = f\left(y_{t-1}, y_{t-2}, ..., y_{t-p}, \omega\right) \qquad (5)$$

where ω is the vector parameters, *f* is a determined function (by the network structure and all parameters from the model).

An ANN is based on a collection of connected units or nodes called artificial neurons (a simplified version of biological neurons in an animal brain). Each connection (a simplified version of a synapse) between artificial neurons can transmit a signal from one to another. The artificial neuron that receives the signal can process it and then signal artificial neurons connected to it. A neural network can be used to predict future values of possibly noisy multivariate time-series based on past histories and can be described as a network of simple processing nodes or neurons that are interconnected to each other in a specific order to perform simple numerical manipulations.

Single hidden layer feed-forward network model used most widely for forecasting. The model is characterized by a network of three layers of simple processing units connected by acyclic links. Can get the output (y_t) from the inputs $(y_{t-1}, y_{t-2}, ..., y_{t-p})$ with the mathematical expression:

$$y_t = \alpha_0 + \sum_{j=1}^{q} \alpha_j g\left(\beta_{0,j} + \sum_{i=1}^{p} \beta_{i,j} y_{t-i}\right) + \varepsilon_t \qquad (6)$$

where $\alpha_j (j = 0, 1, ..., q)$ and $\beta_{i,j}$ $(i = 0, 1, ..., p; j = 0, 1, ..., q)$ are the model parameters, called the connection weights, *p* is the number of input nodes, *q* is the number of hidden nodes. The logistic function uses as the hidden layer transfer function $g(x)$, this can be a certain function. The choice of this function depends on the model that you chose. In this paper, the researcher chose the expression Ψ from WA (Figure 2).

Figure 2. Input variables

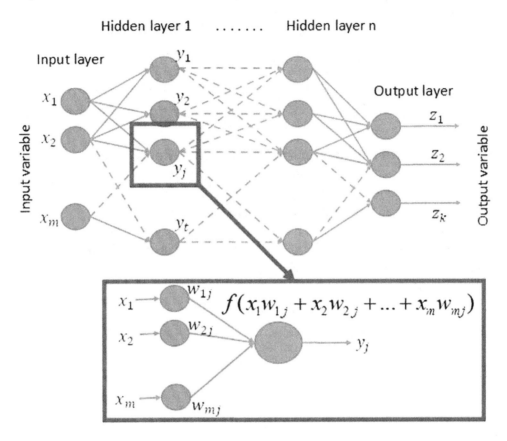

ANN model in (5) can give us the future value y_i from the past observations $(y_{t-1}, y_{t-2}, ..., y_{t-p})$. With the Expression (4), can see that, the neural network model and the nonlinear autoregressive model are equivalent. Thus, one output node in the output layer of Expression (5) can use for one– step– ahead forecasting.

In the representational Expression (5), if q (the number of hidden nodes) is sufficiently large, the result is so best. This expression is able to approximate an arbitrary function. But, with a small number of hidden nodes often works well in forecasting. Depending on the data, can choose a value q, and there is no systematic rule for the choice of this parameter.

Another important task of ANN is the choice of the parameter p, the number of lagged observations. This is the dimension of the input vector. Because there are no rules that can be help the selection of the value of p, experiments are often conducted. And with that, the researcher can select an appropriate p.

After the choice of two parameter p and q, the authors can start the ANN to estimate the output parameter. Use some efficient nonlinear optimization algorithms (such as generalized reduced gradient), the parameters are estimated with an overall accuracy criterion (one of trends is the mean squared error – MSE, that is minimized). In this paper, the authors will use MSE as the accuracy criterion.

In ANN model, you need a relatively large data to build a successful model. Bigger data will give us a better result. Besides that, data transformation is required to get the best results.

2 steps of the ANN model in Table 3:

Table 3. Two steps of the ANN model

Input		Original data (X_{data})
1		*Filter* X_{data}
2		$X_{new} \xrightarrow{\quad ANN \quad} X_{prediction}$
Output		Result

2.3. Wavelet − Artificial Neural Network (WA−ANN) Model

The WA– ANN model, was constructed from the subseries $\{D_1;D_2;D_3;A_3\}$ at time t, are used as the inputs for the ANN and the denoised time series at time t is the output for the ANN.

The data set was divided into two parts: training data and testing data. This can redivide times.

The Levenberg–Marquardt (L–M) algorithm was utilized to train the ANN models because it was fast, accurate, and reliable (*Adamowski and Karapataki, 2010*).

3 steps of the WAANN model in Table 4:

Table 4. Three steps of the WAANN model

Input	Original data (X_{data})
1	$X_{data} \xrightarrow{\quad WA-(n)level \quad} noise$
2	$X_{data} - noise \rightarrow X_{new}$
3	$X_{new} \xrightarrow{\quad ANN \quad} X_{prediction}$
Output	Result

Discrete wavelet transform formula for WAANN model:

$$\{X_l\} \rightarrow \{X'_l\}12$$

with $\{X_l\}$ – original data, and $\{X_l'\}$ – filted data (after using discrete wavelet transform).

ANN formula for WAANN model:

$$\widehat{X}_{t+\alpha} = f\left(X'_t, X'_{t+1}, X'_{t+2}, ..., X'_{t+\beta}\right) \tag{7}$$

with:

$\widehat{X}_{t+\alpha}$ −α^{th} value in future (prediction)

$X'_t, X'_{t+1}, X'_{t+2}, ..., X'_{t+\beta} - \beta$ continuous values was used for prediction

2.4. Time Series (ARIMA)

A time series data $\{x_t, t = 0, 1, 2, ...\}$ is a set of observations on the values that a variable takes at different time t. Time could be continuous or discrete. ARIMA is a linear forecasting model for a stationarity time series. The given time series data are first checked for stationarity. If the data are non-stationary, they are transformed to stationarity by differencing d times. The consequential data are modeled as an autoregressive moving average (ARMA) time series as follows:

$$x_t = c + \varepsilon_t + \sum_{t=1}^{p} \varphi_i x_{t-i} + \sum_{j=1}^{q} \theta_j \varepsilon_{t-j} \tag{8}$$

where x_t represents actual value at t^{th} time period, ε_t represents the error sequence which is assumed to be white nose and is Gaussian distribution with zero mean. The coefficients in the equation includes the autoregressive (AR) coefficients as ϕ_i, $i = 1,p$ and the moving average (MA) coefficients as θ_j, $j = \overline{1,q}$. Integer numbers p, q are two order parameters of model. Thus the time series model is denoted as ARIMA(p,d,q).

Box and Jenkins gave a realistic approach to estimate the model coefficients. The ARIMA modeling produce contains three steps: (a) determination of model order (b) estimation of model coefficients; and (c) prediction about the data. In the first step, after the time series data is made stationary, p and q are determined by using different approaches such as correction analysis, autocorrelation and partial auto-correction plots. In the next step, the model coefficients are estimated using Gaussian maximum likelihood estimation (GMLE). The model is validated by using Akaike information criterion (AIC). The model ARIMA with the minimum AIC value is the best fit. Last of all, the future value of the time series is forecasted thought running the model with estimated coefficients and available past data.

2.5. Hybrid Model WAANN–TS

All time-series data have three basic parts:

- A trend part (X_{trend})
  - Long term change in mean
- A seasonal part (X_{season})
  - Seasonality: annual values. Can be deseasonalized
- A remainder part $(X_{remainder})$
  - Data series after removal of trend and seasonal values

$X_{data} = X_{trend} + X_{season} + X_{remainder}$

2.5.1. The Trend

Moving averages are one of the most popular method used for smoothing series data. The trend can get from moving averages method. Have three type of this method:

- Simple Moving Average
- Weighted Moving Average
- Exponential smoothing

2.5.1.1. Simple Moving Average

The simple moving average was prevalent before the rise of computers due to the ease in calculating. The increase in processing power has made other types of moving averages and technical indicators easier to use. A simple moving average is calculated from the average of the closing values for the time period being examined.

A simple moving average most often used for series data, but it can also be calculated for other types of data. The value in smoothing data can be used for higher level smoothing parts. At the end of the new values period, that data is added to the calculation, while the oldest values of data in the series are eliminated.

For a simple moving average, the formula is the sum of the data points over a given period divided by the number of periods.

$$X_1 \quad X_2 \quad X_3 \quad X_4 \quad X_5 \quad X_6 \quad X_7$$

$$\underbrace{\frac{1}{n}\left(X_1 + \ldots + X_n\right)=X_{1\,trend}}$$

$$\frac{1}{n}\left(X_1 + \ldots + X_n\right) = X_{2\,trend}$$

Example: in this example, $N_{SME} = 4$

2.5.1.2. Weighted

Weighted moving averages assign a heavier weighting to more current data points since they are more relevant than data points in the distant past. The sum of the weighting should add up to 1. The weighting is equally distributed in the case of the simple moving average (the simple moving average method has only 1 weighting).

The weighted average can be calculated by multiplying the given values by its associated weighting and totaling the values. The denominator of the weighted moving averages is the sum of the number of values periods as a triangular number.

In the data series of this paper, each value has no more relevance than other values, so that, this method cannot be used in this paper.

2.5.1.3. Exponential Moving Averages

Exponential moving averages are also weighted toward the recent values, but the rate of decrease between the one value and its preceding value is not consistent. The difference in the decrease is exponential. Rather than every preceding weight being 1.0 smaller than the weight in front of it, you might have a difference between the first two period weights of 1.0, a difference of other parameter (maybe 1.2) for the two periods after those, and so on.

Calculating an exponential moving average involves a couple of steps.

- The first step is to determine the simple moving average for the data period, which is the first data point in the exponential moving averages formula.
- Then, a multiplier is calculated by taking 2, divided by the number of time periods plus 1.
- The final step is to take the closing values minus the prior day exponential moving averages, times the multiplier plus the prior day exponential moving averages.

An exponential moving average uses an exponentially weighted multiplier to give more weight to recent values, it can provide a better effective indicator to determine trend data when compared with the weighted moving average or the simple moving average. That the exponential moving average is more effective to get the trend data. On the other side, the basic smoothing method (in the simple moving average) may make it better for finding simple support and resistance. In general, moving averages smooth series data that can otherwise be visually noisy.

2.5.2 Season Series (X_{season})

The seasonal can get by the ratio-to-moving average (RMA) method. The basic idea of the ratio to moving average method is to separate a time series into two components, the trend-cycle-irregular series and the seasonal series. The seasonal series from ratio to moving average method is fixed and invariable between different periods. To get seasonal decomposition, this study chose the multiplicative forms of the ratio to moving average (Joy & Thomas, 1928).

2.5.3 Remainder Series ($X_{remainder}$)

The remainder series can get by removal of trend and seasonal values

2.5.4 Decomposition

The data set was decomposed by TS to three parts: the trend series, the season series and the remainder series.

- The season X_{season} part is found by smoothing of the seasonal
- X_{trend} is smoothed to find the trend data: used simple moving average method
- X_{trend} (new) is fusion of X_{trend} (old) and X_{season}.
- Overall level subtracted from seasonal series and added to the X_{trend} (new)
- This process can be repeated $n-$ times until convergence (in this paper, $n = 1$)

- $X_{remainder}$ is the residuals of the trend + seasonal parts
  ○ Data series after removal of trend and seasonal values

Next, Table 5 shows 4 steps of the WAANN–TS model

Table 5. Four steps of the WAANN-TS model

Input	Original data (X_{data})
1	$X_{data}\ Time\_series \to X_{trend\,(old)} + X_{season} + X_{remainder}$
2	$X_{trend\,(old)} + X_{season} \to X_{trend\,(new)}$
3	$X_{trend\,(new)ARIMA} \to Y_{trend}$
4	$X_{remainder}\ WAANN \to Y_{remainder}$
Output	Combining results

2.6. Evaluate Model

The mean square error (MSE), the mean absolute deviation (MAD) used for comparison:

$$MSE = \sum_{i=1}^{n} \frac{\left(X_i - \widehat{X}_{i,prediction}\right)^2}{n} \qquad (6)$$

$$MAD = \sum_{i=1}^{m} \frac{\left|X_i - \widehat{X}_{mean,prediction}\right|}{m} \qquad (7)$$

with:

$\{X_i\}$ is original data in test set.

$\{\widehat{X}_{i,prediction}\}$ is predictive values.

$\{\widehat{X}_{mean,\ prediction}\}$ is the mean of predictive values.

m, n, l – the length of test set.

3. EXPERIMENTS AND RESULTS

3.1. Result for Sunspot Data and Comparison with Zhang's Model

In 2003, Zhang (Zhang G. P., 2003) build a hybrid model from the ARIMA model and the ANN model. The result of the hybrid model was better than the single ARIMA model and better than the single ANN model, too.

The sunspot data, from 1700 to 1987, were considered for Zhang's model (Babu & Reddy, 2014). This data has 288 values. In this paper, rebuilding model of Zhang's model used one – step – ahead prediction and predict value of 25 data points in future (Babu & Reddy, 2014). And for the new ARIMA-WAANN model will predict 25th value (in future), too.

In Zhang's model A, parameters (p, d, q) in ARIMA model is (3, 1, 2), and ANN model used 4 x 4 x 1 model (Zhang G. P., 2003). In this model, the auto-fix program shows that the parameters' set (3, 1, 2) is best (p, d, q) parameters.

In Zhang's model B, parameters (p, d, q) in ARIMA model is (6, 2, 4), and ANN model used model 4 x 4 x 1. This model used parameters $(p, d, q) = (6, 2, 4)$ from best values of the proposed hybrid model.

In WAANN-TS model A, parameters (p, d, q) in ARIMA model is (3, 1, 2) (the (p, d, q) parameters from Zhang's model A), and ANN model used model 4 x 4 x 1.

In WAANN-TS model B, parameters (p, d, q) in ARIMA model is (6, 2, 4), and ANN model used model 4 x 4 x 1. These parameters are picked from Table 6 of results in subsection **3.3.**

Comparison for results of Zhang's model and new model in Table 6:

Table 6. Comparison for results of Zhang's model and new model

Model	MSE	MAD
ARIMA	308.6630	15.7601
ANN	288.0001	14.4203
Zhang's model A	300.1016	14.5022
Proposed model A	298.4051	14.2000
Zhang's model B	305.2960	14.5107
Proposed model B	296.1400	14.1086

3.2. Study Area and Used Data for Proposed Hybrid Method

Red river, in the North Vietnam, is the second largest river (after Mekong) in Vietnam, one third of the country's population (30 million) are provided water by this river. It is very important river because it provides water for the inhabitants of the capital Hanoi. The Red river basin is 143,700 km^2 and the main length is 1,149 km. In this paper, water level of Hanoi station is chosen in our case study for prediction.

This study, to predict water level of Red river. The water level is measured in the stations. The rainy season is focused study the data 2015, 2016, 2017. Total, the series has 3402 values. The first 3000 values (in dataset) are used for training model, and the last 402 values (in dataset) used for testing the model.

The researchers considered data on rainy season from June to September each year (Junes, Julys, Augusts and Septembers of years 2015, 2016 and 2017) (Table 7).

Table 7. 3 data sets (in period June 11 to Sep 16)

Series	Data size	Training	Test
2015	1108	1000	108
2016	1120	1000	120
2017	1174	1000	174
All data	3402	3000	402

3.3. Prediction Results of Single Models: ARIMA

In this model, parameters (p, d, q) and their MSE and MAD were showed in Table 8.

Table 8. Parameters (p, d, q) and their MSE and MAD

	N°	p	D	q	MSE	MAD
	1	1	0	1	1.945223031914350E−04	2.07980732496066E−05
	21	7	2	1	1.927364767083160E−04	3.45766998447464E−05
	41	5	1	2	1.968573229657890E−04	1.96087303494654E−05
	61	3	0	4	1.976273804160430E−04	1.93905614023771E−05
	81	9	2	4	1.986129704031790E−04	2.00383331030387E−05
	101	7	1	5	1.988649684116720E−04	1.95149063541498E−05
	121	5	0	6	1.993988531587980E−04	1.93204574261010E−05
	141	2	2	7	2.011904613539030E−04	5.13125394465020E−05
	161	9	1	7	2.611888649532650E−04	1.97275087447128E−05
	181	7	0	8	3.238642779215270E−04	1.99589768235006E−05
	201	4	2	9	4.311771357526170E−04	2.81939367320099E−05
	216	9	2	9	3.448032990954940E−04	1.73972287838558E−05
Min	72	6	2	4	1.835632382451900E−04	1.32864007539485E−05
Max	9	3	2	1	1.854328044154660E−04	1.48669101853349E−04

The best model is model with parameters $(p, d, q) = (6, 2, 4)$
The result of this model is shown in Table 9:

Table 9. Result of the model ARIMA

	MSE (scaled-original data)	MAD (scaled-original data)
6h	145.5924×10^{-4}	12.0627×10^{-2}

3.4. Prediction Results of Single Models: ANN

The ANN model uses a network with form 4 x 4 x 1 (Groot & Wurtz, 1991). 3 continued values are used for predicting the future value (Figure 3).

Figure 3. Result data of the ANN model (compare with original data)

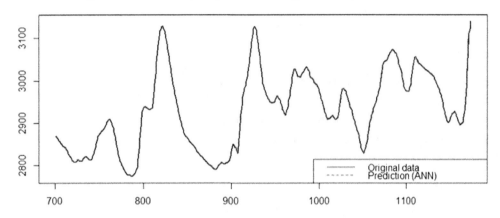

For ANN model, the result is showed in Table 10:

Table 10. Result of the model ANN

	MSE (scaled-original data)	MAD (scaled-original data)
6h	3.7158×10^{-4}	0.4767×10^{-2}

3.5. Prediction Results of Hybrid Models: WAANN

For this model, model discrete wavelet transform was used for pre−processing data set, and model artificial neural network was used for prediction (Table 11 and Figure 4).

Table 11. Result of the model WAANN

	MSE (scaled-original data)	MAD (scaled-original data)
6h	2.5027×10^{-4}	0.4768×10^{-2}

Figure 4. Result data of the WAANN model (compare with original data)

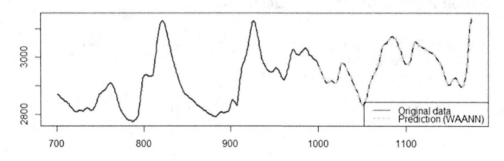

3.6. Prediction Results of Hybrid Models: WAANN–TS (Scaling Data)

The data was decomposed into two parts: trend part and remained part.

Trend part got by simple moving average method. The trend part needs to be a stationary for ARIMA method (Table 12).

Table 12. ARIMA

N_{SME}	Stationary or non-stationary?
1	Yes
2	Yes
...	...
14	Yes
15	No
16	No
...	...
100	No
...	...

If the trend part is stationary, the ARIMA method is used, and if the trend part is nonstationary, the ANN method is used.

In this paper, parameter $N_{SME} = 14$ is used.

With this decomposition, the model ANN (WAANN) was used (Table 13-15 and Figure 5).

And with the remainder series, the model ARIMA was used.

Table 13. Result for trend series of the model WAANN – TS. The model WAANN was used forscaled-trend part.

	MSE (scaled-trend part)	MAD (scaled-trend part)
6h	2.8997×10^{-4}	1.4457×10^{-2}

Table 14. Result for remainder series of the model WAANN – TS. The model ARIMA was used for the remainder part

	MSE (remainder part)	MAD (remainder part)
6h	0.0806×10^{-4}	0.2737×10^{-2}

Table 15. Result of the model WAANN – TS

	MSE (scaled-original data)	MAD (scaled-original data)
6h	2.4460×10^{-4}	1.2063×10^{-2}

Figure 5. Result data of the WAANN – TS model (compare withscaled-original data)

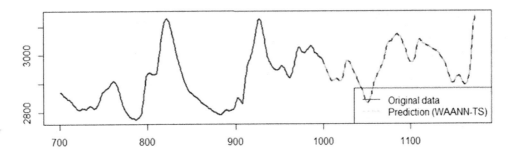

3.7. Comparison Results of Models (ARIMA, ANN, WAANN and WAANN – TS)

(MSE and MAD were computed by scaling data) (Table 16)

3.8. Prediction Results of Hybrid Models: WAANN – TS in Original Data

In this paper, a new method and model was designed, used for short-term prediction. Proposed model was used for forecasting water level and flood in the Red river in North Vietnam, station "Hanoi city". The result of the proposed model is better than results of current models, these are using in Hanoi station (ARIMA and ANN) (Table 17).

In the test (with the Wolf's Sunspot data), the proposed model has given better results, than that of Zhang's hybrid model 3% (for MSE criterion).

Table 16. Compare results of the model ARIMA, ANN, WAANN, Zhang's model and WAANN – TS (inscaled-original data)

	MSE (scaled-original data)	MAD (scaled-original data)
ARIMA	145.5924×10^{-4}	12.0627×10^{-2}
ANN	3.7158×10^{-4}	0.4768×10^{-2}
WAANN	2.5027×10^{-4}	0.4767×10^{-2}
Zhang's model	3.0912×10^{-4}	0.48×10^{-2}
WAANN–TS	2.4460×10^{-4}	0.4063×10^{-2}

Table 17. compare results of the model ARIMA, ANN, WAANN and WAANN – TS (in original data)

	Mean error (by centimeter)	Proposed model better than...
ARIMA	87.8165	2867%
ANN	3.4711	17.3%
WAANN	3.4704	17%
Zhang's model	3.4944	18.1%
WAANN–TS	2.9579	–

In the real time series data, this paper showed the prediction results for water level in 6 hours in future in Hanoi station.

For MSE criterion, the proposed model is better than the ARIMA model 5841%, better than the ANN model 51.4%, better than WAANN model 2%, and better than Zhang's model 12.6%. The comparison was showed in Table 16.

For original data (water level) criterion, the proposed model gave results that is better than ARIMA model 2867%, better than ANN model 17.3%, better than WAANN model 17%, and better than Zhang's model 18.1%. This comparison was showed in Table 17.

The results of the proposed hybrid model WAANN – TS show that it is more accurate than the single models (the ANN model and the ARIMA model) and the current hybrid models (Zhang's model and the WAANN model) in forecasting water level in our case study. The authors have found that in case of training data set, for the model WAANN – TS having MSE is the smallest.

4. CONCLUSION

1. In this paper, the authors have successfully integrated WAANN and time series to a new hybrid model.
2. Well applying new proposal hybrid model for case study Hanoi station, northwest Vietnam.
3. The result was better than result from current models in Hanoi station (ANN model).
4. Results were more accurate when using our hybrid model in forecasting water level.

The propose method has better prediction than current models (used in stations in North Vietnam) because the new model removes noise with the wavelet model. Those noises are non-predictable.

With the results were got, the proposed method will be tested in Hanoi station for the prediction of the water level of Red river in Hanoi. This method will also be tested in other stations (on Red river) for prediction flood in Red river's delta (North Vietnam).

In the future, the proposed hybrid method can use some little upgrades:

1. Use other machine learning methods in hybrid model (for time series) such as LSTM, RNN, CNN, etc. or update hybrid method which combines the strength of more single models.
2. Add some other data series such as rainfall, water level of neighboring stations, etc. to analyses and predict data series.
3. Add spatial factors in the forecasting method in the next paper: Red river's delta has some stations in Red river and in other river. The data series from those station
4. is useful for forecasting water level (and flood) of rivers in the Red river's delta.

ACKNOWLEDGMENT

The authors are gratefully acknowledged the editor-in-chief, associate editors and anonymous reviewers' constructive comments on an earlier version of the paper. The comments have given a good scope to improve the manuscript. This research was partly supported by Hanoi University of Science and Technology, Vietnam.

REFERENCES

Adamowski, J., & Chan, H. F. (2011). A wavelet neural network conjunction model for groundwater level forecasting. *Journal of Hydrology (Amsterdam)*, *407*(1-4), 28–40. doi:10.1016/j.jhydrol.2011.06.013

Babu, C. N., & Reddy, B. E. (2014). A moving-average filter based hybrid ARIMA–ANN model for forecasting time series data. *Applied Soft Computing*, *23*, 27–38. doi:10.1016/j.asoc.2014.05.028

Behera, H., & Biswal, P. D. (2010). Power quality time series data mining using S-transform and fuzzy expert system. *Applied Soft Computing*, *10*(3), 945–955. doi:10.1016/j.asoc.2009.10.013

Belayneh, A., Adamowski, J., Khalil, B., & Ozga-Zielinski, B. (2014). Long-term SPI drought forecasting in the Awash River Basin in Ethiopia using wavelet neural network and wavelet support vector regression models. *Journal of Hydrology (Amsterdam)*, *508*, 418–429. doi:10.1016/j.jhydrol.2013.10.052

Cleveland, R. B., Cleveland, W. S., McRae, J. E., & Terpenning, I. (1990). A seasonal - trend decomposition procedure based on Loess. *Journal of Official Statistics*, *6*(1), 3–73.

Dogan, K., & Goetschalckx, M. (1999). A primal decomposition method for the integrated design of multi-period production-distribution systems. *IISE Transactions*, *31*(11), 1027–1036. doi:10.1080/07408179908969904

Gerbing, D. (2016). Time Series Components. School of Business Administration, Portland State University.

Groot, C. D., & Wurtz, D. (1991). Analysis of univariate time series with connectionist nets: A case study of two. *Neurocomputing, 3,* 177–192. doi:10.1016/0925-2312(91)90040-I

Hyndman, R. J., & Khandakar, Y. (2008). Automatic time series forecasting: The forecast package for R. *Journal of Statistical Software, 27*(3), 1–22. doi:10.18637/jss.v027.i03

Joy, A., & Thomas, W. (1928). The use of Moving Averages in the Measurement of Seasonal Variations. *Journal of the American Statistical Association, 23*(163), 241–252. doi:10.1080/01621459.1928.10503019

Khandelwal, I., Adhikari, R., & Verma, G. (2015). Time Series Forecasting using Hybrid ARIMA and ANN Models based on DWT Decomposition. *Procedia Computer Science, 48,* 173–179. doi:10.1016/j.procs.2015.04.167

Liu, H., Tian, H., Pan, D., & Li, Y. (2013). Forecasting models for wind speed using wavelet, wavelet packet, time series and Artificial Neural Networks. *Applied Energy, 107,* 191–208. doi:10.1016/j.apenergy.2013.02.002

Mukherjee, A., & Ramachandran, P. (2018). Prediction of GWL with the help of grace TWS for unevenly spaced time series data in India: Analysis of comparative performances of SVR, ANN and LRM. *Journal of Hydrology, 558,* 647–658. doi:10.1016/j.jhydrol.2018.02.005

Niu, C., & Ji, L. (2012). A hybrid method based on Wavelet Analysis for short-term load forecasting. *Journal of Convergence Information Technology, 7*(17), 540–547. doi:10.4156/jcit.vol7.issue17.63

Nury, A. H., Hasan, K., & Alam, M. J. (2017). Comparative study of Wavelet-ARIMA and Wavelet-ANN models for temperature time series data in northeastern Bangladesh. *Journal of King Saud University - Science, 29*(1), 47-61.

Panigrahi, S., & Behera, H. (2017). A hybrid ETS–ANN model for time series forecasting. *Engineering Applications of Artificial Intelligence, 66,* 49–59. doi:10.1016/j.engappai.2017.07.007

Raza, M., & Khosravi, A. (2015). A review on artificial intelligence based load demand forecasting techniques for smart grid and buildings. *Renewable & Sustainable Energy Reviews, 50,* 1352–1372. doi:10.1016/j.rser.2015.04.065

Tran, H. D., Muttil, N., & Perera, B. J. (2016). Enhancing accuracy of autoregressive time series forecasting with input selection and wavelet transformation. *Journal of Hydroinformatics, 18*(5), 791–802. doi:10.2166/hydro.2016.145

Tseng, F. M., Yu, H. C., & Tzeng, G. H. (2002). Combining neural network model with seasonal time series ARIMA model. *Technological Forecasting and Social Change, 69*(1), 71–87. doi:10.1016/S0040-1625(00)00113-X

Wang, S., Yu, L., Tang, L., & Wang, S. (2011). A novel seasonal decomposition based least squares support vector regression ensemble learning approach for hydropower consumption forecasting in China. *Energy, 36*(11), 6542–6554. doi:10.1016/j.energy.2011.09.010

Yadav, B., & Eliza, K. (2017). A hybrid wavelet-support vector machine model for prediction of lake water level fluctuations using hydro-meteorological data. *Measurement, 103,* 294–301. doi:10.1016/j.measurement.2017.03.003

Zhang, G. P. (2003). Time series forecasting using a hybrid ARIMA and neural network model. *Neuro-computing, 50*, 159–175. doi:10.1016/S0925-2312(01)00702-0

Zhang, G. P., & Qi, M. (2005). Neural network forecasting for seasonal and trend time series. *European Journal of Operational Research, 160*(2), 501–514. doi:10.1016/j.ejor.2003.08.037

This research was previously published in the International Journal of Information Retrieval Research (IJIRR), 10(3); pages 1-19, copyright year 2020 by IGI Publishing (an imprint of IGI Global).

Chapter 51

Drought Estimation–and–Projection Using Standardized Supply–Demand–Water Index and Artificial Neural Networks for Upper Tana River Basin in Kenya

Raphael Muli Wambua

Egerton University Department of Agricultural Engineering, Nakuru, Kenya

ABSTRACT

Drought occurrence, frequency and severity in the Upper Tana River basin (UTaRB) have critically affected water resource systems. To minimize the undesirable effects of drought, there is a need to quantify and project the drought trend. In this research, the drought was estimated and projected using Standardized Supply-Demand-Water Index (SSDI) and an Artificial Neural Network (ANN). Field meteorological data was used in which interpolated was conducted using kriging interpolation technique within ArcGIS environment. The results indicate those moderate, severe and extreme droughts at varying magnitudes as detected by the SSDI during 1972-2010 at different meteorological stations, with SSDI values equal or less than -2.0. In a spatial domain, the areas in south-eastern parts of the UTaRB exhibit the highest drought severity. Time-series forecasts and projection show that the best networks for SSDI exhibit respective ANNs architecture. The projected extreme droughts (values less than -2.00) and abundant water availability (SSDI values ^{3} 2.00) were estimated using Recursive Multi-Step Neural Networks (RMSNN). The findings can be integrated into planning the drought-mitigation-adaptation and early-warning systems in the UTaRB.

DOI: 10.4018/978-1-6684-2408-7.ch051

INTRODUCTION

The Upper Tana River Basin (UTaRB) has an area of 17,420 km². According to TNC (2015), approximately 5.3 million persons live in the UTaRB. Generally, the area receives two rainy seasons annually with annual average amount of 2000 mm at the high altitudes adjacent to Mount Kenya, which is at highest elevation above sea level. The lowest areas receive lower amounts of rainfall. The hydrology of the UTaRB is critical to Kenyan economy (Hiho and Mugalavai, 2010). Hydrological processes in the basin when affected by drought greatly influence agricultural activities, hydro-power generation, water supply to the City of Nairobi and the national parks and reserves located within the basin. The occurrence of drought in a river basin or any area adversely affects socio-economic development. Different drought indices can be used for drought estimation. In this study, Standardized supply-demand water index (SSDI) that combines effective precipitation and crop evapo-transpiration is used to detect drought within the UTaRB.

Drought is a condition on land characterised by scarcity of water that falls below a defined threshold level. It is a disaster linked to climate that may affect a wide range of land (Ali et al., 2018). Drought may be categorized into four types; climatological, agricultural hydrological and the socio-economic. Any type of drought can last for short period of time such as weeks and months, or long periods as in seasons, years and decades. Each drought type lasting for specific period of time may exhibit specific spatio-temporal characteristics (Peters et al., 2006; Tallaksen et al., 2009; Wang et al., 2016). Droughts may be expressed in terms of indices that depend on precipitation deficit, soil-water deficit, low stream flow, low reservoir levels and low groundwater (Hao et al., 2018; Sanmartín et al., 2018). Hydrological drought adversely affects various aspects of human interest such as food security, water supply and hydropower generation (Karamouz et al., 2009; Belayneh and Adamowski, 2013). Globally, drought has become more frequent and severe due to climate variability with some regions experiencing droughts at varying scales and times. Therefore, global impacts of drought on environmental, agricultural and socio-economic aspects are great. Droughts have either direct or indirect impacts on river basins and human lives (IPCC 2014; Hao et al., 2018). Direct impacts include degradation of water resources in terms of quantity and quality, reduced crop productivity, increased livestock and wildlife mortality rates, increased soil erosion and land degradation, and increased plant diseases and insect attacks (UN, 2008; Scheffran et al., 2012). On the other hand, the indirect impacts of drought comprise reduced income, unemployment, and migration of people and animals. Worldwide, more than eleven million persons have died since 1900 as a result of drought related impacts. In addition, two billion persons have been critically affected by the impacts (FAO, 2013). The main challenges associated with drought are that it causes ill health through water scarcity, malnutrition and famine (UN, 2008; Mcevoy, 2018). The extent of the effect of drought depends on its characteristics which may be described using an index.

A drought index (DI) is a function used for assessing, quantifying, detecting occurrence and severity of droughts. The Drought Indices (DIs) were developed for specific regions using specific structures and forms of data input. There is limited information in the application of drought indices that combines both temporal and spatial drought evaluation at river basin scales. Drought has been assessed in terms of temporal and spatial domain using evapotranspiration mapping as illustrated by Eden (2012). There are two broad categories of drought indices; satellite based and the data driven drought indices (Belayneh and Adamowski, 2013). In addition, drought may be forecasted using the index in conjunction with some modelling techniques such as application of Artificial Neural Networks (ANNs) (Ali et al., 2018).

Drought forecasting has received a new approach especially with the development of the ANNs. An ANN is a computing system made up of a number of simple and highly interconnected information processing elements. Such a system has performance characteristics that resemble biological neural networks of human brain. ANN has numerous merits when used for data processing. The system processes information based on their dynamic state response to external input (Morid, 2007). ANNs have the capacity to model relationships that are quite dynamic and can capture many kinds of relationships including non-linear functions which are difficult or impossible to determine using other approaches (Mustafa et al., 2012). The ANNs have recently been used in water resources engineering (WRE) and drought forecasting (Ali et al., 2018; Halagundegowda and Singh, 2018). WRE comprises the study of hydraulics, hydrology, environment and geological related variables. Drought indices and ANNs may be applied to describe, forecast or project drought characteristics in any river basin. In the present research drought was estimated and projected using SSDI and ANNs for UTaRB.

DESCRIPTION OF STUDY AREA

The study was conducted in the upper Tana River basin (UTaRB) (Figure 1). The study area is part of the larger Tana River basin, the largest river basin in Kenya (Jacobs et al., 2004; WRMA, 2010). According to IFAD (2012), the upper Tana River basin has huge forest and land resources located along the eastern slopes of Mount Kenya and Aberdares range which influence the hydrological processes of the entire basin. The UTaRB lies between latitudes 00° 05' and 01° 30' south and longitudes 36° 20' and 37° 60' east. The elevation of the upper Tana River basin ranges from approximately 730 m to 5,190 m above mean sea level (a.m.s.l.) at These elevations are at Kindaruma hydropower dam and Mount Kenya and respectively.

Figure 1. Map of the upper Tana River basin

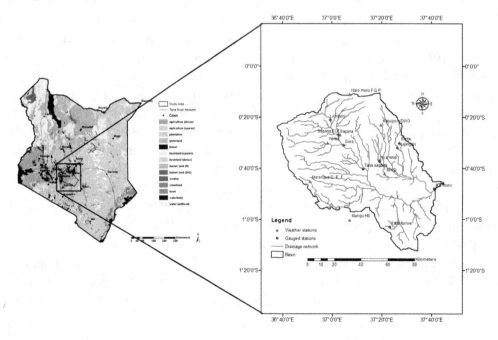

Precipitation Data

In the upper Tana River basin, data from meteorological stations were obtained from the Ministry of Water and Irrigation. The meteorological data included precipitation, temperature and evaporation data. The data were then subjected to exploratory data processing. It was found out that only eight stations had reliable and consistent and sufficient data. Where the available data contained less than 20% data gaps, then these data were selected for computation the SSDI. The eight stations used in the study (Table 1) are located within the low (LE), lower middle (LME), middle (ME) and high (HE) elevations. The stations are located at different agro-ecological zones.

Table 1. Meteorological stations within the UTaRB used for in this study

S.No	Station Name	Station ID	Coordinates		Elevation (m)
			Longitude (Deg)	Latitude (Deg)	
1	MIAD	9037112	37.350	-0.700	1246
2	Embu	9037202	37.450	-0.500	1494
3	Kerugoya DWO	9037031	37.327	-0.382	1598
4	Sagana FCF	9037096	37.054	-0.448	1234
5	Nyeri	9036288	36.970	-0.500	1780
6	Maragua G. E. F.	9036212	36.850	-0.750	2296
7	Naro-moru F.G.P.	9037064	37.117	-0.183	2296
8	Mangu HS	9137123	37.033	-1.100	1630

'Deg' means Degrees

Time-Series Drought Detection Using SSDI

The standardized supply-demand water index (SSDI) combined effective precipitation and crop evapotranspiration. The monthly difference between effective precipitation and the crop evapotranspiration was used as input data. The result is a simple climatic water balance computed at defined time scales to give SSDI. In the present research, effective precipitation was considered as that portion of precipitation that infiltrates into the soil and is available for crop production. It excluded the fraction of precipitation that led to runoff, interception, and direct evaporation before infiltration. Effective precipitation (P_e) was estimated using simplified USDA-SCS function stated as:

$$P_e = \begin{cases} P - 0.048P^2 & For \ P < 8.3 \\ 4.17 + 0.1P & For \ P \geq 8.3 \end{cases} \tag{1}$$

where:

P=Daily precipitation (mm/day)

On the other hand, crop-evapotranspiration (ET_c) was estimated indirectly using the reference evapotranspiration and the crop coefficient. The ET_c was determined using the following relation:

$$ET_c = ET_0 \times K_c \tag{2}$$

where:

ET_c = crop evapo-transpiration (mm/day)

K_c = crop coefficient (dimensionless)

ET_0 = reference evapotranspiration (mm/day)

The K_c value for major crop (Maize) in UTaRB for different growing stages were adopted from Food and Agriculture Organization (FAO). Both the P and ET_c were computed per day then summed up for all the days in the respective month.

Blaney-Criddle Method

Blaney-Criddle method is suitable for areas with limited records of climatic data and the only available data is air temperature. This method is considered to be one of the best temperature-based methods for humid areas (Jensen et. al. 1990). Although, Hargreaves and Blaney-Criddle methods have also been developed for areas with limited data (Sivaprakasam et al., 2011), the latter remains to be simpler than the former, and this is why it was selected in this study. The Blaney Criddle function adapted for calculation of reference evapotranspiration (ET_0) in this study is shown in Equation (3) whose detailed procedure is illustrated in Doorenbos and Pruitt (1977):

$$ET_o = p(0.46T_{mean} + 8) \tag{3}$$

where:

ET_o = Reference evapotranspiration (mm/day)

T_{mean} = Mean daily temperature (°C)

P = Mean daily percentage of annual daytime hours (%)

After computation of the daily ET0, the data was converted into the monthly ET0.
The SSDI was expressed as a function defined in the following equation:

$$SSDI = \begin{cases} W - \dfrac{c_0 + c_1 W + c_2 W_2}{1 - d_1 W + d_2 W_2 + d_3 W_3} & For \ P \le 0.5, \ W = \sqrt{-2\ln(P)} \\[4mm] \dfrac{c_0 + c_1 W + c_2 W_2}{1 - d_1 W + d_2 W_2 + d_3 W_3} - W & For \ P > 0.5 \ and \ W = \sqrt{-2\ln(1-P)} \end{cases} \tag{4}$$

where:

$c_0 = 2.515517$

$c_1 = 0.802853$

$c_2 = 0.010328$

$d_1 = 1.432788$

$d_2 = 0.189269$

$d_3 = 0.001308$

which were adopted for the present calculation (Yuan et al., 2017):

$$P = 1 - F(x) \tag{5}$$

The standardized $F(x)$ values were computed using the relation:

$$F(x) = \left[1 + \left(\frac{\alpha}{x - \gamma}\right)^{\beta}\right]^{-1} \tag{6}$$

where α, β and γ are respectively the scale, shape and location parameters. These parameters were estimated using the following functions:

$$\beta = \frac{2w_1 - w_0}{6w_1 - w_0 - 6w_2} \tag{7}$$

$$\alpha = \frac{(w_0 - 2w_1)\beta}{\Gamma(1 + 1/\beta)\Gamma(1 - 1/\beta)} \tag{8}$$

$$\gamma = w_0 - \alpha \Gamma \left(1 + \frac{1}{\beta} \right) \Gamma \left(1 - \frac{1}{\beta} \right) \tag{9}$$

where, $\Gamma(\beta)$ is the gamma function of β. The w0, w1 and w2 are probability parameters of defined orders which are computed as:

$$w_s = \frac{1}{N} \sum_{i=1}^{N} \left(1 - F_i \right)^s \times D_i \tag{10}$$

where:

S = the order of the parameter

N = number of data points

F_i = the frequency estimator

The equation estimator was computed from the following function:

$$F_i = \frac{i - K}{N} \tag{11}$$

where:

I = range of observations arranged in ascending order

K = constant (= 0.35 citation)

Using Equations 5 to 11, the function F(x) was modelled and then used to determine the SSDI as per Equation 4.

Drought Forecasting

The data for different stations within the upper Tana River basin were used by applying the SSDs modelling programme within the Matrices Laboratory (MATLAB). The first step involved defining the input neurons in the input layer. In this step, different input neurons with different time delays of *t, t-1, t-2, ..., t-n*, for each hydro-meteorological station were applied. Secondly, the number of Hidden Neurons (HN) was set as equal to 2n+1 in the architecture of the ANN. By trial and error method, the hidden neurons were increased or decreased by a value of one and this was used to evaluate the value of forecasts using the following relation:

$$E_F = \left| 1.0 - \frac{SSDI_{Obs} - SSDI_{For}}{SSDI_{Obs}} \right| \times 100\% \qquad (12)$$

where:

E_F = Efficiency of forecasting

$SSDI_{Obs}$ = Observed magnitude of SSDI

$SSDI_{For}$ = Forecasted magnitude of the SSDI

For each hydro-meteorological station, the FFN and RNN structures of the ANN models were trained using the Levernberg-Marquardt (LM) algorithm. Preliminary results at each station showed that a three-layer Feed Forward Neural Network (FFN) with different input and HN performed best in terms of efficiency based on coefficient of determination (R). In this case, the FFN were considered as the best for the detailed drought studies.

The output layer neurons in all the networks were equal to the forecast of the respective lead short-term forecast of SSDI. For instance, a $SSDI_{t+1}$ and $SSDI_{t+3}$ into the future was calculated for 1 and 3 months lead times using the Neural Networks within the GUI of the MATLAB toolbox. In this research, the SSDI values of 1 and 3 were considered to reflect relatively short-term conditions. On a monthly temporal domain, the DI_{t+1} and DI_{t+3} were calculated as the drought forecasts for lead times of 1 and 3 months respectively. Table 5 presents a summary of the forecasting inputs for various SSDI as modified from Belayneh (2012). In this study, the initial number of HN was determined using the relation adapted from Belayneh (2013) given as $2n+1$, where n is the number of input neurons. The trial and error method was applied in which the number of HN was altered by either decreasing or increasing by 1 the computed HN, and testing the performance efficiency for each trial using Equation 14. The best ANN was selected by picking the model architecture that gave the best level of performance in forecasting efficiency. This process was repeated for all the meteorological stations.

Performance Evaluation

Three performance measures; correlation coefficient, modified index of agreement and Nash–Sutcliffe efficiency were adopted for model evaluation. The data for the period 1970 to 1990 was used for calibration purpose while the remaining data set for 1991 to 2010 was used for validation of the models. The functions adapted for model evaluation are as described below.

The correlation coefficient (R) was used to determine the statistical relationship between the observed and the predicated drought conditions within the upper Tana River basin. The fundamental function was customised to the respective SSDI values using the relation:

$$R = \frac{\sum\limits_{i=1}^{n}\left(SSDI_{Obs} - \overline{SSDI}_{Obs}\right)\left(SSDI_{For} - \overline{SSDI}_{For}\right)}{\sum\limits_{i=1}^{n}\left(SSDI_{Obs} - \overline{SSDI}_{Obs}\right)\left(SSDI_{For} - \overline{SSDI}_{For}\right)^{2}} \tag{13}$$

where:

R = correlation coefficient

$SSDI_{Obs}$ = observed value of the drought index

$\overline{SSDI}_{Obs}$ = mean of the observed values of the drought index

$SSDI_{For}$ = forecasted value of the drought index

$\overline{SSDI}_{For}$ = mean of the forecasted values of the drought index

n = number of data points considered

The R is a measure of the strength of the linear relationship between the observed and forecasted SSDI values. It varies from 0 to 1. The values of 0 and 1 indicate a poor and perfect forecasting capability of the model respectively.

The modified index of agreement was applied in performance testing. This method was used because it is quite sensitive to the differences on forecasted and observed hydro-meteorological values than correlation coefficient (R) (Krause et al., 2005). This index gives the ratio of mean square error and the potential error and is mathematically expressed as:

$$d_{SSDI} = 1.0 - \frac{\sum\limits_{i=1}^{n}\left|SSDI_{Obs} - SSDI_{For}\right|}{\sum\limits_{i=1}^{n}\left(\left|SSDI_{For} - \overline{SSDI}_{Obs}\right| + \left|SSDI_{Obs} - \overline{SSDI}_{Obs}\right|\right)} \tag{14}$$

where:

d_{I} = modified index of agreement

$SSDI_{obs}$ = observed value of the drought index

$SSDI_{for}$ = forecasted value of the drought index

$\overline{SSDI}_{Obs}$ = mean of the measured values

n = number of observations

The Nash–Sutcliffe Efficiency (NSE) statistical approach was used effectively to evaluate observed and predicted hydrologic data (Nash and Sutcliffe, 1970; Biamah et al., 2002). The NSE was used to indicate how well the plot of observed versus simulated data fits the 1: 1 line: Its value ranges from -¥ to 1.0. Mathematically NSE adapted for this study is given as:

$$NSE = 1.0 - \left[\frac{\sum_{i=1}^{n} \left(SSDI_i^{obs} - SSDI_i^{for} \right)^2}{\sum_{i=1}^{n} \left(SSDI_i^{obs} - \overline{SSDI}_{Obs} \right)^2} \right] \qquad (15)$$

where:

NSE = Nash–Sutcliffe Efficiency

DI_i^{obs} = observed value of the drought index

DI_i^{for} = forecasted value of the drought index

$\overline{SSDI}^{Obs}$ = mean value of the drought index

n = total number of observations

The resulting values of NSE were compared with those given as acceptable levels of the efficiency as per Nash-Sutcliffe (1970) criterion.

Assessment of Drought Characteristics Using the Formulated SSDI

The SSDI values were computed from which time series plot was created based on truncation levels. The SSDI values were then characterized into different drought ranks as shown in Table 2 as adapted from Barua (2010).

From the time series graph, the duration, maximum and median magnitude of each drought condition were extracted. The SSDI was also used to detect the on-set and end months of the drought period by selecting the times in months when the SSDI values were below or above the truncation level. The SSDI values below and above the truncation level indicated the on-set and end time of the drought respectively. The severity of the drought in the UTaRB was then computed using the relation:

$$S_{SSDI} = \sum_{N=1}^{N} SSDI_d \times P_{SSDI} \qquad (16)$$

where:

S_{SSDI} = annual drought severity based on SSDI for a defined year

$SSDI_d$ = sum of drought severity values below zero during a particular year

P = probability of drought occurrence for the defined year

Table 2. Drought classification based on SSDI

State	Criterion	Drought Description
0	2.00 or more	Abudant water availability
1	1.99 to 0	Wet
2	0 to -0.99	Near normal
3	-1.00 to -1.49	Moderate drought
4	-1.50 to -1.99	Severe drought
5	-2.00 and less	Extreme drought

Once the station based SSDI severity values were calculated, they were the used for development of Severity maps. For each year, the drought severity at each station is assessment using severity Equation (16). The spatial distribution of the drought severity within the ArcGIS 10.1 environment was conducted using the kriging method.

Projection of Time-Series Drought Using SSDI and ANNs

Future drought events were projected using Recursive multi-step neural networks (RMSNN) as per [24]. RMSNN with multiple neurons within the input and hidden layers adapted from [14] was used to project time-series drought in the river basin from the year 2010 to 2097 (87 years). The RMSNN consisted of a single neuron in the output layer which represents a one month lead time projection and was conducted for k months. Using the available data from 1970 to 2010, the RMSNN was first designed and calibrated considering only one month lead time using present and several months of the past SSDI values as inputs. The resulting neural network with the same number of input combination was then used for projection of SSDI values for a multiple lead times in a recursive process as described in Figure 2. The drought projection $(t+1)$ was first calculated based on n months of the past SSDI values including the SSDI at month t. This projected value $SSDI_{(t+1)}$ was then used with past SSDI values of t, $t-1$, …, $t-n$ months to project $SSDI_{(t+2)}$. This process was repeated recursively to obtain the drought projection for k months (k=1044) to represent the total period from the year 2011 to 2097. The whole process led to drought projection at month t for k time steps from $(t+1)$ to $(t+k)$. By using the projection it is assumed that the drought trend and associated hydro-meteorological variables within the basin is the same both for the data period (1970 to 2010) and the projection period (2011 to 2097).

Figure 2. Three Layer RMSNN used for drought projection in conjunction with SSDI

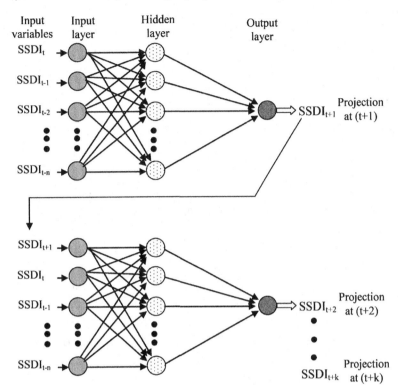

RESULTS AND DISCUSSIONS

Time Series Drought Based on SSDI

The effective precipitation (P_e) and reference evapotranspiration (ET_0) were computed for all the stations. The resulting data was used for the SSDI water balanced estimation. For the purpose of illustration, two data sets; Pe and ET_0 for Embu (ID 9037202) meteorological station is presented in Tables 3 and 4 respectively for a typical year of 2008.

Table 3. Computed effective precipitation (Pe) for a typical year of 2008

Month	J	F	M	A	M	J	J	A	S	O	N	D
P day(mean)	2.161	0	5.370	11.366	0.435	0.686	1.803	0.674	0.26	7.212	3.316	0.064
P_e (mm/day)	1.937	0	3.986	5.306	0.426	0.664	1.647	0.652	0.256	4.715	2.788	0.064
Days	31	29	30	30	31	30	31	31	30	31	30	31
P_e(mm/month)	60.050	0	119.575	159.2	13.218	19.921	51.062	20.224	7.7027	146.185	83.659	1.994

Table 4. Computed ET$_0$ based on Blaney-Criddle method for typical year of 2008

Month	J	F	M	A	M	J	J	A	S	O	N	D
T$_{mean}$	4.8	5.1	5.1	4.3	3.5	2.8	2.2	2.9	3.5	4.2	4.5	5.1
P	0.28	0.28	0.28	0.28	0.27	0.27	0.27	0.27	0.27	0.28	0.28	0.28
p(0.46T+8)	2.858	2.897	2.897	2.794	2.595	2.508	2.433	2.520	2.595	2.781	2.820	2.897
ET$_0$(mm/day)	3.1	3.1	3	3.2	2.7	2.6	2.6	2.5	2.7	3	3	3.2
Days	31	29	30	30	31	30	31	31	30	31	30	31
ET$_0$(mm/month)	96.1	89.9	90	96	83.7	78	80.6	77.5	81	93	90	99.2

The computed ET$_0$ was then used to determine crop evapotranspiration (ET$_c$) based on Equation (2). Then the P$_e$ and ET$_c$ were then integrated into Equation 4 for determination of SSDI values at a monthly Temporal resolution.

For the purpose of representation, time-series plots from four meteorological stations are described. The time series SSDI results of the four stations namely; Naro-moru (ID 9037064), Nyeri (ID 9036288), Embu (ID 9037202) and Sagana FCF (ID 9037096) are summarized in Figures 3 to 6. From these results, it is observed that the drought magnitude varied from station to station with major droughts episodes of different durations occurring between 1990 and 1997 for all the gauging stations. The results show that the SSDI values were consistently below -2.0 in all the stations for the period 1990 to 1997. This means that most areas in the basin experienced extreme drought in the stated years. The results also indicate that moderate, severe and extreme droughts at varying magnitudes as detected by the SSDI were experienced in 1973, 1978, 1984, 1994, 2000 and 2010 at different meteorological stations and for the entire basin (Figure 7), with the SSDI values equal or less than -2.0. Any value greater than 0, indicate near normal, wet and abundant water availability in the basin.

Figure 3. Time-series drought for Naro-Moru FGP (9037064) meteorological station

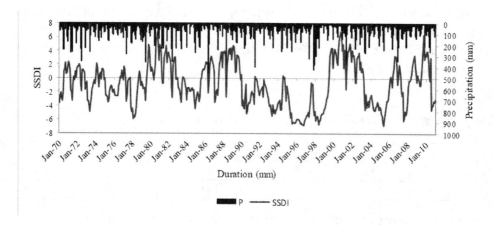

Figure 4. Time-series drought for Nyeri (9036288) meteorological station

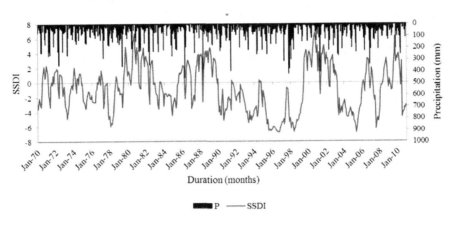

Figure 5. Time-series drought for Embu (9037202) meteorological station

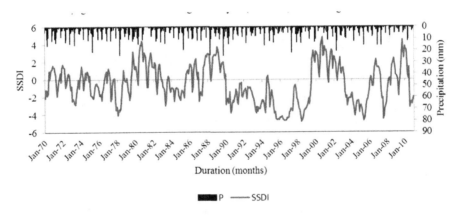

Figure 6. Time-series drought for Sagana FCF (9037096) meteorological station

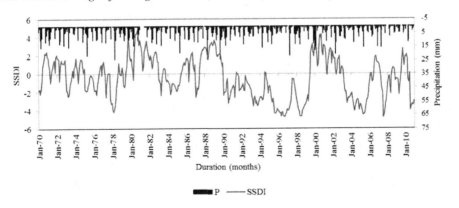

Figure 7. Average time-series drought for the entire UTaRB

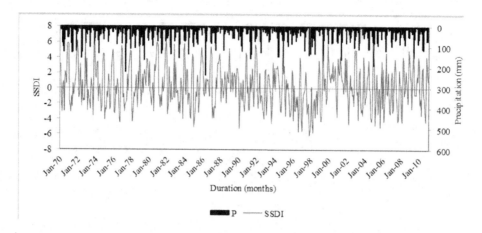

Spatially Distributed Drought Severity Based on SSDI

Results for 1970 to 2010 show that the temporal and spatial drought severities have been increasing over the years. Referring to Figure 8(a) the values range from 1.69 to 2.22 and 3.59 to 4.17 in 1970 and 3.74 to 6.29 and 4.37 to 4.96 (Figure 8e) in 2010. The areas in south-eastern side of the basin experience the highest drought severity. These south-eastern areas with the highest decadal drought severities are considered to be the most drought-risk prone areas. In formulation of drought mitigation areas, these risk areas should be prioritized.

SSDI Drought Forecasts

Different ANN architectures were tested for the meteorological SSDI. For the meteorological drought forecasting, SSDI was used to formulate the network models. From the results (Table 5) the ANN architectures 6-10-1 gave the best R, d_{SSDI} and NSE values for 1-month drought forecasting, at Nyeri (9036288) meteorological stations. Different ANNs architectures with unique combination can also be extracted from the data for the 3-minth drought forecasting.

Drought Projections Based on SSDI and RMSNN

The most notable average drought events expected for the entire UTaRB is as presented in Figure 9. The average drought for observed period (1970 to 2010) and projection period (2010-2055) for entire basin was used because it a representation of correct image of what happens in the basin as far as drought is concerned. Thus an output representative of drought for the whole basin; the projected extreme droughts (Values of SSDI less than -2.00) include the years 2019 to 2020, 2028 to 2030, 2040 to 2041, 2050, 2053 to 2054, 2060 to 2063, 2070 to 2073 and 2081 to 2083. In addition the projected abudant water supply (SSDI values ^{3} 2.00) events are in the years 2017, 2026, 2033, 2046 and 2055 as shown in Figure 9.

Figure 8. (a to e) Spatial drought for UTaRB as detected using SSDI for the period 1980-2010

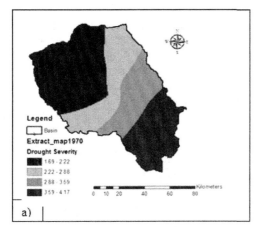

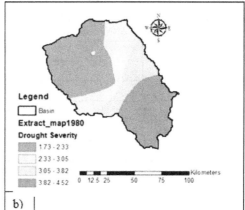

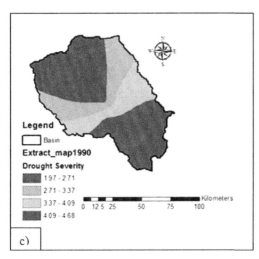

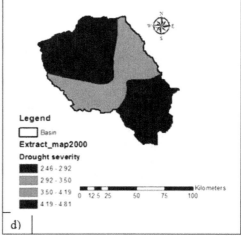

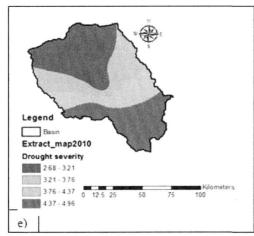

Table 5. Best ANNs for 1-month and 3-month drought forecasting of SSDI

Station ID[a]	SSDI				SSDI			
	ANN Arch[b]	R	d1	NSE	ANN Arch[b]	R	d1	NSE
	1-Month Lead Time				3-Months Lead Time			
9037112	6-5-1	0.753	0.805	0.698	6-7-1	0.664	0.718	0.607
9037096	6-3-1	0.724	0.773	0.665	6-9-1	0.643	0.696	0.591
9037202	6-5-1	0.748	0.799	0.695	6-5-1	0.657	0.715	0.606
9037031	6-9-1	0.685	0.735	0.633	6-5-1	0.612	0.667	0.555
9036288	6-10-1	0.852	0.924	0.822	6-10-1	0.764	0.816	0.712
9137123	6-3-1	0.787	0.833	0.734	6-3-1	0.688	0.745	0.636
9037212	6-7-1	0.762	0.814	0.709	6-10-1	0.669	0.721	0.619
9037064	6-10-1	0.855	0.907	0.806	6-10-1	0.776	0.787	0.694

[a]The station IDs defined as 9037112, 9037096, 9037202, 9037031, 9036288, 9137123, 9037212 and 9037064 refer to MIAD, Sagana FCF, Embu, Kerugoya DWO, Nyeri, Mangu HS, Maragua GEF and Naro-moru FGP weather stations respectively

[b]The short form of 'Architecture'

Figure 9. Time-series drought for the observed and projected periods in the UTaRB

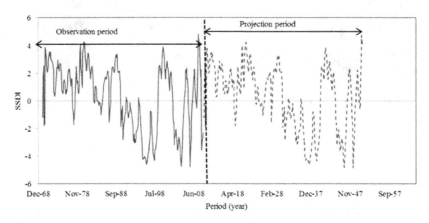

CONCLUSION

The Standardized Supply-Demand-Water Index (SSDI) applied in the present research integrated effective precipitation and crop evapo-transpiration in a water balance approach. Time-series results of drought estimation period (1972 to 2010) indicate that moderate, severe and extreme droughts at different degrees were detected by the SSDI. These droughts were experienced in 1973, 1978, 1984, 1994, 2000 and 2010 at different meteorological stations and for the entire basin, with the SSDI values equal or less than -2.0. SSDI values around 0, 0 to1.99 and greater than 2.0 indicate near normal, wet and abundant water availability in the basin respectively. Spatial drought revealed that the south-eastern areas of the UTaRB had the highest decadal drought severities and is considered to be most drought-risk prone areas compared to the other parts. Within the basin, drought was projected ahead using the SSDI in conjunction with Recursive Multi-step Neural Networks (RMNN). the findings indicate projected extreme droughts

(Values of SSDI less than -2.00) and abudant water supply (SSDI values ³ 2.00) events for forthcoming years (2010 to 2097). From this study, the proposed drought estimation-and-projection will provide a tool for water managers to formulate a long-term drought, preparedness and mitigation strategies as well as regional water plan for future drought resilience.

REFERENCES

Ali, Z., Hussain, I., Faisal, M., Nazir, H. M., Hussain, T., Yousaf, M., ... Gani, S. H. (2018). Forecasting Drought Using Multilayer Perceptron Artificial Neural Network Model. *Advances in Meteorology*, 1–9.

Belayneh, A. and Adamowski, J. (2012). Standard precipitation index drought forecasting using neural networks, wavelet neural networks and support vector regression, *Journal of applied computational intelligence and soft computing,* 1-13.

Belayneh, A. and Adamowski, J. (2013). Drought forecasting using new machine learning methods, *Journal of Water and Land Development,* 18 (I-IV), 3-12.

FAO. (2013). Crop evapo-transpiration guidelines for computing crop water requirements; cooperate document repository report.

FAO. (2013). Report on land and water. Retrieved from www.fao.org/nrl/aboutnr/nrl

Halagundegowda, G. R., & Singh, A. (2018). Multilayer perceptron Method of Artificial Neural Network for Classification of farmers Based on Adoption of Drought Coping Mechanisms. *International Journal of Pure and Applied Bioscience*, *6*(2), 1408–1414. doi:10.18782/2320-7051.6405

Hao, Z, Singh, V. P. Xia, Y. (2018). Seasonal drought prediction; advances, challenges and future prospects, a *Review of Geophysics*, *56*, 108-141.

Hiho, J. M., Mugalavai, E. M. (2018). The effect of droughts on food security in Kenya, *The International Journal of Climate Change- impacts and responses*, *2*(2), 1-17.

IFAD. (2012). Upper Tana catchment natural resource management project report, east and southern Africa division, project management department.

IPCC. (2014). Climate Change 2014, fifth assessment report on impacts, adaptation and vulnerability, WGII AR5, Summary for policy makers.

Jacobs, J. Angerer, J., Vitale, J., Srinivasan, R., Kaitho, J. and Stuth, J. (2004). Exploring the Potential Impact of Restoration on Hydrology of the Upper Tana RiverCatchment and Masinga Dam, Kenya. Texas A & M University.

Karamouz, M., Rasouli, K., & Nazi, S. (2009). Development of a hybrid index for drought prediction: Case study. *Journal of Hydrologic Engineering*, *14*(6), 617–627. doi:10.1061/(ASCE)HE.1943-5584.0000022

Krause, P., Boyle, D. P., & Base, F. (2005). Comparison of different efficiency criteria for hydrological model assessment. *Advances in Geosciences*, *5*, 89–97. doi:10.5194/adgeo-5-89-2005

McEvoy, J., Bathke, D. J., Burkardt, N., Cravens, A. E., Haigh, T., Hall, K. R., ... Wickham, E. (2018). Ecological Drought: Accounting for the Non-Human Impacts of Water Shortage in the Upper Missouri Headwaters Basin, Montana, USA. *Resources Journal, 7*(14), 1–16.

Morid, S., Smakhtin, V., & Bagherzadeh, K. (2007). Drought forecasting using artificial neural networks and time series of drought indices. *International Journal of Climatology, 27*(15), 2103–2111. doi:10.1002/joc.1498

Mustafa, M. R., Isa, M. H., & Rezaur, R. B. (2012). Artificial neural networks in Water Resources Engineering; Infrastructure and applications, *Journal of World Academy of Science. Engineering and Technology, 6*, 2–24.

Peters, E. G., Bier, H. A. J., van Lanen, H. A. J., & Torfs, P. J. J. F. (2006). Propagation and spatial distribution of drought in a groundwater catchment. *Journal of Hydrology (Amsterdam), 321*(1–4), 257–275. doi:10.1016/j.jhydrol.2005.08.004

Sanmartín, J. F., Pan, D., Fischer, L., Orlowsky, B., Hernández, J. G., Jordan, F., ... Xu, J. (2018). Searching for the optimal drought index and timescale combination to detect drought: A case study from the lower Jinsha River basin, China. *Hydrology and Earth System Sciences, 22*(1), 889–910. doi:10.5194/hess-22-889-2018

Scheffran, J., Marmer, E., & Show, P. (2012). Migration as a contribution to resilience and innovation in climate adaptation: Social networks and co-development in North West Africa. *Applied Geography (Sevenoaks, England), 33*, 119–127. doi:10.1016/j.apgeog.2011.10.002

Sivaprakasam, S., Murugappan, A., & Mohan, S. (2011). Modified Hargreaves equation for estimation of ET_o in a hot and humid location in Tamilnadu state, India. *International Journal of Engineering Science and Technology, 3*(1), 592–600.

Tallaksen, L. M., Hisdal, H., & Lanen, H. A. J. V. (2009). Space-time modelling of catchment scale drought characteristics. *Journal of Hydrology (Amsterdam), 375*(3-4), 363–372. doi:10.1016/j.jhydrol.2009.06.032

The Nature Conservancy (TNC). (2015). *Upper Tana-Nairobi water fund business case, Version 2.* Nairobi, Kenya: The Nature Conservancy.

UN. (2008). *Trends in sustainable development, agriculture, rural development, land desertification and drought. Department of economic and social affairs.* New York: United Nations.

UNDP. (2012). Kenya: adapting to climate variability in Arid and Semi-Arid Lands (KACCAL), project report

Wang, W, & Ertsen, M. W., Svoboda M, D. & Hafeez, M. (2016). Propagation of drought: From meteorological to Agricultural and Hydrological Drought. *Advances in Meteorology*, 1–5.

Wilby, R. L., Orr, H. G., Hedger, M., Forrow, D., & Blakmore, M. (2006a). Risks posed by climate variability to delivery of water framework directive objectives. *Environment International, 32*(8), 1043–1055. doi:10.1016/j.envint.2006.06.017

WRMA. (2010). *Physiological survey in the upper Tana catchment, a natural resources management project report*. Nairobi.

Yuan, Z., Xu, J., Chen, J., Huo, J., Yu, Y., Locher, P., & Xu, B. (2017). Drought assessment and projection under climate change; A case study in Middle and lower Lower Jinsha River Basin. *Advances in Meteorology*, 1–17.

Chapter 52
Dead Sea Water Levels Analysis Using Artificial Neural Networks and Firefly Algorithm

Nawaf N. Hamadneh

iD https://orcid.org/0000-0002-2170-2074

Saudi Electronic University, Saudi Arabia

ABSTRACT

In this study, the performance of adaptive multilayer perceptron neural network (MLPNN) for predicting the Dead Sea water level is discussed. Firefly Algorithm (FFA), as an optimization algorithm is used for training the neural networks. To propose the MLPNN-FFA model, Dead Sea water levels over the period 1810–2005 are applied to train MLPNN. Statistical tests evaluate the accuracy of the hybrid MLPNN-FFA model. The predicted values of the proposed model were compared with the results obtained by another method. The results reveal that the artificial neural network (ANN) models exhibit high accuracy and reliability for the prediction of the Dead Sea water levels. The results also reveal that the Dead Sea water level would be around -450 until 2050.

1. INTRODUCTION

A key aspect of water resources management activities is to predict the level of water bodies such as seas, rivers, and lakes (Ghorbani, Deo, Karimi, Yaseen, & Terzi, 2018; Yaseen et al., 2018). Artificial neural networks (ANNs) models were used successfully to model the lakes and the river systems without using experimental apparatuses(Buyukyildiz, Tezel, & Yilmaz, 2014; Esbati, Khanesar, & Shahzadi, 2017; Kakahaji, Banadaki, Kakahaji, & Kakahaji, 2013; Yaseen et al., 2018). Also, using an optimization scheme in a predictive model can thus improve the performance of the NN models(Asteris & Nikoo, 2019; Ghorbani et al., 2018; Walczak, 2019).

The Dead Sea consists of the world's biggest lakes and the water lakes threatened by drought due to several factors such as lack of rain and exploitation of sea water (Al Rawashdeh, Ruzouq, Pradhan, Ziad, & Ghayda, 2013; Dente, Lensky, Morin, Dunne, & Enzel, 2018). The Dead Sea is a unique and

DOI: 10.4018/978-1-6684-2408-7.ch052

essential environment from an economic, environmental and tourist point of view (Kiro et al., 2017). Numerous scientific studies have been published on the degradation of the Dead Sea water level using radar interference (Al-Hanbali, Al-Bilbisi, & Kondoh, 2005; Closson et al., 2003). After that, Landsat images for the period 1810–2005 was used to study the fluctuation level of the Dead Sea surface area (Al Rawashdeh et al., 2013). In their study, the geographic information system (GIS) and Global Positioning System were used to predict of Dead Sea water level. In recent years, the intelligent methods have been largely used in prediction of water level fluctuations in lakes (Esbati et al., 2017; Ghorbani et al., 2018; Kakahaji et al., 2013). They have used hybrid artificial intelligence approaches and statistical analysis or water level prediction. Moreover, no one used artificial intelligence models to estimate the Dead Sea water levels.

In this study, the prediction of the future water level of the Dead Sea is investigated using multilayer perceptron neural network (MLPNN) which is trained using the firefly algorithm (FFA). One of the main advantages of MLPNN-FFA method is that FFA can easily optimally estimate the parameters of MLPNN. Furthermore, the accuracy of the used methods is evaluated using various statistical parameters. Using an optimization scheme in a predictive model can thus utilize the best NN parameters.

This paper is organized as follows. In Section 2, different methods including MLPNN and FFA are described. In Section 3, the experimental results are discussed. Finally, Section 4 concludes this study.

2. METHODS

2.1. Multilayer Perceptron Neural Network

ANNs are mathematical models which are *inspired* by the way the *biological* nervous systems (Ghorbani et al., 2018; N. Hamadneh, Khan, & Tilahun, 2018; N. N. Hamadneh, Khan, & Khan, 2018; Heidari, Faris, Aljarah, & Mirjalili, 2018; Pham, Bui, Prakash, & Dholakia, 2017). MLPNN is one of the widely known of feedforward artificial neural networks(Ghiasi, Irani Jam, Teimourian, Zarrabi, & Yousefi, 2019). In this study, MLPNN has used for prediction the water level of the Dead Sea, where Figure 1 shows the location of the Dead Sea (https://www.nationsonline.org/oneworld/map/jordan_map.htm, 2018).

MLPNNs have three types of layers, which include the input layers, hidden layers, and the output layer. Figure 2 shows a structure of MLPNN (Jadidi, Menezes, de Souza, & de Castro Lima, 2018; Mefoued, 2013; Yeung, Li, Ng, & Chan, 2016).

The activation function (sigmoid function) in the hidden layer can be written as:

$$y = tanhx = \frac{1 - e^{-2x}}{1 + e^{-2x}} \tag{1}$$

Figure 1. The location of Dead Sea

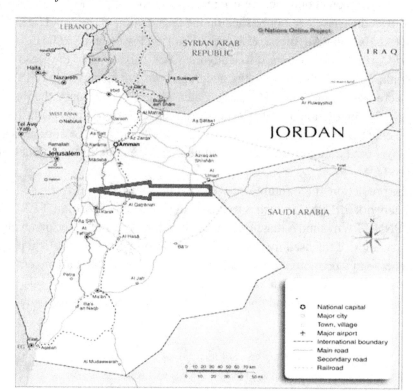

Figure 2. Structure of a multilayer perceptron neural network

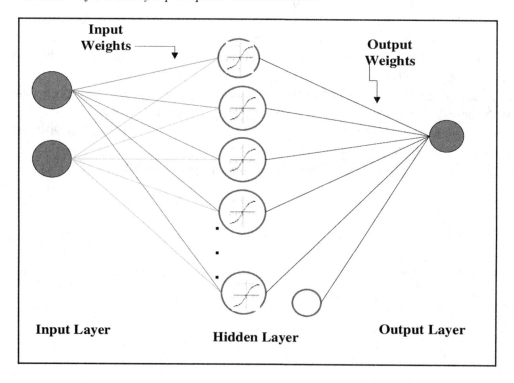

Training methods are used to improve the performance of artificial neural networks (ANNs) by determining the best parameters of ANNs. Metaheuristic algorithms are widely used for training ANNs, providing a sufficiently good ANN model(N. N. Hamadneh et al., 2018; Normah, Oh, Chien, Choi, & Robiah, 2015; Tilahun, Ngnotchouye, & Hamadneh, 2017). Because of the properties of optimization algorithms, several algorithms are used for training ANNs to find the best parameters, such as Particle swarm optimization (PSO) algorithm, Genetic algorithm (GA), and FFA (Amanifard, Nariman-Zadeh, Borji, Khalkhali, & Habibdoust, 2008; Ghorbani et al., 2018; N. Hamadneh, Sathasivam, Tilahun, & Choon, 2012; Han, Lu, Hou, & Qiao, 2018). The parameters of MLPNNs are the input and the output weights of the neural models. In this study, the PSO algorithm is used to train ANNs, because it is one of the most effective metaheuristic algorithms is used for optimization problems. Equation (2) is the root mean squared error (*RMSE*) function which we have used as an objective function to test the performance of ANNs (Mefoued, 2013; Motlagh & Taghipour-Gorjikolaie, 2018):

$$RMSE = \sum_i^N \frac{\left(Actual\,output - target\,output \right)^2}{N} \tag{2}$$

where the target output values are determined by Equation (3), while the actual output values are the NN output values:

$$Output\left(y_k\right) = \sum_{j=1}^m \sum_{i=1}^n w_{jk} \sum_{k=1}^s w'_{ki} tanh x_j \tag{3}$$

where:

n: Number of the neurons in the hidden layer.
m: Number of input values.
s: Number of the neurons in the input layer.
k: Number of the neurons in the hidden layer.
w_{jk}: Input weight between input layer and hidden layer.
w'_{ki} : Output weight between hidden layer and output layer.

2.2. Firefly Algorithm

FFA is one of the metaheuristic algorithms that are very effective for applying in many scientific fields. (Le, Bui, Ngo, Nguyen, & Nguyen-Xuan, 2019; Tilahun et al., 2017; Yang, Hosseini, & Gandomi, 2012). The algorithm simulates the relationship between fireflies using their flashing lights. The algorithm assumes that any other firefly can attract each firefly. Note that, the attractiveness of a firefly is directly proportional to its brightness which depends on the objective function. Figure 3 is the flowchart of FFA (Ghorbani et al., 2018; N. N. Hamadneh, 2018; Tilahun et al., 2017; Yang et al., 2012). Fireflies updates continue to be repeated until a termination criterion is met. Note that, the termination criterion is the maximum number of iterations or tolerance from the optimum value if it is known.

Figure 3. Flowchart of firefly algorithm on artificial neural networks

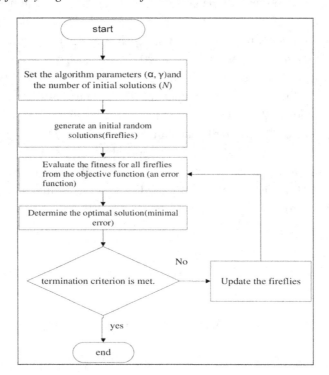

Like any optimization algorithm, modifying FFA parameter is the best forward idea to improve the performance of the results. Besides, changing the values of the parameters according to the search state is efficient. Moreover, when the search continues, to get a good accuracy conversion, the randomness movement must decrease.

3. RESULTS AND DISCUSSION

In this study, the water levels data of the Dead Sea from 1880 to 2005 are utilized for training the ANNs. I have taken one value of dead sea water level every five years from 1880 to 2005. FFA is used 50 times to train the neural networks, and then we have selected the best NN model that has minimal error as shown in Figure 4. The architecture of the neural networks which we used as one input neuron, six hidden neurons, and one output neuron. In parallel to that, FFA is used for the training process to determine the input and the output weights of NNs by determining the minimal error between the actual values and target values. The MATLAB software has been used to implement FFA and ANNs.

As a result of training the neural networks, the NN model representing successfully the experimental testing data set, as shown in Figure 5. I have also used the regression equation to test the experimental data with the corresponding values of the NN model, as shown in Figure 6. The correlation coefficient is ($r =0.987$). Then we used the t-statistical test and critical correlation value formula to test the correlation coefficient. The correlation coefficient r is greater than the critical correlation value r_c which equal to 0.26 for a significance level of 0.05. Accordingly, we have sufficient evidence to support NN model for the prediction of the Dead sea water level:

$$t = r \sqrt{\frac{n-2}{1-r^2}} \tag{4a}$$

$$r_C = \sqrt{\frac{\dfrac{t^2}{n-2}}{\dfrac{t^2}{n_{-2}}+1}} \tag{4b}$$

where n is the size of data, r is correlation coefficient, and r_C is critical correlation value.

Figure 4. Best performance of FFA based on RMSE

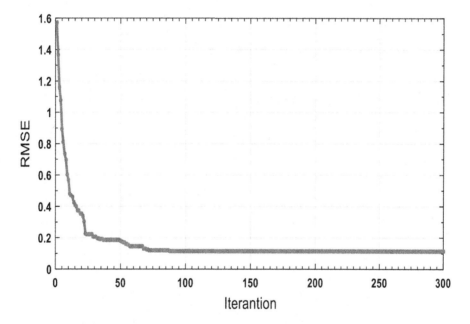

In Figure **7**, the Dead Sea water levels from 2008 to 2017 are utilized as testing data with the corresponding NN model values. The correlation coefficient r for the testing data is 0.97, see Figure 8. Additionally, we have used the NN model to predate the dead sea water level from 2018 to 2015, as shown in Figure 9. Moreover, the comparison of the expected results of the model with the results of (Al Rawashdeh et al., 2013) shows that the results are in good agreement.

Figure 5. Experimental testing data (target data) with corresponding neural network data (actual data)

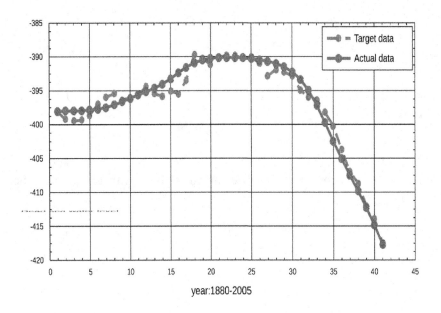

Figure 6. Scatter plot of NN model values with the experimental training values

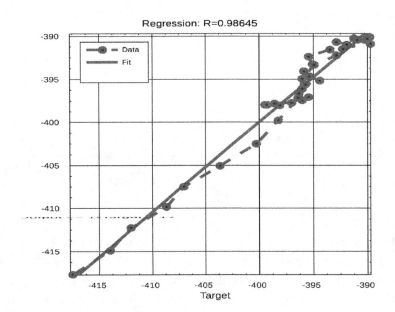

Figure 7. Experimental testing data (target data) with corresponding neural network data (actual data)

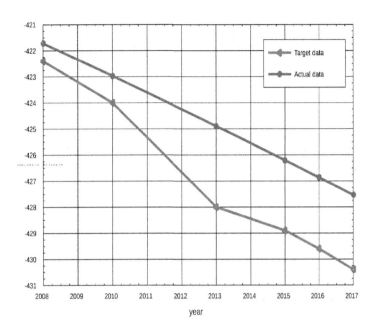

Figure 8. Scatter plot of NN model values with the experimental training values

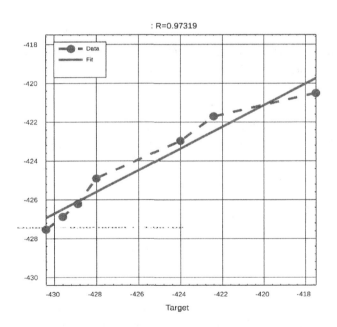

Figure 9. The prediction of Dead Sea water level from 2018 to 2050

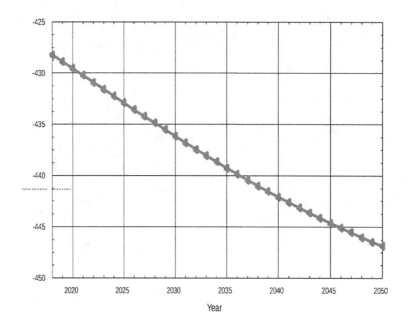

4. CONCLUSION

This study enables the prediction of the Dead Sea water levels until 2050 using artificial neural networks(ANNs) integrated with the firefly algorithm (FFA). It is important to note that this study is the first one to use ANNs to predict the Dead Sea water level. Using FFA, ANNs enabled us to find the best models by creating optimal solutions with minimal errors. In accordance with the results, FFA is a useful optimization algorithm for enhancing the accuracy of applied for Dead Sea water level models. Also, the use of the model showed that the Dead Sea water level would remain continually decreasing. One of the main advantages of the use of ANNs is that one can adjust the model depending on the variables that can occur at any time. It is worth noting that the accuracy of the performance of neural models can be improved by incorporating more information into the learning process. The rate of precipitation, temperature and the Dead sea water levels, which may contain more information to help improve the accuracy of the neural models, could be subject of the future work.

REFERENCES

Al-Hanbali, A., Al-Bilbisi, H., & Kondoh, A. (2005). The environmental problem of the Dead Sea using remote sensing and GIS techniques. Paper presented at the 11th CEReS International Symposium on Remote Sensing, Chiba University, Chiba, Japan. Academic Press. Retrieved from http://www2.cr.chiba-u.jp/symp2005/documents/Postersession/p017_AAlHanbali_paper.pdf

Al Rawashdeh, S., Ruzouq, R., Pradhan, B., Ziad, S. A.-H., & Ghayda, A. R. (2013). Monitoring of Dead Sea water surface variation using multi-temporal satellite data and GIS. *Arabian Journal of Geosciences*, *6*(9), 3241–3248. doi:10.100712517-012-0630-6

Amanifard, N., Nariman-Zadeh, N., Borji, M., Khalkhali, A., & Habibdoust, A. (2008). Modelling and Pareto optimization of heat transfer and flow coefficients in microchannels using GMDH type neural networks and genetic algorithms. *Energy Conversion and Management*, *49*(2), 311–325. doi:10.1016/j.enconman.2007.06.002

Asteris, P. G., & Nikoo, M. (2019). Artificial bee colony-based neural network for the prediction of the fundamental period of infilled frame structures. *Neural Computing & Applications*, 1–11.

Buyukyildiz, M., Tezel, G., & Yilmaz, V. (2014). Estimation of the change in lake water level by artificial intelligence methods. *Water Resources Management*, *28*(13), 4747–4763. doi:10.100711269-014-0773-1

Closson, D., Karaki, N. A., Hansen, H., Derauw, D., Barbier, C., & Ozer, A. (2003). Space-borne radar interferometric mapping of precursory deformations of a dyke collapse, Dead Sea area, Jordan. *International Journal of Remote Sensing*, *24*(4), 843–849. doi:10.1080/01431160210147388

Dente, E., Lensky, N. G., Morin, E., Dunne, T., & Enzel, Y. (2018). Sinuosity evolution along an incising channel: New insights from the Jordan River response to the Dead Sea level fall. *Earth Surface Processes and Landforms*.

Esbati, M., Khanesar, M. A., & Shahzadi, A. (2017). Modeling level change in Lake Urmia using hybrid artificial intelligence approaches. *Theoretical and Applied Climatology*, 1–12.

Ghiasi, M., Irani Jam, M., Teimourian, M., Zarrabi, H., & Yousefi, N. (2019). A new prediction model of electricity load based on hybrid forecast engine. *International Journal of Ambient Energy*, *40*(2), 179–186. doi:10.1080/01430750.2017.1381157

Ghorbani, M. A., Deo, R. C., Karimi, V., Yaseen, Z. M., & Terzi, O. (2018). Implementation of a hybrid MLP-FFA model for water level prediction of Lake Egirdir, Turkey. *Stochastic Environmental Research and Risk Assessment*, *32*(6), 1683–1697. doi:10.100700477-017-1474-0

Hamadneh, N., Khan, W., & Tilahun, S. (2018). Optimization of microchannel heat sinks using prey-predator algorithm and artificial neural networks. *MACHINES*, *6*(2), 26. doi:10.3390/machines6020026

Hamadneh, N., Sathasivam, S., Tilahun, S. L., & Choon, O. H. (2012). Learning logic programming in radial basis function network via genetic algorithm. *Journal of Applied Sciences (Faisalabad)*, *12*(9), 840–847. doi:10.3923/jas.2012.840.847

Hamadneh, N. N. (2018). A Comparison between Firefly and Prey-Predator Algorithms Based on Artificial Neural Networks. *Applied Mathematical Sciences*, *12*(24), 1157–1165. doi:10.12988/ams.2018.8346

Hamadneh, N. N., Khan, W. S., & Khan, W. A. (2018). Prediction of thermal conductivities of polyacrylonitrile electrospun nanocomposite fibers using artificial neural network and prey predator algorithm. *Journal of King Saud University-Science*.

Han, H.-G., Lu, W., Hou, Y., & Qiao, J.-F. (2018). An adaptive-PSO-based self-organizing RBF neural network. *IEEE Transactions on Neural Networks and Learning Systems*, 29(1), 104–117. doi:10.1109/TNNLS.2016.2616413 PMID:28113788

Heidari, A. A., Faris, H., Aljarah, I., & Mirjalili, S. (2018). An efficient hybrid multilayer perceptron neural network with grasshopper optimization. *Soft Computing*, 1–18. Retrieved from https://www.nationsonline.org/oneworld/map/jordan_map.htm

Jadidi, A., Menezes, R., de Souza, N., & de Castro Lima, A. (2018). A hybrid ga–mlpnn model for one-hour-ahead forecasting of the global horizontal irradiance in Elizabeth city, North Carolina. *Energies*, 11(10), 2641. doi:10.3390/en11102641

Kakahaji, H., Banadaki, H. D., Kakahaji, A., & Kakahaji, A. (2013). Prediction of Urmia Lake water-level fluctuations by using analytical, linear statistic and intelligent methods. *Water Resources Management*, 27(13), 4469–4492. doi:10.100711269-013-0420-2

Kiro, Y., Goldstein, S. L., Garcia-Veigas, J., Levy, E., Kushnir, Y., Stein, M., & Lazar, B. (2017). Relationships between lake-level changes and water and salt budgets in the Dead Sea during extreme aridities in the Eastern Mediterranean. *Earth and Planetary Science Letters*, 464, 211–226. doi:10.1016/j.epsl.2017.01.043

Le, D. T., Bui, D.-K., Ngo, T. D., Nguyen, Q.-H., & Nguyen-Xuan, H. (2019). A novel hybrid method combining electromagnetism-like mechanism and firefly algorithms for constrained design optimization of discrete truss structures. *Computers & Structures*, 212, 20–42. doi:10.1016/j.compstruc.2018.10.017

Mefoued, S. (2013). Assistance of knee movements using an actuated orthosis through subject's intention based on MLPNN approximators. *Paper presented at the 2013 International Joint Conference on Neural Networks (IJCNN)*. Academic Press. 10.1109/IJCNN.2013.6706827

Motlagh, N. V., & Taghipour-Gorjikolaie, M. (2018). Comparison of heuristic methods for developing optimized neural network based models to predict amphiphobic behavior of fluorosilica coated surfaces. *Surface and Coatings Technology*.

Normah, G.-M., Oh, J.-T., Chien, N. B., Choi, K.-I., & Robiah, A. (2015). Comparison of the optimized thermal performance of square and circular ammonia-cooled microchannel heat sink with genetic algorithm. *Energy Conversion and Management*, 102, 59–65. doi:10.1016/j.enconman.2015.02.008

Pham, B. T., Bui, D. T., Prakash, I., & Dholakia, M. (2017). Hybrid integration of Multilayer Perceptron Neural Networks and machine learning ensembles for landslide susceptibility assessment at Himalayan area (India) using GIS. *Catena*, 149, 52–63. doi:10.1016/j.catena.2016.09.007

Tilahun, S. L., Ngnotchouye, J. M. T., & Hamadneh, N. N. (2017). Continuous versions of firefly algorithm: A review. *Artificial Intelligence Review*, 1–48.

Walczak, S. (2019). Artificial neural networks. In Advanced Methodologies and Technologies in Artificial Intelligence, Computer Simulation, and Human-Computer Interaction (pp. 40-53). Hershey, PA: IGI Global. doi:10.4018/978-1-5225-7368-5.ch004

Yang, X.-S., Hosseini, S. S. S., & Gandomi, A. H. (2012). Firefly algorithm for solving non-convex economic dispatch problems with valve loading effect. *Applied Soft Computing*, *12*(3), 1180–1186. doi:10.1016/j.asoc.2011.09.017

Yaseen, Z. M., Ghareb, M. I., Ebtehaj, I., Bonakdari, H., Siddique, R., Heddam, S., ... Deo, R. (2018). Rainfall pattern forecasting using novel hybrid intelligent model based ANFIS-FFA. *Water Resources Management*, *32*(1), 105–122. doi:10.100711269-017-1797-0

Yeung, D. S., Li, J.-C., Ng, W. W., & Chan, P. P. (2016). MLPNN training via a multiobjective optimization of training error and stochastic sensitivity. *IEEE Transactions on Neural Networks and Learning Systems*, *27*(5), 978–992. doi:10.1109/TNNLS.2015.2431251 PMID:26054075

This research was previously published in the International Journal of Swarm Intelligence Research (IJSIR), 11(3); pages 19-29, copyright year 2020 by IGI Publishing (an imprint of IGI Global).

Chapter 53
Artificial Neural Network for Markov Chaining of Rainfall Over India

Kavita Pabreja

(iD) https://orcid.org/0000-0001-9856-0900

Maharaja Surajmal Institute, GGSIP University, India

ABSTRACT

Rainfall forecasting plays a significant role in water management for agriculture in a country like India where the economy depends heavily upon agriculture. In this paper, a feed forward artificial neural network (ANN) and a multiple linear regression model has been utilized for lagged time series data of monthly rainfall. The data for 23 years from 1990 to 2012 over Indian region has been used in this study. Convincing values of root mean squared error between actual monthly rainfall and that predicted by ANN has been found. It has been found that during monsoon months, rainfall of every n+3rd month can be predicted using last three months' (n, n+1, n+2) rainfall data with an excellent correlation coefficient that is more than 0.9 between actual and predicted rainfall. The probabilities of dry seasonal month, wet seasonal month for monsoon and non-monsoon months have been found.

INTRODUCTION

Water resource planning is one of the most important activities for the growth of a country like India where economy is too much dependent on agriculture. The prediction of hydrological variables *viz.* precipitation, flood stream and runoff flow play an important role for the growth and development of a nation. In India, irrigation is not common and primarily rainfall water is used for supplying water to crops by farmers. When rainfall is not sufficient, irrigation is utilized as supplement. The forecasting of probability of occurrence of rainfall is one of the most important factors for planning and management of crops and decisions related to water management, following which the liability in economy due to unpredictability of water can be reduced. Hence forecasting, modeling and monitoring of rainfall are of

DOI: 10.4018/978-1-6684-2408-7.ch053

great significance in the field of agriculture as also emphasized by (Geng et al., 1986); (Hoogenboom, 2000); (Sentelhas, et al., 2001).

Weather forecasting can be defined as daily progress and advancement of the weather up to several days ahead, and seasonal forecasting is related to the average weather conditions for a few months to about a year as stated by Chang and Yeung (2003). Since seasonal forecasts provide knowledge of weather for a few months in advance, they are important for all government sectors to increase productivity and minimize losses as mentioned by Ansari (2013).

The hydrological variables vary on a scale of space and time. Spatial and time series analysis of occurrence of rainfall on monthly basis is vital for observation of the hydrological behavior. There are many contributing factors on which hydrological cycle depends and rainfall is considered as the most important of them as stated by Mimikou (1983); Hamlin and Rees (1987).

Various statistical and soft-computing techniques have been used by meteorologists in past for predicting weather variables. The purpose of this piece of research is to predict rainfall data with an accuracy which is better than previous studies and based on lesser number of training datasets. The other dimension is to find important correlations between various months' rainfall. Also, the probabilities of dry seasonal month, wet seasonal month for monsoon and non-monsoon months has been calculated.

BACKGROUND

Synoptic, numerical and statistical methods have been used for forecasting of rainfall by various authors *viz.* (Tyagi et al., 2011); (Chatterjee et al., 2009); (Iyengar & Basak,1994). Time series technique which is one of the important statistical techniques has been used by many authors as stated in (Sengupta & Basak, 1998); (Iyengaer, 1991).

Markov model, a statistical approach, has been applied to provide forecasts of weather states (dry or wet day) for some future time depending upon values of weather variables given by current and some previous states. Markov chains specify the state of each day as wet or dry and generate a relation between the state of current day and the states of preceding days. The order of Markov chain depends upon the number of preceding days under consideration. Sorup et al. (2011) observed that the first order Markov chain is quite important whereas the second order Markov Chain is even more significant. The authors also found that that there is no noticeable difference between the model parameters of first and second order. It has been observed that the wet day of previous two time periods affect positively the wet day of current time period in the rainy season as compared to the dry day of previous two time period as explained by Hossain and Anam (2012). A 3-state Markov chain model with five independent variables for rainfall forecasting in Haryana, India, has been applied by Aneja and Srivastava (1999). Dash (2012) has found that the first order Markov chain is able to provide value for the precipitation occurrence for all months in Odisha, India.

A hidden state Markov model has been developed to explain the long-term persistence in annual rainfall by Thyer and Kuzcera (1999). In another work, Selvi and Selvaraj (2011) used first order Markov Chain modeling for annual basis of rainfall measurements over Tamil Nadu. The authors have used the annual rainfall for the years 1901 to 2000 and formed the frequency distribution table. The states correspond to class interval and then a transition probability matrix is formed. The authors demonstrated that Markov Chain approach is one of the best options to model future rainfall.

Recent technique for seasonal forecasting is based on Numerical Weather Prediction model which works on principle of dynamic modelling. Dynamic models apply prognostic physical equations. As mentioned by Ousmane, Neil Ward and Wassila (2011), there are two-tiered coupled ocean atmosphere climate models (capable of predicting Sea surface temperature followed by climate), fully coupled ocean-atmosphere-land-ice general circulation models (CGCMs) that provide features of predicting atmosphere and ocean collectively. Dynamic models use non-linear equations of mass conservation, motion, and energy to predict the complex atmosphere-ocean processes. Though they require huge computing resources to produce results, they are able to simulate the physical phenomena and are capable of producing more accurate forecasts. There is a growth in usage of dynamic models at a global scale which is primarily because of increasing power and reducing costs of computing machines.

ANN technique has been widely used by meteorologists since 1986 as explained by Rumelhart et al. (1986) as it can handle the complex and non-linear behaviour in a better way as compared to earlier statistical techniques. It is capable of predicting the future value of the time series from itself. ANN can predict even the chaotic time series such as rainfall as explained by Elsner and Tsonis (1992). Hence it can overcome the shortcomings of commonly used standard statistical and dynamical models.

ANN has also demonstrated encouraging results for predicting maximum and minimum temperatures for all twelve months, in study by Guhathakurta et al. (2013). The authors have used geographical information like latitude, longitude, and elevation as inputs to generate maximum and minimum temperatures at a place where there is no observatory. In more recent development, Feed forward Neural Network has been used by Guhathakurta (2008) for prediction of monsoon rainfall in 36 sub-division levels of India by using the rainfall data from years 1941-2005.

Other soft computing techniques *viz.* Fuzzy Inference System (FIS) have also been adapted for simulating and modeling of the systems behavior that are generally non-linear multivariate, and noisy, as mentioned by various authors *viz.* (ASCE Task committee, 2000; El-Shafie et al., 2007, 2008, 2009,2010, 2011; Fallah-Ghalhary et al., 2009; French et al., 1992; Galambosi et al., 1999; Hadli et al., 2002; Halff et al., 1993; Karamouz et al., 2004; Kumarasiri et al.,2006; Maria et al., 2005; Ozelkan et al., 1996; Sahai et al., 2000; Suwardi et al., 2006; Wong et al., 2003).

Regardless of the fact that there has been a large number of researches using empirical statistic and dynamic models for prediction of seasonal and annual rainfall, there is a scope of improvement so as to increase the accuracy in prediction of rainfall. In this paper, rainfall over Indian region has been analyzed from three different aspects. First, a deterministic Artificial Neural Network model and a linear regression model has been utilized for prediction of monsoon rainfall based on lagged time series data of rainfall on monthly basis for 23 years from 1990 to 2012 over Indian region. The predicted value of rainfall by both techniques has been compared and it has been found that ANN model has proved to be one of the best and demonstrated convincing Root Mean Squared Error (RMSE) between actual monthly rainfall and that predicted. RMSE is a frequently used measure of the differences between values predicted by a model and the values observed.

ANN is a novel technique and it has been found that the rainfall of n+3rd month can be predicted using last three months rainfall i.e. n+2, n+1 and n months' rainfall data with an excellent correlation coefficient which is more than 0.9 between actual and predicted rainfall. Secondly, the Pearson's correlation coefficient between consecutive month's rainfall has been calculated which is more than 0.75 that validates the fact that the rainfall of consecutive months is strongly correlated. Thirdly, the probability of dry and wet months, for monsoon and non-monsoon months has also been calculated that would help for proper planning of crops plantation.

DATA COLLECTION AND PRE-PROCESSING

India is in the northern hemisphere and its region is nearly 3.287 million square kilometres. In order to carry out the study the monthly rainfall, the data for the years 1990 to 2012 has been downloaded from "The World Bank data's climate description" site. The variation in annual rainfall over Indian region for 23 years is shown in Figure 1 and a sample of original data has been shown in Table 1.

Figure 1. Variation in annual rainfall over Indian region for 23 years

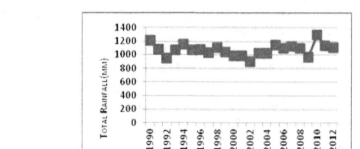

Table 1. A sample of monthly rainfall over Indian region

S.No.	Year	Month	Rainfall (mm)
1	1990	1	6
2	1990	2	19
3	1990	3	24
4	1990	4	35
5	1990	5	75
6	1990	6	185
7	1990	7	290
8	1990	8	283
9	1990	9	177
10	1990	10	84
11	1990	11	24
12	1990	12	11
13	1991	1	10
14	1991	2	11
15	1991	3	15

A time series based on three month lagged rainfall data has been created by pre-processing data in such a way that every three months' rainfall data, r_n, r_{n+1}, r_{n+2} used as predictors can predict the following i.e. r_{n+3} month's rainfall data, called predictand. For this purpose, a program in Java language has been written that accepts Table 1 data as input and after pre-processing generates the data in the format of Table 2 so that a lagged time series can be developed. A sample of this pre-processed data is shown in Table 2.

ABOUT TECHNIQUE USED

The most important contribution of this paper is that the prediction of rainfall for monsoon months over Indian region *viz.* May to October, has been done. The data shown in Table 2 has been filtered again by writing a program in Java language, so as to select only the rainfall for monsoon months of India and is shown in Table 3 where in first row, n=5 means month of May, n+1 means month of June, n+2 means July; and n+3 means August.

Corresponding to first row, the input dataset comprises of rainfall of three consecutive months (r_n, r_{n+1}, r_{n+2}) of Monsoon season e.g. May, June, July rainfall to predict August rainfall (r_{n+3}) as mentioned in Table 3. Similarly, the chain is developed for all monsoon months. The prediction of rainfall has been experimented with two techniques of Matlab viz. Artificial Neural Network and Linear regression.

Table 2. A sample of lagged three months (r_n, r_{n+1}, r_{n+2}) rainfall data to forecast fourth month(r_{n+3} rainfall, for all months of year

S. No	Predictor						Predictand	
	Rainfall for Month n in mm (r_n)		Rainfall for Month n+1 in mm (r_{n+1})		Rainfall for Month n+2 in mm (r_{n+2})		Rainfall for Month n+3 in mm (r_{n+3})	
1	Jan'90	6	Feb'90	19	Mar'90	24	Apr'90	35
2	Feb'90	19	Mar'90	24	Apr'90	35	May'90	75
3	Mar'90	24	Apr'90	35	May'90	75	Jun'90	185
4	Apr'90	35	May'90	75	Jun'90	185	Jul'90	290
5	May'90	75	Jun'90	185	Jul'90	290	Aug'90	283
6	Jun'90	185	Jul'90	290	Aug'90	283	Sep'90	177
7	Jul'90	290	Aug'90	283	Sep'90	177	Oct'90	84
8	Aug'90	283	Sep'90	177	Oct'90	84	Nov'90	24
9	Sep'90	177	Oct'90	84	Nov'90	24	Dec'90	11
10	Oct'90	84	Nov'90	24	Dec'90	11	Jan'91	10

An Artificial Neural Network is based on a mathematical approach that resembles the way the biological neural networks of living beings work. There are a large number of artificial neurons that perform processing of information, as explained by Sivanandam et al. (2009) and Kosko (2005).

Table 3. A sample of lagged three months (r_n, r_{n+1}, r_{n+2}) rainfall data to forecast fourth month(r_{n+3} rainfall, for monsoon months only

S. No.	Predictor						Predictand	
	Rainfall for Month n in mm (r_n)		Rainfall for Month n+1 in mm (r_{n+1})		Rainfall for Month n+2 in mm (r_{n+2})		Rainfall for Month n+3 in mm (r_{n+3})	
1	May'90	75	Jun'90	185	Jul'90	290	Aug'90	283
2	Jun'90	185	Jul'90	290	Aug'90	283	Sep'90	177
3	Jul'90	290	Aug'90	283	Sep'90	177	Oct'90	84
4	May'91	63	Jun'91	214	Jul'91	250	Aug'91	248
5	Jun'91	214	Jul'91	250	Aug'91	248	Sep'91	134
6	Jul'91	250	Aug'91	248	Sep'91	134	Oct'91	63
7	May'92	52	Jun'92	123	Jul'92	223	Aug'92	239
8	Jun'92	123	Jul'92	223	Aug'92	239	Sep'92	164
9	Jul'92	223	Aug'92	239	Sep'92	164	Oct'92	55
10	May'93	59	Jun'93	167	Jul'93	270	Aug'93	184

In this paper, we have trained and tested the Artificial Neural Network by deploying a two-layer Multi-Layer Perceptron (MLP) Back Propagation network, with default settings of all parameters, except learning algorithm. In the hidden layer, Tangent-sigmoid transfer function is deployed and in the output layer, a pure linear transfer function is used. Eleven Back propagation learning algorithms available in NNtoolbox, have been experimented for prediction of monthly rainfall in mm and out of them trainRP (Resilient Backpropagation) and trainSCG (Scaled Conjugate Gradient) algorithms have produced the most convincing results with minimum Root Mean Squared Error.

The other statistical technique that has been experimented with is Linear regression that is used for finding linear relationship between target and one or more predictors. The data of Table 3 has been used for developing a multiple linear regression model to predict rainfall (r_{n+3}) based on predictor months' rainfall (r_n, r_{n+1}, r_{n+2}). The records were partitioned into three sets, randomly; as training, validation and testing sets with 60%, 20% and 20% records, respectively.

Secondly, Pearson's correlation coefficient between rainfall of month n (r_n) and month n+1 (r_{n+1}); between Rainfall of month n (r_n) and month n+2 (r_{n+2}); between Rainfall of month n (r_n) and month n+3 (r_{n+3}) has been calculated for the sample data shown in Table 2. This is done for all 276 months (that includes monsoon as well as non-monsoon months).

Thirdly, the probability of dry and wet months, for monsoon months and non-monsoon months separately was calculated separately. For monsoon months (May to October) and non-monsoon months (November, December, January to April), this analysis was done using monthly rainfall, by using a program developed in Java programming language, considering less than 60mm rainfall in a month as dry month and otherwise wet month.

RESULTS AND DISCUSSIONS

Rainfall Prediction Results Based on Artificial Neural Network

Related to prediction of rainfall based on lagged three consecutive months' rainfall (r_n, r_{n+1}, r_{n+2}) as input to ANN to predict n+3 month rainfall (r_{n+3}), convincing results have been demonstrated. The correlation coefficient between actual and forecasted rainfall is observed as more than 0.9 for training, testing and validating using trainSCG and trainRP algorithm respectively as depicted in Figure 2 and Figure 3.

Figure 2. Correlation analysis between actual rainfall and predicted rainfall for monthly time series lagged data, using trainSCG learning algorithm

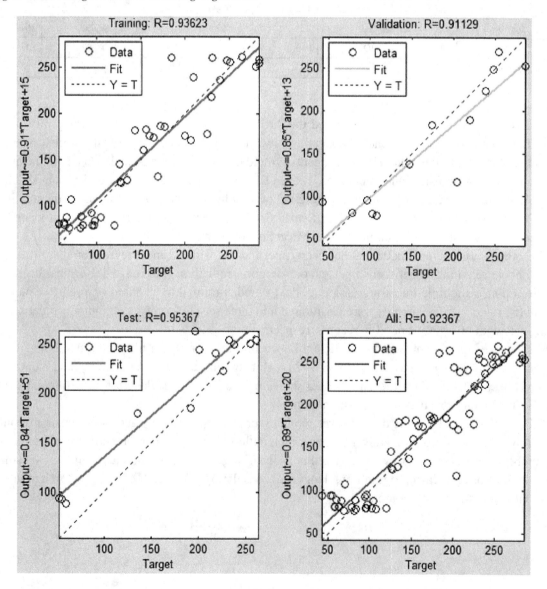

Figure 3. Correlation analysis between actual rainfall and predicted rainfall for monthly time series lagged data, using trainRP learning algorithm

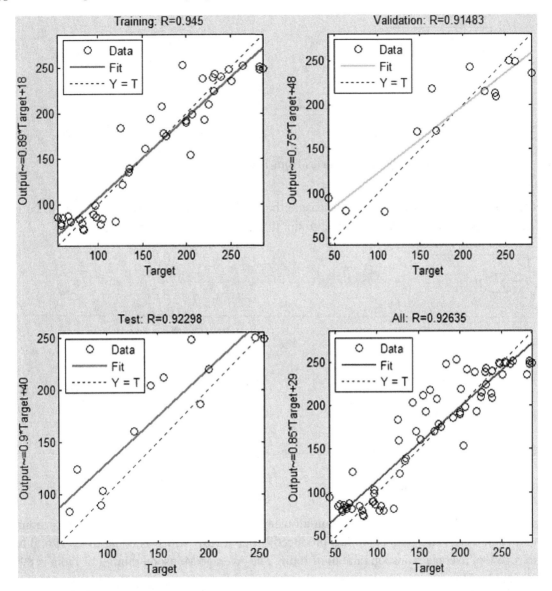

Table 4. Details of values of correlation coefficient R corresponding to different datasets under consideration

S.No.	Datasets	R Between Predicted and Actual Rainfall Using trainSCG Algorithm	R Between Predicted and Actual Rainfall Using trainRP Algorithm
1	Training	0.93623	0.945
2	Testing	0.95367	0.92298
3	Validation	0.91129	0.91483
4	All	0.92367	0.92635

The Root Mean Squared Error (RMSE) depicts the error between the actual output and the model's predicted output:

$$RMSE = \sqrt{\frac{\sum_{i=1}^{n}\left(\hat{y_i} - y_i\right)^2}{n}}$$

where:

$\hat{y_i}$ = a set of actual values of an output, i varies from 1 to n

The standard deviation (STDEV) is a measure that gives insight into variation of individual group member values from the mean value for the group. It is given by following equation:

$$\sigma = \sqrt{\frac{1}{N}\sum_{i=1}^{N}\left(y_i - \overline{y}\right)^2}$$

where:

σ = standard deviation

N = number of values/ predictions in dataset

y_i = each actual output value of dataset

$\overline{y}$ = the arithmetic mean of the data.

The RMSE and STDEV of predicted rainfall using trainSCG and trainRP learning algorithms are shown in Table 5. TrainRP algorithm has produced lower RMSE which is equal to 28.19mm and is equal to 3.16% of average monsoon rainfall of India. The Average Monsoon rainfall of India is 890mm as mentioned by Skymet.

Table 5. Values of RMSE and STDEV for different training algorithms

S.No.	Training Algorithm	RMSE	STDEV
1	trainSCG	28.52mm	66.63mm
2	trainRP	28.19mm	72.65mm

A 2-D line graph to visualize the relation between predicted and actual rainfall values has been created and shown in Figure 4 (as a sample for monsoon months of 1990 to 1993). The graph clearly shows how closely the two curves follow each other. These results are based on trainRP learning algorithm as the RMSE of this algorithm is the minimum among all other learning algorithms.

Figure 4. Relation between months and actual/predicted rainfall using ANN trainRP learning algorithm

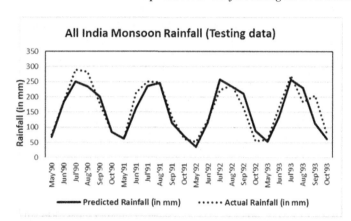

Rainfall Prediction Results Based on Multiple Linear Regression Model

The relationship between rainfall of predictor months and predictand month has been estimated by using multiple linear regression model. The RMSE has been found to be 59.99mm which is 6.74% of average monsoon rainfall of India. Standard deviation with this technique is 80.51mm. The plot in Figure 5 shows the predicted and actual rainfall vs. month. It can be observed clearly that ANN is capable of predicting monsoon rainfall more accurately than conventional statistical approach of linear regression.

Figure 5. Relation between months and actual/predicted rainfall using linear regression model

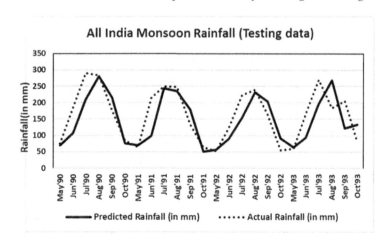

Correlation Between Rainfall of Various Months

The Pearson's correlation coefficient (R) signifies the degree of linear relationship between Rainfall of month n (r_n) and month n+1 (r_{n+1}); between Rainfall of month n (r_n) and month n+2 (r_{n+2}); between Rainfall of month n (r_n) and month n+3 (r_{n+3}) have been calculated and shown in Table 6.

Table 6. Correlation coefficient between rainfall of month n (r_n) and month n+1 (r_{n+1}); between rainfall of month n (r_n) and month n+2 (r_{n+2}); between rainfall of month n (r_n) and month n+3 (r_{n+3}), for all 276 months

	r_n	r_{n+1}	r_{n+2}	r_{n+3}
r_n	1.0000	0.7638	0.331	0.1353
r_{n+1}	0.7638	1.0000	0.7631	0.3297
r_{n+2}	0.331	0.7631	1.0000	0.7631
r_{n+3}	0.1353	0.3297	0.7631	1.0000

The results showed that rainfall of any two consecutive months (monsoon/ non-monsoon) i.e. month n (r_n) and month n+1 (r_{n+1}) where n varies from 1 to 275, are strongly correlated having R>0.75. So, every next month's rainfall is positively correlated with its previous month's rainfall whereas this correlation coefficient reduces corresponding to rainfall of month n (r_n) and month n+2 (r_{n+2}); rainfall of month n (r_n) and month n+3 (r_{n+3}).

Probability of Dry and Wet Months

Different probabilities of dry month, wet month for monsoon and non-monsoon months separately have been found, shown in Table 7. P_D is probability of the month being dry i.e. monthly rainfall less than 60mm, P_W is probability of the month being wet, F_D is Number of dry months, F_W is number of wet months, n is number of months of data.

Table 7. Probability of dry and wet months in monsoon and non-monsoon months

Season	Total No. of Months, n	No. of Dry Months, F_D	No. of Wet Months, F_W	Prob. of Dry Months, $P_D=F_D/n$	Prob. of Wet Months, $P_W=F_W/n$
Monsoon	138	19	119	0.14	0.86
Non-monsoon	138	137	1	0.99	0.01

These findings clearly support the fact that that in India there are a greater number of dry season months as compared to wet months. Rainfall takes place mainly in monsoon months i.e. May, June, July, August, September, October. The yield of crop specifically in rain fed fields directly depends on rainfall patterns. The sequential process of wet and dry months can certainly be used for planning and management of crops and other agricultural operations as also mentioned by Dasgupta and De (2001).

CONCLUSION

Rainfall forecasting plays a significant role in water management for agriculture in a country like India where economy depends heavily upon agriculture. The forecasting of probability of occurrence of monthly rainfall is significant for planning and management of crops and decisions related to water management following which the risk due to uncertainty of water can be reduced. Therefore forecasting, modeling and monitoring of rainfall are of a high importance in agricultural activities. Forecasting rainfall has always been difficult because of its inherent high spatio-temporal variability. Given below are the conclusions:

- A prediction model has been designed that is a complementary technique for markov chain model yet simple, applicable and accurate. Feedforward backpropagation artificial neural network has performed reasonably well to forecast monthly rainfall based on three months lagged time series monsoon rainfall for the Indian region. A statistical method of multiple linear regression to predict the monsoon rainfall has also been evaluated.

A summary of RMSE, % of mean monsoon rainfall and standard deviation using the two best performing learning algorithms of ANN and using linear regression is shown in Table 8.

Table 8. A comparison between performance of ANN and multiple linear regression model

S.No.	Technique Used	RMSE (in mm)	% of Mean Monsoon Rainfall	STDEV (in mm)
1	ANN (using trainSCG)	28.52	3.20	66.63
2	ANN (using trainRP)	28.19	3.16	72.65
3	Multiple linear regression	59.99	6.74	80.51

It is concluded that ANN has provided better results for forecasting rainfall using three months lagged rainfall data. This study has markedly confirmed that application of Soft Computing techniques can complement the forecasting of rainfall. Earlier studies by Guhathakurta (2008) based on huge data of rainfall of 36 sub-divisions of India for 65 years, have demonstrated RMSE equal to 46.5mm which is 5.3% of mean monsoon rainfall of India. The results shown by our method of lagged time series are quite convincing.

- Important correlations between various months' rainfall has been found and discussed. It is observed that rainfall of any two consecutive months is strongly positively correlated with each other and value of correlation coefficient being greater than 0.75 always. This is valid for all 12 months of rainfall data over Indian region for a period of 23 years;
- The probabilities of dry seasonal month, wet seasonal month for monsoon and non-monsoon months, have been found and it has been witnessed that these probabilities are very important as far as planning of crops having different requirement of wet/ dry season is concerned.

This paper varies from other previous researches explained in Background section, as it is based not on daily rainfall but on monthly rainfall of 23years. Three different aspects related to rainfall over Indian region have been addressed *viz.* forecasting of rainfall based on last three months' monthly rainfall, finding correlations between consecutive months' rainfall, finding probability for dry and wet seasonal months for monsoon and non-monsoon seasons. The study can be extended to include techniques like Fuzzy Inference System, Adaptive Neuro Fuzzy Inference System and for other geographical regions in future.

REFERENCES

Aneja, D. R., & Srivastava, O. P. (1999). Markov chain model for rainfall occurrence. *Journal of the Indian Society of Agricultural Statistics*, *52*, 169–175.

Ansari, H. (2013). Forecasting Seasonal and Annual Rainfall Based on Nonlinear Modeling with Gamma Test in North of Iran. *International Journal of Engineering Practical Research, 2*(1).

ASCE Task Committee. (2000). Artificial Neural Networks in Hydrology I: Preliminary Concepts. *Journal of Hydrologic Engineering*, *5*(2), 115–123. doi:10.1061/(ASCE)1084-0699(2000)5:2(115)

Chang, W.L., & Yeung, K.H. (2003). *Seasonal Forecasting for Hong Kong, A Pilot Study*. Hong Kong Observatory. Technical Note, No. 104.

Chatterjee, S., Ghosh, S., & De, U. K. (2009). Reduction of number of parameters and forecasting convective developments at Kolkata (22.53^{0}N, 88.33^{0}E), India during pre-monsoon season: An application of multivariate techniques. *Indian Journal of Radio & Space Physics*, *38*, 275–282.

Dasgupta, S., & De, U. K. (2001). Markov chain model for pre monsoon thunderstorm in Calcutta, India. *Indian Journal of Radio & Space Physics*, *30*, 138–142.

Dash, P. R. (2012). A markov chain modelling of daily precipitation occurrences of Odisha. *International Journal of Adv Comp Math Sci (India)*, *3*, 482–486.

El-Shafie, A., Abdalla, O., Noureldin, A., & Aini, H. (2010). Performance Evaluation of a Nonlinear Error Model for Underwater Range Computation Utilizing GPS Sonobuoys. *Neural Computing & Applications*, *19*(5), 272–283.

El-Shafie, A., Alaa, E. A., Noureldin, A., & Mohd, R. T. (2009). Enhancing Inflow Forecasting Model at Aswan High Dam Utilizing Radial Basis Neural Network and Upstream Monitoring Stations Measurements. *Water Resources Management*, *23*(11), 2289–2315. doi:10.100711269-008-9382-1

El-Shafie, A., Noureldin, A., Mohd, R. T., & Hassan, B. (2008). Neural Network Model for Nile River Inflow Forecasting Based on Correlation Analysis of Historical Inflow Data. *Journal of Applied Sciences (Faisalabad)*, *8*(24), 4487–4499. doi:10.3923/jas.2008.4487.4499

El-Shafie, A., Reda, T. M., & Noureldin, A. (2007). A Neuro-Fuzzy Model for Inflow Forecasting of the Nile River at Aswan High Dam. *Water Resources Management*, *21*(3), 533–556. doi:10.100711269-006-9027-1

El-Shafie, A. H., El-Shafie, A., El-Mazoghi, G. H., Shehata, A., & Taha, M. R. (2011). Artificial Neural Network Technique for Rainfall Forecasting Applied to Alexandria, Egypt. *International Journal of Physical Sciences*, *6*(6), 1306–1316.

Elsner, J. B., & Tsonis, A. A. (1992). Nonlinear prediction, chaos and noise. *Bulletin of the American Meteorological Society*, *73*(1), 49–60. doi:10.1175/1520-0477(1992)073<0049:NPCAN>2.0.CO;2

Fallah-Ghallhary, G. A., Mousavi-Baygi, M., & Habibi Nokhandan, M. (2009). Annual Rainfall Forecasting by Using Mamdani Fuzzy Inference System. *Journal of Environmental Sciences (China)*, *3*(4), 400–413.

French, M. N., Krajewski, W. F., & Cuykendal, R. R. (1992). Rainfall Forecasting in Space and Time Using a Neural Network. *Journal of Hydrology (Amsterdam)*, *137*(1-4), 1–37. doi:10.1016/0022-1694(92)90046-X

Galambosi, A., Duckstein, L., Ozelkan, E., & Bogardi, I. (1999). Fuzzified Effect of ENSO and Macro Circulation Patterns on Precipitation: An Arizona Case Study. *International Journal of Climatology*, *19*(13), 1411–1426. doi:10.1002/(SICI)1097-0088(19991115)19:13<1411::AID-JOC423>3.0.CO;2-H

Geng, S., Penning-de-Vries, F. W. T., & Supit, I. (1986). A Simple Method for Generating Daily Rainfall Data. *Agricultural and Forest Meteorology*, *36*(4), 363–376. doi:10.1016/0168-1923(86)90014-6

Guhathakurta, P. (2008). Long lead monsoon rainfall prediction for meteorological sub-divisions of India using deterministic artificial neural network model. *Meteorology and Atmospheric Physics*, *101*(1-2), 93–108. doi:10.100700703-008-0335-2

Guhathakurta, P., Tyagi, A., & Mukhopadhyay, B. (2013). Climatology at any point: A neural network solution. *Mausam (New Delhi)*, *64*, 231–250.

Hadli, H., & Ridd, P. (2002). Modeling Inter-Annual Variation of a Local Rainfall Data Using a Fuzzy Logic Technique. In *Proceedings of international Forum on Climate Prediction*. James Coo University.

Halff, A. H., Halff, H. M., & Azmoodeh, M. (1993). *Predicting Runoff from Rainfall Using Neural Networks. In Proc. Engineering hydrology* (pp. 760–765). New York: ASCE.

Hamlin, M. J., & Rees, D. H. (1987). Use of Rainfall Forecasts in the Optimal Management of Smallholder Rice Irrigation, A case study. *Hydrological Sciences Journal*, *32*(1), 15–29. doi:10.1080/02626668709491159

Hoogenboom, G. (2000). Contribution of Agrometeorology to the Simulation of Crop Production and its Applications. *Agricultural and Forest Meteorology*, *103*(1-2), 137–157. doi:10.1016/S0168-1923(00)00108-8

Hossain, M. M., & Anam, S. (2012). Identifying the dependency pattern of daily rainfall of Dhaka station in Bangladesh using Markov chain and logistic regression model. *Agriculture Science (Ghana)*, *3*(03), 385–391. doi:10.4236/as.2012.33045

Iyengaer, R. N. (1991). Application of principle component analysis to understand variability of rainfall. *Proceedings Indian Academy Science (Earth & Planet Science)*, *100*, 105-126.

Iyengar, R. N., & Basak, P. (1994). Regionalization of Indian monsoon rainfall and long term variability signals. *International journal of climatology(UK)*, *14*(10), 1095–1114. doi:10.1002/joc.3370141003

Karamouz, M., Zahraie, B., & Eghdamirad, S. (2004). Seasonal Rainfall Forecasting Using Meteorological Signals. In *Proceedings of the 1st Conference of Iran Water Sources Management*. Technological Faculty, Tehran University.

Kosko, B. (2005). *Neural Networks and Fuzzy Systems*. Prentice Hall of India Ltd.

Kumarasiri, A. D., & Sonnadara, D. U. J. (2006). Rainfall Forecasting: An Artificial Neural Network Approach. *Institute of Physics – Sri Lanka. Proceedings of the Technical Sessions*, *22*, 1–13.

Maria, C., Valverde, R., Haroldo Fraga de Campos, V., & Nelson Jesus, F. (2005). Artificial Neural Network Technique for Rainfall Forecasting Applied to the Sao Paulo Region. *Journal of Hydrology (Amsterdam)*, *301*(1-4), 146–162. doi:10.1016/j.jhydrol.2004.06.028

Mimikou, M. (1983). Forecasting Daily Precipitation Occurrence with Markov Chain of Seasonal Order. *J Am Water Resour. As.*, 219-224.

Moller, M. F. (1993). A Scaled Conjugate Gradient Algorithm for Fast Supervised Learning. *Neural Networks*, *6*(4), 525–533. doi:10.1016/S0893-6080(05)80056-5

Monthly rainfall data for India. (n.d.). Available from https://data.worldbank.org/indicator/AG.LND.PRCP.MM

Ousmane, N., Neil Ward, M., & Wassila, M. (2011). Predictability of Seasonal Sahel Rainfall Using GCMs and Lead-Time Improvements Through the Use of a Coupled Model. *Journal of Climate*, *24*(7), 1931–1949. doi:10.1175/2010JCLI3557.1

Ozelkan, E. C., Ni, F., & Duckestin, L. (1996). Relationship Between Monthly Atmospheric Circulation Patterns and Prediction: Fuzzy Logic and Regression Approaches. *Water Resources Research*, *32*(7), 2097–2103. doi:10.1029/96WR00289

Rumelhart, D., Hinton, G. E., & Williams, R. J. (1986). *Learning internal representation by error propagation. In Parallel distributed processing: exploration in the microstructure of cognition* (Vol. 1, pp. 318–362). Cambridge: MIT Press.

Sahai, A. K., Somann, M. K., & Satyan, V. (2000). All India Summer Monsoon Rainfall Prediction Using an Artificial Neural Netw. *Climate Dynamics*, *16*(4), 291–302. doi:10.1007003820050328

Selvi, S. T., & Selvaraj, R. S. (2011). Stochastic Modelling of Annual Rainfall at Tamil Nadu. *Universal Journal of Environmental Research and Technology*, *1*(4), 566–570.

Sengupta, P. R., & Basak, P. (1998). Some studies of southwest monsoon rainfall. Proceedings Indian National Science Academy, 737-745.

Sentelhas, P. C., de Faria, R. T., Chaves, M. O., & Hoogenboom, G. (2001). Evaluation of the WGEN and SIMMETEO Weather Generators for the Brazilian Tropics and Subtropics, Using Crop Simulation Models. *Revista Brasileira de Agrometeorologia*, *9*(2), 357–376.

Sivanandam, S. N., Sumathi, S., & Deepa, S. N. (2009). *Introduction to Neural Networks using Matlab.* Tata McGraw Hill Education Private Ltd.

Sorup, H. J. D., Madsen, H., & Arnbjerg-Nielsen, K. (2011). Markov Chain Modelling of precipitation time sries: Modelling waiting times between tipping bucket rain gauge tips. *Proceedings of 12th International conference on urban drainage*, 11-16.

Suwardi, A., Takenori, K., & Shuhei, K. (2006). Neuro-Fuzzy Approaches for Modelling the Wet Season Tropical Rainfall. *J. Agric. Inforam. Research*, *15*, 331–334.

Thyer, M., & Kuzcera, G. (1999). Modelling long term persistence in rainfall time series: Sydney rainfall case study. *Hydrology and Water Resources Symposium,* 550-555.

Tyagi, B., Naresh Krishna, V., & Satyanarayana, N. V. (2011). Study of thermodynamic indices in forecasting pre-monsoon thunderstorm over Kolkata during STORM pilot phase 2006-08. *Nat Hazards (Netherlands)*, *56*(3), 681–698. doi:10.100711069-010-9582-x

Wong, K. W., Wong, P. M., Gedeon, T. D., & Fung, C. C. (2003). Rainfall Prediction Model Using Soft Computing Technique. *Soft Computing. Foundation. Methodologies and Applications*, *7*, 434–438.

This research was previously published in the International Journal of Business Analytics (IJBAN), 7(3); pages 71-84, copyright year 2020 by IGI Publishing (an imprint of IGI Global).

Chapter 54
Emotion Recognition From Speech Using Perceptual Filter and Neural Network

Revathi A.
SASTRA University, India

Sasikaladevi N.
SASTRA University, India

ABSTRACT

This chapter on multi speaker independent emotion recognition encompasses the use of perceptual features with filters spaced in Equivalent rectangular bandwidth (ERB) and BARK scale and vector quantization (VQ) classifier for classifying groups and artificial neural network with back propagation algorithm for emotion classification in a group. Performance can be improved by using the large amount of data in a pertinent emotion to adequately train the system. With the limited set of data, this proposed system has provided consistently better accuracy for the perceptual feature with critical band analysis done in ERB scale.

INTRODUCTION

Speech signal is considered as the acoustic signal obtained by exciting the vocal tract by quasi periodic pulses of air for voiced sounds and noise like excitation for unvoiced sounds. Speech utterances reveal the linguistic content, accent, slang and emotional state of a speaker. It is really cumbersome to recognize the emotions from speech with limited set of data. Emotion recognition from speech has found applications in call centers and unmanned control of risky processes. This system would be useful for treating the mentally retarded patients and patients with depression and anxiety. Web related services, retrieval of information and synthesis of data would use this automated emotion recognition system. These systems will find place in operating robots for the speech commands given by the emotional operator. Modulation spectral feature is used as a new feature by Siging Wu et.al (Wu, 2011) for emo-

DOI: 10.4018/978-1-6684-2408-7.ch054

tion recognition. Chi-Chun Lee et.al (Lee, 2011) have used hierarchical binary classifier and acoustic & statistical feature for emotion recognition. K. Sreenivasa Rao et.al (Rao, 2012) have used MFCC and GMM for recognizing emotions. Ankur Sapra et.al (Sapra, 2013) has used modified MFCC feature and NN classifier for emotion recognition. Shashidar G. Koolakudi et.al (Koolagudi, 2012) have used MFCC and GMM for speaker recognition in emotional environment. In this chapter on speaker independent emotion recognition, SVM is used to create templates for all emotions and system is evaluated with the speeches of a speaker not considered for training. Training speeches are converted into set of features and SVM models are developed as representative of emotions. During testing, group classification is done using minimum distance classifier and subsequently individual emotion classification is done in a group containing pertinent emotion models using linear binary classifier. Perceptual linear predictive cepstrum with critical band analysis done in BARK and ERB scale are used as features in this work and they provide complimentary evidence in assessing the performance of the system based on ANN modeling technique. ANN modeling technique is based on the selection of hidden layers and number of neurons in hidden layer. Weights between the layers are optimized using iterative procedure and output layer with two neurons to choose one of the two emotions in a group. This chapter also deals with the comparative analysis between the features and analysis is done comprehensively to assess the performance of the speaker independent and dependent emotion recognition system.

Affective computing has played a pivotal role in acting as an interface between humans and machines. Speech based emotion recognition system is difficult to be implemented because of the dataset which is containing limited set of speech utterances spoken limited set of speakers. Emotion recognition from speech is performed by using various databases. This chapter on multi speaker independent emotion recognition encompasses the use of perceptual features with filters spaced in Equivalent rectangular bandwidth (ERB) and BARK scale and vector quantization (VQ) classifier for classifying groups and artificial neural network with back propagation algorithm for emotion classification in a group. Performance can be improved by using the large amount of data in a pertinent emotion to adequately train the system. With the limited set of data, this proposed system has provided consistently better accuracy for the perceptual feature with critical band analysis done in ERB scale with overall accuracy as 76% and decision level fusion classification yielded 100% as accuracy for all emotions except FEAR and BOREDOM. Overall accuracy of the decision level fusion classifier is 78%. Speaker dependent emotion recognition system has provided 100% as accuracy for all the emotions for perceptual feature with critical band analysis done in ERB scale and perceptual linear predictive cepstrum has given 100% as accuracy for all emotions except anger and fear emotions.

MATERIALS AND METHODS

PLPC and ERBPLPC Extraction

The extraction of perceptual linear predictive cepstrum deals with computation of spectrum using FFT technique, wrap the spectrum along the BARK and ERB frequency scales, performing convolution between the warped spectrum and power spectrum of the simulated critical band masking curve, performing pre-emphasis by simulated loudness equalization, mapping between the intensity and the perceived loudness done by cube root compression, generation linear predictive (LP) coefficients and conversion into LP derived cepstrum. Probability is computed by counting the number of samples whose spectral energy is greater than the threshold by total number of samples in a frame of 16 msecs duration. Procedure (Revathi, 2018) used for Mel frequency perceptual feature extraction is detailed below.

1. Compute power spectrum on windowed speech.
2. Perform grouping to 21 critical bands in BARK scale and 35 critical bands in ERB scale for the sampling frequency of 16 kHz.
3. Perform loudness equalization and cube root compression to simulate the power law of hearing.
4. Perform IFFT
5. Perform LP analysis by Levinson -Durbin procedure.
6. Convert LP coefficients into PLP and ERBPLP Ccpstral coefficients.

The relationship between frequency in BARK and ERB with frequency in Hz is specified as in (1) &(2)

$$f(bark) = 6 * \sinh^{-1} f((Hz)/600) \tag{1}$$

$$f(erb) = 21.4 * \log10(4.37e^{-3} * Hz + 1) \tag{2}$$

Experimental Analysis Based on Clustering Technique

The way in which L training vectors can be clustered into a set of M code book vectors is by K-means clustering algorithm (Jeyalakshmi, 2016). Classification procedure for arbitrary spectral analysis vectors that chooses the codebook vector is by computing Euclidean distance between each of the test vectors and the M cluster centroids. The spectral distance measure for comparing test feature vector v_i and cluster centroid v_j is as in (3).

$$d(v_i, v_j) = d_{ij} = 0 \text{ when } v_i = v_j \tag{3}$$

If codebook vectors of an M-vector codebook are taken as y_m. $1 \leq m \leq M$ and new spectral vector to be classified is denoted as v, then the index m^* of the best codebook entry is as in (4)

$$m^* = \arg(\min(d(v, y_m))) \text{ for } 1 \leq m \leq M \tag{4}$$

Clusters are formed in such a way that they capture the characteristics of the training data distribution. It is observed that Euclidean distance is small for the most frequently occurring vectors and large for the least frequently occurring ones.

Emotion Recognition Based on ANN Modeling Technique

Performance of the any recognition system mainly depends on the database used. EMO-DB Berlin database used in this work contains only ten speeches uttered by ten speakers in the age group 21 to 35 years in different emotions such as Anger, Boredom, Disgust, Fear, Happy, Neutral and Sad. Robustness of the system depends on the amount of data considered for training to create templates for emotions. This work on emotion recognition from speech contains two phases namely training and testing. During training phase, speech signal is generated by concatenating the utterances in pertinent emotion from nine speakers and speech vector is allowed to pass through the conventional pre-processing stages namely pre-emphasis, frame blocking and windowing. Then perceptual features and probability are extracted for each speech frame of 16 msecs duration. Neural network models are created for emotions in a group. ANN is one of the types of supervised learning neural network. In the back propagation neural network, the network weights are updated on the basis of the error between the target output and the actual output by means of the back-propagation of the errors (Scanzio, 2010). This network has input layer, hidden layer and output layer. The training of the back propagation neural network (Fausett, 1994) proceeds as follows:

- Initialize the network weights with small random values.
- The input pattern is assigned to input neurons x_i, $i=1,2...n$ and broadcast to the next layer. In hidden layer z_j, $j=1,2...p$, each node sums the weighted inputs and applies its sigmoid activation function to compute its output signal as in equation (5).

$$z_{in\,j} = a_{0j} + \sum_{i=1}^{n} x_i \, a_{ij}$$

$$z_j = Activation(z_{in\,j})$$

$$Activation(z_{in\,j}) = \frac{1}{1 + \exp^{(-z_{in\,j})}} \tag{5}$$

- The z_j is broadcast to the next layer. In output layer y_k, $k=1,2...m$, each node sums the weighted inputs and applies its sigmoid activation function to compute its output signal as in equation (6).

$$y_{in\,k} = b_{0k} + \sum_{j=1}^{p} z_j \, b_{jk}$$

$$y_k = Activation(y_{in\,k})$$

$$Activation(y_{in\,k}) = \frac{1}{1 + \exp^{(-y_{in\,k})}} \tag{6}$$

- The output layer computes the error between target output and actual output.

$$e_k = t_k - y_k$$

- Compute error information term and propagate back as in equation(7)

$$\delta_k = e_k \, F'(y_{in\,k})$$

$$F'(y_{in\,k}) = Activation(y_{in\,k})[1 - Activation(y_{in\,k})] \tag{7}$$

- Compute its weight correction term as in equation (8), which is used to update weights a_{ij} and b_{jk}

$$\Delta b_{0k} = \alpha\,\delta_k$$

$$\Delta b_{jk} = \alpha\,\delta_k\,z_j \tag{8}$$

α- Learning rate
- The hidden layer sums the weighted output data as in equation (9)

$$\delta_{in\,j} = \sum_{k=1}^{m} \delta_k b_{jk} \tag{9}$$

$\delta_{in\,j}$ is multiplied by the derivative of its sigmoid activation function to compute its error information term as in equation (10)

$$\delta_j = \delta_{in\,j}\,F'(z_{in\,j}) \tag{10}$$

- Calculate its weights correction term as in equation (11)

$$\Delta a_{0j} = \alpha\,\delta_j$$

$$\Delta a_{ij} = \alpha\,\delta_j\,x_i \tag{11}$$

- The hidden layer updates its bias and weights as in equation (12)

$$a_{ij}(\text{new}) = a_{ij}(\text{old}) + \Delta a_{ij} \tag{12}$$

- The output layer updates its bias and weights as in equation (13)

$$b_{jk}(\text{new}) = b_{jk}(\text{old}) + \Delta b_{jk} \tag{13}$$

The flow diagram shown in Fig.1 indicates the process used for back propagation training algorithm using artificial neural network

Test speech vector is pre-emphasized by using single order high pass filter so that flattening of speech spectrum is done. After getting speech vector passing through the pre-emphasis stage, speech vector is divided into overlapping frames of 16 msecs duration with 50% overlap between frames enabling no loss of information. Each speech frame is windowed by using Hamming window so that signal discontinuity at the beginning and end of the speech frame is eliminated. Speech frame after pre-processing would undergo FFT filtering, critical band analysis, Loudness equalization, cube root compression, LP coefficients extraction and deriving cepstrum from the LP coefficients. These extracted features are applied to the group specific models and group is identified correctly based on minimum distance classifier. Then, the features are given to the emotion specific models in a group and emotion recognition accuracy is computed by counting the number of speech segments correctly classified out of total number of segments considered for each emotion.

Figure 1. Flow diagram – BPNN algorithm

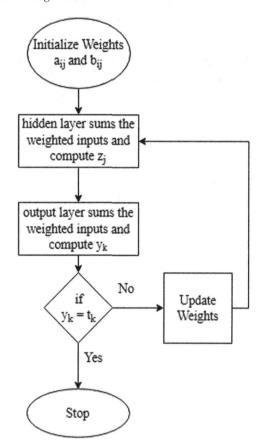

RESULTS AND DISCUSSION

This multi-speaker independent emotion recognition system from noisy test speeches is evaluated by using the implementation of the parallel group classifier and parallel specific emotional pattern classifier [7] to improve the accuracy of the system. Parallel group classifier and parallel emotion specific classifier is indicated in Figure 5.The concatenated test speech vector is applied to the pre-processing techniques namely pre-emphasis, frame blocking and windowing and the extracted feature vectors are applied to the vector quantization (VQ) templates for identifying a group and applied to the ANN templates and based on the minimum error criterion test speech is classified as association with pertinent emotion. Group classification is done based on minimum distance classifier and individual emotion in a group is classified based on ANN based minimum mean squared error classifier. After conventional pre-processing stages, extracted perceptual features are applied to the group models and group should be correctly classified based on minimum distance classifier. Then the features are applied to the emotion specific ANN models as shown in Figures (2 -4) and classification of the pertinent emotion is done by calculating the mean squared error for each feature vector with neural network models. This process is repeated for all feature vectors and indices are extracted. Finally, classification is done pertaining to the model which provides maximum of the index selection among the emotions in a group. For creating ANN templates by using back propagation algorithm, fourteen frames with 13 coefficients are concatenated and normalized. These features are applied to the neural network with one hidden layer containing half the number of neurons as compared to the input layer. Output layer contains the number of neurons corresponding to the number of classes. Weights between the layers are initialized with random values. Using iterative procedure, weights are optimized to march toward the target error. For testing using ANN, feature vectors extracted for the test speech utterances in pertinent emotion after group classification are applied to the ANN templates, and based on the minimum mean squared error criterion, emotions are classified.

Figure 2. BPNN structure – classification of Anger and Fear

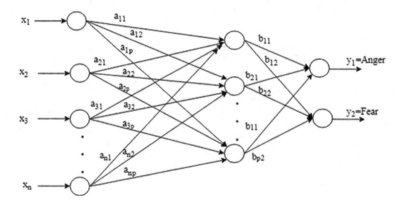

Figure 3. BPNN structure – classification of Boredom and Disgust

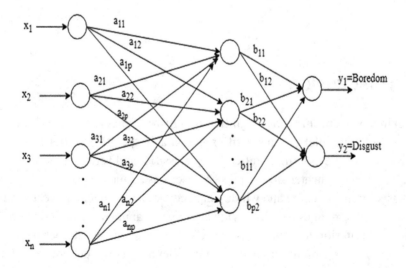

Figure 4. BPNN structure – classification of Neutral and Sad

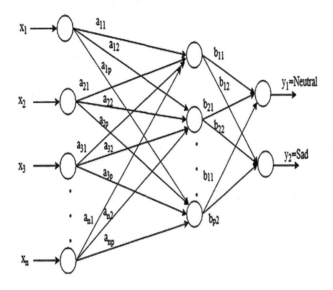

Figure 5. Decision level fusion classifier using ANN

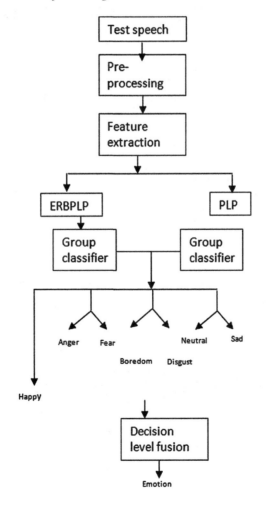

Evaluation of the multi-speaker independent emotion recognition using ANN for ERBPLP is shown in Table 1.

Table 1. Performance evaluation of speaker independent system – ERBPLP based ANN

Emotion	Anger	Fear	Emotion	Boredom	Disgust	Emotion	Neutral	Sad
Anger	25	0	Boredom	8	17	Neutral	8	0
Fear	5	0	*Disgust*	*0*	*26*	Sad	0	22

Multi speaker independent emotion recognition from speech is evaluated using PLP as a feature and ANN as a modeling technique. Performance is depicted in Table2

Table 2. Performance evaluation of speaker independent system – PLP based ANN

Emotion	Anger	Fear	Emotion	Boredom	Disgust	Emotion	Neutral	Sad
Anger	25	0	Boredom	5	20	Neutral	8	0
Fear	5	0	*Disgust*	*0*	*26*	Sad	0	22

Decision level fusion classifier is evaluated using both features and ANN as a modeling technique. Table 3 depicts the performance of the system using decision level fusion classifier.

Table 3. Performance evaluation of speaker independent system – Decision level fusion classifier

Emotion	Anger	Fear	Emotion	Boredom	Disgust	Emotion	Neutral	Sad
Anger	25	0	Boredom	11	14	Neutral	8	0
Fear	5	0	*Disgust*	*0*	*26*	Sad	0	22

Table 4 indicates the performance of the speaker dependent emotion recognition system for perceptual features with filters spaced in ERB scale.

Table 4. Performance evaluation of speaker dependent system – ERBPLP based ANN

Emotion	Anger	Fear	Emotion	Boredom	Disgust	Emotion	Neutral	Sad
Anger	243	0	Boredom	149	0	Neutral	136	0
Fear	0	109	*Disgust*	*0*	*91*	Sad	0	172

Multi speaker dependent emotion recognition from speech is evaluated using PLP as a feature and ANN as a modeling technique. Performance is depicted in Table 5

Table 5. Performance evaluation of speaker dependent system – PLP based ANN

Emotion	Anger	Fear	Emotion	Boredom	Disgust	Emotion	Neutral	Sad
Anger	154	89	Boredom	149	0	Neutral	136	0
Fear	50	59	*Disgust*	*0*	*91*	Sad	0	172

Decision level fusion classifier is evaluated using both features and ANN as a modeling technique. Table 6 depicts the performance of the speaker dependent system using decision level fusion classifier.

Table 6. Performance evaluation of speaker dependent system – Decision level fusion classifier

Emotion	Anger	Fear	Emotion	Boredom	Disgust	Emotion	Neutral	Sad
Anger	243	0	Boredom	149	0	Neutral	136	0
Fear	0	109	*Disgust*	*0*	*91*	Sad	0	172

From the tables, it is understood that perceptual features with critical band analysis done in ERB scale performs better than that of the features with filters spaced in BARK scale for both speaker independent and dependent emotion recognition system.

CONCLUSION

This chapter discusses the use of perceptual features with critical band analysis done in ERB and BARK scale and artificial neural network for creating templates as representative models for emotions. Features are extracted from the concatenated training speeches pertaining to the emotions. Extracted features pertaining to arousal and soft emotions are used to create set of clusters representing group models. Features extracted using pertinent emotional speech utterances are neural networks with initialization of random weights between the layers. Back propagation algorithm is used to optimize the weights between the layers by using minimization of mean squared error criterion. Iterative procedure is used to update the weights by fixing the target error and neural network models are created for each emotion. During testing, test speeches are concatenated to form a test vector and features are extracted after applying initial pre-processing stages namely pre-emphasis, frame blocking and windowing. Pre-emphasis stage is done to spectrally flatten the test speech signal. Frame blocking is used to convert the speech vector into frames of 16msecs duration with 8msecs overlapping in order to avoid the information loss. Windowing is done to remove the signal discontinuities at the beginning and end of speech frames. Features extracted from the pre-processed speech vector are applied to the group models to identify a group based on minimum distance classifier and further classification is done in a group containing pertinent emotion models based on minimum mean squared error criterion. Perceptual features with filters spaced in ERB scale has provided the better accuracy of 76% as compared to the perceptual features with filters spaced in BARK scale for which the accuracy is found to be 74%. Decision level fusion classifier has yielded the accuracy as 78%. Speaker dependent emotion recognition system is implemented by using same set of utterances for training and testing. Perceptual features with critical band analysis done in ERB scale has provided 100% as accuracy for all emotions and perceptual features with filters spaced in BARK has given 100% as individual accuracy for all emotions except Anger and Fear. Decision level fusion classifier using both the features and ANN as modeling technique has given the accuracy as 100% for all emotions. Emotion recognition from speech would find applications in business processing centers, web analysis, medical diagnosis of patients, and automated services based on the emotional state of a speaker.

REFERENCES

Fausett, L. (1994). *Fundamentals of neural networks: architectures, algorithms, and applications.* Prentice-Hall.

Jeyalakshmi, C., Revathi, A., & Yenkataramani, Y. (2016). Integrated models and features-based speaker independent emotion recognition. *International Journal of Telemedicine and Clinical Practices*, *1*(3), 277–291. doi:10.1504/IJTMCP.2016.077920

Koolagudi, S. G., Sharma, K., & Rao, K. S. (2012, August). Speaker recognition in emotional environment. In *International Conference on Eco-friendly Computing and Communication Systems* (pp. 117-124). Berlin, Germany: Springer.

Lee, C. C., Mower, E., Busso, C., Lee, S., & Narayanan, S. (2011). Emotion recognition using a hierarchical binary decision tree approach. *Speech communication*, *53*(9-10), 1162–1171. doi:10.1016/j.specom.2011.06.004

Rao, K. S., Kumar, T. P., Anusha, K., Leela, B., Bhavana, I., & Gowtham, S. V. S. K. (2012). Emotion recognition from speech. *International Journal of Computer Science and Information Technologies*, *3*(2), 3603–3607.

Revathi, A., & Jeyalakshmi, C. (2018). Emotions recognition: different sets of features and models. *International Journal of Speech Technology, 1-10.*

Sapra, A., Panwar, N., & Panwar, S. (2013). Emotion recognition from speech. *International Journal of Emerging Technology and Advanced Engineering*, *3*(2), 341–345.

Scanzio, S., Cumani, S., Gemello, R., Mana, F., & Laface, P. (2010). Parallel implementation of Artificial Neural Network training for speech recognition. *Pattern Recognition Letters*, *31*(11), 1302–1309. doi:10.1016/j.patrec.2010.02.003

Wu, S., Falk, T. H., & Chan, W. Y. (2011). Automatic speech emotion recognition using modulation spectral features. *Speech communication*, *53*(5), 768–785. doi:10.1016/j.specom.2010.08.013

This research was previously published in Neural Networks for Natural Language Processing; pages 78-91, copyright year 2020 by Engineering Science Reference (an imprint of IGI Global).

Chapter 55
An Efficient Random Valued Impulse Noise Suppression Technique Using Artificial Neural Network and Non-Local Mean Filter

Bibekananda Jena
Anil Neerukonda Institute of Technology & Sciences, Visakhapatnam, India

Punyaban Patel
Malla Reddy Institute of Technology, Secunderabad, India

G.R. Sinha
CMR Technical Campus, Secunderabad, India

ABSTRACT

A new technique for suppression of Random valued impulse noise from the contaminated digital image using Back Propagation Neural Network is proposed in this paper. The algorithms consist of two stages i.e. Detection of Impulse noise and Filtering of identified noisy pixels. To classify between noisy and non-noisy element present in the image a feed-forward neural network has been trained with well-known back propagation algorithm in the first stage. To make the detection method more accurate, Emphasis has been given on selection of proper input and generation of training patterns. The corrupted pixels are undergoing non-local mean filtering employed in the second stage. The effectiveness of the proposed technique is evaluated using well known standard digital images at different level of impulse noise. Experiments show that the method proposed here has excellent impulse noise suppression capability.

DOI: 10.4018/978-1-6684-2408-7.ch055

INTRODUCTION

Image denoising is one of the widely studied unsolved problems and plays a significant role in the research area of image processing and computer vision. Most of the time images are contaminated by impulse noise during the process of image acquisition or at the time of transmission due to malfunctioning image pixels in the camera sensors, channel transmission errors or faulty storage hardware. Therefore, a pre-processing stage is always required before processing an image for any application. Noise filtering is one of the important parts of this stage. The objectives of image denoising algorithms are to detect and suppress the unhealthy pixel elements in the test image without harming the fine details of the image. Impulse noise found in digital images is a spark that disturbs the information contain in the images. It distorts the pixels of a digital image by replacing the original value either by fixed value or any random value within the available dynamic range. So there are two categories of impulse noise as per the distribution of noise in an image: salt and pepper noise (SPN) and Random valued impulse noise (RVIN) (Dey, Ashour, Beagum et al., 2015) (Ikeda, Gupta, Dey et al., 2015). Impulse noises can be mathematically described by the following model (Patel, Jena, Majhi & Tripathy, 2012):

$$s\left(u,v\right) = \begin{cases} \gamma\left(u,v\right) & \text{with probability } P \\ x\left(u,v\right) & \text{with probability } 1-P \end{cases} \tag{1}$$

where, $s(i,j)$ specifies a certain location of a pixel in the test noisy image, $x(i,j)$ indicates an original healthy image pixel element and $\gamma(u,v)$ represents a location where a pixel element is contaminated by impulse noise. In salt-and-pepper noise(SPN), the corrupted pixels either obtain the minimum value or the maximum value of the available dynamic range i.e. $\eta(i,j)\hat{I}\{\text{Sm}i_{n,S}\text{ma}_{x\}}$, and in random-valued impulse noise(RVIN), the corrupted pixel element can attain any possible value of the available dynamic range i.e. $y(i,j)\hat{I}\{\text{Sm}i_{n,S}\text{ma}_{x\}}$ where, $\text{Sm}i_{n,S}\text{ma}_{x}$ denote the minimum and the maximum pixel intensity within the available dynamic range of the image respectively. Therefore, the detection and suppression of presence of RVIN in an image is a challenging work (Gonzalez & Wood, 2002; Chanda & Majumder, 2002; Kang & Wang, 2009). Figure 1 shows the result of image corrupted by RVIN and SPN noise. Most of the existing algorithm performs very well for suppression of salt and pepper noise (SPN), whereas the performance towards random valued impulse noise (RVIN) is quite miserable (Jena, Patel &Majhi, 2014).

Noise removal from images is a prominent field of research and many authors have proposed a large number of methods and explained their effectiveness with other methods. The main thrust on all such methods is to detect and suppress unhealthy pixels present in the image while keeping the image details unaffected. Initially the most common and popular filters used for impulse noise suppression is the simple median filter as in Chanda and Majumder (2002) Jena, Patel, Majhi, and Tripathy (2013) and its modifications. But it could not differentiate between noisy and noise free pixels. Due to the above case, all the pixels i.e. both healthy and unhealthy are allowed in taking part in the filtering stage which causes absence of fine details in the restored images and producing blotches. To avoid such problem an impulse noise detection stage must be included in the algorithm before filtering process, which can only allow the identified corrupted pixels only to be filtered. In last few year some improved noise removal process with advanced noise detection algorithm have been proposed, such as: Space Variant Median Filters for the Restoration of Impulse Noise Corrupted Images (Kang & Wang, 2009), Adaptive Impulse Detection Using Center-Weighted Median Filters ACWM (Chen & Wu, 2001), A New Detector for Switching Median Filter ASWMF (AKKOUL, LEDEE, LECONGE & HARBA, 2009), Advanced impulse detection based on pixel-wise MAD (PWMAD) (Crnogavic, Chand, Senk & Trpovski, 2004), Impulse Noise Filter With Adaptive Mad-Based Threshold ADMAD (Crnojevi´c, 2005), An Efficient Detail-Preserving Approach for Removing Impulse Noise in Images ATBMF(Luo,2006) and A Signal-Dependent Rank Ordered Mean SDROM (Abreu, Lightstone, Mitra, & Arakawa,1996). These filters work well for suppressing Salt and Pepper noise and also give satisfactory results for image corrupted with low density of RVIN. But when noise increases these method fails to give appropriate value for a corrupted pixel, because the median of the filtering window easily falls to the value of impulse noise. A slightly different method which uses the directional information in the filtering window to detect and restore the corrupted pixels was employed in Directional weighted median (DWM) filter (Dong & Xu, 2007) a few years back. In the restoration process this filter applied to the corrupted image recursively for 7 to 10 iterations. Even though its results are encouraging at high density of RVIN, but found not suitable for real time application due to its high computational overhead.

Recently a universal noise filter (ROR-NLM) (Xiong & Zhouping, 2012) has been proposed by introducing a new impulse detector called the robust Outlyingness ratio (ROR) with the non-local means (NLM) filtering method. The use of NLM in noise removal process, enhance its filtering capability and has attracted a lot of attention of researchers, works in the area of signal and image processing. The NLM algorithm exploits the self-similarity or information redundancy within images and restores the corrupted pixel by computing the weighted mean of all identified similar pixels in the filtering window. But this method doesn't perform well when images are corrupted by less noise density. Guangyu Xu currently proposed a universal noise filter in (Xu & Tan, 2013) by combining the robust local image statistics called the extreme compression rank order absolute difference (ECROAD) with the nonlocal means. The filter is capable of suppressing any type of impulse noise efficiently by varying some parameters discussed in the method. Another filtering technique is the Adaptive rank weighted switching filter RWASF (Smolka, Malik & Malik, 2012), this filter is based on order statistics and uses the weighted cumulative distances between pixels for the detection of corrupted pixel elements. Some techniques using the fuzzy rule for denoising methods for finding out corrupted pixels and uncorrupted pixels more effectively for removal of RVIN have also been introduced in the last two years. One of such methods is a new weighted mean filter ANWMF (Liu, Chen, Zhou & You, 2015) method, the noise detector proposed in this case identifies a noisy pixel by some fuzzy rule that matches the stochastic nature of impulse noise and highly improve the restoring ability. In addition to this, a local image statistic minimum edge pixels difference (MEPD) is used to identify edge pixels from noisy pixel element. Muhammad Habib proposed another fuzzy based method called adaptive fuzzy inference system based directional median filter (AFIDM) (Habib, Ayyazhussain, Rashsed & Ali, 2016) method for impulse noise removal. The algorithm uses fuzzy logic to construct a membership function adaptively for robust fuzzy inference based impulse noise detector which can efficiently distinguish between original pixels and noisy pixel element without affecting the edges and detail information present in the image. However, at higher noise densities, it fails to restore fine details due to improper classification of noisy and non-noisy pixel elements.

The learning ability of the Neural Network (NN) makes it more popular for classification of noisy and non-noisy element in the field of denoising of image in the last few years. Liang, Lu, Chang and Lin (2008) proposed a method that uses an adaptive two-level feed-forward neural network (NN) trained by back-propagation algorithm to filter the noisy pixels effectively and keep the original information unaffected. In (Sa & Majhi, 2010) a neural network is employed, which used ROAD and PWMAD value of each pixel in the image to classify the noisy and non-noisy pixels. As the ROAD and PWMAD can only detect noisy pixels at low noise density, when the noise density increases beyond 25% the filters fails to identify corrupted pixels and noise removal capability goes down. In predictive-based adaptive switching median filter (PASMF) (Nair & Vijur, 2013) Madhu trained a neural network which can effectively remove impulse noise. In Pushpavalli and Sivaradje (2013), Pushpavalli also trained a Feed Forward neural network using Back Propagation Algorithm to make the filter more robust to suppress the effect of that long-tailed impulse noise and short tailed uniform noise keeping image features unaffected. Majhi and Fathi (2005) used a Functional Link Artificial Neural Network along with an improved spatial filter to restore corrupted image. However, the performance of these filters is miserable at high noise density (Patel, Jena, Majhi & Tripathy, 2012). Therefore, a robust technique is required which not only classify the noisy and non-noisy pixels efficiently but also the filtering process can restore the corrupted pixels with appropriate value.

In this paper, we proposed a new two stage noise removal algorithm using neural network for suppression of random valued impulse noise. To make an efficient impulse detector, we have used two different features extracted from the image and based on this data the detector takes decision. In the first stage, a well-trained ANN is used for fast and accurate classification of noisy and non-noisy element including edge pixels in the image at different noise level. The input parameters, to the neural network are derived from two different statistical parameters namely, robust outlyingness ratio (ROR) (Xiong & Zhouping, 2012) and Rank Based Weighted Distance Measures (RBWDM) (Smolka, Malik, & Malik, 2012). Subsequently, the identified noisy pixels are filtered with a modified version of the non-local mean filter. The different sections of this paper are organized in a sequence as initially the introduction, then the review of the ROLD and RBWDM, followed by the proposed method, simulation, results, and finally, concluding remarks.

REVIEW OF ROR AND RBWDM STATISTICS

Robust Outlyingness Ratio (ROR) (Xiong & Zhouping, 2012):

This is a newly proposed parameter for detection of RVIN noise in images. ROR measures how much each pixel gets affected by impulse noise i.e. how much a pixel looks like an impulse noise. Some pixels look more like noisy pixels, and some do not look like noisy pixels. The computation of ROR is involves the following steps.

Step 1: Consider a 5 x 5 window, W with center pixel as the test pixel 'u'
Step 2: Compute $med(u)$ as the median of the window
Step 3: Compute the median of absolute deviation, *MAD* as,

$$MAD\left(u\right) = med\left\{\left|v - \text{Med}\left(u\right)\right|, \ v \in \text{W}\right\} \tag{2}$$

Step 4: Compute

$$MADN(u) = MAD(u) \, / \, 0.6457 \tag{3}$$

Step 5: Compute

$$ROR(u) = \left| \frac{\left| (u - med(u)) \right|}{MADN(u)} \right| \tag{4}$$

Figure 1. Original and Noisy Lena Image with SPN and RVIN

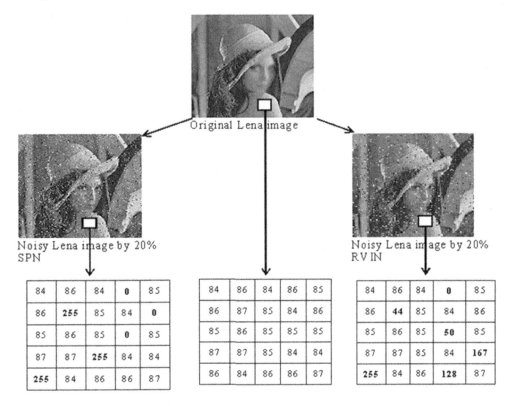

The Median operator in the above equation represents the median value of all the observations and the coefficient "0.6457" is the median absolute deviation (MAD) of a standard normal random variable.

Figures 2 and 3 show examples for illustrating the ROR value calculations. The same intensity values have been used for neighbor pixels in both examples but central pixel values are different. In example 1, the gray level of center pixel greatly differs from its all neighbors. In this case, we can observe that ROR value is 20.53, which is a significantly higher ROLD value indicates most likely impulse. But in example 2, the central pixel is very close to its most of the neighboring pixels. The ROLD value obtained in this particular case is 1.03, which is a significantly lower value

Figure 2. Example 1: Demonstration for ROR Value Calculation. (a) Intensity Values in 5× 5 Sliding Window W, (b) Median Value of the Window, 'W', (c) Absolute Differences Between Median Value and all Pixels in 'W', (d) Median of Absolute Deviation, MAD, (e) Normalized MAD, (f) ROR Value

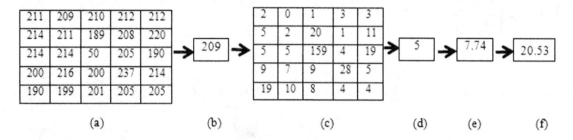

(a) (b) (c) (d) (e) (f)

Figure 3. Example 2: Demonstration for ROR Value Calculation. (a) Intensity Values in 5× 5 Sliding Window W, (b) Median Value of the Window, 'W', (c) Absolute Differences Between Median Value and all Pixels in 'W', (d) Median of absolute Deviation, MAD, (e) Normalized MAD, (f) ROR Value

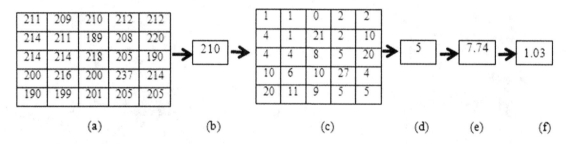

(a) (b) (c) (d) (e) (f)

Rank Based Weighted Distance Measures (RBWDM) (Smolka, Malik, & Malik, 2012)

Rank Based Weighted Distance Measures (RBWDM) is the difference between weighted distances assigned to the center pixel and the minimum value of the weighted distances of the filtering window W. The steps to calculate RBWDM are given below.

Step 1: Let's consider a window 'W'of size (N×N) and find out the distance between each pixel in the window from other pixels i.e.

$$d_{uv} = x_u - x_v \tag{5}$$

Where $u = 1.2.3.....N^2$ and $v = 1, 2 ... (N^2 -1)$

Step 2: Arrange the distance matrix in ascending order

$$d_{u1}, d_{u2}, ... d_{un} \rightarrow d_{u(1)}, \leq d_{u(2)} \leq, ... \leq d_{u(n)} \tag{6}$$

If 'r' indicates the rank of a given distance, then $d_{u(t)}$ will represent the corresponding distance value, i.e. the minimum distance has rank '1' and the maximum has rank $(N^2 - 1)$.

Step 3: Calculate the weighted sum of distance as given by the equation below

$$\Delta_u = \sum_{r=1}^{N^2-1} f(r) \cdot d_{u(r)} \tag{7}$$

$f(r)$ is a monotonically decreasing function and can be taken as $1/r$ or $1/r^2$

Step 4: Denote the weighted sum assigned to the central pixel as Δ_c

Step 5: Then, the rank weighted sum of distances calculated for each pixel belonging to Win Step: 3 are arranged in ascending order to determine the minimum weighted distance Δ_{min} as given below

$$\Delta_1 \leq \Delta_2 \leq, \dots \leq \Delta_n \rightarrow \Delta_{r1} \leq \Delta_{r2} \leq, \dots \leq \Delta_{rn} \tag{8}$$

$$\Delta_{min} = \Delta_{r1} \tag{9}$$

Step 6: The Rank Based Weighted Distance Measures (RBWDM) can be estimated as

$$RBWDM = \| \Delta_c - \Delta_{min} \| \tag{10}$$

Figures 4 and 5 show the calculation of the RBWDM value from a given window. The same window has been taken here but the deviation of center pixel in presence of impulse noise is less from the original value. In example 3, the intensity of center pixel differs from its all neighbors. In this case, we can see that RBWDM value is 55.15, which is considered as a higher RBWDM indicates the presence of noisy pixel. But in example 4, the central pixel is very close to its most of the neighboring pixels. The RBWDM value obtained in this particular case is 10.57, which is a lower value. RBWDM value greater than 15 is considered as noisy element in the image.

PROPOSED METHOD

The proposed method consists of two stages for suppressing impulse noise, the first stage is the noise detection stage used to identify the corrupted pixels in the image. In this paper, a back propagation neural network is trained with a set of known training parameters and produced a binary map of the corrupted image of the output. A value '1' at any location in the binary image indicates that the neural networks identify a pixel in the corresponding location in the stage as noisy elements and '0' represent a noise free pixel in the corresponding location. The detection stage is followed by the filtering process which restored the valued of the detector noisy candidate. The different steps of the proposed algorithm are discussed below.

Figure 4. Example 3: Demonstration for RBWDM Value Calculation. (a) Intensity Values in 5× 5 Sliding Window W, (b) Sum of Weighted Difference of Each Pixels from Other Pixels in 'W', (c) Weighted Differences Arranged in Ascending Order, (d)Minimum Weighted Difference and Weighted Difference Corresponds to Center Pixel, (e) RBWDM Value

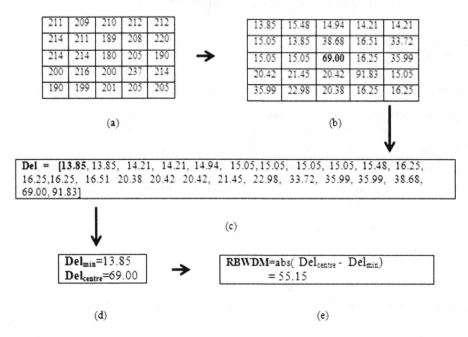

Figure 5. Example 4: Demonstration for RBWDM Value Calculation. (a) Intensity Values in 5× 5 Sliding Window W, (b) Sum of Weighted Difference of Each Pixels from Other Pixels in 'W', (c) Weighted Differences Arranged in Ascending Order, (d) Minimum Weighted Difference and Weighted Difference Corresponds to Center Pixel, (e) RBWDM Value

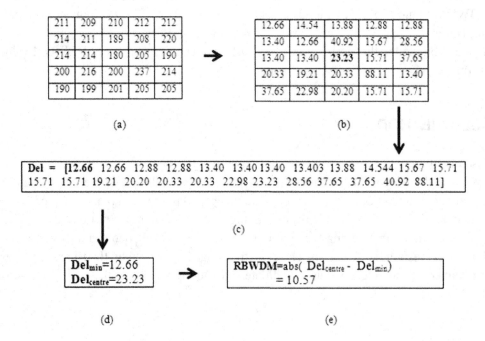

1. Compute ROR statistic for every pixel element in the corrupted test image.
2. Compute RBWDM statistic for every pixel element.
3. The ROR and RBWDM parameters extracted for each pixel of corrupted test image applied to the trained neural network to test the pixel whether i.e. noisy or non- noisy pixel
4. Apply the modified NLM filter to restore the value of identified noisy element only.

Figure 6. Architecture of the Proposed Neural Detector

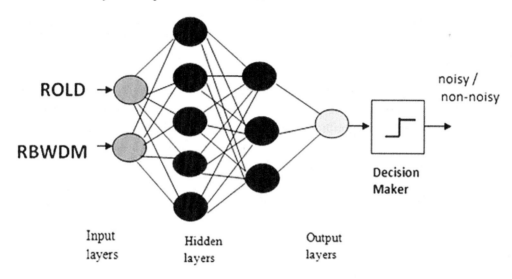

Figure 7. Lena Image

Neural Network Based Impulse Detection

In this paper, a neural network with two hidden layers and decision maker as shown in Figure 6 is used for detection of RVIN. The ANN has two input nodes corresponding to the two training parameters ROR and RBWDM compute 5×5 windows around the pixel, the two hidden layers with 5 neurons in the first stage and 3 neurons in the second stage layer. The output layer consists of 1 neuron to distinguish between healthy and unhealthy pixels, the activation function is used in the hidden layer and output layer are 'tansig' and 'logsig' respectively. The output neural network applied to a decision maker round of output to the neural integer value, efficient detector of noisy pixel the ANN (Hore, Bhattacharya, Dey, Hassanien, Banerjee & Chaudhuri, 2016) used in the proposed algorithm needs to be trained properly, to train neural network 2000 patterns (1000 noisy and 1000 noise-free) are selected at a random from Lena image as shown in Figure 7 corrupted with 30% of RVIN. The normalized ROR and RBWDM computed for each training pixel by considering a 5×5 window. The target output of healthy pixel is taken as '0' and that of the corrupted pixel taken as '1'. The proposed 2-5-3-1 ANN is then undergoing training using back-propagation algorithm. The error goal is set to 0 and maximum number of epochs as 200, once the neural network trained properly, then it can be used for classification of noisy element from the original pixels in any image (Chatterjee, Sarkar, Hore et al., 2016; Dey, Ashour, Chakraborty et al., 2016).

Filtering Process

Most of the schemes discussed in the introduction section used median value for restoring the corrupted pixels which blurs the image due to loss of image details. To overcome this limitation, a trilateral filtering scheme as discussed in (Garnett, 2005) is used here on the corrupted pixel identified in the detection stage. This filter is the modified form of bilateral filtering scheme proposed by Tomasi and Manduchi (1998). The trilateral filtering technique used here applies a nonlinear filtering to suppress noise while sharpness of edges is unaffected. Here each identified noisy pixel element is replaced by a weighted average of the neighborhood pixels gray level in a $(2M+1) \times (2M+1)$ filtering window. The weight of each neighbor pixel with respect to center pixel is the product of its spatial, radiometric and impulsive component. The weight function derives from spatial component gives higher value for the pixels near to the center pixel and decreases with increase in spatial distance of the center and neighbor pixel. Similarly, the radiometric function related to the similarity of the neighboring pixels to the center pixel. The third weighting function is defined from the impulsive nature of a pixel that is how much a pixel deviated from the original value in presence of impulse noise.

For effective use of filter in removal of impulse noise, a switching function known as Joint impulsivity (Garnett, 2005) is necessary to introduced, which determine how much to use the radiometric component and impulsive component for weight calculation of neighboring pixels. The radiometric weight is used more heavily than impulsive weight to smooth impulses that are only slightly different from the surrounding, whereas high impulsive weight is required to remove larger outlier. It may be noted that the trained neural network proposed in noise detection stage not only classify the image pixels but also states its impulsivity. So, the output of the neural network (not the output of the decision maker) can be used to define the switching function. The Noise filtering algorithm is presented below.

Step 1: Consider a $(2M+1) \times (2M+1)$ window W with center pixel as the test pixel 'α'in an image Y.

Step 2: Calculate the spatial weight of each neighboring pixel 'β' with respect to u as

$$w_s\left(\alpha, \beta\right) = exp\left(\frac{|\alpha - \beta|^2}{2\sigma_s^2}\right) \tag{11}$$

Step 3: Calculate the radiometric weight of each neighboring pixel 'β' with respect to u as

$$w_r\left(\alpha, \beta\right) = exp\left(\frac{|f_\alpha - f_\beta|^2}{2\sigma_r^2}\right) \tag{12}$$

where, f_α and fβ denote the gray value at α and β.

Step 4: Calculate the Impulsive weight of each neighboring pixel 'β' with respect to u as

$$W_I\left(\alpha\right) = exp\left[-\frac{\left(P\left(\alpha\right)Q\left(\alpha\right)\right)}{2\left(\sigma_{RD}\sigma_{RB}\right)}\right] \tag{13}$$

where, $P(\alpha)$ and $Q(\alpha)$ are respectively represent ROR and RBWDM values of α. The spread of ROR and RBWDM parameters are given by σRD a$_{nd}$ σRB, r$_{es}$pectively.

Step 5: Calculate the switching function Joint impulsivity each neighboring pixel 'β' with respect to α as

$$J\left(\alpha, \beta\right) = 1 - exp\left[-\frac{\left(\frac{T\left(\alpha\right) + T\left(\beta\right)}{2}\right)^2}{2\sigma_J^2}\right] \tag{14}$$

where T($\bullet$) indicates output of the neural network for each test pixel in the input.

Step 6: Calculate net weight each β with respect to α is given as

$$w\left(\alpha, \beta\right) = w_s\left(\alpha, \beta\right)w_r\left(\alpha, \beta\right)^{1-J\left(\alpha, \beta\right)}w_I\left(\beta\right)^{J\left(\alpha, \beta\right)} \tag{15}$$

Step 7: Now restore the corrupted pixel with the value given in the expression below

$$\hat{f}_\alpha = \frac{\sum_{\beta \in ¥} w(\alpha, \beta) f_\beta}{\sum_{\beta \in ¥} w(\alpha, \beta)} \tag{16}$$

SIMULATIONS AND RESULTS

The restoration ability of the proposed method is evaluated by extensive simulations on well-known standard 8-bit images of size 512×512. The results obtained for Pepper, Pentagon, House, Bridge, and Gold hill is present in this paper. The above image is corrupted with RVIN from 30% to 60% compared to the efficient, the proposed method along with the well-known impulse noise with restored algorithm such as ACWM, PWMAD, DWM, SDOOD, ROR-NLM, ENLM, AFIDM, ANWMF, and RWASF are applied to the above noisy images. It has been observed that the performance of the algorithm varies with change in size of the filtering window. After number of trials we got satisfactory for the filtering window $5 \times 5(M = 2)$, which perform better in both noise suppression and preserving image detail. Apart of above case, there are five other parameters, σ_s, σ_r, σ_{RD}, σ_{RB} and σ_J that need to be adjusted to make the proposed method more reliable and efficient. Again, through numbers of trials, the optimal values of $\{\sigma_s, \sigma_r, \sigma_{RD}, \sigma_{RB}$ and $\sigma_J\}$ for suppressing random-value impulse noise are taken as, 0.4, 10, 0.1, 0.4 and 0.1 respectively. Peak Signal to Noise Ratio (PSNR) (Dey, Samanta, Yang, Das & Chaudhuri, 2013) (Dey, Samanta, Chakraborty, Das, Chaudhuri & Suri, 2014) (Dey, Roy & Dey, 2012) is taken as the performance metric defined in (17) used for comparison. For getting best result the image is processed iteratively. It has been observed that the algorithm required one iteration for low noise and maximum three iterations for removing high- density impulse noise.

$$PSNR = 10 \log_{10} \left(\frac{255^2}{\frac{1}{M x N} \sum_{i=1}^{M} \sum_{j=1}^{N} \left(f_{i,j} - \hat{f}_{i,j} \right)^2} \right) \tag{17}$$

Where (M×N) indicates test image size and $f_{i,j}$ & $\hat{f}_{i,j}$ represented the gray level l values at (i,j)th location of original uncorrupted test image and restored version of the corrupted image respectively. Table 1 represents the comparison analysis of the PSNR of Peppers, Gold hill, Pentagon, and House. It can be observed from the result that the proposed technique performance better than standard and existing algorithm discussed above. The simulated PSNR for the Bridge image plotted in Figure 8, it is clear from the graph that signification improvement of proposed method over other methods. The restored Pepper image from the different scheme is shown in Figure 9 at 50% Noise level. It can be observed from that the visual quality of filtered image using proposed method is superior to the quality of the filtered image using existing standard method.

Table 1. Comparative Analysis of PSNR for Various Restoration Techniques

Images	% of Noise	ACWM	PWMAD	DWM	SDOOD	ROR NLM	RWASF	ENLM	ANWMF	AFIDM	PROPOSED
	30	30.03	32.12	29.23	25.78	22.78	32.75	30.34	32.39	31.25	**33.13**
	40	27.35	23.33	28.84	27.92	31.21	29.80	28.38	31.22	30.58	**31.82**
Peppers	50	24.60	19.97	26.80	24.53	29.04	26.14	26.50	30.12	28.21	**30.52**
	60	21.43	17.35	23.65	21.08	26.26	22.17	23.80	28.21	25.31	**29.01**
	30	28.27	26.90	30.90	30.15	27.51	28.23	27.47	28.02	30.20	**31.51**
	40	26.63	24.53	27.86	26.98	26.78	27.21	26.50	27.52	29.78	**30.52**
Pentagon	50	24.93	22.03	26.97	25.91	26.03	25.45	25.45	26.25	29.02	**29.93**
	60	23.23	19.78	25.90	24.47	25.10	23.33	24.13	25.35	27.28	**28.57**
	30	34.91	29.69	37.40	34.21	38.54	37.85	35.64	29.68	34.13	**39.42**
	40	31.30	25.13	34.43	31.33	35.66	33.32	33.05	28.00	32.71	**37.25**
House	50	27.51	21.36	31.41	28.01	33.30	28.56	29.20	27.48	30.77	**35.14**
	60	24.088	18.53	27.24	23.84	30.55	24.12	26.38	26.13	26.61	**32.39**
	30	32.12	27.25	32.23	31.12	31.50	33.15	31.00	27.02	30.50	**34.81**
	40	29.23	24.55	30.64	29.03	30.43	30.64	29.36	25.30	29.08	**33.24**
Goldhill	50	25.78	20.12	28.60	26.11	29.27	26.82	27.29	24.95	27.81	**30.67**
	60	22.78	17.15	25.30	22.31	27.64	22.77	24.65	23.66	27.78	**28.79**

Figure 8. Comparative Analysis of PSNR at Various Noise Densities of Bridge Image

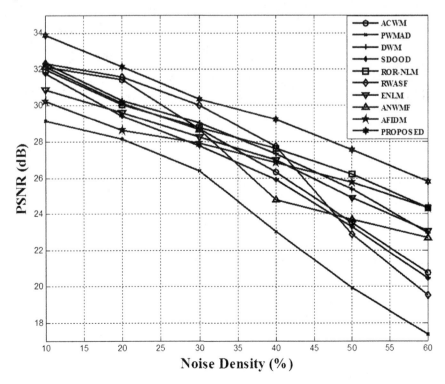

Figure 9. Restored Pepper Images of Various Filters for Image Corrupted with 50% Random Valued Impulse Noise (a) Original Pepper Image (b) Noisy Image (c) Proposed Method (d) ACWMF (e)PWMAD (f) DWM (g)SDOOD (h) ROR-NLM (i) RWASF (j) ENLM (k)ANWMF (l)AFIDM

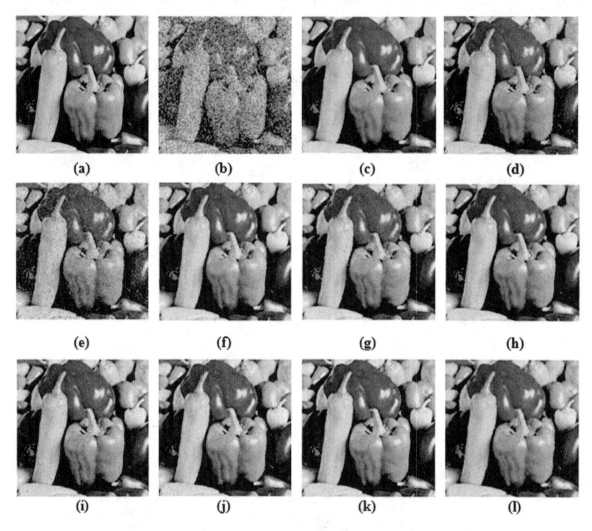

CONCLUSION

In this paper, a new innovative restoration method is proposed to recover images corrupted with RVIN effectively. The method used a neural network based detection method taking the ROR and RBWDM value of each pixel of the image as its input. The two features extracted from training image used as the input to the neural network make the detection accuracy high enough and generalized for which the designed structure of the network neither required to be trained every time for different noise ratio or different images. The modified Nonlocal means filtering process is applied to the selected noisy candidates without affecting the healthy pixels. The effectiveness of the proposed algorithm has been compared with some well-known existing method. It has been observed from the comparative analysis that proposed technique outperforms the existing state of art methods both in terms of noise suppression and preserving the images details.

REFERENCES

Abreu, E., Lightstone, M., Mitra, S., & Arakawa, K. (1996). A new efficient approach for the removal of impulse noise from highly corrupted images. *IEEE Transactions on Image Processing, 5*(6), 1012–1025. doi:10.1109/83.503916 PMID:18285188

Akkoul, S., Ledee, R., Leconge, R., & Harba, R. (2009). A new detector for switching median filter. In *Proceedings of the 6th International Symposium on Image and Signal Processing and Analysis.*

Chanda, B., & Majumder, D. Dutta. (2002). Digital Image Processing and Analysis (1st ed.). Prentice-Hall of India.

Chatterjee, S., Sarkar, S., Hore, S., Dey, N., Ashour, A. S., & Balas, V. E. (2016). Particle swarm optimization trained neural network for structural failure prediction of multistoried RC buildings. *Neural Computing & Applications.*

Chen, T., & Wu, H.R. (2001). Adaptive impulse detection using center-weighted median filters. *IEEE Signal Processing Letters, 8*(1).

Crnogavic, V. (2004). Advanced impulse detection based on pixel-wise MAD. *IEEE Signal Processing Letters, 11*(7), 589–592. doi:10.1109/LSP.2004.830117

Crnojevi'c, V. (2005). Impulse Noise Filter With Adaptive Mad-Based Threshold. In *Proceedings of the IEEE International Conference on Image Processing*, Genova (Vol. 3). 10.1109/ICIP.2005.1530397

Dey, N., Ashour, A. S., Beagum, S., Pistola, D. S., Gospodinov, M., Gospodinova, E. P., & Tavares, J. M. R. (2015). Parameter optimization for local polynomial approximation based intersection confidence interval filter using genetic algorithm: An application for brain MRI image de-noising. *Journal of Imaging, 1*(1), 60–84. doi:10.3390/jimaging1010060

Dey, N., Ashour, A. S., Chakraborty, S., Samanta, S., Sifaki-Pistolla, D., Ashour, A. S., ... Nguyen, G. N. (2016). Healthy and unhealthy rat hippocampus cells classification: A neural based automated system for Alzheimer disease classification. *Journal of Advanced Microscopy Research, 11*(1), 1–10. doi:10.1166/jamr.2016.1282

Dey, N., Roy, A. B., & Dey, S. (2012). A novel approach of color image hiding using RGB color planes and DWT. *arXiv preprint arXiv:1208.0803.*

Dey, N., Samanta, S., Chakraborty, S., Das, A., Chaudhuri, S. S., & Suri, J. S. (2014). Firefly algorithm for optimization of scaling factors during embedding of manifold medical information: An application in ophthalmology imaging. *Journal of Medical Imaging and Health Informatics, 4*(3), 384–394. doi:10.1166/jmihi.2014.1265

Dey, N., Samanta, S., Yang, X. S., Das, A., & Chaudhuri, S. S. (2013). Optimisation of scaling factors in electrocardiogram signal watermarking using cuckoo search. *International Journal of Bio-inspired Computation, 5*(5), 315–326. doi:10.1504/IJBIC.2013.057193

Dong, Y., & Xu, S. (2007). A new Directional Weighted Median Filter for Removal of Random-Valued Impulse Noise. *IEEE Signal Processing Letters, 14*(3), 193–196. doi:10.1109/LSP.2006.884014

Garnett, R., Huegerich, T., Chui, C., & Wenjie He. (2005). A Universal Noise Removal Algorithm with an Impulse Detector. *IEEE Transactions on Image Processing*, *14*(11), 1747–1754. doi:10.1109/TIP.2005.857261 PMID:16279175

Gonzalez, R. C., & Woods, R. E. (2002). *Digital Image Processing. Engle-wood cliffs*. NJ: Prentice-Hall.

Habib, M., Hussain, A., Rasheed, S., & Ali, M. (2016). Adaptive fuzzy inference system based directional median filter for impulse noise removal. *Int. J. Electron Commun*, *70*, 689-697.

Hore, S., Bhattacharya, T., Dey, N., Hassanien, A. E., Banerjee, A., & Chaudhuri, S. B. (2016). A real time dactylology based feature extraction for selective image encryption and artificial neural network. In *Image Feature Detectors and Descriptors* (pp. 203–226). Springer International Publishing. doi:10.1007/978-3-319-28854-3_8

Hore, S., Chatterjee, S., Sarkar, S., Dey, N., Ashour, A. S., Balas-Timar, D., & Balas, V. E. (2016). Neural-based prediction of structural failure of multistoried RC buildings. *Structural Engineering & Mechanics*, *58*(3), 459–473. doi:10.12989em.2016.58.3.459

Ikeda, N., Gupta, A., Dey, N., Bose, S., Shafique, S., Arak, T., ... Suri, J. S. (2015). Improved correlation between carotid and coronary atherosclerosis SYNTAX score using automated ultrasound carotid bulb plaque IMT measurement. *Ultrasound in Medicine & Biology*, *41*(5), 1247–1262. doi:10.1016/j.ultrasmedbio.2014.12.024 PMID:25638311

Jeba, Y. P., & Sandra, M. P. R. (2013). Image Denoising Techniques for Salt and Pepper Noise: A Comparative Study. *International Journal of Research In Computer Applications And Robotics*, *1*(8), 27-33.

Jena, B., Patel, P., & Majhi, B. (2014). Fuzzy based random valued Impulse noise suppression using optimal direction method. *Elixir International Journal*, *71*, 24729–24734.

Kang, C.-C., & Wang, W.-J. (2009). Modified Switching Median Filter with One More Noise Detector for Impulse Noise Removal. *Int. J. Electron. Commun.*, *63*(11), 998–1004. doi:10.1016/j.aeue.2008.08.009

Liang, S. F., Lu, S. M., Chang, J. Y., & Lin, C. T. (2008). A novel two-stage impulse noise removal technique based on neural networks and fuzzy decision. *IEEE Transactions on Fuzzy Systems*, *16*(4), 863 – 873.

Liu, L., Chen, C. L. P., Zhou, Y., & You, X. (2015). A new weighted mean filter with a two-phase detector for removing impulse noise. *Information Sciences*, *315*, 1–16. doi:10.1016/j.ins.2015.03.067

Luo, W. (2006). An efficient detail-preserving approach for removing impulse noise in images. *IEEE Signal Processing Letters*, *13*(7), 413–416. doi:10.1109/LSP.2006.873144

Majhi, B., & Fathi, M. (2005). FLANN detector based filtering of images corrupted by impulse noise. *Journal of Computer Science*, *1*(3), 332–336. doi:10.3844/jcssp.2005.332.336

Nair, M. S., & Vijur, S. (2013). Predictive-based adaptive switching median filter for impulse noise removal using neural network-based noise detector. Signal. *Image and Video Processing*, *7*(6), 1041–1070. doi:10.100711760-012-0310-8

Patel, P. (2012). Dynamic adaptive median filter (damf) for removal of high density impulse noise., International Journal Image. *Graphics and Signal Processing*, *11*(11), 53–62. doi:10.5815/ijigsp.2012.11.08

Patel, P., Jena, B., Majhi, B., & Tripathy, C. (2012). Fuzzy based adaptive mean filtering technique for removal of impulse noise from images. *International Journal of Computer Vision and Signal Processing*, *1*(1), 15-21. Retrieved from http://www.ijcvsp.com

Pushpavalli, R., & Sivaradje, G. (2013). Feed forward back propagation algorithm for eliminating uniform noise and impulse noise. *European Journal of Natural and Applied Sciences*, *1*(1), 10–27.

Sa, P. K., & Majhi, B. (2010). An Improved Adaptive Impulsive Noise Suppression Scheme for Digital Images. *Elsevier International Journal of Electronics and Communications*, *64*(4), 322–328. doi:10.1016/j.aeue.2009.01.005

Smolka, B., Malik, K., & Malik, D. (2012). Adaptive rank weighted switching filter for impulsive noise removal in color images. Springerlink.com.

Tomasi, C., & Manduchi, R. (1998). Bilateral filtering for gray and color images. In *Proc. IEEE Int. Conf. Computer Vision* (pp. 839–846). 10.1109/ICCV.1998.710815

Xiong, B. (2012). A Universal Denoising Framework with a New Impulse Detector and Nonlocal Means. *IEEE Transactions on Image Processing*, *21*(4), 1663–1275. doi:10.1109/TIP.2011.2172804 PMID:22020688

Xu, G., & Tan, J. (2013). A universal impulse noise filter with an impulse detector and nonlocal means. *Circuits Syst. Signal Process.* New York: Springer Science + Business Media. .doi:10.100700034-013-9640-1

This research was previously published in the International Journal of Rough Sets and Data Analysis (IJRSDA), 5(2); pages 148-163, copyright year 2018 by IGI Publishing (an imprint of IGI Global).

Chapter 56
Health Insurance Claim Prediction Using Artificial Neural Networks

Sam Goundar
The University of the South Pacific, Suva, Fiji

Suneet Prakash
The University of the South Pacific, Suva, Fiji

Pranil Sadal
The University of the South Pacific, Suva, Fiji

Akashdeep Bhardwaj
iD https://orcid.org/0000-0001-7361-0465
University of Petroleum and Energy Studies, India

ABSTRACT

A number of numerical practices exist that actuaries use to predict annual medical claim expense in an insurance company. This amount needs to be included in the yearly financial budgets. Inappropriate estimating generally has negative effects on the overall performance of the business. This study presents the development of artificial neural network model that is appropriate for predicting the anticipated annual medical claims. Once the implementation of the neural network models was finished, the focus was to decrease the mean absolute percentage error by adjusting the parameters, such as epoch, learning rate, and neurons in different layers. Both feed forward and recurrent neural networks were implemented to forecast the yearly claims amount. In conclusion, the artificial neural network model that was implemented proved to be an effective tool for forecasting the anticipated annual medical claims for BSP Life. Recurrent neural network outperformed the feed forward neural network in terms of accuracy and computation power required to carry out the forecasting.

DOI: 10.4018/978-1-6684-2408-7.ch056

1. INTRODUCTION

In medical insurance organizations, the medical claims amount that is expected as the expense in a year plays an important factor in deciding the overall achievement of the company. BSP Life (Fiji) Ltd. provides both Health and Life Insurance in Fiji. Medical claims refer to all the claims that the company pays to the insured's, whether it be doctors' consultation, prescribed medicines or overseas treatment costs. Claims received in a year are usually large which needs to be accurately considered when preparing annual financial budgets. These claim amounts are usually high in millions of dollars every year. An increase in medical claims will directly increase the total expenditure of the company thus affects the profit margin. Currently utilizing existing or traditional methods of forecasting with variance. This research study targets the development and application of an Artificial Neural Network model as proposed by Chapko et al. (2011) and El-said et al. (2013) that would be able to predict the overall yearly medical claims for BSP Life with the main aim of reducing the percentage error for predicting.

According to Rizal et al. (2016), neural network is very similar to biological neural networks. Neural networks can be distinguished into distinct types based on the architecture. Two main types of neural networks are namely feed forward neural network and recurrent neural network (RNN). Artificial neural networks (ANN) have proven to be very useful in helping many organizations with business decision making. Example, Sangwan et al. (2020) proposed artificial neural network is commonly utilized by organizations for forecasting bankruptcy, customer churning, stock price forecasting and in many other applications and areas. This research focusses on the implementation of multi-layer feed forward neural network with back propagation algorithm based on gradient descent method. The network was trained using immediate past 12 years of medical yearly claims data. Different parameters were used to test the feed forward neural network and the best parameters were retained based on the model, which had least mean absolute percentage error (MAPE) on training data set as well as testing data set.

In the insurance business, two things are considered when analysing losses: frequency of loss and severity of loss. Previous research investigated the use of artificial neural networks (NNs) to develop models as aids to the insurance underwriter when determining acceptability and price on insurance policies. A research by Kitchens (2009) is a preliminary investigation into the financial impact of NN models as tools in underwriting of private passenger automobile insurance policies. Results indicate that an artificial NN underwriting model outperformed a linear model and a logistic model. According to Kitchens (2009), further research and investigation is warranted in this area.

In the past, research by Mahmoud et al. (2013) and Majhi (2018) on recurrent neural networks (RNNs) have also demonstrated that it is an improved forecasting model for time series. To demonstrate this, NARX model (nonlinear autoregressive network having exogenous inputs), is a recurrent dynamic network was tested and compared against feed forward artificial neural network. Abhigna et al. (2017) state that artificial neural network (ANN) has been constructed on the human brain structure with very useful and effective pattern classification capabilities. ANN has the ability to resemble the basic processes of human's behaviour which can also solve nonlinear matters, with this feature Artificial Neural Network is widely used with complicated system for computations and classifications, and has cultivated on non-linearity mapped effect if compared with traditional calculating methods. According to Zhang et al. (2016), ANN has the proficiency to learn and generalize from their experience. The authors Motlagh et al. (2016) emphasize that the idea behind forecasting is previous know and observed information together with model outputs will be very useful in predicting future values. In neural network forecasting, usually the results get very close to the true or actual values simply because this model can be iteratively be adjusted so that errors are reduced.

Viaene et al. (2005) explored the explicative capabilities of neural network classifiers with automatic relevance determination weight regularization. Reports the findings from applying these networks for personal injury protection automobile insurance claim fraud detection. The automatic relevance objective function scheme provides us with a way to determine which inputs are most informative to the trained neural network model. An implementation of MacKay's (1992) evidence framework approach to Bayesian learning is proposed as a practical way of training such networks. The empirical evaluation was based on a data set of closed claims from accidents that occurred in Massachusetts, USA, in 1993.

The first type of artificial neural network is a feed forward neural network. The basic layout of multi-layer feed forward neural network has three layers, which are input layer, middle layer is known as hidden layer and one output layer. Input layer, which is independent, receives the data as input. Hidden layer transforms the input into objects (Abdel et al., 2013) that the output layer can utilize. Output layer converts the hidden layer activations into the scale that has been specified by the user. According to Abhishek et al. (2012) Multi-layer networks utilize a number of learning techniques as proposed by Salama et al. (2014), with the most common being back-propagation. The output values are usually compared with the actual value to get the error rate. The calculated value is then put through the network as the input. This way the network adjusts the weight of each connector so that the error could be reduced. After several iterations, the values will eventually come to a state where the error is very small. Some other factors, which needs to be thoroughly considered in the process of designing the neural network, are Epoch (iterations), weight initialization, Neurons in the hidden layer, learning rate and the momentum constant or bias value. Training process usually involves adjusting these parameters for maximum accuracy.

Ajibola et al. (2012) looks at using artificial neural network's primary role of providing financial protection for other industries by the insurance industry. In spite of the harsh economic environment in Nigeria, the insurance industry has been crucial to the consummation of business plans and wealth creation. However, the continued downturn experienced by many countries, in the last decade, seems to have affected negatively on the financial health of the industry, thereby rendering many insurance companies inherently distressed. Although there is a regulator to monitor the insurance companies in order to prevent insolvency and protect the right of consumers this oversight function has been made difficult because the regulators appeared to lack the necessary tools that would adequately equip them to perform their oversight functions. One such critical tool is a decision-making model that provides early warning signal of distressed firms. Their research constructs an insolvency prediction model based on artificial neural network approach, which could be used to evaluate the financial capability of insurance companies.

The second type of artificial neural network is known as recurrent neural network (RNN). The authors Zhang et al. (2016) state that unlike feed forward neural networks, recurrent neural networks (RNN) are bi-directional where the output is fed back to the previous units. The feedback enables the neural network models to be trained and process sequences dynamically, which would have better prediction. According to Khan et al. (2013) recurrent neural networks have inbuilt dynamic behaviour, which is why it is, referred as special neural networks. The main difference between the feed forward neural networks is the feedback path (s) where the output is fed back into the system as an input. The inter-relationship between the inputs and the internal state is processed for creating the output after the training. Learning process is supervised, where the target values are always the second source of information.

This research has been organized as follows. Section 2 presents literature survey of previously published research on the same domain and topic. Section 3 illustrates initial investigation and raw data collection process. Section 4 presents the Research Methods followed which includes performing an auto-correlation, data normalization, algorithm training of the test data and then checking the design for network accuracy and the stopping criteria. Section 5 is based on actual implementation and compares two models Feed Forward Neural Network and Recurrent Models. Section 6 compares the neural network models and the Human Prediction.

2. LITERATURE SURVEY

Dong et al. (2019) presented the computational framework for Reservoir Computing using Recurrent Neural Network (RNN) having fixed weights. The authors proposed several physical implementations to improve the energy efficiency and speed using a scattering model.

Dumas et al. (2019) performed a review for a set of neural network architectures for intra image predictions. The authors proved that fully connected neural networks tend to provide better performance for small block sizes, while convolutional neural networks had better predictions for large complex textures blocks.

Liu et al. (2019) proposed deep learning-based neural network prediction model for image compression. The authors initially articulated prediction of multi-class classification problem and a framework that transformed the multi-class classification into binary classification problem solved by just one binary classifier. Then the authors constructed the deep learning based binary classifier to predict if an image is lossy with another or not. The authors also proposed a sliding window search strategy. This helped predict results for the lossless predictor. Experimental results show that the mean accuracy of the perceptually lossless predictor. The research displayed superior results for the proposed neural model as compared to the conventional models.

Random rough subspace based neural network ensemble method was proposed by Xu, Wang, Zhang, and Yang (2011) for insurance fraud detection. In this method, rough set reduction is firstly employed to generate a set of reductions, which can keep the consistency of data information. Secondly, the reductions are randomly selected to construct a subset of reductions. Thirdly, each of the selected reductions is used to train a neural network classifier based on the insurance data. Finally, the trained neural network classifiers are combined using ensemble strategies. For validation, a real automobile insurance case is used to test the effectiveness and efficiency of our proposed method with two popular evaluation criteria including the percentage correctly classified (PCC) and the receive operating characteristic (ROC) curve. The experimental results show that our proposed model outperforms single classifier and other models used in comparison. The findings of this study reseal that the random rough subspace based neural network ensemble method can provide a faster and more accurate way to find suspicious insurance claims, and it is a promising tool for insurance fraud detection.

Dong et al. (2019) proposed a novel neural network model for health-related prediction model for whole population and individuals for blood glucose fluctuations. The authors integrated pre-training and fine-tuned processes to overcome the problem of insufficient data for individual patient and making full use of the population and individual differences and fluctuations. When compared with other machine learning and neural network approaches, the numerical results suggest that the proposed approach gains significant improvements on prediction accuracy.

Dong et al. (2019) proposed a new neural prediction approach based on recurrent neural networks (RNN). The authors incorporated pre-processing of clustering into the classical RNNs. Numerical results suggested that the proposed approach utilized more than one cluster for both type I and type II datasets and has gained improvements compared with support vector regression (SVR) and other RNN methods in terms of prediction accuracy.

Epilepsy is a neurological disorder associated with abnormal electrical activity in the brain, which causes seizures. The occurrence of seizure is not predictable; the duration between seizures, as well as the symptoms, varies from patient to another. Nashaat et al. (2019) designed and implemented a monitoring system for epileptic patients; the system should continuously check some vital signs, analyse the measurements, and decide whether the patient is nearly to have a seizure or not. Whenever a seizure is predicted, the system initiates an alarm. In addition, a notification should be sent to the health care responsible, as well as one preferred contact. By implementing the monitoring system, people who suffer from epilepsy will have more chance to work and live a normal life. Thus, this research study presents the concept of the overall system and shows results of the implemented systems: EEG, ECG and Fall Detection system. Results have shown that the fall detection accuracy reached 99.89% whereas the accuracy of the prediction using the ANN was about 97.34%.

Liou, Tang, and Chen (2008) looked at the usage of artificial neural networks in hospitals and health care providers. Because of the exaggerated and fraudulent medical claims initiated by national insurance schemes, artificial neural networks can be applied for detection. Their study applied data mining techniques to detect fraudulent or abusive reporting by healthcare providers using their invoices for diabetic outpatient services. This research was pursued in the context of Taiwan's National Health Insurance system. We compare the identification accuracy of three algorithms: logistic regression, neural network, and classification trees. While all three are quite accurate, the classification tree model performs the best with an overall correct identification rate of 99%. The neural network (96%) and the logistic regression model (92%) follow it.

Predicting indoor air quality becomes a global public health issue. Commercial organizations have developed a smart connected object, which is able to measure different physical parameters including concentration of pollutants (volatile organic compounds, carbon dioxide and fine particles). This smart object must embed prediction capacities in order to avoid the exceedance of an air quality threshold. This task is actually performed by neural network models. However, when some events occur (change of people's behaviours, change of place of the smart connected object as example), the embedded neural models become less accurate. So, a relearning step is needed in order to refit the models. The smart connected object must perform this relearning, and therefore, it must use the less computing time as possible. Thomas et al. (2019) proposed combining a control chart in order to limit the frequency of relearning, and to compare three learning algorithms (backpropagation, Levenberg-Marquardt, neural network with random weights) in order to choose the more adapted to this situation.

Jun et al. (2019) proposed a general framework that incorporates effective missing data imputation using VAE and multivariate time series prediction. We utilize the uncertainty obtained from the generative network of the VAE and employ uncertainty-aware attention in imputing the missing values. We evaluated the performance of our architecture on real-world clinical dataset (MIMIC-III) for in-hospital mortality prediction task. Our results showed higher performance than other competing methods in mortality prediction task.

Mahdi et al. (2019) presented Deep Learning technique called long short term memory (LSTM) recurrent neural networks to find sessions that are prone to code failure in applications that rely on telemetry data for system health monitoring. The authors used LSTM networks to extract telemetry patterns that lead to a specific code failure. For code failure prediction, treating the telemetry events, sequence of telemetry events and the outcome of each sequence as words, sentence and sentiment in the context of sentiment analysis, respectively. The proposed method is able to process a large set of data and can automatically handle edge cases in code failure prediction. The authors took advantage of Bayesian optimization technique to find the optimal hyperactive parameters as well as the type of LSTM cells that leads to the best prediction performance. The authors introduced the Contributors and Blockers concepts. In this research, contributors are the set of events that cause a code failure, while blockers are the set of events that each of them individually prevents a code failure from happening, even in presence of one or multiple contributor(s). Once the proposed LSTM model is trained, we use a greedy approach to find the contributors and blockers. To develop and test our proposed method, we use synthetic (simulated) data in the first step. The synthetic data is generated using a number of rules for code failures, as well as a number of rules for preventing a code failure from happening. The trained LSTM model shows over 99% accuracy for detecting code failures in the synthetic data. The results from the proposed method outperform the classical learning models such as Decision Tree and Random Forest. Using the proposed greedy method, we are able to find the contributors and blockers in the synthetic data in more than 90% of the cases, with a performance better than sequential rule and pattern mining algorithms.

According to Yunos et al. (2016), expected claim frequency and the expected claim severity were used in predictive modelling for motor insurance claims. There are two categories of claims were considered, namely, third party property damage (TPPD) and own damage (OD). Data sets from the year 2001 to 2003 are used to develop the predictive model (Mnasser et al., 2014). The main issues in modelling the motor insurance claims are related to the nature of insurance data, such as huge information, uncertainty, imprecise and incomplete information; and classical statistical technique (Azar et al., 2014) which cannot handle the extreme value in the insurance data. Their research proposes the back propagation neural network (BPNN) model as a tool to model the problem. A detailed explanation of how the BPNN model solves the issues is provided.

Zhang et al. (2019) proposed a hybrid neural network model, which combines convolutional neural network (CNN) and recurrent neural network (RNN). The proposed model extracted local features and captured the degradation process. In order to show the effectiveness of the proposed approach, tests on the NASA Commercial Modular Aero-Propulsion System Simulation (C-MAPSS) dataset of turbofan engine. The experimental results show that the proposed CNN-RNN hybrid model achieves better score values than the multilayer perceptron (MLP), support vector regression (SVR) and (CNN) on FDOOI, FD003 and FD004 data sets.

Kurtah et al. (2019) presented their research to provide a system that displays in real time the disease status. The system also predicts the propagation of diseases allowing the concerned health ministry to better plan remedial actions. The system consists of three mobile crowdsourcing applications that allow the public, doctors and pharmacies to report diseases and drugs sales in real time. Data regarding diseases for the year 2017 were retrieved and the corresponding daily weather information namely as temperature, humidity and wind for that year was then extracted and added to this dataset. An Artificial Neural Network (ANN) was then trained with this dataset and then used to predict the propagation of the diseases, which can be monitored, by the Ministry of Health and Quality of Life through another application. The prediction was performed based on the number of reported diseases on the current day along with weather forecasts for the forthcoming days and the results were promising. The model has been evaluated resulting in an accuracy of 90%. Finally, we believe that such a system can be very beneficial to the ministry, which can then take informed decisions to counteract the possible propagation of diseases.

Chuanchai et al. (2019) proposed a framework for spatially predicting the particulate matter concentration in the area without monitoring station. The proposed framework consisted of two components. One is a particulate matter monitoring station deployed in a reference location, and other is a spatial prediction model to apply spatial interpolation technique and machine learning technique to provide the particulate matter concentration value in the area without monitoring station. This study also explores the results from the variety of components in the model. Two spatial interpolation techniques, namely IDW: Inverse Distance Weigh and Kriging are compared. The evaluation results show that the model can spatially predict particulate matter concentration value with the average 10.16% error by using the Kriging technique with seven inputs for machine learning.

Decaro et al. (2019) illustrated application of machine learning techniques to predict hematic parameters using blood visible spectra during ex-vivo treatments. A spectroscopic setup was prepared for acquisition of blood absorbance spectrum and tested in an operational environment. This setup is non-invasive and can be applied during dialysis sessions. A support vector machine and an artificial neural network, trained with a dataset of spectra, have been implemented for the prediction of haematocrit and oxygen saturation. Results of different machine learning algorithms are compared, showing that support vector machine is the best technique for the prediction of haematocrit and oxygen saturation.

3. INITIAL INVESTIGATION

Before the actual implementation of the models, there was a need to carry out some analysis on the raw data and have formal research methods. BSP LIFE (Fiji) Ltd provided the raw claims data, relationships between the data sets needed to be identified. The raw data was summarized yearly to explore the trends in the yearly claimed amount paid. To understand and observe the overall trend between the annual medical claims figure, the aggregated sum of medical claims amount paid for each year was calculated. Figure 1 highlights the yearly trend of medical claims paid out.

Figure 1. Medical claims amount paid for each year

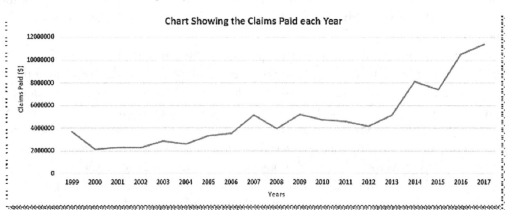

The yearly medical claims amount was divided into the 4 quarters as the next step of analysis. After dividing and summarizing the results into quarters, observations concluded that quarterly series had noise and could not be used as the input for forecasting. The accuracy of the prediction model that would be designed later would also be affected negatively if quarterly amount were to be used. Figure 2 shows the trends of quarterly medical claims series.

Figure 2. Medical claims paid for each quarter

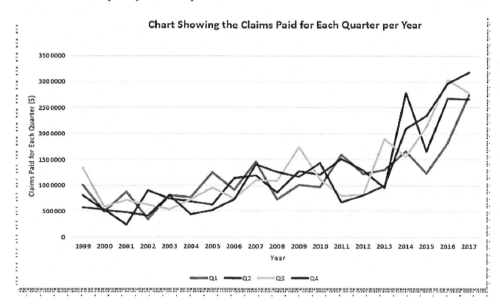

A number of features are extracted from the raw data, which encompassed of average age of the insured, acute disease amount and chronic disease amount for each year. Table 1 shows the summary of features extracted.

4. RESEARCH METHODS

The research methods initiated by taking the raw data, performing an auto-correlation and then initiating the data normalization followed by training the test data. Finally, network design was checked for network accuracy and the stopping criteria. The below section illustrates the implementation process in form of figures and graphs.

4.1 Auto-Correlation

Auto- Correlation is a depiction of the extent of similarity between a time series and a lagged version of itself over consecutive time intervals. In this research, Correlation was used to determine the window size of the input to the network model that would be developed. MatLab software was used to plot the auto-correlation of the series, which highlighted the positive correlation in 1, 2 and 3 lag variables.

The Lags were used to identify the number of input to the network i.e. the number of years of claims amount needed as the input. Figure 3 shows the plot from Mat-Lab which was achieved by using the correlation function.

Table 1. Yearly claims figure and feature summary

Year	Claims Paid	Data	Average Age	Acute	Chronic
2001	3724016.038	Training	37.86	1677712.204	2046303.834
2002	2137491.717	Training	38.73	372907.245	1764584.472
2003	2318647.2	Training	41.48	128182.3	2190464.9
2004	2289772.26	Training	40.9	263764.24	2026008.02
2005	2892552.57	Training	39.85	125446.68	2767105.89
2006	2630915.71	Training	40.41	235286.64	2395629.07
2007	3337894.81	Training	40.78	243860.186	3094034.626
2008	3528283.74	Training	38.44	556824.34	2971459.4
2009	5161877.31	Training	40.73	921796.24	4240081.07
2010	3936563.29	Training	38.79	1217478.56	2719084.73
2011	5181380.24	Training	39.58	1014753.33	4166626.91
2012	4731157.85	Training	40.37	1159020.06	3572137.79
2013	4581545.17	Training	39.81	896958.86	3684586.31
2014	4140205.86	Test	36.35	1370092.91	2770112.95
2015	5159114.67	Test	31.48	1868632.78	3290481.89
2016	8094810.18	Test	31.89	3028274.76	5066535.42
2017	7378419.19	Test	31.35	1681138.83	5697280.36
2018	10483842.3	Test	32.72	3766492.5	6717349.8
2019	1362799.91	Test	32.16	4859328.41	6503471.5

4.2 Data Normalization

The process of scaling numeric data into a new range of values which are usually between [-1, 1] or [0, 1] is known as Data normalization. According to the authors Abhigna, Jerritta, Srinivasan, and Rajendran (2017), a number of normalization methods exists which can be used for data normalization such as Min- Max Normalization, Median normalization, Statiscal or Z-Score Normalization, Statistical Column Normalization and Sigmoid Normalization. In this research, Min-Max Normalization technique was utilized so that the claims value is scaled between the range of [0, 1]. Since sigmoid activation function was used at the hidden and output layer where the inputs were required to be normalized between 0 to 1, the authors used data normalization. The formula that was used to carry out the normalization was:

$$X_{norm} = (X - X_{min}) / (X_{max} - X_{min})$$

Figure 3. Auto-correlation plot of the yearly claims series

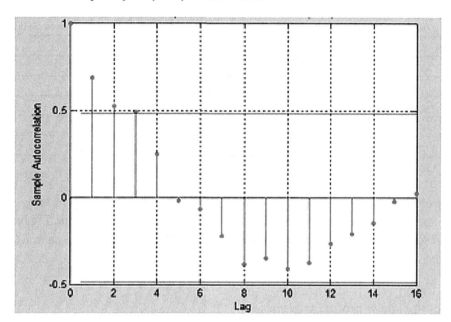

X in the formula denotes the actual value to be normalised, X_{min} refers to the minimum value in the data set and X_{max} refers to the maximum value. Min-Max normalization had the advantage of retaining exactly all relationships in the data after the scaling which is why this is used. After the pre- processing of medical raw claims data were successfully completed, the next step required the actual model to be built.

4.3 Training and Test Data

The claim records provided had past 20 years of raw data, which was then, divided into training and test data. The split ratio between the training and test data was approximately 70% and 30%. For training, claim records from 1999 to 2011 were used and for testing, records from 2012 to 2018 were used.

4.4 Network Design

Training algorithm together with activation function needed to be determined before the actual implementation of the networks. Back propagation algorithm based on gradient descent method was chosen. The hidden layer and the output layer had activation function as sigmoid or logistic function, which was used at each neuron in these layers with the formula as:

$\{Sigmoid\ Activation\} = 1 / (1 + e^{-x})$

There were three instances of the initial network model implemented with having 1, 2 and 3 input. There were three instances built with 3 different input simply because there was positive correlation with 1,2 and 3 lag variables. Separate bias units were used which connected to every neuron in the hidden and output layer. Table 2 shows the structure of the input to the model and the desired output for training.

Table 2. Input structure to and from network

Input Values to Network	Estimated Output Value from Network
x_1, x_2, x_3	x_4
X_2, x_3, x_4	X_5
X_3, x_4, x_5	X_6
......	......
x_n, x_{n+1}, x_{n+2}	X_{n+3}
$x_{n+1}, x_{n+2}, x_{n+3}$	X_{n+4}

An example of the illustration of inputs from Table 2, consider the first case of training, claims figure for 1999,2000 and 2001 which will be used to predict 2002 yearly claims amount. Figure 4 shows the basic layout and structure of the feed forward neural network implementation. The neurons in the hidden layer were adjusted during the training process.

Figure 4. Basic structure of network implemented

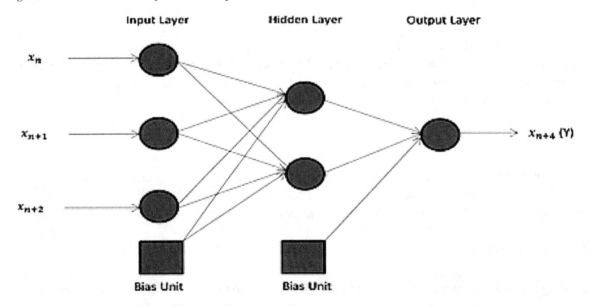

4.5 Network Parameters

The parameters such as the learning rate, number neurons in the hidden layer, bias unit value and Epochs were adjusted during the training process. There was no confined method of identifying the parameters that would yield the best result in terms of actual vs predicted. The only way of adjusting these parameters were on a trial and error basis and observing the accuracy of the network. The method that worked well was adjusting these parameters on a trial and error basis, observing which parameters achieved lower error in the training, and testing process.

4.6 Network Accuracy

The accuracy of the models was measured through Mean Absolute Percentage Error (MAPE). Root Mean Squared Error (RMSE) was also used at some instances just too see the accuracy of the network. The following was the formula used for calculating MAPE:

$$MAPE = \frac{100}{n} \sum_{t=1}^{n} \left(\frac{\left[Yn - Yt \right]}{\left[Yt \right]} \right)$$

Where Y_n is the actual value and Y_t is the predicted value.

4.7 Stopping Criteria

Epochs and MAPE was used to stop the training and testing process. The neural network models were tested with a number of different Epochs where MAPE is observed. For each Epoch size, MAPE was observed and eventually reached a point where the lowest MAPE was observed. Root Mean Squared Error on the training data was also used as the stopping criteria and worked well.

5. IMPLEMENTATION PROCESS

5.1 Model 1 – Feed Forward Neural Network

To find out which input size was best, the initial feed forward neural network had one input, 1 hidden and 1 output layer. The network was implemented in C++ to have better picture of how the actual algorithms worked and to observe how the weights were updated while training to reach a lower MAPE. During training, a number of neurons were chosen to observe the impact on MAPE of the network. During the initial runs, the model generated random weights, which were modified while training. Inputs fed to the neural network consisted of 1, 2 and 3 years of medical annual claims paid amount. From the observations, it was concluded that 3 years of data or 3 inputs had much accurate results compared to 1 and 2 inputs. Table 3 shows how the RMS error was reduced when the number of inputs were increased.

Table 3. Summary of RMS Errors with different network inputs

Epoc Count	Learning Rate	Hidden Neurons	RMS Error (1 Input)	RMS Erro3 (2 Input)	RMS Error (3 Input)
2000	0.15	5	0.08965	0.0704	0.0208
2000	0.15	6	0.0982	0.0707	0.0332
2000	0.15	7	0.09043	0.0711	0.0415
2000	0.15	8	0.09065	0.717	0.0448
2000	0.15	9	0.0909	0.0722	0.0541

Now that the input to the network was confirmed, another feed forward neural network model was implemented which consisted of all features i.e. chronic claimed amount, acute claimed amount, average age and annual claimed amount. Including all features as inputs did had positive impact on the MAPE on the training data set but failed on the test data set. The initial model (3-5-1) with three inputs, 5 neurons in the hidden layer and 1 output layer had the training data accuracy of 93% and test accuracy of 87.9%. Learning rate and the bias value were also adjusted during training. The neural network model that came to this accuracy had the learning rate as 0.15 and bias value of 1. The most appropriate Epoch size was found to be 50000. Figures 5 and 6 show how MAPE was reduced during the training process.

Figure 5. MAPE against different epocs on training set

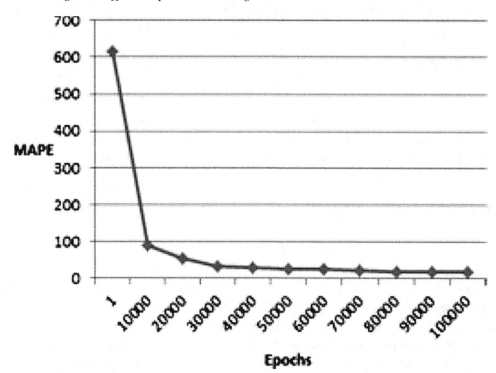

Figure 6. Actual vs predicted on training set and on test data set

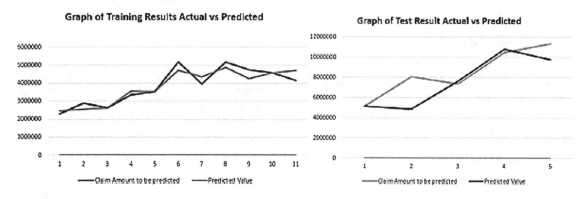

5.2 Model 2 – Recurrent Neural Network

After the successful implementation of Feed Forward Neural Network, it was time to test the network using Recurrent Neural Network. NARX (Non-Linear Autoregressive Network) is implemented as part of this research. NARX is a recurrent dynamic network. The number of inputs to the network remained the same as three. The accuracy of the network was MAPE. This network was implemented using MATLAB software.

The parameters such as the learning rate, number of neurons in the hidden layer were adjusted to obtain the least MAPE on both training and test data sets. The network managed to achieve 90.38% as the accuracy on the training set and 93.58% on test set. The number of neurons in the hidden layer was 50 and the learning rate was 2.5, which was used to achieve this. Figures 7 and 8 illustrate the layout of the recurrent network.

Figure 7. Recurrent neural network layout

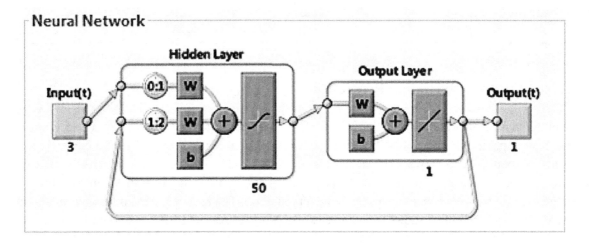

Figure 8. Actuals vs predicted on training set and test data set

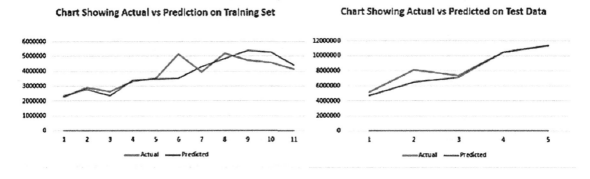

6. MODEL COMPARISION

6.1 Neural Network Models

After the actual implementation of both models and observing the accuracy and performance, a quick comparison was carried out. In terms of performance of the networks, Recurrent was much faster and required very low computation resources to complete the runs. Feed Forward on the other hand was very resource intensive and took a while to run, sometimes took 15 minutes to complete one run. Recurrent neural network model also outperformed Feed forward neural network in terms of the accuracy. Table 4 shows the summary of accuracy between the two models.

Table 4. Summary of accuracy between the two neural networks

Neural Network	MAPE on Training Set	Accuracy on Training Set	MAPE on Test Set	Accuracy on Test Set
Feed Forward	7.00	93.00	12.15	87.85
Recurrent	9.62	90.38	6.42	93.58

6.2 Comparing with Human Prediction

One of the main aim of the research carried out was to compare and contrast the level of accuracy between human prediction and Artificial Neural Network Prediction. BSP Life (Fiji) Ltd currently has a variance of about 18.10% between the actuals and forecasted value. After implementing the two models and observing the accuracy, there was a reduction of about 11.5% in the overall Mean Absolute Percentage Error (MAPE) when compared to human prediction. The recurrent neural network model had an MAPE of 6.42%. Table 5 shows the comparison of MAPE between BSP Life and the ANN models.

Table 5. Comparison of MAPE between BSP Life and the ANN models

Year	BSP Life Forecast % Error	ANN % Error	Difference %
2015	17.5	7.99	9.51
2016	8.5	19.47	-10.97
2017	4.5	3.9	0.6
2018	22.5	0.5	22
2019	37.5	0.22	37.28
MAPE	**18.1**	**6.42**	**11.68**

7. CONCLUSION

This research focused on forecasting yearly claims amount for BSP Life (Fiji) Ltd. Neural network model has been trained using the data from 1999 to 2017. After observing the results from the implementation, it can be concluded that forecasting medical claims figure is possible and provided strong results of forecasting using Artificial Neural Network Models. The ANN model outperformed the human prediction that is used now. The ANN model reduced the error rate by about 11.5%. NARX model outperformed the overall accuracy of the Feed Forward ANN together with the computational resources that is required for forecasting. Longer periods were required to train the Feed Forward Neural Network when compared to NARX recurrent model. Training the network with larger Epoch size resulted in the network being over trained where the results in the training set was very pleasing but did not perform well on the test data set.

REFERENCES

Abdel Alim, O., Shoukry, A., Elboughdadly, N., & Abouelseoud, G. (2013). A Probabilistic Neural Network-Based Module for Recognition of Objects from their 3-D Images. *International Journal of System Dynamics Applications*, 2(2), 66–79. doi:10.4018/ijsda.2013040105

Abhigna, P., Jerritta, S., Srinivasan, R., & Rajendran, V. (2017). Analysis of feed forward and recurrent neural networks in predicting the significant wave height at the moored buoys in Bay of Bengal. In *Proceedings of the International Conference on Communication and Signal Processing (ICCSP)*. Academic Press; . doi:10.1109/ICCSP.2017.8286717

Abhishek, K., Kumar, A., Ranjan, R., & Kumar, S. (2012). Rainfall prediction of a maritime state (Kerala), India using SLFN and ELM techniques. In *Proceedings of the International Conference on Intelligent Computing, Instrumentation and Control Technologies (ICICICT)*. Academic Press. doi:10.1109/ICICICT1.2017.8342829

Abroyan, N. (2017). Convolutional and recurrent neural networks for real-time data classification. In *Proceedings of the Seventh International Conference on Innovative Computing Technology (INTECH)*. Academic Press; . doi:10.1109/INTECH.2017.8102422

Azar, A., & Balas, V. (2012). Statistical Methods and Artificial Neural Networks Techniques in Electromyography. *International Journal of System Dynamics Applications*, 1(1), 39–47. doi:10.4018/ijsda.2012010103

Banerjee, S., Chaudhuri, S. S., & Roy, S. (2017). Fuzzy logic based vision enhancement using sigmoid function. In *Proceedings of the IEEE Calcutta Conference (CALCON)*. IEEE Press; . doi:10.1109/CALCON.2017.8280692

Chapko, A., Emrich, A., Flake, S., Golatowski, F., Gräßle, M., Kohlos, A., ... Zoth, C. (2011). uRun: A Framework for User-Generated Mobile Services in the Health and Fitness Domain. *International Journal of Service Science, Management, Engineering, and Technology*, 2(4), 79–97. doi:10.4018/ijssmet.2011100108

Chuanchai, P., Champrasert, P., & Rattanadoung, K. (2019). Particulate Matter Concentration Spatial Prediction using Interpolation Techniques with Machine Learning. In *Proceedings of the 7th IEEE International Conference on Information and Communication Technology (ICoICT)*. IEEE Press; . doi:10.1109/ICoICT.2019.8835214

Decaro, C., Montanari, G., Molinariz, R., Gilberti, A., & Bagno, A. (2019). Machine learning approach for prediction of Hematic parameters in Hemodialysis patients. *IEEE Journal of Translational Engineering in Health and Medicine*, 7, 1–8. doi:10.1109/JTEHM.2019.2938951

Din, G. M. U., & Marnerides, A. K. (2017). Shor Term power load forecasting using Deep Neural Networks. In *Proceedings of the International Conference on Computing, Networking and Communications (ICNC)*. Academic Press; . doi:10.1109/ICCNC.2017.7876196

Dong, J., Rafayelyan, M., Krzakala, F., & Gigan, S. (2019). Optical Reservoir Computing Using Multiple Light Scattering for Chaotic Systems Prediction. *IEEE Journal of Selected Topics in Quantum Electronics*, 26(1), 1–12. doi:10.1109/JSTQE.2019.2936281

Dong, Y., Wen, R., Li, Z., Zhang, K., & Zhang, L. (2019). A New RNN Based Approach to Diabetic Blood Glucose Prediction. In *Proceedings of the 7th IEEE International Conference on Bioinformatics and Computational Biology (ICBCB)*. IEEE Press; . doi:10.1109/ICBCB.2019.8854670

Dong, Y., Wen, R., Zhang, K., & Zhang, L. (2019). A Novel RNN-Based Blood Glucose Prediction Approach Using Population and Individual Characteristics. In *Proceedings of the 7th IEEE International Conference on Bioinformatics and Computational Biology (ICBCB)*. IEEE Press; . doi:10.1109/ICBCB.2019.8854657

Dumas, T., Roumy, A., & Guillemot, C. (2019). Context-Adaptive Neural Network-Based Prediction for Image Compression. *IEEE Transactions on Image Processing*, 29, 679–693. doi:10.1109/TIP.2019.2934565

El-said, S. (2013). Reliable Face Recognition Using Artificial Neural Network. *International Journal of System Dynamics Applications*, 2(2). doi:10.4018/ijsda.2013040102

Hajiaghayi, M., & Vahedi, E. (2019, April). Code Failure Prediction and Pattern Extraction using LSTM Networks. In *Proceedings of the 2019 IEEE Fifth International Conference on Big Data Computing Service and Applications (BigDataService)* (pp. 55-62). IEEE. doi:10.1109/BigDataService.2019.00014

Ibiwoye, A., Ajibola, O. O., & Sogunro, A. B. (2012). Artificial Neural Network Model for Predicting Insurance Insolvency. *International Journal of Management and Business Research*, 2(1).

Jun, E., Mulyadi, A., & Suk, H. (2019). Stochastic Imputation and Uncertainty-Aware Attention to EHR for Mortality Prediction. In *Proceedings of the IEEE International Joint Conference on Neural Networks (IJCNN)*. IEEE Press; . doi:10.1109/IJCNN.2019.8852132

Khan, M., Khattak, A., Zafari, F., & Mahmud, S. A. (2013). Electrical load forecasting using fast learning recurrent neural networks. In *Proceedings of the International Joint Conference on Neural Networks (IJCNN)*. Academic Press; . doi:10.1109/IJCNN.2013.6706998

Khatri, S. K., Singhal, H., & Johri, P. (2014). Sentiment analysis to predict Bombay stock exchange using artificial neural network. In *Proceedings of the 3rd International Conference on Reliability, Infocom Technologies and Optimization*. Academic Press; . doi:10.1109/ICRITO.2014.7014714

Kitchens, F. L. (2009). Financial implications of artificial Neural Networks in automobile insurance underwriting. *International Journal of Electronic Finance, 3*(3), 311–319. doi:10.1504/IJEF.2009.027853

Kurtah, P., Takun, Y., & Nagowah, L. (2019, July). Disease Propagation Prediction using Machine Learning for Crowdsourcing Mobile Applications. In *Proceedings of the 2019 7th International Conference on Information and Communication Technology (ICoICT)* (pp. 1-6). IEEE. doi:10.1109/ICoICT.2019.8835381

Liou, F.-M., Tang, Y.-C., & Chen, J.-Y. (2008). Detecting hospital fraud and claim abuse through diabetic outpatient services. *Health Care Management Science, 11*(4), 353–358. doi:10.100710729-008-9054-y

Liu, H., Zhang, Y., Zhang, H., Fan, C., Kwong, S., Kuo, C., & Fan, X. (2019). Deep Learning-Based Picture-Wise Just Noticeable Distortion Prediction Model for Image Compression. *IEEE Transactions on Image Processing, 29*, 641–656. doi:10.1109/TIP.2019.2933743

Mahmoud, M., & Sunni, F. (2012). Stability of Discrete Recurrent Neural Networks with Interval Delays: Global Results. *International Journal of System Dynamics Applications, 1*(2), 1–14. doi:10.4018/ijsda.2012040101

Majhi, S. (2018). An Efficient Feed Foreword Network Model with Sine Cosine Algorithm for Breast Cancer. *International Journal of System Dynamics Applications, 7*(2), 1–14. doi:10.4018/IJSDA.2018040101

Mnasser, A., Bouani, F., & Ksouri, M. (2014). Neural Networks Predictive Controller Using an Adaptive Control Rate. *International Journal of System Dynamics Applications, 3*(3), 127–147. doi:10.4018/ijsda.2014070106

Motlagh, T., & Khaloozadeh, H. (2016). A new architecture for modelling and prediction of dynamic systems using neural networks: Application in Tehran stock exchange. In *Proceedings of the 4th International Conference on Control, Instrumentation, and Automation (ICCIA)*. Academic Press. doi:10.1109/ICCIAutom.2016.7483160

Pei, S., Tong, L., Li, X., Jiang, J., & Huang, J. (2017). Feed-forward network for cancer detection. In *Proceedings of the 13th International Conference on Natural Computation, Fuzzy Systems and Knowledge Discovery (ICNC-FSKD)*. Academic Press. doi:10.1109/FSKD.2017.8393356

Petrescu, L., Cazacu, E., & Petrescu, C. (2015). Sigmoid functions used in hysteresis phenomenon modelling. In *Proceedings of the 9th International Symposium on Advanced Topics in Electrical Engineering (ATEE)*. Academic Press. doi:10.1109/ATEE.2015.7133863

Pun, T. B., & Shahi, T. B. (2018). Nepal Stock Exchange Prediction Using Support Vector Regression and Neural Networks. In *Proceedings of the 2018 Second International Conference on Advances in Electronics, Computers and Communications (ICAECC)*. Academic Press. doi:10.1109/ICAECC.2018.8479456

Rizal, A., & Hartati, S. (2016). Recurrent neural network with Extended Kalman Filter for prediction of the number of tourist arrival in Lombok. In *Proceedings of the International Conference on Informatics and Computing (ICIC)*. Academic Press; . doi:10.1109/IAC.2016.7905712

Safarinejadian, B., Tajeddini, A., & Ramezani, A. (2013). Predict time series using extended, unscented, and cubature Kalman filters based on feed-forward neural network algorithm. In *Proceedings of the 3rd International Conference on Control, Instrumentation, and Automation*. Academic Press; . doi:10.1109/ICCIAutom.2013.6912827

Salama, M., & Hassanien, A. (2014). Fuzzification of Euclidean Space Approach in Machine Learning Techniques. *International Journal of Service Science, Management, Engineering, and Technology*, 5(4), 29–43. doi:10.4018/ijssmet.2014100103

Samarawickrama, A. J. P., & Fernando, T. G. I. (2017). A recurrent neural network approach in predicting daily stock prices an application to the Sri Lankan stock market. In *Proceedings of the IEEE International Conference on Industrial and Information Systems (ICIIS)*. IEEE Press; . doi:10.1109/ICIINFS.2017.8300345

Sangwan, N., & Bhatnagar, V. (2020). Comprehensive Contemplation of Probabilistic Aspects in Intelligent Analytics. *International Journal of Service Science, Management, Engineering, and Technology*, 11(1), 116–141. doi:10.4018/IJSSMET.2020010108

Seo, J., Lee, J., & Kim, K. (2018). Decoding of Polar Code by Using Deep Feed-Forward Neural Networks. In *Proceedings of the International Conference on Computing, Networking and Communications (ICNC)*. Academic Press; . doi:10.1109/ICCNC.2018.8390279

Solovyeva, A. B. (2017). Types of recurrent neural networks for non-linear dynamic system modelling. In *Proceedings of the XX IEEE International Conference on Soft Computing and Measurements (SCM)*. IEEE Press; . doi:10.1109/SCM.2017.7970552

Tang, T. A., Mhamdi, L., McLernon, D., Zaidi, S. A. R., & Ghogho, M. (2018). Deep Recurrent Neural Network for Intrusion Detection in SDN-based Networks. In *Proceedings of the 4th IEEE Conference on Network Softwarization and Workshops (NetSoft)*. IEEE Press; . doi:10.1109/NETSOFT.2018.8460090

Thomas, P., Suhner, M., & Derigent, W. (2019). Relearning procedure to adapt pollutant prediction neural model: Choice of relearning algorithm. In *Proceedings of the IEEE International Joint Conference on Neural Networks (IJCNN)*. IEEE Press; . doi:10.1109/IJCNN.2019.8852193

Venkadesan, A., Bhavana, G., Haneesha, D., & Sedhuraman, K. (2017). Comparison of feed forward and cascade neural network for harmonic current estimation in power electronic converter. In *Proceedings of the International Conference on Innovative Research in Electrical Sciences (IICIRES)*. Academic Press; . doi:10.1109/IICIRES.2017.8078295

Viaene, S., Dedene, G., & Derrig, R. A. (2005). Auto claim fraud detection using Bayesian learning neural networks. *Expert Systems with Applications*, 29(3), 653–666. doi:10.1016/j.eswa.2005.04.030

Wang, S., Ning, C., & Cui, W. (2015). Time series prediction of bank cash flow based on grey neural network algorithm. In *Proceedings of the International Conference on Estimation, Detection and Information Fusion (ICEDIF)*. Academic Press; . doi:10.1109/ICEDIF.2015.7280205

Wu, B., Li, K., Yang, M., & Lee, C. H. (2016). A study on target feature activation and normalization and their impacts on the performance of DNN based speech dereverberation systems. In *Proceedings of the Asia-Pacific Signal and Information Processing Association Annual Summit and Conference (APSIPA)*. Academic Press; . doi:10.1109/APSIPA.2016.7820875

Xiao, D., Li, X., Lin, X., & Shi, C. (2015). A time Series Prediction method based on self-adaptive RBF neural network. In *Proceedings of the 4th International Conference on Computer Science and Network Technology (ICCSNT)*. Academic Press. doi:10.1109/ICCSNT.2015.7490837

Xu, W., Wang, S., Zhang, D., & Yang, B. (2011, April). Random rough subspace based neural network ensemble for insurance fraud detection. In *Proceedings of the 2011 Fourth International Joint Conference on Computational Sciences and Optimization* (pp. 1276-1280). IEEE. doi:10.1109/CSO.2011.213

Yunos, Z. M., Ali, A., Shamsyuddin, S. M., Ismail, N., & Sallehuddin, R. S. (2016). Predictive Modelling for Motor Insurance Claims Using Artificial Neural Networks. *International Journal of Advances in Soft Computing and its Applications, 8*(3), 160-172.

Zhang, W., Li, B., Zhao, D., Gong, F., & Lu, Q. (2016). Workload Prediction for Cloud Cluster Using a Recurrent Neural Network. In *Proceedings of the International Conference on Identification, Information and Knowledge in the Internet of Things (IIKI)*. Academic Press; . doi:10.1109/IIKI.2016.39

Zhang, X., Dong, Y., Wen, L., Lu, F., & Li, W. (2019). Remaining Useful Life Estimation Based on a New Convolutional and Recurrent Neural Network. In *Proceedings of the 15th IEEE International Conference on Automation Science and Engineering (CASE)*. IEEE Press; . doi:10.1109/COASE.2019.8843078

This research was previously published in the International Journal of System Dynamics Applications (IJSDA), 9(3); pages 40-57, copyright year 2020 by IGI Publishing (an imprint of IGI Global).

Chapter 57
Forecasting and Technical Comparison of Inflation in Turkey With Box–Jenkins (ARIMA) Models and the Artificial Neural Network

Erkan Işığıçok
Bursa Uludağ University, Turkey

Ramazan Öz
Uludağ University, Turkey

Savaş Tarkun
Uludağ University, Turkey

ABSTRACT

Inflation refers to an ongoing and overall comprehensive increase in the overall level of goods and services price in the economy. Today, inflation, which is attempted to be kept under control by central banks or, in the same way, whose price stability is attempted, consists of continuous price changes that occur in all the goods and services used by the consumers. Undoubtedly, in terms of economy, in addition to the realized inflation, inflation expectations are also gaining importance. This situation requires forecasting the future rates of inflation. Therefore, reliable forecasting of the future rates of inflation in a country will determine the policies to be applied by the decision-makers in the economy. The aim of this study is to predict inflation in the next period based on the consumer price index (CPI) data with two alternative techniques and to examine the predictive performance of these two techniques comparatively. Thus, the first of the two main objectives of the study are to forecast the future rates of inflation with two alternative techniques, while the second is to compare the two techniques with respect to statistical and econometric criteria and determine which technique performs better in comparison. In this context, the

DOI: 10.4018/978-1-6684-2408-7.ch057

9-month inflation in April-December 2019 was forecast by Box-Jenkins (ARIMA) models and Artificial Neural Networks (ANN), using the CPI data which consist of 207 data from January 2002 to March 2019 and the predictive performance of both techniques was examined comparatively. It was observed that the results obtained from both techniques were close to each other.

1. INTRODUCTION

With the most general meaning, inflation refers to the increase in the overall level of prices. Today, inflation is tried to be kept under control by central banks. Inflation, which is attempted to be kept under control, is not only addressed in terms of firms or individuals, but it also has a significant meaning for the general population. At this point, the cost of inflation is seen on investors and consumers in making decisions at the basic level. The high inflation environment in the countries also puts investors and consumers into an environment of instability. In this context, inflation constitutes an input at the decision-making stage for both investors and consumers. On the other hand, accurate predictions of the future inflation rates are of great importance for decision makers.

2. FORECASTING METHODS

Today, time series analysis and artificial neural network methods are frequently used in inflation forecasting. Considering the preliminary reporting in terms of time series, Box-Jenkins (ARIMA) method is used in the literature. In the time series analysis, past observations of data are interdependent. Therefore, it is possible to make future estimations with ARIMA models by using the information in the past observations. In this respect, the most basic point in working with time series models is that the series should show a static structure. If the average, variance and co-variance of a time series do not change over time, it can be said that the series exhibits a static structure. If the series is static, a suitable model is established in accordance with the Box-Jenkins method and the future predictions can be performed.

On the other hand, recently Artificial Neural Network (ANN) for nonlinear time series has also been widely used to make future estimates. In the studies conducted with ANN, it was found that the economic series presents successful results in the future estimations thanks to the advantages such as learning and generalizing information from the data presented to the network.

In Turkey, inflation targeting was started in 2002 by the implicit inflation regime. Figure 1 shows the time path graph of the actual and targeted inflation for the period of 2002-2018.

When Figure 1 is analyzed, it is seen that the inflation rate which had been realized until 2005 followed a path below the targeted inflation level. A similar situation occurred in 2009 and 2010. However, in the periods other than those periods, the actual inflation rate was higher than the targeted inflation rate. Thus, the difference between the actual inflation and the targeted inflation in recent years in Turkey is increasing gradually. Hence, estimating the future rates of inflation in our country has become important in terms of the targeted inflation rate.

Figure 1. Time path graph of actual and targeted inflation

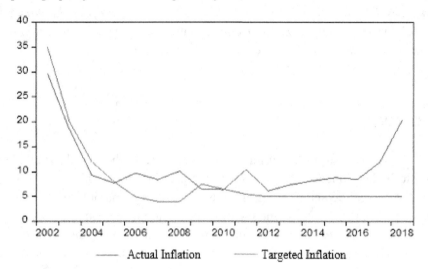

3. LITERATURE REVIEW

In the literature, there are many studies in which future predictions of inflation were made by using the Box-Jenkins (ARIMA) models with different economic variables in different periods. Alnair and Ahiakpor (2011) in Gana, Meçik, and Karabacak (2011) in Turkey, in their studies covering the 2000-2010 period, achieved successful results in inflation forecasts by using only ARIMA models.

Işığıçok (1994), in his book "Analysis of Causality in Time Series", found that there was a two-way causality between money supply and inflation in Turkey bu using ARIMA models in addition to Granger causality. Also, Işığıçok (1999), found in his study called the estimation of variance of inflation in Turkey by ARCH and GARCH models that inflation in Turkey had no ARCH influence depending on the Q1 data of 1982and Q2 data of 1999,and he found that the variance of inflation did not change significantly and it was random except for the fluctuation in 1994 Q2. Furthermore, Işığıçok and Parasız (1993), in their study called "the Mark-Up Pricing Policy and Inflation in Turkey" found that one of the causes of inflation in our country during the period from 1980 to 1992 was the mark-up inflation.

Among the studies comparing the performance of more than one model instead of a single model, Bokhari and Feridun (2006) compared the VAR and ARIMA models for Pakistan and concluded that the ARIMA model had a better predictive power. Önder (2004), in his study, in which he compared the inflation forecast success of Phillips Curve, ARIMA, VAR and VECM models, concluded that the Phillips Curve Model yielded better results than other models. Domaç (2004), in his study in which he predicted inflation for Turkey showed that among Mark-Up Models, Monetary Open Models, Phillips Curve Model and ARIMA Model, Philips Curve Model gave the best result. Ugurlu and Saracoglu (2010) used naive model, exponential smoothing model and the ARIMA model for the inflation forecast in Turkey, and as a result they found that the method which gave the minimum deviation was the ARIMA model. In their study, Akdogan et al. (2012) compared short-term inflation estimation success of random walk, SARIMA, Kalman Filtering, VAR and Bayesian VAR models. They concluded that the most successful model for inflation forecast was the Bayesian VAR model. In their study, Bayramoğlu et al. (2014), used ARMA, Generalized Phillips Curve, New Keynesian Phillips Curve, the Hodrick-Prescott and Kalman

Filtering methods for the inflation forecast in Turkey, The most successful prediction model was revealed to to be a triangular model of inflation using Hodrick-Prescott filtering and natural unemployment rate (NAIRU). Akdag, and Yigit (2016), in their study using 2004-2013 data for Turkey, compared the predictive inflation success of ARIMA and Neural Network models and concluded that ARIMA method gave better results. Bayramoglu and Ozturk (2017) in their study compared the predictive performances of ARIMA and gray system and obtained mainly two results. The first result was that ARIMA model gave better results for CPI and that the gray system model predicted better for PPI.

On the other hand, there are many studies in the literature for future predictions with artificial neural networks or ARIMA models. Among these, Tang et al. (1991), in their study using monthly business data, found that ANN and ARIMA models gave similar results in the long-term series, whereas in ANN, the short-term series showed better results. Caire et al. (1992) compared the results of ANN and ARIMA prediction using daily electricity consumption data. As a result of this study, while ANN gave better results than ARIMA, the long-term predictions were found to be much better. Refenes (1993), in his study of hourly exchange rate time series data, found that ANN gave better predictive values than exponential correction and ARIMA models. Shabri (2001), in his study of the time series he compiled on five different topics, found that ANN and ARIMA models gave close results in the seasonal time series, and ARIMA showed better predictive results in the irregular time series. Montanes et al. (2002) as a result of their analysis with nuclear energy data, concluded that ANN had better predictive performance and that ARIMA models could not predict systematic changes in time series. Kamruzzaman and Sarker (2003) conducted a study in which they made predictions using artificial neural network models and ARIMA formed by six different cross exchange rates related to the Australian dollar. As a result of this study, they determined that the predictions made with ANN were better than those with ARIMA. Binner et al. (2005), in their study using GNP and the deflator, Divisia Euro M3 data, found that in the analyses conducted with VAR, ARIMA and ANN, ANN made more accurate predictions. Zou et al. (2007) made a prediction about the wheat prices in the Chinese economy with ARIMA, YSA and the models they obtained with the combination of these two models and compared the predictive performance of these models. The comparison results showed that ANN had the best predictive performance among the models used in the study. Abdelmouez et al. (2007) compared ARIMA, multiple regression and ANN methods using a data set of 3429 observations compiled from the US stock market. As a result of the analyses, it was observed that ANN had better predictive results. Insel et al. (2010) compared the predictive performances of ARMA and ANN by using the annual change in nominal dollar exchange rate index in Turkey's economy in the years from 1987 to 2007, the annual inflation rate, the nominal interest rate for twelve-month deposit accounts and monthly data belonging to the logarithm of real GDP. As a result of the predictions made in the study, it was understood that ANN yielded better prediction rates for the inflation rate, interest rate and foreign exchange rate, and that ARMA functioned better in the prediction of the real GDP. Eğrioğlu et al. (2011), evaluated that the hybrid approach in which the prediction results of forward and backward propagation artificial neural network are combined using artificial neural networks would be appropriate in the inflation rate forecast in Turkey. Choudhary and Haider (2012) reported that artificial neural networks would be appropriate for short-term forecasts for inflation estimation in their study for 28 member countries of the Organization for Economic Co-operation and Development (OECD).

Recently, a constant increase in the inflation level in our country and its negative effects on the market are noteworthy. In this respect, the purpose of this study is to predict the future inflation series with

Box-Jenkins (ARIMA) and ANN models and to compare the predictive performance of both methods technically.

Since the studies using Turkey inflation data are generally designed on the inflation uncertainty and there is a limited number of prediction studies, this study is expected to contribute to the literature.

4. METHODOLOGY

In the time series analysis, there are many unit root tests in the literature in order to determine whether the series are stable. The most commonly used unit root test is the Dickey-Fuller (1979) unit root test. The general form of the Augmented Dickey Fuller unit root test is as in Equation (1):

$$\Delta Y_t = \mu + \beta t + \delta Y_{t-1} + \sum_{j=1}^{p} \delta_j \Delta Y_{t-j} + \varepsilon_t \tag{1}$$

In Equation (1), the delayed values of the dependent variable are included in the model in order to eliminate the auto-correlation existing in the error term. In order to determine the k value of delay time for the dependent variable, information criteria such as Akaike information criterion (AIC) and Schwarz information criterion (SIC) are used (Çınar & Öz, 2017). The hypotheses used in decision making in order to determine the stability in the ADF unit root test state that the null hypothesis series is not stationary and that the alternative hypothesis shows a stable structure.

The other unit root tests to be used in the study are the Phillips-Perron test and the KPSS unit root tests developed by Kwiatkowski, Phillips, Schmidt, and Shin (1992). In the KPSS test, the hypotheses that are established while investigating the stability of the series reveal that the hypothesis of the ADF unit root test is taken in a different way and the null hypothesis series are stable while the alternative hypothesis reveal that the series follow a non-stable form and there is a unit root in the series. In fact, the absence of a unit root in the series shows that there is a trend-free state, which means that the trend is stagnant.

4.1. Box-Jenkins Methodology

Box-Jenkins (1976) approach is a method of finding the most appropriate ARIMA data generation process in accordance with the realized data in the modeling of time series. (Sevüktekin & Çınar, 2017). The Box - Jenkins approach is one of the statistical estimation methods used in the realization and control of prospective estimates in the analysis of one-variable time series (Kaynar & Taştan, 2009). The basis of the Box-Jenkins technique is the selection of the ARIMA model that best suits the structure of the data among alternative models (Işığıçok, 1994).

In the Box-Jenkins approach, the prediction is carried out in four stages. The basic steps taken in the four stages are to define the time series model, to estimate, to perform the test or to perform the distinctive checks and to make preliminary reporting (the forecast) (Işığıçok, 1994):

1. The current set of models is determined, the stability of the data is searched, unit root tests are performed for being stationary, and the difference is taken if necessary. In addition, to identify the potential models, the correlogram including the ACP and PACF values is used;
2. Models that match the structure of the data are identified. For this purpose, ACF and PACF are calculated;
3. The parameters of the alternative models considered to be appropriate are estimated. Then, the best model is selected according to statistical and econometric criteria;
4. The model is checked for conformity. Future term estimates are made for the most appropriate model selected.

Time series including a linear, discrete and stochastic process are called Box-Jenkins or ARIMA models. Linear stationary Box-Jenkins models are classified as AR (Autoregressive) MA (Moving Average) and autoregressive moving average (ARMA), which is a combination of the two. The non-stationary series are called the integrated auto regressive moving average (ARIMA, Auto Regressive Integrated Moving Average) model which are applied to the series rendered stationary as a result of a difference (Ataseven, 2013). It might be useful to provide information on these models.

Representation of an autoregressive AR (p) model with a finite number of degrees (p), as a linear function of the past values of the variable in the current period:

$$Y_t = \delta + 1Y_{t-1} + 2Y_{t-2} + \dots + pY_{t-p} + \varepsilon_t \tag{2}$$

is written as (2) and p. degree is called autoregressive model (process) and $p(L)Y_t=\varepsilon_t$ is shown as (3). In the equation δ shows the cutting term and the stochastic process of the average for Y_t $i = 1, 2, \dots$, for p p the autoregressive parameters for the lagged values of the dependent variable and εt shows the error term. Model $i = 1, 2, \dots$ is expressed as AR (1), AR (2) and AR (p) for p respectively.

With the same logic, the representation of the moving average MA (q) model, which contains a finite number of degrees (q), as the linear function of the present value of the variable in the present:

$$Y_t = \mu + \varepsilon_t + \theta_1\varepsilon_{t-1} + \theta_2\varepsilon_{t-2} + \dots + \theta_q\varepsilon_{t-q} \tag{3}$$

is written as (3) and is called q. degree-moving average model (process) and shown as $Y_t=\theta_q(L)\varepsilon_t$ (Işığıçok, 1994). In the equation μ is the cutting term and shows the average of Y_t which is the stochastic process, $j = 1, 2, \dots$ for q θ_q values indicate the moving average parameters for the delayed values of the error term. The model $j=1, 2, \dots$ is expressed as MA (1), MA (2) and MA (q) respectively for q.

Finally, mixed models including both autoregressive and moving average ARMA (p, q) models can also be used. Thus, the representation of the autoregressive moving average ARMA (p, q) model, which contains a finite number of degrees (p and q), as the current value of the variable with its past values and as a linear function of the present and past values of the error term and the values of the past is:

$$Y_t = \delta + {}_1Y_{t-1} + \dots + {}_pY_{t-p} + \varepsilon_t + \theta_1\varepsilon_{t-1} + \dots + \theta_q\varepsilon_{t-q} \tag{4}$$

written as (4) is called p. degree autoregressive and q. degree-moving average model (process) and shown as $p(L)Y_t = \theta_q(L)\varepsilon_t$. Model i = 1, 2, ... is stated as AR, p and j = 1, 2,), q, ARMA (1,1), ARMA (1,2), ARMA (2,1), ARMA (2,2) and ARMA (p, q) respectively.

On the other hand, many of the real-life time series have an extra-stationary or non-stationary structure because they contain a certain stochastic process over time. Undoubtedly, economic time series are generally non-stationary due to the random walking process (Atasen, 2013). Even though some time series exhibit a non-stationary structure, it is possible to convert the series to a stationary state. For this purpose, although different approaches are applied, different degrees of difference can be applied to the series. Thus, the time series from which difference is taken is defined as the integrated process. In the process of ARIMA (p, d, q) I is expressed as integrated and d is the number of difference that must be taken for the time series stabilization.

4.2. Artificial Neural Network (ANN)

Artificial neural network is the computer algorithms which have the skills of learning from the properties of the human brain and producing new functions with this information and the ability to find new information (Fausett (1994) and Öztemel (2003). The artificial neural network has many different characteristics based on these models such as imitating the working principle of the human brain, making generalizations from data, learning and working with many variables. The smallest units that serve as the basis for the operation of artificial neural networks are called artificial nerve cells or process elements (Akdağ, 2015).

Artificial neural networks (ANN), which can model both linear and non-linear series due to their structure, have become one of the alternative methods used in time series analysis. One of the most important advantages of the ANN is that in cases where the functional structure of the data set cannot be determined precisely, ANN, which is also known as different function convergent based on data, does not need any presuppositions on the data set unlike statistical techniques (Kaynar & Taştan, 2009).

In the most basic ANN cell, there are different components, such as inputs, weights, aggregation function, activation function, and output, as can be seen in Figure 2.

Figure 2. A simple artificial neural network

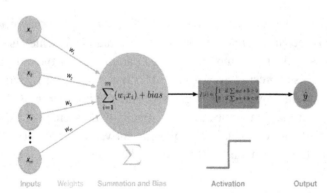

1200

A back-propagation algorithm is an algorithm that performs a general learning on the neural network. In this type of learning, synaptic weights are reduced to update (Haykin, 1998):

$$E_{av} = \frac{1}{2} \sum_{n=1}^{N} \sum_{j \in C} e_j^2 (n) \tag{5}$$

Here, the cluster C is a set of indices of output neurons, and for this function minimization, Equation (6) is attempted to be minimized:

$$E(n) = \frac{1}{2} \sum_{j \in C} e_j^2 (n) \tag{6}$$

This function is minimized and follows the chain rule in mathematics and Equation (7) is obtained:

$$\frac{\partial E(n)}{\partial w_{ji}(n)} = \frac{\partial E(n)}{\partial e_{ji}(n)} \frac{\partial e_j(n)}{\partial y_j(n)} \frac{\partial y_j(n)}{\partial v_j(n)} \frac{\partial v_j(n)}{\partial w_{ji}(n)} \tag{7}$$

Equation (7) becomes Equation (8) as a result of certain operations (Haykin, 1998):

$$\frac{\partial E(n)}{\partial w_{ji}(n)} = -e(n) \varphi_j' \left(v_j(n) \right) y_i(n) \tag{8}$$

$$\Delta W_{ji}(n) = -\eta \frac{\partial E(n)}{\partial w_{ji}(n)} \tag{9}$$

Here, η expresses the speed of learning. In general, the formula of weight changes in the back-propagation algorithm $\delta_j(n)$ is expressed as Equation (10) to express the local gradient function (Haykin, 1998):

$$\Delta W_{ji}(n) = \delta_j(n) \, y_i(n) \tag{10}$$

The data set used in the study was trained with the Levenberg-Marquardt back propagation algorithm preferred owing to the stability and speed in the training of artificial neural networks Çavuşoğlu et.al (2012). This algorithm is derived from the steep descent and Newton algorithms and is as follows Önder et al. (2013):

$$\Delta w = (J^T J + \mu I)^{-1} J^T e \tag{11}$$

Here:

- W, weight vector;
- I, unit matrix;
- μ is the coefficient of combination;
- J shows (PxM) xN size Jacobian Matrix;
- e shows (PXM) xI size error vector;
- P shows the number of training sample;
- M, the number of outputs;
- N denotes the number of weights;
- μ is an adjustable parameter, and if this parameter is too large, the method behaves like a steep descent, and if it is too small, it acts like the Newton method.

An adaptive structure for this parameter is as follows:

$$\mu(n) = \begin{cases} \mu(n-1)kE(n) > E(n-1) \\ \mu(n-1)/kE(n) \le E(n-1) \end{cases} \tag{12}$$

In the equation, k is a constant number and E is the conformity value. The reason for choosing Levenberg-Marquardt back propagation algorithm which is frequently preferred among optimization algorithms is because it helps to achieve a fast, stable and consistent result in short-term or medium-term data sets. The hidden layer number of the network constructed during application is determined by the user. The number of hidden layers applied in the study, the number of neurons in these layers and the activation function used are found by trial and error.

5. APPLICATION AND FINDINGS

In this study, inflation estimation was made by using ARIMA models with ANN model and the estimated models were examined comparatively. For this purpose, the TRCB data on the consumer price index (CPI) variable representing inflation covers the period 2002:01 - 2019:03, which includes annual change compared to the same month of the previous year.

The aim of the selection of Box-Jenkins ARIMA models in the prediction of inflation was to produce more successful results in the short term, while the aim of selecting artificial neural networks used for nonlinear time series was the widespread use in the literature lately. One of the two main objectives of the study was to estimate inflation, while the other was to technically compare the predictive performance of the Artificial Neural Network with Box-Jenkins ARIMA models. When comparing, criteria realized by both methods including Mean Error (ME), Mean Absolute Error (MAE), Mean Error Square (MSE), Average Error Percentage (MPE) and Average Absolute Error Percent (MAPE) were used. The formulas of these criteria are as follows:

$$ME = \frac{1}{n}\sum_{t=1}^{n} e_t \tag{13}$$

$$MAE = \frac{1}{n}\sum_{t=1}^{n} |e_t| \tag{14}$$

$$MSE = \frac{1}{n}\sum_{t=1}^{n} |e_t^2| \tag{15}$$

$$MPE = \frac{1}{n}\sum_{t=1}^{n} \frac{e_t}{Y_t} \tag{16}$$

$$MAPE = \left[\frac{1}{n}\sum_{t=1}^{n} \left|\frac{e_t}{Y_t}\right|\right] \cdot 100 \tag{17}$$

5.1. Box-Jenkins (ARIMA) Models and Findings

The progress of inflation series as of the period discussed is as in Figure 3. In Figure 3, while inflation was decreasing until 2004, it was close to each other in the period of 2004-2017 and has increased in recent years.

Figure 3. Time path graph of inflation

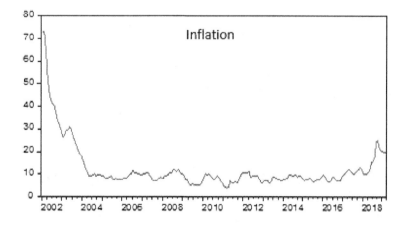

In the estimation of ARIMA models, firstly, the variable of interest should display a static structure. When Figure 3 is examined, it can be said that the series spread around a certain average especially after 2004, thus exhibiting a static structure. However, the course of the series does not give a definitive result about being stationary. Various unit root tests and models were applied in order to determine whether the inflation series is stationary or not. The unit root test results are as in Table 1.

Table 1. Unit root test results

Augmented Dickey - Fuller Unit Root Test Results				
Inflation		Intercept	Trend and intercept	None
		Level	Level	Level
Delay		1	1	1
ADF Test Statistics		-8.683344[a]	-8.060824	-5.850789
MacKinnon Critical values	1%	-3.452253	-4.003449	-2.576291
	5%	-2.875468	-3.431896	-1.942383
	10%	-2.574271	-3.139664	-1.615669
Philips-Perron Unit Root Test Results				
Inflation		Intercept	Trend and intercept	None
		Level	Level	Level
Bandwidth		1	2	6
PP Test Statistics		-9.281831[a]	-7.698644	-6.080404
MacKinnon Critical values	1%	-3.452095	-4.003226	-2.576236
	5%	-2.875398	-3.431789	-1.942376
	10%	-2.574234	-3.139601	-1.615674
KPPS Unit Root Test Results				
Inflation		Intercept	Trend and intercept	None
		Level	Level	Level
Bandwidth		10	10	-
KPSS Test (LM) Statistics.		0.610900[a]	0.308643	-
	1%	0.739000	0.216000	-
	5%	0.463000	0.146000	-
	10%	0.347000	0.119000	-

Note: Values in parentheses indicate the number of delayed values of the dependent variable added to the model. a is significant at the level of 0.01, b is significant at the level of 0.05 and c is significant at the level of 0.10.

As a result of the ADF and PP unit root tests conducted in order to reveal whether the inflation variable display a stationary structure or not, it was demonstrated that the inflation variable exhibits a static structure for the cutting model. As the hypotheses were established in the reverse test in the KPSS unit root test, the result showed that the ADF and PP unit root tests were supported, i.e., the series was stable.

After the original inflation series was determined to be stationary, the model estimates were made to determine the appropriate ARIMA model. While making model estimations, it was revealed that inflation variable did not show trend and seasonality in the period covered. In this case, ARIMA (5,0,3) model, which was one of the predicted models, was determined as the most suitable model. The results of this model were obtained as in Table 2.

Table 2. ARIMA (5,0,3) model forecast result

	Coefficient	t Stat.	Prob.
Intercept	36.34275	0.661106	0.5093
AR (1)	0.950410	11.50898	0.0000
AR (2)	0.856052	7.829076	0.0000
AR (3)	-0.229652	-2.332181	0.0207
AR (4)	-0.935160	-9.435961	0.0000
AR(5)	0.357451	4.384467	0.0000
MA (1)	0.684587	9.295865	0.0000
MA (2)	-0.599799	-6.808387	0.0000
MA (3)	-0.897945	-14.11015	0.0000
SIGMASQ	1.614686	13.33761	0.0000
Criteria	Finding	Criteria	Finding
R^2	0.985546	R^2_{adj}	0.984886
SE of Reg.	1.302555	SSR	334.2401
AIC	3.458635	SIC	3.619636
F Stat.	1492.492	F Prob.	0.000000

When the model estimation results are examined, the parameters other than the cutting parameter are statistically significant. The F statistic which expresses the general significance of the model also states that there is a general fit in the model. AIC and SIC values were at low levels. Corrected coefficient of determination which indicates the explanatory power of the model (R^{2nd}), was realized approximately at 98%. The error statistics calculated for the residues of the model are as in Table 3.

Table 3. Error statistics of the model

Mistakes	ARIMA (5,0,3)
ME	-0.057616
MAE	0.845697
MSE	1.614687
MPE	-0.004227
MAPE	7.872748

On the other hand, the actual values of the inflation (model), the estimated values and the course of the residues (the first and the last part of the data) are as in Figure 4.

Figure 4. Actual and estimated values of inflation series and the course of the residues

obs	Actual	Fitted	Residual	Residual Plot	obs	Actual	Fitted	Residual	Residual Plot
2002M01	73.1570	72.0276	1.12936		2016M11	7.00000	6.90458	0.09542	
2002M02	73.0788	73.1131	-0.03432		2016M12	8.53000	7.16141	1.36859	
2002M03	65.1131	72.4142	-7.30112		2017M01	9.22000	9.73978	-0.51978	
2002M04	52.7234	59.6740	-6.95053		2017M02	10.1300	9.13412	0.99588	
2002M05	46.2186	46.1470	0.07162		2017M03	11.2900	11.3720	-0.08204	
2002M06	42.6039	42.1301	0.47384		2017M04	11.8700	11.6557	0.21430	
2002M07	41.2771	39.3842	1.89300		2017M05	11.7200	12.3810	-0.66105	
2002M08	40.2414	40.0690	0.17245		2017M06	10.9000	12.0552	-1.15517	
2002M09	37.0480	38.0171	-0.96911		2017M07	9.79000	10.1754	-0.38539	
2002M10	33.4486	34.4623	-1.01369		2017M08	10.6800	9.93453	0.74547	
2002M11	31.7660	30.6911	1.07487		2017M09	11.2000	11.1222	0.07777	
2002M12	29.7488	29.6597	0.08909		2017M10	11.9000	11.5199	0.38015	
2003M01	26.3839	27.8167	-1.43271		2017M11	12.9800	12.7629	0.21714	
2003M02	27.0106	23.3740	3.63651		2017M12	11.9200	13.3467	-1.42666	
2003M03	29.4084	27.0243	2.38411		2018M01	10.3500	11.6358	-1.28578	
2003M04	29.4503	29.2806	0.16972		2018M02	10.2600	9.74823	0.51177	
2003M05	30.7415	28.4911	2.25039		2018M03	10.2300	10.4245	-0.19449	
2003M06	29.7593	31.1926	-1.43330		2018M04	10.8500	10.3686	0.48137	
2003M07	27.4382	27.5393	-0.10108		2018M05	12.1500	11.3144	0.83564	
2003M08	24.9072	26.2846	-1.37740		2018M06	15.3900	13.0818	2.30816	
2003M09	22.9997	22.5329	0.46678		2018M07	15.8500	17.3162	-1.46624	
2003M10	20.7804	21.3056	-0.52522		2018M08	17.9000	15.8527	2.04727	
2003M11	19.2547	19.3076	-0.05288		2018M09	24.5200	19.8036	4.71637	
2003M12	18.3555	17.2364	1.11911		2018M10	25.2400	28.2884	-3.04841	
2004M01	16.2205	17.8250	-1.60449		2018M11	21.6200	24.8254	-3.20543	
2004M02	14.2822	13.8143	0.46792		2018M12	20.3000	20.8815	-0.58147	
2004M03	11.8287	12.9834	-1.15472		2019M01	20.3500	19.7675	0.58247	
2004M04	10.1825	9.85234	0.33016		2019M02	19.6700	20.5734	-0.90337	
2004M05	8.88027	8.45879	0.42147		2019M03	19.7100	19.8442	-0.13419	

In addition, the relation between the actual values of the model and the estimated values and the distribution of residues (remnants) are as in Figure 5. According to the findings, it can be said that the actual and estimated values are close to each other. Of course, the fact that the residual remains within the desired confidence limits increases the prefer ability of the model.

Figure 5. Relationship between actual and estimated values of inflation series and distribution of residuals

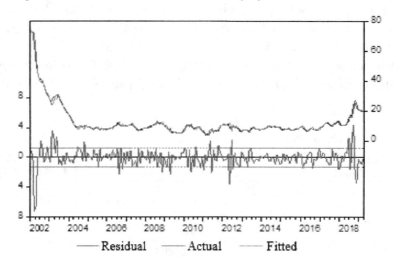

After the model estimation, the expost and exante predictions of the inflation series were realized as in Table 4.

Table 4. Estimated Expost and Exante prediction results for inflation series

Period	Actual	Expost	Residual	Period	Exante	LL	UL
2018M07	15.85	17,32	-1.47	2019M04	19.98	17.43	22.53
2018M08	17.90	15.85	2.05	2019M05	20.37	17.82	22.92
2018M09	24.52	19,80	4.72	2019M06	20.80	18.25	23.35
2018M10	25.24	28,29	-3.05	2019M07	21.31	18.76	23.86
2018M11	21.62	24.83	-3.21	2019M08	21.81	19.26	24.36
2018M12	20.30	20.88	-0.58	2019M09	22.25	19.70	24.80
2019M01	20.35	19.77	0.58	2019M10	22.76	20.21	25.31
2019M02	19.67	20.57	-0,90	2019M11	23.29	20.74	25.84
2019M03	19.71	19,84	-0,13	2019M12	23.81	21.26	26.36

SEy = 1.302555. According to ARIMA, the future 9 months of Inflation figures will show an increase even if a little.

95% confidence intervals for exante periods are as follows:

2019M04: $19.98\pm1.96 * 1.302555 = 17.43 - 22.53$

...

2019M12: $23.81\pm1.96 * 1.302555 = 21.26 - 26.36$

When the findings in Table 4 are analyzed, it is seen that the actual inflation figures and the expost estimation results are at similar levels. The fact that retrospective estimates are close to actual values may be the evidence of the reliability of the future forecast. On the other hand, according to the exante estimation results for the next 9 periods with ARIMA model, it is estimated that the inflation rate will be between 21.26% and 26.36% in December 2019 with 95% probability.

Figure 6. Artificial neural network algorithm established in the model

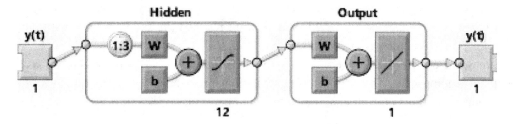

5.2. Artificial Neural Network (ANN) and Findings

MATLAB program was used to analyze the data in the study, which was established as an ANN model by using the CPI data for the period of January 2002 - March 2019. The ANN algorithm established in the model is as in Figure 6.

The data set between 01.2002-03.2019 is divided into categories of 70%, 20% and 10%. Of the 207 data related, 145 were used for training, 41 for verification and 21 for testing. The data set is trained with the Levenberg-Marquardt back propagation algorithm. After the experiments, it was seen that the number of hidden layers was taken as 12 and the number of delays as 3 as shown in Figure 7. If few hidden layers are selected, it is seen that the generalization capability of the network is increased. If a large number of neurons are selected, an increase in the ability of the network to memorize is observed. Adding a large number of secret neurons or hidden layers to the network, however, causes an enormous increase in the number of accounts.

Figure 7. ANN performance (mean squared error-MSE)

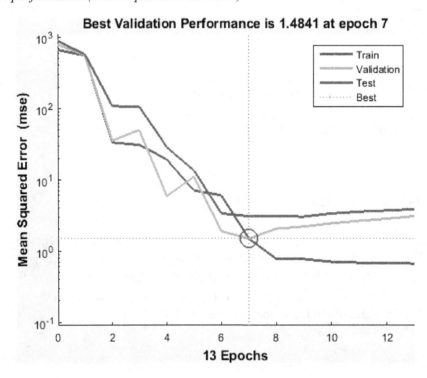

The turnover performance of the established network reached the smallest MSE with the smallest value of 1.4841 and 13 iterations in 7 cycles.

In Figure 8, the error values convergent to zero at the training, verification and test phase confirm that the model is compatible. The errors in this calculation are the result of subtracting the outputs from the targets, and the outliers indicate that they mostly fall between -1.514 and 1.708. Figure 9 shows the model adaptation graph of data in training, verification, and testing stages. Accordingly, convergence to the alignment line increases the accuracy of the model.

Figure 8. Error histogram chart

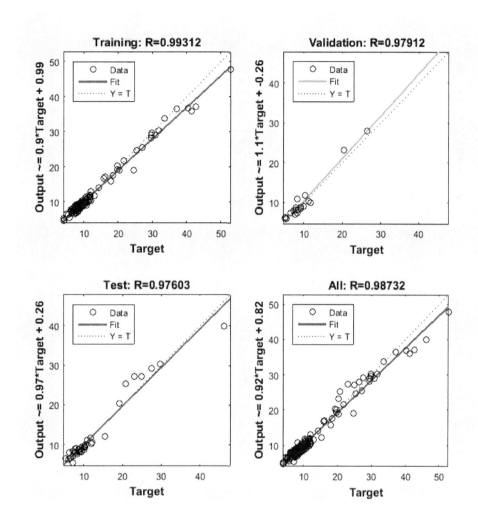

Figure 10 shows the course of errors between training, verification and test objectives and outcomes as a result of the training of the network. When the section showing the total of errors is examined, it can be seen that since the errors of the model are within the required confidence interval limits (-5,+5) the network reaches the desired performance.

SEy = 1.348558. According to ANN, the future 9 months of Inflation figures will decrease even if a little.

95% confidence intervals for exante periods are as follows:

2019M04: 19.55±1.96 * 1.348558 = 16.91 - 22.19

...

2019M12: 15.82±1.96 * 1.348558 = 13.18 – 18.46

Figure 9. Training success of network

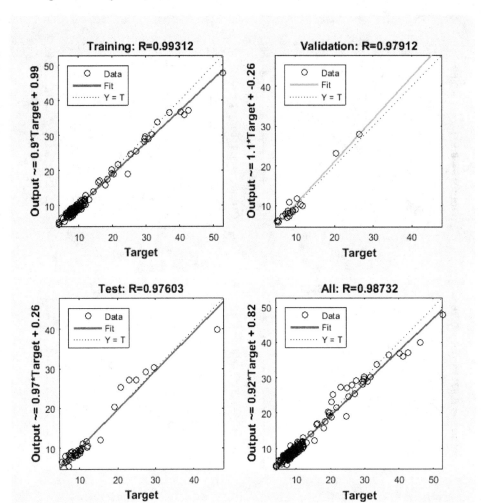

Table 5. Estimated Expost and Exante prediction results for inflation series

Period	Actual	Expost	Residual	Period	Exante	LL	UL
2018M07	15.85	16.71	0.86	2019M04	19.55	16.91	22.19
2018M08	17.90	15.79	2.11	2019M05	19.42	16.78	22.06
2018M09	24.52	19.06	5.46	2019M06	19.25	16.61	21.89
2018M10	25.24	24.67	0.57	2019M07	19.02	16.38	21.66
2018M11	21.62	21.61	0.01	2019M08	18.72	16.08	21.36
2018M12	20.30	23.11	-2.81	2019M09	18.31	15.67	20.95
2019M01	20.35	18.89	1.46	2019M10	17.74	15.10	20.38
2019M02	19.67	20.14	-0.47	2019M11	16.95	14.31	19.59
2019M03	19.71	19.24	0.47	2019M12	15.82	13.18	18.46

Figure 10. Artificial neural network regression performance (training result time series response graph)

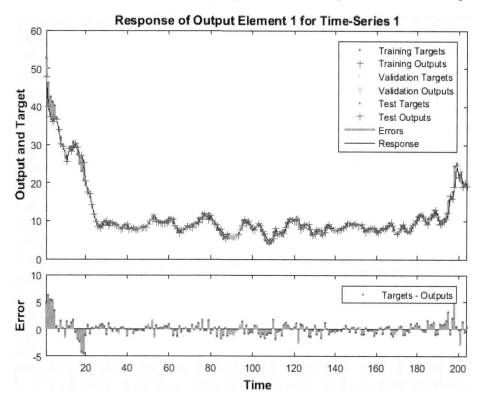

When the expost values are analysed in Table 5, it is seen that the actual inflation values and the expost estimation values are close to each other (Difference was realized between -2.81 and 5.46). The fact that the difference between the prediction values for the past period and the actual values are not high increases the adequacy and reliability of the predictions for the next period with ANN.

On the other hand, the exante estimation results for the 9-month period are given in Table 5. At this point, it was predicted that the estimation results found with ANN would be around 15.82-19.55% for the period of 2019M04-2019M12. The results which were close to these results were also obtained by ARIMA models. However, the estimation results obtained according to both techniques are based on previous period data. Undoubtedly, it can be said that, apart from the fragile structure in our economy and the volatility of the dollar in the current period, the Istanbul Municipality election, which was canceled by the Higher Court for Elections, and the re-experienced election environment would have an impact on inflation and the inflation results would be larger than those estimates.

Figure 11 presents the inflation forecast and the actual rates graph together. When the graph is examined, it can be said that the process which continued with the collapse of Lehmann Brothers in September 2008 could be considered as the beginning of the economic crisis. Accordingly, ANN successfully predicted (with a difference of -0.17) the volatility in the markets stemming from the exchange rate fluctuations in 2018 (with a difference of 2.11).

Finally, Table 6 shows the results of the ARIMA model and the results obtained from the ANN model and the criteria for the residues (remnants) of both models. The comparisons of the findings are in the conclusion section.

Figure 11. Inflation realization with ANN model prediction

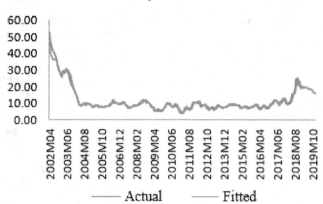

Table 6. Comparison of estimation values of models

Period	ARIMA(5,0,3)	ANN(NAR(t-3)	Jointly	LL	UL
2019:04	19.98	19.55	19.76	17.17	22.36
2019:05	20.37	19.42	19.89	17.29	22.49
2019:06	20.80	19.25	20.01	17.41	22.61
2019:07	21.31	19.02	20.13	17.53	22.73
2019:08	21.81	18.72	20.21	17.61	22.80
2019:09	22.25	18.31	20.18	17.59	22.78
2019:10	22.76	17.74	20.09	17.50	22.69
2019:11	23.29	16.95	19.87	17.27	22.47
2019:12	23.81	15.82	19.41	16.81	22.01
Criteria					
R^2	0.985546	0.974798			
SE_Y	1.302555	1.348558			
ME	-0.04974	0.109858			
MAE	0.865488	0.886689			
MSE	1.630975	1.791864			
MPE	-0.00535	-0.010060			
MAPE	8.198722	8.042681			

There is a slight difference between the values obtained from both methods. According to Box-Jenkins ARIMA, inflation figures are predicted higher in the next three months, while according to YSA findings are at a lower level. Although the arithmetic averages of these values can be taken, it is more appropriate to obtain a geometric mean due to the proportionality of the values. In this case, when the square root of the multiplication of the two values is taken:

2019M04: $\sqrt{(19,98)(19,55)} \cong 19.76$

...

2019M12: $\sqrt{(23,81)(15,82)} \cong 19.41$

$$\sqrt{(SE_{Y,ARIMA})(SE_{Y,YSA})} = \sqrt{(1,302555)(1,348558)}$$

$SE_{Y,ORTAK} \cong 1.325357$

Based on the combined results of the two techniques, the interval estimate results for the next three periods are as follows:

2019M04: $19,76 \pm 1.96 * 1.325357 = 17.17 - 22.36$

...

2019M12: $19,41 \pm 1.96 * 1.325357 = 16.81 - 22.01$

CONCLUSION

The predictions from various linear and nonlinear time series models can be combined with different prediction studies. In this study, Box-Jenkins ARIMA and back propagation ANN were used for inflation variable and Eviews 10, MATLAB and Excel programs were used as package programs. In the model preparation stage, the CPI data in the period 2002:01-2019:03 were used to represent the inflation.

The results obtained from ARIMA and ANN models were found to be very close to each other. While the coefficient of determination of ARIMA model was found higher, the standard error, mean error, mean absolute error, mean square error and mean percentage error of estimation were lower than ANN model. In contrast, the mean absolute percentage error value was lower in the ANN model.

By taking the geometric mean of both results, it was concluded that the inflation rate in April 2019 would be between 17.17% and 22.36% with 95% probability and in December 2019 between 16.81% and 22.01%.

There are 426 items in the CPI, which is the main inflation indicator (TUIK, 2015). Among these items, the two most important items that lead to deviations of estimates are the energy prices linked to the foreign markets and the alcohol and tobacco prices controlled by the Ministry of Finance. In order to benefit the state budget, upward and downward movement in alcohol and tobacco prices is reflected reversely in the same way as the inflation indicator. This in turn prevents the correct estimation of inflation.

In addition, future-based estimations were made with the help of the model obtained from the study. In the Exante phase, the estimates were made for short-term (9-month) periods. This is because short term exante predictions are reliable when working with time series for inflation, while, on the other hand, the margin of error in long term forecasts can be increased significantly.

When the success performance of Box-Jenkins ARIMA and ANN models are compared, in case the ANN model is not successful in solving the short-term variance problem, since ARIMA model displays a successful performance with its stationary structure, the models exhibited performances close to each other. For this reason, different models should be tried in the prediction phase and the most suitable model for the data set should be investigated separately, and at the same time as the data set changes, it should be checked as well.

REFERENCES

Abdelmouez, G., Hashem, S. R., & Atiya, A. F., & El-Gamal, M.A. (2007). Neural network vs. linear models for stock market sectors forecasting. In *Neural Networks 2007* (pp. 1365-1369). Academic Press.

Akdag, M. (2015). Inflation Forecast with Box-Jenkis and Artificial Neural Network Models [Master's Thesis]. Atatürk University, Institute of Science and Technology.

Akdağ, M., & Yiğit, V. (2016). Inflation forecast with Box-Jenkins and artificial neural network models. *Atatürk University Journal of Economics and Administrative Sciences*, *30*(2).

Akdoğan, K., Başer, S., Chadwick, M. G., Ertuğ, D., Hülagü, T., Kösem, S., . . . Tekatlı, N. (2012). Short term inflation forecasting models for Turkey and a forecast combination analysis. TCMB.

Alnaa, S. E., & Ahiakpor, F. (2011). ARIMA (autoregressive integrated moving average) approach to predicting inflation in Ghana. *Journal of Economics and International Finance*, *3*(5), 328–336.

Ataseven B (2013). Foresight Modeling with Artificial Neural Networks. *Öneri Magazine*, *10*(19), 101-115.

Bayramoğlu, T., & Öztürk, Z. (2017). Inflation Forecast with ARIMA and Gray System Models. *Journal of Human and Social Sciences Research*, *6*(2), 760–776.

Binner, J. M., Bissoondeeal, R. K., Elger, T., Gazely, A. M., & Mullineux, A. W. (2005). A comparison of linear forecasting models and neural networks: an application to Euro inflation and Euro Divisia. *Applied Economics*, *37*(6), 665 680.

Bokhari, S. M. H., & Feridun, M. (2006). Forecasting inflation through econometric models: An empirical study on Pakistani data. *Doğuş University Journal*, *7*(1), 39–47.

Box, G. E. P., & Jenkins, G. M. (1976). *Time series analysis: „Forecasting and control*. San Francisco, CA: Holden-Day.

Caire, P., & Hatabian, G., & Muller, C. (1992). Progress in forecasting by neural networks. In *Neural Networks 1992* (pp. 540 545). Academic Press.

Çavuşlu, A., Yasar, M., & Cihan, B. (2012). Hardware Implementation of the Levenberg-Marquardt ANN training with Algorithm. Turkey Informatics Foundation of Computer Science and Engineering Journal, 5(1). Retrieved from http://dergipark.gov.tis

Choudhary, M. A., & Haider, A. (2012). Neural network models for inflation forecasting: An appraisal. *Applied Economics*, *44*(20), 2631–2635. doi:10.1080/00036846.2011.566190

Çınar, M. & Öz, R. (2017). A Proposal in the Context of Renewable Energy for Energy Consumption and Economic Growth. *Journal of academic value studies*, *3*(13), 40-54.

Dickey, D.A. & Fuller, W.A. (1979). Distribution of the estimators for autoregressive time series with a unit root. *Journal of the American Statistical Association, 74*, 427–431.

Domaç, İ. (2004). Explaining and forecasting inflation in Turkey. World Bank.

Fausett, L. (1994). *Fundamentals of Neural Networks: Architectures, Algorithms and Applications.* USA: Prentice Hall.

Haykin, S. (1998). Neural Networks: A Comprehensive Foundation (2nd ed.). Prentice-Hall.

Eğrioğlu, E., Yolcu, U., Aladağ, Ç. H., & Uslu, V. R. (2011). Hybrid approach to prediction of inflation in the forward and backward propagation artificial neural network in Turkey. *Doğuş University Journal, 11*(1), 42–55.

İnsel, A., Karakas, M., & Süalp, M.N. (2010). A Comparative Analysis Of The Arma And Neural Networks Models: A Case Of Turkish Economy. *İktisat İşletme ve Finans, 25*(290), 35-64.

Işığıçok, E. (1994). *Causality Analysis in Time Series: An Empirical Research on Money Supply and Inflation on in Turkey.* Bursa: Uludag University Press.

Işığıçok, E. & Parasız İ. (1993). Mark-Up Pricing Policy and Inflation in Turkey. *Journal of Economic Approach, 4*(8), 83-95.

Kamruzzamman, J. & Sarker, R. A. (2003). Forecasting of Currency Exchange Rates using ANN: A Case Study. In *Neural Networks & Signal Processing (ICNNSP03)* (pp. 793 797). Academic Press.

Kaynar, O., & Taştan, S. (2009, July-December). Comparison of MLP Artificial Neural Networks and ARIMA Model in Time Series Analysis. *Erciyes University Faculty of Economics and Administrative Sciences Journal,* (33), 161-172.

Kaynar, O., Taştan, S., & Demirkoparan, F. (2011). Estimation of Natural Gas Consumption by Artificial Neural Networks. *Ataturk University Journal of Economics and Administrative Sciences, 10*, 463-474.

Kwiatkowski, D., & Phillips, P. C. B., Schmidt, P., & Shin, Y. (1992). Testing the Null Hypothesis of Stationarity Against the Alternative of a Unit Root. Journal of Econometrics, 54(1-3).

Meçik, O., & Karabacak, M. (2011). Inflation forecasting with ARIMA models: Turkey application. *Selcuk University Journal of Social and Economic Research, 22*, 177–198.

Montañés, E., Quevedo, J. R., Prieto, M. M., & Menéndez, C.O. (2002). Forecasting time series combining machine learning and Box-Jenkins time series Advances in Artificial Intelligence. In *Advances in Artificial Intelligence* (pp. 491 499). Springer.

Önder, A. Ö. (2004). Forecasting inflation in emerging markets by using the Phillips curve and alternative time series models. *Emerging Markets Finance & Trade, 40*(2), 71–82. doi:10.1080/154049 6X.2004.11052566

Önder, E., Bayır, F., & Hepsen, A. (2013). Forecasting Macroeconomic Variables Using Artificial Neural Network and Traditional Smoothing Techniques. *Journal of Applied Finance and Banking, 3*(4), 73–104.

Öztemel, E. (2003). *Artificial Neural Networks.* Istanbul: Papatya Publishing.

Refenes, A. N., Azema-Barac, M., Chen, L., & Karoussos, S. (1993). Currency exchange rate prediction and neural network design strategies", Neural Computing & Applications, Springer, 1(1), ss.46 58.

Sevüktekin, M. & Çınar, M. (2017). Econometric Time Series Analysis: EViews Applied. Bursa: Dora Yayıncılık.

Shabri, A. (2001). Comparison of time series forecasting methods using neural networks and Box-Jenkins model. *Matematika, 17*(1), 1–6.

Tang, Z., de Almeida, C., & Fishwick, P. A. (1991). Time series forecasting using neural networks vs. Box-Jenkins methodology. *Simulation, 57*(5), 303–310.

The Central Bank of the Republic of Turkey. (n.d.). Electronic Data Distribution System. Retrieved from https://evds2.tcmb.gov.tr/

Zou, H., Xia, G., Yang, F., & Wang, H. (2007). An investigation and comparison of artificial neural network and time series models for Chinese food grain price forecasting. *Neurocomputing, 70*(16), 2913.

ENDNOTE

[1]   It was presented in International Data Science & Engineering Symposium (IDSES19).

This research was previously published in the International Journal of Energy Optimization and Engineering (IJEOE), 9(4); pages 84-103, copyright year 2020 by IGI Publishing (an imprint of IGI Global).

Section 5
Organizational and Social Implications

Chapter 58

Comparative Analysis of Proposed Artificial Neural Network (ANN) Algorithm With Other Techniques

Deepak Chatha

Department of Computer Science and Engineering, Panipat Institute of Engineering and Technology, Samalkha, India

Alankrita Aggarwal

https://orcid.org/0000-0002-0931-1118

Department of Computer Science and Engineering, Panipat Institute of Engineering and Technology, Samalkha, India

Rajender Kumar

https://orcid.org/0000-0001-7334-729X

Department of Computer Science and Engineering, Panipat Institute of Engineering and Technology, Samalkha, India

ABSTRACT

The mortality rate among women is increasing progressively due to cancer. Generally, women around 45 years old are vulnerable from this disease. Early detection is hope for patients to survive otherwise it may reach to unrecoverable stage. Currently, there are numerous techniques available for diagnosis of such a disease out of which mammography is the most trustworthy method for detecting early cancer stage. The analysis of these mammogram images are difficult to analyze due to low contrast and nonuniform background. The mammogram images are scanned and digitized for processing that further reduces the contrast between Region of Interest and background. Presence of noise, glands and muscles leads to background contrast variations. Boundaries of suspected tumor area are fuzzy & improper. Aim of paper is to develop robust edge detection technique which works optimally on mammogram images to segment tumor area. Output results of proposed technique on different mammogram images of MIAS database are presented and compared with existing techniques in terms of both Qualitative & Quantitative parameters.

DOI: 10.4018/978-1-6684-2408-7.ch058

INTRODUCTION

The edges are feature points characterizes boundary between two dissimilar objects present in an image. Edge detection is one of the distinguished image processing technique used extensively in many applications like Segmentation, Machine Vision and learning, Analysis, Feature Extraction etc. Edge detection filters relevant information, by preserving crucial structural details. Any edge detection technique copes with various challenges i.e. false positives, Noise, poor contrast and in appropriate thresholding. There exist several edge detectors, but our literature survey confirms that none of them performs optimally on mammogram images for tumor segmentation.

ARTIFICIAL NEURAL NETWORK (ANN)

In recent years, it has also been observed that the artificial neural network (ANN) is used to resolve problems related to complex scenarios and logical thinking. Therefore, this article works investigates the capability of ANN to restore the edge information from the digital mammogram images for the detection of tumor in earlier stages. In this paper, a robust edge detection algorithm based on Artificial Neural Networks is proposed. The first stage of algorithm involves Bilateral filtration and Multi-Thresholding using entropy technique to ensure least loss of details in input image during binarization. This Binary image is disintegrated into 3×3 windows and is applied as an input to a supervised BPNNto determine weights and bias for another feed-forward neural network. Finally, the output of feed-forward neural network is used to detect the presence of edge in input centre pixel of the window.

EVALUATE THE PERFORMANCE OF ANN WITH EXISTING TECHNIQUES

Quantitative Comparison

The Qualitative comparison is basically done by visual inspection. The few parameters which are kept in mind while declaring best technique among different edge detector are: True Edges, Thin Boundaries, Lost detail, Noise and Broken Edges.

TEST IMAGE 1

The Qualitative comparison of Artificial Neural Network (ANN) technique with other existing techniques for test image 1 is shown in Figure 1. It is clear by visual inspection that Artificial Neural Network (ANN) algorithm gives best results among all other competing detectors as it is manifesting maximum accurate tumor details with minimum structural loss. Also, it is observed that there is high continuity among all edge pixels along with almost true and thin edges.

The Quantitative results are color coded to differentiate top three performing technique among others as shown in Table 2.

Figure 1. Edge detection of test image1: (a) Original; (b) Sobel; (c) Robert; (d) Prewitt; (e) Canny; (f) Artificial Neural Network (ANN)

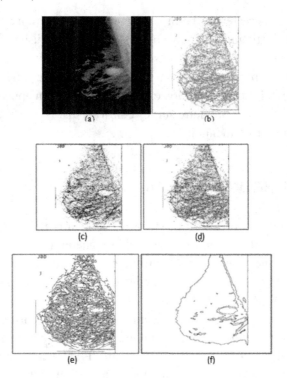

Table 1. Quantitative analysis of test image 1

S.No	Parameter	Sobel	Robert	Prewitt	Canny	Artificial Neural Network (ANN)
1	Fmeasure	0.013483	0.083679	0.018052	0.017473	1.483634
2	Accuracy	0.533251	0.535400	0.535196	0.530701	0.585468
3	BER	54.991246	54.803575	54.826640	55.206117	50.465731
4	NRM	0.549912	0.548036	0.548266	0.552061	0.504657
5	PSNR	3.309164	3.329212	3.327304	3.285501	3.824400
6	DRD	1376.641093	1370.416079	1370.885555	1384.757273	1222.405677
7	MPM	0.149743	0.147927	0.148037	0.150739	0.105539

The Quantitative analysis for test image 1 is given in Table 1. The Quantitative results shows that Artificial Neural Network (ANN) technique is performing excellently than all other competing techniques. The Artificial Neural Network (ANN) technique offers maximum (F-Measure, Accuracy & PSNR) and lowest (NRM, DRD, BER & MPM), which is required for any optimal technique (Figures 2-6).

Table 2. Quantitative results

	Best Result 1
	Best Result 2
	Best Result 3

Figure 2. Quantitative comparison (Fmeasure) for test image 1

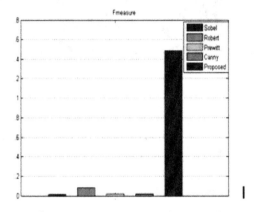

Figure 3. Quantitative comparison (NRM) for test image 1

Figure 4. Quantitative comparison (PSNR) for test image 1

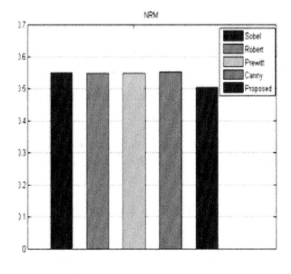

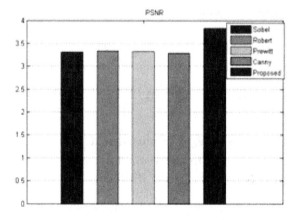

Figure 5. Quantitative comparison (DRD) for test image 1

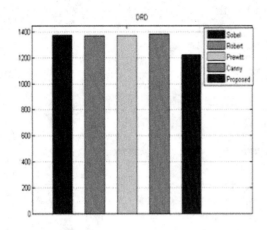

Figure 6. Quantitative comparison (MPM)for test image 1

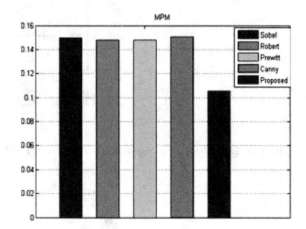

CONCLUSION

The comparative results show the superiority of proposed technique, which outperforms all other comparative techniques by providing visually better output images. The remarkable quantitative results clearly unveil the ability of proposed technique to reject noises by filtering out informative pixels. Therefore, it may be concluded that the strategy of using efficiently trained ANN for the detection of edges in mammogram input image results in a design of highly robust & adaptive edge detector; thereby making it an optimal choice among all detectors.

REFERENCES

Shrivakshan, G. T., & Chandrasekar, C. (2012). A Comparison of Various Edge Detection Techniques Used In Image Processing. *International Journal of Computer Science Issues*, *9*(5), 269–276.

Akila, K., & Sumathy, P. (2015). Early Breast Cancer Tumor Detection on Mammogram and Images. *IJCSET*, *5*(9), 334–336.

Chickanosky, V., & Mirchandani, G. (1998, May). Wreath products for edge detection. In *Proceedings of the 1998 IEEE International Conference on Acoustics, Speech and Signal Processing ICASSP'98* (Vol. 5, pp. 2953-2956). IEEE.

Gotas, B., Ntirogiannis, K., & Pratikakis, I. (2011). DIBCO 2009: Document Binarization Contest. *IJDAR*, *14*(1), 35–44. doi:10.100710032-010-0115-7

Goubalan, S. R. T. J., Goussard, Y., & Maaref, H. (2016). Unsupervised Malignant Mammographic Breast Mass Segmentation Algorithm Based On Pickard Markov Random Field. In *Proceedings of the 2016 IEEE International Conference on Image Processing (ICIP)* (pp. 2653-2657). IEEE Press. 10.1109/ICIP.2016.7532840

Heindel, A., Wige, E., & Kaup, A. (2016). Low- Complexity Enhancement Layer Compression For Scalable Lossless Video Coding Based HEVC. *IEEE Transactions on Circuits and Systems for Video Technology, 99*, 1.

Joshi, K., Yadav, R., & Allwadhi, S. (2016). PSNR and MSE Based Investigation of LSB. In *Proceedings of the International Conference on Computational Techniques in Information and Communication Technologies (ICCTICT)* (pp. 280-285). Academic Press. 10.1109/ICCTICT.2016.7514593

Lakshminarayana, M., & Sarvagya, M. (2015). Random sample measurement and reconstruction of medical image signal using compressive sensing. In *Proceedings of the IEEE International Conference on Computing and Network Communications* (pp. 255-262). IEEE Press. 10.1109/CoCoNet.2015.7411195

Liu, A. (2009). Evaluation of Gray Image Definition Based on Edge Kurtosis in Spatial Domain. In *Proceedings of the First International Workshop on Education and Computer Science* (pp. 472-475). Academic Press. 10.1109/ETCS.2009.634

Lu, H., Kot, A. C., & Shi, Y. Q. (2004). Distance-Reciprocal Distortion Measure For Binary Document Images. *IEEE Signal Processing Letters, 11*(2), 228–231. doi:10.1109/LSP.2003.821748

Neil, R. O. (1963). Convolution Operators And L(P, Q) Spaces. *Duke Mathematical Journal, 30*(1), 129–142. doi:10.1215/S0012-7094-63-03015-1

Radha, M., & Adaekalavan, S. (2016). Mammogram of Breast Cancer Detection Based Using Image Enhancement Algorithm. *International Journal of Advanced Research in Computer and Communication Engineering, 5*(7).

Sharifi, M., Fathy, M., & Mahmoudi, M. T. (2002). A Classified and Comparative Study of Edge Detection Algorithms. In *Proceedings of IEEE International Conference on Information Technology: Coding and Computing (ITCC)* (pp. 117 – 120). IEEE Press. 10.1109/ITCC.2002.1000371

Shastri, M., Roy, S., & Mittal, M. (2019). Stock Price Prediction using Artificial Neural Model: An Application of Big Data. EAI Endorsed Transactions on Scalable Information Systems, 6(20). doi:10.4108/eai.19-12-2018.156085

Sun, W., & Wang, Y. (2005). Segmentation Method of MRI Using Fuzzy Gaussian Basis Neural Network Neural Information Processing. *Letters and Reviews, 8*(2), 19–24.

Tian, J., Wang, Y., Dai, X., & Zhang, X. (2013). Medical image processing and analysis. In *Molecular Imaging* (pp. 415–469). Springer.

Umbaugh, S. E. (2005). *Computer Imaging: Digital Image Analysis and Processing*. CRC Press.

Yadav, M., Purwar, R. K., & Mittal, M. (2018). Handwritten Hind Character Recognition-A Review. *IET Image Processing, 12*(11), 1919–1933. doi:10.1049/iet-ipr.2017.0184

This research was previously published in the International Journal of Security and Privacy in Pervasive Computing (IJSPPC), 12(1); pages 29-35, copyright year 2020 by IGI Publishing (an imprint of IGI Global).

Chapter 59
Developing Strategies in the Sharing Economy:
Human Influence on Artificial Neural Networks

Ramona Diana Leon

ⓘD https://orcid.org/0000-0002-1448-0522

National School of Political and Administrative Studies, Romania

ABSTRACT

The sharing economy is challenging the traditional business models and strategies by encouraging collaboration, non-ownership, temporal access, and redistribution of goods and/or services. Within this framework, the current chapter aims to examine how managers influence, voluntarily or involuntarily, the reliability of a managerial early warning system, based on an artificial neural network. The analysis focuses on seven Romanian sustainable knowledge-based organizations and brings forward that managers tend to influence the results provided by a managerial early warning system based on artificial neural network, voluntarily and involuntarily. On the one hand, they are the ones who consciously decide which departments and persons are involved in establishing the structure of the managerial early warning system. On the other hand, they unconsciously influence the structure of the managerial early warning system through the authority they exercise during the managerial debate.

INTRODUCTION

The concept of "sustainability" has its roots in the social sciences, more exactly, in the ecological paradigm (O'Riordan, 1976), and it is used for the first time by George Ludwig Hartig, in 1785. He argues that forestry can be sustainable only if the future generations will be able to obtain the same benefits from its exploitation as the current generation. However, the perspective from which it is approached changed radically in the last centuries (Table 1). Thus, the theories developed in the 19th and the early 20th centuries (namely, the classical theory, the stakeholder theory, etc.) adopt an economic perspective

DOI: 10.4018/978-1-6684-2408-7.ch059

and claim that a firm's sustainability is ensured through profit maximization and shareholders' satisfaction. Furthermore, the theories promoted during the 20th and 21st centuries (like, neo-institutional theory, the knowledge-based theory of the firm, the holistic theory etc.) bring forward two more perspectives, namely: the social and ecological ones; as a consequence, three pillars of company's sustainability are emphasized, such as: profitability, stakeholders' satisfaction, and natural environment (Fiksel, 2006; Leon, 2018a; Lozano, 2008). Nevertheless, these perspectives are combined and the borders of sustainability are extended by the sharing economy which describes a socio-economic environment dominated by non-ownership (Belk, 2014; Botsman & Rogers, 2011), intra- and inter-organizational collaboration (Leon, Rodriguez-Rodriguez, Gomez-Gasquet, & Mula, 2017; Mantymaki, Baiyere, & Islam, 2019; Sthapit, 2019), temporary access (Habibi, Davidson, & Laroche, 2017; Yang, Bi, & Liu, 2020), and sharing of under-utilized or idle goods and/or services (Hong, Kim, & Park, 2019; Lee & Kim, 2019).

Within this framework, managers realize that the traditional strategies and business models, such as: the powerful input of resources into the supply sector (Böcker & Meelen, 2017; Fan, Xia, Zhang, & Chen, 2019), platform competition and price-setting (Armstrong, 2006; Eisenmann, Parker, & van Alstyne, 2006), and network externalities (Parker & van Alstyne, 2005) are no longer viable. Therefore, they have to focus not only on increasing shareholders' satisfaction but also on augmenting their internal and external stakeholders' satisfaction, improving the quality of life, and protecting the environment. In other words, they have to address the challenges from the micro- and macro-environment, having their stakeholders' best interest in mind.

Table 1. The perspectives from which the concept of "sustainability" is approached

Perspective	Sustainability as...	Author/-s (Year)
Environmental	*A duty*	Barkemeyer, Holt, Preuss, and Tsang (2011); Pearce, Markandya, and Barbier (1989)
	A process	Braat (1991)
	An ability	Bansal (2005); Jennings and Zandbergen (1995)
	A capacity	Ariansen (1999)
	A component of the social and ethical responsibility	Landrum and Ohsowski (2018); Ng and Burke (2010); Richardson (2009); Schwartz and Carroll (2008)
Social	*A condition*	Torjman (2000)
	A level	Black (2004)
Economic	*A general goal*	Anderson (1991); Saunila, Nasiri, Ukko, and Rantala (2019)
	A specific objective	Daily and Walker (2000); Maddox (2000)
	A change factor	Blum-Kusterer and Hussain (2001); Bos-Brouwers (2010)
	A way to satisfy stakeholders' needs	Dyllick and Hockerts (2002); Hahn, Figge, Pinkse, and Preuss (2010)
	An image of productivity	Dunphy, Griffiths, and Benn (2003); Holliday, Schmidheiny, and Watts (2002)
	An adaptive capacity	Kira and van Eijnatten (2008)
	A stage of development	Ketola (2010)
	A process	Cândea (2006)
	A result	Vaida and Cândea (2010)

Against this backdrop, managers look for potential solutions and tools that could provide them some "early warnings". Therefore, for the last 50 years, various early warning systems have been developed. Some of them use abstract tools, like: statistical analysis (Laitinen & Chong, 1999; Salzano, Garcia Agreda, Di Carluccio, & Fabbrocino, 2009) or artificial neural networks (Yang, 2012; Zheng, Zhu, Tim, Chen, & Sun, 2012) while others focus on managers' involvement and mitigate for the use of managerial debates (Day & Schoemaker, 2005; Kotler & Caslione, 2009). Only a few researchers (Bertoncel, Erenda, Pejić Bach, Roblek, & Meško, 2018; Haji-Kazemi & Andersen, 2013; Leon, 2018b) take into account the challenges brought forward by the sharing economy and the fact that this is usually focusing on the external stakeholders (Frenken & Schor, 2017; Li, Ding, Cui, Lei, & Mou, 2019; Niemimaa, Järveläinen, Heikkilä, & Heikkilä, 2019; Stofberg & Bridoux, 2019). Thus, they state that, in the current environment, a successful strategic tool should combine the subjective character of a managerial debate with the abstract character of various business intelligence tools.

Despite the valuable insights provided by this mixt approach of the managerial early warning system, its findings may be limited by several biases. According to Elbanna (2010), managers can influence strategy's development through coalition formation, agenda control, tactics of timing, and tactics concerning the control and manipulation of information. Besides, several scholars (Curşeu, Schruijer, & Fodor, 2016; Hollenbeck, Beersma, & Schouten, 2012; Parayitam & Papenhausen, 2016) argue that the results of a managerial early warning system can also be influenced by company's size, group diversity, agreement-seeking behavior, and knowledge sharing behavior. Each of these may have an impact on the identification of weak signals since they limit managers' perspective, and influence the way in which managers act during debates, factors selection, scenarios development, and strategy development. Starting from these, the current chapter aims to examine how managers influence, voluntarily or involuntarily, the reliability of a managerial early warning system, based on an artificial neural network.

The content of this chapter is organized around four sections. Section 2 describes the conceptual framework, emphasizing the tools used by the management teams to foresight the company's potential threats and opportunities. Then, the research design is highlighted; a qualitative-quantitative approach is employed in order to examine how the managers from 7 Romanian sustainable knowledge organizations influence, voluntarily or involuntarily, the reliability of a managerial early warning system, based on an artificial neural network. The results of this analysis are presented in Section 4 and they prove that managers influence, consciously and unconsciously, the reliability of a managerial early warning system. On the one hand, they are the ones who consciously decide which departments and persons are involved in establishing the structure of the managerial early warning system. On the other hand, they unconsciously influence the structure of the managerial early warning system through the authority they exercise during the managerial debate. Last but not least, the chapter closes by synthesizing the main findings and providing further research directions.

MANAGERIAL EARLY WARNING SYSTEMS – NEW SOLUTIONS TO OLD PROBLEMS

A managerial early warning system is a strategic tool that fosters the anticipation of the weak signals and the development of various responses to turbulence. Thus, it is seen as a specific information system, based on a cause-effect analysis (Ohatka & Fukazawa, 2009; Williams, Klakegg, Walker, Andersen,

& Magnussen, 2012) and capable of extending the time available to react to unforeseen events (Genc, Duffie, & Reinhart, 2014).

The development of a managerial early warning system includes three phases, namely:

1. *Environment scanning* – focuses on selecting the elements from the micro- and macro-environment that could influence directly or indirectly the company's evolution and sustainability. At this level, managers tend to choose between adopting an inside or outside approach. The former reduces the volume of information that has to be processed further while offering a limited perspective on what may happen. The latter provides a complete image of the environment due to its 360° perspective while generating information overload. Although managers tend to choose between the two approaches, they neglect the fact that these are complementary and a state of equilibrium can be achieved between them.

2. *Diagnosis* – concentrates on collecting and analyzing historical data in order to determine trends and patterns. Several scholars recommend adopting an abstract approach and applying statistical methods and techniques (Bisson & Diner, 2017; Cao et al., 2011; Laitinen & Chong, 1999; Li & Davies, 2001; Schwarz, 2005; Tsai, 2013) while others state that the solution lies in adopting a subjective approach and using a managerial debate (Day & Schoemaker, 2005; Kotler & Caslione, 2009). Only a few researchers emphasize the advantages provided by both perspectives and argue that these could be combined (Bertoncel et al., 2018; Haji-Kazemi & Andersen, 2013; Leon, 2018b).

3. *Strategy formulation* – is the most subjective phase of the managerial early warning system and it involves using long-term orientation, strategic thinking, creativity and thinking outside the box. Within this framework, future evolutions are predicted, scenarios are built and strategic response is provided for what may come.

Against the backdrop of the sharing economy and the increased interest in developing smart firms, economies, communities, and cities, various abstract models of managerial early warning systems are developed (Table 2). These models use classical statistical techniques (such as, logit regression, fragility analysis, structural modeling, Kolmogorov – Smirnov test, Mann – Whitney – Wilcoxon test, etc.), are excellent when it comes to evaluating the influence factors from the environment but they do not comply with all the requirements for being labeled as a "managerial early warning system". Thus, they support the identification of weak signals and neglect the importance of developing various strategic responses. In other words, they lack a strategic approach; therefore, their utility stops at the second phase of the managerial early warning system. Furthermore, they tend to focus on financial performance and ignore the indicators that describe a company's social and environmental perspective.

The managerial early warning systems based on artificial neural networks take the advantage of the faster pace of the technological progress and try to fill the gap by using modern statistical techniques, like fuzzy logic or neural networks (Table 3). These work similar to the human brain and facilitate not only data analysis and patterns identification but also the development of potential strategic responses. Although these models aim to provide valuable insights and to ensure a high level of objectivity, the process is still under managers' influence due to the fact that the inputs describing the decisional situation are selected either by the management team (Li & Davies, 2001) or an employee (Cao, Chen, Wu, & Mao, 2011; Schwarz, 2005). These studies support the idea that people should be involved in strategy development since a strategy is implemented by human resources, its success depends on their involvement and is reflected by stakeholders' satisfaction. As Leon (2018b, p.105) state, *a managerial early warning system can provide fabulous solutions for what may come and plans may look great on paper but if human resources do not know what is expected from them and why should they do it, then it would be very difficult for the management team to exploit their full potential. Company's efforts for being sustainable, satisfying the interest of all the categories of stakeholders, may prove to be a real fiasco.*

Table 2. Abstract models of managerial early warning systems, based on classical statistical techniques

Author/-s (Year)	Managerial Early Warning System	
	Goal	**Tools**
Laitinen and Chong (1999)	To predict the firm's bankruptcy.	- time-series analysis
Schwarz (2005)	To anticipate the challenges from the internal and external business environment.	- trend analysis
Lieu, Lin, and Yu (2008)	To forecast the probability of a company experiencing financial distress.	- Kolmogorov – Smirnov test; - Mann-Whitney-Wilcoxon test; - logit regression.
Dikmen, Talat Birgonul, Ozorhon, and Egilmezer Sapci (2010)	To predict the failure likelihood of construction companies by assessing their current situation based on both company-specific and external factors.	- analytical network process; - Delphi method.
Tsai (2013)	To predict the company's financial distress.	- multinomial logit model; - probability forecast; - bootstrapping.
Li, Xia, Li, and Zheng (2015)	To forecast the evolution of the vegetable price.	- regression analysis
Hernandez Ticono, Holmes, and Wilson (2018)	To predict corporate financial distress/bankruptcy.	- polytonomous response logit regression
Boonnnan, Jacobs, Kuper, and Romero (2019)	To predict the financial crisis.	- the logit model.
Dekker, Panja, Dijkstra, and Dekker (2019)	To identify the "rest" and "disrupted" states of the Dutch railways.	- Principal Component Analysis; - Louvain model and Bries score.

Although the development of sharing economy encourages communication and collaboration among stakeholders (Abhari, Davidson, & Xiao, 2019; Davlembayeva, Papagiannidis, & Alamanos, 2019; Mishra, Chiwenga, & Ali, 2019) and treats information and communication technologies as a means to achieve organizational goals, only a few researchers state that the managerial early warning systems should be based on debates (Day & Schoemaker, 2005; Kotler & Caslione, 2009; Philip & Schwabe, 2018). They argue that in order to determine the weak signals, to react properly to the challenges that occur in the internal and external environment, the management team has to answer to the following questions:

1. What were our past blind spots? What is happening in these areas now?
2. Is there any instructive analogy for us in another sector?
3. Which important signals are we ignoring without having a rational argument?
4. In our business sector, who is the best at identifying the weak signals and at reacting to these ahead of everyone else?
5. What are our mavericks and outliers trying to tell us?

6.   What future surprises could really affect (help) us?

7.   What emerging technologies could change the business rules that we know?

8.   *Is there any unbelievable scenario?* (Day & Schoemaker, 2005)

Table 3. Abstract models of managerial early warning systems, based on modern statistical techniques

Author/-s (Year)	Managerial Early Warning System	
	Goal	**Tools**
Li and Davies (2001)	To build an intelligent hybrid system for developing global marketing strategies.	- expert system; - fuzzy logic; - artificial neural network.
Tan and Dihardjo (2001)	To predict financial distress in Australian credit unions.	- artificial neural network.
Cao et al. (2011)	To anticipate the moment when a firm will enter into the decline stage.	- Pawlak rough set theory; - artificial neural network.
Li, Qin, Li, and Hou (2016)	To prevent accidents from iron and steel enterprises.	- Analytic Hierarchy Process; - Entropy Weight Method; - Grey System Theory GM (1,1)
Bisson and Diner (2017)	To determine the drivers of change from the milk market competitive environment.	- Delphi method; - graph analysis.
Huang, Wang, and Kochenberger (2017)	To detect the financial deterioration of Chinese companies.	- random-forest; - support vector machine; - neural network.
Li, Wei, and Zhou (2017)	To predict delayed customer orders that will allow for measures to be taken to minimize the risk.	- active learning transductive support vector machine
Hu and Liu (2019)	To anticipate the crisis situation of the supply chain quality.	- fuzzy inference system
Vafaei, Ribeiro, and Camarinha-Matos (2019)	To improve proactive decision making in condition-based maintenance strategies.	- fuzzy logic

Using a managerial debate as an early warning system provides the proper framework for increasing the quality of managers' decision (Raes, Heijltjes, Glunk, & Roe, 2011), improving resource allocations (Cadez & Guilding, 2008), and augmenting managers' involvement in strategy development and implementation (Olsson, Aronsson, & Sandberg, 2017; Ogbeide & Harrington, 2011; Sölvell, 2018). In other words, a managerial debate allows them to explore and manipulate the environment (Vansteenkiste, Niemiec, & Soenens, 2010), to adapt strategic foresight based on their assumptions and mental models (Ringland, 2010), and to understand how and why things are done (Leon, 2018b). However, this model is time-consuming and strongly influenced by the organizational culture and climate. Last but not least, it can be influenced by the company's size. As García Martín and Herrero (2018) and Rashid (2018) show, the size of the company is directly related to the characteristics of the board and the company's performance. Starting from the aforementioned aspects, it can be stated that:

Hypothesis 1: The company's size has an impact on the reliability of the managerial early warning system.

Furthermore, only a few researchers (Bertoncel et al, 2018; Haji-Kazemi & Andersen, 2013; Leon, 2018b) use the development of the sharing economy as a cornerstone and claim that the abstract and subjective approaches of a managerial early warning system could be combined in a strategic tool.

Haji-Kazemi and Andersen (2013) combine the debate with post-mortem analysis while Bertoncel et al. (2018) and Leon (2018b) use a managerial debate and an intelligent business system in the diagnosis phase and place the strategy formulation under the responsibility of the management team. Despite the various advantages provided by this type of managerial early warning system, one issue remains under-explored, namely: managers' influence on the system's reliability.

Managerial groups are considered to be the cornerstone of modern organizations (Curşeu et al., 2016; Hollenbeck et al., 2012) due to the fact that they are able to integrate the explicit and tacit knowledge of the members, to make rational decisions, and to foster strategies implementation. Nevertheless, several issues remain debatable among academics and practitioners, and they tend to focus on group diversity, knowledge sharing behavior, and agreement-seeking behavior.

First of all, most studies (Goyal, Kakabadse, & Kakabadse, 2019; Kipkirong Tarus & Aime, 2014; Parayitam & Papenhausen, 2016; Van der Walt, Ingley, Shergill, & Townsend, 2006) emphasize the positive effect of group diversity on decision quality. Thus, Parayitam and Papenhausen (2016) argue that managers who have different functional backgrounds focus more on decision outcomes than on members' satisfaction; in other words, they are more oriented to tasks than relationships. However, group diversity does not guarantee decision quality since various variables mediate this relationship. On the one hand, individuals' variables like personality, emotional intelligence, etc. should be taken into account; thus, Tuwey and Tarus (2016) prove that chairman's leadership efficacy, members' personal motivation and background have a positive effect on board strategy involvement while Azouzi and Jarboui (2013) reveal that a CEO emotional intelligence is not always positively correlated with board efficiency. On the other hand, organizational variables like size, organizational culture, and climate must be considered; hence, Bridges (2018) claim that the organizations led by more outcome-oriented managers have strong paternalistic cultures while the ones led by more process-oriented managers value diversity. Taking these into account, it can be stated that:

Hypothesis 2: Company's size has an impact on managers' influence.

Secondly, the knowledge sharing behavior is usually brought forward when it comes to managerial group decisions since the group's main purpose is to foster knowledge dissemination and re-combination. Nevertheless, Mojzisch, Grouneva, and Schultz-Hardt (2010) state that three biases may affect this process, namely: (i) manager's preferences, (ii) the importance of external validation, and (iii) uncertainty avoidance. The former highlights the fact that managers evaluate new information based on their initial preferences and discharge everything that is not consistent with these; in other words, managers' mental models which represent the main *sources of expertise, action, and cooperation of individuals in the group* (Hautala, 2011, p.603) are challenged. Furthermore, Mojzisch et al. (2010) prove that the information that can be corroborated by others is considered to be more accurate and relevant than un-corroborated information. Managers' tendency to avoid uncertainty affects the way they perceive and process information; thus, they trust existing information more than the new one (Eisenbart, Garbuio, Mascia, & Morandi, 2016).

Last but not least, the knowledge sharing behavior is linked with agreement-seeking behavior. According to Parayitam and Papenhausen (2016), this provides a solid platform behavior and lowers the levels of process conflict. Still, Finkelstein et al. (2010) state that, at this level, several pitfalls may appear due to inappropriate prejudgments, inappropriate experience, and attachments. These influence the perspective from which managers approach the discussed issues and also the choices they make. They can rarely be objective and impartial when it comes to scanning the environment, identifying the weak signals, and deciding the firm's future. For example, during debates, they may feel the need to align with the CEO's opinion if their past experiences have taught them that this is the right thing to do. As Curşeu et al. (2016) claim, when the responsibility resides with the group leader, the members may exhibit less escalating tendencies. Besides, they can also be tempted to align to the opinion of the majority if they do not experience high psychological safety and they have noticed that the outsiders (those who "dare" to disagree with the majority) are treated differently. As a consequence, they will not share their opinions, ideas, thoughts; instead, they will agree with whatever the majority of the CEO decides. Given these, the following assumption can be made:

Hypothesis 3: Managers' influence affects the reliability of the managerial early warning system.

RESEARCH METHODOLOGY

This chapter aims to examine how managers influence, voluntarily or involuntarily, the reliability of a managerial early warning system, based on an artificial neural network.

Since the research deals with "how" issues, a case-study strategy is employed (Yin, 2014). According to Mariotto, Zanni, and Marcondes de Moraes (2014), this can facilitate theory development if *the particulars of the case are seen as opportunities to make further adjustments in an already crystallized understanding of reality.* Furthermore, a multiple case study approach is developed and the focus is on the sustainable knowledge-based organization which is described as *a complex and adaptive economic entity in which managers are oriented towards achieving multiple objectives (knowledge, economic, environmental and social) by planning on short, medium and long term, adapting to the economic environment challenges in a timely manner, and by adopting an ethic attitude towards all the stakeholders* (Leon, 2013a, 2018a).

In order to select the case study units, a documentary study is employed. According to the Chamber of Commerce, there are 49 potentials sustainable knowledge-based organizations in Iasi. Further, the annual informs of each of these companies is analyzed in order to determine if they meet all the required conditions; the documentary study concentrates on the following criteria: (i) establishing multiple objectives (economic, social, environmental, etc.); (ii) planning on short, medium and long term; (iii) developing an open organizational culture; (iv) investing in human resources; (v) collaborating with other firms; and (vi) reduced number of first-line and middle managers (Leon, 2013b, 2018a). After applying these selection criteria, the research population was reduced to 7 companies.

Further, following Leon (2018b) approach, a multi-stage process is developed, where the outputs of one serve as inputs for the next one. First of all, the external consultant reunites with the person(s) encharged with developing the company's strategy. At this stage, the following variables are considered: (i) the number of persons involved; (ii) the number of departments involved in the process; (iii) CEO's impact on establishing the strategic factors; and (iv) the share of factors that belong to the already validated structure of the managerial early warning system, designed for sustainable knowledge-based organizations. The third variable is codified as a dummy variable where "1" signifies that the CEO decides which factors should be taken into consideration and the others (if any) align to CEO's opinion, and "0" reflects that the list including the strategic factors is the result of a debate. For measuring the last variable, the structure proposed by Leon (2013b) is used as a starting point since it proves that a managerial early warning system should include at least 28 factors (Table 4), describing various events from the micro- and macro-environment.

After choosing the strategic factors that should be taken into consideration, data regarding their evolution are collected from internal and external sources and included in a multi-layer artificial neural network, based on the back-propagation principle. The network is trained using a learning rate of 0.7, a momentum of 0.8 and a target error of 0.01. Further, the artificial neural network is used for forecasting the company's profitability for the next three years.

Table 4. The cornerstone of a managerial early warning system

Factors	Artificial neural network layer	Code
Inflation	Input	F1
Legal system efficiency	Input	F2
Interest rate	Hidden	F3
Foreign direct investment	Hidden	F4
Unemployment	Hidden	F5
Corruption	Hidden	F6
Market deregulation	Hidden	F7
Economic growth	Hidden	F8
Fiscal pressure	Hidden	F9
Bureaucracy	Hidden	F10
Population distribution by age and education	Hidden	F11
Industry atomization	Hidden	F12
Investments in education and research, development and innovation	Hidden	F13
Entrance barriers	Hidden	F14
Employees' professional development	Hidden	F15
Minimum wage	Hidden	F16
Innovations' growth rate	Hidden	F17
Market size	Hidden	F18
Human resources expenses	Hidden	F19
Quality – price ratio	Hidden	F20
Market share	Hidden	F21
Sales variation	Hidden	F22
Customers' satisfaction	Hidden	F23
Dependency of certain clients	Hidden	F24
Variable expenses	Hidden	F25
Revenues	Hidden	F26
Total expenses	Hidden	F27
Profit	Output	F28

Source: (Leon, 2018b)

Once the forecasted values are obtained, the relationships established among the company's size, managers' influence and system's reliability are tested using structural equation modeling, especially partial least square technique (PLS-SEM). This is recommended whenever: (i) the sample size is small; (ii) the research is exploratory; (iii) the predictive accuracy is paramount; and (iv) a correct model specification cannot be provided (Gatautis, Vaiciukynaite, & Tarute, 2019; Shmueli et al., 2019; Wong, 2013).

MAIN RESULTS

According to data presented in Table 5, strategic planning and development are treated as a collective action in both types of companies, SME and large firms; thus, in each organization, more than 2 people are involved in deciding the strategic factors from the micro- and macro-environment. Apparently, all the analyzed firms try to avoid having a limited perspective upon their future and the factors that may influence it; therefore, various people from different departments are involved in strategic planning.

Nevertheless, there is an exception; in a large company from the textile industry, the company's future is decided by two persons who work in the Strategic Management department. The activities are organized based on a matrix organizational chart and the manager and vice-manager of the department are scanning the environment, identifying the weak signals, building scenarios, finding potential solutions, and establishing the most appropriate strategy. Although their analysis is based on the reports delivered by other departments and the CEO is not actively involved in the process, they do not debate; they are more likely to complement each other than to oppose one another.

The situation is different in SMEs where the CEO is practically the one who decides what is important and what is not. For example, in one of the analyzed SMEs, from the consulting services industry, the strategic factors and the relationships established among them were discussed with the management team in a reunion that lasted more than 2 hours. Four persons attended the reunion, namely: the external consultant, the CEO, and two members of the administrative department (the manager of the administrative department, and the human resources specialist), and the discussions concentrated on determining the elements that may influence firm's profitability, based on a "cause-effect" approach. During the reunion, the managers focused mainly on the factors from the internal environment and neglected the influence of the external factors. As the CEO stated right from the beginning:

Table 5. Managers' involvement in strategic planning

Company	Size	No. of persons involved	No. of departments involved	CEO's impact	Share of common factors (%)
1	SME	3	3	1	100.00
2	Large	7	5	0	71.43
3	SME	3	2	1	53.57
4	SME	2	2	0	96.43
5	Large	2	1	0	67.86
6	Large	5	5	1	82.14
7	Large	9	9	1	100.00

Source: (Leon, 2018b)

We are protected from what happens outside ... we are too small to be affected by the macro-economic events and we are protected from the national crises since all our contracts are negotiated in euro. Besides, our success depends on our employees' capacity to work on various projects at the same time and satisfying customers' expectations.

For almost 2 hours, the other two participants were eager to support the CEO's opinion. As a consequence, several factors from the standard version were removed (almost 50%) and other elements were proposed; however, most of the factors that were removed described elements from the external environment while most of the ones that were proposed belonged to the internal environment.

Synthesizing, at the end of each reunion that the external consultant had with the management team, the structure of the managerial early warning system is developed. Then, data regarding factors evolution during 1998 – 2015 are collected from internal and external sources. Information upon the external factors is retrieved from Eurostat, National Institute of Statistics, World Bank and OECD databases while data regarding the evolution of the internal factors are collected from the annual reports and confidential internal documents, such as marketing studies, employees' evaluation, etc.

Further, the information is included in an artificial neural network, designed using Alyuda NeuroIntelligence®, in order to forecast the company's profitability during 2016 – 2018 and to identify the potential weak signals. The system's reliability (Table 6) is reflected by the learning cycles, the probability of obtaining the forecasted values and the average error. The first one brings forward how fast does the learning occur; in this case, the output values are computed and compared with the correct answers until the value of the error function is reduced significantly. In other words, when the number of learning cycles is higher, it means that it takes longer for the managerial early warning system to identify the patterns.

Table 6. The reliability of the managerial early warning system

Company	Learning cycles	Probability	Average error
1	732	95.00	0.00323
2	3176	92.30	0.00429
3	4174	86.50	0.00736
4	111	95.00	0.00418
5	3245	89.45	0.00672
6	3275	93.50	0.00451
7	1786	97.40	0.00372

Source: (Leon, 2018b)

As it can be observed from Table 7, the managerial early warning system developed for Company number 3 registered the highest number of learning cycles (4174), almost 40 times higher than Company number 1, and the lowest confidence interval; thus, after 4174 learning cycles, the forecasted results provided by the managerial early warning system can be guaranteed with an 86.50% probability. On the other hand, the best situation encountered is Company number 1; this time, after 111 learning cycles, the forecasted results can be guaranteed with a 95.00% probability.

Once all the variables of the model's constructs (company's size, managers' influence, and the reliability of the managerial early warning system) are measured, the relationships established among them are tested using the PLS-SEM technique. In line with Hair, Black, and Babin (2012), convergent validity is used for ensuring the correlation between formative and reflective, theoretical and empirical models. Furthermore, the reflective model's validity is highlighted by the convergent and discriminant validity. Thus, the proposed model is valid since Cronbach's Alpha and the composite reliability (CR) are higher than 0.7, and the average variance extracted (AVE) is higher than 0.5 (Table 7). The former proves the internal consistency of the analyzed constructs while the latter emphasizes that the variance explained by the analyzed indicators exceeds the variance generated by the error.

Last but not least, as it can be remarked in Figure 1, the reliability of the managerial early warning system is influenced by both the company's size and managers' influence. In fact, 78.10% of the variability of the managerial early warning system reliability can be explained by managers' influence and company size while 13.30% of managers' influence is positively correlated with the company's size.

Table 7. Convergent validity analysis

Variable	Item	Cronbach's Alpha	CR	AVE
Managers' influence	No. of persons involved	0.736	0.825	0.561
	No. of departments involved			
	CEO's impact			
	Share of common factors			
Managerial early warning system reliability	Learning cycles	0.785	0.875	0.701
	Probability			
	Average error			
Company size	Company size	1.000	1.000	1.000

Source: (Leon, 2018b)

Figure 1. The relationships established among the company's size, managers' influence and the reliability of the managerial early warning system

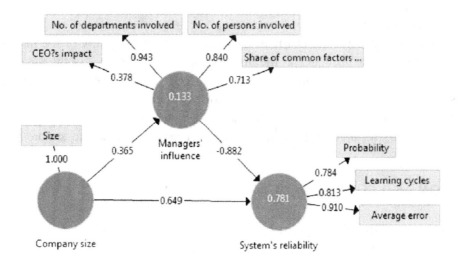

When analyzing the relationships established among the company's size, managers' influence and the reliability of the managerial early warning system, the following elements should be taken into consideration:

- there is a weak positive correlation between company's size and managers' influence ($\beta = 0.365$; $p < 0.05$); therefore, if the company size increases by one standard deviation from its mean, managers' influence would be expected to increase by 0.365 its own standard deviation from its own meanwhile all the other constructs remain constant. In other words, the larger the company gets, the powerful managers' influence becomes.

- there is a strong positive correlation between company's size and the reliability of the managerial early warning system ($\beta = 0.649$; $p < 0.05$); therefore, if the company size increases by one standard deviation from its mean, the reliability of the managerial early warning system would be expected to increase by 0.649 its own standard deviation from its own meanwhile all the other constructs remain constant. Therefore, the larger the company gets, the more reliable the managerial early warning system becomes. As the firm grows, managers' perspective enlarges; they are forced to analyze more elements in order to ensure the company's sustainability. Therefore, various factors are included in the structure of the managerial early warning system which becomes more reliable; it manages to better reflect what is happening inside and outside the organizational boundaries.

- there is a strong negative correlation between managers' influence and the reliability of the managerial early warning system ($\beta = -0.882$; $p < 0.05$); therefore, if managers' influence increases by one standard deviation from its mean, the reliability of the managerial early warning system would be expected to decrease by 0.882 its own standard deviation from its own meanwhile all the other constructs remain constant. As mentioned before, when it comes to making decisions, managers tend to depart from rationality and to adopt a political behavior. In other words, if managers' influence increases so does their thirst for power and their desire to control the environment. Due to these, they will be tempted to modify the structure of the managerial early warning system by including only those factors that they consider to be appropriate. The situation will be similar to the one encountered in the SME from the consulting services industry where almost 50% of the managerial early warning system's structure was radically changed. As a consequence, the reliability of the managerial early warning system will decrease and the future strategy will be defined based on inappropriate results.

- the company's size has a direct and indirect influence on the reliability of the managerial early warning system. On the one hand, as the firm gets larger, the influence of the management team becomes more powerful; as mentioned previously, as the influence of the management team increases, the reliability of the managerial early warning system decreases. However, the company's size also has a positive impact on the reliability of the managerial early warning system; in other words, as the firm gets larger, the managerial early warning system becomes more reliable.

CONCLUSION AND FUTURE RESEARCH DIRECTIONS

The analysis focuses on 7 Romanian sustainable knowledge-based organizations and brings forward that managers tend to influence the results provided by a managerial early warning system based on artificial neural network, voluntarily and involuntarily. On the one hand, they are the ones who consciously decide which departments and persons are involved in establishing the structure of the managerial early warning system. On the other hand, they unconsciously influence the structure of the managerial early warning system through the authority they exercise during the managerial debate. Thus, it was emphasized that 78.10% of the variability of the managerial early warning system reliability can be explained by managers' influence and the company's size; the former is negatively correlated with the system's reliability while the latter is positively correlated with system's reliability.

These findings have both theoretical and practical implications. On the one hand, they extend the literature from the strategic management field by emphasizing how CEOs may influence the process of strategic planning even when an artificial neural network is used for identifying the future weak signals. On the other hand, they offer a better understanding of how managers may influence, voluntarily and involuntarily, strategic planning and development.

REFERENCES

Abhari, K., Davidson, E., & Xiao, B. (2019). Collaborative innovation in the sharing economy. *Internet Research*, *29*(5), 1014–1039. doi:10.1108/INTR-03-2018-0129

Anderson, V. (1991). *Alternative Economic Indicators*. Routledge.

Ariansen, P. (1999). Sustainability, morality and future generations. In W. M. Lafferty & O. Langhelle (Eds.), *Towards Sustainable Development and the Conditions of Sustainability* (pp. 84–96). McMillian. doi:10.1057/9780230378797_5

Armstrong, M. (2006). Competition in two-sided markets. *The RAND Journal of Economics*, *37*(3), 668–691. doi:10.1111/j.1756-2171.2006.tb00037.x

Azouzi, M., & Jarboui, A. (2013). CEO emotional intelligence and board of directors' efficiency. *Corporate Governance*, *13*(4), 365–383. doi:10.1108/CG-10-2011-0081

Bansal, P. (2005). Evolving sustainability: A longitudinal study of corporate sustainable development. *Strategic Management Journal*, *26*(3), 197–218. doi:10.1002mj.441

Barkemeyer, R., Holt, D., Preuss, L., & Tsang, S. (2011). What Happened to the 'Development' in Sustainable Development? Business Guidelines Two Decades after Brundtland. *Sustainable Development*. Retrieved on August 15, 2011 from http://onlinelibrary.wiley.com.ux4ll8xu6v.useaccesscontrol.com/ doi /10.1002/sd.521/pdf

Belk, R. (2014). You are what you can access: Sharing and collaborative consumption online. *Journal of Business Research*, *67*(8), 1595–1600. doi:10.1016/j.jbusres.2013.10.001

Bertoncel, T., Erenda, I., Pejić Bach, M., Roblek, V., & Meško, M. (2018). A Managerial Early Warning System at a Smart Factory: An Intuitive Decision-making Perspective. *Systems Research and Behavioral Science*, *35*(4), 406–416. doi:10.1002res.2542

Bisson, C., & Diner, O. Y. (2017). Strategic Early Warning System for the French milk market: A graph theoretical approach to foresee volatility. *Futures*, *87*, 10–23. doi:10.1016/j.futures.2017.01.004

Black, A. (2004). *The quest for sustainable, healthy communities*. Paper presented at the Effective Sustainability Education Conference, NSW Council on Environmental Education, UNSW, Sydney.

Blum-Kusterer, M., & Husain, S. S. (2001). Innovation and corporate sustainability: An investigation into the process of change in the pharmaceutical industry. *Business Strategy and the Environment, 10*(5), 300–316. doi:10.1002/bse.300

Böcker, L., & Meelen, T. (2017). Sharing for people, planet or profit? Analysing motivations for intended sharing economy participation. *Environmental Innovation and Societal Transitions, 23*, 28–39. doi:10.1016/j.eist.2016.09.004

Boonnnan, T. M., Jacobs, J. P. A. M., Kuper, G. H., & Romero, A. (2019). Early Warning Systems for Currency Crises with Real-Time Data. *Open Economies Review, 30*(4), 813–835. doi:10.100711079-019-09530-0

Bos-Brouwers, H. E. J. (2010). Corporate Sustainability and Innovation in SMEs: Evidence of Themes and Activities in Practice. *Business Strategy and the Environment, 19*(7), 417–435. doi:10.1002/bse.652

Botsman, R., & Rogers, R. (2011). *What's mine is yours: How collaborative consumption is changing the way we live*. Collins.

Braat, L. (1991). The Predictive Meaning of Sustainability Indicators. In O. Kuik & H. Verbruggen (Eds.), *Search of Indicators of Sustainable Development* (pp. 57–70). Kluwer Academic Publishers. doi:10.1007/978-94-011-3246-6_6

Bridges, E. (2018). Executive ethical decisions initiating organizational culture and values. *Journal of Service Theory and Practice, 28*(5), 576–608. doi:10.1108/JSTP-07-2017-0106

Cadez, S., & Guilding, C. (2008). An exploratory investigation of an integrated contingency model of strategic management accounting. *Accounting, Organizations and Society, 33*(7-8), 836–863. doi:10.1016/j.aos.2008.01.003

Cândea, D. (2006). De la dezvoltarea durabilă la întreprinderea sustenabilă. *Întreprinderea sustenabilă, 1*, iii-vi.

Cao, Y., Chen, X., Wu, D. D., & Mao, M. (2011). Early warning of enterprise decline in a life cycle using neural networks and rough set theory. *Expert Systems with Applications, 38*(6), 6424–6429. doi:10.1016/j.eswa.2010.09.138

Curşeu, P. L., Schruijer, S. G. L., & Fodor, O. C. (2016). The influences of knowledge loss and knowledge retention mechanisms on the absorptive capacity and performance of a MIS department. *Management Decision, 54*(7), 1757–1787. doi:10.1108/MD-02-2016-0117

Daily, G. C., & Walker, B. H. (2000). Seeking the great transition. *Nature, 403*(6767), 243–245. doi:10.1038/35002194 PMID:10659827

Davlembayeva, D., Papagiannidis, S., & Alamanos, E. (2019). Mapping the economics, social and technological attributes of the sharing economy. *Information Technology & People*, ITP-02-2018-0085. Advance online publication. doi:10.1108/ITP-02-2018-0085

Day, G. S., & Schoemaker, P. J. H. (2005). Scanning the Periphery. *Harvard Business Review*, *83*(11), 135–150. PMID:16299966

Dekker, M. M., Panja, D., Dijkstra, H. A., & Dekker, S. C. (2019). Predicting transitions across macroscopic states for railway systems. *PLoS One*, *14*(6), e0217710. doi:10.1371/journal.pone.0217710 PMID:31170230

Dikmen, I., Talat Birgonul, M., Ozorhon, B., & Egilmezer Sapci, N. (2010). Using analytic network process to assess business failure risks of construction firms. *Engineering, Construction, and Architectural Management*, *17*(4), 369–386. doi:10.1108/09699981011056574

Dunphy, D., Griffiths, A., & Benn, S. (2003). *Organizational Change for Corporate Sustainability*. Routledge.

Dyllick, T., & Hockerts, K. (2002). Beyond the business case for corporate sustainability. *Business Strategy and the Environment*, *11*(2), 130–141. doi:10.1002/bse.323

Eisenbart, B., Garbuio, M., Mascia, D., & Morandi, F. (2016). Does scheduling matter? When unscheduled decision making results in more effective meetings. *Journal of Strategy and Management*, *9*(1), 15–38. doi:10.1108/JSMA-03-2014-0017

Eisenmann, T., Parker, G., & van Alstyne, M. W. (2006). Strategies for two-sided markets. *Harvard Business Review*, *84*(10), 92–101.

Fan, Y., Xia, M., Zhang, Y., & Chen, Y. (2019). The influence of social embeddedness on organizational legitimacy and the sustainability of the globalization of the sharing economic platform: Evidence from Uber China. *Resources, Conservation and Recycling*, *151*, 104490. doi:10.1016/j.resconrec.2019.104490

Fiksel, J. (2006). Sustainability and resilience: toward a system approach. *Sustainability: Science. Practice & Police*, *2*, 14–21.

Frenken, K., & Schor, J. (2017). Putting the sharing economy into perspective. *Environmental Innovation and Societal Transitions*, *23*, 3–10. doi:10.1016/j.eist.2017.01.003

García Martín, J. C., & Herrero, B. (2018). Boards of directors: Composition and effects on the performance of the firm. *Economic Research-Ekonomska Istraživanja*, *31*(1), 1015–1041. doi:10.1080/1331 677X.2018.1436454

Gatautis, R., Vaiciukynaite, E., & Tarute, A. (2019). Impact of business model innovations on SME's innovativeness and performance. *Baltic Journal of Management*, *14*(4), 521–539. doi:10.1108/BJM-01-2018-0035

Genc, E., Duffie, N., & Reinhart, G. (2014). Event-based supply chain early warning system for an adaptive production control. *Procedia CIRP*, *19*, 39–44. doi:10.1016/j.procir.2014.04.076

Goyal, R., Kakabadse, N., & Kakabadse, A. (2019). Improving corporate governance with functional diversity on FTSE 350 boards: Directors' perspective. *Journal of Capital Markets Studies*, *3*(2), 113–136. doi:10.1108/JCMS-09-2019-0044

Habibi, M. R., Davidson, A., & Laroche, M. (2017). What managers should know about the sharing economy? *Business Horizons*, 60(1), 113–121. doi:10.1016/j.bushor.2016.09.007

Hahn, T., Figge, F., Pinkse, J., & Preuss, L. (2010). Trade-Offs in Corporate Sustainability: You can't Have Your Cake and Eat It. *Business Strategy and the Environment*, 19(4), 217–229. doi:10.1002/bse.674

Hair, J. F. Jr, Black, W. C., & Babin, B. J. (2012). *Multivariate data analysis*. Prentice Hall.

Haji-Kazemi, S., & Andersen, B. (2013). Application of performance measurement as an early warning system. *International Journal of Managing Projects in Business*, 6(4), 714–738. doi:10.1108/IJMPB-04-2012-0015

Hautala, J. (2011). Cognitive proximity in international research groups. *Journal of Knowledge Management*, 15(4), 601–624. doi:10.1108/13673271111151983

Hernandez Ticono, M., Holmes, P., & Wilson, N. (2018). Polytomous response financial distress models: The role of accounting, market and macroeconomic variables. *International Review of Financial Analysis*, 59, 276–289. doi:10.1016/j.irfa.2018.03.017

Hollenbeck, J. R., Beersma, B., & Schouten, M. E. (2012). Beyond team types and taxonomies: A dimensional scaling conceptualization for team description. *Academy of Management Review*, 37(1), 82–106. doi:10.5465/amr.2010.0181

Holliday, C. O. J., Schmidheiny, S., & Watts, S. P. (2002). *Walking the Talk: The Business Case for Sustainable Development*. World Business Council for Sustainable Development.

Hong, J. H., Kim, B. C., & Park, K. S. (2019). Optimal risk management for the sharing economy with stranger danger and service quality. *European Journal of Operational Research*, 279(3), 1024–1035. doi:10.1016/j.ejor.2019.06.020

Hu, X., & Liu, D. (2019). The research into screening crisis early warning indicators of supply chain quality based on fuzzy inference system. *Journal of Intelligent & Fuzzy Systems*, 36(2), 935–942. doi:10.3233/JIFS-169870

Huang, J., Wang, H., & Kochenberger, G. (2017). Distressed Chinese firm prediction with discretized data. *Management Decision*, 55(5), 786–807. doi:10.1108/MD-08-2016-0546

Jennings, P. D., & Zandbergen, P. A. (1995). Ecologically sustainable organizations: An institutional approach. *Academy of Management Review*, 20(4), 1015–1052. doi:10.5465/amr.1995.9512280034

Ketola, T. (2010). Five Leaps to Corporate Sustainability through a Corporate Responsibility Portfolio Matrix. *Corporate Social Responsibility and Environmental Management*, 17(6), 320–336. doi:10.1002/csr.219

Kipkirong Tarus, D., & Aime, F. (2014). Board demographic diversity, firm performance and strategic change: A test of moderation. *Management Research Review*, 37(12), 1110–1136. doi:10.1108/MRR-03-2013-0056

Kira, M., & van Eijnatten, F. M. (2008). Socially Sustainable Work Organizations: A Chaordic System Approach. *Systems Research and Behavioral Science*, 25(6), 743–756. doi:10.1002res.896

Kotler, P., & Caslione, J. A. (2009). *Chaotics: The Business of Managing and Marketing in the Age of Turbulence*. AMACOM.

Laitinen, E. K., & Chong, H. G. (1999). Early warning system for crisis in SMEs: Preliminary evidence from Finland and the UK. *Journal of Small Business and Enterprise Development*, 6(1), 89–102. doi:10.1108/EUM0000000006665

Landrum, N. E., & Ohsowski, B. (2018). Identifying Worldviews on Corporate Sustainability: A Content Analysis of Corporate Sustainability Reports. *Business Strategy and the Environment*, 27(1), 128–151. doi:10.1002/bse.1989

Lee, K.-H., & Kim, D. (2019). A peer-to-peer (P2P) platform business model: The case of Airbnb. *Service Business*, 13(4), 647–669. doi:10.100711628-019-00399-0

Leon, R. D. (2013a). Sustainable knowledge based organization from an international perspective. *International Journal of Management Science and Information Technology*, 10, 166–181.

Leon, R. D. (2013b). A managerial early warning system for the sustainable knowledge based organization. *Ovidius University Annals. Economic Sciences Series*, 13(1), 842–847.

Leon, R. D. (2018a). The sustainable knowledge based organizations – definitions and characteristics. *Environmental Engineering and Management Journal*, 17(6), 1425–1437. doi:10.30638/eemj.2018.141

Leon, R. D. (2018b). A Managerial Early Warning System: From an Abstract to a Subjective Approach. In R. D. Leon (Ed.), *Managerial Strategies for Business Sustainability during Turbulent Times* (pp. 100–121). Information Science Publishing., doi:10.4018/978-1-5225-2716-9.ch006

Leon, R. D., Rodriguez-Rodriguez, R., Gomez-Gasquet, P., & Mula, J. (2017). Social network analysis: A tool for evaluating and predicting future knowledge flows from an insurance organization. *Technological Forecasting and Social Change*, 114, 103–118. doi:10.1016/j.techfore.2016.07.032

Li, C. P., Qin, J. X., Li, J. J., & Hou, Q. (2016). The accident early warning system for iron and steel enterprises based on combination weighting and Grey Prediction Model GM (1,1). *Safety Science*, 89, 19–27. doi:10.1016/j.ssci.2016.05.015

Li, Q., Wei, F., & Zhou, S. (2017). Early warning systems for multi-variety and small batch manufacturing based on active learning. *Journal of Intelligent & Fuzzy Systems*, 33(5), 2945–2952. doi:10.3233/JIFS-169345

Li, S., & Davies, B. J. (2001). GloStra – a hybrid system for developing global strategy and associated Internet strategy. *Industrial Management & Data Systems*, 101(3), 132–140. doi:10.1108/02635570110386643

Li, Y., Ding, R., Cui, L., Lei, Z., & Mou, J. (2019). The impact of sharing economy practices on sustainability performance in the Chinese construction industry. *Resources, Conservation and Recycling*, 150, 104409. doi:10.1016/j.resconrec.2019.104409

Li, Y. Z., Xia, J. B., Li, C. G., & Zheng, M. Y. (2015). Construction of an Early-Warning System for Vegetable Prices Based on Index Contribution Analysis. *Sustainability*, 7(4), 3823–3837. doi:10.3390u7043823

Lieu, P. T., Lin, C. W., & Yu, H. F. (2008). Financial early-warning models on cross-holding groups. *Industrial Management & Data Systems*, *108*(8), 1060–1080. doi:10.1108/02635570810904613

Lozano, R. (2008). Developing collaborative and sustainable organizations. *Journal of Cleaner Production*, *16*(4), 499–509. doi:10.1016/j.jclepro.2007.01.002

Maddox, J. (2000). Positioning the goalposts. *Nature*, *403*(6766), 139–140. doi:10.1038/35003065 PMID:10646578

Mantymaki, M., Baiyere, A., & Islam, A. K. M. N. (2019). Digital platforms and the changing nature of physical work: Insights from ride-hailing. *International Journal of Information Management*, *49*, 452–460. doi:10.1016/j.ijinfomgt.2019.08.007

Mariotto, F. L., Zanni, P. P., & Marcondes de Moraes, G. H. S. (2014). What is the use of a single-case study in management research? *Revista de Administração de Empresas*, *54*(4), 358–369. doi:10.1590/S0034-759020140402

Mishra, J., Chiwenga, K., & Ali, K. (2019). Collaboration as an enabler for circular economy: A case study of a developing country. *Management Decision*, MD-10-2018-1111. Advance online publication. doi:10.1108/MD-10-2018-1111

Mojzisch, A., Grouneva, L., & Schultz-Hardt, S. (2010). Biased evaluation of information during discussion: Disentangling the effects of preference consistency, social validation, and ownership of information. *European Journal of Social Psychology*, *40*(6), 946–956. doi:10.1002/ejsp.660

Ng, E. S., & Burke, R. J. (2010). Predictor of Business Student's Attitudes toward Sustainable Business Practices. *Journal of Business Ethics*, *95*(4), 603–615. doi:10.100710551-010-0442-0

Niemimaa, M., Järveläinen, J., Heikkilä, M., & Heikkilä, J. (2019). Business continuity of business models: Evaluating the resilience of business models for contingencies. *International Journal of Information Management*, *49*, 208–216. doi:10.1016/j.ijinfomgt.2019.04.010

O'Riordan, T. (1976). *Environmentalism*. Pion Limited.

Ogbeide, G., & Harrington, R. (2011). The relationship among participative management style, strategy implementation success, and financial performance in the foodservice industry. *International Journal of Contemporary Hospitality Management*, *23*(6), 719–738. doi:10.1108/09596111111153448

Ohatka, F., & Fukazawa, Y. (2009). Managing risks symptom: A method to identify major risks of serious problem projects in SI environment using cyclic causal model. *Project Management Journal*, *41*(1), 51–60. doi:10.1002/pmj.20144

Olsson, O., Aronsson, H., & Sandberg, E. (2017). Middle management involvement in handling variable patient flows. *Management Research Review*, *40*(9), 1007–1024. doi:10.1108/MRR-05-2016-0114

Parayitam, S., & Papenhausen, C. (2016). Agreement-seeking behavior, trust, and cognitive diversity in strategic decision making teams: Process conflict as a moderator. *Journal of Advances in Management Research*, *13*(3), 292–315. doi:10.1108/JAMR-10-2015-0072

Parker, G., & van Alstyne, M. W. (2005). Two-sided network effects: A theory of information product design. *Management Science*, *51*(10), 1494–1504. doi:10.1287/mnsc.1050.0400

Pearce, D., Markandya, A., & Barbier, E. B. (1989). *Blueprint for a Green Economy*. Earthscan.

Philip, T., & Schwabe, G. (2018). Understanding early warning signs of failure in offshore-outsourced software projects at team level. *Journal of Global Operations and Strategic Sourcing*, *11*(3), 337–356. doi:10.1108/JGOSS-12-2017-0057

Raes, A. M. L., Heijltjes, M. G., Glunk, U., & Roe, R. A. (2011). The interface of the top management team and middle managers: A process model. *Academy of Management Review*, *36*(1), 192–126. doi:10.5465/amr.2009.0088

Rashid, A. (2018). Board independence and firm performance: Evidence from Bangladesh. *Future Business Journal*, *4*(1), 34–49. doi:10.1016/j.fbj.2017.11.003

Richardson, B. J. (2009). Keeping Ethical Investment Ethical: Regulatory Issues for Investing for Sustainability. *Journal of Business Ethics*, *87*(4), 555–572. doi:10.100710551-008-9958-y

Ringland, G. (2010). The role of scenarios in strategic foresight. *Technological Forecasting and Social Change*, *77*(9), 1493–1498. doi:10.1016/j.techfore.2010.06.010

Salzano, E., Garcia Agreda, A., Di Carluccio, A., & Fabbrocino, G. (2009). Risk assessment and early warning systems for industrial facilities in seismic zones. *Reliability Engineering & System Safety*, *94*(10), 1577–1584. doi:10.1016/j.ress.2009.02.023

Saunila, M., Nasiri, M., Ukko, J., & Rantala, T. (2019). Smart technologies and corporate sustainability: The mediation effect of corporate sustainability strategy. *Computers in Industry*, *108*, 178–185. doi:10.1016/j.compind.2019.03.003

Schwartz, M. S., & Carroll, A. B. (2008). Integrating and Unifying Competing and Complementary Frameworks: The Search for a Common core in the Business and Society Field. *Business & Society*, *47*(2), 148–186. doi:10.1177/0007650306297942

Schwarz, J. O. (2005). Pitfalls in implementing a strategic early warning system. *Foresight*, *7*(4), 22–30. doi:10.1108/14636680510611813

Shmueli, G., Sarstedt, M., Hair, J. F., Cheah, J. H., Ting, H., Vaithilingam, S., & Ringle, C. M. (2019). Predictive model assessment in PLS-SEM: Guidelines for using PLSpredict. *European Journal of Marketing*, *53*(11), 2322–2347. doi:10.1108/EJM-02-2019-0189

Sölvell, I. (2018). Managers' silent whisper innovation involvement and role-modeling in service firms. *European Journal of Innovation Management*, *21*(1), 2–19. doi:10.1108/EJIM-02-2017-0020

Sthapit, E. (2019). My bad for wanting to try something unique: Sources of value co-destruction in the Airbnb context. *Current Issues in Tourism*, *22*(20), 2462–2465. doi:10.1080/13683500.2018.1525340

Stofberg, N., & Bridoux, F. (2019). Consumers' choice among peer-to-peer sharing platforms: The other side of the coin. *Psychology and Marketing*, *36*(12), 1176–1195. doi:10.1002/mar.21265

Tan, C., & Dihardjo, H. (2001). A study of using artificial neural networks to develop an early warning predictor for credit union financial distress with comparison to the probit model. *Managerial Finance*, *27*(4), 56–77. doi:10.1108/03074350110767141

Torjman, S. (2000). *The social dimension of sustainable development*. Caledon Institute of Social Policy.

Tsai, B. H. (2013). An Early Warning System of Financial Distress Using Multinomial Logit Models and a Bootstrapping Approach. *Emerging Markets Finance & Trade*, *49*(2), 43–69. doi:10.2753/REE1540-496X4902S203

Tuwey, J., & Tarus, D. (2016). Does CEO power moderate the relationship between board leadership and strategy involvement in private firms? Evidence from Kenya. *Corporate Governance*, *16*(5), 906–922. doi:10.1108/CG-01-2016-0010

Vafaei, N., Ribeiro, R. A., & Camarinha-Matos, L. M. (2019). Fuzzy Early Warning Systems for Condition Based Maintenance. *Computers & Industrial Engineering*, *128*, 736–746. doi:10.1016/j.cie.2018.12.056

Vaida, A., & Cândea, D. (2010). Model pentru internalizarea sustenabilității în organizații. *Întreprinderea sustenabilă, 5*, 1-62.

Van der Walt, N., Ingley, C., Shergill, G., & Townsend, A. (2006). Board configuration: Are diverse boards better boards? *Corporate Governance*, *6*(2), 129–147. doi:10.1108/14720700610655141

Vansteenkiste, M., Niemiec, C. P., & Soenens, B. (2010). The development of the five mini-theories of self-determination theory: an historical overview, emerging trends, and future directions. In T. C. Urdan & S. A. Karabenick (Eds.), *The decade ahead: theoretical perspectives on motivation and achievement* (Vol. 16, pp. 105–165). Emerald Group Publishing., doi:10.1108/S0749-7423(2010)000016A007

Williams, T., Klakegg, O. J., Walker, D. H. T., Andersen, B., & Magnussen, O. M. (2012). Identifying and acting on early warning signs in complex projects. *Project Management Journal*, *43*(2), 37–53. doi:10.1002/pmj.21259

Wong, K. K.-K. (2013). Partial Least Squares Structural Equation Modeling (PLS-SEM) Techniques Using SmartPLS. *Marketing Bulletin*, *24*, 1–32.

Yang, C. (2012). Research on internet public opinion detection system based on domain ontology. In F. L. Wang, J. Lei, Z. Gong, & X. Luo (Eds.), *WISM'12 Proceedings of the 2012 international conference on Web Information Systems and Mining* (pp. 105-110). Berlin: Springer-Verlag. 10.1007/978-3-642-33469-6_15

Yang, Y., Bi, G. B., & Liu, L. D. (2020). Profit allocation in investment-based crowdfunding with investors of dynamic entry times. *European Journal of Operational Research*, *280*(1), 323–337. doi:10.1016/j.ejor.2019.07.016

Yin, R. K. (2014). *Case Study Research Design and Methods*. Sage.

Zheng, G., Zhu, N., Tim, Z., Chen, Y., & Sun, B. (2012). Application of a trapezoidal fuzzy AHP method for work safety evaluation and early warning rating of hot and humid environments. *Safety Science*, *50*(2), 228–239. doi:10.1016/j.ssci.2011.08.042

KEY TERMS AND DEFINITIONS

Artificial Neural Network: An ICT tool that imitates the real environment, providing various estimations and emphasizing how the system could react under certain circumstances.

Inappropriate Experience: The use of standard rules in various situations with the hope that they will always provide the same result. It goes hand in hand with individuals' resistance to change.

Inappropriate Prejudgments: A belief that one's assumption is the most appropriate one and all the other ideas that may contradict it should be ignored. It supports managerial myopia.

Managerial Early Warning System: An organizational tool based on data collection, analysis, and communication that supports the anticipated identification of weak signals and the development of the future business strategy. It involves analyzing the micro- and macro-environment, diagnosing the situation and determining the best way to react to the identified challenges.

Sustainability: The capacity of a system to develop various activities on short and long term without negatively influencing the systems with which it is connected.

Sustainable Knowledge-Based Organization: A complex and adaptive economic entity in which managers are oriented towards achieving multiple objectives (knowledge, economic, environmental and social) by planning on short, medium and long term, adapting to the economic environment challenges in timely manner, and by adopting an ethic attitude towards all the stakeholders.

Sustainable Organization: An ethic and authentic firm that is able to achieve its economic, social and environmental objectives, on short, medium, and long term through the rational use of its resources.

Weak Signal: An element from the micro- or macro-environment that comes out of the blue and forces the organization to react one way or another.

This research was previously published in Strategies for Business Sustainability in a Collaborative Economy; pages 199-221, copyright year 2020 by Business Science Reference (an imprint of IGI Global).

Chapter 60
Wavelet Packet Analysis of ECG Signals to Understand the Effect of Cannabis Abuse on Cardiac Electrophysiology of Indian Women Working in Paddy Fields

Suraj Kumar Nayak
National Institute of Technology Rourkela, India

Soumanti Das
National Institute of Technology Rourkela, India

Ashirbad Pradhan
National Institute of Technology Rourkela, India

Gitika Yadu
National Institute of Technology Rourkela, India

Salman Siddique Khan
National Institute of Technology Rourkela, India

Shankar Jaykishan Patel
Jagnyaseni Hospital, India

Shikshya Nayak
Veer Surendra Sai University of Technology, India

Champak Bhattacharyya
National Institute of Technology Rourkela, India

Kunal Pal
National Institute of Technology Rourkela, India

ABSTRACT

This chapter is aimed at identifying the variation in the cardiac electrophysiology due to the abuse of the cannabis products (bhang) in a non-invasive manner. ECG signals were acquired from 25 Indian women working in the paddy fields. Amongst them, 10 women regularly abused bhang and the rest 15 women never abused bhang. The ECG signals were preprocessed and subjected to wavelet packet decomposition (WPD) up to the level 3 using db04 wavelet. Ninety-six statistical features were extracted from the wavelet packet coefficients and analyzed using linear and non-linear statistical methods. The

DOI: 10.4018/978-1-6684-2408-7.ch060

results suggested a variation in the cardiac electrophysiology due to the abuse of bhang. Artificial neural networks (ANNs), namely, radial basis function (RBF) and multilayer perceptron (MLP) were able to classify the ECG signals with an accuracy of ≥95%. This supported the hypothesis that abuse of bhang may alter the cardiac electrophysiology. The results of the study may be used to increase awareness among people to avoid the abuse of cannabis products.

INTRODUCTION

The abuse of *Cannabis sativa* based products for recreational purposes is common across the globe (Bachs & Mørland, 2001). Although severe restrictions have been imposed by the Government of India (GoI) on many of the cannabis products such as Marijuana, and Hashish, the restrictions on bhang (a recreational product made from the leaves of cannabis plant) is not so strong. It is widely abused by the common people (especially in villages) due to its low cost. Further, it is also used to make drinks by people belonging to Hindu religion during certain carnivals (Nayak et al., 2016). However, some recent studies have reported the onset of cardiovascular diseases in the people abusing cannabis, which may even lead to mortality (Menahem, 2013). Although the effect of cannabis products on human health has been much reviewed, not much work was found to analyze the effect of cannabis on the cardiac electro-physiology (Nayak et al., 2016). The physiology of the heart can be non-invasively analyzed using ECG signal analysis (Opie, 2004). Feature extraction is one of the important steps in the analysis of the ECG signals. The features should be extracted in such a way that they can contain the essential information about the original data in a reduced dimension. Thus, the features can be used, instead of the original signal, for performing desired signal processing operations. In some cases, the features have been reported to provide better interpretation than the original signals (Guyon & Elisseeff, 2006; Li & Zhou, 2016). In recent years, wavelet-based feature extraction methods such as discrete wavelet transform (DWT) and its recent extension WPD are gaining popularity among the researchers for the extraction of features from the ECG signals (Gokhale & Khanduja, 2010; Mahapatra, Mohanta, Mohanty, kumar Nayak, & kumar Behari, 2016; Rai, Trivedi, & Shukla, 2013). Amongst them, WPD has been reported to be superior as it decomposes not only the approximation coefficients (AC) but also the detailed coefficients (DCs) in contrast to the DWT, which decomposes only the ACs. As a result, both the DCs and the ACs can be used to extract features to provide more information (Li & Zhou, 2016). Numerous methods have been proposed for the classification of the ECG signals such as Fuzzy Logic (Kundu, Nasipuri, & Basu, 1998), Support Vector Machine (SVM) (Maldonado, Leija, Vera, & Alvarado, 2016), K-Nearest Neighbor (K-NN) method (Faziludeen & Sankaran, 2016) and Artificial Neural Network (ANN) (Gautam & Giri, 2016). Amongst them, the ANN-based algorithms are gaining popularity in recent years (Roza, de Almeida, & Postolache, 2017). This may be attributed to the fact that ANN provides the facility to improve the classification accuracy easily because of its multi-parametric nature (Alexakis et al., 2003). Taking the motivation from the above-mentioned discussion, we have attempted to investigate the effect of regular bhang abuse on the cardiac electrophysiology of Indian women working in the paddy fields. The ECG signals were acquired from the volunteers, and WPD analysis of the ECG signals was performed to ex-tract features. Statistical significance of the features was analyzed using linear and non-linear statistical methods, and ANN classification was carried out using the statistically significant features.

BACKGROUND

The rhythmic electrical activity within the heart results in the rhythmic contraction of the heart muscles. Initially, the electrical impulse is generated at the sinoatrial node (SA node), located on the right atrium close to the superior vena cava (Boyett, Honjo, & Kodama, 2000). The SA node is 15 mm long, 3 mm wide and 1 mm thick. It is made up of specialized cardiac muscles. A connection exists between the SA node and the atrial muscle fibers allowing the transmission of the electrical impulse (Monfredi, Dobrzynski, Mondal, Boyett, & Morris, 2010). The impulse gets transmitted to the atrioventricular node (AV node) within an interval of 0.03 msec. A bundle of fibers called AV bundle is associated with the AV node. The bundle is capable of providing an unidirectional flow of the impulse i.e. from the atrium to the ventricles due to its property of restricting the backward flow of the impulse (Hall, 2015). The bundle adds a delay of 1.3 msec to the impulse that allows the proper contraction of the atria to finish the flow of blood to the ventricles (Burns, 2013). A specialized cardiac muscle called Purkinje fiber is present between AV node and ventricles, which helps in the instantaneous distribution of the impulse across the endocardial surfaces of the ventricle within a time interval of 0.03 msec (Rentschler et al., 2001). Then it is transmitted to the epicardial surface of the ventricle by the ventricular muscle fiber (Torrent-Guasp et al., 2001). The impulse passing through the heart spreads to the surrounding environment and small amplitude of it reaches the surface of the body. The impulse reaching the skin surface is detected by placing electrodes on the skin, and provides an indication of the cardiac electrophysiology (Barr & Van Oosterom, 2010). A graphical illustration of this cardiac electrophysiology is called the electrocardiogram (ECG) (Harland, Clark, Peters, Everitt, & Stiffell, 2005). A physiologically standard ECG wave is comprised of different types of waves, namely, the P wave, the QRS complex and the T wave (Hurst, 1998). The P wave is defined as the electrical potential resulting from the depolarization of atria. The QRS complex denotes the electrical potential resulting from the depolarization of the ventricles (Dilaveris & Gialafos, 2001). The T wave is caused by the electrical potential resulting from the repolarization of the ventricles (Wellens, Bär, & Lie, 1978). Thus, the P wave and the QRS complex are often called the depolarization waves, whereas the T wave is called the repolarization wave (Opthof et al., 2007). The amplitude of these ECG constituent waves depends on the locations of the electrodes, placed on the skin surface, and their closeness to the heart (Schijvenaars, Kors, van Herpen, Kornreich, & van Bemmel, 1997). The QRS complex amplitude of 3-4 mV has been reported in the cases where one electrode is placed directly over the left ventricle and the other electrode is placed anywhere else on the body, away from the heart. This amplitude is, however, very less as compared to the electrode potential measured directly from the heart membrane, i.e. 110 mV. For electrodes placed on forearms of the two hands or on one forearm and one leg as per the Einthoven's triangle, the QRS complex has been reported to vary from 1 to 1.5 mV (Bacharova, Selvester, Engblom, & Wagner, 2005). For the same arrangement of the electrodes, the amplitude of the P wave ranges between 0.1 and 0.3 mV and the amplitude of the T wave ranges from 0.2 to 0.3 mV. An important parameter of the ECG signal is the PQ interval, which is defined as the time interval between the inception of the P wave and the inception of the Q wave. Physiologically it represents the time gap between the beginning of the atrial contraction and the ventricular contraction, with an average value of 0.16 sec. In case, the Q wave is absent, the time interval between the beginning of the atrial contraction and the ventricular contraction is depicted by the PR interval (Gervais et al., 2009). The ventricles contract for about 0.35 sec, and in a standard ECG signal, it is represented by the time interval between the inception of the Q wave and the completion of the T wave, also called as the QT interval (Okin et al., 2000). ECG signals have been widely explored for the diagnosis of various cardiological diseases (Desai, Martis, Nayak, Sarika, & Seshikala, 2015) as well as for understanding the effect of various stimuli (e.g., music, smoking, and exercise) on the cardiac electrophysiology (Hajizadeh, Abbasi, & Goshvarpour, 2015). Elhaj *et al.* (2016) reported the recognition and classification of five types of beat classes of arrhythmia (as per the recommendation of the Association for Advancement of Medical Instrumentation), namely, non-ectopic beats, supra-ventricular ectopic beats, ventricular ectopic beats, fusion beats, and unclassifiable paced beats using linear and non-linear features of ECG signals (Elhaj, Salim, Harris, Swee, & Ahmed, 2016). The linear features included the outcomes of the principal component analysis of the discrete wavelet transform coefficients, whereas the non-linear features included the higher order statistics and cumulants. The different classes of arrhythmia could be classified with a maximum classification accuracy of 98.91% using a composite method employing both SVM and ANN. Abedi *et al.* (2017) performed ECG signal analysis to understand the effect of a Persian music on the heart of young women. In their study, the ECG signals were acquired from 22 healthy females in resting condition and while listening to music (Abedi, Abbasi, & Goshvarpour, 2017). The ECG signals were processed to extract 20 morphological and DWT-based features. These features were subjected to classification using ANN and probabilistic neural network (PNN) by dividing the whole data into training and testing datasets. The training data set could be classified with the accuracy of 88% and 97% using ANN and PNN, respectively. On the other hand, the testing data set was classified with the accuracy of 84% and 93% using ANN and PNN, respectively. Fujita *et al.* (2017) reported the use of WPD analysis of ECG signals for the diagnosis of coronary artery disease, myocardial infarction, and congestive heart failure. The ECG signals were decomposed into 30 WPD coefficients and 12 nonlinear features were extracted from each coefficient. The KNN classifier was used to provide the classification accuracy of 97.98%, sensitivity of 99.61% and specificity of 94.84% using 8 ReliefF ranked features as the input.

The abuse of cannabis-based products (e.g., Marijuana, and Hashish) for recreational purposes is growing day-by-day (Bachs & Mørland, 2001), although the abuse of most of these products is strictly abandoned by the Government of India. Bhang is a recreational product made from the leaves of cannabis plant. It is widely abused by the people residing in the villages apart from people following Hindu religion. In the last few decades, many researchers have reported the incidence of cardiovascular diseases or even death in people abusing cannabis products (Menahem, 2013; Wolff, Rouyer, & Gény, 2013). However, not much research has been performed on understanding the cardiac physiology in people abusing cannabis regularly (Nayak et al., 2016). Based on the facts mentioned above, the present work aims at identifying the changes in the cardiac electrophysiology due to the cannabis abuse using WPD analysis of the ECG signals.

MAIN FOCUS OF THE CHAPTER

The main focus of this study is to analyze the effect of the abuse of cannabis-based products such as bhang on the cardiac electrophysiology of Indian women in a non-invasive manner using ECG signal analysis. The study was motivated by the fact that most of the Indian women, working in the paddy fields, abuse cannabis. The understanding of the effect of cannabis abuse on the electrical activity of the heart can be used enhance the awareness of these women regarding the negative impact of cannabis products on the cardiac health.

METHODOLOGY

Acquisition of ECG Signals

This study involved ECG signal acquisition from Indian women (volunteers), who have been working in the paddy field for at least last 5 years. 30 volunteers were invited for the study. The details of the study was explained to them, and they were requested to sign an informed consent form if they generated interested to take part in the study. Out of the 30 volunteers, 25 volunteers provided their consent to participate in this study. They belonged to the age group of 20 to 50 years. Amongst the 25 volunteers, 15 volunteers never abused bhang and were categorized under the Category-A. The rest 10 volunteers regularly abused bhang and were put under the Category-B. The ECG signals were acquired from the volunteers for 6 min using ECG clamp electrodes placed in the lead-1 configuration. The ECG signals were amplified using a commercially available ECG amplifier (Vernier EKG, Vernier Software & Technology, USA). The amplified ECG signals were then digitized using a data acquisition device (NI USB 6009, National Instruments, USA) and recorded into a computer using a LabVIEW (V13.0, National instruments, USA) program. The sampling frequency of the data acquisition device was set at 1000 Hz.

Wavelet Packet Analysis

In this study, the 6 min ECG signal was processed using a LabVIEW program to extract a 5 sec portion. This signal was band-limited using a low-pass filter of cut-off frequency 50 Hz and resampled at 360 Hz using a Spline interpolation function prior to WPD (Li & Zhou, 2016). The resampled ECG signals were subjected to WPD up to level 3 with Daubechies (db04) as the mother wavelet. The reason for choosing Daubechies wavelet may be attributed to its similarity with the shape of the QRS complex of the ECG wave (Ray, Nayak, Champaty, Tibarewala, & Pal, 2016). The WPD analysis resulted in the formation of 8 wavelet packet coefficients, representing the frequency sub-bands. Each of these 8 wavelet packet coefficients was used to extract 12 statistical parameters. As a result, 96 statistical parameters were extracted from each ECG signal. The entire wavelet packet analysis was implemented using in-lab designed LabVIEW programs.

Statistical Analysis and ANN Classification

These 96 wavelet-based statistical parameters were subjected to statistical analysis for identification of the important predictors, having significantly different values in Category-A and Category-B. The linear method t-test (p-value $\leq$ 0.05) and the decision tree-based non-linear methods (predictor importance $\geq$0.95), namely, Classification And Regression Tree (CART), Boosted Tree (BT) and Random Forest (RF) were employed for this purpose using Statistica software (trial V13.2, Dell Inc., USA). The statistically significant parameters obtained from the afore-mentioned statistical analysis were used as input for further analysis using ANN. The conventional ANN networks, namely, RBF and MLP were implemented using Statistical Data Miner toolkit to classify the ECG signals into Category-A and Category-B.

RESULTS AND DISCUSSION

The 3 level WPD analysis of each ECG signal resulted in the formation 8 wavelet packet coefficients (Figure 1). These coefficients were named as 000, 001, 010, 011, 100, 101, 110 and 111. The 12 parameters extracted from each wavelet packet coefficient include Arithmetic Mean (AM), Mode (MOD), Median (MED), Summation (SUM), Standard Deviation (SD), Variance, Root Mean Square value (RMS), Kurtosis, Skewness (SKNS), Energy Density (ED), Log Energy (LE), and Shannon Entropy (SE). Thus, the finally extracted 96 parameters were named as P-E, where P stands for the name of the statistical parameter and E represents the name of the wavelet packet coefficient. Out of the statistical parameters, none was found to be statistically significant from the t-test analysis. The t-test is a linear statistical method that can be used to detect the occurrence of any significant variation in the mean values of the parameters of two populations (Ray et al., 2016). CART is a decision tree algorithm mainly used to design models for prediction from a given set of data (Lewis, 2000). In this method, the dataset is broken down into segments, and a prediction model is fitted for each segment. The problems which involve discrete values for the target variable would prefer a classification tree, whereas a regression tree would be useful for the problems involving continuous target variable. The misclassification cost is used to derive the classification error in the classification trees (Lemon, Roy, Clark, Friedmann, & Rakowski, 2003). However, in the case of regression trees, the prediction error is calculated as the square of the difference between predicted and measured values (Harrell Jr, 2015). The CART analysis suggested that Skewness of the 1st wavelet packet coefficient (SKNS000) is an important predictor, having a higher value in Category-B as compared to Category-A (Table 1). Skewness measures the asymmetry of the frequency distribution curve of a variable with respect to its mean. This suggested that the frequency distribution curve of the first wavelet packet coefficient was more deviated from its mean value in Category-B as compared to Category-A. Boosted tree is considered as one of the most robust and efficient data mining tools for making predictions. It is used both for regression and classification problems, depending on whether the target variable is continuous or discrete (Windeatt & Ardeshir, 2002). The idea of boosted trees originated from the application of boosting methods to regression trees (Elith, Leathwick, & Hastie, 2008). This method involves the generation of a sequence of binary trees, and each successive tree is generated based on the prediction residuals of the previous tree. Mode of the 4th wavelet packet coefficient (MOD011) was found to be the only important predictor from BT analysis. RF is also a powerful decision tree algorithm, used for both classification and regression problems. It was first introduced by Breiman (Svetnik et al., 2003). It involves some simple tree predictors (Strobl, Malley, & Tutz, 2009), in which each tree predictor generates an outcome when a group of predictor variables is provided. The group of predictor variables is chosen independently and is responsible for the outcome of the tree predictor. The Median of the 4th wavelet packet coefficient (MED011) was identified as the important predictor from RF analysis. The occurrence of these important predictors suggested that the properties of the ECG signals acquired from the volunteers belonging to Category-A and Category-B varied significantly.

To further ascertain the variation in the characteristics of the ECG signals of the volunteers belonging to Category-A and Category-B, ANN classification was performed. ANN is a non-linear, supervised, computational method inspired by the working of the biological neural networks (Jain, Mao, & Mohiuddin, 1996). It consists of nodes (neurons), which are connected to each other. ANN uses multiple inputs with weights acting upon them, a threshold function and an activation function for finding the output. The weights are calculated during training, thus, generating the model (Agatonovic-Kustrin &

Beresford, 2000). In our study, the important predictors, in various combinations, were used as the input for the widely used neural networks, namely, MLP and RBF. The MLP network is regarded as one of the best-known class of neural network. It is characterized by one or more hidden layer of neurons and does not generate closed class boundaries (Markou & Singh, 2003). On the other hand, the RBF network represents another important class of neural network containing only a single layer of hidden neurons. In a RBF network, the distance between an input vector and prototype vector determines the activation of the hidden unit. The MLP 2-8-2 network was able to classify the important predictors with an overall classification efficiency of 100% when SKNS000 and MED011 were used as the inputs (Table 2). The network used BFGS 50 algorithm for its training and Entropy was used as the error function. The hidden activation function and the output activation function were logistic function and Softmax function, respectively. On the other hand, the RBF 2-20-2 network was able to provide a classification efficiency of 95% with the same variables as the inputs and RBFT as the training algorithm. Gaussian function was used as the hidden activation function. The error function and the output activation function were same as that of the MLP 2-8-2 network. The classification summary of the MLP 2-8-2 and the RBF 2-20-2 networks has been tabulated in Table 3 and 4.

Figure 1. WPD of an ECG signal into level-3 using db04 wavelet

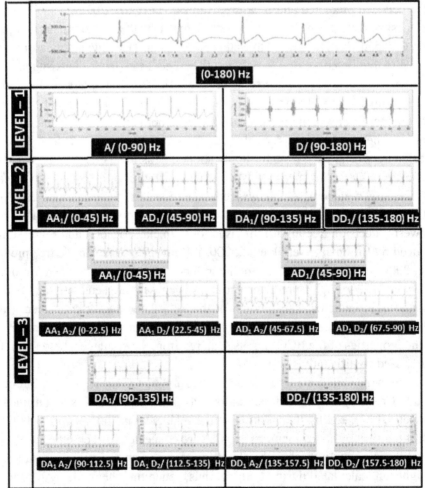

The Association for the Advancement of Medical Instrumentation (AAMI) recommends the evaluation of the performance of the neural networks using four benchmark statistical indices, i.e., sensitivity (SE), positive predictivity (+P), false positive rate (FPR) and accuracy (ACC) (Li & Zhou, 2016). These performance indices can be computed from the analysis of the true positive (TP), false negative (FN), true negative (TN) and false positive (FP) results of the test as given Equation 1-4 (Li & Zhou, 2016). TP indicates the number of cases of a particular class correctly classified, whereas, FN signifies the number of cases of a particular class incorrectly classified, respectively. TN is used to identify the number of cases, which do not belong to a particular class and are classified as not belonging to the considered class and FP represents the number of the cases incorrectly classified as belonging to a particular class, which in actuality do not belong that class (Luz, Nunes, De Albuquerque, Papa, & Menotti, 2013). The values of SE, +P, FPR and ACC were calculated for both the MLP 2-8-2 and RBF 2-20-2 networks and have been tabulated in Table 5. In summary, both the MLP and RBF ANN networks were able to classify the important ECG predictors with an accuracy $\geq 95\%$. This, in turn, supported the inference drawn from the statistical analysis of the wavelet packet based ECG parameters that significant variation has occurred in the ECG signals (i.e., cardiac electrophysiology) due to the abuse of bhang.

$$SE = \frac{TP}{TP + FN} \times 100\ \% \tag{1}$$

$$+P = \frac{TP}{TP + FP} \times 100\ \% \tag{2}$$

$$FPR = \frac{FP}{TN + FP} \times 100\ \% \tag{3}$$

$$ACC = \frac{TP + TN}{TP + TN + FP + FN} \times 100\ \% \tag{4}$$

Table 1. Important predictors obtained from statistical analysis of the wavelet packet coefficient parameters

Methods	Features	Mean ± SD		Predictor Importance
		Category-A	Category-B	
CART	SKNS000	1.862 ± 0.715	2.184 ± 0.568	1.000
BT	MOD011	0.000 ± 0.001	-0.0003 ± 0.002	1.000
RF	MED011	0.000 ± 0.0003	-0.0001 ± 0.0003	1.000

Table 2. Architecture details of MLP 2-8-2 and RBF 2-20-2 networks

Networks	Features Used	Classification Efficiency (%)	Training Performance (%)	Testing Performance (%)	Algorithm	Error Function	Hidden Activation Function	Output Activation Function
MLP 2-8-2	SKNS000, MED011	100	100	100	BFGS 50	Entropy	Logistic	Softmax
RBF 2-20-2	SKNS000, MED011	95	100	80	RBFT	Entropy	Gaussian	Softmax

Table 3. Classification summary of MLP 2-8-2 network

	Category-A	Category-B	Overall
Total	15.000	10.000	25.000
Correct	15.000	10.000	25.000
Incorrect	0.000	0.000	0.000
Correct (%)	100.000	100.000	100.000
Incorrect (%)	0.000	0.000	0.000

Table 4. Classification summary of RBF 2-20-2 network

	Category-A	Category-B	Overall
Total	15.000	10.000	25.000
Correct	15.000	9.000	24.000
Incorrect	0.0000	1.000	1.000
Correct (%)	100.0000	90.000	95.000
Incorrect (%)	0.000	10.000	5.000

Table 5. Performance evaluation of the RBF AND MLP networks

Networks Used	Sensitivity (SE)	Positive Predictivity (+P)	False Positive Rate (FPR)	Accuracy (ACC)
MLP 5-8-2	100%	100%	0%	100%
RBF 5-7-2	95%	95%	5%	95%

FUTURE RESEARCH DIRECTIONS

The present research was devoted to the detection of the alteration in the cardiac electrophysiology in Indian women due to cannabis abuse using WPD-based analysis of ECG signals. Future studies may be performed using other ECG signal analysis techniques (e.g., empirical mode decomposition (EMD), recurrence quantification analysis (RQA), and autoregression moving average (ARMA) modeling) to identify the most suitable method. The RR intervals can be extracted from the ECG signals to perform heart rate variability (HRV) analysis, which can divulge information about the autonomic nervous system in a non-invasive manner.

CONCLUSION

ECG signals were acquired for 6 min from 25 female volunteers belonging to Category-A (volunteers not abusing bhang) and Category-B (volunteers abusing bhang). 5 sec portion of the ECG signals were extracted and preprocessed before subjecting to WPD analysis. WPD of the ECG signals was performed up to level 3 using db04 wavelet, resulting in the formation of 8 wavelet packet coefficients from each ECG signal. A total of 96 statistical parameters were computed from these 8 wavelet packet coefficients.

Linear and non-linear statistical methods indicated 3 parameters (i.e., SKNS000, MOD011, and MED011) as statistically important. These parameters suggested a variation in the cardiac electrophysiology due to the abuse of bhang. However, ANN classification was performed to further ascertain the variation. Both MLP and RBF ANN networks were able to provide a classification accuracy of ≥95%. This confirmed the variation the cardiac electrophysiology because of bhang abuse. An in-depth analysis can be performed in future to identify the exact changes in the cardiac electrophysiology.

REFERENCES

Abedi, B., Abbasi, A., & Goshvarpour, A. (2017). Investigating the effect of traditional Persian music on ECG signals in young women using wavelet transform and neural networks. *Anatolian Journal of Cardiology. Anadolu Kardiyoloji Dergisi, 17*(5).

Agatonovic-Kustrin, S., & Beresford, R. (2000). Basic concepts of artificial neural network (ANN) modeling and its application in pharmaceutical research. *Journal of Pharmaceutical and Biomedical Analysis, 22*(5), 717–727. doi:10.1016/S0731-7085(99)00272-1 PMID:10815714

Alexakis, C., Nyongesa, H., Saatchi, R., Harris, N., Davies, C., & Emery, C. (2003). *Feature extraction and classification of electrocardiogram (ECG) signals related to hypoglycaemia.* Paper presented at the Computers in Cardiology.

Bacharova, L., Selvester, R. H., Engblom, H., & Wagner, G. S. (2005). Where is the central terminal located?: In search of understanding the use of the Wilson central terminal for production of 9 of the standard 12 electrocardiogram leads. *Journal of Electrocardiology, 38*(2), 119–127. doi:10.1016/j. jelectrocard.2005.01.002 PMID:15892021

Bachs, L., & Mørland, H. (2001). Acute cardiovascular fatalities following cannabis use. *Forensic Science International, 124*(2), 200–203. doi:10.1016/S0379-0738(01)00609-0 PMID:11792512

Barr, R. C., & Van Oosterom, A. (2010). Genesis of the electrocardiogram. In *Comprehensive electrocardiology* (pp. 167–190). Springer. doi:10.1007/978-1-84882-046-3_5

Boyett, M. R., Honjo, H., & Kodama, I. (2000). The sinoatrial node, a heterogeneous pacemaker structure. *Cardiovascular Research, 47*(4), 658–687. doi:10.1016/S0008-6363(00)00135-8 PMID:10974216

Burns, N. (2013). Cardiovascular Physiology. School of Medicine, Trinity College.

Camm, A. J., Malik, M., Bigger, J., Breithardt, G., Cerutti, S., & Cohen, R. J. (1996). Heart rate variability: Standards of measurement, physiological interpretation and clinical use. Task Force of the European Society of Cardiology and the North American Society of Pacing and Electrophysiology. *Circulation, 93*(5), 1043–1065. doi:10.1161/01.CIR.93.5.1043 PMID:8598068

Desai, U., Martis, R. J., Nayak, C. G., Sarika, K., & Seshikala, G. (2015). *Machine intelligent diagnosis of ECG for arrhythmia classification using DWT, ICA and SVM techniques.* Paper presented at the India Conference (INDICON), 2015 Annual IEEE. 10.1109/INDICON.2015.7443220

Dilaveris, P. E., & Gialafos, J. E. (2001). P-wave dispersion: A novel predictor of paroxysmal atrial fibrillation. *Annals of Noninvasive Electrocardiology*, 6(2), 159–165. doi:10.1111/j.1542-474X.2001. tb00101.x PMID:11333174

Elhaj, F. A., Salim, N., Harris, A. R., Swee, T. T., & Ahmed, T. (2016). Arrhythmia recognition and classification using combined linear and nonlinear features of ECG signals. *Computer Methods and Programs in Biomedicine*, 127, 52–63. doi:10.1016/j.cmpb.2015.12.024 PMID:27000289

Elith, J., Leathwick, J. R., & Hastie, T. (2008). A working guide to boosted regression trees. *Journal of Animal Ecology*, 77(4), 802–813. doi:10.1111/j.1365-2656.2008.01390.x PMID:18397250

Faziludeen, S., & Sankaran, P. (2016). ECG Beat Classification Using Evidential K-Nearest Neighbours. *Procedia Computer Science*, 89, 499–505. doi:10.1016/j.procs.2016.06.106

Gautam, M. K., & Giri, V. K. (2016). An Approach of Neural Network For Electrocardiogram Classification. *APTIKOM Journal on Computer Science and Information Technologies*, 1(3), 115–123.

Gervais, R., Leclercq, C., Shankar, A., Jacobs, S., Eiskjaer, H., Johannessen, A., ... Daubert, C. (2009). Surface electrocardiogram to predict outcome in candidates for cardiac resynchronization therapy: A sub-analysis of the CARE-HF trial. *European Journal of Heart Failure*, 11(7), 699–705. doi:10.1093/eurjhf/hfp074 PMID:19505883

Gokhale, M., & Khanduja, D. K. (2010). Time domain signal analysis using wavelet packet decomposition approach. *International Journal of Communications. Network and System Sciences*, 3(03), 321–329. doi:10.4236/ijcns.2010.33041

Guyon, I., & Elisseeff, A. (2006). An introduction to feature extraction. *Feature Extraction*, 1-25.

Hajizadeh, S., Abbasi, A., & Goshvarpour, A. (2015). *Intelligent classification of ECG signals to distinguish between pre and on-music states.* Paper presented at the Information and Knowledge Technology (IKT), 2015 7th Conference on. 10.1109/IKT.2015.7288790

Hall, J. E. (2015). *Guyton and Hall Textbook of Medical Physiology E-Book.* Elsevier Health Sciences.

Harland, C., Clark, T., Peters, N., Everitt, M. J., & Stiffell, P. (2005). A compact electric potential sensor array for the acquisition and reconstruction of the 7-lead electrocardiogram without electrical charge contact with the skin. *Physiological Measurement*, 26(6), 939–950. doi:10.1088/0967-3334/26/6/005 PMID:16311443

Harrell, F. E. Jr. (2015). *Regression modeling strategies: with applications to linear models, logistic and ordinal regression, and survival analysis.* Springer. doi:10.1007/978-3-319-19425-7

Hurst, J. W. (1998). Naming of the waves in the ECG, with a brief account of their genesis. *Circulation*, 98(18), 1937–1942. doi:10.1161/01.CIR.98.18.1937 PMID:9799216

Jain, A. K., Mao, J., & Mohiuddin, K. M. (1996). Artificial neural networks: A tutorial. *Computer*, 29(3), 31–44. doi:10.1109/2.485891

Kundu, M., Nasipuri, M., & Basu, D. K. (1998). A knowledge-based approach to ECG interpretation using fuzzy logic. *IEEE Transactions on Systems, Man, and Cybernetics. Part B, Cybernetics*, *28*(2), 237–243. doi:10.1109/3477.662764 PMID:18255941

Lemon, S. C., Roy, J., Clark, M. A., Friedmann, P. D., & Rakowski, W. (2003). Classification and regression tree analysis in public health: Methodological review and comparison with logistic regression. *Annals of Behavioral Medicine*, *26*(3), 172–181. doi:10.1207/S15324796ABM2603_02 PMID:14644693

Lewis, R. J. (2000). *An Introduction to Classification and Regression Tree (CART) Analysis*. Paper presented at the Annual Meeting of the Society of Academic Emergency Medicine in.

Li, T., & Zhou, M. (2016). ECG classification using wavelet packet entropy and random forests. *Entropy (Basel, Switzerland)*, *18*(8), 285. doi:10.3390/e18080285

Luz, E. J. D. S., Nunes, T. M., De Albuquerque, V. H. C., Papa, J. P., & Menotti, D. (2013). ECG arrhythmia classification based on optimum-path forest. *Expert Systems with Applications*, *40*(9), 3561–3573. doi:10.1016/j.eswa.2012.12.063

Mahapatra, S., Mohanta, D., Mohanty, P., Nayak, S., & Behari, P. (2016). A Neuro-fuzzy Based Model for Analysis of an ECG Signal Using Wavelet Packet Tree. *Procedia Computer Science*, *92*, 175–180. doi:10.1016/j.procs.2016.07.343

Maldonado, H., Leija, L., Vera, A., & Alvarado, C. (2016). *Post myocardial infarct detection with support vector machine and ECG intervals ratios JTp/JT, Tpe/JTp and Tpe/JT*. Paper presented at the Medical Engineering Physics Exchanges/Pan American Health Care Exchanges (GMEPE/PAHCE), 2016 Global.

Markou, M., & Singh, S. (2003). Novelty detection: a review—part 2: neural network based approaches. *Signal Processing*, *83*(12), 2499–2521. doi:10.1016/j.sigpro.2003.07.019

Menahem, S. (2013). Cardiac asystole following cannabis (marijuana) usage–Additional mechanism for sudden death? *Forensic Science International*, *233*(1), e3–e5. doi:10.1016/j.forsciint.2013.10.007 PMID:24200372

Monfredi, O., Dobrzynski, H., Mondal, T., Boyett, M. R., & Morris, G. M. (2010). The anatomy and physiology of the sinoatrial node—a contemporary review. *Pacing and Clinical Electrophysiology*, *33*(11), 1392–1406. doi:10.1111/j.1540-8159.2010.02838.x PMID:20946278

Nayak, S. K., Suman, S., Nayak, B. M., Banerjee, I., Pal, K., & Champaty, B. (2016). *Effect of Cannabis consumption on ANS and conduction pathway of heart of Indian paddy field workers*. Paper presented at the India Conference (INDICON), 2016 IEEE Annual. 10.1109/INDICON.2016.7839018

Okin, P. M., Devereux, R. B., Howard, B. V., Fabsitz, R. R., Lee, E. T., & Welty, T. K. (2000). Assessment of QT interval and QT dispersion for prediction of all-cause and cardiovascular mortality in American Indians. *Circulation*, *101*(1), 61–66. doi:10.1161/01.CIR.101.1.61 PMID:10618305

Opie, L. H. (2004). *Heart physiology: from cell to circulation*. Lippincott Williams & Wilkins.

Opthof, T., Coronel, R., Wilms-Schopman, F. J., Plotnikov, A. N., Shlapakova, I. N., Danilo, P. Jr, ... Janse, M. J. (2007). Dispersion of repolarization in canine ventricle and the electrocardiographic T wave: T pe interval does not reflect transmural dispersion. *Heart Rhythm, 4*(3), 341–348. doi:10.1016/j.hrthm.2006.11.022 PMID:17341400

Pal, K., Goel, R., Champaty, B., Samantray, S., & Tibarewala, D. (2013). Heart rate variability and wavelet-based studies on ECG signals from smokers and non-smokers. *Journal of The Institution of Engineers (India): Series B, 94*(4), 275-283.

Rai, H. M., Trivedi, A., & Shukla, S. (2013). ECG signal processing for abnormalities detection using multi-resolution wavelet transform and Artificial Neural Network classifier. *Measurement, 46*(9), 3238–3246. doi:10.1016/j.measurement.2013.05.021

Ray, A., Nayak, S. K., Champaty, B., Tibarewala, D., & Pal, K. (2016). Non-Linear Analysis of Heart Rate Variability and ECG Signal Features of Swimmers from NIT-Rourkela: A Case Study. *Computational Tools and Techniques for Biomedical Signal Processing*, 56.

Rentschler, S., Vaidya, D. M., Tamaddon, H., Degenhardt, K., Sassoon, D., & Morley, G. E. (2001). Visualization and functional characterization of the developing murine cardiac conduction system. *Development, 128*(10), 1785–1792. PMID:11311159

Roza, V. C. C., de Almeida, A. M., & Postolache, O. A. (2017). *Design of an artificial neural network and feature extraction to identify arrhythmias from ECG.* Paper presented at the Medical Measurements and Applications (MeMeA), 2017 IEEE International Symposium on.

Schijvenaars, B. J., Kors, J. A., van Herpen, G., Kornreich, F., & van Bemmel, J. H. (1997). Effect of electrode positioning on ECG interpretation by computer. *Journal of Electrocardiology, 30*(3), 247–256. doi:10.1016/S0022-0736(97)80010-6 PMID:9261733

Strobl, C., Malley, J., & Tutz, G. (2009). An introduction to recursive partitioning: Rationale, application, and characteristics of classification and regression trees, bagging, and random forests. *Psychological Methods, 14*(4), 323–348. doi:10.1037/a0016973 PMID:19968396

Svetnik, V., Liaw, A., Tong, C., Culberson, J. C., Sheridan, R. P., & Feuston, B. P. (2003). Random forest: A classification and regression tool for compound classification and QSAR modeling. *Journal of Chemical Information and Computer Sciences, 43*(6), 1947–1958. doi:10.1021/ci034160g PMID:14632445

Torrent-Guasp, F., Ballester, M., Buckberg, G. D., Carreras, F., Flotats, A., Carrió, I., ... Narula, J. (2001). Spatial orientation of the ventricular muscle band: Physiologic contribution and surgical implications. *The Journal of Thoracic and Cardiovascular Surgery, 122*(2), 389–392. doi:10.1067/mtc.2001.113745 PMID:11479518

Wellens, H. J., Bär, F. W., & Lie, K. (1978). The value of the electrocardiogram in the differential diagnosis of a tachycardia with a widened QRS complex. *The American Journal of Medicine, 64*(1), 27–33. doi:10.1016/0002-9343(78)90176-6 PMID:623134

Windeatt, T., & Ardeshir, G. (2002). Boosted tree ensembles for solving multiclass problems. *Multiple Classifier Systems*, 179-182.

Wolff, V., Rouyer, O., & Gény, B. (2013). Response to letter regarding article,"cannabis-related stroke: Myth or reality? *Stroke*, *44*(5), e57–e57. doi:10.1161/STROKEAHA.113.001094 PMID:23741740

ADDITIONAL READING

Abo-Zahhad, M., Ahmed, S. M., & Abbas, S. N. (2015). *A new biometric authentication system using heart sounds based on wavelet packet features*. Paper presented at the Electronics, Circuits, and Systems (ICECS), 2015 IEEE International Conference on. 10.1109/ICECS.2015.7440238

Acharya, U. R., Sudarshan, V. K., Rong, S. Q., Tan, Z., Lim, C. M., Koh, J. E., ... Bhandary, S. V. (2017). Automated detection of premature delivery using empirical mode and wavelet packet decomposition techniques with uterine electromyogram signals. *Computers in Biology and Medicine*, *85*, 33–42. doi:10.1016/j.compbiomed.2017.04.013 PMID:28433870

Ai, D., Yang, J., Wang, Z., Fan, J., Ai, C., & Wang, Y. (2015). Fast multi-scale feature fusion for ECG heartbeat classification. *EURASIP Journal on Advances in Signal Processing*, *2015*(1), 46. doi:10.118613634-015-0231-0

Akar, S. A., Kara, S., & Bilgiç, V. (2016). Investigation of heart rate variability in major depression patients using wavelet packet transform. *Psychiatry Research*, *238*, 326–332. doi:10.1016/j.psychres.2016.02.058 PMID:27086252

Alickovic, E., Kevric, J., & Subasi, A. (2018). Performance evaluation of empirical mode decomposition, discrete wavelet transform, and wavelet packed decomposition for automated epileptic seizure detection and prediction. *Biomedical Signal Processing and Control*, *39*, 94–102. doi:10.1016/j.bspc.2017.07.022

Arvanaghi, R., Daneshvar, S., Seyedarabi, H., & Goshvarpour, A. (2017). Fusion of ECG and ABP signals based on wavelet transform for cardiac arrhythmias classification. *Computer Methods and Programs in Biomedicine*, *151*, 71–78. doi:10.1016/j.cmpb.2017.08.013 PMID:28947007

Bensafia, K., Mansour, A., & Haddab, S. (2017). Blind Source Subspace Separation and Classification of ECG Signals. 5th Internationale Confernce en Automatique & Traitement de Signal, Sousse, Tunisia.

Chandra, S., & Sharma, A. (2017). *A computationally efficient approach for ECG signal denoising and data compression*. Paper presented at the Control and System Graduate Research Colloquium (ICSGRC), 2017 IEEE 8th. 10.1109/ICSGRC.2017.8070561

Desai, U., Martis, R. J., Nayak, C. G., Sarika, K., & Seshikala, G. (2015). *Machine intelligent diagnosis of ECG for arrhythmia classification using DWT, ICA and SVM techniques*. Paper presented at the India Conference (INDICON), 2015 Annual IEEE. 10.1109/INDICON.2015.7443220

Deshmukh, S. V., & Dehzangi, O. (2017). *ECG-Based Driver Distraction Identification Using Wavelet Packet Transform and Discriminative Kernel-Based Features*. Paper presented at the Smart Computing (SMARTCOMP), 2017 IEEE International Conference on. 10.1109/SMARTCOMP.2017.7947003

Ergin, S., Uysal, A. K., Gunal, E. S., Gunal, S., & Gulmezoglu, M. B. (2014). *ECG based biometric authentication using ensemble of features.* Paper presented at the Information Systems and Technologies (CISTI), 2014 9th Iberian Conference on. 10.1109/CISTI.2014.6877089

Fraiwan, L. (2016). Predicting Preterm Delivery Based on Wavelet Packet Analysis of a Single Electrohysterography Channel. *Journal of Medical Imaging and Health Informatics, 6*(6), 1419–1425. doi:10.1166/jmihi.2016.1821

Gayani, K., Jacob, V., & Nair, K. N. (2014). Automation of ECG heart beat detection using Morphological filtering and Daubechies wavelet transform. *IOSR Journal of Engineering, 4*, 53–58. doi:10.9790/3021-041215358

Hassan, Z., Gilani, S. O., & Jamil, M. (2016). Improvement in ECG based biometric systems using Wavelet Packet Decomposition (WPD) algorithm. *Indian Journal of Science and Technology, 9*(30). doi:10.17485/ijst/2016/v9i30/97958

He, H., Tan, Y., & Liu, X. (2013). *Feature extraction of ECG signals in meridian systems using wavelet packet transform and clustering algorithms.* Paper presented at the Networking, Sensing and Control (ICNSC), 2013 10th IEEE International Conference on.

Jegan, R., Anusuya, K., & George, E. M. (2015). Real-time ECG peak detection for heart rate measurement using wavelet packet transform. *International Journal of Biomedical Engineering and Technology, 19*(3), 244–254. doi:10.1504/IJBET.2015.072994

Kearley, K., Selwood, M., Van den Bruel, A., Thompson, M., Mant, D., Hobbs, F. R., ... Heneghan, C. (2014). Triage tests for identifying atrial fibrillation in primary care: A diagnostic accuracy study comparing single-lead ECG and modified BP monitors. *BMJ Open, 4*(5), e004565. doi:10.1136/bmjopen-2013-004565 PMID:24793250

Li, H., Feng, X., Cao, L., Li, E., Liang, H., & Chen, X. (2016). A new ECG signal classification based on WPD and ApEn feature extraction. *Circuits, Systems, and Signal Processing, 35*(1), 339–352. doi:10.100700034-015-0068-7

Li, H., Yuan, D., Ma, X., Cui, D., & Cao, L. (2017). Genetic algorithm for the optimization of features and neural networks in ECG signals classification. *Scientific Reports, 7*, 41011. doi:10.1038rep41011 PMID:28139677

Lin, C.-Y., Chang, S.-L., Lin, Y.-J., Lo, L.-W., Chung, F.-P., Chen, Y.-Y., ... Chen, S.-A. (2015). Long-term outcome of multiform premature ventricular complexes in structurally normal heart. *International Journal of Cardiology, 180*, 80–85. doi:10.1016/j.ijcard.2014.11.110 PMID:25438221

Lowres, N., Freedman, S. B., Gallagher, R., Kirkness, A., Marshman, D., Orchard, J., & Neubeck, L. (2015). Identifying postoperative atrial fibrillation in cardiac surgical patients posthospital discharge, using iPhone ECG: A study protocol. *BMJ Open, 5*(1), e006849. doi:10.1136/bmjopen-2014-006849 PMID:25586373

Maharaj, E. A., & Alonso, A. M. (2014). Discriminant analysis of multivariate time series: Application to diagnosis based on ECG signals. *Computational Statistics & Data Analysis, 70*, 67–87. doi:10.1016/j.csda.2013.09.006

Raj, A. A. S., Dheetsith, N., Nair, S. S., & Ghosh, D. (2014). *Auto analysis of ECG signals using artificial neural network.* Paper presented at the Science Engineering and Management Research (ICSEMR), 2014 International Conference on. 10.1109/ICSEMR.2014.7043597

Raja, C., & Gangatharan, N. (2015). Appropriate sub-band selection in wavelet packet decomposition for automated glaucoma diagnoses. *Int. J. Autom. Comput..*

Safara, F., Doraisamy, S., Azman, A., Jantan, A., & Ramaiah, A. R. A. (2013). Multi-level basis selection of wavelet packet decomposition tree for heart sound classification. *Computers in Biology and Medicine*, *43*(10), 1407–1414. doi:10.1016/j.compbiomed.2013.06.016 PMID:24034732

Shao, R., Hu, W., Wang, Y., & Qi, X. (2014). The fault feature extraction and classification of gear using principal component analysis and kernel principal component analysis based on the wavelet packet transform. *Measurement*, *54*, 118–132. doi:10.1016/j.measurement.2014.04.016

Singh, O., & Sunkaria, R. K. (2015). *The utility of wavelet packet transform in QRS complex detection-a comparative study of different mother wavelets.* Paper presented at the Computing for Sustainable Global Development (INDIACom), 2015 2nd International Conference on.

Singh, T., & Misal, A. (2015). Detection of Cardiac Abnormality from PCG Signal Using Wavelet Packet. *i-Manager's Journal on Digital Signal Processing, 3*(1), 12.

Wang, X., Gui, Q., Liu, B., Jin, Z., & Chen, Y. (2014). Enabling smart personalized healthcare: A hybrid mobile-cloud approach for ECG telemonitoring. *IEEE Journal of Biomedical and Health Informatics*, *18*(3), 739–745. doi:10.1109/JBHI.2013.2286157 PMID:24144678

Wess, M., Manoj, P. S., & Jantsch, A. (2017). *Neural network based ECG anomaly detection on FPGA and trade-off analysis.* Paper presented at the Circuits and Systems (ISCAS), 2017 IEEE International Symposium on. 10.1109/ISCAS.2017.8050805

Yan, J., & Lu, L. (2014). Improved Hilbert–Huang transform based weak signal detection methodology and its application on incipient fault diagnosis and ECG signal analysis. *Signal Processing*, *98*, 74–87. doi:10.1016/j.sigpro.2013.11.012

KEY TERMS AND DEFINITIONS

Artificial Neural Network (ANN): ANN is an electronic computational model that tries to mimic the functionalities of the biological neural networks.

Boosted Tree (BT): BT is one of the most robust and efficient decision tree method that uses a sequence of binary trees in which every new tree is generated based on the prediction residuals of the previous tree.

*Cannabis Sativa***:** *Cannabis sativa* is a flowering plant of the Cannabaceae family. It is used to develop a diverse group of products including industrial fiber, medicine, oil and recreational products.

Classification and Regression Tree (CART): CART is a conventional decision tree method used to design models for prediction from a given set of data.

Random Forest (RF): RF is a powerful ensemble learning method that can be used for both classification and regression problems.

Sinoatrial (SA) Node: SA node is a part of the heart, located in the upper side of the right atrium that is responsible for the generation of electrical impulse within it.

Wavelet Packet Decomposition (WPD): WPD is a special case of DWT that decomposes both the approximation coefficients and the detailed coefficients at each level of decomposition.

This research was previously published in Design and Development of Affordable Healthcare Technologies; pages 257-273, copyright year 2018 by Medical Information Science Reference (an imprint of IGI Global).

Chapter 61
Classifying Diabetes Disease Using Feedforward MLP Neural Networks

Ahmad Al-Khasawneh
Hashemite University, Jordan

Haneen Hijazi
Hashemite University, Jordan

ABSTRACT

Diagnosing chronic diseases is about making accurate and quick decisions based on contradictory information and constantly evolving knowledge. Hence, there has been a persistent need to help health practitioners in making correct decisions. Diabetes is a common chronic disease. It is a global health-care threat and the eighth leading cause of death in the world. Modern artificial intelligence techniques are being used in diagnosing chronic diseases including artificial neural networks. In this chapter, a feedforward multilayer-perceptron neural network has been implemented to help health practitioners in classifying diabetes. Through the work, an algorithm was proposed in purpose of determining the number of hidden layers and neurons in a MLP. Based on the algorithm, two topologies have been introduced. Both topologies exhibited good classification accuracies with a slightly higher accuracy for the MLP with only one hidden layer. The data set was obtained from King Abdullah University Hospital in Jordan.

INTRODUCTION

Healthcare is a major concern of communities and individuals. It significantly contributes in countries' economies. Information technology has spread widely in health care industry in the last few decades. Healthcare Information Technology or e-Health is the application of information processing involving both computer hardware and software that deals with the storage, retrieval, sharing, and use of health care information, data, and knowledge for communication and decision making (Brailer & Thompson, 2004). Despite the dramatic growth in the last few decades, the continuous research and the nonstopping

DOI: 10.4018/978-1-6684-2408-7.ch061

achievements in the health care information technology industry proof that this field still in its infancy and many other several research could be conducted. Health-care Information Technology systems employ several different methods. These systems can be electronic medical records (EMRS), electronic health records (EHRS), personal health record (PHR), payer-based health record, computerized physician order entry (CPOE), clinical decision support, and E-prescribing (Bray, 2010). Nowadays, Clinical Decision Support Systems (CDSSs) are mostly in demand by healthcare practitioners as they usually perform intelligently and helps in early detection of chronic diseases (Sharma & Virmani, 2017).

The medical domain is characterized by contradictory information and constantly evolving knowledge. Hence, it was of utmost important to help diagnosticians to make correct decisions (El-Sappagh & Elmogy, 2016). Generally, Decision Support Systems (DSS) enable decision makers to utilize knowledge and data to support and meet their demands for decision-making (El-Gayar, Deokar, & Tao, 2011).

CDSSs are information systems that help healthcare practitioners in making medical deci-sions about patients using relative patient and clinical data (Dinevski, Bele, Šarenac, Rajkovič, Šušteršic, 2011). The use of such systems helps in reducing medical errors, minimizing treatment cost, and improving patient's health (Golemati, Mougiakakou, Stoitsis, Valavanis, Nikita, 2005). In 2005, Garg et al. Stated that CDSSs improved practitioners' performance in 64% of the studies, and patients' outcomes in 13% of them (Garg, et al., 2005). In CDSSs, Artificial intelligence plays a vital role in the applied techniques. These techniques falls under one of two categories; knowledge-based and non-knowledge based systems (Abbasi & Kashiyarndi, 2006). Knowledge-based systems contain knowledge about very specific tasks and facts, and consist of knowledge base, infer-ence engine, and a mechanism to communicate (Abbasi & Kashiyarndi, 2006). Rule-based expert systems and Bayesian Network are examples on the knowledge-based systems. Non-knowledge-based systems employ Machine learning techniques instead, like neural Networks and genetic Algorithms. Unfortunately, there is no mutual model that can be adjusted for the diagnosis of all kinds of diseases (Mokeddem, Atmani, & Mokaddem, 2014). In health care systems, Machine learning used to learn from description of previously treated patients and help practitioners to diagnose objectively and reliably.

In sum, various intelligent techniques could be used to implement CDSS, which one to select depends on the problem domain, the probable solution, the amount of data available, the cost of the system, the required efficiency, researcher choice and purpose, and many other parameters (Abbasi & Kashiyarndi, 2006). In medicine, CDSS can help in monitoring, alerting, interpreting, assisting, diagnosing, and managing decision support (Pestotnik, 2005).

Neural networks are one of the best solutions in complex, multiple variable systems wherein applying ordinary rule-based programming and following an algorithmic solution is an improbable task. Moreover, The ANNs are suitable where traditional classification methods fail due to noisy or incomplete data. In medicine, Artificial Neural Networks (ANNs) are a hot area of concern in the fields of diagnosis, bio-medical analysis, image analysis, and drug development (Tsakona, Paschali, Tsolis, & Skapetis, 2013).

Diagnosis, in medicine, is the recognition of a disease. In traditional methods, clinical practitioners need to deal with huge amount of data of various types which cannot be handled by the human experts. Being the first step in the treatment process, diagnosis is critical and any error in this step can lead to catastrophic consequences, beside the probable delay where conventional methods may last for weeks or even months. What makes things worse is the lack of inexperienced specialists in the diagnosis of a specific disease especially in the developing countries. To summarize, incorrect diagnosis may waste time, resources, quality of health, and even human life (Wasyluk & Raś, 2010). Hence, computer-based methods are becoming inevitable in the diagnosis process due to its efficiency, accuracy, reliability, repeatability, pragmatism, and avoidance of other human being factors such as fatigue, stress, and diminished attention (Panchal & Shah, 2011). A clinical DSS that is developed mainly for diagnosing process is usually called Diagnosing Decision Support Systems (DDSS). Being such a complex real world problem, diagnosing process is best handled using ANNs.

Diabetes is a global healthcare threat and the eighth leading cause of death in the world. Indeed, it is a major health care problem that is becoming more serious over time. Its sever-ty does not reside in the disease itself solely, but also in its complex complications on the diabetic's body. According to the international diabetes federation statistics in 2017, 425 million adult have diabetes worldwide (5.6% of the population). This number is expected to rise to 629 million in 2045 (IDF, 2017). By the end 2017, 4 million deaths are expected as a result of diabetes and its complications. The vast majority of the overall cases are in the developing countries. As of 2013, Jordan ranked 37th globally and 10th in the Arab world in diabetes prevalence (IDF Diabetes Atlas, 2013). These numbers indicate a very high prevalence both locally and globally, which makes it of utmost importance to manage the disease successfully. Due to its importance and critical role in the treatment process, managing the diagnosing phase correctly and on time would reflect positively on the treatment process. In this aid developing a CDSS for the diagnosis step would help remarkably.

In this paper, a DDSS for the diabetes mellitus has been implemented using a multi-layer perceptron artificial neural network. The paper opens with an introductory section to health care, CDSS, ANNs, and diabetes. Section 2 provides a necessary theoretical background on both diabetes as an illness and ANNs as an implementation technique. Section 3 summarizes those works in literature that are relevant to this work. Section 4 explains the implementation method in details. Last but not least, the verification technique and the experimental results are discussed in section 5.

BACKGROUND

Diabetes Mellitus

A chronic disease is a long-lasting, persistent disease or a disease that comes with time. Arthritis, asthma, cancer, COPD, diabetes, hepatitis C and HIV/AIDS are common examples on chronic diseases (Ward & Black, 2016). The incidence of chronic diseases is increasing globally due to pollution and poor life habits (Woo, Yang, Lee, & Kang, 2014).

In order to produce energy, cells need to absorb sugar from blood. This is accomplished by a hormone made by the pancreas gland in the human body called insulin. For whatever reason, if sugar is not absorbed well by body cells, its percentage in blood stream will increase (hyperglycaemia) and exceed the normal level causing what is called Diabetes Mellitus (DM) or in short (Diabetes) (National Institute of Diabetes and Digestive and Kidney Disease, 2017). Diabetes is a metabolic disorder that can be classified into two main categories: type 1 and type 2 (Nichols, 2014). Type 1 and type 2 diabetes may have similar names, but they are different diseases with unique causes. Type 2 diabetes is much more common that type 1 (National Diabetes Statistics Report, 2017).

Type 1 diabetes or the "juvenile diabetes" is an insulin-dependent diabetes (IDDM), this form of diabetes results when the pancreas fails to produce enough insulin, this could happen when defence system attacks the beta cells which produces insulin in the pancreas. The reason behind this situation is still ambiguous, but viral infections such as mumps and rubella cytomegalovirus may play role

(MayoClinic, 2013). This type of diabetes infects mostly children, but it can also target people at any ages. Type 1 diabetes develops rapidly; its signs and symptoms arise rapidly within weeks or months. A diabetic person may suffer from polydipsia (increased thirst), polyphagia (constant hunger), polyuria (frequent urination), extreme tiredness, sudden weight loss, slow healing wounds, recurrent infection, and blurred vision (MayoClinic, 2013). Exclusively in type 1, patient experiences diabetic ketoacidosis (a type of metabolic problems characterized by nausea, vomiting, abdominal pain, the smell of acetone on the breath, kussamul or deep breathing, and decreased level of consciousness. In order to make accurate diagnosis, several blood tests could be conducted such as A1C (although it is not recommended for type1), FPG, and OGTT (National Institute of Diabetes, Digestive and Kidney Disease, 2017). These types of tests are explained in details later. Another two types of test are conducted to differentiate type1 from type 2. The first is a blood test to check autoantibodies in the blood. The other is a urine test to check the presence of ketones. If the result of any of these tests is positive then it is type 1 diabetes. In order to control it, a patient with diabetes 1 needs insulin injection daily, healthy diet, close monitoring, and regular physical exercises (MayoClinic, 2013).

Type 2 diabetes or the (adult-onset diabetes) is a non-insulin-dependent diabetes (NIDDM), it results when body cells are unable to respond to the produced insulin. The main cause for this condition is still unknown, but primarily it might be a consequence of life style factors and genetics, it can be effected with obesity, poor diet, physical inactivity, aging, family history, ethnicity, high blood pregnancy affecting the unborn child (National Diabetes Statistics Report, 2017). Type 2 is the most common type with a percentage of 90-95% of the cases. This type can be managed with or without insulin. Thus, type 1 and type 2 are different in several aspects, Table 1 compares between these two types of diabetes.

Table 1. Comparing type 1 and Type 2 diabetes

	Type 1	Type 2
Cause	insufficient produced insulin	Insulin resistance
Genetic basis (family history)	Possible	Strongly possible
Other Risk factors	viral infection	Lifestyle factors, obesity and aging
Body size	Thin or normal	Obese
Onset	Rapidly (in weeks)	Slowly (in months or years)
Ages at onset (often)	In children	In adults
Ketoacidosis	Common	Rare
Autoantibodies	Present	Absent
Endogenous insulin	Low or absent	Normal, low or high
Concordance in identical twins	50%	90%
Gestational diabetes	---	May develop type2 later on.
Afflicted ethnics	All	African-American, Latino, Native
		American, Asian, Pacific Islander
Medical tests	A1C test	A1C test
	Random plasma glucose	Random plasma glucose
	Fasting plasma glucose	Fasting plasma glucose
	Genetic test	Oral glucose tolerance test

The condition wherein the level of glucose in blood is very high, but not high enough for a diagnosis of diabetes is called "prediabetes". A prediabetes person often suffers from diabetes type 2 later on (National Diabetes Statistics Report, 2017). Many other risk factors are considered as indicators on the presence of diabetes (National Diabetes Statistics Report, 2017):

- Waist measurement, despite the BMI value, above 40 cm for men, and above 35 cm for women
- High blood pressure: above 140/90
- High Density Lipoprotein (HDL): cholesterol—"good" cholesterol—level below 35 mg/dL, or a triglyceride Level above 250 mg/dL.
- Polycystic ovary syndrome
- History of giving birth to at least one baby weighing more than 9 pounds

Blood Tests

In order to diagnose diabetes type 1, type 2, and prediabetes accurately and early, since symptoms may arise too late especially for type 2, several blood tests could be used:

- **A1C Test:** It's called also hemoglobin A1C, HBA1C, or glycohemoglobin. It measures average blood sugar level for the past 2 or 3 months. Its result is expressed in percentages. The higher the percentage, the higher amount of sugar in blood. If this test scores 6.5% or above, then the person (National Diabetes Statistics Report, 2017). As this type of test might be not available, and as it is not recommended for diagnosing type 1 and Gestational Diabetes (although it may give correct results), and as it may cause interference and give inaccurate results for people with upnormalities like those with hemoglobin variant, or people of African, Mediterranean, or Southeast Asian descent, or people with family members with sickle cell anemia or a thalassemia, other types of tests should be conducted.
- **Fasting Plasma Glucose (FPG):** Measures sugar in a blood sample after overnight (or at least 8 hours) fasting. Blood sugar values are expressed in milligram per deciliter (mg/dl) or in millimoles per liters (mmol/L). A person with FPG equals or above 126 gm/dl is a diabetic person. This test is more convenient and less expensive than OGTT (National Diabetes Statistics Report, 2017).
- **Random Plasma Glucose (RPG):** This test is used usually for regular checkups. Blood sample is taken at a random time. If this test reports a value of sugar blood above 200 mg/dl, then the person suffers from diabetes (Nichols, 2014).
- **Oral Glucose Tolerance Test (OGTT):** This test measures blood glucose after fasting 8 hours and 2 hours after the person drinks a liquid containing 75 gm of glucose dissolved in water. If this test scored a value between 140 and 199, the person suffers from a special prediabetes called Impaired Glucose Tolerance (IGT). If the result arises to 200 gm/dl or above at two hours, then there is diabetes. The ranges of values of these tests for each of diabetic, prediabetic, and normal cases are presented in Table 2 (National Diabetes Statistics Report, 2017).

Another type of diabetes is the Gestational Diabetes. Pregnant shows resistance to insulin in week 24 and disappears after birth. Gestational Diabetes and their babies may develop type 2 diabetes on the long term. For babies, immediate risk is not as for those who had type 1 and type 2 before (National Diabetes Statistics Report, 2017). On the long term, diabetes can cause many dangerous complications which might reach to disabling and life threatening. It may cause cardiovascular disease, kidney disease, eye disease, nerve damage, diabetic foot, and pregnancy complications (National Diabetes Statistics Report, 2017).

Table 2. Blood test levels for diagnosing diabetes

	A1C (percent)	Fasting Plasma Glucose (mg/dL)	Oral Glucose Tolerance Test (mg/dL)
Diabetes	6.5 or above	126 or above	200 or above
Prediabetes	5.7 to 6.4	100 to 125	140 to 199
Normal	About 5	99 or below	139 or below

Artificial Neural Networks (ANNs)

Artificial Neural Network is a computational model inspired by the human brain. It is a system of interconnected processing elements resemble the "neurons" that can compute values from inputs by feeding the information through the network. Figure 1 clarifies the similarity between the biological and artificial neurons. It is capable of both machine learning and pattern recognition. As mentioned before, ANNs are best suitable to resolve nonlinear problems which cannot be expressed using ordinary rule based techniques including diagnosis problems (Aleksander & Morton, 1995).

Figure 1. Biological and artificial neurons

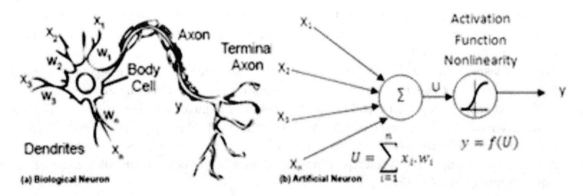

The artificial neurons are organized in layers. The structure of a typical neural network involves input layer, at least one hidden layer, and the output layer. The majority of ANNs have at least one hidden layer between the in-\put and the output layers (Fausett, 2001). The number of hidden layers will be discussed later. ANN is defined by the interconnection pattern between neurons, the learning process, and the activation function. Neurons in any ANN are fully connected; this means that each neuron in a layer is connected with each neuron in next layer through a weighted connection or synapses, these weights manipulate the data in the calculations and indicate the connection strength between the connected neurons (Fausett, 2001).

When the neural network receives data, its input layer neurons are activated. Then, the activations are transferred to the first hidden layer, processed and transferred to the next layer. This process is repeated till a neuron in the last layer is activated which resembles the output. Neural networks vary in the number of layers and directions. Several types of neural networks exist: feed forward neural network, recurrent neural network, radial basis function network, cohune self-organizing network, modular neural network, physical neural network, and learning vector quantization (Fausett, 2001).

Feedforward is the simplest type of neural network which was first described by (Rumelhart & Mc-Clelland, 1986). In this neural network information is transferred in one direction from input through hidden layers to output. A feedforward network can be single layer perceptron with only one output layer, or a multilayer perceptron MLP. A MLP is a one direction feedforward neural network with multiple layers (i.e. input, hidden layers, and output). A MLP has a non-linear activation function, and is trained using backpropagation algorithm (Haykin, 1994).

Determining the number of hidden layers in a neural network is the network designer task. Indeed, it is not a trivial task, there is no precisely defined rule to follow in order to determine the number of hidden layers, but by all the odds, the number of hidden layers should increase with the increased complexity of the system (Mahesh, Suresh, & Babu, 2013). Moreover, more hidden layers are required for multi-staged model. Practically, the majority of real world problems are satisfied with only one hidden layer (Ganesan, Venkatesh, & Rama, 2010). Not only that but also, having more than one hidden layer may slow down the performance of the system. On the other hand, most studies suggest determining the number of hidden layers and nodes empirically to optimize the network performance (Wahyunggoro, Permanasari, & Chamsudin, 2013). This is usually accomplished by performing training on different topologies with different number of layers and neurons then select the topology with the highest accuracy (i.e. the minimum value of mean square error).

Determining the number of neurons in the hidden layer is also a very important issue. Using too few neurons makes it difficult to adequately detect the signals in a complicated data set, which is called "underfitting" (Heaton, 2013). On the other hand, using too many neurons makes the limited amount of information contained in the training set not enough to train all of the neurons in the hidden layers, which is called (overfitting) (Haykin, 1994). Even if the training data is sufficient, large number of hidden neurons may increase the neural network training time. Different rules-of-thumb were suggested to determine the number of neurons in hidden layers (Heaton, 2013). One suggests that it should be between the number of neurons in the input layer and the number of neurons in the output layer. Another rule suggests that the number of neurons in the hidden layer should be 2/3 the size of the input layer, plus the size of the output layer. A third rule suggests that it should be less than twice the number of neurons in the input layer (Haykin, 1994). For networks with multi-hidden layers, it was suggested that the number of neurons in each hidden layer except the first one will be the number of neurons in the previous layer divided by two (Xu & Chen, 2008).

The activation function is a function that specifies the output of the neuron to a given input. Neural networks support several forms of activation functions such as step functions, linear functions, and sigmoid (i.e. Logistic function and hyperbolic tangent function) (Karlik & Olgac, 2011). Step function is commonly used with simple network (i.e. perceptron). Using linear activation functions with multiple layers neural network would be equivalent to a single layer linear network (McClelland, 2013). Hyperbolic tangent function is a symmetric sigmoid nonlinear curve what makes it an ideal activation of MLP and in the hidden layers particularly. Its output ranges between (-1, +1) and its mathematical definition is (Karlik & Olgac, 2011):

$$\tanh(x) = e^{x} - e^{-x} \tag{1}$$

$$e^{x} + e^{-x}$$

Neural networks are trained via learning algorithms. To train a neural network means to allow it to learn by example. Learning algorithms could be supervised and unsupervised. In the supervised learning each vector (input) and its classification (output) in the training set is known previously. In the unsupervised learning (clustering), the output is not known before. Classification of input vectors is done automatically during the formation of the classifier (Mohri, Rostamizadeh, & Talwalkar, 2012). In this context, the authors are interested in the supervised learning process using neural networks. Large variety of supervised training algorithms exists. Backward propagation of errors or the backpropagation algorithm is the most common training algorithm to be used with multi-layer network.

Once the optimal network architecture is found, the training process starts. The training is done using pairs of predefined pairs of inputs and outputs. Herein, for each input (i.e. usually a vector or record in the training data set) the output is calculated using the weights and functions in the hidden layers (initial weights are chosen randomly). Then the resultant output is compared with the desired predefined output, the error is then propagated back to the network to adjust weights for the next input in order to hopefully get an output that is closer to the desired one. The training process performed iteratively on the same dataset until the minimum value of mean square error between the actual output and the desired output is reached (Fausett, 2001). Actually, the best performance of the system on the training dataset occurs early, thus it is not necessary to continue training until the training error stops decreasing. Thus training is usually performed for 30-45 iterations (Ganesan et al., 2010). Having finished training, the neural network needs to be verified with new examples other than those were used in the training process. If the overall accuracy of the network is acceptable, then it could be used to predict the output of any new input.

A multilayer perceptron is a feedforward neural network that utilizes a backpropagation learning algorithm and a nonlinear activation function. It is the most common neural network architecture in use today (Haykin, 1994). As its name suggests, a MLP consists of more than two layers (input, output, and one or more hidden layers), any number of neurons in each layer, any number of inputs representing the features and any number of outputs representing the classifications (Haykin, 1994). A MLP is used in complex, multivariable applications such as medical diagnosis (Abbasi & Kashiyarndi, 2006).

RELATED WORK

Applying artificial intelligent techniques in solving clinical problems has attracted many researchers especially in the diagnosis process. In this section, the authors introduce significant works wherein artificial neural networks are utilized to help in disease diagnosis process, specifically, the diabetes illness. Some of these works are listed below:

Cheruku, Edla, Kuppili, Dharavath, & Beechu (2017) Proposed an architecture for weightless neural networks (WNNs) that uses variable sized random access memories to optimise the memory usage and a modified binary TRIE data structure for reducing the test time. The results of the proposed architecture outperforms in terms of accuracy as compared to conventional neural network-based classifiers.

El-Sappagh & Elmogy (2016) introduced a systematic review that examines the current state of Case-Based Reasoning (CBR) and its limitations in the medical domain, especially for diabetes mellitus.

Ngan & Li (2015) combined the strengths of both domain-knowledge-based and machine-learning-based approaches to propose a Hypoglycemic Expert Query Parametric Estimation (H-EQPE) model and a Linear Checkpoint (L-Checkpoint) algorithm to detect hypoglycemia of diabetes patients. The paper focuses on determining the BGL monitoring threshold to prevent the patients from suffering hypoglycemic events.

Farahmand, You, Shi, & Wadhwa (2015) Compared between of two data mining techniques (i.e. Decision Tree and logistic regression modelling) for predicting diabetes. Results show that both methods present a good prediction for pre-diabetes and that Decision Tree modelling is a better indicator to predict pre-diabetes.

Fashoto, Adeyeye, Owolabi, & Odim (2015) Modelled a feedforward neural network to solve the problem associated with the medical diagnosis of acute inflammations and acute nephrises of the urinary system. The output shows that the classification accuracy of the model to be approximately 90%.

Al-Khasawneh & Hijazi (2014) developed a clinical decision support system that helps in diagnosing diabetes mellitus using a multilayer perceptron artificial neural network.

Temurtas, Yumusak, & Temurtas (2009) presented a comparative study on Pima Indian diabetes disease diagnostic by using multilayer neural network which was trained by LM algorithm and probabilistic neural network. They compared the results they obtained with other related studies conducted on the same database. (Sumathy, Mythili, Kumar, Jishnujit, & Kumar, 2010) proposed a method for diagnosing diabetes using newly designed inputs parameters and backpropagation algorithm.

Acar, Özerdem, & Akpolat (2011) trained four types of neural networks (i.e. perceptron, MLP, Elman and ART1) to forecast whether someone has diabetes or not. Finally, the best performance was observed as 82.10% in the MLP network with 8-20-1 structure. (Robert-son, Lehmann, Sandham, & Hamilton, 2011) used Elman recurrent artificial neural networks (ANNs) to make BGL predictions based on a history of Blood Glucose Level (BGLs), meal intake, and insulin injections. (Giveki, 2012) introduced an automatic approach to diagnose diabetes based on Feature Weighted Support Vector Machines (FW-SVMs) and Modified Cuckoo Search (MCS).

Karan, Bayraktar, Haluk, & Karlık (2012) presented a neural network algorithm that classifies diabetes illness data on client/server architecture. (Mahesh et al., 2013) proposed a Generalized Regression Neural Network (GRNN) based expert system to help in diagnosing the hepatitis B disease. Their system classifies each patient into infected and non-infected. If infected then how severe it is in terms of intensity rate. (Amato et al., 2013) discussed and summarized the philosophy, capabilities, and limitations of artificial neural networks in medical diagnosis through selected examples including diabetes disease.

METHOD

In this research a MLP neural network was used to diagnose diabetes and to determine its type. The system was implemented using Matlab 7.8. During the development phase the authors passed by the phases summarized in Figure 2.

Figure 2. Diagnosing diabetes mellitus method

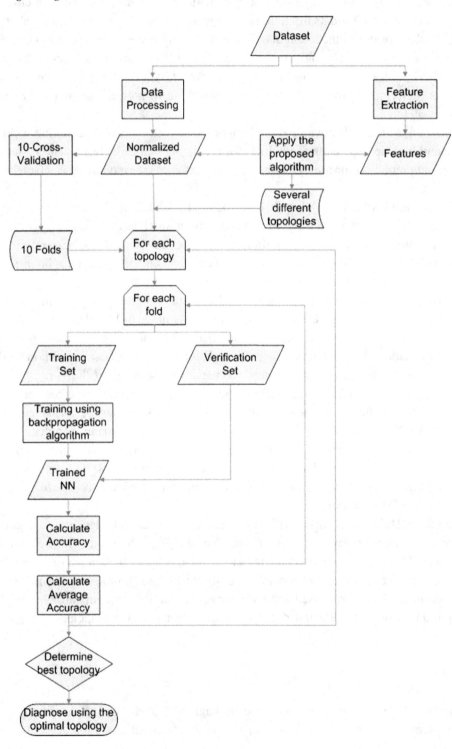

Dataset

Clinical data was obtained from King Abdullah University Hospital in Jordan. The dataset contains information about 730 patients. For each patient, a set of 18 features and the diabetic diagnosis (i.e. non diabetic, prediabetes, type1 diabetes, type2 diabetes, and gestational diabetes) is stated. These pieces of information constitute the basis of the training database which will be discussed later. This sample consists of 200 prediabetes, 70 type 1 diabetic, 280 type 2 diabetic, 80 gestational diabetic, and the remaining are non-diabetic.

Features Selection

Correct diagnosis depends largely on the features selected to train the network. Redundant, insufficient features should be avoided since it may make a noise affecting the output. This requires some medical experience. Herein, the features were decided upon with consultation of clinicians at King Abdullah University Hospital. The training database was built with respect to those features. A list of the selected features is displayed in Table 3.

Table 3. Diabetes features, types, and encodings

	Feature	Type	Encoding
Symptoms	Polydipsia	Boolean	Presences =1, Absence=0
	Polyphagia	Boolean	Presences =1, Absence=0
	Polyuria	Boolean	Presences =1, Absence=0
	Ketoacidosis	Boolean	Presences =1, Absence=0
	Polycystic ovary	Boolean	Presences =1, Absence=0
	A1C	Numerical	-------
	FPF	Numerical	-------
Biomedical Analysis	RPG	Numerical	-------
	OGTT	Numerical	-------
	Autoantibodies test	Boolean	Positive = 1, Negative =0
	Ketones test	Boolean	Positive = 1, Negative =0
	HDL cholesterol	Numerical	-------
	Family history	Boolean	Presences =1, Absence=0
	Age	numerical	-------
Risk Factors	Pregnancy	Boolean	Pregnancy =1, non-pregnancy=0
	BMI	Numerical	-------
	Affected twins	Boolean	Presences =1, Absence=0
	Physical activity	Boolean	Practice =0, no practice= 1

Construct the Optimal Structure of the Neural Network

Being a MLP neural network, this network has a one input layer with 18 neurons which represent the features. Being a classification problem rather than regression, the output layer has N neurons rather than a single neuron, one for each of the N categories of the target variable. Thus this network has one output layer with 5 neurons which represent the diabetic diagnosis (i.e. non-diabetic, prediabetic, type 1 diabetic, type 2 diabetic, and gestational diabetic). A MLP should also have at least one hidden layer. As highlighted before, determining the number of hidden layers and neurons is not a trivial task. There is no way to determine the optimal number of the hidden layers and neurons. As mentioned before, many rules-of-thumb were suggested to help in this aid. In addition, a MLP with only one hidden layer is usually sufficient to solve the majority of real life problems. Nevertheless, most research recommends that determining the number of hidden layers and neurons should be determined experimentally. Therefore, in this research, neural networks of different topologies were implemented. To determine the number of topologies, the number of hidden layers in each topology, and the number of neurons in each layer, the authors proposed the algorithm 1 based on the rules-of-thumb mentioned earlier.

According to this algorithm, two topologies for the neural network were implemented, displayed in Figure 3 and Figure 4. In both topologies, each layer neuron is fully connected to the neurons in the next layer through connection weights.

Preprocessing Dataset

As any neural network input should be numerical. Non-numerical input features should be encoded so that its value is expressed using numerical data. The encoding for each feature is displayed in Table 3. Since the range of input data in a neural network may vary widely, and in order to remove any influence of the units of measure, dataset should be pre-processed and scaled. One way to this is to perform feature standardization. This makes the values for each feature have a zero-mean and a unit variance. This could be achieved by firstly calculating the mean and the standard deviation for each feature, then for each feature value the mean is subtracted and the resultant value is divided by the calculated standard deviation (Pedregosa, et al., 2011).

Preparing the Training Dataset

For subsequent 10-fold-cross-validation purposes, the dataset (760 patients) is partitioned into 10 equal size subsets (each of 76 patients). In each fold, nine of the ten partitions (i.e. 648 patients) are used as a training set and the one remaining partition is left for verification purposes (i.e. verification set or test set). This assures that all values are used for both training and validation, and each value is used for validation exactly once. Neural network learns by a series of examples called (training data-base). The structure of our training database is shown in Table 4. Our training database has 18 fields representing the features and another field represents the diagnosis. It also has 648 records; a record for each patient.

Table 4. The structure of our training database

Patient ID	Medical Data						Diagnosis
	Feature 1	Feature 2	...	Feature j	....	Feature	18	
1	Data 1,1	Data 1,2		Data 1,j		Data 1,18		Diabetes 2
2	Data 2,1	Data 2,2		Data 2,j		Data 2,18		Nondiabetes
...	...	...	...	...	...	...		...
p	Data p,1	Data p,2		Data p,j		Data p,18		Diabetes 1
P+1	Data p+1,1	Data p+1,2		Data p+1,j		Data p+1,18		Diabetes 1
...	...	...	...	...	...	...		...
648	Data 730,1	Data 730,2		Data 730,j		Data 730,18		Nondiabetes

Training the Network

For each topology, the neural network is trained 10 rounds over the 10 folds training sets. After each round, the network is verified against the verification set of that fold. For training purposes, the authors adapted a back-propagation algorithm and a sigmoid (non-linear) activation function (i.e. tangh(x)). The goal behind the training process is to adjust the weights to minimize the output error function E. In other words, to make the actual output and the target output similar as much as possible. The success of using back-propagation algorithm in training MLPs depends largely on the learning rate and the momentum value to be used. The learning rate controls the size of the weight and the bias changes during the learning process, while the momentum prevents the system from converging to a local minimum. There is no systematic way to determine the most appropriate values; overall, they are both real numbers in the range [0, 1]. Herein, a value of 0.9 was used for the momentum, 0.1 for the training rate, and 10000 for the number of iteration (epochs). Initial weights were also chosen randomly in order to break symmetry and small to avoid intermediate saturation of the activation function; usually in the range [-a, a] where $0.1 < a < 2$.

EXPERIMENTAL RESULTS

Verification

In order to examine how the proposed neural network model will generalize to an independent data set, cross validation technique was applied. In the cross-validation (or sometimes referred to as rotation validation) the original data set is partitioned into k partitions. One partition is used as verification set while the remaining k-1 partitions are used as a training set. The verification partition is rotated over the K partitions and thus the process is repeated K times (i.e. folds) (Poole & Mackworth, 2010).

Figure 3. Topology 1: A MLP with one hidden layer for diagnosing diabetes

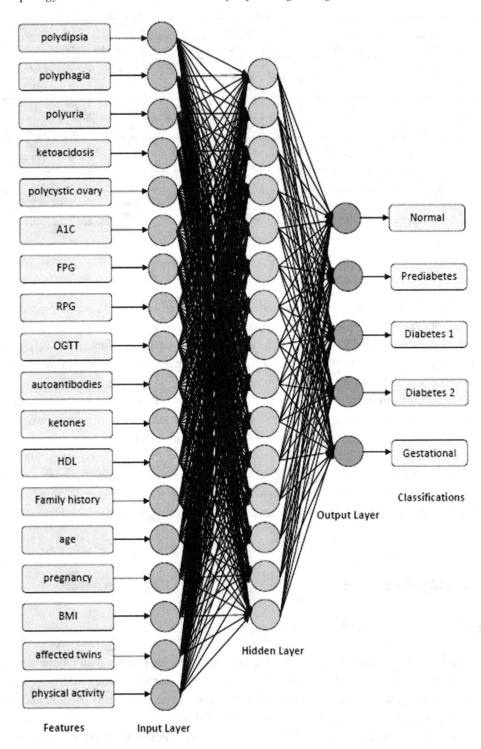

Figure 4. Topology 2: A MLP with Two Hidden Layers for Diagnosing Diabetes

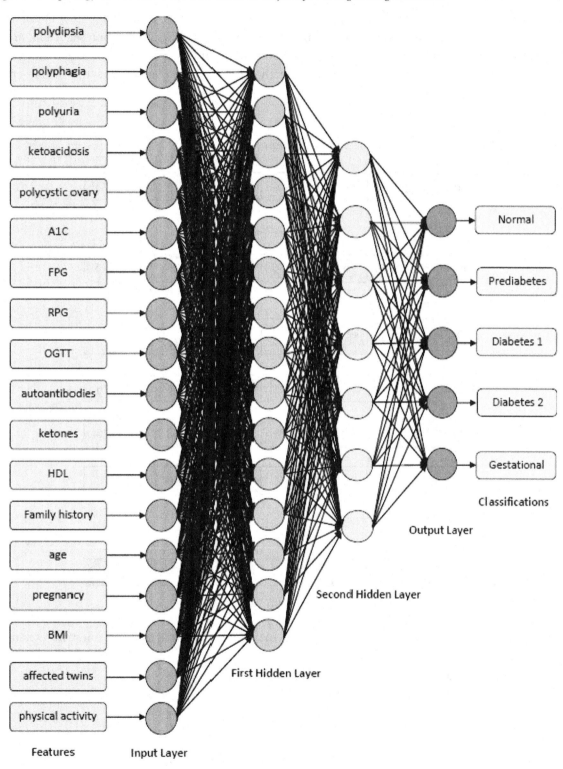

In this system, a 10-fold cross validation was used. The original data set (760 patients) was splitted randomly into 10 equal subsets. Each topology was presented to 10 folds. At each fold, 9 of the subsets were used as training dataset, and the other remaining subset was used as verification set. Then, in the next fold, the verification subset is rotated. This guarantees that all values are used for both training and validation, and each value is used for validation exactly once. Figure 5 clarifies how the 10-fold-cross validation technique was applied in this research.

Figure 5. Applying 10-fold-cross validation on the dataset

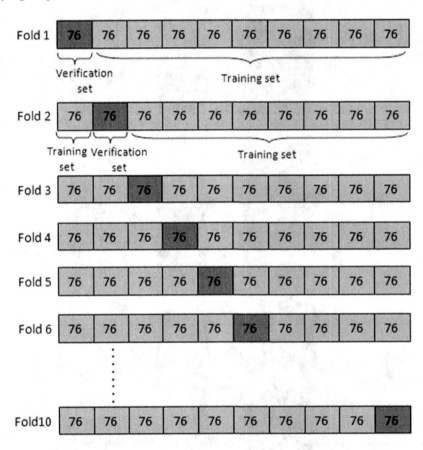

For each topology, the classification accuracy was measured at each fold using the following equation:

$$FCA = \frac{number\ of\ correct\ classifications\ in\ the\ classification\ set}{verification\ set\ size} \tag{2}$$

Then, the average of all observations for all folds was calculated. Table 5 summarizes the experimental results for topology 1 (one hidden layer) and the experimental results for topology 2 (two hidden layers). The results revealed that diagnosing diabetes using neural network models achieves a very good classification Accuracy. A comparison between the two topologies (18-15-6) and (18-15-7-5) in classification accuracy for each fold is shown in figure 6. Figure 7 shows a comparison of the general average classification accuracy for both topologies. The figure implies that a MLP with either a single hidden layer (topology-1) or multi-hidden layer (topology-2) gives a good classification results with a slightly higher average classification accuracy for the MLP with single hidden layer.

From these observations, it can be concluded that a neural network with one hidden layer (with a classification accuracy of (91.5%)) performs better than the network with two hidden layers (with a classification accuracy of (89.1%)). This result advocates the claims that one hidden layer is sufficient for majority of real life problems. The neural network with the highest classification accuracy (i.e. one hidden layer network) was chosen.

Table 5. Classification accuracy for topology 1 and topology 2

Fold	Topology 1	Topology 2
1	0.92	0.91
2	0.86	0.86
3	0.88	0.88
4	0.97	0.93
5	0.95	0.92
6	0.82	0.82
7	0.89	0.85
8	0.93	0.91
9	0.97	0.93
10	0.96	0.9
Average Accuracy	91.50%	89.10%

Figure 6. Classification Accuracy for 10-Folds

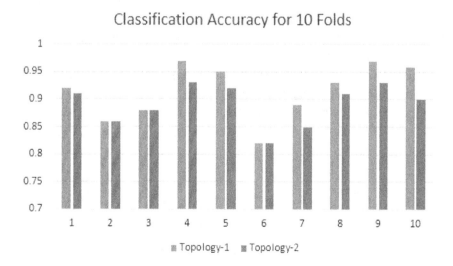

Figure 7. A Comparison between the Average Classification Accuracy between Topology-1 and Topology-2

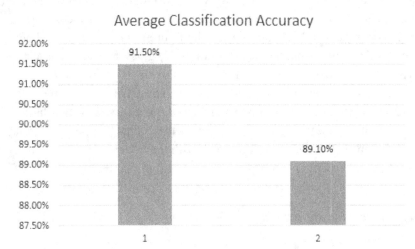

CONCLUSION AND FUTURE WORK

In this paper, a MLP based clinical decision support system was introduced. The system takes in 18 variables as an input. These variables represent the symptoms, biomedical analysis, and other risk factors of the diabetes illness. The output of the system classifies the diabetic status of the patient into five categories (i.e. normal, prediabetes, type1, type2, and gestational diabetes). To determine the number of hidden layers, the authors proposed an algorithm based on the already known rules of thumb. Hence, two different topologies were trained and verified using feed forward backpropagation algorithm and 10-fold cross-validation technique. The first topology (18-15-6) gave higher averaged accuracy (91.5%) than the second topology (18-15-7-5) with an averaged accuracy (89.1%). This result is consistent with the trend which says that a MLP with a single hidden layer is sufficient for the majority of real life problems.

According to these results, the implemented system seems to be a promising diabetes diagnostic tool. Practically, several barriers and obstacles to their implementation exist. One barrier is the incomplete medical knowledge base. Another barrier is the lack of electronic medical records (EMRs) in the clinical environments. Sometimes, the use of such EMRs that include computerized decision support system capabilities can be considered another barrier. High clinicians' resistance and low motivation to use such computerized systems is another challenging issue. On the other hand, the system is expected to give higher accuracy on larger data set. In future, the followed method could be applied on other chronic diseases like hepatitis, hypertension, and coronary. For general purposes systems, those systems could be integrated into a single general purpose diagnostic system using feature extraction techniques.

REFERENCES

Abbasi, M., & Kashiyarndi, S. (2006). *Clinical decision support systems: A discussion on different methodologies used in Health Care.* Academic Press.

Acar, E., Özerdem, M. S., & Akpolat, V. (2011). Diabetes Mellitus Forcast Using Various Types of Artificial Neural Networks. *6th International Advanced Technologies Symposium*, 196-201.

Aleksander, I., & Morton, H. (1995). *An introduc-tion to neural.* London: Int Thomson Comput Press.

Al-Khasawneh, A., & Hijazi, H. (2014). A Predictive E-Health Information System: Diagnosing Diabetes Mellitus Using Neural Network Based Decision Support System. *International Journal of Decision Support System Technology, 6*(4), 31–48. doi:10.4018/ijdsst.2014100103

Amato, F., López, A., Peña-Méndez, E. M., Vaňhara, P., Hampl, A., & Havel, J. (2013). Artificial neural networks in medical diagnosis. *Journal of Applied Biomedicine, 11*(2), 47–58. doi:10.2478/v10136-012-0031-x

Brailer, D., & Thompson, T. (2004). *Health IT strategic framework.* Academic Press.

Bray, O. (2010). *Health Care Information Technology: A Key to Quality and Cost Issues.* LWVUS.

Health Care Education Task Force. (2012). *Diagnosis of Diabetes and Prediabetes.* National Institute of Diabetes and Digestive and Kidney Disease.

Cheruku, R., Edla, D. R., Kuppili, V., Dharavath, R., & Beechu, N. R. (2017). Automatic disease diagnosis using optimised weightless neural networks for low-power wearable devices. *Healthcare Technology Letters, 4*(4), 122–128. doi:10.1049/htl.2017.0003 PMID:28868148

Dinevski, D., Bele, U., Šarenac, T., Rajkovič, U., & Šušteršic, O. (2011). Telemedicine Techniques and Applications. In G. Graschew (Ed.), Clinical Decision Support Systems (pp. 185-210). InTech.

El-Gayar, O. F., Deokar, A. V., & Tao, J. (2011). DSS-CMM: A Capability Maturity Model for DSS Development Processes. *International Journal of Decision Support System Technology, 3*(4), 14–34. doi:10.4018/jdsst.2011100102

El-Sappagh, S., & Elmogy, M. M. (2016). Medical Case Based Reasoning Frameworks: Current Developments and Future Directions. *International Journal of Decision Support System Technology, 8*(3), 31–62. doi:10.4018/IJDSST.2016070103

Farahmand, K., You, G., Shi, J., & Wadhwa, S. S. (2015). Data Mining for Predicting Pre-diabetes: Comparing Two Approaches. *International Journal of User-Driven Healthcare, 5*(2), 26–46. doi:10.4018/IJUDH.2015070103

Fashoto, S. G., Adeyeye, M., Owolabi, O., & Odim, M. (2015). Modelling of the Feed Forward Neural Network with its Application in Medical Diagnosis. *International Journal of Advances in Engineering and Technology, 8*(4), 507–520.

Fausett, L. L. (2001). *Fundamentals of Neural Net-works: Architectures, Algorithms, and Applications.* New York: Addison-Wesley Inc.

Ganesan, N., Venkatesh, K., & Rama, M. A. (2010). Application of Neural Networks in Diagnosing Cancer Disease Using Demographic Data. *International Journal of Computers and Applications, 1*(26), 76–85.

Garg, A., Adhikari, N., McDonald, H., Rosas-Arel-lano, M., Devereaux, P., Beyene, J., ... Haynes, R. B. (2005). Effects of computerized clinical decision support systems on practitioner performance and patient outcomes: A systematic review. *Journal of the American Medical Association, 293*(10), 1223–1238. doi:10.1001/jama.293.10.1223 PMID:15755945

Giveki, D. (2012). *Automatic detection of diabetes diagnosis using feature weighted support vector machines based on mutual information and modified cuckoo search*. Academic Press.

Golemati, S., Mougiakakou, S., Stoitsis, J., Valavanis, I., & Nikita, K. S. (2005). Clinical Decision Support Systems: Basic Principles and Applications in Diagnosis and Therapy. In Clinical Decision Support Systems (pp. 250-296). Idea Group Inc.

Haykin, S. (1994). Neural Networks: A Comprehensive Foundation (2nd ed.). Pearson Education, Inc.

Heaton, J. (2013). Feedforward Backpropagation Neural Networks. In J. Heaton (Ed.), Introduction to Neural Networks for Java (2nd ed.). Heaton Research, Inc.

International Diabetes Federation. (2013). *IDF Diabetes Atlas*. Author.

International Diabetes Federation. (2017). *IDF Diabetes Atlas*. Author.

Karan, O., Bayraktar, C., Gümüşkaya, H., & Karlık, B. (2012). Diagnosing diabetes using neural networks on small mobile devices. *Expert Systems with Applications, 39*(1), 54–60. doi:.eswa.2011.06.046 doi:10.1016/j

Karlik, B., & Olgac, A. V. (2011). Performance Analysis of Various Activation Functions in Gen-eralized MLP Architectures of Neural Networks. *International Journal of Artificial Intelligence And Expert Systems, 1*(4), 111–122.

M. C. (2013, June 23). *Type 1 diabetes Diagnosis at Mayo Clinic*. Retrieved May 15, 2014, from Mayo Clinic: http://www.mayoclinic.org/diseases-con-ditions/type-1-diabetes/basics/tests-diagnosis/con-

Mahesh, C., Suresh, V. G., & Babu, M. (2013). Diagnosing Hepatitis B Using Artificial Neural Net-work Based Expert System. *International Journal of Engineering and Innovative Technology, 3*(6), 139–144.

McClelland, J. L. (2013, February 6). *Explorations in parallel distributed processing: A handbook of models, programs, and exercises*. Stanford, CA: Academic Press.

Mohri, M., Rostamizadeh, A., & Talwalkar, A. (2012). *Foundations of Machine Learning*. MIT Press.

Mokeddem, S., Atmani, B., & Mokaddem, M. (2014). A New Approach for Coronary Artery Diseases Diagnosis Based on Genetic Algorithm. *International Journal of Decision Support System Technology, 6*(4), 1–15. doi:10.4018/ijdsst.2014100101

Ngan, C.-K., & Li, L. (2015). H-EQPE Model and L-Checkpoint Algorithm: A Decision-Guidance Approach for Detecting Hypoglycemia of Diabetes Patients. *International Journal of Decision Support System Technology, 7*(4), 20–35. doi:10.4018/IJDSST.2015100102

Nichols, H. (2014, March 3). *What is the difference between diabetes type 1 and diabetes*. Retrieved May 15, 2014, from Medical News Today: http://www. medicalnewstoday.com/articles/7504.php

Panchal, D., & Shah, S. (2011). Artificial Intelligence Based Expert System For Hepatitis B Diagnosis. *International Journal of Modeling and Optimiza-tion, 1*(4), 362–366. doi:10.7763/IJMO.2011.V1.61

Pedregosa, F., Varoquaux, G., Gramfort, A., Michel, V., Thirion, B., Grisel, O., & ... . (2011). Scikit-learn: Machine Learning in {P}ython. *Journal of Machine Learning Research, 12*, 2825–2830.

Pestotnik, S. L. (2005). Expert Clinical Decision Support Systems to Enhance Antimicrobial Steward-ship Programs. *Pharmacotherapy*, 25(8), 1116–1125. doi:10.1592/phco.2005.25.8.1116 PMID:16207103

Poole, D., & Mackworth, A. (2010). Avoiding Overfitting. In D. Poole & A. Mackworth (Eds.), Artificial Intelligence: Foundations of Computational Agents. Cambridge University Press.

Robertson, G., Lehmann, E. D., Sandham, W., & Hamilton, D. (2011). Blood Glucose Prediction Using Artificial Neural Networks Trained with the AIDA Diabetes Simulator: A Proof-of-Concept Pilot Study. *Journal of Electrical and Computer Engineering*, 2011, 1–11. doi:10.1155/2011/681786

Rumelhart, D. E., & McClelland, J. L. (1986). Parallel distributed processing: explorations in the mi-crostructure of cognition: Vol. 1. *Foundations*. Cambridge, MA: MIT Press.

Sharma, K., & Virmani, J. (2017). A Decision Support System for Classification of Normal and Medical Renal Disease Using Ultrasound Images: A Decision Support System for Medical Renal Diseases. *International Journal of Ambient Computing and Intelligence*, 8(2), 52–69. doi:10.4018/IJACI.2017040104

Sumathy, M., Kumar, P., Jishnujit, T. M., & Kumar, K. R. (2010). Diagnosis of Diabetes Mel-litus based on Risk Factors. *International Journal of Computers and Applications*, 10(4).

Temurtas, H., Yumusak, N., & Temurtas, F. (2009). A comparative study on diabetes disease diagnosis using neural networks. *Expert Systems with Applications*, 36(4), 8610–8615. doi:10.1016/j.eswa.2008.10.032

Tsakona, A., Paschali, K., Tsolis, D., & Skapetis, G. (2013). Proposed Electronic Medical Record with Emphasis on Hepatitis Diagnosis. *International Journal of Caring Sciences*, 6(2), 138–145.

Wahyunggoro, O., Permanasari, A. E., & Chamsudin, A. (2013). Utilization of Neural Network for Disease Forecasting. *59th ISI World Statistics Congress*, 549-554.

Ward, B. W., & Black, L. I. (2016). State and Regional Prevalence of Diagnosed Multiple Chronic Con-ditions Among Adults Aged ≥18 Years — United States, 2014. *Morbidity and Mortality Weekly Report*, 65(29), 735–738. doi:10.15585/mmwr.mm6529a3 PMID:27467707

Wasyluk, H. A., & Raś, Z. W. (2010). Action Rules Approach to Solving Diagnostic Problems in Clinical Medicine. In G. Devlin (Ed.), Decision Support Systems Advances (pp. 99-106). InTech.

Woo, J.-I., Yang, J.-G., Lee, Y.-H., & Kang, U.-G. (2014). Healthcare Decision Support System for Administration of Chronic Diseases. *Healthcare Informatics Research*, 20(3), 173–182. doi:10.4258/hir.2014.20.3.173 PMID:25152830

Xu, S., & Chen, L. (2008). A Novel Approach for Determining the Optimal Number of Hidden Layer Neurons for FNN's and Its Application in Data Mining. Proceedings of the 5th International Conference on Information Technology and Applications, 683-686.

ADDITIONAL READING

Ahmed, S. S., Dey, N., Ashour, A. S., Sifaki-Pistolla, D., Bălas-Timar, D., Balas, V. E., & Tavares, J. M. R. (2017). Effect of fuzzy partitioning in Crohn's disease classification: A neuro-fuzzy-based approach. *Medical & Biological Engineering & Computing*, *55*(1), 101–115. doi:10.100711517-016-1508-7 PMID:27106754

Ben Abdessalem Karaa, W., Ben Azzouz, Z., Singh, A., Dey, N., & Ashour, S, A., & Ben Ghazala, H. (. (2016). Automatic builder of class diagram (ABCD): An application of UML generation from functional requirements. *Software, Practice & Experience*, *46*(11), 1443–1458. doi:10.1002pe.2384

Bose, S., Mukherjee, A., Chakraborty, S., Samanta, S., & Dey, N. (2013, December). Parallel image segmentation using multi-threading and k-means algorithm. In *Computational Intelligence and Computing Research (ICCIC), 2013 IEEE International Conference on* (pp. 1-5). IEEE. 10.1109/ICCIC.2013.6724171

Chatterjee, S., Chakraborty, R., Dey, N., & Hore, S. (2015). A quality prediction method for weight lifting activity.

Kamal, S., Dey, N., Ashour, A. S., Ripon, S., Balas, V. E., & Kaysar, M. S. (2017). FbMapping: an automated system for monitoring facebook data. *Neural Network World*, *27*(1), 27–57. doi:10.14311/NNW.2017.27.002

Kamal, S., Dey, N., Nimmy, S. F., Ripon, S. H., Ali, N. Y., Ashour, A. S., ... Shi, F. (2016). Evolutionary framework for coding area selection from cancer data. *Neural Computing & Applications*, 1–23.

Kamal, S., Ripon, S. H., Dey, N., Ashour, A. S., & Santhi, V. (2016). A MapReduce approach to diminish imbalance parameters for big deoxyribonucleic acid dataset. *Computer Methods and Programs in Biomedicine*, *131*, 191–206. doi:10.1016/j.cmpb.2016.04.005 PMID:27265059

Li, Z., Shi, K., Dey, N., Ashour, A. S., Wang, D., Balas, V. E., ... Shi, F. (2017). Rule-based back propagation neural networks for various precision rough set presented KANSEI knowledge prediction: A case study on shoe product form features extraction. *Neural Computing & Applications*, *28*(3), 613–630. doi:10.100700521-016-2707-8

Karaa, W. B. A., Ashour, A. S., Sassi, D. B., Roy, P., Kausar, N., & Dey, N. (2016). Medline text mining: an enhancement genetic algorithm based approach for document clustering. In *Applications of Intelligent Optimization in Biology and Medicine* (pp. 267–287). Springer International Publishing. doi:10.1007/978-3-319-21212-8_12

Karaa, W. B. A., Mannai, M., Dey, N., Ashour, A. S., & Olariu, I. (2016, August). Gene-disease-food relation extraction from biomedical database. In *International Workshop Soft Computing Applications* (pp. 394-407). Springer, Cham.

Kausar, N., Abdullah, A., Samir, B. B., Palaniappan, S., AlGhamdi, B. S., & Dey, N. (2016). Ensemble clustering algorithm with supervised classification of clinical data for early diagnosis of coronary artery disease. *Journal of Medical Imaging and Health Informatics*, *6*(1), 78–87. doi:10.1166/jmihi.2016.1593

Kausar, N., Palaniappan, S., Samir, B. B., Abdullah, A., & Dey, N. (2016). Systematic analysis of applied data mining based optimization algorithms in clinical attribute extraction and classification for diagnosis of cardiac patients. In *Applications of intelligent optimization in biology and medicine* (pp. 217–231). Springer International Publishing. doi:10.1007/978-3-319-21212-8_9

Ngan, T. T., Tuan, T. M., Minh, N. H., & Dey, N. (2016). Decision Making Based on Fuzzy Aggregation Operators for Medical Diagnosis from Dental X-ray images. *Journal of Medical Systems*, *40*(12), 280. doi:10.100710916-016-0634-y PMID:27787784

Nimmy, S. F., Kamal, M. S., Hossain, M. I., Dey, N., Ashour, A. S., & Shi, F. (2017). Neural Skyline Filtering for Imbalance Features Classification. *International Journal of Computational Intelligence and Applications*, *16*(03), 1750019. doi:10.1142/S1469026817500195

Wang, D., He, T., Li, Z., Cao, L., Dey, N., Ashour, A. S., ... Shi, F. (2016). Image feature-based affective retrieval employing improved parameter and structure identification of adaptive neuro-fuzzy inference system. *Neural Computing & Applications*, 1–16.

Roy, P., Goswami, S., Chakraborty, S., Azar, A. T., & Dey, N. (2014). Image segmentation using rough set theory: A review. *International Journal of Rough Sets and Data Analysis*, *1*(2), 62–74. doi:10.4018/ijrsda.2014070105

Tang, R., Fong, S., Dey, N., Wong, R. K., & Mohammed, S. (2017). Cross Entropy Method Based Hybridization of Dynamic Group Optimization Algorithm. *Entropy (Basel, Switzerland)*, *19*(10), 533. doi:10.3390/e19100533

Wang, D., Li, Z., Cao, L., Balas, V. E., Dey, N., Ashour, A. S., ... Shi, F. (2016). Image Fusion Incorporating Parameter Estimation Optimized Gaussian Mixture Model and Fuzzy Weighted Evaluation System: A Case Study in Time-Series Plantar Pressure Data Set. *IEEE Sensors Journal*, *17*(5), 1407–1420. doi:10.1109/JSEN.2016.2641501

Wang, D., Li, Z., Dey, N., Ashour, A. S., Sherratt, R. S., & Shi, F. (2017). Case-Based Reasoning for Product Style Construction and Fuzzy Analytic Hierarchy Process Evaluation Modeling Using Consumers Linguistic Variables. *IEEE Access : Practical Innovations, Open Solutions*, *5*, 4900–4912. doi:10.1109/ACCESS.2017.2677950

KEY TERMS AND DEFINITIONS

Artificial Neural Network: Is a computational model inspired by the human brain that consists of interconnected processing elements resemble the "neurons" that can compute values from inputs by feeding the information through the network.

Classification Accuracy: Is the percentage of correct predictions.

Clinical Decision Support System: Is a health information system that helps health practitioners in making decisions especially in the diagnosis process.

Cross Validation: Is a technique to evaluate predictive models by partitioning the original sample into a training set to train the model, and a test set to evaluate it.

Diabetes: Is a chronic disease that results when the percentage of sugar in blood increases and exceeds the normal level.

Multilayer Perceptron: Is feedforward artificial neural network that utilizes backpropagation supervised learning for training.

This research was previously published in Technological Innovations in Knowledge Management and Decision Support; pages 127-149, copyright year 2019 by Information Science Reference (an imprint of IGI Global).

Chapter 62
Computational Performance Analysis of Neural Network and Regression Models in Forecasting the Societal Demand for Agricultural Food Harvests

Balaji Prabhu B. V.
B.M.S College of Engineering, Bengaluru, VTU, Belgaum, India

M. Dakshayini
B.M.S College of Engineering, Bengaluru, VTU, Belgaum, India

ABSTRACT

Demand forecasting plays an important role in the field of agriculture, where a farmer can plan for the crop production according to the demand in future and make a profitable crop business. There exist a various statistical and machine learning methods for forecasting the demand, selecting the best forecasting model is desirable. In this work, a multiple linear regression (MLR) and an artificial neural network (ANN) model have been implemented for forecasting an optimum societal demand for various food crops that are commonly used in day to day life. The models are implemented using R toll, linear model and neuralnet packages for training and optimization of the MLR and ANN models. Then, the results obtained by the ANN were compared with the results obtained with MLR models. The results obtained indicated that the designed models are useful, reliable, and quite an effective tool for optimizing the effects of demand prediction in controlling the supply of food harvests to match the societal needs satisfactorily.

DOI: 10.4018/978-1-6684-2408-7.ch062

1. INTRODUCTION

Demand planning plays a very strategic role in improving the performance of every business, as the planning for a whole lot of other activities depends on the accuracy and validity of this exercise (Sultana & Shathi, 2010). The field of agriculture is not an exception; demand forecasting plays an important role in this area also, where a farmer can plan for the crop production according to the demand in future. Hence, a system which could forecasts the demand for day-to-day food harvests and assists the farmers in planning the crop production accordingly may lead to beneficial farming business. The agricultural or farming system generates massive collections of data with the potential to reveal insights into optimizing costs and outcomes if analyzed with the proper tools.

Over the last few decades, statistical methods have been used largely to solve predictions and classifications problems. Some of the commonly used statistical techniques for predictions and classifications are multiple regression, logistic regression, discriminant analysis etc. Most of the researchers have been used regression models to solve the prediction problems in various scenarios. These days, neural network (NN) methods have been extensively used in prediction and classification problems. Neural network methods have become very significant models for a wide variety of applications across many disciplines where the statistical methods were being used. This has led many researchers to compare the traditional statistical methods with neural network methods in several of applications (Ali Aydın Koç, 2013). Many studies have shown the relationship between neural networks and statistical models in many disciplines.

This work is focusing on the power of modern predictive data analytics in educating the farmers towards the demand-based supply of food crops to reduce the loss and price variations. These problems have risen mainly due to the unsynchronized demand and supply of food crops (Balaji Prabhu & Dakshayini, 2018). Forecasting the needs of various food harvests may help us to build an effective analytical system in instructing the farmers for cultivating the food crops according to the actual necessity and make the agriculture as a successful business. Despite the availability of huge historical data about the crop demand, a gap between the demand for and supply of food harvests has resulted in significant loss for farmers and varied market prices causing the substantial encumbrance to the agriculture system.

The aim of this work is to find the best method for forecasting the societal demand for various food harvests by analyzing the computation performances of ANN and MLR forecasting methods. Forecasting is done using MLR and ANN forecasting models and also analyzed the computational performance in forecasting of these models using different performance parameters. A cloud-based system could be developed based on the selected model through which the developed system could effectively assist the farmers in cultivating the crops based on the forecasted demand. So that, the supply of the food harvest could be map with the demand avoiding the loss for farmers leading to sustainable farming.

The main contribution of this work is a novel ANN and MLR based high-performance computing models to forecast the demand for different food crops and select the best amongst them by comparing their performances in demand forecasting.

Rest of the paper is organized as follows; Section 2 gives a survey on ANN and MLR model, Section 3 briefs about the regression and neural network models. System architecture and methodology are explained in Section 4. Section 5 discusses the implementation and performance analysis of the models. Section 6 concludes the paper.

2. LITERATURE SURVEY

Demand forecasting is critical in managing the demand of electricity. Authors have used the data from Kaggle competition and developed a neural network model to predict the energy loads across different grids of the network. The results show that, neural network model was able to perform well in predicting the electricity load across the network grid (Busseti, Osband, & Wong, 2012).

The authors have studied the forecasting of financial price movements using feed forward and recurrent neural networks. Authors have developed an ANN model to predict the financial time series value. The model has considered the feed forward non-deep networks with more neurons and deep networks with fewer neurons for analysis. The developed model has generated better estimates than the reference methods (Widegren, 2017).

The work has reviewed some of neural network model, and the recent work on them. Additionally, authors have discussed some of the main tasks performed with time series data using neural network model. Finally, the work has concluded that the model developed using neural networks has yielded better results in most of the scenarios (Gamboa, 2017).

S. Makridakis et al. have evaluated the performance of statistical methods with ML methods using a large subset of 1045 monthly time series used in the M3 Competition. The analysis shows that, accuracy of the statistical models is better compared to ML methods. Authors have discussed the reasons being the low accuracy of ML models over the statistical ones and also proposed some possible ways of forwarding (Makridakis, Spiliotis, & Assimakopoulos, 2018).

S. Tiryaki et al. (Tiryaki, Özşahin, & Yildirim, 2014) have developed ANN and MLR models for predicting an optimum bonding strength of heat-treated woods. The ANN model was developed using mat lab neural network toolbox. The performance of the ANN model in predicting the best results are analysed by implementing various networks. Then, the results of ANN models were compared with the results of MLR model. The results have shown that the ANN model gives the better results compared to MLR model.

Several studies have been carried out to analyze the dynamic and statistical downscaling for climate variability and climate change. D. Mendes et al. has introduced ANNs and MLR models to predict the rainfall in South America. The work has examined the usage of ANNs and MLR analysis with principal component analysis as temporal downscaling methods for the generation of monthly rainfall. Both the ANN and MLR method performed well with the observed data sets. The authors have concluded that ANNs are worthwhile substitutes for the demonstrating the rainfall using time series data (Soares Dos Santos, Mendes, & Rodrigues Torres, 2016).

The paper (Paswan & Begum, 2017) has reviewed the studies on ANN and traditional statistical methods used in the prediction of agricultural crop production. The study has revealed that ANN models will perform well in the process of predictions compared to statistical methods. However, the identification of various network parameters in ANN models such as the levels of hidden layers, number of neurons in each hidden layer to optimize the network configuration is a time-consuming process compared to statistical model. The paper concludes that both models have their own advantages and disadvantages.

The performance of ANN and MLR models in estimating the solar radiation over Turkey was studied by (Mehmet, 2013). Authors have considered NOAA satellite data and month wise meteorological data about temperature, longitude, latitude, altitude for modeling and testing the models. The results obtained indicated that, the ANN model could achieve a better performance compared to MLR model in estimating the monthly average solar radiation values. The results were also revealed that more accurate results could be obtained with the satellite data compared to meteorological data values.

Ann and MLR models are developed by (Patel & Brahmbhatt, 2015) to predict the consumption of fuel in pyrolysis oil blended with diesel used in a single cylinder diesel engine. The parameters such as ratio of compression, pressure, timing, and load are considered for building and training the models. The ANN model has performed well even with the small data sets. The results show that accuracy of ANN model is more in predicting the fuel consumption of a cylinder compared to MLR model.

M Zaefizadeh et al. (Zaefizadeh & Khayatnezhad, 2011) have performed the comparison of ANN and MLR models in predicting the yield. The "farm experiments and numerical resources" data sets were used for training and testing the models. The statistical methods based on the F test using the mathematical expectancy mean squares (EMS) was carried out to build MLR model, whereas ANN was developed in the Matlab software. The parameters such as numbers of fertile tillers, grains per main spike, and grain weight were used to build the models. The results show that MLR model could able to predict better results compared to ANN model.

There has no substantial work been done in forecasting the societal demand for food crops that has led to a gap between Demand and supply of food crops. Hence, this work proposes a forecasting mode based on MLR and ANN and also compares the accuracy of both models in forecasting the demand with the actual demand values.

3. BACKGROUND WORKS

Regression is one of the most commonly used statistical methods to build any forecasting models. Regression models will foresee the value of response variable using the preceding values of explanatory variables. The model computes the value of response variable by establishing a relationship between response and explanatory variables with the help of linear line. The model will fit the line along the values of explanatory variables with the possible minimal error between the line and values. Based on the number of explanatory variables used to foresee the value of the response variable, regression model could be categorized into simple linear regression (one explanatory variable) or multiple linear regression (more than one explanatory variable).

3.1 Multiple Linear Regressions

A Regression model with more than one explanatory variable used to predict the value of response variable is called a multiple linear regression model. A multiple linear regression equation can be written as shown in Equation 1.

$$R_i = I + B_1 * X_{i,1} + B_2 * X_{i,2} + \ldots + B_n * X_{i,n} + e_i \qquad (1)$$

Where

R_i is an ith response variable

X_i is the ith explanatory variables

I is the Intercept of the line

B_i is the slope of the line

e_i is the error in the ith value of X

The slope and intercept values need to be calculated with respect to the explanatory variables in order to predict the future values.

The slope of the equation can be calculated using the formula 2

$$Slope(B) = (N\Sigma X * R - (\Sigma X)(\Sigma R)) / (N\Sigma X^2 - (\Sigma X)^2) \tag{2}$$

The intercept of a line is calculated using the Formula 3

$$Intercept (I) = (\Sigma R - B(\Sigma X) / N) \tag{3}$$

Substituting the value of intercept, I and a slope B in the equation with the set of X values gives the prediction for the response variable R.

3.2 Artificial Neural Networks

ANNs have been used in various application ranges from prediction to pattern recognition. The network architecture of ANNs contains numerous neurons as processing elements placed at different layers of the network. The network of the ANN model can be categorized in to 3 main layers such as an input layer, an output layer and one or more hidden layers as shown in Figure 1. The neurons of all the 3 layers are interrelated by the means of weights "w_i". Each neuron in the layer "n" gets the facts from all the neurons present in the layer "n-1" (Paliwal & Kumar, 2009). The received fact is added with the weights and the bias of the layer (θn). The activation function f() is applied to computed value and transmits to all neurons of the subsequent layer "n+1".

The number of neurons in the network regulates the performance of the ANN network. The neurons in the input layers relate to number of input variables, and the neurons in the output layers relates to number of output variables. The levels of hidden layers and the neurons in each level of the hidden layers are defined by trial and error mode considering the performance of the network as a metric.

4. IMPLIMENTATION AND METHODOLOGY

The demand of any product depends on several factors ("Factors of Supply and Demand") such as income of people, taste, price, willing to buy a product etc. Food commodities belong to the category of necessary products, the demand of a necessary products mainly depends on the factors such as per capita demand D_b, income growth I_G, expenditure elasticity E_e and population P_y for the year 'y' (Mittal, 2008). The data sets required for the demand forecasting and analysis are gathered from the Agmarknet

("Agmarknet"), NSS (Government of Karnataka, 2012; India National Sample Survey Office, 2010), and other authorized websites.

Figure 1. A multi-layer feed-forward back-propagation ANN model

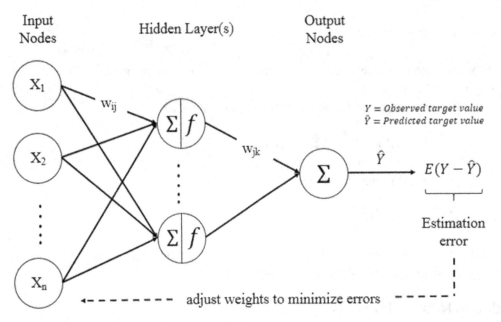

4.1 MLR Model

The demand of a food commodity for the year 'y' represented as D_y depends on several explanatory variables. So, the demand D_y can be expressed as a linear combination of response (D_y) and explanatory (D_b, I_G, E_e, P_y) variables as shown in Equation 4, using regression Equation 1.

$$D_y = \beta_0 + \beta_1 D_b + \beta_2 I_G + \beta_3 E_e + \beta_4 P_y + e \qquad (4)$$

Where β_0, β_1, β_2, β_3 and β_4 are the unknown parameters of the equation and 'e' is the error term.

Figure 2 shows the system architecture for the proposed MLR demand forecasting model. The data-sets containing the values of per capita demand for different commodities, per capita income, and the expenditure elasticity for different commodities and the population growth for the previous ten years are stored in the database. The proposed MLR model is applied to all the data sets stored to forecast the demand for the year 'y'. The "per capita demand", "per capita income", "expenditure elasticity", and the "population growth" are the explanatory parameters and demand as the response parameter of the model.

In general, this regression demand equation can be written as in the Equation 5.

$$Y_i = \beta_0 + \beta_1 {}^* X_{i,1} + \beta_2 {}^* X_{i,2} + \ldots + \beta_3 {}^* X_{i,n} + e_i, \ i := 1, 2, \ldots, m \qquad (5)$$

Figure 2. Multiple linear regression based demand forecasting model

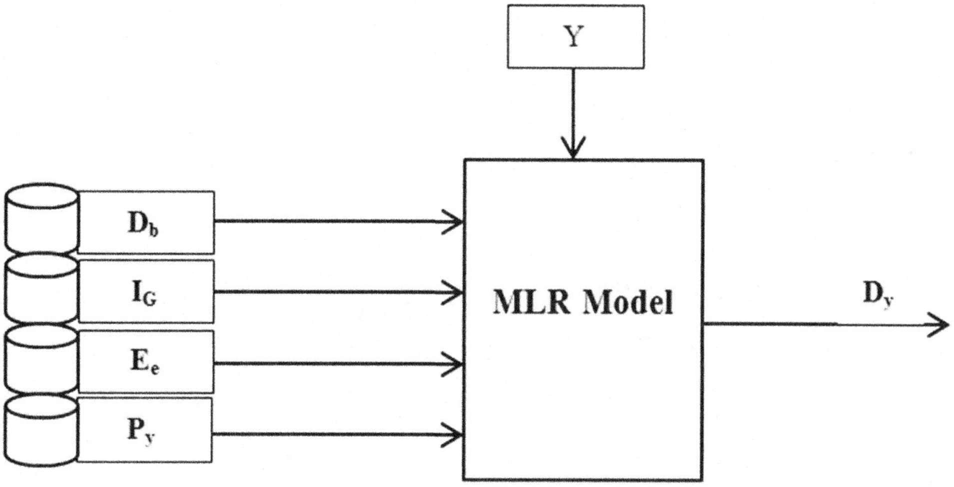

Where m: number of observations and n: number of variables.

Y_i (i = 1,2, …, m) is the dependent variable- D_y

$X_{i,k}$ (k = 1,2, …, n) are the independent variables measured without error- D_b, I_G, E_e P_y

β_0, β_1, β_2, …, β_n are the unknown parameters of the model

e_i is the random error term, i=1, 2, …, n

The least squares approach is used in order to estimate the slope vector S and intercept I, which minimizes the overall possible computations of the intercept and slopes calculation (Miller, 2013).

4.2 ANN Model

In this work, the values of the explanatory variables D_b, I_G, E_e, P_y are used as an input layer variable and the response variable D_y is used as a output layer variable in the ANN model. The data set is partitioned in to training and testing data set to train and test the model. To configure the hidden layers and the neurons in each hidden layer, the model was trained with the training data set by considering the MSE value as a decisive parameter. Trial and error method were applied until the error between the measured and the predicted values was minimized.

The model was trained with the feed forward and back propagation multilayer ANN and "trainlm" algorithm was used as a training algorithm. The Rectified Linear units (relu) is used as an activation function in hidden layers and linear transfer function (purelin) as an output layer activation function. The damped least-squares method algorithm (nls.lm) was used as the learning rule. The training of the ANN model was stopped after 39 epochs as the minimal MSE value of "0.00050" has obtained.

A four-layered ANN architecture has been proposed with the 1 input layer with 5 neurons, 2 hidden layers with 4 and 2 neurons, and 1 output layer with 1 neuron as shown in the Figure 3.

Figure 3. Proposed ANN network architecture

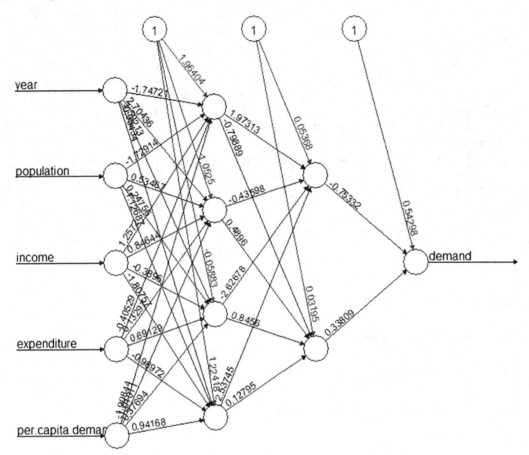

5. IMPLEMENTATION AND PERFORMANCE ANALYSIS

The proposed MLR and ANN models are implemented in R using "linear model" and "neuralnet" packages respectively. Before applying the proposed forecasting model, it is necessary to check whether there exists any linear relationship between the dependent and independent variables. The relation between the response and predictor variables can be analysed through several ways such as compute the simple summary function to check the means standard deviation, correlation etc. The relationship can be visualized using the scatter plots, which shows the existence of a linear relationship between the response variables and predictor variables, outliers, data-entry errors and skewed or unusual distributions.

Figure 4 is the scatter plot for analysing the relationship between the dependent and independent variables used in the demand forecasting model for the rice crop. From the figure it can be determined that, there exists a linear relationship between the variables of the model. So, the preferred variables could be used in implementing the model. Table 1 shows the correlation between the variables of the model, from the table it is observed that there exists a strong correlation between the variables of the model. As the independent variables exhibits a strong correlation with the dependent variable, used independent variables are more significant in model development.

The scatter plot is drawn to analyse the relationship between the variables of the model and the resultant scatter plot that shows the existence of relationships with the variables of the model so that we can use the variables in the implementation of the model. The proposed model gives the most significant values with the correlation coefficients and the R-squared values are indicates the efficiency of the developed model with the considered independent variables.

Figure 4. Scatter Plots showing the relationship between the dependent and independent variable for the crop rice

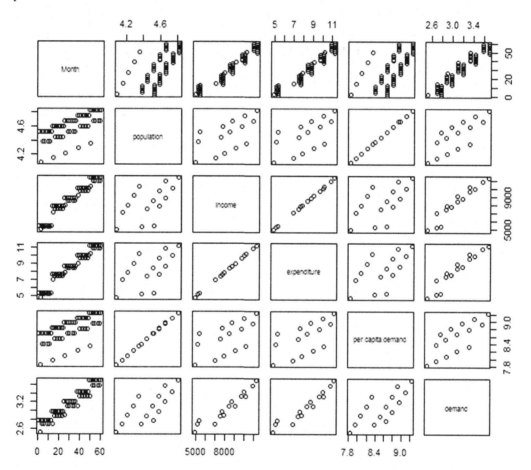

Table 1. Correlation between dependent and independent variables

Variable	population	income	expenditure	Per capita	Demand
population	1.000000	0.70402	0.7040245	0.9997	0.8121
income	0.704024	1.00000	1.0000000	0.6928	0.8696
expenditure	0.704024	1.00000	1.000000	0.6928	0.8674
Percapita	0.999791	0.69281	0.692818	1.0000	0.8012
demand	0.812161	0.96962	0.969623	0.8012	1.0000

The Model shows the high significance with the 'p' (0.0204) value and R-squared (0.895) values. So, the model could be used effectively in forecasting the demand for the crop Rice. The demand for the rice crop is forecasted using the proposed models and compared with the actual demand values as shown in Table 2. From the table it can be conclude that, the predicted values of ANN model are more accurate compared to MLR model values. Figure 5 plots the graph for the Table 2 values and visualizes the comparison of the models.

Table 2. Comparison of the Actual Demand and Forecasted Demand by MLR and ANN models for the crop Rice for the year 2015 to 2021. (Values in lakh tons)

year	Actual Demand	Demand Prediction using MLR model	Demand Prediction using ANN model
2015	39.8	39.36	39.83007
2016	42.9	43.92	42.8294
2017	46.2	47.87	46.02664
2018	46.4	46.67	49.4002
2019	NA	54.08	53.07025
2020	NA	57.22	56.93376
2021	NA	62.91	61.04997

Figure 5. Comparison of MLR vs. ANN model prediction with respect to actual values

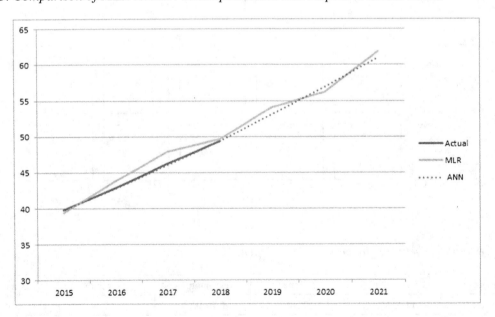

5.1 Performance Evaluation

The training and testing data sets were normalized to the range between 0 and 1 using the minimum and maximum values of the data sets to level the significance of variables. Upon training the model, the output values are de-normalized to the actual values using a reverse normalization process to evaluate the results. The normalization of the values is done using the Equation (6).

$$X_n = \frac{X - X_{min}}{X_{max} - X_{min}} \tag{6}$$

where X_n is the normalized value of a variable, X is actual value of the variable, X_{min} is the minimum value of the X and X_{max} is the maximum values of X.

To evaluate the performance of the prediction models, the mean square error (MSE), the mean absolute percentage error (MAPE), the root means square error (RMSE) and coefficients of determination (R^2) were used as evaluation parameters. The MSE, MAPE, RMSE and R^2 values were calculated using Equations (7), (8), (9) and (10) respectively.

$$MSE = \frac{1}{N} \sum_{i=1}^{N} \left(tm_i - tp_i \right)^2 \tag{7}$$

$$MAPE\left(Y, \widehat{Y}\right) = \frac{1}{N} \sum_{1}^{N} \left| \frac{Yi, \widehat{Y}_i}{yi} \right| \tag{8}$$

$$RMSE\left(Y, \widehat{Y}\right) = \sqrt{\frac{1}{N} \sum_{i=1}^{n} \left(Yi, \widehat{Yi}\right)^2} \tag{9}$$

$$R^2 = 1 - \frac{\sum_{i=1}^{N} \left(tm_i - tp_i \right)^2}{\sum_{i=1}^{N} \left(tm_i - tp_i^- \right)^2} \tag{10}$$

Where,

tm_i is the measured value.

tp_i is the predicted value.

N is the total number of samples.

Y is the actual value.

$\hat{Y}$ is the predicted value.

The performance of the MLR and ANN models in the prediction of demand values are measured with the performance evaluation parameters and tabulated in Table 3.

Table 3. Performance Evaluation of MLR and ANN models

Model	Data set	MSE	MAPE	RMSE	R²
ANN	Training set	0.0050	1.35	0.16	0.994
	Testing set	0.0083	2.82	0.32	0.982
MLR	All data set	0.0070	2.02	0.28	0.983

From the Table 3 it can be observed that, ANN records better values compared to MLR model in all the cases. The mean standard error values for ANN model in testing (0.050) and training (0.083) are lower than MLR model (0.007) value. Ann archives a lesser value for MAPE as 1.35% and 2.82% in training and testing cases respectively, whereas MAPE value for MLR model is 2.02% which is slightly higher than ANN value. Furthermore, the RMSE values for ANN are 0.16 and 0.32 for training and testing data sets respectively and MLR model records 0.28 with RMSE estimation. In the estimation of R² value also, the ANN model archives better values compared to MLR model.

From the results, it can be concluded that the ANN model performs better in forecasting the demand values for food commodities compared to MLR model. So, the ANN could be used for effective forecasting of the demand for different food crops. Using the ANN model developed, the demand of Rice, Wheat, Tomato and Onion for the state of Karnataka from the year 2018 to 2021are predicted as shown Table 4.

Table 4. Demand forecasting for different crops using the developed model from the year 2018 to 2021. (Values in lakh tons)

Year	Vegetables		Cereals	
	Onion	Tomato	Rice	Wheat
2018	70.36804	62.59364	49.4002	10.32
2019	73.61138	64.74002	53.07025	11.06
2020	76.85473	67.34063	56.93376	11.67
2021	80.09808	71.25701	61.04997	12.33

Results obtained from experimental studies illustrated that regulating the supply of food harvests according to the forecasted demand significantly affect in reducing the gap between demand for and supply of food harvests and there by achieving the expected profit for farmers and price for consumers.

6. CONCLUSION

Demand forecasting of societal food crops plays an important role in the field of agriculture, based on which a data analytical system could be developed in the direction of educating the farmers to harvest the food crops based on this demand, so that farmers could get the expected profit. Hence, identifying an effective forecasting model that could forecasts the demand of various food crops that are commonly used in day to day life very near to the actual demand is essential. So, in this work, a Multiple Linear regression (MLR) and an artificial neural network (ANN) models have been used for forecasting the demand considering the historical data about demand supply and price values taken from authorized govt. websites. Computation performance of both the methods is analysed based on the input given and demand predicted to find the best forecasting method. It has been revealed that both ANN and MLR models produces accurate results in all cases. ANN model performs slightly better compared to MLR model. So ANN forecasting method could be used to predict the demand of the food harvests and supply of the same could be controlled accordingly leading to successful agricultural system. In future, a cloud based analytics system could be developed as a service to help the farmers in selecting the best suitable crops for their land and having a demand in future. The system could regulate the supply according to the demand and helps the farmers in avoiding the loss and also makes the consumers happy by satisfying their needs.

REFERENCES

Agmarknet. (n.d.). Price trends. Retrieved from http://agmarknet.gov.in/PriceTrends/Default.aspx

Ali Aydın Koç, Ö. Y. (2013). A comparative study of artificial neural networks and logistic regression for classification of marketing campaign results. *Mathematical and Computational Applications*, *18*(3), 392–398. doi:10.3390/mca18030392

Balaji Prabhu, B.VDakshayini, M. (2018). Performance Analysis of the Regression and Time Series Predictive Models using Parallel Implementation for Agricultural Data. *Procedia Computer Science*, *132*, 198–207. doi:10.1016/j.procs.2018.05.187

Busseti, E., Osband, I., & Wong, S. (2012). Deep learning for time series modeling. Stanford. Retrieved from http://cs229.stanford.edu/proj2012/BussetiOsbandWong-DeepLearningForTimeSeriesModeling.pdf

Factors of Supply and Demand. (n.d.). Grain PHD. Retrieved from http://www.grainphd.com/wp-content/uploads/2017/07/Supply-and-Demand.pdf

Gamboa, J. C. B. (2017). Deep Learning for Time-Series Analysis. Retrieved from http://arxiv.org/abs/1701.01887

Government of Karnataka. (2012). Household Consumer Expenditure in [State Sample] NSS 64 th Round (July 2007 – June 2008). Directorate of Economics and Statistics, (4).

India National Sample Survey Office. (2010). Household Consumption of Various Goods and Services in India. NSS 66th Round July-2009 June-2010.

Makridakis, S., Spiliotis, E., & Assimakopoulos, V. (2018). Statistical and Machine Learning forecasting methods: Concerns and ways forward. *PLoS One, 13*(3), 1–26. doi:10.1371/journal.pone.0194889 PMID:29584784

Mehmet, S. (2013). Comparison of ANN and MLR models for estimating solar radiation in Turkey using NOAA / AVHRR data. *Advances in Space Research, 51*(5), 891-904.

Miller, T. (2013). Modeling techniques in predictive analytics. Business problems and solutions with r.

Mittal, S. (2008). Demand-Supply Trends and Projections of Food in India. Indian Council for Research on International Economics Relations, (209).

Paliwal, M., & Kumar, U. A. (2009). Neural networks and statistical techniques: A review of applications. *Expert Systems with Applications, 36*(1), 2–17. doi:10.1016/j.eswa.2007.10.005

Paswan, R. P., & Begum, S. A. (2017). *Regression and Neural Networks Models for Prediction of Crop Production.*

Patel, S. C. & Brahmbhatt, P. K. (2015). ANN and MLR Model of Specific Fuel Consumption for Pyrolysis Oil Blended with Diesel used in a Single Cylinder Diesel Engine: A Comparative Study.

Soares Dos Santos, T., Mendes, D., & Rodrigues Torres, R. (2016). Artificial neural networks and multiple linear regression model using principal components to estimate rainfall over South America. *Nonlinear Processes in Geophysics, 23*(1), 13–20. doi:10.5194/npg-23-13-2016

Sultana, N., & Shathi, S. R. (2010). Demand Planning Methodology in Supply Chain Management. *Proceedings of the 2010 International Conference on Industrial Engineering and Operations Management.* Academic Press.

Tiryaki, S., Özşahin, Ş., & Yildirim, I. (2014). Comparison of artificial neural network and multiple linear regression models to predict optimum bonding strength of heat treated woods. *International Journal of Adhesion and Adhesives, 55*, 29–36. doi:10.1016/j.ijadhadh.2014.07.005

Widegren, P. (2017). Deep learning-based forecasting of financial assets.

Zaefizadeh, M., Jalili, A., Khayatnezhad, M., Gholamin, R., & Mokhtari, T. (2011). Comparison of multiple linear regressions (MLR) and artificial neural network (ANN) in predicting the yield using its components in the hulless barley. In Advances in Environmental Biology (pp. 109-114). Academic Press.

This research was previously published in the International Journal of Grid and High Performance Computing (IJGHPC), 12(4); pages 35-47, copyright year 2020 by IGI Publishing (an imprint of IGI Global).

Chapter 63
Particle Swarm Optimization of BP–ANN Based Soft Sensor for Greenhouse Climate

M. Outanoute

Sensors Electronic & Instrumentation Group, Physics Department, Faculty of Sciences, Moulay Ismaïl University, Meknes, Morocco

A. Lachhab

Modelling, Systems Control and Telecommunications Team, Department of Electrical Engineering, High School of Technology, Moulay Ismaïl University, Meknes, Morocco

A. Selmani

Sensors Electronic & Instrumentation Group, Physics Department, Faculty of Sciences, Moulay Ismaïl University, Meknes, Morocco

H. Oubehar

Sensors Electronic & Instrumentation Group, Physics Department, Faculty of Sciences, Moulay Ismaïl University, Meknes, Morocco

A. Snoussi

Modelling, Systems Control and Telecommunications Team, Department of Electrical Engineering, High School of Technology, Moulay Ismaïl University, Meknes, Morocco

M. Guerbaoui

Modelling, Systems Control and Telecommunications Team, Department of Electrical Engineering, High School of Technology, Moulay Ismaïl University, Meknes, Morocco

A. Ed-dahhak

Modelling, Systems Control and Telecommunications Team, Department of Electrical Engineering, High School of Technology, Moulay Ismaïl University, Meknes, Morocco

B. Bouchikhi

Sensors Electronic & Instrumentation Group, Physics Department, Faculty of Sciences, Moulay Ismaïl University, Meknes, Morocco

DOI: 10.4018/978-1-6684-2408-7.ch063

ABSTRACT

In this article, the authors develop the Particle Swarm Optimization algorithm (PSO) in order to optimise the BP network in order to elaborate an accurate dynamic model that can describe the behavior of the temperature and the relative humidity under an experimental greenhouse system. The PSO algorithm is applied to the Back-Propagation Neural Network (BP-NN) in the training phase to search optimal weights baded on neural networks. This approach consists of minimising the reel function which is the mean squared difference between the real measured values of the outputs of the model and the values estimated by the elaborated neural network model. In order to select the model which possess higher generalization ability, various models of different complexity are examined by the test-error procedure. The best performance is produced by the usage of one hidden layer with fourteen nodes. A comparison of measured and simulated data regarding the generalization ability of the trained BP-NN model for both temperature and relative humidity under greenhouse have been performed and showed that the elaborated model was able to identify the inside greenhouse temperature and humidity with a good accurately.

1. INTRODUCTION

A greenhouse system is a closed environment where some climate variables can be manipulated in order to obtain adequate climatic conditions, for the development and growth of the cultures, using automatic control strategies (Shamshiri & Ismail 2013). The greenhouse environmental control involves the field of control technology, as the way to optimize inside greenhouse climate based on measured variables and acting on greenhouse equipment (Lu et al., 2015). The dynamics of the climatic variables in a greenhouse are very complex. That is due to the presence of nonlinearities, subjected to strong disturbances (measurable and non-measurable ones) and a high degree of correlation among variables (Frausto & Pieters, 2004; Bennis et al., 2008).

Due to the complexity of the real engineering systems, like the greenhouse system, some importance has been put into implementing Artificial Intelligence (AI) techniques including neural networks, fuzzy logic, neuro-fuzzy, evolutionary algorithms, or some combination among them. Although artificial intelligent methods offer the advantage of the capability of capturing essential functional relationships among the data when such relationships are not a priori known or are very difficult to describe mathematically in situations of the collected data are corrupted by noise. Therefore, they had gained importance and successfully applied in large areas, such as modelling, prediction, control, optimization, business, and financial engineering (He & Ma, 2010).

For plants of high complexity, like greenhouse process, it is of main importance to develop accurate models of the plant which will be used to describe the system behaviour. Furthermore, a perfect model is significant for the parmaters tuning of the controller based on the system's dynamic model, to design a performance control law (Kiranyaz et al., 2009). In this way, neural networks algorithms are a very sophisticated nonlinear modelling techniques used to perform an accurate modelling of the greenhouse system dynamics for temperature or both air temperature and relative humidity, due to its capability of learning and generalization from examples using the data-driven self-adaptive approach, as long as enough data are presented in the training process (Lai & Zhang, 2009).

Normally, when designing and training a neural network, different architectures must be tried before the one that seems effective is found. Obviously, there is no guarantee that the final selected architecture is the best possible one and for large problems this method becomes impractical. In addition, change in other network parameters such as the learning algorithm or the number of epochs affect the best choice of architecture. This interdependence makes it difficult to find optimal architectures for a given problem (Zhang et al., 2007).

Hence, the heuristic optimization methods which evolve network architectures can solve these problems (Chen et al., 2016; Meng et al., 2016). One of the main advantages of heuristic methods is that they convergence to the optimum solution in more short time than others and convergence fewer to local minimum (Shan Ngan &Wei Tan, 2016).

Particle Swarm Optimization (PSO) algorithm is a new population based heuristic optimization method first proposed by Kennedy and Eberhart (Bas, 2016). It's an effective swarm intelligence optimization algorithm featuring high search speed and high efficiency. Recently, successful applications of PSO algorithm to the optimization problems attract much attention in various problems intelligence optimization (Aladag et al., 2012). Although, PSO algorithm can be used in terms of the learning algorithm to assist in network training phase in order to adapt connection weight and biases adaptation. This benefits to the ANN since its generalization capability can be improved (Mohammadi & Mirabedini, 2014).

Thus, this paper investigates the use of PSO algorithm as a heuristic optimization method to search optimal weights and biases by using a neural network model for identifying the behaviour of the temperature and relative humidity under greenhouse system.

2. MATERIALS AND METHODS

2.1. Experimental Setup

Measurements of climate parameters were obtained from an experimental greenhouse located at the Faculty of Sciences of Meknes (Morocco). This system is automated with several sensors and actuators that are connected respectively to a control and acquisition system based on a personal computer (Guerbaoui et al., 2013). This system allows the measurement of the different climatic parameters inside and outside the greenhouse. The acquisition of data collected from the sensors and the different actuators order are assured by the use of a data acquisition card NI-PCI6024E. All the cards of interface, conditioning of the sensors, card of protection, and of cards of power are connected to a PC via the data acquisition. This system has the proficiency to serve as the basis for research and testing of various advanced control strategies (Ed-Dahhak et al., 2013; El Afou et al., 2014).

2.2. Collecting and Preprocessing of Experiment Data

For modelling purposes, experiment measurement were collected for three days, acquired with a sampling time of 10 seconds. Figure 1 (a-f) show the data profile of input and output climate variables.

First of all, all the data were carried on normalization processing to scale the inputs and targets so that they fall within the interval [-1, 1]. The used formula is as follows:

$$\overline{x}_i = 0.01 + 0.99 * \left(\frac{x_i - x_{min}}{x_{max} - x_{min}} \right)$$

(1)

Where $\overline{x}_i$ is a value after normalization, x_i is the measured value, x_{max} and x_{min} are the maximum and the minimum of the measured values.

Figure 1. Data Profile of Input and Output Variables: (a) Command Heater, (b) Command Ventilator, (c) External Temperature, (d) External Relative Humidity, (e) Internal Temperature And (f) Internal Relative Humidity

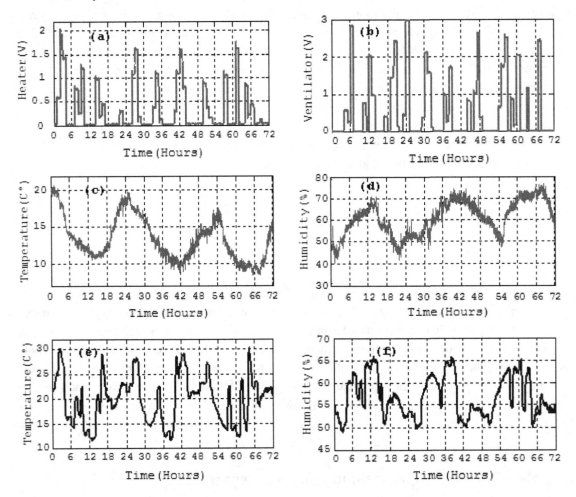

The multi-layer perceptron (MLP) architecture adopted for ANN model for identifying dynamic responses of the temperature and relative humidity under greenhouse is depicted in Figure 2. The external temperature, the external relative humidity, command of heater and ventilator, the previous values of internal temperature and relative humidity were defined as input nodes whereas the internal temperature and the internal relative humidity were the output nodes.

Figure 2. Topology Structure of BP-NN for Identifying Dynamic Responses of the Temperature Interne and Relative Humidity Interne

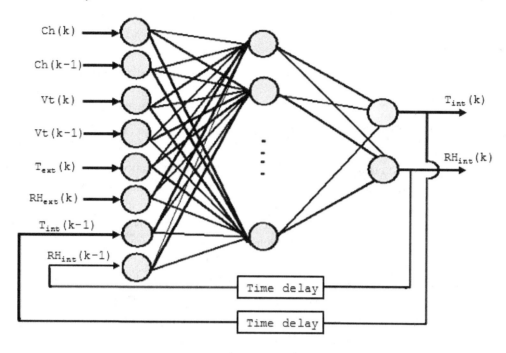

A tang sigmoid function of the equation (2) was used as a transfer function in the hidden layer of the network.

$$Transig(n) = \frac{2}{\left(1 + exp\left(-2 * n\right)\right)} - 1 \tag{2}$$

Three different performance criteria have been computed. Namely, the Mean Square Error (MSE), the Variance Accounted For (VAF), and the best FIT criterion between the predicted values of the network and the experimental values are given by the following expressions, respectively:

$$Fit = \sum_{i=1}^{N} \sum_{j=1}^{K} (y_j(i) - \hat{y}_j(i)))^2 \tag{3}$$

$$MSE = \frac{1}{N} \sum_{k=1}^{N} (y(k) - \hat{y}(k))^2 \tag{4}$$

Where $y_j(i)$ denotes the real output, $\hat{y}_j(i)$ denotes the simulated output of the model, and N is the total number of data observation.

$$VAF = \left(1 - \frac{\text{var}\left(y - \hat{y}\right)}{\text{var}(y)}\right).100\% \tag{5}$$

Where y is a vector containing the actual output data, $\hat{y}$ is a vector with the simulated output data of the model.

2.3. Particle Swarm Optimization Algorithm

Particle Swarm Optimization (PSO) is one of the evolutionary optimization technique, inspired by the social behaviour of the swarm in nature, developed by Eberhart and Kennedy in 1995. In this technique, there is a population of particles which move through the solution space to find the optimal solution.

The algorithm starts by initializing a population of random solutions called particles and searches for optima by updating generations. If the ith particle of the swarm is represented by the D–dimensional vector $X_i = (x_{i1}, x_{i2}, ..., x_{iD})$. The best previous position of the ith particle (giving the minimum fitness value) is recorded and represented as $P_i = (p_{i1}, p_{i2,} ... p_{iD})$, called pbest, and the location change (velocity) of the ith particle is $V_i = (v_{i1}, v_{i2}, ..., v_{iD})$. The best particle among all particles in the swarm is denoted by the gbest. Each particle tracks its previous best position and the global best position by continuously updating its velocity and position until the number of iterations exceeds the maximum or a pre-defined fitness function value is reached. To achieve convergence, the particles are manipulated according to the equations (6) and (7) (Das et al. 2013):

- The velocity update equation:

$$v_i(k+1) = wv_i(k) + c_1 r_1(pbest_i(k) - x_i(k)) + c_2 r_2(gbest(k) - x_i(k)) \tag{6}$$

- The position update equation:

$$x_i(k+1) = x_i(k) + vi_i k + 1) \tag{7}$$

Where

$v_i(k)$ is the kth current velocity of the ith particle,
$x_i(k)$ is the kth current position of the ith particle,
w is the inertia weight;
k is the kth current iteration of the algorithm,
i is the ith particle of the swarm,
c_1 and c_2 are two positive constants,
r_1 and r_2 are random values between 0 and 1.

Figure 3 shows the flow chart of PSO algorithm.

Figure 3. The Flow Chart of PSO Algorithm

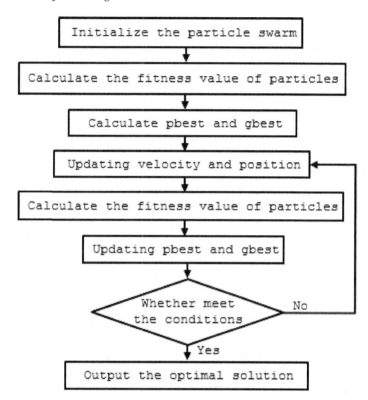

3. MODEL RESULTS AND DISCUSSION

ANN model where its weight and biases parameters are optimized using particle swarm optimization technique which was investigated in order to estimate the temperature and relative humidity under greenhouse based on the collected data.

The implementation parameters of the ANN and PSO algorithm are summarized in Table 1 and Table 2, respectively. The number of hidden neurones constitutes the hidden layer is determined by a test-error procedure based on several simulations running.

Table 1. ANN parameters

ANN Parameters	values
Goal (MSE)	0.001
Inputs	8
Hidden layer	1
Training data	17200
Testing data	8640
Hidden layer neurons	14
Output layer neurons	2

Table 2. Parameters of PSO Algorithm

PSO parameters	Values
Population Size	40
Number of Iterations	120
w_{max}	1
w_{min}	0
$c_1 = c_2$	2

Figure 4 shows the convergence rates PSO-ANN based on the fitness values in 120 iterations.

Figure 4. Best Fitness Evolution Curve versus the Iterations Step Number during Training

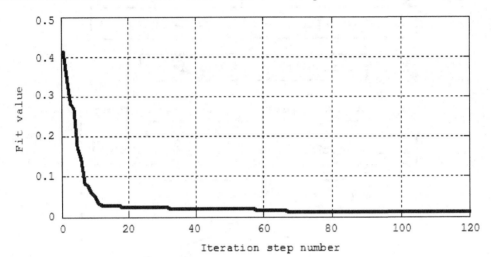

From this fitness curves it is clearly seen that during the initial iterations the convergence of the PSO-ANN was very fast; however, in the last iterations. According to this graph, confirms that the PSO-ANN had a trade-off between avoiding premature converge and walk around the whole search space for all values of weights and biases values. Thus, the optimal values of weights and biases are which achieved corresponding to the fitness value of 0.0089 as the best fitness.

Figure 5 and Figure 6 depict the curves of the simulated values of temperature and the relative humidity and its measured values, respectively, for the training dataset.

Figure 5. Temperature Curve Fitting with the Desired Temperature on the Training Dataset

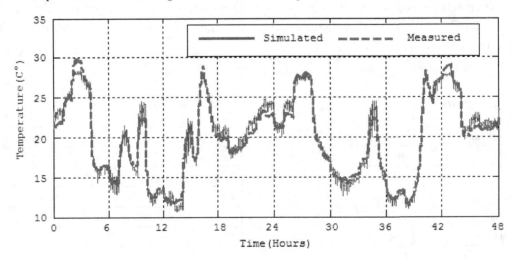

Figure 6. Relative Humidity Curve Fitting with the Desired Relative Humidity on the Training Dataset

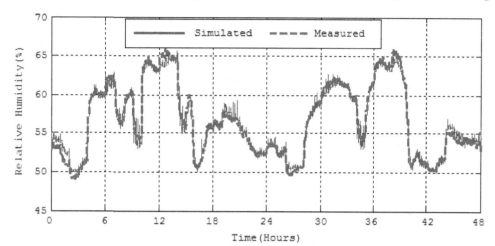

It can be seen that the estimated internal temperature and internal relative humidity obtained from the proposed PSO-ANN training algorithm based on the system identification technique follow the measured values ones, respectively. The obtained results in the training stage, show clearly the excellent performance of training the neural network model by using PSO-ANN algorithm.

To illustrate the accuracy of the proposed neural network approach, we represent in Figure 7 and Figure 8 the results of of simulated and measured temperature and relative humidity, respectively.

Figure 7. Temperature Curve Fitting with the Desired Temperature on the Test Dataset

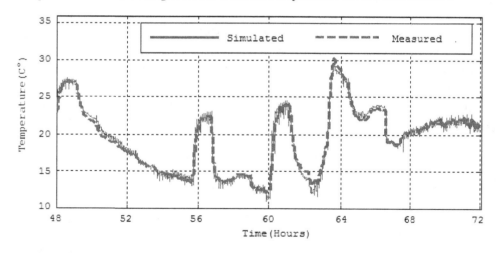

It can be seen that the outputs estimated values closely follows the pattern of the measured temperature with a VAF of 98.78% and MSE of 0.023 and for relative humidity values we obtain a VAF of 98.00% and MSE of 0.062. This confirms that the proposed neural network model is high accuracy.

Figure 8. Relative Humidity Curve Fitting with the Desired Relative Humidity on the Test Dataset

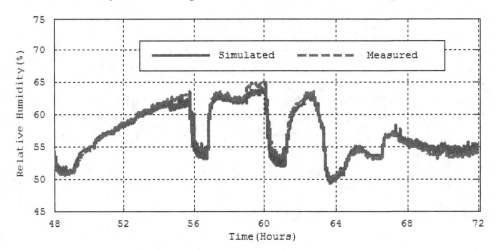

Based on the obtained results, we concluded that PSO-ANN outperforms the modelling of the temperature and relative humidity under greenhouse system owing to the good learning efficiency and generalization ability of the PSO algorithm compared to the standard neural network algorithm based model for the greenhouse climate model.

4. CONCLUSION

In this paper, we used a very efficient procedure based on Particle Swarm Optimization technique in order to outperform the training stage of a BP-ANN model to achieve an accurate model for temperature and relative humidity under greenhouse. The obtained results shown that the PSO-ANN neural network can identify successfully its outputs due to optimal weight matrices between input and output which were produced. Therefore, it can be noticed that the proposed PSO algorithm which was characterized by a low complexity is suitable for use as a training algorithm tool for ANNs models. So, they can be used in decision-making and automatic control in real-time applications for greenhouse system computing optimal control strategies.

REFERENCES

Zhang, J. R., Zhang, J., Lok, T. M., & Lyu, M. R. (2007). A hybrid particle swarm optimization–back-propagation algorithm for feedforward neural network training. *Applied Mathematics and Computation*, *185*, 1026–1037. doi:10.1016/j.amc.2006.07.025

Aladag, C. H. E., Yolcu, U., Egrioglu, E., & Dalar, A. Z. (2012). A new time invariant fuzzy time series forecasting method based on particle swarm optimization. *Applied Soft Computing*, *12*(10), 3291–3299. doi:10.1016/j.asoc.2012.05.002

Das, G., Pattnaik, P. K., & Padhy, S. K. (2013). Artificial Neural Network trained by Particle Swarm Optimization for non-linear channel equalization. *Expert Systems with Applications*, *41*, 491–3496.

Bas, E. (2016). The training of multiplicative neuron model based artificial neural networks with differential evolution algorithm for forecasting. *J. Artif. Intell. Soft Comput. Res*, *6*(1), 5–11. doi:10.1515/jaiscr-2016-0001

Bennis, N., Duplaix, J., Enéa, G., Haloua, M., & Youlal, H. (2008). Greenhouse climate modelling and robust control. *Computers and Electronics in Agriculture*, *61*(2), 96–107. doi:10.1016/j.compag.2007.09.014

Chen, X. T., Wang, T., & Liang, W. (2016). General aircraft material demand forecast based on PSO-BP neural network. *International Journal of Control and Automation*, *9*(5), 407–418. doi:10.14257/ijca.2016.9.5.39

El Afou, Y., Belkoura, L., Outanoute, M., Guerbaoui, M., Rahali, A., Ed-Dahhak, A., ... & Bouchikhi, B. (2014). Feedback Techniques Using PID and PI Intelligent For Greenhouse Temperature Control. *International Journal of Advanced Research in Electrical, Electronics and Instrumentation Engineering*, *3*(6), 9779–9792.

Frausto, H. U., & Pieters, J. G. (2004). Modelling greenhouse temperature using system identification by means of neural networks. *Neurocomputing*, *56*, 423–428. doi:10.1016/j.neucom.2003.08.001

He, F., & Ma, C. (2010). Modeling greenhouse air humidity by means of artificial neural network and principal component analysis. *Computers and Electronics in Agriculture*, *71*, 19–23. doi:10.1016/j.compag.2009.07.011

Ed-Dahhak, A., Guerbaoui, M., ElAfou, Y., Outanoute, M., Lachhab, A., Belkoura, L., & Bouchikhi, B. (2013). Implementation of fuzzy controller to reduce water irrigation in greenhouse using LabVIEW. *International Journal of Engineering and Advanced Technology Studies*, *1*(2), 12–22.

Kiranyaz, S., Ince, T., Yildirim, A., & Gabbouj, M. (2009). Evolutionary artificial neural networks by multi-dimensional particle swarm optimization. *Neural Networks*, *22*(10), 1448–1462. doi:10.1016/j.neunet.2009.05.013 PMID:19556105

Lai, X. M. Z. (2009). An efficient ensemble of GA and PSO for real function optimization. In *Proceedings of 2nd IEEE International Conference on Computer Science and Information Technology*, Beijing, China, August 8-11 (pp. 651-655).

Lu, H. G., Li, C. Y., & Jiang, J. P. (2015). application of intelligence control in agriculture greenhouses. *Applied Mechanics and Materials*, *719*, 293–297. doi:10.4028/www.scientific.net/AMM.719-720.293

Meng, L., Yin, S., & Hu, X. (2016). An improved mamdani fuzzy neural networks based on PSO algorithm and new parameter optimization. *Indonesian Journal of Electrical Engineering and Computer Science*, *1*(1), 201–206. doi:10.11591/ijeecs.v1.i1.pp201-206

Mohammadi, N., & Mirabedini, S. (2014). Comparison of particle swarm optimization and backproagation algorithms for training feedforward neural network. *Journal of Mathematics and Computer Science*, *12*, 113–123.

Guerbaoui, M., El Afou, Y., Ed-Dahhak, A., Lachhab, A., & Bouchikhi, B. (2013). PC-based automated drip irrigation system. *International Journal of Engineering Science and Technology*, 5(1), 221–225.

Shamshiri, R., & Ismail, W. I. W. (2013). A review of greenhouse climate control and automation systems in tropical regions. *Journal of Agricultural Science and Applications*, 2(3), 175–182. doi:10.14511/jasa.2013.020307

Shan Ngan, M., & Tan, W. C. (2016). Photovoltaic multiple peaks power tracking using particle swarm optimization with artificial neural network algorithm. In Advances in Solar Photovoltaic Power Plants (pp. 107–138). Springer.

This research was previously published in the Journal of Electronic Commerce in Organizations (JECO), 16(1); pages 72-81, copyright year 2018 by IGI Publishing (an imprint of IGI Global).

Chapter 64
An Innovative Air Purification Method and Neural Network Algorithm Applied to Urban Streets

Meryeme Boumahdi
University Abdelmalek Essaadi, Tétouan, Morocco

Chaker El Amrani
University Abdelmalek Essaadi, Tétouan, Morocco

Siegfried Denys
University of Antwerp, Research Group Sustainable Energy, Air and Water Technology, Antwerp, Belgium

ABSTRACT

In the present work, multiphysics modeling was used to investigate the feasibility of a photocatalysis-based outdoor air purifying solution that could be used in high polluted streets, especially street canyons. The article focuses on the use of a semi-active photocatalysis in the surfaces of the street as a solution to remove anthropogenic pollutants from the air. The solution is based on lamellae arranged horizontally on the wall of the street, coated with a photocatalyst (TiO_2), lightened with UV light, with a dimension of 8 cm × 48 cm × 1 m. Fans were used in the system to create airflow. A high purification percentage was obtained. An artificial neural network (ANN) was used to predict the optimal purification method based on previous simulations, to design purification strategies considering the energy cost. The ANN was used to forecast the amount of purified with a feed-forward neural network and a backpropagation algorithm to train the model.

DOI: 10.4018/978-1-6684-2408-7.ch064

INTRODUCTION

Most cities in the world suffer from air pollution, due several many factors such as burning fuel, industry and release of chemicals (Kurt, 2016, Li, 2012, Li, 2017). Many studies have focused on reducing emissions of pollutants, with significant progress being made. So far, large part of the population in urban areas breathe air, that does not meet European standards nor the World Health Organisation Air Quality Guidelines (Kelly, 2015). Currently, there is no ready-to-use technology available for a sustainable removal of particulate matter (PM), Nitric Oxides (NOx), nor volatile organic compounds (VOCs), in an urban environment. The photocatalytic oxidation (PCO) has been the focus of increasing attention in recent years, to abate pollutants, with possible applications in several areas, including environmental and energy related areas. The Titanium dioxide (TiO_2) used as photocatalysts, is almost the only material suitable in industry at present and also probably in the future (Paz, 2010; Mamaghani, 2017). The choice of TiO2 is based on the highest stability, low cost, and transparency to visible light and a highly efficient photoactivity (Ribeiro, 2013). PCO is particularly useful for volatile organic compounds (VOC's), but according to the literature, the NOx can also be degraded to a lesser extent (to nitrogen). Furthermore, TiO_2 is also known to degrade the organic fraction of particulate matter (black carbon, soot). The latter is proven by many papers evidencing the self-cleaning properties of TiO2 (Bianchi, 2015).

In the last decades, thanks to advances made in computational resources, numerical simulation approaches have become increasingly popular. Nowadays, simulations with Computational Fluid Dynamics (CFD) is frequently used to assess urban microclimate.

Several research in artificial neural networks (ANNs) show that ANNs have powerful pattern classification and pattern recognition capabilities and they are used in many fields. They have become well established as viable, multipurpose, robust computational methodologies with solid theoretic support and with strong potential to be effective in any discipline (Dayhoff, 2001). Inspired by the biological system, especially the sophisticated functionality of human brains where hundreds of billions of interconnected neurons process information in parallel (Wang, 2003). ANNs algorithms are able to learn and generalize from examples and experiences as they have the ability to capture functional relationships among the data, even if the relationships are hard to describe or they are unknown. The advantage of using ANNs is that they minimize the error compared to other forecasting methods, and they provide results that are approximately close to analytical values.

Recent studies focusing on outdoor pollution show that the most important problem in the urban environment is the lack of urban ventilation. In this context, the proposed solution in this work focuses on the improvement of the contact with photocatalytic surfaces, taking advantage from the self-cleaning properties of TiO_2. In this paper, a new solution for outdoor air purification based on semi-active photocatalysis is described. We present an innovative solution for outdoor air purification, using photocatalysis technology. This technology is based on coated lamellas with TiO_2, lighted with UV light and placed horizontally on the buildings, in streets, using forced convection with a fan to force polluted air over the system. Natural convection was tested to in order to reduce the energy cost. It replaces the airflow generated by the fans, with an airflow produced by the density difference of the air between the lamellas. Considering the complexity of the interactions involved, a modelling approach is the designated approach to follow. In the present work, air flow, adsorption / desorption and photocatalytic reactions were studied using commercial computational fluid dynamics (CFD) software (Table 1).

The first section of the paper provides a literature review and related work on photocatalysis properties and its use on air purification. The multiphysics modeling section explains in detail the use of CFD and the geometry that was used for the model, the airflow modeling, and adsorption and desorption equations used to model the system. The next section presents the use of the simulation, not only to test the efficiency of the method but also to train other machine learning algorithms to predict the purification behavior for other streets. It explains the reason why IA was used in this study and some mathematical formulas that were used in the feed-forward neural network. Finally, results are presented obtained from the simulations using CFD, and the results obtained from the neural network model.

Table 1. Nomenclature

D mass diffusion coefficient of acetaldehyde in air ($m^2 s^{-1}$) **u** stationary velocity field vector ($m s^{-1}$) **n** normal vector pointing outward on the boundaries of the geometry θ_{Acal} fractional surface coverage Γ_s maximum surface coverage ($mol\ m^2$) C_{ads} surface concentration of acetaldehyde ($mol\ m^{-2}$)	K Langmuir equilibrium constant ($m^3\ mol^{-1}$) K_{ads} adsorption rate constant ($m s^{-1}$) K_{des} desorption rate constant ($mol\ m^{-2}\ s^{-1}$) k_{pco} photocatalytic reaction rate constant (s^{-1}) R_{pco} photocatalytic reaction rate ($mol\ m^{-2}s^{-1}$) N_{ads} adsorption flux of acetaldehyde ($mol\ m^{-2}s^{-1}$) N_{des} desorption flux of acetaldehyde ($mol\ m^{-2}s^{-1}$) C_{VOCs} concentration of ($mol\ m^{-3}$)

RELATED WORK

The PCO principle is based on a semiconductor type of reaction: photons with sufficient energy in the UV range, hitting the TiO_2, causes electrons from the valence band to move to the conduction band. So, when photocatalyst titanium dioxide (TiO_2) absorbs Ultraviolet (UV) radiation from sunlight or illuminated light sources (fluorescent lamps), it will produce pairs of electrons and holes. The electron of the valence band of titanium dioxide becomes excited when illuminated by light. The excess energy of this excited electron promoted the electron to the conduction band of titanium dioxide, therefore, creating the negative-electron (e-) and positive-hole (h+) pair. Both electrons and holes can then cause oxidation and reduction reactions, causing both water and oxygen molecules to form very reactive radicals such as the hydroxyl radical (HO•) and •O_2– radicals. These oxidation / reduction reactions take place at the surface (in fact, H_2O and O_2 should be adsorbed on the surface, hence the O_{2ads} notation). In the presence of air or oxygen, UV-irradiated TiO_2 is capable of destructing many organic contaminants completely (Zhao 2003). The activation of TiO_2 by UV light can be written as:

$$TiO_2 + h\nu \rightarrow h+ + e-$$

In this reaction, h+ and e– are powerful oxidizing and reductive agents, respectively. The oxidative and reductive reactions are expressed as:

- Oxidative reaction:
  $$h+ + H_2O \rightarrow H+ + •OH$$

- Reductive reaction:
  $$O_{2ads} + e- \rightarrow •O_2-$$

For a complete PCO reaction, the final products of reactions are CO_2 and H_2O:

OH* + pollutant $+O_2$ → Products (CO_2; H_2O; etc.)

Today, the main application field of PCO lies in end-of-pipe active PCO reactors in which polluted air is forced over a photocatalytic surface. Unfortunately, contradicting results exist concerning the efficiency of passive decontamination surfaces (paving, walls and facades treated with a photocatalyst to clean air) in the real urban atmosphere (so-called passive PCO). Concluded from different field data of the Life+ project PhotoPAQ that a realistic annual average NOx reduction of 2% can be expected in main urban street canyons exceeding the European annual NO_2 threshold limit value of 40 µg.m^{-3}. The limitations of passive decontamination surfaces in urban environments are not surprising. Firstly, as mass transport is often limited, only a fraction of the photocatalytic degradation potential is used (Paz 2010). Secondly, passive systems are often based on solar light, and thus depend on the sun cycle. Furthermore, common photocatalysts are primarily metal oxides and sulphides and require UV light for their activation. A lot of research is being done to shift the activity of photocatalysts to the visible light spectrum, with varying success.

Compared to conventional air cleaning technologies, such as adsorption and filtration, PCO can target several air pollutants, does not pose a disposal issue and uses a sustainable energy source. Furthermore, the process is operated at ambient conditions, i.e. room temperature, and works best at typical low concentration levels (ppb or ppm) of polluted air. Several air cleaning methods are available on the market. Technologies as condensation ionization and incineration cannot control emissions and improve air quality, thus, these technologies degrade air quality (Ranjit 2016). Filtration technologies are the most widely used methods for air cleaning, they are known by the low cost and high pollutant removal effectiveness. But they are associated with health issues by increasing the pollutant concentration. In this context Heterogeneous photocatalysis with titanium dioxide (TiO_2) as a catalyst is a rapidly developing field in environmental engineering, as it has a great potential to cope with the increasing pollution, besides its self-cleaning properties.

A solution for the air by traffic can be found in the treatment of the pollutants as close as possible from the source (Chen, 2009). There are different steps for the air purification through heterogeneous photocatalysis: under the influence of UV-light, the photoactive TiO_2 at the surface of the material is activated. One of the solutions that applied the photocatalysis in outdoor air purification using titanium dioxide was based on photocatalytic concrete paving blocks. Finally, they can be removed from the surface by the rain or cleaning/washing with water. This technology removes around 15% of NO (Boonen, 2014; Srivastava, 2015).

MULTIPHYSICS MODELING

Geometry

The proposed method in this work is based on lamellae coated with TiO_2 with the dimension of 8 cm × 48 cm × 1 m. Lightened with UV light. The rotation of the lamellae is 45° to guarantee the air flow in the system. A constant VOCs background concentration was used 10^{-4}mol/m^3. Three different flow rates were tested at 0.1 m^3/s, 0.5 m^3/s and 1 m^3/s with a pressure of 100 Pa, to see the difference between the air velocity and the VOCs concentration. A concentration equal to the initial condition was considered in the open boundaries. On the top, open boundaries are considered (air can leave or enter the geometry through open boundaries). The boundary condition there is a specific pressure and should be chosen sufficiently far from the buildings Figure 1.

Figure 1. Geometry of the proposed method based on coated lamellae

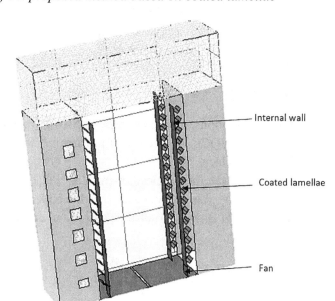

Air Flow Modeling

The commercial software package Comsol Multiphysics v.5.3 was used to perform all theoretical simulations. In this work, several models provided by Comsol were used. Computational fluid dynamics model was used to simulate the air flow generated by the fans (Hanna, 2006; Buccolieri, 2011; Toparlar, 2017; Whong, 2016; Blocken, 2016; García-Sánchez, 2018) . Transport of diluted species model was used for the chemical reactions happened in the coated surfaces. LiveLink for Matlab model was used in order to connect Comsol to Matlab and to transfer all the simulation data to Matlab. A 2D model was used instant of a 3D model to reduce computational time and also resources. A test mesh was used in the model; the meshes used were gradually refined until they do not affect the results. The finer mesh was required in certain places to guarantee the efficiency in the model and all the chemical and photocatalysis reactions happened in the surface of the lamellae. A user-defined mesh was used there to guarantee good results and a total number of 53,680 triangles were needed to guarantee a sufficiently fine mesh for the model (Figure 2).

Local Reynolds numbers were low under the studied conditions, between 30 and 190. As a result, a laminar air flow model for incompressible fluid could be used. A steady state for the air flow velocities in the street was generated using a stationary solver using a fan. The transport of the VOCs in the street was modeled by coupling the time-dependent advection and diffusion equation to the stationary velocity field vector u (Walsem, 2016):

$$\frac{\partial C_{vocs}}{\partial t} = \nabla \cdot \left(D \nabla C_{VOCs} \right) - u \cdot \nabla C_{VOCs}$$

With C_{VOCs} is the concentration of the VOCs [mol.m^{-3}] and D is the mass diffusion coefficient of the acetaldehyde as a component of VOCs in the air [m^2 s^{-1}] (Sherwood, 1975; Salvadores, 2016). The latter was set to 10^{-4}m^2 s^{-1} and it can be found in the literature.

Adsorption Desorption of VOCs

For more in-depth description of the equations, refer to (Walsem, 2016). Some equations will present to explain the adsorption/ desorption of VOCs. An important precursory step in photocatalysis is the adsorption of pollutants on the TiO$_2$ surface. The fractional surface coverage θ_{Acal} is determined as the ratio of the surface concentration of adsorbed molecules [mol/m^{-2}] $C_{VOCs,ads}$ and Γ_s, as defined the maximum surface coverage. In addition, θ_{Acal} can be determined by the bulk concentration C_{VOCs} and the Langmuir equilibrium constant K, with K is the ratio of the adsorption and desorption rate constants k_{ads}/k_{des} (Walsem, 2016; Vorontsov, 2004):

$$\theta_{Acal} = \frac{K.C_{VOC}}{1 + K.C_{VOC}} = \frac{C_{ads}}{\Gamma_s}$$

Knowing only the value of Langmuir equilibrium constant K is not sufficient for an accurate modeling, for this reason it was important to use independent value for both K_{ads} and K_{des} to simulate the evolution of the pollutant concentration in the system. VOCs adsorption was modeled as a species flux N_{ads} across the coated surface of the lamellae [mol m^{-2} s^{-1}] from the street to the surface; desorption, on the other hand, was a species flux N_{des} across the same boundaries but in opposite direction:

$$-n.\left(-D \nabla C_{vocs} + u.C_{vocs} \right) = -N_{ads} + N_{des}$$

With n is the normal vector pointing outward on the boundaries. To ensure the conservation of mass, the same rate expressions were used for the new species Cads. The only difference is that desorption is a sink term with a negative sign and adsorption is a source term with a positive sign:

$$\frac{\partial C_{ads}}{\partial t} = N_{ads} - N_{des}$$

A uniform UV intensity distribution on the coated surfaces of the lamellae was assumed. Also, a straightforward approach was followed in which the photocatalytic reaction rate is expressed by an order one with respect to the surface concentration of adsorbed molecules (Mo, 2009):

$$R_{pco} = k_{pco} C_{ads}$$

where k_{pco}[s^{-1}] is the photocatalytic reaction rate constant. The photocatalytic reaction rate R_{pco} [mol m^{-2} s^{-1}] was added to the expression for the time derivative of adsorbed acetaldehyde as an extra sink term to account for the degradation of acetaldehyde on the coated surfaces of the glass tubes during illumination:

$$\frac{\partial C_{ads}}{\partial t} = N_{ads} - N_{des} - R_{pco}$$

Figure 2. Representation of the mesh used in the CFD simulations

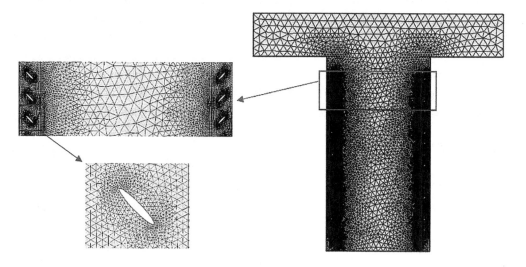

Simulation Scenarios

A large number of research studies have focused on street canyons, where the highest levels of air pollution often occur and the larger targets of impact are concentrated. Most authors have adopted different combinations of monitoring and modelling techniques for assessing air quality in urban street. There are several methods for monitoring roadside particulate and gaseous pollutants, each one of them having a number of advantages and drawbacks. Passive sampling can be used to obtain air quality data of high spatial resolution (both vertically and horizontally). On the other hand, active sampling can provide high temporal resolution. Literature and recent studies focusing on traffic related pollution show that the most important problem in urban environments such as street canyons is the lack of 'urban ventilation', causing pollutants to remain in the streets. Solutions to this are very drastic: urban design can help (but requires removing buildings, creating open space in cities). Locally, solutions using PCO might be promising. However, when using PCO one should also invest in methods to improve contact with photocatalytic surfaces. We expect that the solution to the problem is a trade-off between energy use (fans etc.) and air quality. Other systems like natural convection and solar energy (e.g., PV cells for powering fans and heating surfaces) could be a solution also. In an urban context removing the pollutants from one to another location is not a solution, hence the need for purification.

In this context, the aim of this work is to simulate a new technology for air cleaning in street canyons. In this purpose four different streets were simulated. Those streets are known as one of the most polluted streets in the city and they have different aspect ratio. For each street aspect ratio, two scenarios were tested. In the first approach, only a constant concentration background was taking in consideration. We modeled the polluted air as a constant concentration avoiding any other pollution sources as traffic, a concentration of 10^{-4} mol.m^{-3} was taking into account, it is about 2.4 ppm (for an average molecular weight of VOC 80g/mol). This is a high value, but not unusual for contaminated urban streets. This concentration could be found in the principal streets in big cities or industrial areas. Indoors, mostly values of a few 100's ppb (up to 500 ppb = 0.5 ppm) are encountered. The VOC's concentration is not constant all the time, it depends also on the traffic in the streets, car emissions, industrial activities etc.

In the second approach, car emission was introduced in the simulation as a source continuously emitting pollutants with a concentration of 10^{-6}mol.m^{-3}.s^{-1}. By doing so, it was important to simulate under the same conditions (boundary condition and car emission) without photocatalysis reaction, in order to compare the efficiency of the model in the two cases. The simulation without air cleaning present the evolution of the concentration of the VOC's in the normal case. In both cases, open boundaries also had the same concentrations as the initial concentration. Open boundaries represent the area outside the street.

Application of AI as a Forecasting Tool

Artificial neural networks (ANNs), are networks of simple processing elements (called 'neurons') operating on their local data and communicating with other elements. ANNs learns from training data to discover patterns and relationships between the input and the output. There are many types of ANNs but the principe is similar, each ANN consists of an input layer, one or more hidden layers of neurons and a final layer of output neurons. The input layer passes the information to the next layer. Each neuron in a particular layer is connected with all neurons in the next layer. The connection between the ith and jth neuron is characterized by the weight coefficient w_{ij} and the i_{th} neuron by the threshold coefficient ϑi (Figure 3). The weight coefficient is the degree of importance of the connection in the neural network. In the hidden layer, all the processing and computation are done. ANNs are formed from several neurons, depending on the model. Each neuron is connected with a coefficient (weight). They are known also as processing elements as they process information (Li, 2017; Schmidhuber, 2015). Each neuron has also a transfer function (1,2) (Srivastava 2014) and one output. The inputs of each neuron are multiplied by the connection weights, then combined and passed through a transfer function (3) (Srivastava 2014) to make the output of the neuron (Figure 3). There are many transfer functions in the literature. The output value (activity) of the ith neuron xi is determined by the equations below (Wilamowski, 2010; Fu, 2015):

$$x_i = s(\xi_i) \tag{1}$$

$$\xi_i = \vartheta_i + \Sigma\omega_{ij}x_j \tag{2}$$

$$\psi(x) = \frac{1}{1 + e^{-x}} \tag{3}$$

where ξ_i is the potential of the ith neuron and $\psi(x)$ is the sigmoid function.

Figure 3. Typical structure of a feed-forward neural network

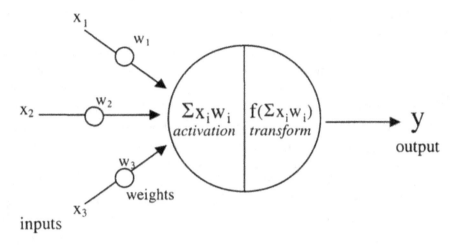

Neural Network Model

The model is based on a feed-forward neural network, with back propagation, it's a simple model from the literature. That kind of ANNs should at least have three layers, an input layer, a hidden layer, and an output layer. Appropriate selection of the number of hidden layers, and neurons in each of them needs experimentation. In this network, there no cycles nor loops, and the information moves in only one direction. Given a dataset with N distinct samples $\{x_i, t_i\}_{i=1}^{N}$ where the inputs $x_i \in Rn$ and the outputs t_i $\in Rm$, the NN with K hidden nodes and activation function $\psi(.)$ for approximating the N samples can be expressed by (Wan 2015):

$$f_k\left(x_j\right) = \sum_{i=1}^{k} \beta_i \psi\left(a_i.x_j + b_i\right), \quad j = 1,2....,N \qquad (4)$$

where a_i denotes the weight vector between the ith hidden neuron and the input neurons, β_i is the weight vector between the ith hidden neuron and the output neurons, bi represents the threshold of the ith hidden node, and $\psi(a_i x_j + b_i)$ is the output of the ith hidden node with respect to the input x_j. Theoretically, the parameters of NN can be optimized through different algorithms, among which the back propagation (BP) algorithm is the most common gradient-based algorithm with the objective function defined by (Wan 15):

$$C = \sum_{j=1}^{N} \left(\sum_{i=1}^{K} \beta_i \psi\left(a_i.x_j + b_i\right) - t_j \right)^2 \qquad (5)$$

Once the error is less or equal to the threshold value, the test set of data is used by the trained neural network with the new weights to test the performance of the neural network. This step is important to see how well the network is good and to test the ability to predict the output with the minimum error possible using the adjusted weight of the network. After that, the network is trained (with the training set) and tested (with the test set), then it becomes ready to make predictions. It's possible to feed it with some new input to produce the predicted output.

In order to minimize the error, the weight of each node needs to be updated. Back propagation algorithm looks for the minimum value of the error function in weight space using a technique called the delta rule or gradient descent through calculating the derivative of the error function. For more in-depth description of the backpropagation rule refers to (Lippmann, 1987; Srivastava, 2014; Basheer, 2000). The ANN was trained using the Levenverg-Marquardt algorithm, a standard training algorithm from the literature. It is fast and has stable convergence, as it combines the gradient descent and the Gauss-Newton algorithms. The Levenberg–Marquardt (LM) algorithm is remarkably efficient and strongly recommended for neural network training (Wilamowski, 2010; Fu, 2015). Eight training algorithms were used to compare the results based on the training time, number of iterations and Mean Squared Error (MSE). One single hidden layer was used in this network with a number of neurons (5, 10, 20). The hyperbolic-tangent-sigmoid function was used as a transfer function. Levenberg-Marquardt algorithms gives the less error comparing to other algorithms, so it was used to train the model. The Mean Squared Error is the minimization criteria:

$$MSE = \frac{1}{N} \sum_{i=1}^{N} \left(\widehat{X}_i - X_i \right)^2$$

To avoid the problem of overfitting, cross-validation can be used. The main idea is to use the initial training data to generate mini train-test splits where those splits will be used to tune the model. Cross-validation is a powerful preventative measure against overfitting because it allows tuning hyper parameters with only the original training test. Early stopping is also a solution for the overfitting problem, and it is based on dividing data into two sets, training and validation, and computing the validation error periodically during training. Training is stopped when the validation error rate starts to go up (Khryashchev et al., 2018).

Three neurons in the input layer were used, two for the coordinate of each point of the street and the third for the time step. The output consists of one neuron presenting the concentration of the VOCs, and five neurons was used in the hidden layers for calculations (4, 5) (Figure 4).

Dataset Details

The training data of then model was collected from the simulation results in Comsol Multiphysics. Only one simulation was taken into account, because of the amount of data. The simulation of a street with an aspect ratio of 1.8 with a constant concentration was used to feed the model. Comsol software was used to create a mesh to export data, with a distance of 10 cm between two points. Different Comsol models were used in this work, computational fluid dynamics (CFD) model was used to simulate the air flow in the system, then, transport of diluted species (tds) was used for the chemical reactions and the photocatalysis reactions. Afterwards the data was exported to Matlab using LiveLink for Matlab.

LiveLink for Matlab is a model provided by Comsol to make a link between the two software, in order to export the simulation models, data and also use Matlab functions in Comsol. The choice of Matlab can be explained by the tools provided by Comsol to export the data, also Matlab provides tools to create ANN models with different training algorithms; The final dataset consists of the coordinate x and y of each point and the concentration of VOCs recorded for six hours, with a time step of 1 minute. The dataset was randomly divided into three sets. Training set consists of 70% of the data used to train the model, 15% samples as validation data to measure the generalization of the network by feeding it with data it has not seen before. The rest of the data is called test data; it is used for an independent measure of the performance of the neural network in terms of MSE (Mean Squared Error). It is the square difference between the predicted value and the target and it is always a positive value.

Figure 4. Artificial neural network architecture used for five neurons in a single hidden layer

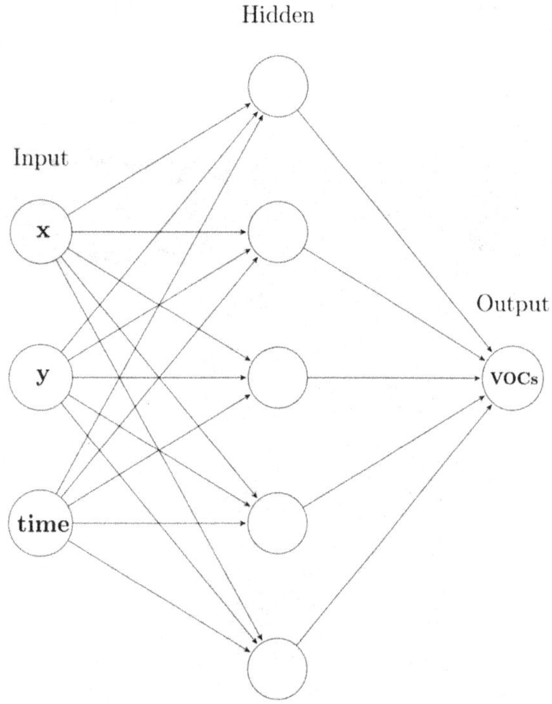

Learning and Forecasting Procedures

The Neural Network Fitting Tool GUI nn tool available in MATLAB (R2017a) is used to carry out the analysis on the purification data from the previous simulations. The only simulation data that was used is the case of a street with an aspect ratio of 1.8 with a constant VOCs concentration background. An artificial Feed-Forward neural network was used and it was trained with Levenberg-Marquardt algorithm for back propagation. The network contained three neurons in the input layers, one hidden layer with 10 neurons and the output layer contained one neuron, and the concentration of VOCs presented the target of the network.

DISCUSSION AND RESULTS

Simulation Results

Air Flow

A stationary solver was used to simulate the air flow generated by forced convection. A typical steady-state is plotted (Figure 5). Three different flow rates were used in this work 0.1 m³/s, 0.5 m³/s and 1m³/s to test the impact of the air flow in the process. The highest velocity was recorded near to the fans in two sides; it can be explained by the fact that in these places the air flow did not get in touch with any obstacle yet to reduce the velocity. The maximum velocity in the sides of the fans was (resp. 0.4, 2.3, 3.92 m/s). The lowest velocity was located inside the street; less than 0.4 m/s was recorded and the velocity in the system varies between 0.5m/s and 1.5 m/s. The velocity profile depends on the location, the distance from the fan, the fan used, the pressure and also the flow rate.

Figure 5. Modeled velocity profile in the street using a fan for the air flow

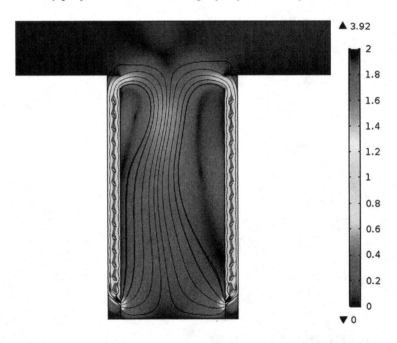

VOC's Concentration Modelling

The evolution of the VOCs concentration is modeled by coupling the time dependent advection and diffusion equation to the stationary velocity. Four different street aspect ratios with both constant concentration background and car emission were tested but only one case will be presented. A street with an aspect ratio of 1.8 (the dimensions of the street are height = 18 m and width = 10 m). We mention that a full-scale simulation was made.

Figure 6 presents the evolution of the concentration of VOCs in the street for different time steps. At the beginning of the simulation, the concentration was the same 10^{-4} mol.m-3 in each point of the street and the system. After running the fans in the two sides, the fans create an air flow in the street, but especially between the lamellae. Once the air gets in contact with the coated surfaces, with the presence of the UV light, the molecules are broken down into water and CO_2. This process reduces the VOCs concentration and makes the air more purified. The purified air follows the same velocity streamline, and it turns back to the street, minimizing the amount the VOCs there. By the time the purified air gradually replaces the polluted air (4 hours), after that a steady state is achieved. The velocity of the air flow affects the results, for this reason it was important to test different fans with different flow rate. The more the air gets in contact with the coated surfaces, the more it reduces the VOCs by breaking them down.

Figure 7 presents the average concentration in the street during the simulation time using the three fans flow rate. The concentration average decreases differently with each case. A low percentage of purification can be achieved with a low flow rate of 38%, while a high flow rate can provide more purification 65% which can be explained by the amount of the VOCs molecules adsorbed by the coated lamellae and the movement of the air in the street and between the lamellae that moves the pollutants molecules. In all the cases, the concentration average gets lower and lower until a stationary state is established. A balance between open boundaries, fan and purification were found after several hours of simulation.

Figure 8 presents a summary of all the simulations made with a constant concentration background. It presents the concentration averages for each aspect ratio testing different methods. Comsol Multiphysics provides a tool to calculate the average of each species in every time step. For every aspect ratio, the flow rate affects the purification percentage. It increases the number of absorbed molecules by the coated surfaces, thus break down more VOCs molecules. The purified air returns back to the street creating a loop that reduces the concentration of the polluted in the street.

Figure 9 shows the average concentration of the VOCs in all the simulations that introduce the car emissions as a source continuously emitting pollutant. The velocity of the air flow also affects, in this case, the purification percentage for the same reason explained before. In all the aspect ratio, high flow rates result high purification percentage, due to the high amount of air get in contact with the coated lamellae. In all case, over 60% of purification could be achieved if we used a powerful fan.

The goal of this work is to find the method that gives the best purification percentage. But this method needs to be environmentally friendly by reducing the energy cost of the solution. So, it was required to take into account the energy consumption of the method. A comparison was made based on the efficiency of the method and the energy cost. In both cases, commercial fans with the same characteristics were used in the comparison. A high purification percentage 65% cost around 780W. While reducing the energy cost of the method to 250W reduces the purification percentage to only 38%.

Artificial Intelligence Methods Results

In the first approach, polynomial regression was used to predict the best purification method. Regression analysis is usually carried out under the hypothesis that one of the variables is normally distributed with constant variance, its mean being a function of the other variables. Polynomial of Degree n would look like:

$$Y = b_0 + b_1 x_1 + b_2 x_2^2 \ldots + b_n x_n^n$$

where Y caret is the predicted outcome value for the polynomial model with regression coefficients b1 to bn for each degree and Y intercept b0. The model is simply a general linear regression model with n predictors raised to the power of i where i = 1 to n.

Figure 6. Evolution of the concentration during the simulation time

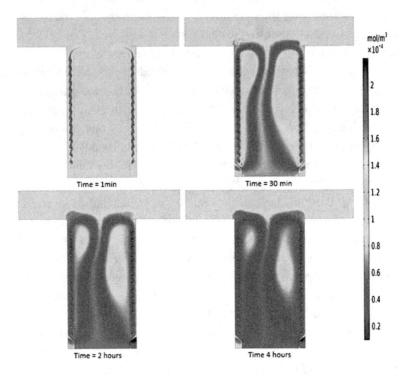

Figure 7. Average concentration of VOCs with different flow rate for a street with an aspect ratio of 1.8

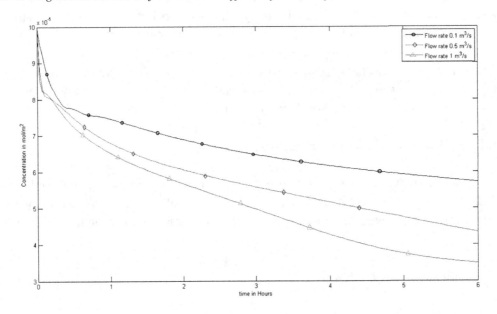

Figure 8. Purification percentage for different street aspect ratio testing different flow rate, with a constant concentration

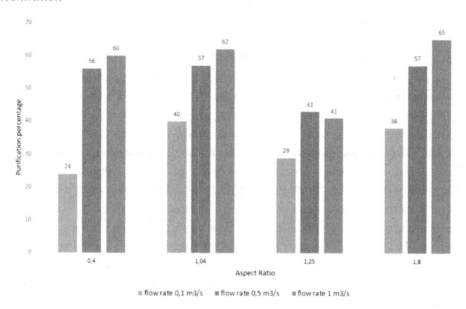

Figure 9. Purification percentage for different street aspect ratio test different flow rate, with a continuous emitting source

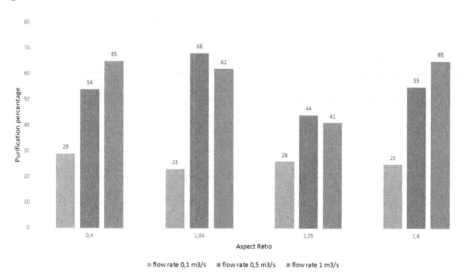

The steady-state concentration is modeled as an nth degree polynomial. 15 polynomials were tested. The optimal polynomial was chosen based on the error. The degree 13 gives the best results. The choice was validated by comparing the given results from polynomial regression with other results from Comsol. By running a simulation for a new aspect ratio, the model gives error between 0.1% and 0.3%. The results were used to decide the best purification method, by comparing the efficiency of the solution and the consumed energy. (Figure 10) presents the graphical interface developed with Matlab for this solution. The graphical interface shows the predicted purification percentage of the new street aspect ratio and the energy cost. The blue lines present the simulation data and the red dotes are the predicted percentage. The interface calculi also the energy cost of the solution based on similar fan in the market with the same characteristics.

In the second approach, different training algorithms could be used to train the neuron network. The ANN was used to investigate the possibility of reduction of the calculation time, which is long if we want to simulate the solution for a city with hundred streets. (Figure 11) presents a comparison between nine training algorithms. The Levenberg-Marquardt algorithm gives less Mean Square Error (MSE) comparing to others. But it takes around 38 minutes to train the model, using a computer with 4 cores and 12 GB in RAM. The Levenberg-Marquardt algorithm was used to train the model and then, used to predict the concentration for a new aspect ratio. The choice of this algorithm was based on the MSE. LM algorithm combines the advantages of gradient-descent and Gauss-Newton methods. The use of artificial neural network to predict the evolution of the concentration is beneficial to reduce the calculation time. It allows reducing extremely the simulation time. For example, to simulate 2 hours of outdoor air purification will take at least 50 minutes using Comsol Multiphysics. But using a trained network with Levenberg-Marquardt algorithm the prediction will take only 20 seconds with a mean square error of $3.1.10^{-8}$. Time reduction present 144 times acceleration ratio. Therefore, the use of ANN to simulate emission concentration would be an original and good option to design an air purification strategy for different streets aspect ratio and to propose consequently an optimal solution for a cleaner city.

Figure 10. Prediction of the steady-state concentration after purification with the best purification method and the energy cost

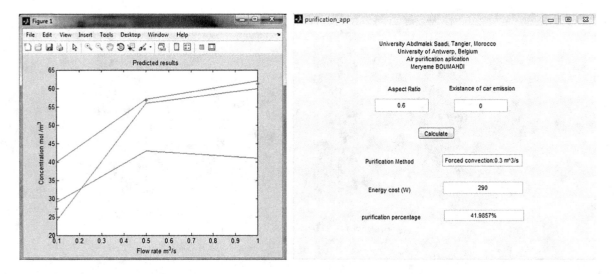

Figure 11. Training algorithms and related performance

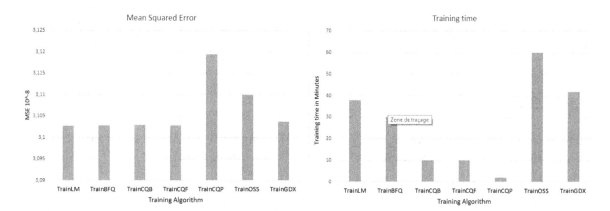

CONCLUSION

The aim of this work was to present a new and innovative outdoor air purification solution. The solution was based on TiO2 coated lamellae. Photocatalysis was used to break down the molecules of VOCs, reduce concentration and clean the air. Different strategies and cases have been tested and car traffic as a continuous source of emission has also been taken into account. In this system, several physics and chemistry equations have been combined. The results of the simulations showed a good percentage of purification. The percentage depends on the air velocity where a high percentage of air flow is required. High flow rate fans are required in order to achieve this airflow. The air cleaning percentage can achieve 65% of clearing with a fan with a flow rate of $1 \ m^3s^{-1}$.

At the end of the simulation tasks, polynomial regression and artificial neuron network were used to predict the purification percentage for new streets and to choose the best purification strategy based on the efficiency and the energy cost. Polynomial regression has been used to determine an optimized new aspect ratio purification scenario.

The artificial neural network was used to predict the development of new street concentration. The simulation output has been used to train the forecasting model. The model is based on a neural feed-forward network with back spread. In this work, nine different training algorithms were tested. The model was trained with the ML algorithm, based on the MSE and the training.

The network could be used to predict the concentration for a new aspect ratio as the mean square error obtained is $3.1.10^{-8}$. The ANN model also reduces the calculation time, the time reduction has a speed ratio of 144 times. This study was the first attempt to model a new outdoor air pollution solution.

For future research, real weather conditions and pollution concentrations, obtained from soil sensors or satellite data, could be taken into account in the purification process and other artificial intelligence methods as a deep leaning to obtain better results.

ACKNOWLEDGMENT

The authors of this work are thankful to VLIR-UOS for the financial support provided within the project ZEIN 2016Z193.

REFERENCES

Adebiyi, A. A., Adewumi, A. O., & Ayo, C. K. (2014). Comparison of ARIMA and artificial neural networks models for stock price prediction. *Journal of Applied Mathematics*.

Agatonovic-Kustrin, S., & Beresford, R. (2000). Basic concepts of artificial neural network (ANN) modeling and its application in pharmaceutical research. *Journal of Pharmaceutical and Biomedical Analysis*, *22*(5), 717–727. doi:10.1016/S0731-7085(99)00272-1 PMID:10815714

Basheer, I. A., & Hajmeer, M. (2000). Artificial neural networks: Fundamentals, computing, design, and application. *Journal of Microbiological Methods*, *43*(1), 3–31. doi:10.1016/S0167-7012(00)00201-3 PMID:11084225

Bianchi, C. L., Pirola, C., Galli, F., Cerrato, G., Morandi, S., & Capucci, V. (2015). Pigmentary TiO_2: A challenge for its use as photocatalyst in NOx air purification. *Chemical Engineering Journal*, *261*, 76–82. doi:10.1016/j.cej.2014.03.078

Blocken, B. (2018). LES over RANS in building simulation for outdoor and indoor applications : A foregone conclusion? *Building Simulation*, *11*(5), 821–870. doi:10.100712273-018-0459-3

Blocken, B., Stathopoulos, T., & van Beeck, J. P. A. J. (2016). Pedestrian-level wind conditions around buildings: Review of wind-tunnel and CFD techniques and their accuracy for wind comfort assessment. *Building and Environment*, *100*, 50–81. doi:10.1016/j.buildenv.2016.02.004

Boonen, E., & Beeldens, A. (2014). Recent photocatalytic applications for air purification in Belgium. *Coatings*, *4*(3), 553–573. doi:10.3390/coatings4030553

Brunekreef, B., & Holgate, S. T. (2002). Air pollution and health. *Lancet*, *360*(9341), 1233–1242. doi:10.1016/S0140-6736(02)11274-8 PMID:12401268

Buccolieri, R., Salim, S. M., Leo, L. S., Di Sabatino, S., Chan, A., Ielpo, P., ... Gromke, C. (2011). Analysis of local scale tree-atmosphere interaction on pollutant concentration in idealized street canyons and application to a real urban junction. *Atmospheric Environment*, *45*(9), 1702–1713. doi:10.1016/j.atmosenv.2010.12.058

Chen, J., & Poon, C. S. (2009). Photocatalytic construction and building materials: From fundamentals to applications. *Building and Environment*, *44*(9), 1899–1906. doi:10.1016/j.buildenv.2009.01.002

D'Amato, G., Pawankar, R., Vitale, C., Lanza, M., Molino, A., Stanziola, A., ... D'Amato, M. (2016). Climate change and air pollution: Effects on respiratory allergy. *Allergy, Asthma & Immunology Research*, *8*(5), 391–395. doi:10.4168/aair.2016.8.5.391 PMID:27334776

Dayhoff, J. E., & DeLeo, J. M. (2001). Artificial neural networks. *Cancer, 91*(S8), 1615–1635. doi:10.1002/1097-0142(20010415)91:8+<1615::AID-CNCR1175>3.0.CO;2-L PMID:11309760

Fu, X., Li, S., Fairbank, M., Wunsch, D. C., & Alonso, E. (2015). Training recurrent neural networks with the Levenberg–Marquardt algorithm for optimal control of a grid-connected converter. *IEEE Transactions on Neural Networks and Learning Systems, 26*(9), 1900–1912. doi:10.1109/TNNLS.2014.2361267 PMID:25330496

García-Sánchez, C., van Beeck, J., & Gorlé, C. (2018). Predictive large eddy simulations for urban flows: Challenges and opportunities. *Building and Environment, 139*, 146–156. doi:10.1016/j.buildenv.2018.05.007

Hanna, S. R., Brown, M. J., Camelli, F. E., Chan, S. T., Coirier, W. J., Hansen, O. R., ... Reynolds, R. M. (2006). Detailed Simulations of Atmospheric Flow and Dispersion in Downtown Manhattan: An Application of Five Computational Fluid Dynamics Models. *Bulletin of the American Meteorological Society, 87*(12), 1713–1726. doi:10.1175/BAMS-87-12-1713

Ivanovsky, L., Khryashchev, V., Lebedev, A., & Kosterin, I. (2017, November). Facial expression recognition algorithm based on deep convolution neural network. In *Proceedings of the 2017 21st Conference of Open Innovations Association (FRUCT)* (pp. 141-147). IEEE. 10.23919/FRUCT.2017.8250176

Kelly, F. J., & Fussell, J. C. (2015). Air pollution and public health: Emerging hazards and improved understanding of risk. *Environmental Geochemistry and Health, 37*(4), 631–649. doi:10.100710653-015-9720-1 PMID:26040976

Khryashchev, V., Pavlov, V., Priorov, A., & Kazina, E. (2018, May). Convolutional Neural Network for Satellite Imagery. In *Proceedings of the 22th Conference of Open Innovations Association FRUCT'22* (pp. 344-347).

Kurt, O. K., Zhang, J., & Pinkerton, K. E. (2016). Pulmonary health effects of air pollution. *Current Opinion in Pulmonary Medicine, 22*(2), 138–143. doi:10.1097/MCP.0000000000000248 PMID:26761628

Lapedes, A., & Farber, R. (1987). Nonlinear signal processing using neural networks: Prediction and system modelling.

Li, H., Zhang, Z., & Liu, Z. (2017). Application of artificial neural networks for catalysis: A review. *Catalysts, 7*(10), 306. doi:10.3390/catal7100306

Li, X., Qiao, Y., & Shi, L. (2017). The aggregate effect of air pollution regulation on CO2 mitigation in China's manufacturing industry: An econometric analysis. *Journal of Cleaner Production, 142*, 976–984. doi:10.1016/j.jclepro.2016.03.015

Li, Y., Li, Y., Zhou, Y., Shi, Y., & Zhu, X. (2012). Investigation of a coupling model of coordination between urbanization and the environment. *Journal of Environmental Management, 98*, 127–133. doi:10.1016/j.jenvman.2011.12.025 PMID:22265813

Lippmann, R. (1987). An introduction to computing with neural nets. *IEEE ASSP Magazine, 4*(2), 4–22. doi:10.1109/MASSP.1987.1165576

Mamaghani, A. H., Haghighat, F., & Lee, C. S. (2017). Photocatalytic oxidation technology for indoor environment air purification: The state-of-the-art. *Applied Catalysis B: Environmental*, *203*, 247–269. doi:10.1016/j.apcatb.2016.10.037

Mo, J., Zhang, Y., Xu, Q., Lamson, J. J., & Zhao, R. (2009). Photocatalytic purification of volatile organic compounds in indoor air: A literature review. *Atmospheric Environment*, *43*(14), 2229–2246. doi:10.1016/j.atmosenv.2009.01.034

Murakami, S. (1997). Current status and future trends in computational wind engineering. *Journal of Wind Engineering and Industrial Aerodynamics*, *67-68*, 3–34. doi:10.1016/S0167-6105(97)00230-4

Nath, R. K., Zain, M. F. M., & Jamil, M. (2016). An environment-friendly solution for indoor air purification by using renewable photocatalysts in concrete: A review. *Renewable & Sustainable Energy Reviews*, *62*, 1184–1194. doi:10.1016/j.rser.2016.05.018

Paz, Y. (2010). Application of TiO_2 photocatalysis for air treatment: Patents' overview. *Applied Catalysis B: Environmental*, *99*(3-4), 448–460. doi:10.1016/j.apcatb.2010.05.011

Ribeiro, P. C., Costa, A. C. F. M., Kiminami, R. H. G. A., Sasaki, J. M., & Lira, H. L. (2013). Synthesis of tio2 by the pechini method and photocatalytic degradation of methyl red. *Materials Research*, *16*(2), 468–472. doi:10.1590/S1516-14392012005000176

Salvadores, F., Minen, R. I., Carballada, J., Alfano, O. M., & Ballari, M. M. (2016). Kinetic study of acetaldehyde degradation applying visible light photocatalysis. *Chemical Engineering & Technology*, *39*(1), 166–174. doi:10.1002/ceat.201500507

Schatzmann, M. (Ed.). (2010). *COST 732 model evaluation case studies: approach and results*. Meteorological Inst.

Schmidhuber, J. (2015). Deep learning in neural networks: An overview. *Neural Networks*, *61*, 85–117. doi:10.1016/j.neunet.2014.09.003 PMID:25462637

Sherwood, T. K., Pigford, R. L., & Wilke, C. R. (1975). *Mass transfer*. McGraw-Hill.

Sottile, F., Caceres, M. A., & Spirito, M. A. (2012). A Simulation Tool for Real-Time Hybrid-Cooperative Positioning Algorithms. *International Journal of Embedded and Real-Time Communication Systems*, *3*(3), 67–87. doi:10.4018/jertcs.2012070105

Srivastava, A. (2015). Photocatalytic application of titanium dioxide in architectural concrete: A review. *International Journal of Scientific Research & Chemical Engineering*, *1*(1).

Srivastava, N., Hinton, G., Krizhevsky, A., Sutskever, I., & Salakhutdinov, R. (2014). Dropout: A simple way to prevent neural networks from overfitting. *Journal of Machine Learning Research*, *15*(1), 1929–1958.

Toparlar, Y., Blocken, B., Maiheu, B., & van Heijst, G. J. F. (2017). A review on the CFD analysis of urban microclimate. *Renewable & Sustainable Energy Reviews*, *80*, 1613–1640. doi:10.1016/j.rser.2017.05.248

van Walsem, J., Verbruggen, S. W., Modde, B., Lenaerts, S., & Denys, S. (2016). Cfd investigation of a multi-tube photocatalytic reactor in non-steady-state conditions. *Chemical Engineering Journal*, *304*, 808–816. doi:10.1016/j.cej.2016.07.028

Vorontsov, A. V., & Dubovitskaya, V. P. (2004). Selectivity of photocatalytic oxidation of gaseous ethanol over pure and modified TiO_2. *Journal of Catalysis*, *221*(1), 102–109. doi:10.1016/j.jcat.2003.09.011

Wan, C., Zhao, J., Song, Y., Xu, Z., Lin, J., & Hu, Z. (2015). Photovoltaic and solar power forecasting for smart grid energy management. *CSEE Journal of Power and Energy Systems*, *1*(4), 38–46. doi:10.17775/CSEEJPES.2015.00046

Wang, S. C. (2003). Artificial neural network. In *Interdisciplinary computing in java programming* (pp. 81–100). Boston, MA: Springer. doi:10.1007/978-1-4615-0377-4_5

White, H. (1989). Learning in artificial neural networks: A statistical perspective. *Neural Computation*, *1*(4), 425–464. doi:10.1162/neco.1989.1.4.425

Wilamowski, B. M., & Yu, H. (2010). Improved computation for Levenberg–Marquardt training. *IEEE Transactions on Neural Networks*, *21*(6), 930–937. doi:10.1109/TNN.2010.2045657 PMID:20409991

Zhao, J., & Yang, X. (2003). Photocatalytic oxidation for indoor air purification: A literature review. *Building and Environment*, *38*(5), 645–654. doi:10.1016/S0360-1323(02)00212-3

Zhong, J., Cai, X. M., & Bloss, W. J. (2016). Coupling dynamics and chemistry in the air pollution modelling of street canyons: A review. *Environ. Pollut.* PMID:27149146

This research was previously published in the International Journal of Embedded and Real-Time Communication Systems (IJERTCS), 10(4); pages 1-19, copyright year 2019 by IGI Publishing (an imprint of IGI Global).

Chapter 65
Artificial Neural Network for Pre-Simulation Training of Air Traffic Controller

Tetiana Shmelova
https://orcid.org/0000-0002-9737-6906
National Aviation University, Ukraine

Yuliya Sikirda
https://orcid.org/0000-0002-7303-0441
National Aviation University, Ukraine

Togrul Rauf Oglu Jafarzade
National Aviation Academy, Azerbaijan

EXECUTIVE SUMMARY

In this chapter, the four layers neural network model for evaluating correctness and timeliness of decision making by the specialist of air traffic services during the pre-simulation training has been presented. The first layer (input) includes exercises that cadet/listener performs to solve a potential conflict situation; the second layer (hidden) depends physiological characteristics of cadet/listener; the third layer (hidden) takes into account the complexity of the exercise depending on the number of potential conflict situations; the fourth layer (output) is assessment of cadet/listener during performance of exercise. Neural network model also has additional inputs (bias) that including restrictions on calculating parameters. The program "Fusion" of visualization of the state of execution of an exercise by a cadet/listener has been developed. Three types of simulation training exercises for CTR (control zone), TMA (terminal control area), and CTA (control area) with different complexity have been analyzed.

DOI: 10.4018/978-1-6684-2408-7.ch065

INTRODUCTION

Statistics data (Leychenko, Malishevskiy, & Mikhalic, 2006; Allianz Global Corporate & Specialty. EMBRY-RIDDLE Aeronautical University, 2014; Aviation Accident Statistics, 2018; Statistics of the World's the Largest Aircraft Accidents for the Years 1974-2014, 2018) show us, that causality of aviation accidents didn't change over the past decade: 70-80% of accidents and disasters happened due to human factor, and only 15-20% – through constructive and productive deficiencies of the aircraft. It is important to pay more attention to the training of aviation specialists because they are dealing with equipment that is becoming more complicated from year to year. Modern recommendations of International Civil Aviation Organization (ICAO) are to use information technology in aviation systems as in training as in operation (International Civil Aviation Organization [ICAO], 2007, 2008). Automation is seen as one of many resources available to the human operators, controllers and pilots alike, who retain the responsibility for management and direction of the overall Air Traffic Management (ATM) system. Additionally, unexpected or unplanned events must be a required part of planning and design when considering the systems that would replace the cognitive and adaptive capabilities of controllers or pilots. The development of training for automated systems is more difficult than for non-automated systems. One of the primary challenges in developing training for automated systems is to determine how much a trainee will need to know about the underlying technologies in order to use automation safely and efficiently. Course development based on a task analysis can be more effectiveness than traditional training development techniques.

BACKGROUND

Quality training of aviation experts, including specialists in Air Traffic Services (ATS), occupied the important part in reducing the influence of the human factor (European Organisation for the Safety of Air Navigation [Eurocontrol], 2004a). There are three types of air traffic controller (ATC) training, leading towards the issue and maintenance of an ATC license and associated unit endorsements. Initial training is the first type. ATC training phases (Figure 1) (Eurocontrol, 2004b, 2015):

1. Initial Training.
    a. Basic Training.
    b. Rating Training.
2. Unit Training.
    a. Transitional Training.
    b. Pre-On-the-Job Training (Pre-OJT).
    c. On-the-Job Training (OJT).
3. Continuation Training.
    a. Refresher Training.
    b. Conversion Training.

Simulation Training is an important part of ATC training. It is a complex of existing forms and methods of training, in which cadets / listeners through the implementation of appropriately formulated complex tasks and exercises under the guidance of the instructor develop skills and practical application

Figure 1. Progression of ATC training
(Eurocontrol, 2015)

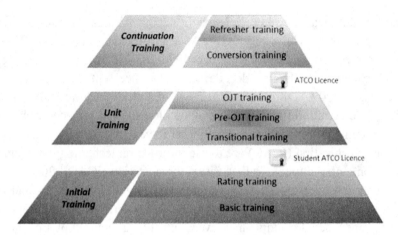

of the theoretical provisions of several disciplines (Eurocontrol, 2004b, 2015). The aim of training is to improve ATC work and refinement practical skills of ATS in standard situations, potential conflict situations (PCS), in the special conditions and in the flight emergencies. The quality and number of exercises, objective evaluation of exercises influence on the effectiveness of Simulation Training.

Simulation Training is a model of communication where cadet / listener, either individually or in the group receives information through a media at a rate (Eurocontrol, 2000). The combination of these elements defines the training event.

Media is the physical means by which an instructor or a training designer communicates a message. One media can use several supports we are going to define the media related to simulation but shall not attempt to make an exhaustive list of the many types of support and educational materials. It has defined the following five media:

1.   Real Equipment.
2.   High-fidelity Simulator (HI FI SIM).
3.   Simulator (SIM).
4.   Part-Task Trainer (PTT).
5.   Other Training Device (OTD).

It is used any of the three rates of learning although most of the exercises are in real time:

1.   Self-paced Learning.
2.   Time-restricted learning.
3.   Real Time.

According to the recommendations of Eurocontrol (2004b, 2015) and to optimize the effectiveness of Simulation Training, theoretical and practical training combine from the beginning of the training using the Pre-Simulation (Pre-SIMUL). The process of learning starts with getting by the cadet / listener Skill Acquisitions, then performance Part-Task Practice and continues Simulation.

Eurocontrol has defined several types of Simulation and has differentiated between pre-simulation and simulation exercises, and it has added the notion of Guided Simulation. Simulation (SIMUL) is a provision of knowledge, skills, and attitudes by means of a representation of air traffic responding to the cadet / listener action as real air traffic. Types of Simulation include Individual Simulation (IND SIMUL), Team Simulation (TEAM SIMUL) and Group Simulation (GROUP SIMUL). Simulation always includes Briefing (Brief), Debriefing (Debrief) and Tutoring. Guided Simulation (GSIMUL – Guided SIMUL) is the extensive interaction between the cadet / listener and the computer in the form of questions, feedback, comments, instructions, and assessment. This guidance assumes the existence of a theoretical model against which the cadet / listener can be compared. Guided Skills Acquisitions (GSA – Guided SA) – Skill Acquisitions (SA) with interactive assessment, comments and guidance – are actual at this time. Guided PTP (GPTP) is a Part-Task Practice (PTP), accompanied by comments, display results, assessment of the cadet / listener and the ability of feedback.

The system of ATC Simulation Training is characterized by low level of objective evaluation of exercises (Eurocontrol, 2004b, 2015). It's connected with the development of sufficient exercises at a given difficulty level. Increasing the number of exercises leading to significant growth an amount of instructional and methodical staff and requirements for their professional skills as well as time for developing the appropriate exercises of a given complexity. The most time spent on modeling of air situation in accordance with the set of objectives in the exercise, verification of exercise to meet at a given level of difficulty, verification graph to meet a planned workload and the possibility of conflict-free exercises.

In modeling of the air situation using inverse task of generating dynamic air situation at a given exercise intensity, takes into account the complexity of air traffic, presence, and quantity of PCS, flight emergencies (Ministry of Transport and Communications of Ukraine, 2007). The correctness and the timeliness are important criteria for evaluating the quality of the exercises (Eurocontrol, 2000, 2004b, 2015). Taking into account as correctness as timeliness can be done with the help of Artificial Neural Network (ANN). Automation of process of exercise verification can reduce the time for its preparation (saving up to 80% of the time).

A hybrid neural-expert system is a perspective direction of development of a neuron-information technology (Komashynskiy & Smirnov, 2002). ANN has many advantages compared to traditions and knowledge-based of diagnostic systems (Arkhangelskiy, Bohaenko, Grabowskiy, & Ryumshyn, 1999; Suzuki, 2013). It can be trained on examples, work in real-time, secure and tolerant to errors. With the help of ANN diagnoses state of the patient, performs the prediction on the stock market and the weather forecast, makes decision on granting the loan, diagnoses condition of equipment, guided operation of the engine, etc. (Komashynskiy & Smirnov, 2002; Gardner & Dorling, 1998; Goedeking, 2010). ANN is being created by the serial and parallel association of individual neurons. The neural network is grouped in two classes according to the type of connections: straight directional network (which links don't have loops) and recurrent network (with feedback connections). (Komashynskiy & Smirnov, 2002; Arkhangelskiy et al., 1999; Suzuki, 2013; Gardner & Dorling, 1998; Goedeking, 2010; Borovikov, 2008). The most common among straight directional networks are single-layer and multi-layer perceptrons, cognitron and Radial Basis Function (RBF) networks; among the recurrent network can be distinguished Hopfield, Boltzmann and Kohonen networks (Arkhangelskiy et al., 1999; Suzuki, 2013).

Using of neural networks and neuro-fuzzy systems is appropriate for solutions many problems in aviation, where it is necessary to process a large amount of fuzzy information and solving difficult formalized multiparameter nonlinear tasks (which) and problems, namely in the case of: decision making about departure and selection of an optimum alternate aerodrome landing (Kharchenko, Shmelova,

Artemenko, & Otryazhiy, 2011); choosing the optimum place of forced landing (Kharchenko, Shmelova, Sikirda, & Gerasimenko, 2011); estimation of efficiency of alternative variants of flight completion in the event of an extraordinary situation (Shmelova, Yakunina, & Yakunin, 2013); diagnostic erroneous actions of the operator of ergatic aviation system in flight emergencies (Shmelova, Yakunina, Moyseenko, & Grinchuk, 2014), etc.

It is proposed to use a neural network model of evaluation correctness and timeliness of decision making by ATC in the case of PCS during the performance of exercises in the Simulation Training through pre-training studying.

ESTIMATION OF SITUATION'S COMPLEXITY IN CASE OF POTENTIAL CONFLICT SITUATION WITH THE HELP OF FUZZY SETS METHOD

There is well-known concept of Threat and Error Management (TEM), which allows determining links between safety and operability of operator in fleeting difficult operating conditions (ICAO, 2008; Kharchenko, Chynchenko, & Raychev, 2007). Conception has descriptive character and can be used as means of diagnosis both characteristics of human efficiency and effectiveness of the system. Despite the fact that the TEM was originally developed for use in the cockpit, but it can also be used in various organizations of the aviation industry, including services for ATS.

Regarding ATC, TEM consists of three components:

- Threats;
- Errors;
- Undesirable conditions.

According to TEM, threats and errors are the routine parts of aviation activity. ATC should control undesirable conditions because it led to dangerous consequences. One of the main components of TEM is the control of undesirable conditions, and it has the same meaning as factors of threats and errors. Control of undesirable conditions is the last opportunity to avoid dangerous consequences and thus provide maintaining at a given level of aviation safety in ATS.

The concept, according to the problem of determining the timeliness of decision making in solving PCS by ATC, was developed classification stages of conflict situation evolution (Shmelova, Sikirda, Zemlyanskiy, & Danilenko, 2015).

The threat of conflict situation is the first stage of the PCS. The threat comes from the moment when the time of remaining to the conflict situation equal time, which needed to perform all elements for solving PCS, taking into account the required buffer time.

The pre-conflict situation is the second stage of the PCS. The pre-conflict situation occurs from the moment when the time of remaining until the conflict situation equal time, which needed to perform all elements to solve the PCS without buffer time. In this situation, the violation of the separation intervals is not yet come, but the probability of resolving the situation is extremely small.

The conflict situation is a stage when happens violation of the separation intervals. Since the classification shows, that for determining the timeliness in dealing with decision-making during PCS should determine when there is a transition stage to the current situation the threat of conflict and pre-conflict situation.

In order to get the quantitative indicators of the level of the situation's complexity in the developing of PCS, was used the method of fuzzy sets (Zade, 1965; Borisov, Krumberh, & Fedorov, 1990).

There are values of the linguistic variable on the scale:

- The threat of conflict;
- The pre-conflict situation;
- The conflict situation.

The minimum level of situation's complexity equal zero (0), maximum – one (1). The resulting range is divided into five intervals.

The degree of membership of linguistic variable at a certain interval defined as the ratio of answers number (where it occurs in this range) to the maximum value of this number for all intervals. There was conducted survey of 30 experts from the air traffic service training center of Flight Academy of the National Aviation University by Delphi method in two rounds. Getting results shown in Table 1.

Table 1. Survey results

Meaning of Membership Functions of the Complexity of the Situation in Case of PCS, μ	Interval, Units				
	0-0.2	0.2-0.4	0.4-0.6	0.6-0.8	0.8-1.0
The threat of conflict, μ_1	1	1	22	6	0
The pre-conflict situation, μ_2	0	0	8	20	2
The conflict situation, μ_3	0	0	1	12	17

Membership functions of the situation's complexity μ (threat of conflict, pre-conflict situation, conflict situation) in the case of PCS are in Table 2 and shown in Figure 2.

Figure 2. Membership functions of the situation's complexity in case of PCS

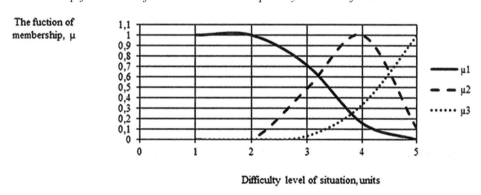

There is a system of transitions between components of TEM concept (stages of development of PCS) in the graph of states (Figure 3).

Table 2. Classification of conflict situation by the criterion of timeliness

Classification by the TEM	Classification by Timeliness	Description of Situation	Level of Complexity of Situation, Units
Threat	Threat of conflict situation	Fixed PCS which requires solving	1-2
Error	Pre-conflict situation	Parry of PCS is difficult or impossible	4
Undesirable condition	Conflict situation	Violation of separation intervals, the conflict situation has happened	5

Figure 3. Transitions between stages of PCS: T_0 – is a state, which characterized by presence of threat in PCS; T_1 – is a pre-conflict situation, happen in result of erroneous or inaction of operator (cadet / listener) ; T_2 – is a conflict situation (violation of separation intervals); t_{01} – is a transition from T_0 to T_1, characterized by time of parry of PCS and buffer time; t_{12} – is a transition from T_1 to T_2, characterized by the time of parry of PCS at stage T_1, in case of transition to stage T_2 happen critical situation; t_{10} – is a transition from T_1 to T_0, characterized by the ability of the operator to resolve the PCS; t_{21} – is a transition from T_2 to T_1, characterized by the appearance of conflict due to T_2 (violations of separation's rules), but in case of successful resolution of problem by operator during allowable time – a return to pre-conflict situation ($T_{sim} = T_2$)

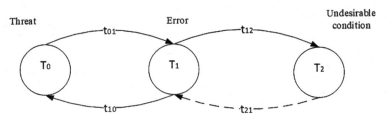

Determine the state of the exercise as (1):

$$y = \begin{cases} 1; t_{01} + t_{12} \le T_2 \\ 0; t_{01} + t_{12} > T_2 \end{cases}.$$ (1)

The time to solve conflict depends on the individual characteristics of the operator (cadet / listener) (c), the numbers of PCS (n) and time of PCS (T_s) (2):

$$T_{sc} = T_c \times c + T_n \times n + T_s,$$ (2)

where c – is a coefficient, which defines the individual characteristics of the operator (cadet / listener); n – is an amount of PCS; T_s – is a time of developing PCS, if $n=1$, $c=1$, then $T_{sc} = T_c + T_n + T_s$.

NEURAL NETWORK MODEL OF EVALUATION CORRECTNESS AND TIMELINESS OF AIR TRAFFIC CONTROLLER'S DECISION MAKING DURING PRE-SIMULATION TRAINING

To automate the evaluation of pre-training stage of Initial Training of ATC at the stage of pre-training studying the Multilayer Perceptron Network (MPN) has been developed (Shmelova, Sikirda, Zemlyanskiy, Danilenko, & Lazorenko, 2016). It has four layers, two of which are hidden. Each neuron is characterized by the input value (dendrite) and the output value (axon), weight coefficients (synapses), threshold function. The network has additional inputs, called the Bias (offset) that takes into account additional restrictions on calculating parameters (3):

$$\sum_{i=1}^{n} w_i x_i - \theta \geq 0 .$$ (3)

where w_i – are the weight coefficients; x_i – are the neural network inputs; $\bar{\theta}$ – is a Bias (shift).
General view of the ANN shown in Figure 4 (4):

$$\bar{Y} = f(\overline{net} - \bar{\theta}),$$ (4)

where f – is a non-linear function (active function); $\overline{net}$ – is a weighted sum of inputs.

Figure 4. General view of the ANN

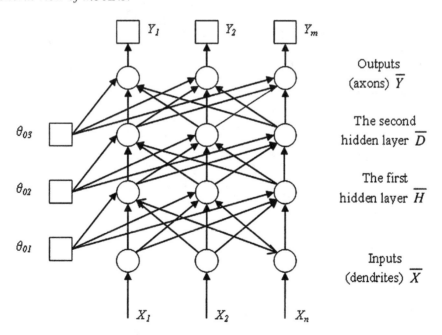

Characteristics of ANN's layers:

- **The First Layer (Input):** Are the exercises that perform cadets / listeners to solve PCS ($\overline{X}$);
- **The Second Layer (Hidden):** Are the physiological characteristics of cadets / listeners ($\overline{H}$);
- **The Third Layer (Hidden):** Is the complexity of the exercises, which is determined by the number of PCS ($\overline{D}$);
- **The Fourth Layer (Output):** Is an assessment of cadets / listeners during the performance of exercises ($\overline{Y}$).

Consider in more detail the topology of the neural network as an example, if three cadets / listeners (Y_1, Y_2, Y_3) perform two tasks (X_1 and X_2) (Figure 5).

Figure 5. Example of ANN when three cadets / listeners perform two tasks

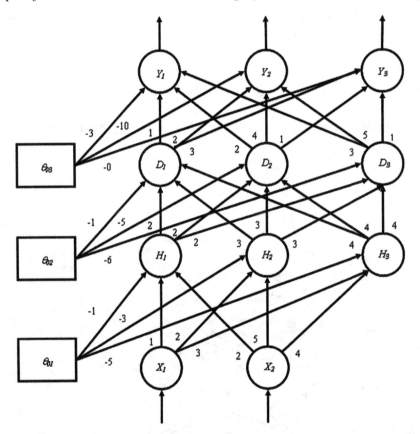

The first layer (input) are the inputs x_1, x_2, ..., x_n that meet the tasks that perform by cadets / listeners to solve PCS ($\overline{X}$).

The second layer (hidden) defines the physiological characteristics of cadets / listeners ($\overline{H}$) using additional input Bias, which specifies limits on individual solving of exercises (T_{01}).

The output vector of the second layer (5):

$$\overline{H} = f(\overline{W}_1, \overline{X}) = f(\overline{net}_1 - \bar{\theta}_{01}), \tag{5}$$

where $\overline{net}_1 = \overline{W}_1 \overline{X}$;

- $\overline{W}_1 = \begin{pmatrix} w_{01} & w_{11} & w_{21} \\ w_{02} & w_{12} & w_{22} \\ w_{03} & w_{13} & w_{23} \end{pmatrix}$: Are the weight coefficients, for example for studying the situation when
  two exercises are doing by three cadets / listeners;

- $X = \begin{pmatrix} X_1 \\ X_2 \\ 1 \end{pmatrix}$: Are the tasks that perform by cadets / listeners to solve PCS;

- $\bar{\theta}_{01}$: Is a time to solve individual training exercises.
- **The Third Layer (Hidden):** Is a complexity of the exercise, which is determined by the number of PCS ($\overline{D}$) and characterized by dynamic air situation. Auxiliary input Bias indicates the total limit of time for resolving PCS (T_{02}).

The output vector of the third layer (6):

$$\overline{D} = f(\overline{W}_2, \overline{H}) = f(\overline{net}_2 - \bar{\theta}_{02}), \tag{6}$$

where $\overline{net}_2 = \overline{W}_2 \overline{H}$;

- $\overline{W}_2 = \begin{pmatrix} d_{01} & d_{11} & d_{21} \\ d_{02} & d_{12} & d_{22} \\ d_{03} & d_{13} & d_{23} \end{pmatrix}$: Are the weight coefficients, which takes into account the complexity of
  dynamic air situation;

- $\bar{\theta}_{02}$: Is a time to solve training exercise that takes into account the complexity of the dynamic air situation.
- **The Fourth Layer (Output):** Is a direct assessment of cadet during the performance of exercises ($\overline{Y}$). Auxiliary input Bias limits the number of attempts for solving the PCS (T_{03}).

The output vector of the fourth layer (7):

$$\overline{Y} = f(\overline{W}_3, \overline{D}) = f(\overline{net}_3 - \bar{\theta}_{03}), \tag{7}$$

where $\overline{net}_3 = \overline{W}_3 \overline{D}$;

- $\overline{W}_3 = \begin{pmatrix} y_{01} & y_{11} & y_{21} \\ y_{02} & y_{12} & y_{22} \\ y_{03} & y_{13} & y_{23} \end{pmatrix}$: Are the weight coefficients, taking into account the quality of the exercise

  by the timeliness;

- $\overline{\theta}_{03}$: Are the attempts to solve the exercise.

Provides the following outputs vectors layers of neurons $\overline{H}, \overline{D}, \overline{Y}$ (8):

$$H_i D_k Y_m = \begin{cases} 1; \text{if } f(x) > 0 \\ 0; \text{if } f(x) \le 0 \end{cases}, \tag{8}$$

where f – is a non-linear function of activation.

Consider the following set of values of weight coefficients ($\overline{W} = \overline{W}_1, \overline{W}_2, \overline{W}_3$), that take into account the performance of individual training exercises by cadet / listener depending on the physiological characteristics, the complexity of dynamic air situation, the quality of the exercise according to the timeliness:

$$H_1 = f(1x_1 + 2x_2 - 1);$$

$$H_2 = f(2x_1 + 5x_2 - 3);$$

$$H_3 = f(3x_1 + 4x_2 - 5);$$

$$D_1 = f(2d_1 + 2d_2 + 2d_3 - 1);$$

$$D_2 = f(3d_1 + 3d_2 + 3d_3 - 5);$$

$$D_2 = f(4d_1 + 4d_2 + 4d_3 - 6);$$

$$Y_1 = f(1y_1 + 3y_2 + 2y_3 - 3);$$

$$Y_2 = f(2y_1 + 4y_2 + 1y_3 - 10);$$

$$Y_3 = f(3y_1 + 5y_2 + 1y_3 - 0).$$

Present an example in vector form:

$$\begin{pmatrix} H_1 \\ H_2 \\ H_3 \\ 1 \end{pmatrix} = f\left(\begin{pmatrix} 1 & 2 & -1 \\ 2 & 5 & -3 \\ 3 & 4 & -5 \\ 0 & 0 & 1 \end{pmatrix} \cdot \begin{pmatrix} X_1 \\ X_2 \\ 1 \end{pmatrix} \right);$$

$$\begin{pmatrix} D_1 \\ D_2 \\ D_3 \\ 1 \end{pmatrix} = f \begin{pmatrix} \begin{pmatrix} 2 & 2 & 2 & -1 \\ 3 & 3 & 3 & -5 \\ 4 & 4 & 4 & -6 \\ 0 & 0 & 0 & 1 \end{pmatrix} \cdot \begin{pmatrix} H_1 \\ H_2 \\ H_3 \\ 1 \end{pmatrix} \end{pmatrix};$$

$$\begin{pmatrix} Y_1 \\ Y_2 \\ Y_3 \end{pmatrix} = f \begin{pmatrix} \begin{pmatrix} 1 & 3 & 2 & -3 \\ 2 & 4 & 1 & -10 \\ 3 & 5 & 1 & 0 \end{pmatrix} \cdot \begin{pmatrix} D_1 \\ D_2 \\ D_3 \\ 1 \end{pmatrix} \end{pmatrix}.$$

The result of the functioning with different initial data ($X = (0;0)$, $(0;1)$, $(1;0)$, $(1;1)$), taking into account the coefficients and conditions of performed exercises (time, attempts, characteristics of cadet / listener), are as follows (Table 3).

Table 3. Results of the functioning of the ANN

X_1	X_2	H_1	H_2	H_3	D_1	D_2	D_3	Y_1	Y_2	Y_3
0	0	0	0	0	0	0	0	0	0	0
0	1	1	1	0	1	0	0	0	1	1
1	0	0	0	0	0	0	0	0	0	0
1	1	1	1	1	1	1	1	1	0	1

In general, the ANN can be represented as follows:

$$\overline{H} = f(\overline{W}_1, \overline{X});$$

$$\overline{D} = f(\overline{W}_2, \overline{H});$$

$$\overline{Y} = f(\overline{W}_3, \overline{D}).$$

From the equations we've to get the definition of fourth-layer ANN (9):

$$\overline{Y} = f(W_1 f(W_2 f(W_3(\overline{X})))), \tag{9}$$

where $\overline{X}$ – is a network input vector (exercises); $\overline{W}$ – are the coefficients of individual cadet's / listener's characteristics.

For example, for vector $\overline{H}$, which determines the physiological characteristics of cadet / listener, we have:

$H_1 - w_{11}, w_{21}$ – are the coefficients, which characterized by the ability of cadet / listener N°1;
$H_2 - w_{12}, w_{22}$ – are the coefficients, which characterized by the ability of cadet / listener N°2;
$H_3 - w_{13}, w_{23}$ – are the coefficients, which characterized by the ability of cadet / listener N°3.

Similarly, weighing coefficients that characterize the complexity of the dynamic air situation (vector $\overline{D}$) and the quality of the exercise according to the timeliness (vector $\overline{Y}$) have been taken into account.

The Table 4 shows that during performance of exercise N°2 ($X_2 = 1$) cadets / listeners N°2 and N°3 have completed the task in time (N°1 – have not complied). During solving exercise N°1 – nobody has completed the task. During simultaneously performing of two tasks ($X_1 = 1$, $X_2 = 1$) cadets / listeners N°1 and N°3 have completed the task, cadet / listener N°2 – have not coped with the task.

Visualization of Results of Training Exercise Performance by Air Traffic Controller

The computer program for visualization of the status of exercise performance by cadet / listener under timeliness criterion has been developed (Shmelova et al., 2016). The instructor has information about ATC's stage of solving the problem: threats, pre-conflict or conflict. Threats should be seen as a warning that it is necessary to take immediate measures to resolve the PCS. Pre-conflict stage shows that to avoid conflict is difficult or impossible. Displays information about the origin of these steps will allow those who are taught to pay attention to the necessary taking actions to resolve PCS.

To increase the effect have been proposed to duplicate the information data on those aircraft, between which is predicted PCS. For the instructor, such information will help draw the attention of the learner on the need for measures to resolve the PCS. In conducting group sessions, such information will help the instructor to know which cadet / listener cannot cope with the task.

The Institute of Air Navigation of Flight Academy of National Aviation University has developed modeling complex "Fusion", which provides the multimodal system of predicted PCS (Figure 6).

Figure 6. The block scheme and algorithm of advanced modeling MC Fusion

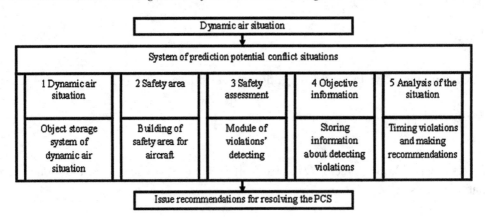

Information from the display of dynamic air situation, with regularity in one second ($t = 1$ sec), is transmitted to the objective system for storing information as to dynamic air situation. Then, considering the parameters of aircraft's movement and its relative positions can determine the type of PCS.

After determining the type of PCS, this information comes to the module of construction safety zone of aircraft. The security zones in MODELING COMPLEX "Fusion" are built in compliance with the regulations to maintain separation intervals (longitudinal, lateral and vertical) (ICAO, 2007). The size of the security zone depends on airspace structure and the relative position of the aircraft (for which the calculation is performed). Security zone is built along the motion vector of aircraft at each time when providing recalculation of the relative position of the aircraft. Ingestion of the aircraft in the security zone of another aircraft clearly regarded as a violation of separation intervals and recorded as the violation.

The module of detection violation's system, including the type of conflict and an active situation of security zone, defines the fact of violation of the intervals.

In cases where the system has detected a violation of safe intervals, this information comes in the system of storage information about violations. Storage information system about violations is able to keep three types of information about the conflict that took place, namely:

- Callsigns of couples aircraft, between which there was conflict;
- Time of conflict;
- Type of conflict.

The visual form of information presentation is the most appropriate form about occurrence phases of PCS for understanding by cadet / listener or instructor.

According to the developed classification, proposed to output the formula of three elements, each of which will show the number of potential conflicting situations at each stage of development. Figure 7 shows the exterior form of the output of such information.

Figure 7. Forms of indication: a – there are predicting four PCS (identified by yellow – the first column); b – one of the PCS has passed the stage of "pre-conflict situation" (identified by the crimson colour – the second column), c – one of the PCS has passed the stage of "conflict" (violation of separation intervals), one more of the PCS has passed the stage of "pre-conflict situation" (crimson (second column) and red (third column) colors have identified)

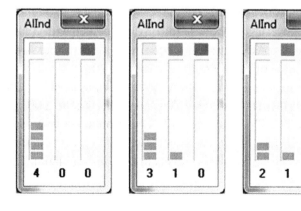

There are elements which are colored yellow, crimson and red colors correspond to stages of conflict situation (have shown in Figure 7). The yellow element corresponds to stage "threat of conflict", crimson – "pre-conflict situation," red – "conflict situation".

Table 4. Implementation of airspace classes in Ukrainian airspace

Nº	Class of Airspace	Zones of Airspace	Restrictions
1	D	CTR	1500-2900 m
2	D (except Boryspil TMA, where class C is applied due to high traffic volumes)	TMA	D (1500-2900 m) and C (2900 m – Fl 660)
3	D and C	CTA	D (1500-2900 m) and C (2900 m – Fl 660)

Indicators, which are located under the color elements, are designed to display information about the number of PCS at an appropriate stage of development. The use of the proposed indicators stages of the PCS at the workplace of future ATS specialist recommended at the stages of training, which will allow cadets / listeners gain the necessary skills to identify and resolve PCS. The similar indication at the workplace of instructor (teacher), can do the group sessions with cadets / listeners is more easier, because that will promptly identify problems in the detecting and resolution of PCS during the performance of training exercises.

Estimation of Pre-Simulation Training Tasks Complexity

The organization of the airspace over the definite area should be arranged so that it corresponds to operational and technical considerations only. In addition, aerodromes, where ATC is provided, should be designated as controlled aerodromes (Ministry of Transport of Ukraine, 2003).

States are selecting airspace classes which are appropriate to their needs. There are three zones of airspace – very important elements of ATM with individual restrictions: Control Zone (CTR), Terminal Control Area (TMA) and Control Area (CTA) (ICAO, 2007).

Control Area can be formed by TMAs of sufficient size to contain the controlled traffic around the busier aerodromes, interconnecting airways of a lateral extent, determined by the accuracy of track-keeping of aircraft operating on them, as well as the navigation means available to aircraft and their capability to exploit them; a vertical extent, covering all levels require to be provided with control service; or area-type control areas within which specific ATS routes have been defined for the purpose of flight planning and which provide for the organization of an orderly traffic (ICAO, 2007).

According to ICAO requirement, the Ukrainian ATS airspace has been classified and designated for following classes: class C and class D (Ministry of Transport of Ukraine, 2003) (Table 4).

The complexity of zone (CTR, TMA, and CTA) has been obtained with the help of expert assessments method (Beshelev & Gurvich, 1973). The experts were ATC, who operated in training course.

The algorithm of estimation of the complexity tasks in the Pre-Simulation Training with the help of expert assessments method:

1. Questionnaires for experts: m – is a number of experts, $m \geq 30$.
2. The matrix of individual preferences: R_i – is a system of preferences of i-expert, $i = \overline{1, m}$.
3. The matrix of group preferences R_j (10):

$$R = R_j = R_{gr} = \frac{\sum\limits_{i=1}^{m} R_i}{m}.$$ (10)

where $R = R_j = R_{gr}$ – is an experts' group opinion of the complexity of j-zone, $j = \overline{1, n}$; n – is a quality of zones.

4. Coordination of expert's opinion.
   a. Calculation of dispersion D (11):

$$D = \frac{\sum\limits_{i=1}^{m} (R_{gr} - R_i)^2}{m - 1}.$$ (11)

   b. Calculation of square average deviation σ (12):

$$\sigma = \sqrt{D}.$$ (12)

   c. The coefficient of the variation ν (13):

$$\nu = \frac{\sigma}{R_{gr}} \cdot 100\%.$$ (13)

If $\nu_{\text{CTR, TMA, CTA}} \leq 33\%$ then the opinion is concerted and system of expert group has been obtained. If $\nu_{\text{CTR, TMA, CTA}} > 33\%$ then it is necessary to calculate Kendal's concordation coefficient W (14):

$$W = \frac{12S}{m^2(n^3 - n) - m\sum\limits_{i=1}^{m} T_i};$$ (14)

$$S = \sum\limits_{j=1}^{n} \left(\sum\limits_{i=1}^{m} R_{ij} - \overline{R} \right)^2;$$

$$T_i = \sum\limits_{i=1}^{m} (t_i^3 - t_i);$$

$$\overline{R} = \frac{1}{n} \sum_{j=1}^{n} \left(\sum_{i=1}^{m} R_{ij} \right),$$

where S – is a generalized dispersion; t_i – is a number of the same ranks in the i-row which fixed the i-expert.

Kendal's concordation coefficient must be within the limits $0,7 < W \leq 1$. If $W < 0,7$ it is necessary to repeat the interrogation.

5. Compare the system of preferences R_{gr} and R_i, $i = \overline{1, m}$ with the help of rating correlation coefficient R_s (Spearman's coefficient) (15):

$$R_s = 1 - \frac{6 \sum_{j=1}^{n} (R_{gr} - R_i)^2}{n(n^2 - 1)}. \tag{15}$$

6. The significance of the calculations.

   a. The significance of the calculation of Kendal's coordination coefficient W, criterion $-\chi^2$ (16):

$$\chi_f^2 = \frac{S}{\frac{1}{2} m(n+1) - \frac{1}{12(n-1)} \sum_{j=1}^{n} R_j} > \chi_t^2, \tag{16}$$

where χ_f^2 – is a factual value of variable; χ_t^2 – is a table value of variable.

   b. The significance of the calculation of Spearman's coefficient R_s with using Student's t-criterion (17):

$$t_{critical} = R_s \sqrt{\frac{n-2}{1 - R_s^2}} > t_{st}, . \tag{17}$$

where n – is a quality of zones; t_{st} – is a tabulated value while the number of degrees of freedom $f = n-2$ and error $\alpha = 5\%$.

7. Weight coefficients w_j of j-zone complexity (18):

$$w_j = \frac{C_j}{\sum_{j=1}^{n} C_j}; \tag{18}$$

$$\sum_{j=1}^{n} w_j = 1,$$

where n – is a quality of zones; $C_j = 1 - \dfrac{R_j - 1}{n}$ – are the estimates, $j = \overline{1, n}$.

8. Graphical presentation of weight coefficients.

For estimation complexity of the exercises in the system of Pre-Simulation Training, it is necessary to find weight coefficients, which characterize the complexity of airspace zones. Assessments of the complexity of airspace zones with using the algorithm of estimation of the complexity tasks in the Pre-Simulation Training have been obtained (Shmelova, Lazorenko, & Bilko, 2014):

1. Questionnaires for experts – ATC with working experience.
2. The matrix of individual preferences. Evaluation of complexity of airspace zones (CTR, TMA, and CTA): R.

R_i has been obtained, $i = \overline{1, m}$, where m – is a number of experts; R_i – is a system of preferences of i-expert.

For example, $R_i = R_{iTMA} > R_{iCTA}, R_{iCTR}, \overline{1, m}$

3. The matrix of group preferences for CTR has been obtained:

$$R_{grCTR} = \frac{\sum_{i=1}^{m} R_{iCTR}}{m} = 2,64.$$

Average value R_{gr} for TMA and CTA have the similar calculations (Table 5).

4. Concordance of expert's opinion.
    a. Calculation of dispersion D:

$$D_{\bullet TR} = \frac{\sum_{i=1}^{m}(R_{grCTR} - R_{iCTR})^2}{m - 1} = 0,401099.$$

Calculations for TMA and CTA would be the same variant (Table 5).

    b. Calculation of square average deviation σ:

$$\sigma_{CTR} = \sqrt{D_{CTR}} = 0,633324.$$

Calculations for TMA and CTA would be the same variant (Table 5).

    c.   The coefficient of the variation ν:

$$\nu_{CTR} = \frac{\sigma_{CTR}}{R_{grCTR}} \cdot 100\% = 23{,}9636\%.$$

Variation for TMA and CTA have the similar calculations (Table 5).

If $\nu_{CTR,TMA,CTA} \leq 33\%$ then the opinion is concerted and the system of expert group has been obtained. For example, $R_{gr} = R_{TMA} > R_{CTR} > R_{CTA}$.

Table 5. The matrix of group preferences

Coordination of Expert's Opinion	CTR	TMA	CTA
	x_1	x_2	x_3
R_{gr}	2.642857	1.142857	2.214286
D_i	0.401099288976	0.131868480769	0.335164576356
σ_i	0.633324	0.363137	0.578934
$\nu_i, \%$	23.9636	31.77445	26.14542

Calculations show that opinion is concerted and it is necessary to obtain weight coefficients of complexity for airspace zones.

5.   Weight coefficients of complexity (Table 6):

$w_1 = w_{CTR}$ – weight coefficient for CTR zone;

$w_2 = w_{TMA}$ – weight coefficient for TMA zone;

$w_3 = w_{CTA}$ – weight coefficient for CTA zone.

6.   Graphical presentation of weight coefficients of CTR, TMA and CTA (Figure 8).

Table 6. The results of the calculation of weight coefficients

N°	Zone	R_{gr}	C_j	w_j
1	CTR	2.642857	0.453333	0.226161
2	TMA	1.142857143	0.953333	0.475786
3	CTA	2.214285714	0.596667	0.298053

Figure 8. Weight coefficients of zones' importance

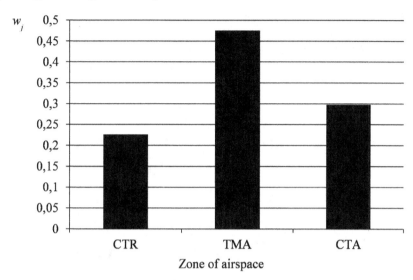

Calculations have been performed with using computer program MS Excel.

Integrated estimation of tasks Q_{jl} with j-level of complexity in air traffic control for n-zones (19):

$$Q_{jl} = \sum_{j=1}^{n} \sum_{l=1}^{L} w_j q_l, \tag{19}$$

where q_l – is an estimation of the task with given complexity and type of airspace zone (CTR, TMA, and CTA); w_j – is a weight coefficient (complexity of airspace zone); l – is a level of the task.

So, we can see that the most difficult zone of airspace according to the opinion of the expert is the Terminal Control Area ($w_{TMA} = 0.475786$).

In the future, ATC instructor would take into account this expert's opinion for the definition of a task according to difficulty.

Integrated estimation for implementation of the task with complexity characteristic of airspace zone has been calculated with the help of additive aggregation method.

For automating estimation of Pre-Simulation Training on initial stage the neural network of multi-layer type has been built (Shmelova et al., 2014). Figure 9 represents the neural network for Simulator Training of cadets / listeners with the specified number of hours and level of training. It is the multilayer perceptron with two hidden layers:

- **The First Layer:** Is a calculation of hours on theoretical training in accordance with the cadets' / listeners' knowledge evaluation;
- **The Second Layer:** Are the restrictions on the given number of hours (hidden layer);
- **The Third Layer:** Are the restrictions on passing hours (hidden layer);
- **The Fourth Layer:** Is an assessment of cadet / listener.

Threshold activation functions have been obtained according to requirements of hours and level of training marks (discipline) in compliance with the assessment criterion of tasks.

Figure 9. Neural network for Pre-Simulation Training of cadets / listeners with the specified number of hours and level of training

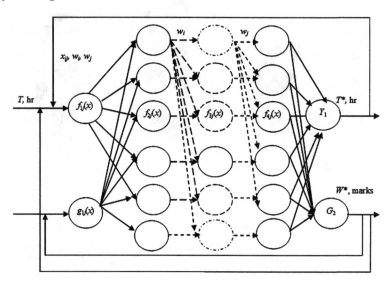

All positions of assessment criteria have been prescribed and must be used in a proper way as given below:

1. To take a duty and workplace preparation.
2. An ability to follow the prescribed standard phraseology (excepting tasks with emergency and urgency situations).
3. Coordination with adjacent ATC units and other kinds of aerodrome service provision units.
4. Handling of procedural control.
5. Handling of visual control.
6. Daily flight plan conduction.
7. Execution of traffic massages timesheets.
8. Timeliness and accuracy of decision making in ATC.
9. Compliance with safety in ATC.
10. Performing of console operations.

Some of the criteria might not be used in order to which are chosen by a supervisor before training.

During Pre-Simulation Training it is necessary to take into account that the abilities and skills of ATC are evaluating feedback.

We cannot apply general assessment criteria as they exist for the time of operation actions evaluation. However, some of them might be useful to apply. So, Pre-Simulation Training assessment criteria are:

- The retelling of the given situation;
- Phraseology to be used;
- Taking a duty and workplace preparation;
- information about traffic;
- Level change proposal;
- Vectoring and heading guidance.

The retelling of the given situation and expected phraseology is a fully individual criterion for supervisors. They must define elements which are necessary to be retail as well as to evaluate proposed phraseology.

Information about traffic must be a reflection of an ability of a student to define/detect through the plan all conflict situations. Evaluation of this element depends on the whole number of conflicts regarding the number of missed.

Level change proposal is a kind of a feedback that defines a degree of suitably given flight levels or altitudes by a student. Evaluation of this element is performed in percentage terms. Deviation of each level is equal to loss of one point.

The accuracy of a heading designation is a three degrees deviation from the desired direction. If we are out of limits we are losing one point within a criterion.

Every element has a five-point system basis. Evidently, missing all points of procedural elements by a student should be considered as non-completed element and the non-completed task correspondingly. Positively given marks are output into the mean value.

FUTURE RESEARCH DIRECTIONS

It is relevant to adapt the development artificial neural network for ATC Pre-Simulation Training of others Air Navigation System's human-operators: pilots, Unmanned Aerial Vehicles operators, flight dispatchers, rescuers, specialists of aviation security, etc. that will allow increasing the quality of their professional study.

It is our belief, that the neural network models can be used for improving the professional training of specialists in any technogenous production (hydraulic engineering, chemical and military industries, gas and oil pipelines, nuclear power plants and transport, etc.).

What's Next?

On the next steps we are planning to use neural network in the System for control and forecasting the development of emergency situations on the base of Artificial Intelligence System / Decision Support System that taking into account the influence of the professional factors (knowledge, habits, skills, experience) as well as the factors of non-professional nature (individual-psychological, psycho-physiological and socio-psychological) on the decision making process by human-operator of Air Navigation System.

CONCLUSION

On the base of the basic concepts of Threat and Error Management in air traffic control the stages of the developing conflict situation have been classified (threat – error – undesirable condition) and quantitative indicators of the complexity level at each stage using fuzzy logic have been defined. The neural network model of assessment the timeliness and correctness of the decision making by the specialist of ATS during the Pre-Simulation Training has been developed and its parameters have been obtained. The block diagram of MODELING COMPLEX "Fusion" with the ability to display phases of PCS, which simplifies the process of ATC training, as well as evaluating their actions in the performance of educational tasks by the instructor, has been presented.

Taking into account the timeliness and correctness of instructor's tasks performed during the Pre-Simulation Training with the help of using ANN will allow determining the possibility of access of specialist of ATS to Simulator Training. Multimodal system "Fusion" will give the possibility to improve the process of training of cadets / listeners through automated assessment of their actions.

With the help of methods of expert assessment, the difficulty of ATC operations (tasks) has been determined. Using the expert's opinion and criterion of weight coefficient, the hard zone for operation on Initial Training, such as simulator practice, has been defined. According to interrogation, the graph, based on preliminary calculation, has been built. The analysis of the graph has shown that TMA is in the first position according to the complexity of operation and procedure in air traffic control. The neural network for Pre-Simulation Training of cadets / listeners with the specified number of hours and level of training has been built. Automation of estimation of Pre-Simulation Training on the phase of Initial Training increases the efficiency of Simulation Training through interactive evaluation of the tasks performed by cadets / listeners. Performance of exercises is accompanying by comments, displaying results, assessments of the cadets / listeners and feedback.

REFERENCES

Allianz Global Corporate & Specialty, Embry-Riddle Aeronautical University. (2014). *Global Aviation Safety Study: A Review of 60 Years of Improvement in Aviation Safety*. Authors.

Arkhangelskiy, V., Bohaenko, I., Grabowskiy, G., & Ryumshyn, N. (1999). *Neural networks in systems of automation*. Kiev: Techniques.

Aviation Accident Statistics. (2018). *National Transportation Safety Board*. Retrieved from www.ntsb. gov/aviation/aviation.htm

Beshelev, S. D., & Gurvich, F. G. (1973). *Expert assessment*. Moscow: Science.

Borisov, A., Krumberh, O., & Fedorov, I. (1990). *Decision Making Based on Fuzzy Models: Examples of Using*. Riga: Zynatne.

Borovikov, V. P. (2008). *Neural Networks. STATISTICA Neural Networks: Methodology and Technology of Modern Data Processing* (2nd ed.). Moscow: Hotline-Telecom.

European Organisation for the Safety of Air Navigation (Eurocontrol). (2000). *Simulations Facilities for Air Traffic Control Training. HUM.ET1.ST07.3000-REP-02*. Brussels, Belgium: Author.

European Organisation for the Safety of Air Navigation (Eurocontrol). (2004a). ATM Services' Personnel (2nd ed.). ESARR 5. Belgium, Brussels: Author.

European Organisation for the Safety of Air Navigation (Eurocontrol). (2004b). *EATM Training Progression and Concepts*. Brussels, Belgium: Author.

European Organisation for the Safety of Air Navigation (Eurocontrol). (2015). *Specifications for the ATCO Common Core Content Initial Training* (2nd ed.). Brussels, Belgium: Author.

Gardner, M. W., & Dorling, S. R. (1998). Survey and Critique of Techniques for Extracting Rules from Trained Artificial Neural Networks. *Atmospheric Environment, 32*(14–15), 2627–2636. doi:10.1016/S1352-2310(97)00447-0

Goedeking, P. (2010). *Networks in Aviation: Strategies and Structures*. Springer. doi:10.1007/978-3-642-13764-8

International Civil Aviation Organization. (2007). Air Traffic Management (15th ed.). Doc. ICAO 4444-ATM/501. Montreal: Author.

International Civil Aviation Organization. (2007). Procedures for Air Navigation Services. Air Traffic Management (15th ed.). Doc. ICAO 4444-ATM/501. Montreal: Author.

International Civil Aviation Organization. (2008). *Threat and Error Management (TEM) in Air Traffic Control. Cir. ICAO 314-AN/178*. Montreal, Canada: Author.

Kharchenko, V., Chynchenko, Yu., & Raychev, S. (2007). Threat and Error Management in Air Traffic Control. *Proceedings of the National Aviation University, 3–4*, 24-29.

Kharchenko, V., Shmelova, T., Artemenko, O., & Otryazhiy, V. (2011). *A. r. Computer Program "Choosing the Pre-Flight Information and Decision Making about Departure for Automated System of Pre-Flight Information Preparation (AS PIP)"*. Kyiv: State Department of Intellectual Property.

Kharchenko, V., Shmelova, T., Sikirda, Yu., & Gerasimenko, O. (2011). *A. r. Computer Program "Optimizing the Choice of Alternative Variant of Aircraft Flight Completion in Flight Emergencies "Prompt"*. Kyiv: State Department of Intellectual Property.

Komashynskiy, V., & Smirnov, D. (2002). *Neural Networks and Its Use in Systems of Management and Communication*. Moscow: Hotline-Telecom.

Leychenko, S., Malishevskiy, A., & Mikhalic, N. (2006). *Human Factors in Aviation: monograph in two books*. Kirovograd: YMEKS.

Ministry of Transport and Communications of Ukraine. (2007). *The Rules for Issuing Certificates of Aviation Personnel in Ukraine*. Kyiv: Author.

Ministry of Transport of Ukraine. (2003). *About Approving the Flight Rules of Aircraft and Air Traffic Services in the Classified Airspace of Ukraine*. Kyiv: Author.

Shmelova, T., Lazorenko, V., & Bilko, A. (2014). Estimation of Pre-Simulating Training Tasks Complexity. *Proceedings of the National Aviation University, No., 1*(62), 17–22.

Shmelova, T., Sikirda, Yu., Zemlyanskiy, A., & Danilenko, O. (2015). Fuzzy Assessment of the Situation's Complexity during Simulation Training of Specialists in Air Traffic Services. In *Materials of International Scientific-Practical Conference "Problems of Energy Efficiency and automation in industry and agriculture"*. Kirovohrad: Kirovohrad National Technical University.

Shmelova, T., Sikirda, Yu., Zemlyanskiy, A., Danilenko, O., & Lazorenko, V. (2016). Artificial Neural Network for Air Traffic Controller's Pre-Simulator Training. *Proceedings of the National Aviation University, No.*, *3*(68), 13–23.

Shmelova, T., Yakunina, I., Moyseenko, V., & Grinchuk, M. (2014). *A. r. Computer Program "Network Analysis of Flight Emergency"*. Kyiv: State Intellectual Property Service of Ukraine.

Shmelova, T., Yakunina, I., & Yakunin, R. (2013). *A. r. Computer Program "Test Extraordinary Incident"*. Kyiv: State Intellectual Property Service of Ukraine.

Statistics of the World's the Largest Aircraft Accidents for the Years 1974-2014. (2018). Foringshurer Insurance. Retrieved from https://forinsurer.com/public/17/01/10/3824

Suzuki, K. (2013). *Artificial Neural Networks – Architectures and Applications*. InTech. doi:10.5772/3409

Zade, L. (1965). Fuzzy sets. *Information and Control*, *8*(3), 338–353. doi:10.1016/S0019-9958(65)90241-X

This research was previously published in Cases on Modern Computer Systems in Aviation; pages 27-51, copyright year 2019 by Engineering Science Reference (an imprint of IGI Global).

Chapter 66
Financial Asset Management Using Artificial Neural Networks

Roohollah Younes Sinaki
https://orcid.org/0000-0001-5358-3711
Ohio University, USA

Azadeh Sadeghi
https://orcid.org/0000-0002-2831-7048
Ohio University, USA

Dustin S. Lynch
Ohio University, USA

William A. Young II
Ohio University, USA

Gary R. Weckman
https://orcid.org/0000-0002-2445-4934
Ohio University, USA

ABSTRACT

Investors typically build portfolios for retirement. Investment portfolios are typically based on four asset classes that are commonly managed by large investment firms. The research presented in this article involves the development of an artificial neural network-based methodology that investors can use to support decisions related to determining how assets are allocated within an investment portfolio. The machine learning-based methodology was applied during a time period that included the stock market crash of 2008. Even though this time period was highly volatile, the methodology produced desirable results. Methodologies such as the one presented in this article should be considered by investors because they have produced promising results, especially within unstable markets.

DOI: 10.4018/978-1-6684-2408-7.ch066

INTRODUCTION

A typical investment portfolio contains four main asset classes. The four main asset classes are U.S. stocks, bonds, international stocks, and hedge positions. Each of these asset classes has multiple stock indices. A successful investment portfolio is determined by the total return on investment over the course of the portfolio. The strategy of creating investment portfolios will vary depending on several factors. Likewise, the evaluation of the success of a portfolio can also vary by client. For example, a conservative client might be satisfied with a 5% return on investment, while an aggressive investor might not be satisfied with a 7% return on investment. The portfolio is an investment in the owner's future; therefore, the return over a long time period is a better determination of the portfolio's success. The time period that is often used to evaluate the performance of a portfolio is five years.

The diversification of a portfolio is an important part of deciding whether a portfolio is performing well. Although many strategies exist, in general, portfolios that are more diverse are considered more resilient to changes in the market and therefore, they are more desired. Another determination of the success of a portfolio is its variance. As was explained earlier, this will change depending on the owner of the portfolio. Investors range from being risk-averse to those who seek risk when it comes to their preferred investment strategy. If the variance in a portfolio is high, the risk is high, which means that there is an increased probability that the return on investment will be minimal or produces a loss. The amount of risk often depends on the age of the portfolio's owner. Given the risk associated with this type of portfolio, it is often difficult to satisfy the owner of an investment. For example, if the owner has a low-risk tolerance, the client might not be satisfied with the construction of a highly volatile portfolio even it is producing a positive return. Some investors are simply not satisfied with the drastic changes in the portfolio's performance over short periods of time even if the intent is to build a long-term positive gain. For these types of clients, a portfolio that shows a lower positive rate of return with a lower variance might be a better fit for the client's risk tolerance and age. Although most financial advisors would disagree with a risk-averse strategy and recommend a more risk-seeking strategy, ultimately, the final decision resides with the owner of the portfolio.

The traditional approach allocates assets for a diversified investment portfolio consists of a risk-tolerance questionnaire, a life stage assessment, a portfolio-objective-guidance-matrix, and finally, allocation judgments made by a financial advisor with the clients' approval. These questions help the client and advisor decide the best path for the client while keeping the risk at an acceptable level. It will help the advisor determine if the client is willing to accept a higher or lower risk/volatility of returns of their investment. The biggest limitation of the traditional approach is that stock indices are difficult to predict, due to volatile behavior and very complex interaction of multiple variables. The stock market is a complex system and has non-linear behavior making it exceedingly difficult to predict.

This research presented in this article has multiple objectives: first, to show that artificial neural networks (ANNs) are capable of predicting real-world occurrences, and secondly, to provide a decision support aid that financial advisors can consult when determining how assets are allowed when constructing a client's investment portfolio. Many financial firms currently do not use machine learning-based systems because they consider the market to be unpredictable due to its high volatility. The research presented in this article will demonstrate that investors should consider decision support systems built upon machine learning techniques because they are capable of producing high rates of returns even during times when the market is highly volatile.

LITERATURE REVIEW

The goal of creating a diversified portfolio is to perform well in bull and bear markets. A bull market is one in which prices are expected to rise, while in a bear market, prices are expected to decline at a rate of 20% or more (Encyclopedia Britannica, 2015). A market decline of 10-20% is considered a "correction" and investors have different strategies during these periods of time. In bull markets, it is common for investors to purchase securities and commodities in the hope that they can sell their investments for a profit in the future. In a bear market, on the other hand, the investor commonly sells their investments in the hope that they can buy them back later at a lower price. In both markets, there are always examples of clients looking to make quick profits, but diversification has proven to be the most consistent strategy that is used by financial advisors.

Technical trading and risk tolerance can take on multiple definitions, depending upon the source. Risk tolerance will vary from person to person and is an important measure when tied to an investment portfolio. An investment portfolio comprises a client's investments and is a crucial part of their future. Investments are money invested by the client, and therefore, quickly become important. Big swings or shifts in the portfolio's value can be hard for clients to accept; therefore, a measure of risk/variance is an important measure for a firm to consider for their clients.

Many different firms have used risk measurement strategies. Niko Canner in 1997 examined how investors' attitudes toward risk should influence the composition of their portfolios. His research offered a simple answer to the question by using the mutual-fund separation theorem, which states that all investors should hold the same composition of risky assets (Canner, Mankiw, & Weil, 1997). Most financial advisors recommend that the more conservative investor's portfolio should consist of a higher ratio of bonds-to-stocks, while a portfolio of a more aggressive investor should consist of a lower ratio of bonds-to-stocks.

Advisors are trying to help their clients optimize their portfolios, but their advice often contradicts economic theory and is very hard to explain between firms and advisors. With that said, more non-traditional methods are being developed and explored within the financial sector in an effort to help both clients and advisors. Although there are many brokerage firms that maintain traditional approaches, some are utilizing newer technologies and predictive methods. Charles Schwab is a brokerage and banking company that operates in four main divisions: investing, wealth management, banking, and trading (Charles Schwab, 2015). The company is based out of San Francisco, California, and has been in business since 1971. Charles Schwab Corporation added an automated investment portfolio service in 2015. Their technology aims to diversify the client's portfolio across many different asset classes while experts monitor the performance of their clients' portfolios. Their technology also rebalances portfolios so that they remain balanced and diversified appropriately in regard to the client's profile.

Artificial neural networks (ANNs) are primarily used only in academia because of their ability to model complex nonlinear systems, but some are beginning to use them for solving more problems in industry (Young & Weckman, 2009). As Young (2009) states, they are not commonly used in industry because they are hard to implement, usually not understood very well, and have a reputation of being "black-box" models. Although there are few mathematical models that exist that can outperform ANNs, most industries have been reluctant to accept them for solving practical problems in business (Young & Weckman, 2009).

ANNs are nonlinear models consisting of various combinations of simple linear and nonlinear functions that are similar to biological neural networks in the human brain. The integration of mathematical functions enables these types of models to mimic the ability of a human brain in order to solve solving difficult, non-linear problems. ANNs are trained with historic data that is processed through various learning algorithms within the network structure. To many, ANNs are considered "universal approximators" (Neural Networks, 1989) that can learn any pattern hidden within the data being analyzed as long as the sample size of data is rather large and the structure of the ANN is reflecting the complexity of the data being modeled. One of the more significant advantages of using ANNs is that they do not require formal assumptions about data being modeled, which is unlike more traditional models derived from probability and statistics (Skapura, 1996).

The predictive quality and usability of ANNs depend on the quality of data being used to train the model. As with any business application, if the quality of information is high, the quality of the results produced by an ANN will also be higher. In other words, having subject domain experts help to decide what information is used to develop an ANN is always preferred. ANNs have a unique ability to overcome the limitations of noisy data (Burney, 1997). As noted, it is always preferred to have subject matter experts help determine what data is being used to train the model, however; it is not an absolute requirement although some caution practitioners that unwanted bias can be introduced if a model does not consider best practices within predictive analytics (Weckman, et al., 2016). The time required to process an ANN use to be a concern. However, in recent times, the time to develop a process is not a major limitation of their development. ANNs have almost always had the ability to model complex systems and in more recent times, they are capable of producing highly accurate results with a large dataset, which is why ANNs are becoming more popular for real-world business applications.

From a mathematical perspective, there are many ways that synapses can occur inside an ANN. Synapses are simply the ability to connect inputs to neurons, neurons to other neurons, and neurons to the output layer of an ANN. Neurons act as linear or non-linear transfer functions that enable ANNs to model complex data. The most common ANN topology is the multi-layered perceptron (MLP) model. The MLP is considered feed-forward networks that are usually trained with backpropagation algorithms. The architecture of a typical MLP is shown in Figure 1. This ANN includes two hidden layers, 40 neurons (i.e. processing elements) in the first hidden layer, 20 neurons in the second hidden layer, and one output neuron in the last layer. It should be noted that in this particular network, the first two hidden layers utilize a hyperbolic tangent function (i.e. Tanh) neuron while the output neuron utilizes a linear transfer function.

ANNs almost always outperform traditional linear and even other non-linear methods. They produce excellent results for pattern recognition problems through deep learning and preform particularly well with noisy data. ANNs typically perform better than linear methods in terms of predicting and classifying data because systems generally behave in non-linear ways. Principe stated that they provide excellent results for problems across many different fields and categories (Principe, Euliano, & Lefebvre, 1999). For these reasons, Qian (2007) suggested that ANNs are "ideal for stock market prediction."

ANNs and other machine learning techniques are not new when it comes to being used to predict stock market outcomes. Researchers have used them to predict turns in individual stocks and bonds for a number of years. One such example is the work of Chiang (1996), who has used ANN methods to forecast the end-of-year net asset value (NAV) of mutual funds. The method uses ANNs and shows that they significantly outperform regression models in situations where data is limited due to its availability. Their ANN consists of one input layer of 15 inputs and one hidden layer of 20 neurons, with the output

Figure 1. MLP ANN (Akinwale et al., 2009)

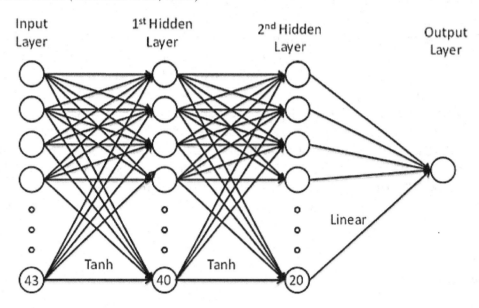

being the NAV of a mutual fund at the year's end. The method utilized a total of 101 datasets and used stepwise regression in SAS to choose the most significant variables for each model. The datasets trained on a range from 1981 to 1985 and were tested on the actual data from 1986. The ANN performed 40% better than the linear regression models (Chiang, 1996).

Vaisla compared linear regression to an ANN and found that the regression models significantly underperformed with respect to the ANNs that were developed (Vaisla, 2010). Akinwale, Arogundade, and Adekoya (2009) also compared regression analysis to the predictive ability of an ANN when predicting Nigeria stock market prices and made similar conclusions.

Many articles and conference papers have been written about ANNs being used to predict portions of the stock market. The majority of articles found in literature attempt to predict the movement of indices, which are composed of many individual stocks. Although this has been a popular use of ANNs, there are other methods that take a broader approach to utilizing ANNs to predict individual stock prices. Weckman et al. (2008) used an ANN model to predict individual stock prices. In addition, Lakshminarayanan (2005) and Hui (2000) also used ANNs to do the same.

The data for this project was a relatively small dataset, which means that additional effort was performed to better understand and improve the prediction performance of the model. Data sets with a limited sample size is a common challenge when developing time series models. This often presents a significant challenge to create useful models for this particular problem domain. This is especially true for ANNs because they typically require a substantial amount of data to "learn" the data properly. Simply put, ANNs normally require a large amount of data in order to discover the underlying patterns of the data that map inputs to the desired output through the machine learning paradigms that are used during the training process. However, methods have been established in order to overcome this limitation. For example, Chawla (2002) developed a popular method called the synthetic minority over-sampling technique (SMOTE). SMOTE was designed in a way that combined the use of random under-sampling of the majority class with the use of random over-sampling of the minority class (Chawla, 2002). This method oversamples the minority class by creating synthetic data examples along with the original data, rather than oversampling that minority class with replacement (Suvarna, 2013).

SMOTE is a method that generates synthetic data examples from the original data in order to improve predictive accuracies in minority classes. SMOTE commonly yields the best results when it comes to re-sampling and can create a larger dataset so that an ANN can learn patterns within datasets that are limited. SMOTE introduces synthetic data along with line segments by joining classes to its nearest neighbor (Chawla, 2002). The SMOTE technique essentially creates a new class sample by interpolating between several class examples that are close to one another. It does this in a "feature space" rather than a "data space." Depending on the amount of synthetic data needed, neighbors from the k nearest neighbors are randomly chosen. Determining the way in which the nearest neighbors are selected is considered a limitation of SMOTE. However, Chawla stated that focusing on the nearest neighbor examples that were classified incorrectly could potentially improve the SMOTE method and overall performance of the technique (Chawla, 2002).

METHODOLOGY

Data Collection

Data is needed to train ANNs in order to predict the different asset classes' performances and trends. The data that was used in the creation of the dataset used for this research consisted of economic data that was used to predict the percent variation of each of the four main asset classes for commonly used within investment portfolios. This data includes factors that affect the economy, such as the unemployment rate, gross domestic product (GDP), the political party in the house, senate, and the resident, just to name a few. A typical example of one of the indices that were examined in this methodology is the large-cap growth index and the percent return for the years 1995 to 2009. It is easy to see that the index varies significantly; during the market crash of 2008, the percent return was -38.44%.

The data associated with the financial market seems to be everywhere, but the data that actually affects how the market acts are more difficult to obtain. The performance of how well each index is performing is reported through the day, but mainstream news outlets often fail to report how well the performance of each of the four asset classes (i.e. U.S. stocks, international stocks, hedges, and bonds) perform throughout the day or even on a daily basis. Thus, one challenge that this research faced was aggregating the data of these four asset classes together so that it could be used to build a predictive model. In order to overcome this obstacle, Morningstar Principia software was used in order to retrieve the desired data for the four asset classes. Morningstar Principia has been a trusted resource for financial professionals for more than 15 years (Morningstar Principia, 2015) and the software provided historical month-to-month performance data for each of the four different asset classes and their historic indices. Table 1 lists the major classes and indices used within the presented research.

The premise of this research is to provide an accurate forecast of an asset class performance so that financial advisors can use this information in order to construct an investment portfolio with higher rates of return on investment for their clients. For this research, the output of the ANN was the percent return on a given investment. Thus, the output was numerical, and the variance of this prediction can help determine if the model produced reliable forecasts. This is because one determination of a good investment portfolio is low volatility. The inputs to the model included both economic factors and politi-

Table 1. Asset classes and indices

Bonds	Hedges	International Stocks	U.S. Stocks
Corporate Short Term	Cash	Emerging Markets	Large Cap Growth
Government Short Term	Commodities	Growth	Large Cap Value
Government Intermediate	Precious Metals	Value	Mid Cap Growth
Government Long Term	Real Estate		Mid Cap Value
High Yield Corporate			Small Cap Growth
International			Small Cap Value
Municipal Intermediate			
Municipal Long Term			
Municipal Short Term			

cal parties. From a data pre-processing standpoint, the historic data was aggregated to the point where it would have been known when a forecast would need to be made. A summary of the inputs used in the ANN developed for this research is listed below:

- Political Party
- Effective Federal Funds Rate (%)
- Corporate Profits After Tax ($B)
- Consumer Price Index-Urban Wage Earners and Clerical Workers
- Industrial Production Index 2007=100
- Consumer Sentiment Index 1966=100
- Unemployment Rate (%)
- Civilian Unemployment Rate
- Consumer Price Index for All Urban Consumers: All Items
- Crude Oil Prices: West Texas Intermediate (WTI)-Cushing, Oklahoma
- Gross Federal Debt
- Housing Starts: Total: New Privately Owned Housing Units Started
- ISM Manufacturing: PMI Composite Index
- M2 Money Stock
- 30-Year Conventional Mortgage Rate
- Producer Price Index: All Commodities
- Real Retail and Food Services Sales
- Total Construction Spending
- Total Vehicle Sales
- Trade Balance: Goods and Services, Balance of Payments Basis
- University of Michigan: Consumer Sentiment
- Real Gross Domestic Product
- S&P/Case-Shiller U.S. National Home Price Index
- Gross Domestic Product
- New Privately-Owned Housing Units Started

- Initial Claims
- Trade Weighted U.S. Dollar Index: Broad

The data found within the Morningstar Principia software was quite extensive, however; at times, the data was incomplete. In other words, missing data was present within the data collected from the software. Since completed records were needed for the ANN, additional resources that are commonly available from simple Internet searches were used in order to complete each and every record where missing data was present during the 1995 to 2009 time period used in this investigation. When the missing data could not be found from simple Internet searches, the Federal Reserve Bank of St. Louis' Economic Research site (2014) was utilized to complete data records. Ultimately, the information collected online, through the Morningstar Principia software, and the data from the Federal Reserve Bank of St. Louis' Economic Research were merged together into a single dataset that was later used to develop and validate the ANN presented in the following sections.

Forecast Time Period

With any predictive model, more data is generally preferred, but unfortunately, only 20 years of data were considered complete from the two primary resources that were used to construct the datasets for this research.

From the 20 years of data, forecasts utilized both a three-month and six-month moving average for each input attribute. Moving averages are a "succession of averages of data from a time series, where each average is calculated by successively shifting the interval by the same period of time" (Dictionary, 2015). In addition to the moving averages, the data was also lagged in order to predict a three-month (i.e., one quarter) window. For example, the data was trained so that the December 1991 output was used to predict March of 1992, then the January 1992 output was used for April 1992, and so on. These moving averages were then added to the database in order to predict the performance of the different asset allocations.

The first attempt in this research was to predict only the average of the four asset classes. ANNs were created and developed for each of the four asset classes and then examined based upon their predictive performances. An example of the variation of values for U.S. Stocks is shown in Figure 2. The figure is provided to simply highlight the complexity of the data being modeled. The data shows some very minor, yet inconsistent seasonality trends with shifting variations through the time series.

Since the variation of each asset's average values was rather large, the models generated for this data were poor. After this experiment was performed, the prediction of a three-month moving average of the output was examined. The three-month moving average was then calculated and added as a new column in the dataset. The ANNs were compared to predict the three-month moving average. The variation of the three-month moving averages for the U.S. Stocks is shown in Figure 3. In comparison to the individual averages found for each asset class, the three-month moving average reduced the overall variation, which results in a more accurate model to be created.

Even though the three-month moving average produced results that outperformed the overall average, the modification did not lead to a statistically significant change in predictive performance measures. Figure 4 shows an example of the six-month moving average for the U.S. Stock class. In comparison to the prior attempts, the six-month moving average showed less variation, which in return, allowed for a more accurate model of the performance of an asset to be created.

Figure 2. U.S. stock monthly variation in value

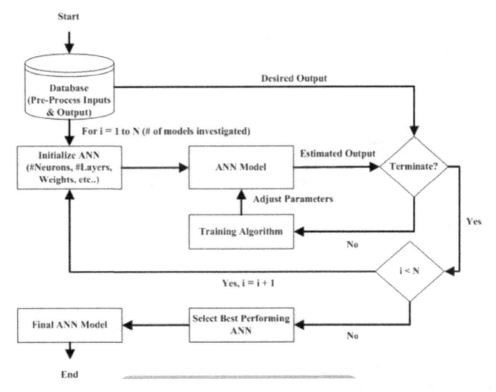

Figure 3. U.S. stock 3-month moving average variation in value

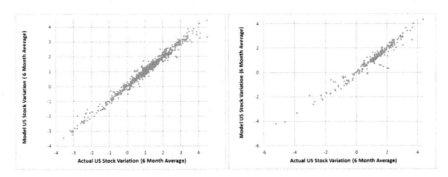

The time-series shown in Figure 4 demonstrates far less erratic behavior due to unexplainable variations within the data than the previous time-series that were analyzed. Thus, after analyzing the capabilities of an ANN's ability to model the performance of each asset class, it was decided that the six-month moving average lagged output would be used for the remainder of the methodology. It should be noted that financial experts were consulted with the development of this model. The experts that were consulted favored the six-month time horizon given the improved quality of the forecast. In addition, they did not react negatively that the time horizon of prediction was longer than three-months since long-term portfolio performance was their primary focus.

Figure 4. U.S. stock 6-month moving average variation in value

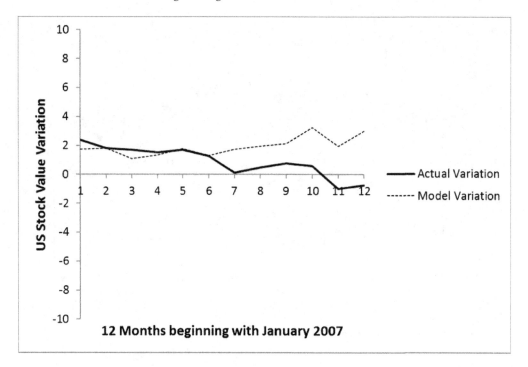

Determining SMOTE and Time Series Forecast

From the aggregated data, a baseline model was created. Other than the pre-processing that has been discussed previously, no other modifications were made to the aggregated data. This data was partitioned into a training, cross-validation, and testing datasets. The training dataset contained 178 records, which left 36 records for cross-validation and 12 records for independent testing. Again, this limited sample-size presents a challenge for ANNs to learn from the data it is presented within the training data. For example, an ANN was developed for Bonds and the results of the training session are shown in Figure 5. The figure for the training session does not show the desired characteristics. For example, the performance for both the training and cross-validation data do not slowly improve over epochs. The lowest average MSE occurs over just a few epochs, which often is an indication that the data is complex, or the architecture of the ANN is not adequate. However, after trying various MLP ANN structures, the accuracy did not improve, which indicates additional pre-processing techniques should be considered.

Figure 6 presents additional evidence of the poor fits that were obtained from the baseline ANN model that was constructed from the aggregated dataset. It is important to mention that the goal of developing a predictive model is to produce a model that generalizes the data well. In order to investigate whether the ANN model generalized the data well, the accuracy of the testing data was explored. Each figure below shows two separate ways to highlight the unexplained variation of the model in terms of modeling the actual data points within the testing data. To investigate this, a 45-degree plot was created, and it is shown as the second figure below. The graph can be interpreted in the following manner. If a model was perfectly accurate, the actual values would fall along a 45-degree line. Visually it is clear that the trend fit and the location of the fit are both poor. Furthermore, the R-value for the testing set was found to be 0.0087, which is extremely poor.

Figure 5. Bonds training and cross-validation results

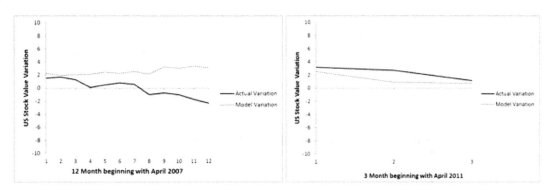

Figure 6. Bonds test results and model versus actual bond variation from test data

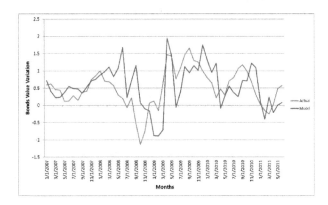

The poor results shown in Figure 6 was not a surprise given the evidence shown in Figure 5. However, to be through with the analysis, the quality of fit was examined for both the training and cross-validation datasets. The 45-degree plots for the training and cross-validation datasets are shown below in Figure 7. These figures show a lot of variation, which is to be expected with complex datasets. The variation in the training and cross-validation data helps to explain why the predictive performances were poor for the testing data found in Figure 6. Simply put, if a model cannot produce a satisfactory quality of fit metrics for training and even more so, cross-validation, then the testing data will not perform well in practice. Thus, additional methods to pre-process the data were necessary in order to create a useful predictive model.

The dataset that was original compiled for this research did not produce reliable and useful results as demonstrated in the previous figures and paragraphs. As noted, the sample size of this dataset was not large, and the quality of fit was directly impacted by the limited sample size. In order to increase the number of records, which was assumed to improve the quality of fit for the model, a method called SMOTE was used to generate synthetic data samples based on the original data (Chawla, 2002). It is important to make the distinction that SMOTE was applied to the original dataset in order to increase the number of records available for training and cross-validation but was not used to generate artificial samples for testing. After creating additional synthetic data samples, the size of the dataset grew to 890 records, which would later be used to create new data partitions for both the training and cross-validation.

The impact of applying this pre-processing method is shown in Figure 8. This figure is much more desirable than the training session that did not use synthetic data points. The learning curve is smooth, and it requires several thousand iterations to arrive at a steady-state. For example, the ANN continued to improve in its predictive performance until the 9,460[th] epoch, versus the earlier method with no synthetic data, which arrived at a steady-state point in only 19 epochs, which is not desirable given the complexity of the data being investigated.

Figure 7. Model versus actual bond variation from training data cross-validation data

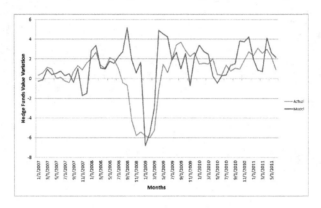

Figure 8. Bonds training and cross-validation results (synthetic data)

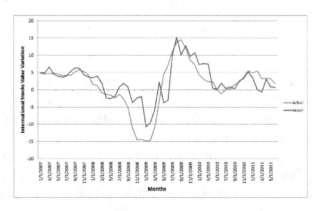

Based on the increased sample size formulated by applying the SMOTE method, Figure 9 shows 45-degree plots for the new training and cross-validation datasets. The figures show a "tight" fit for both the training and cross-validation datasets, which is a desirable characteristic and implies the model should produce accurate fits to the testing data.

The synthetic data created by the SMOTE technique produced results that were very promising. Though the results looked promising after SMOTE was utilized, much more time and experimentation are necessary in order to develop the best performing ANN model. Therefore, the following section will document the process of creating the final ANN model that was used to aid in the process of allocating assets within an investment portfolio.

Figure 9. 45 degree plot of training data (synthetic) and cross-validation (synthetic)

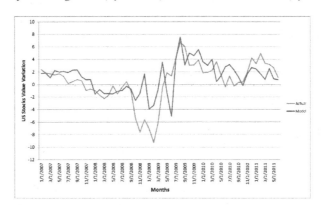

Final ANN Model Creation Based on SMOTE

Various ANN models were developed using many different types of architectures, learning algorithms, training percentages, cross-validation percentages, testing percentages, transfer functions, and hidden layers. Multiple models were developed for each of the four asset classes in order to find the best performing model for each asset class. Figure 10 shows a summary of the process flow utilized to create and find the "best" ANN. It shows three phases, pre-processing, training, and testing (Young, Holland, & Weckman, 2008). Utilizing the key characteristics and the flow chart, the ANNs were initialized and trained in order to make a final decision on which ANN would be used to determine a portfolio's allocation of assets.

Figure 10. Procedural flow for ANN creation

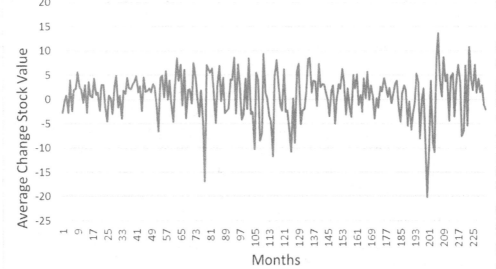

As noted, an ANN model was developed for each of the four asset classes in order to predict the performance of each. Using the dataset created by applying the SMOTE methodology, multiple ANNs were trained and evaluated based upon the six-month moving average, which would give ample time for investors to make decisions for their long-term investment performance goals. As previously described, the ANN models varied in architectures, randomization, learning algorithms, cross-validation and testing percentages, and hidden layers.

Example architectures that were varied for each class include generalized feed-forward (GFF) networks, typical multi-layered perceptron (MLP) networks, and modular networks. All of the ANNs that were developed were tested using different learning algorithms, which included momentum, delta bar delta, and conjugate gradient descent algorithms. The different architectures also utilized different transfer functions, such as Tanh, sigmoid, linear Tanh, and linear sigmoid. The number of hidden layers was also changed for each of the different combinations of architectures, learning algorithms, and transfer functions. The number of hidden layers ranged from one hidden layer to three hidden layers for each of the different combinations. The search to find the best performing ANN for each asset was quite extensive and laborious. An example of the top-four performing models for U.S. Stocks is summarized in Table 2. Determining the top-performing model was determined from models producing the highest R^2 values.

Table 2. Four best performing models

Model #	Architecture	# of Layers	# of Processing Elements by Layer	Activation Function by Layer	Learning Algorithm
1	Multilayer Perceptron	3	100, 75, 50	Hyperbolic Tangent, Hyperbolic Tangent, Linear	Momentum
2	Multilayer Perceptron	3	100, 75, 50	Sigmoid, Sigmoid, Linear	Momentum
3	Multilayer Perceptron	3	30, 20, 10	Hyperbolic Tangent, Hyperbolic Tangent, Linear	Levenberg-Marquardt
4	Multilayer Perceptron	3	30, 20, 10	Sigmoid, Sigmoid, Linear	Levenberg-Marquardt

Training, cross-validation, and testing percentages were examined during the creation of the ANN's forecasting process. ANNs were created using Neurosolutions 6.5. Figure 11 shows that the model's output compared to the actual values for the desired output. The figures suggest that the estimates are fitting closely to the actual data points due to the "tightness" of the 45-degree plot. For example, if a linear regression line was fitted to the cross-validation data appearing below, it would result in an R^2 value of 0.947, which is incredibly high.

Though the model seemed to fit the training and cross-validation well, it is not a true, unbiased evaluation of the model's ability to generalize the data well because of the influence of applying the SMOTE technique to the training and cross-validation data. However, in order to evaluate the generalizability of the model, the testing data, which has not been modified, can be assessed in an unbiased manner. The results of the testing data are shown in Figure 12. Figure 12 describes the output of the first forecasted values which is an evaluation of a 12-month time horizon that started on January 1st in 2007. To capture additional insight, a slightly different time horizon is shown in Figure 13. In this figure, the results of applying the best performing ANN model to U.S. Stocks over a 12-month time period that started on April 1st in 2007. Following this investigation, the last three months of the evaluation period were forecasted. The performance of the final three months of this study resulted in an R-value of 0.752.

Figure 11. Model versus actual training and cross-validation

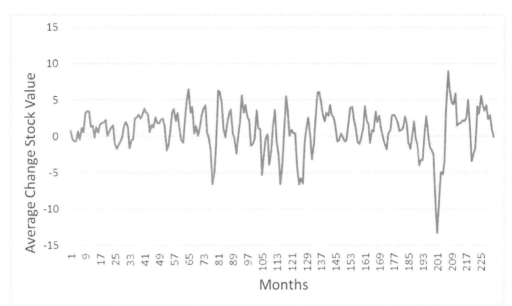

Figure 12. Test results

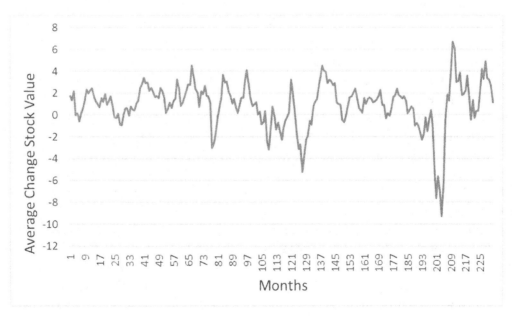

Figure 13. Desired output and actual network output

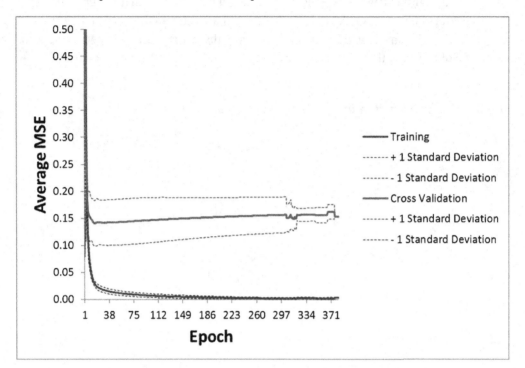

RESULTS

This section presents the results for the ANN models that were developed for the four asset classes (i.e. Bonds, Hedge Funds, International Stocks, and U.S. Stocks) described throughout this article. Before the discussion of the results begins, it is important to remind readers that the U.S. stock market experienced a crash in 2008. Therefore, this time period is of particular interest and the time periods before the crash (BtC) and after the crash (AtC) will be discussed throughout this section.

The results for the Bond asset class are summarized in Figure 14. The overall performance of this asset class resulted in an R^2 of 0.231, which does not imply that the goodness-of-fit is strong. However, an argument could be made that the model is following the actual variation observed within the data well and would still have provided useful information in the process of planning investment portfolios. As noted, the U.S. stock market crashed in 2008. After this time period, the value of R^2 increased slightly to 0.297, which is about a 6% improvement AtC in 2008. Perhaps one could argue that this is not a substantial or statistically significant improvement, but it does at least suggest that the ANN performed as equally well BtC as it did AtC. Thus, the ANNs ability to model the performance of Bonds was consistent and robust to high volatility.

The results of the Hedge class are summarized in Figure 15. The model's predictive ability was similar to the Bond asset class. The overall performance of the model produced an R^2 value of 0.249. This R^2 value shows that the ANN only understood approximately 25% of the variation for the asset class's performance. With respect to BtC and AtC, the ANN model seemed to be resilient to the highly fluctuating market. Likewise, the value of R2 actually improved slightly AtC when the market was more stable.

Figure 14. Final bond performance

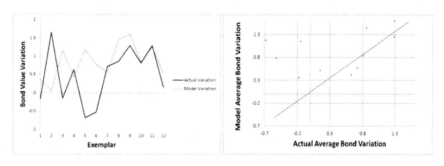

Figure 15. Final hedge performance

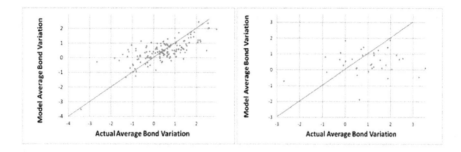

The performance of the International Stock class is summarized in Figure 16. For this asset class, the ANN was able to produce an R2 value of 0.651, which is a drastic improvement over the performance obtained for the Bond and Hedge asset classes. Unlike the previous asset classes that have been described, the ANN for the International Stock class did not improve AtC. In fact, the performance AtC decreased in value to 0.431. However, given the time frame in which decisions are made to allocate assets within an investment portfolio, the ANN is still able to provide useful information because the ANN is able to model the change in trend within the time-series.

The performance of the best performing ANN for the U.S. Stock asset class is shown in Figure 17. For this asset class, the model produced an R^2 value of 0.446, which is nearly the same value for the ANN model for International U.S. Stocks AtC. Thus, approximately 45% of the variation in the U.S. Stock class was explained by the ANN model.

Along with the performance of the ANN model regarding each of the asset classes, the model's ability to model the trend of the data was also investigated. From an adviser's perspective, it is extremely important to know if the performance of a certain asset class is trending down (TD) or trending up (TU) in order to make decisions on how an investment portfolio is allocated. In other words, financial advisers need to know the anticipated change of trajectory of any given asset class to make informed decisions of how an investment portfolio should be constructed. Quarterly averages were calculated based upon the actual observed values over the last three months of a given time period. These values were compared against the last six-month average in order to establish whether the performance of an asset class was actually TU or TD. Thus, by comparing the actual values with the forecasted values for a given ANN, the accuracy of the trend could be determined. An example of the information that could be analyzed by financial advisers for the U.S. Stocks asset class is shown in Table 3.

Figure 16. Final international stock performance

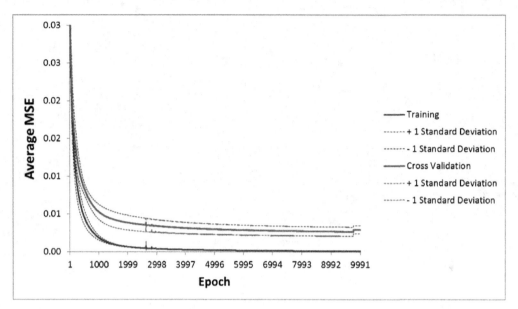

Figure 17. Final U.S. stock performance

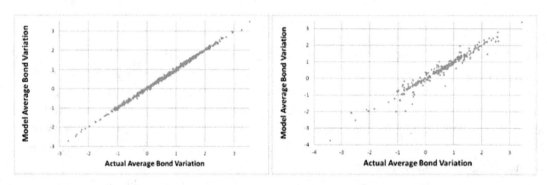

In order to determine how well the trends were modeled by the proposed methodology, the concept shown in Table 3 was applied for all asset classes from 1/1/2007 through 6/1/20011. The results of this study are shown in Table 4. By comparing the actual trend trajectories with the forecasted trend trajectories, the methodology produced an overall accuracy between 64.7% to 70.6% for the four types of asset classes.

Table 3. U.S. stock trend prediction

Date	Actual 6MA	Actual Quarterly Average	Actual Trend	ANN 6MA	ANN Quarterly Average	ANN Trend
1/1/2007	2.388			1.743		
2/1/2007	1.820			1.808		
3/1/2007	1.707	1.972		1.079	1.543	
4/1/2007	1.522			2.224		
5/1/2007	1.696			1.978		
6/1/2007	1.289	1.502	D	2.052	2.085	U
7/1/2007	0.133			1.898		
8/1/2007	0.468			2.303		
9/1/2007	0.788	0.463	D	2.320	2.174	U
10/1/2007	0.575			1.192		
11/1/2007	-0.969			0.732		
12/1/2007	-0.721	-0.372	D	0.782	0.902	D

Table 4. Trend prediction accuracy for each asset class

	Bonds	Hedge	Intl Stocks	US Stocks
Total	64.7%	64.7%	70.6%	64.7%

DISCUSSION

This research methodology was explained approximately 25% of the variation seen in the Hedge asset class. The methodology did not perform as well as anticipated for this particular asset class. The reason why the models for the hedge asset class did not perform to a high degree of accuracy is potentially due to the fact that crash will certainly perform differently from real estate and gold in various markets. After further discussion with the financial advisors, one suggestion for future work was to improve the hedge prediction accuracy by splitting out the hedge asset class and using ANN models to compile an overall hedge asset class prediction.

The ANN models also did not perform as well as one would have wanted for the Bond asset class. At first, this was a concern because bonds typically do not fluctuate as much as stocks. It was assumed that the prediction and understanding of the variance would be much higher in terms of its accuracy. Unfortunately, the models were only capable of understanding approximately 23% of the variation within that asset class. After the crash of 2008, the model improved. The model had virtually no understanding before the crash based upon the inputs that were provided, while after the crash it was able to explain 29% of the variation for that asset class. However, when advisors were consulted about these results, they were concerned with this level of accuracy. They suggested that the prediction for a fixed income bond was less desirable with respect to the other asset classes that were investigated.

Machine learning methods, like the ones presented in this research, are slowly being adopted by financial firms. However, they have not been in practice long enough in order to determine how successful they will be in designing portfolios in the future. However, it does suggest that methodologies, such as the one presented in this article should be at least considered when future methods are explored.

FUTURE RESEARCH

Although this research was considered a success, there are still areas that could be considered for future research in order to improve the performance and usability of the methodology. This section describes a few areas that should be considered by others as a result of the research findings presented in this article.

One avenue for future consideration would be to apply various deep learning models within the scope of financial performances related to investment portfolios. For example, deep learning approaches like convolutional neural networks (CNNs) or recurrent neural networks (RNN) could be one possible methodology to explore. In CNN, the feature extraction and prediction process occur simultaneously. This is not the case for traditional machine learning approaches like MLP ANN where the feature extraction process is implemented manually by an expert in the field. In CNNs, these types of transforms are made inherently and automatically within the framework of the methodology. However, one limitation of applying CNN models is, in contrast to other learning algorithms in which their performance decreases when the amount of data increases, that their performance is highly dependent upon the amount of data that is used. In addition to developing CNN models, recurrent neural network (RNN) models have been shown to be promising for time-series problems. In RNNs, each sample is assumed to be dependent on previous samples. In the context of portfolio management, this could be considered a reliable tool for investors making a decision on how a portfolio should be allocated.

Determining which set of input attributes, as well as the output attribute, of any model is vital to the application and success of a data-driven approach. Thus, additional research could explore a wider set of attributes that were not explored within the research presented. For example, emotional investing plays a critical role in the performance of the market. Thus, one area of future research could be including input attributes that reflect the emotions that influence market behavior. In addition to input attributes that could potentially be integrated into the methodology, the expert opinion could also be considered, which should improve the overall capabilities of a methodology developed for asset allocations within investment portfolios.

Methodologies can evolve with the integration of machine learning methods like CNN or RNNs with the other analytical capabilities such as optimization. Based on the forecasts that could be made with various types of ANNs, optimization could be employed in order to determine an optimal mix of assets to allocate within a client's investment portfolio. Prescriptive analytics could be leveraged in a way that minimizes the variance of the system in order to maximize the highest expected rate of return on the investment portfolio given the client's investment preferences, age, and other characteristics.

Methodologies designed to be used as a decision-making aid for portfolio design should not overlook the expertise of financial advisers. These tools should not be designed with the intent of replacing financial advisors, but they should be designed to help the advisors make more informed, and ultimately, better decisions for their clients. Therefore, with that being said, integrating expert knowledge into the design and implementation of a methodology should always be considered best practice.

REFERENCES

Akinwale, A., Arogundade, O., & Adekoya, A. (2009). Translated Nigeria Stock Market Prices Using Artificial Neural Network for Effective Prediction. *Journal of Theoretical and Applied Information Technology*, *9*, 36–43.

Burney, K. (1997). *Introduction to Neural Networks*. UCL Press.

Canner, N., Mankiw, N., & Weil, D. (1997). An Asset Allocation Puzzle. *The American Economic Review*, *87*(1), 181–191.

Charles Schwab. (2015). *Corporation*. Retrieved from https://en.wikipedia.org/wiki/Charles_Schwab_Corporation

Chawla, N., Bowyer, K. W., Hall, L. O., & Kegelmeyer, W. P. (2002). SMOTE: Synthetic Minority Over-Sampling Technique. *Artificial Intelligence Research*, *16*, 321–357. doi:10.1613/jair.953

Chiang, W. (1996). A Neural Network Approach to Mutual Fund Net Asset Value Forecasting. *Management Science*, *24*(2), 205–215.

Dictionary. (2015). *Moving Average*. Retrieved from http://dictionary.reference.com/browse/moving+average

Economic Research Federal Reserve Bank of St. Louis. (2014). Retrieved from https://research.stlouisfed.org/useraccount/datalists/126909

Encyclopedia Britannica. (2015). *Bear market*. Retrieved from http://www.britannica.com/EBchecked/topic/57332/bear-market

Encyclopedia Britannica. (2015). *Bull market*. Retrieved from http://www.britannica.com/EBchecked/topic/84336/bull-market

Hui, S., Yap, M., & Prakash, P. (2000). A Hybrid Time Lagged Network for Predicting Stock Prices. *International Journal of the Computer, the Internet, and Management, 8*(3).

Jiang, Z., Xu, D., & Liang, J. (2017). *A deep reinforcement learning framework for the financial portfolio management problem.* arXiv preprint.

Lakshminarayanan, S. (2005). *An Integrated Stock Market Forecasting Model Using Neural Networks* (M.S. Thesis). Ohio University.

Morningstar Principia. (2015). *PNR General*. Retrieved from http://advisor.morningstar.com/Principia/pdf/PRN_General_040212.pdf

Neural Networks. (1989). *Multilayer feedforward networks are universal approximators*. Retrieved from http://portal.acm.org/citation.cfm?id=70408

Principe, J., Euliano, N., & Lefebvre, W. (1999). *Neural and adaptive systems: Fundamentals through simulations*. John Wiley & Sons Inc.

Qian, B., & Rasheed, K. (2007). Stock market prediction with multiple classifiers. *Applied Intelligence*, *26*(1), 25–33. doi:10.100710489-006-0001-7

Skapura, D. (1996). *Building Neural Networks*. Addison-Wesley.

Suvarna, V. (2013). SMOTE Based Protein Fold Prediction Classification. *Advances in Computing & Inform. Technology*, 541–550.

Vaisla, K. B. (2010). An Analysis of the Performance of Artificial Neural Network Technique for Stock Market Forecasting. *International Journal on Computer Science and Engineering*, *2*, 2104–2109.

Weckman, G., Dravenstott, R., Young, W. II, Ardjmand, E., Millie, D., & Snow, A. (2016). A Prescriptive Stock Market Investment Strategy for the Restaurant Industry using an Artificial Neural Network Methodology. *International Journal of Business Analytics*, *3*(3), 1–21. doi:10.4018/IJBAN.2016010101

Weckman, G., Lakshminarayanan, S., Snow, A., & Marvel, J. (2008). An Integrated Stock Market Forecasting Model Using Neural Networks. *International Journal of Business Forecasting and Marketing Intelligence*, *1*(1), 30. doi:10.1504/IJBFMI.2008.020813

Young, W., Holland, W., & Weckman, G. (2008). Determining Hall of Fame Status for Major League Baseball Using an Artificial Neural Network. *Journal of Quantitative Analysis in Sports*, *4*(4).

Young, W. II, & Weckman, G. (2009). Using a heuristic approach to derive a grey-box model through an artificial neural network knowledge extraction technique. *Neural Computing & Applications*, *19*(3), 353–366. doi:10.100700521-009-0270-2

This research was previously published in the International Journal of Operations Research and Information Systems (IJORIS), 11(3); pages 66-86, copyright year 2020 by IGI Publishing (an imprint of IGI Global).

Chapter 67
Applying Neural Networks for Modeling of Financial Assets

Dmitry Averchenko
Southern Federal University, Russia

Artem Aldyrev
Southern Federal University, Russia

ABSTRACT

The purpose of this chapter is to develop an analytical system for forecasting prices of financial assets with the use of artificial neural networks technology. Proposed by the authors, the analytical system consists of several neural networks, each of which makes the forecast of financial assets prices. The system includes recurrence (with feedback) neural networks with sigmoidal activation formula. This allows the networks to "remember" a sequence of reactions to the same stimulus. The learning process of neural networks is performed using an algorithm of back propagation of error. The key parameters of forecast for this analytical system are the indicators presented by the terminal MetaTrader 4-broker Forex Club: Average Directional u Movement Index; Bollinger Bands; Envelopes; Ichimoku Kinko Hyo; Moving Average; Parabolic SAR; Standard Deviation; Average True Range; and others.

INTRODUCTION

The main task of the investor is to buy cheaper and to sell more expensively. The higher the asset price variability, the more opportunities to conduct winning trading strategies, even when considering transaction costs. Unfortunately, what appears to be a simple and obvious hindsight is not at all obvious. All forecasting methods and techniques of financial assets prices can be divided on two large groups: fundamental and technical. The concept of fundamental analysis is based primarily on prediction of price behavior as a result of the influence of those or other events in the world economy. The basic methods of fundamental analysis include: benchmarking method, deduction and induction, correlation, grouping and generalization, macroeconomic analysis, industry method, as well as the method of financial coefficients (Schwager & Turner, 1995; Kalmykova, 2007; Chirkova, 2014).

DOI: 10.4018/978-1-6684-2408-7.ch067

Technical analysis is based on three postulates: "the market price takes everything into account", "the market follows the trend", and "the market is the pattern". Technical analysis methods include technical indicators, wave and candle analysis, price charts, and methods of artificial intelligence (neural networks). (Murphy, 1999; Schwager, 1997; Elder, 2007; Kovel, 2007; Nison, 2003). We focus our attention in this chapter on the last method of artificial neural networks.

Neural networks are a class of powerful machine learning algorithms based on statistical methods of analysis. They have been successfully applied for many years in the development of trading strategies and financial models: tasks are determined for developing their own approaches to forecasting the financial market and designing profitable trading systems (Laletina, 2015). New methods and models are being explored to improve the accuracy of forecasts and solve the problems of approximation and classification (Vladimirova, 2014). Despite this situation, neural networks do not have a very good reputation due to frequent failures of their practical application. In most cases, the reasons for failure lie in inadequate design decisions and a general lack of understanding of how they work.

The novelty and relevance of this study is due to the combination of classical approaches of technical analysis and automatic optimization of this model through a neuron network. This excludes cases of inadequacy of the model, and not allowing for the situation of the "black box". The study describes the construction of a neuron network cluster using four networks through which the authors of the study will determine the current phase of the market - trend / flat. Subsequently, the model will use those indicators and approaches that are used for this phase of the market - trend / flat indicators.

The practical significance of the study is to develop a new approach for forecasting prices of financial assets and adopting appropriate investment decisions by combining the classical approaches of the technical analysis and the artificial intelligence. The main target audience of this research can be traders, investors with different investment horizons, and scientists with a similar sphere of scientific interests. We believe the fractal (the neuron analog) is the price of a financial asset, and neural networks are one of the most promising methods of fractal analysis. The key question here is whether it is possible to determine the direction, magnitude, and volatility of future asset price changes by extrapolating the available past data. Adaptive nonlinear systems can be trained to perform technical analysis with minimum possible assumptions.

Lately, the hypothesis of an effective market (EMH) developed by Eugene Fama is seriously criticized as unscientific literature. In its weak form, this hypothesis asserts that the investor cannot receive abnormal rate of return via technical analysis rules, which are based solely on past prices. In other words, information about past prices cannot be useful for extracting abnormal income (Baestaens, Van Den Berg, & Wood D., 1997).

Simultaneously, EMH does not specify the nature and manner of obtaining such information through past prices. Should the simple time-series autocorrelation, methods of Box-Jenkins or Fourier analysis, or many others filtering methods be used? Moreover, EMH is a combined hypothesis.

This means that EMH verification requires preliminary pricing model formation, which in turn depends on the degree of predictability. This circumstance makes the matter even more complicated. The main reason that does not allow the possibility to reject EMH is the presence of the market Index funds (the following strategies of passive management), which are very popular among pension funds. However, recently in the scientific literature there are assumptions that financial markets have some features of predictability (Peters, 1994). However, it should be remembered that the success in applying technical analysis depends entirely on the quality of the optimization method.

Thus, there is a growing need for information systems that can conduct approximation, classify and recognize different types of data over a wide range of their changes and are capable of flexible learning, depending on the changes, goals, and objectives set before them. In such systems, artificial neural networks (NN) are widely used. Currently, there is a large number of various software packages for working with NN, but the implementation of methods and algorithms in most software solutions (for example, algorithms for teaching NN or normalizing input training data) is hidden from the user.

In most cases, the user has no way of knowing which algorithms with which properties the developers of the package used to achieve the best result in teaching NN. Therefore, it is difficult to determine at what expense the properties of the algorithm different software packages demonstrate different results on the same training samples (TS). Additionally, this causes difficulties in the application of the package in own development and in the conduct of research. Consequently, it is impossible to select the optimal software package to work with NN. Modern artificial NNs are often used not as a separate tool, but are instead integrated into information systems that require flexible training depending on the changes of certain tasks. Therefore, to conduct a large amount of computational experiments, NN should be integrated into software complexes, with the use of which these experiments will be conducted.

The software package MatLab provides for working with the NN library Neural Network Toolbox, which allows one to model neural networks of different architectures. During the modeling when trying to scale the network or change for its own purposes, it is necessary to consider the following: The NN topology, weighting coefficients of neural connections, and NN activation functions that cannot be changed without changing the results of NN functioning. This can lead to a violation of the reproduction of results on the same training sample for networks having different structures. The larger the neural network (the greater the number of layers and neurons), the more difficult the evaluation (Turovskiy, 2014, 2015).

THEORETICAL FRAMEWORK

The idea of creating systems for the processing of intellectual information by the image of the device of the nervous system arose in the 1940s. McCulloch and Pitts (1943) created a simplified model of the neural cell – the neuron. NNs are computational structures that, for signal processing, use phenomena similar to those occurring in human brain neurons. The most important feature of the network, providing its broad capabilities, is the parallel processing of information by all links of the network. A large number of inter-neural connections permit speeding up the process of information processing significantly, which provides the possibility of processing signals in real time. In addition, the network becomes resistant to errors that occur (Yahyaeva, 2016).

Another no less important property of the NN is the ability to learn and generalize the accumulated knowledge. The NN has the properties of artificial intelligence. Trained on a limited set of data, the network can summarize the information received and display the results on new data not used in the learning process. The human nervous system is built from elements called neurons. The human brain contains up to 10^{11} neurons, which have approximately 10^{15} compounds among themselves. Each neuron has many properties in common with other organs of the body, but it has unique abilities: to receive, to process and transmit electrochemical signals along the nerve pathways that form the communication system of the brain.

Figure 1. Structure of the biological neuron

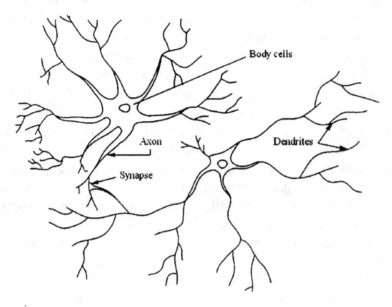

Figure 1 shows the structure of a pair of typical biological neurons. Dendrites go from the body of the nerve cell to other neurons where they take signals at the junction points called synapses. Adopted by the synapses, input signals are transmitted to the neuron's body. Here they are summed and some inputs aim to excite a neuron while others prevent its arousal. When the total excitation in the body of the neuron exceeds a certain threshold, the neuron is excited and sends signal to other neurons through the axon. This basic functional scheme has many complications and exceptions; nevertheless, most of the artificial neural networks simulate only these simple properties.

The artificial neuron imitates, in the first approximation, the properties of a biological neuron. At the input of an artificial neuron comes a set of signals, each of which is the output of another neuron. Each input is multiplied by the corresponding weight, similar to the synaptic force, and all products are summed, determining the activation level of the neuron (Bushuev, 2000).

Figure 2. Model of the simplest artificial neural network

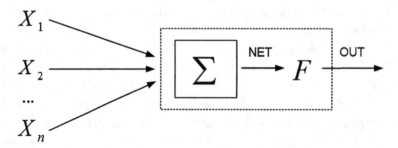

Figure 2 presents a model that realizes this idea. The set of input signals, designated as $X_1, X_2, ..., X_n$, goes to the artificial neuron. These input signals, denoted by the vector X, correspond to the signals arriving at the synapses of the biological neuron. Each signal is multiplied by the corresponding weight $-\omega_1$, $\omega_2, ..., \omega_n$, and supplied on the summing block, designated as Σ each weight corresponds to the "strength" of one biological synaptic connection (the set of weights is denoted by the vector W). The summing block corresponding to the body of the biological element sums the weighted inputs algebraically, thus creating an output which we will call NET. In vector notation this can be compactly written as follows:

$$NET = XW \tag{1}$$

The NET signal is converted by the activation function F and provides an output neural signal OUT. The activation function can be an ordinary linear function

$$OUT = F(NET) \tag{2}$$

where, F - is a constant of threshold function.

$$OUT = \begin{cases} 1, & if\ NET > T \\ 0, & if\ NET \le T \end{cases} \tag{3}$$

where, T is some constant threshold value, or a function that is more accurate simulates the nonlinear transfer characteristic of a biological neuron and provides to the neural network great opportunities.

Figure 3. Graph of the sigmoid function

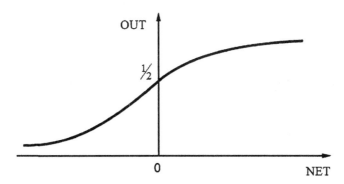

In Figure 2, the block designated F receives the signal NET and issues an OUT signal. If the block F narrows the range changes of quantity NET so that for any values of NET the OUT values belong to some finite interval, then F is called the "compressive" function. As a "compressive" function, the logistic or "sigmoidal" (S-shaped) function is often used (shown in Figure 3). This function is mathematically expressed as:

$$F\left(x\right) = \frac{1}{1+e^{-x}} \qquad (4)$$

Thus, using equations (3) and (4), the authors obtain:

$$OUT = \frac{1}{1+e^{-NET}} \qquad (5)$$

By analogy with electronic systems, the activation function can be considered a nonlinear amplification characteristic of an artificial neuron. The increment factor is calculated as the ratio of the increment of the value of OUT that causes it to become small increment of the NET. It is expressed by the slope of the curve at a certain level of excitation and varies from small values at large negative excitations (the curve is almost horizontal) to the maximum value at zero excitation and again decreases when the excitation becomes large positive.

Grossberg (1973) found that such a nonlinear characteristic solves the dilemma of noising saturation set by him (Wasserman, 1992). How can the same network handle both weak and strong signals? Weak signals require a large network strengthening to give a usable output signal. However, amplifying cascades with high amplification coefficients can lead to saturation of the output by the noise of the amplifiers (random fluctuations), which are present in any physically realized network.

Strong input signals, in turn, will also lead to saturation of amplifying stages, excluding the possibility of a useful utilization of the output. The central area of the logistic function, which has a high gain coefficient, solves the problem of processing weak signals, while areas with a falling gain at the positive and negative ends are suitable for large excitations.

Thus, the neuron operates with a high amplification in a wide range level of input signal.

$$OUT = \frac{1}{1+e^{-NET}} = F\left(NET\right) \qquad (6)$$

Another widely used activation function is the hyperbolic tangent. In form it is similar to the logistic function and is often used by biologists as a mathematical model of nerve cell activation. As an activation function of an artificial neural network, it is written as follows:

$$OUT = th(x) \qquad (7)$$

Similar to a logistic function, the hyperbolic tangent is an S-shaped function; however, it is symmetric about the origin and at the point $NET = 0$, the value of the output signal OUT is zero (see Figure 4). Unlike the logistic function, the hyperbolic tangent takes values of different signs and this property is applied for full number of networks series. The considered simple model of an artificial neuron ignores many properties of its biological twin. For example, it does not take into account the time delays that affect the dynamics of the system. Input signals immediately generate an output signal. And, more importantly, it does not consider the effects of the frequency modulation function or the synchronizing function of the biological neuron, which a number of researchers consider decisive in the nervous activity of the natural brain.

Figure 4. Chart of the hyperbolic tangent

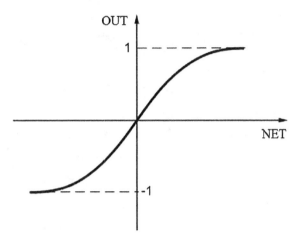

Despite these limitations, networks constructed from such neurons exhibit properties that strongly resemble a biological system. Only time and research will be able to answer the question of whether such coincidences are accidental or they are a consequence of the fact that the most important features of the biological neuron are correctly grasped by the model.

Single-Layer and Multi-Layer Artificial Neural Networks

Although one neuron is capable of performing the simplest recognition procedures, for serious calculations it is necessary to combine neurons in the network. The simplest network is composed of groups of neurons which form a layer, as shown in the right part of Figure 5.

Note that the vertex-circles on the left serve only for the distribution of the input signals. They do not perform any calculations and therefore will not be considered a layer. For greater clarity, let's designate them as circles to distinguish them from computational neurons, denoted by squares. Each element from the set of inputs X by a separate weight is connected to each artificial neuron. And each neuron gives a weighted sum of inputs to the network. There may also be connections between the outputs and the inputs of the elements in the layer.

Figure 5. Model of a single layer artificial neural network

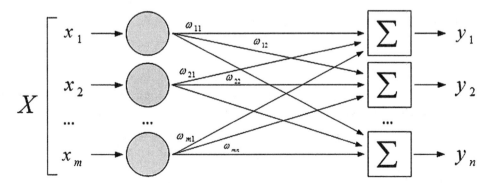

Figure 6. Model of multi-layer artificial neural network

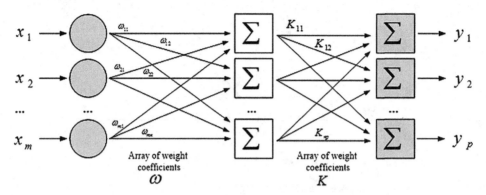

It is convenient to consider the weights as elements of the matrix W. The matrix has m rows and n columns, where m is the number of inputs, and n is the number of neurons. For example, ω_{23} is the weight connecting the second input to the third neuron.

Thus, the calculation of the output vector N, components of which are outputs of OUT-neurons, is reduced to matrix multiplication:

$$N = XW \tag{8}$$

where, N and X are row-vectors.

Larger and more complex neural networks have, as a rule, greater computing power. Although there are networks of all configurations, layered organization of neurons copies the layered structures of certain parts of the brain. It turns out that such multi-layer networks have more possibilities than single-layer networks and in recent years, algorithms have been developed for their training.

Multi-layer networks can be built from cascades of layers. The output of one layer is the input for the subsequent layer. A similar network is shown in Figure 6 and it is displayed with all connections. Multi-layer networks cannot lead to an increase in processing power compared to a single-layer network if the activation function between the layers is linear. The calculation of the layer output consists in multiplying the input vector by the first weight matrix with the subsequent multiplication of the result vector by the second weight matrix (if there is no nonlinear activation function).

$$OUT = (XW_1)W_2 \tag{9}$$

Since the multiplication of matrices is associative, then:

$$(XW_1)W_2 = X(W_1W_2) \tag{10}$$

Figure 6 shows that a two-layer linear network is equivalent to a single-layer matrix, equal to the product of two weight matrices. Therefore, any multi-layer linear network can be replaced by an equivalent single-layer network. However, single-layer networks are very limited in their computing capabilities. Thus, for expansion of the capacity of networks, in comparison with a single-layer network, a nonlinear activation function is needed.

The networks considered so far had no feedbacks (i.e., connections) which are going from the exiting outputs of a certain layer to the inputs of the same layer or previous layers. This special class of networks, called networks without feedbacks or networks of direct distribution, arouse great interest and is widely used. Networks of a more general kind, having connections from output to input, are called networks with feedbacks. Networks without feedbacks have no memory as their output is completely determined by the current inputs and the values of the weights. In some configurations of networks with feedback, the previous output values are returned to the inputs; the output is determined by the current input and the previous outputs. Therefore, networks with feedbacks can have properties similar to short-term human memory, where network outputs also partly depend on previous inputs.

Unfortunately, there is no generally accepted method for counting the number of layers in a network. The multi-layer network consists, as shown in Figure 6, from alternating sets of neurons and weights. In Figure 5, it was already mentioned that the input layer does not perform the summation. These neurons serve only as ramifications for the first set of weights and do not affect to the computing capabilities of the network. Therefore, the first layer is not taken into account when counting layers and the network similar to that depicted in Figure 6 is considered to be two-layer, since only two layers perform calculations. The weights of the layer are connected with the neurons following them. Consequently, the layer consists of a set of weights with the neurons summing the weighted signals following after them.

Training of Artificial Neural Networks

Among all the interesting properties of artificial neural networks, not one captures imagination as much as their ability to train. Their training resembles the process of intellectual development of a human person to such an extent that it might seem that we have achieved a deep understanding of this process. But it is not so. The possibilities of learning artificial neural networks are limited and many difficult tasks need to be solved to determine whether the researchers are on the right track.

The Purpose of Training

The network is trained to give a desired set of outputs (or, at least, equivalent to it) for a set of inputs. Each such input set or output set is a vector. Training is carried out by sequential presentation of input vectors with simultaneous adjustment of weights in accordance with a certain procedure. In the process of learning, weights of the network gradually become such that each input vector produces an output vector.

Teaching With the Teacher

There are learning algorithms with and without a teacher. Training with the teacher assumes that for each input vector there exists a target vector representing the required output. Together they are called a learning pair. Usually the network is trained on a certain number of such training pairs. Presented an output vector, the network output is calculated and compared with the corresponding target vector. The difference (error) is fed into the network with the help of feedback and weights are changed in accordance with the algorithm that seeks to minimize the error. The vectors of the training set are presented sequentially, errors are calculated and weights are adjusted for each vector until the error throughout the training array does not reach an acceptable low level.

Teaching Without a Teacher

Despite numerous applied achievements, training with the teacher was criticized for its biological implausibility. It is difficult to imagine a learning mechanism in the brain, which would compare the desired and actual values of the outputs and performing feedback correction. Teaching without a teacher is a much more plausible model of learning for a biological system. Developed by Kohonen and many others, it does not need a target vector for outputs and consequently, does not require comparison with predefined ideal answers. The training set consists only of input vectors.

The training algorithm adjusts the network weights so that the agreed output vectors are obtained, i.e. the presentation of sufficiently close input vectors will give identical outputs. The learning process, therefore, highlights the statistical properties of the learning set and groups similar vectors into classes. Delivery of a vector to the input from this class will give a certain output vector, but before learning it is impossible to predict which output will be produced by this class of input vectors. Consequently, the outputs of such network must be transformed into some understandable form, conditioned by the learning process. This is not such a serious problem. It is usually not difficult to identify the connection between the input and the output set by the network.

Learning Algorithms

Most modern learning algorithms have grown from the Hebb concept. He proposed a model of teaching without a teacher in which the synaptic force (weight) increases, if both neurons (source and receiver) are activated. In this manner, frequently used paths in the network are amplified and the phenomena of habit and learning through the repetition are explained. In an artificial neural network using the training on the basis of Hebb, the build-up of weights is determined by the product of excitation levels of the transmitting and receiving neurons. This can be written as:

$$\omega_{ij} \bullet (n + 1) = \omega(n) + \alpha \bullet OUT_i \cdot OUT_j \tag{11}$$

where,

$\omega_{ij}(n)$ = the weight value from the neuron i to the neuron j before the tuning,
$\omega_{ij}(n + 1)$ = weight value from neuron i to neuron j after tuning,
α = coefficient of training speed,
OUT_i = output of the neuron i and the input of the neuron j,
OUT_j = output of neuron j.

The networks using the training by the Hebb have developed constructively; however, over the past 20 years more effective learning algorithms have been developed (Haykin, 2006). Therefore, in this investigation the backpropagation algorithm was used to which the authors devoted the following section.

Back Error Propagation Algorithm of Artificial Neural Network

To illustrate this process, we use a neural network consisting of three layers and having two inputs and one output of (Figure 7).

Figure 7. Three-layer neural network

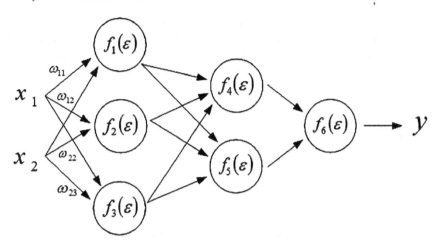

Each neuron consists of two elements. The first element (dendrites) adds weighting coefficient to the input signals. The second element (the body) realizes a non-linear function, the so-called neuron activation function. The signal ε - is the weighted sum of the input signals:

$$y = f\left(\varepsilon\right)$$
$$\varepsilon = x_1 \cdot \omega_1 + x_2 \cdot \omega_2$$

(12)

To train a neural network, we must prepare the data for training (examples). In our case, the training data consists of the input signals (and) and the desired result. Training is a sequence of iterations (repetitions). In each iteration the weights coefficients of the neurons are adjusted with use of new data from training examples. The change in weight coefficients is the essence of the algorithm described below (Melihova, Veprintseva, & Chumichev, 2016).

Figure 8. Distribution in the network of input signals

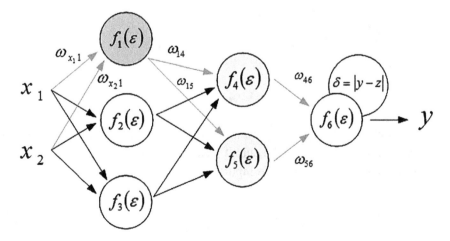

Each step of training begins with the impact of input signals from the training examples. Subsequently, we can determine the values of the output signals for all neurons in each layer of the network. Figure 8 shows how the input signals, acting on the first neuron, are transmitted into the hidden layer. After that, how $f_6(\varepsilon)$ deliver the input signals from $f_4(\varepsilon)$ and $f_5(\varepsilon)$, output signal from $f_6(\varepsilon)$, (i.e., y) is compared with the desired output signal z, which is stored in the training data. The difference between these two signals is called the output network layer error δ.

$$y_i = f_i\left(x_1 \cdot \omega_{x_1 i} + x_2 \cdot \omega_{x_2 i}\right), i = \overline{1,3}$$
$$y_k = f_k\left(y_1 \cdot \omega_{1k} + y_2 \cdot \omega_{2k} + y_3 \cdot \omega_{3k}\right), k = \overline{4,5} \qquad (13)$$
$$y = f_6\left(y_4 \cdot \omega_{46} + y_5 \cdot \omega_{56}\right)$$

It is impossible to directly calculate the error signal for internal neurons, because the output values of these neurons are unknown. For many years, an effective method for learning a multi-layer network was unknown. Only in the mid-1980s was the algorithm for backpropagation of the error was developed. The idea is to propagate the error signal δ back to all neurons whose output signals were input signals for the last neuron (calculated in the learning step, Figure 9).

Figure 9. Back propagation of the error signal

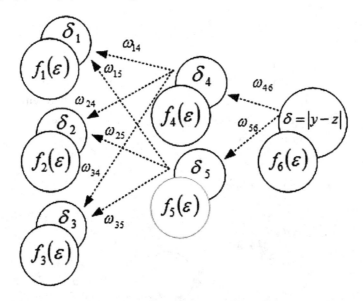

The weight coefficients ω_{mn}, used for backpropagation of the error, are equal to the same coefficients, which were used during the calculation of the output signal. Only the direction of the data flow changes (signals are transmitted from the output to the input). This process is repeated for all layers of the network. If the error has come from several neurons, it is summed up:

$$\delta_i = \omega_{i4} \cdot \delta_4 + \omega_{i5} \cdot \delta_5, i = \overline{1,3}$$
$$\delta_k = \omega_{k6} \cdot \delta, k = \overline{4,5} \tag{14}$$
$$\delta = |z - y|$$

When the value of the signal error is calculated for each neuron, it is possible to correct the coefficient weights of each neuron input (dendrite) node. The authors use the activation function of the sigmoid type (Figure 4):

$$S(x) = \frac{1}{1 + e^{-x}} \tag{15}$$

Then the derivative of the function $S(x)$ is as follows:

$$S'(x) = S(x) \cdot (1 - S(x)) \tag{16}$$

The computation of the derivative is necessary, because to adjust the weighting coefficients when learning NN using the backpropagation algorithm, the gradient descent method is used:

$$\left\{ \begin{array}{l} \omega'_{x_1 i} = \omega_{x_1 i} + \mu \cdot \delta_i \dfrac{df_i(e)}{de} x_1 \\[3mm] \omega'_{x_2 i} = \omega_{x_2 i} + \mu \cdot \delta_i \dfrac{df_i(e)}{de} x_2 \end{array} \right. , i = \overline{1,3} \tag{17}$$

$$\left\{ \begin{array}{l} \omega'_{1k} = \omega_{1k} + \mu \cdot \delta_k \dfrac{df_k(e)}{de} y_1 \\[3mm] \omega'_{2k} = \omega_{2k} + \mu \cdot \delta_k \dfrac{df_k(e)}{de} y_2 \\[3mm] \omega'_{3k} = \omega_{3k} + \mu \cdot \delta_k \dfrac{df_k(e)}{de} y_3 \end{array} \right. , k = \overline{4,5} \tag{18}$$

$$\omega'_{j6} = \omega_{j6} + \mu \cdot \delta \frac{df_6(e)}{de} y_j, j = \overline{4,5} \tag{19}$$

The coefficient μ affects the learning rate of the network. There are several methods for selecting this parameter. The first way is to start the learning process with a large value of the parameter μ. During correction of weight coefficients, the parameter is gradually reduced.

The second is a more complex method of training begins with a small value of the parameter μ. In the learning process, the parameter increases, and then decreases again at the final stage of training. Beginning of the educational process with a low value of the parameter μ makes it possible to determine the sign of the weighting coefficients.

Forecasting the NASDAQ-100 Index Through a Neural Network

In the framework of this study the system for forecasting the rates of financial assets was implemented (based on the NASDAQ-100 index). It is based on four recurrent neural networks of Elman (1990). For calculation, the interval was taken from April 24, 2013 to March 21, 2017. The model was trained on this interval. The 4-hour and daily timeframes were used as a time period. Recurrent neural networks are one of the most complex. In them, in contrast to direct distribution networks, there are feedbacks. Feedbacks allow to provide adaptive memorization of past time events. Recurrent networks are a flexible tool for constructing nonlinear models (Bugorskiy, 2008).

At the heart of the Elman artificial neural network is a multilayer perceptron. The feedback is realized in the Elman network via the transmission on the input layer of baseline data and outputs neurons of the hidden layer. To the original data in this model, the authors use the next set of indicators submitted by the terminal MetaTrader 4, broker Alpari:

Moving Average the simplest and most common indicator of the technical analysis based on which most of the tools for algorithmic trading are built. This indicator allows researchers to determine the average price value of the instrument for the specified time interval. There are several options for calculating a moving average, such as Simple Moving Average (SMA), Exponential Moving Average (EMA), Smoothed Moving Average (SMMA), and Linear Weighted Moving Average (LWMA). In this case, the following period values were used to calculate the EMA:

N= 12, 24, 48, 120;

Ichimoku Kinko Hyo, which can also call an independent trading system, including several different indicators with their time intervals and length.

Tenkan-sen shows the average value of the price for the first period of time, defined as the sum of the maximum and minimum for this time and divided by two. This method allows one to determine the strength of the trend, support and resistance levels. As values of the parameters was used an author's values of constants:

ShPer=9, MidPer=26, LonPer=52;

Average Directional Movement Index allows identifying the presence or absence of a price trend in the market, these indicators were first presented by Wells Wilder. For ADX, the standard period N=14 was used.

Momentum can be used as the leading indicator for forecasting the turn of the market movement, by assumption, that most of the tendencies end with a co-directional sharp price impulse, when most of the participants hastily leave the market (N=14).

Parabolic SAR is like a moving average, but has greater acceleration mainly used to manage the position; namely, its fixation. Where is an index of acceleration, step of price change when closing a position, in our case, has a value of 0.02.

HeikenAshi - is a special type candle, which are somewhat different from Japanese candles. The opening price of such candles is a smoothened quotation period in the range between the opening and the closing of previous HA candle. In other words, the opening and the closing prices are summed up and divided by two. It is important to highlight that in order to calculate the current candles, the values of the previous HA candle are taken. The closing price of the HA – is the average price of the opening, closing, maximum and minimum values of the previous period. Maximum HA candles are defined, as comparison of maximum parameters of ordinary Japanese candle with the price of opening and closing candles HA. Minimum HA are selected by comparing the minimum of an ordinary Japanese candle with the opening and closing of HA candles.

Bollinger Bands are two moving averages, equidistant lines from the price in the distance of some standard inclinations. Indicator lines react to the changes of volatility on the market, thus helping to identify the period of rapid upswing or flat. In the neural network, the following parameters were used: $m = 1, N = 20$.

Commodity Channel Index provides a numerical characteristic of the deviation of the instrument's price from its average value, thus introducing the levels of extreme values. It is possible to identify over-bought or oversold instruments. To calculate the given index classical value of quantity of considered periods $N = 14$ were used.

Relative Strength Index, by the design of the founder, is capable of identifying price peaks and base while the indicator is entering the zones of overbuying and overselling. For the parameter of considered periods value = 9 was taken.

Stochastic Oscillator compares the current price with some price range. The given indicator can be related to the main oscillators which are used in technical analysis, in the base of which underlies the principle of overbuying and overselling of price value of the tool.

The system is presented as a neural network cluster and has the following structure:

Input: Input parameters;

Input for Artificial Neural Network 1: Input parameters, which enter the first neural network (indicators: EMA12, EMA24, EMA48, EMA120, Ichimoku_Span, ADX14_Main);

Input for Artificial Neural Network 2: Input parameters, which enter the second neural network (indicators: ADX14_Di, Momentum14, Ichimoku_tk, EMA12_cl, SAR_0.02_0.2, Ichimoku_Span2);

Input for Artificial Neural Network 3: Input parameters, which enter the third neural network (indicators: Heiken_Ashi, Bollinger_20_1, 38parots, CCI14, RSI9, Stochastic);

Artificial Neural Network 1: Neural network adviser specialized on the forecast of the trend and flat;

Artificial Neural Network 2: Neural network adviser specialized on the forecast of growth and fall of currency, within the conditions of flat;

Artificial Neural Network 3: Neural network adviser specialized on the forecast of growth and fall of currency, within the conditions of the trend;

Artificial Neural Network 3: Neural network, which generalizes the results of previous networks (Artificialneuralnetwork1, Artificialneuralnetwork 2, and Artificialneuralnetwork 3) and general input parameters (Figure 10).

Output: Results of the forecast, expressed in growth and fall of security (Giles & Lawrence, 2006).

Figure 10. Scheme of the neural system

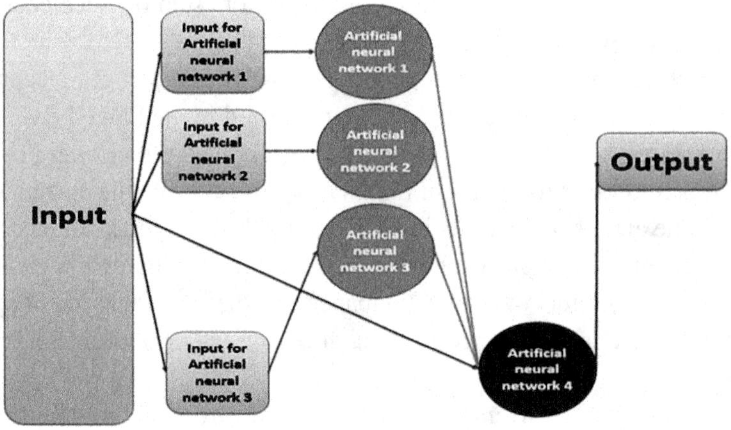

Building a neural network system in a production environment of Matlab:

1. Upload the data from Excel with the name of "Data", from the lists TrainData and TestData (Code block number 1)
2. Creating arrays of training samples for the first three networks (Artificial neural network 1 - neural network adviser specializing in the forecast of a trend or flat. Artificial neural network 2 - a neural network adviser specializing in forecasting the growth or fall of a course in a flat environment. Artificial neural network 3 - a neural network adviser specializing in forecasting the growth or fall course in a trend) (Code block number 2)
3. Creating arrays of testing samples for the first three networks (Artificial neural network 1 - neural network adviser specializing in the forecast of a trend or flat. Artificial neural network 2 - a neural network adviser specializing in forecasting the growth or fall of a course in a flat environment. Artificial neural network 3 - a neural network adviser specializing in forecasting the growth or fall course in a trend.) (Code block number 3)
4. Transpose the arrays for filing into the neural network (Code block number 4)
5. Creating the arrays of outputs for all networks: Artificialneuralnetwork 1, Artificialneuralnetwork 2, Artificialneuralnetwork 3. Output of the fourth network is the output of all the system (Code block number 5)
6. Form an artificial neural network N° 1. (Artificial neural network 1 - a neural network adviser specializing in the forecast of a trend or a flat). (Code block number 6). Elman's neural network has 42 inputs, because transmitted on 6 converted indicators to the input for the last seven days. Output 1. The network has 3 hidden layers, each of which uses a sigmoid activation function; the method of learning is the method of backpropagation of the error. The network stops training either after 10,000 learning epochs (cycles), or on condition that the size of the error is zero. The execution function is the mean absolute error.
7. Teaching the artificial neural network N° 1 and carry out a test on the teaching sampling of data and on the testing sampling of data. (Figure 11, Figure 12) (Code block number 7)Best training performance is 0.37486 at epoch 9996.

8.   Creating the artificial neural network No. 2 (Artificial neural network 2 - a neural network adviser specializing in forecasting the growth or fall of the course in a flat environment) (Code block number 8). Elman's neural network has 42 inputs, because transmitted on 6 converted indicators to the input for the last seven days. Output 1. The network has three hidden layers, each of which uses a sigmoid activation function; the method of learning is the method of backpropagation of the error. The network stops training either after 10,000 learning epochs (cycles), or on condition that the size of the error is zero. The execution function is the mean absolute error.

9.   Training of artificial neural network N° 2 and testing on the learning sample of data and on the testing sample of data(Figure 13, Figure 14) (Code block number 9)Best training performance is 0.40839 at epoch 9996.

10.   Forming an artificial neural network No. 3 (Artificial neural network 3 - a neural network adviser specializing in forecasting the growth or fall of the course in a trend). Elman's neural network has 42 inputs, because transmitted on 6 converted indicators to the input for the last seven days. Output 1. The network has 3 hidden layers, each of which uses a sigmoid activation function; the method of learning is the method of backpropagation of the error. The network stops training either after 10,000 learning epochs (cycles), or on condition that the size of the error is zero. The execution function is the mean absolute error. (Code block number 10).

11.   Training of artificial neural network N° 3 testing on the learning sample of data and on the testing data sample (Figure 15, Figure 16) (Code block number 11).Best training performance is 0.38879 at epoch 9976.

12.   Forming an array of training samples for the 4th network (Artificial neural network 4 - a neural network that summarizes the results of previous networks: Artificial neural network 1, Artificial neural network 2 and Artificial neural network 3 and common input parameters) (Code block number 12)

13.   Transpose the massifs for the feed into the neural network (Artificial neural network 1, Artificial neural network 2 and Artificial neural network 3) (Code block number 13)

14.   Combine the original input parameters and the results of the first 3 networks (Code block number 14)

15.   Forming an array of test samples for 4th network (Artificial neural network 4 - a neural network that summarizes the results of previous networks: Artificial neural network 1, Artificial neural network 2 and Artificial neural network 3 and common input parameters) (Code block number 15)

16.   Integration the original input parameters and the results of the first 3 networks (Code block number 16)

17.   Formation of an artificial neural network No. 4 (Artificial neural network 4 - a neural network that summarizes the results of previous networks: Artificial neural network 1, Artificial neural network 2 and Artificial neural network 3 and common input parameters). (Code block number 17). Elman's neural network has 45 inputs, because transmitted on 6 converted indicators to the input for last 7 days and also the outputs of previous networks (Artificial Neural Network 1, Artificial neural network 2 and Artificial neural network 3).. Output 1. The network has three hidden layers, each of which uses a sigmoid activation function; the method of learning is the method of backpropagation of the error. The network stops training either after 10,000 learning epochs (cycles), or on condition that the size of the error is zero. The execution function is the mean absolute error.

18. Training of artificial neural network N° 4. Artificial neural network 4 - a neural network which summarizes results of previous networks: Artificial neural network1, Artificial neural network 2, Artificial neural network 3 and common input parameters.Then testing artificial neural network 4on the learning data sample and on the testing data sample (Figure 17, Figure 18) (Code block number 18). Best training performance is 0.2284 at epoch 9941.
19. Transpose the output of the network (Code block number 19)
20. Forming a massif for evaluating the results (Code block number 20)
21. Convert an answer of the system response as follows: If on the output the result will be less than 0.5, then 0, if more, then 1 (Code block number 21)
22. If the answers of the system are equal to the correct values, then a unit is placed (Code block number 22)
23. Summation of all correct answers (Code block number 23)
24. The proportion of correct answers in the testing sample of data (Table 1) (Code block number 24)

Figure 11. Window of the process of learning the artificial neural network No. 1

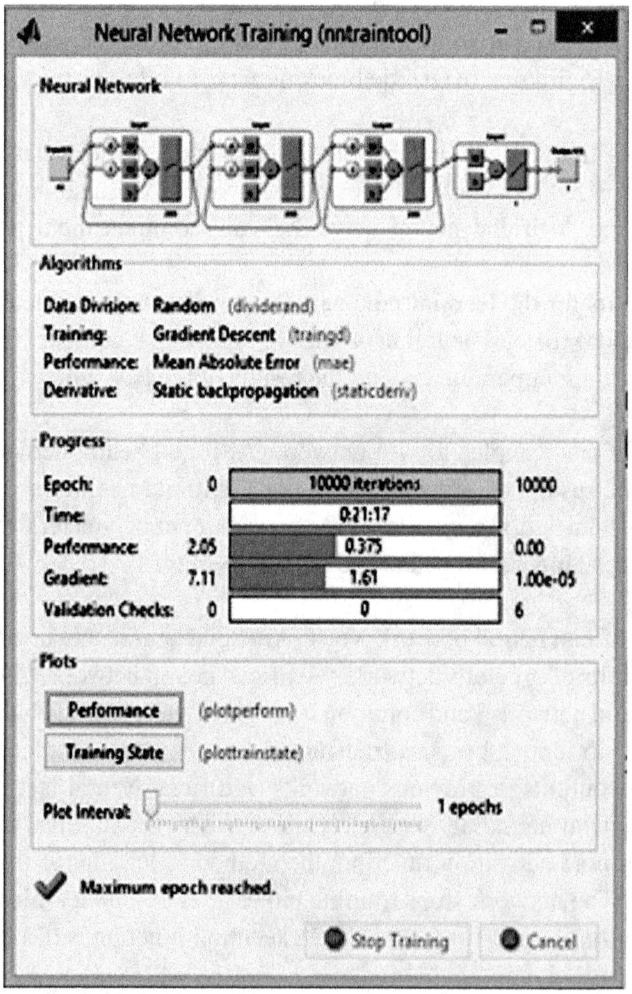

Figure 12. The graph of the learning error of artificial neural network No. 1

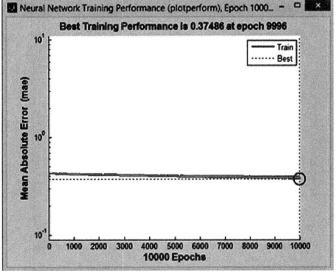

Figure 13. Window of the learning process of artificial neural network No. 2

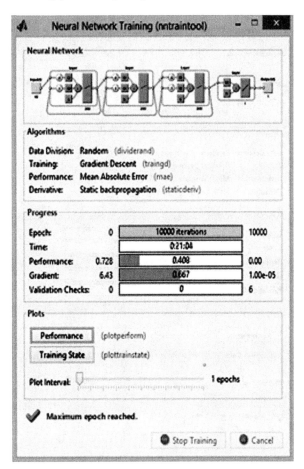

Figure 14. The graph of the learning error of the artificial neural network No. 2

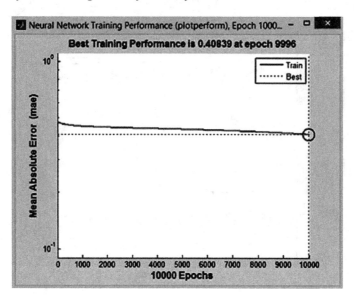

Figure 15. The window of the process of learning the artificial neural network N° 3

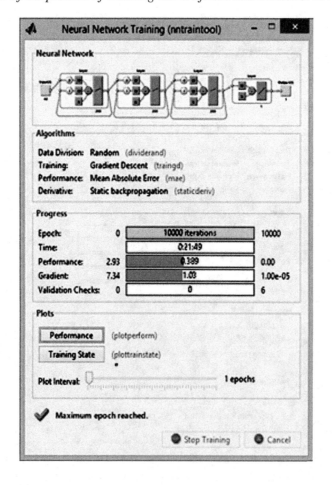

Figure 16. Chart of learning error of artificial neural network No. 3

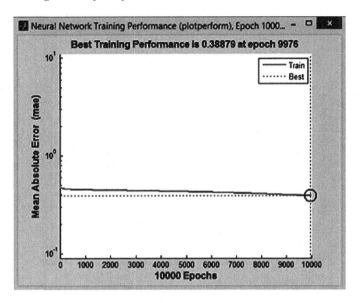

Figure 17. The window of the learning process of an artificial neural network N⁰ 4

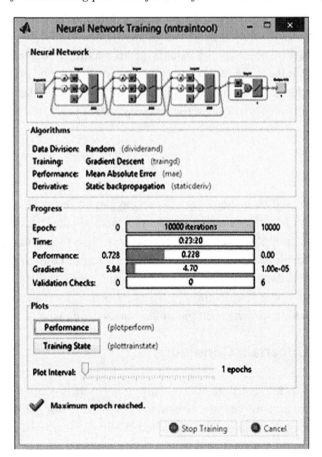

Figure 18. Graph of learning error of artificial neural network No. 4

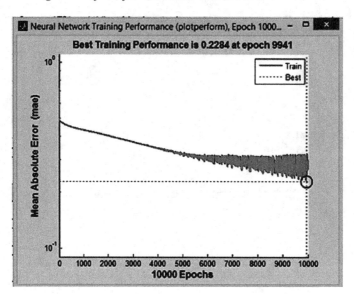

Table 1 presents the results of testing the model for the period March 3, 2017 to May 3, 2017. For convenience, the column names correspond to the names of the variables that were used in the code. The first column characterizes the output values of the model; the third column characterizes the result obtained. In the second and third columns, the value 0 means opening a short sale, and the value 1 means opening the purchase, within the same bar. When the values of the second and third columns coincide, in the fourth column recorded 1 - true, under mismatch of 0 - false. Thus, the constructed model allows to predict the direction of price movement for the next day with a probability of more than 86%.

CONCLUSION

Based on the results of the study the following conclusion can be drawn. Neural networks, unlike the other statistical methods of multidimensional classification analysis, are based on the parallel processing of information and possess the ability to conduct self-learning. This means that neural networks make it possible to obtain a valid result based on data that was not encountered in the learning process.

The ability to model nonlinear processes, adaptability and work with noisy data make it possible to apply neural networks to solve a wide class of financial problems. The main advantages of neural networks, in comparison with traditional computational methods, consist of the following advantages.

Problem Solving in Uncertain Conditions

The ability of a neural network to learning allows them to solve the tasks with unknown variables and dependencies between input and output data. Neural networks can work with incomplete data. In addition, the relationship between the data is not established in advance since the method involves studying the existing relationships on the finished models.

Table 1. Performance indicators of the trained neural network (learning on the interval 24.04.13 - 21.03.17) for the period 22.03.17 - 03.05.17

OutputTestNet4	TestDataTargetForNet4	OutputTestNet4v2	True / False
0.768384871	0	1	0
0.919348023	1	1	1
0.965955128	1	1	1
0.956145818	1	1	1
0.786567834	1	1	1
1.024603642	1	1	1
-0.06389309	0	0	1
1.138041594	1	1	1
0.945113273	1	1	1
0.09343831	0	0	1
0.8953719	1	1	1
0.187533021	0	0	1
0.910185852	1	1	1
-0.015994155	0	0	1
0.760703532	0	1	0
0.22351667	0	0	1
0.99790483	1	1	1
0.323678698	0	0	1
0.959294256	1	1	1
0.989780381	1	1	1
0.052524776	0	0	1
1.030220979	1	1	1
1.005773521	1	1	1
0.900863843	0	1	0
0.902306425	1	1	1
9.73E-05	0	0	1
1.025063458	1	1	1
0.704575764	1	1	1
0.451072272	1	0	0
0.726591368	1	1	1
Number of correct answers			26
Share of correct answers			0.8667

Resistance to Noises in the Input Parameters

The neural network can independently determine non-informative parameters for their analysis and screening.

Adaptation to the Environmental Changes

Neural networks can be retrained in new environmental conditions, described by slight fluctuations of the environment parameters. That is to state it is possible to retrain the neural networks on the basis of minor fluctuations of environment parameters. The possibility of neural network methods for modeling the behavior of prices of the American index NASDAQ-100 is substantiated. It is demonstrated that the model based on four recurrent neural networks of Elman allows predicting the future behavior of prices quite accurately.

As trading signals, the model generated a fractional numerical value. Furthermore, the obtained data were considered already in a discrete representation, where 0 was considered as a sell signal, and 1 - signal for a purchase. A trading solution was generated at the time of the opening of the day bar. Upon its closure, it was possible to compare the predicted results of the model and the actual market data. After training between April 24, 2013 to March 21, 2017, the model showed excellent results during the period from March 22 to May 3, 2017, with a forecast accuracy of 86.7%.

To test this model on other financial instruments, the authors prepared in the application the source code in the MQL4 (Appendix 1) language and applied package MatLab (Appendix 2), through which it is possible to obtain similar trading signals and conduct more detailed studies. It can be concluded that neural networks are a tool that allows solving problems with an unknown beforehand algorithm in advance, initially possessing a strong degree of oscillation and therefore it is difficult to formalize. However, the use of this tool requires a sensible selection of explanatory factors, effective work with data preprocessing. In general, the construction of such models can be used to conduct algorithmic trading (Vladimirova & Koksharova, 2014).

REFERENCES

Baestaens, D.E., Van Den Berg, W.M., & Wood, D. (1997). Neural Network solutions for trading in financial markets. *Pitman Bublished*, 56-77.

Bugorskiy, V.N., & Sergienko, A.G. (2008). Ispolzovanie neyronnyh setey dlya modelirovaniya prognoza kotirovok tsennyh bumag. *Prikladnaya Informatika, 3*.

Bushuev, K. (2000). Primeneniene yrosetevyh metodov pri prognozirovanii dinamiki rynka aktsiy. Modeli ekonomicheskih system I informatsionnye tehnologii. *Finansovay aakademiya pri Pravitelstve RF*, 30-35.

Chirkova, E. (2014). *How to evaluate business by analogy*. Alpina Pablisher.

Elder, A. (2007). *How to play and win on the stock exchange*. Alpina Pablisher.

Elman, J. L. (1990). Finding structure in time. *Cognitive Science, 14*(2), 179–211. doi:10.120715516709cog1402_1

Giles, C.L., Lawrence, S., & Tsoi, A.C. (2006). *Rule inference for financial prediction using recurrent neural networks*. Academic Press.

Haykin, S. (2006). *Neural networks a comprehensive foundations*. Hamilton, Canada: McMaser University.

Kalmykova, L. (2007). *Fundamental analysis of financial markets*. Peter.

Kovel, M. (2007). *Trend Following: How Great Traders Make Millions in Up or Down Markets.* FT Press.

Laletina, A. (2015). Prognozirovanie finansovyh ryncov s ispol'zovaniem iskusstvennyh neyronnyh setey. Elektronnye sredstva I sistemy upravleniya. *Tomskiy gosudarstvennyj universitet system upravleniyai radioelektroniki,* 214-217.

MATLAB. (n.d.). Retrieved from http://www.mathworks.com/products/matlab/

Melihova, O. A., Veprintseva, O. V., & Chumichev, V. S. (2015). *Rezhimyobucheniya v iskusstvennyh neyronnyh setyah.* YUFU.

Murphy, J. (1999). *Technical Analysis of the Financial Markets: A Comprehensive Guide to Trading Methods and Applications.* New York Institute of Finance.

Nison, S. (2003). *The Candlestick Course.* Wiley.

Peters, E. E. (1994). *Fractal Market Analysis.* Wiley.

Schwager, J. (1997). *Technical Analysis.* Wiley.

Schwager, J., & Turner, S. (1995). Futures: Fundamental Analysis. Wiley.

StatSoft. (n.d.). Retrieved from http://www.statsoft.ru/products/STATISTICA_Base/

Turovskiy, Y. A. (2014). O pytmodelirovaniya alternativnyh cheloveko-mashinnyh interfeysov. *Aktualnye napravleniya nauchnyh issledovaniy XXI veka: teoriya I praktika, 5,* 249–252.

Turovskiy, Y. A. (2015). Otsenka skorosti raboty neyrokompyuternogo interfeysa, realizovannogo s ispolzovaniem gibridnogo intellekta. *Biomeditsinskaya radioelektronika, 3,* 61–70.

Vladimirova, D. (2014). Prognozirovanie finansovyh ryncov iskusstvennymi neiyronnymi setyami. Naukaibiznes: Putirazvitiya. *Fond razvitiya nauki I kultury,* 26-42.

Vladimirova, D. B., & Koksharova, A. A. (2014). Prognozirovanie finansovyh rynkov iskusstvennymi neyronnymi setyami. *FGBUVPO Permskiy natsionalnyy issledovatelskiy politehnicheskiy universitet, 3,* 45.

Wasserman, F. (1992). *Neurocomputer Techniques: Theory and Practice.* Moscow: Mir Publ.

Yahyaeva, G. E. (2016). *Osnovy teorii neyronnyh setey.* Natsionalnyy Otkrytyy Universitet.

This research was previously published in Fractal Approaches for Modeling Financial Assets and Predicting Crises; pages 172-204, copyright year 2018 by Business Science Reference (an imprint of IGI Global).

APPENDIX 1

Preliminary Data in MQL4

```
#propertystrict    #propertyshow_inputs
externintN = 1000; // Numberofbars
voidOnStart()
{ int Handle; string   File_Name="Данные-"+Symbol()+".csv"; datetime Data; int
trend, H, result; double Sup, Inf;
Handle=FileOpen(File_Name,FILE_CSV|FILE_WRITE,";");// Open file
 if(Handle<0) { if(GetLastError()==4103) Alert("file not existence ",File_
Name); else Alert("Error open file ",File_Name); return; }
FileWrite(Handle, "Data", "EMA12", "P", "EMA24", "P", "EMA48", "P", "EMA120",
"P", "Ichimoku_Span", "P1", "P2", "ADX14_Main", "P", "TREND", "", "ADX14_Di",
"P1", "P2", "Momentum14", "P", "Ichimoku_tk", "P1", "P2", "EMA12_cl", "P",
"SAR_0.02_0.2", "P", "Ichimoku_Span2", "Result", "", "Heiken_Ashi", "P1",
"P2", "Bollinger_20_1", "P1", "P2", "38parots", "CCI14", "P", "RSI9", "P",
"Stochastic", "P", "Result", "", "Volume", "High", "Low", "Close", "Open");
FileWrite(Handle, "", "X_11", "Pr","X_12", "Pr", "X_13", "Pr", "X_14", "Pr",
"X_15", "Pr1", "Pr2", "X_16", "Pr", "Y_1", "", "X_21", "Pr1", "Pr2", "X_22",
"Pr", "X_23", "Pr1", "Pr2", "X_24", "Pr", "X_25", "Pr", "X_26", "Y_21", "",
"X_27", "Pr1", "Pr2", "X_28", "Pr1", "Pr2", "X_29", "X_210", "Pr", "X_211",
"Pr", "X_212", "Pr", "Y_22", "", "Volume", "High", "Low", "Close", "Open");
for (inti=2; i<=N; i++)
{ Data = iTime(Symbol(), 0, i);  // DateTime
   // find the bar number on H1 for the opening time of the current bar on D1
   H = iBarShift(Symbol(), PERIOD_H4, Data);  // search bar on H1 by time
   Sup = High[iHighest(Symbol(), 0, MODE_HIGH, 3, i)]; Inf =
Low[iLowest(Symbol(), 0, MODE_LOW, 3, i)];  // go beyond the range of 3 can-
dles before
if (Close[i-1] > Sup || Close[i-1] <Inf) trend = 1; else trend = -1;
if (Close[i-1] > Open[i-1]) result = 1; else if (Close[i-1] < Open[i-1]) re-
sult = -1; else result = 0; // the result of closing the candle
FileWrite(Handle, Data, Neiron_1_1MA(H), pNeiron_1_1MA(H), Neiron_1_2MA(H),
pNeiron_1_2MA(H), Neiron_1_3MA(H), pNeiron_1_3MA(H), Neiron_1_4MA(H),
pNeiron_1_4MA(H), Neiron_1_5Ishim(H), pNeiron_1_5Ishim(H),
p2Neiron_1_5Ishim(H), Neiron_1_6ADX(H), pNeiron_1_6ADX(H),trend, " ",
Neiron_2_1ADX(H), pNeiron_2_1ADX(H), p2Neiron_2_1ADX(H), Neiron_2_2Momentum(H),
pNeiron_2_2Momentum(H), Neiron_2_3IshimT(H), pNeiron_2_3IshimT(H),
p2Neiron_2_3IshimT(H), Neiron_2_4MA(H), pNeiron_2_4MA(H), Neiron_2_5SAR(H),
pNeiron_2_5SAR(H), Neiron_2_6Ishim(H), result, " ", Neiron_2_7Heiken_Ashi(H),
pNeiron_2_7Heiken_Ashi(H), p2Neiron_2_7Heiken_Ashi(H), Neiron_2_8Bollinger(H),
pNeiron_2_8Bollinger(H),  p2Neiron_2_8Bollinger(H), Neiron_2_9_38parrots(H),
```

```
Neiron_2_10CCI(H), pNeiron_2_10CCI(H), Neiron_2_11RSI(H), pNeiron_2_11RSI(H),
Neiron_2_12Stoch(H), pNeiron_2_12Stoch(H), result, "", Volume[H], High[H],
Low[H], Close[H], Open[H]); }  FileClose(Handle); // Close and save the re-
cord file return; }
//The first neuron of the first network
int Neiron_1_1MA(inti){intNeir; double MA1=iMA(NULL,PERIOD_H4,12,0,MODE_
EMA,PRICE_CLOSE,i); if(MA1<iHigh(Symbol(), PERIOD_H4, i) && MA1>iLow(Symbol(),
PERIOD_H4, i)) Neir=-1; else Neir=1; return(Neir);}
double pNeiron_1_1MA(inti){  double MA1=iMA(NULL,PERIOD_H4,12,0,MODE_EMA,PRICE_
CLOSE,i);  return(MA1); }
//The second neuron of the first network
int Neiron_1_2MA(inti){intNeir; double MA1=iMA(NULL,PERIOD_H4,24,0,MODE_
EMA,PRICE_CLOSE,i); if(MA1<iHigh(Symbol(), PERIOD_H4, i) && MA1>iLow(Symbol(),
PERIOD_H4, i)) Neir=-1; else Neir=1; return(Neir);}
double pNeiron_1_2MA(inti){double MA1=iMA(NULL,PERIOD_H4,24,0,MODE_EMA,PRICE_
CLOSE,i); return(MA1);}
//The third neuron of the first network
int Neiron_1_3MA(inti){intNeir; double MA1=iMA(NULL,PERIOD_H4,48,0,MODE_
EMA,PRICE_CLOSE,i); if(MA1<iHigh(Symbol(), PERIOD_H4, i) && MA1>iLow(Symbol(),
PERIOD_H4, i)) Neir=-1; else Neir=1; return(Neir);}
double pNeiron_1_3MA(inti){double MA1=iMA(NULL,PERIOD_H4,48,0,MODE_EMA,PRICE_
CLOSE,i); return(MA1);}
//The fourth neuron of the first network
int Neiron_1_4MA(inti){intNeir; double MA1=iMA(NULL,PERIOD_H4,120,0,MODE_
EMA,PRICE_CLOSE,i); if(MA1<iHigh(Symbol(), PERIOD_H4, i) && MA1>iLow(Symbol(),
PERIOD_H4, i)) Neir=-1; else Neir=1; return(Neir);}
double pNeiron_1_4MA(inti){double MA1=iMA(NULL,PERIOD_H4,120,0,MODE_EMA,PRICE_
CLOSE,i); return(MA1);}
//The fifth neuron of the first network
int Neiron_1_5Ishim(inti){ intNeir; double SpanA=iIchimoku(NULL,PERIOD_
H4,9,26,52,MODE_SENKOUSPANA,i); double SpanB=iIchimoku(NULL,PERIOD_
H4,9,26,52,MODE_SENKOUSPANB,i); double Supremum=MathMax(SpanA,SpanB); double
Infinum =MathMin(SpanA,SpanB); if(iClose(Symbol(), PERIOD_H4, i)<Supremum
&&iClose(Symbol(), PERIOD_H4, i)>Infinum) Neir=-1; else Neir=1; return(Neir);}
double pNeiron_1_5Ishim(inti){ double SpanA=iIchimoku(NULL,PERIOD_
H4,9,26,52,MODE_SENKOUSPANA,i); return(SpanA);}
double p2Neiron_1_5Ishim(inti){ double SpanB=iIchimoku(NULL,PERIOD_
H4,9,26,52,MODE_SENKOUSPANB,i); return(SpanB);}
//The sixth neuron of the first network
int Neiron_1_6ADX(inti){ intNeir; double ADX=iADX(NULL,PERIOD_H4,14,PRICE_
CLOSE,MODE_MAIN,i); if(ADX<25) Neir=-1; else Neir=1; return(Neir);}
double pNeiron_1_6ADX(inti){ double ADX=iADX(NULL,PERIOD_H4,14,PRICE_
CLOSE,MODE_MAIN,i); return(ADX);}
```

```
//The first neuron of the second network
int Neiron_2_1ADX(inti){intNeir=0; double DI_Plus =iADX(NULL,PERIOD_
H4,14,PRICE_CLOSE,MODE_PLUSDI,i); double DI_Minus=iADX(NULL,PERIOD_H4,14,PRICE_
CLOSE,MODE_MINUSDI,i); if(DI_Plus>DI_Minus) Neir= 1; if(DI_Plus<DI_Minus)
Neir=-1; return(Neir);}
double pNeiron_2_1ADX(inti){ double DI_Plus =iADX(NULL,PERIOD_H4,14,PRICE_
CLOSE,MODE_PLUSDI,i); return(DI_Plus);}
double p2Neiron_2_1ADX(inti){ double DI_Minus=iADX(NULL,PERIOD_H4,14,PRICE_
CLOSE,MODE_MINUSDI,i); return(DI_Minus);}
//The second neuron of the second network
int Neiron_2_2Momentum(inti){ intNeir=0; double Momentum=iMomentum(NULL,PERIOD_
H4,14,PRICE_CLOSE,i); if(Momentum>100) Neir= 1; if(Momentum<100) Neir=-1;
return(Neir);}
double pNeiron_2_2Momentum(inti){ double Momentum=iMomentum(NULL,PERIOD_
H4,14,PRICE_CLOSE,i); return(Momentum);}
//The third neuron of the second network
int Neiron_2_3IshimT(inti){ intNeir=0; double Fast=iIchimoku(NULL,PERIOD_
H4,9,26,52,MODE_TENKANSEN,i); double Slow=iIchimoku(NULL,PERIOD_
H4,9,26,52,MODE_KIJUNSEN,i); if(Fast>Slow) Neir= 1; if(Fast<Slow) Neir=-1;
return(Neir);}
double pNeiron_2_3IshimT(inti){double Fast=iIchimoku(NULL,PERIOD_
H4,9,26,52,MODE_TENKANSEN,i); return(Fast);}
double p2Neiron_2_3IshimT(inti){ double Slow=iIchimoku(NULL,PERIOD_
H4,9,26,52,MODE_KIJUNSEN,i); return(Slow);}
//The fourth neuron of the second network
int Neiron_2_4MA(inti){ intNeir=0; double MA1=iMA(NULL,PERIOD_H4,12,0,MODE_
EMA,PRICE_CLOSE,i); if(iClose(Symbol(), PERIOD_H4, i)>MA1) Neir= 1;
if(iClose(Symbol(), PERIOD_H4, i)<MA1) Neir=-1; return(Neir);}
double pNeiron_2_4MA(inti){double MA1=iMA(NULL,PERIOD_H4,12,0,MODE_EMA,PRICE_
CLOSE,i); return(MA1);}
//Fifth neuron of the second network
int Neiron_2_5SAR(inti){intNeir=0; double SAR=iSAR(NULL,PERIOD_H4,0.02,0.2,i);
if(iClose(Symbol(), PERIOD_H4, i)> SAR) Neir= 1; if(iClose(Symbol(), PERIOD_
H4, i)< SAR) Neir=-1; return(Neir);}
double pNeiron_2_5SAR(inti){ double SAR=iSAR(NULL,PERIOD_H4,0.02,0.2,i);
return(SAR);}
//The sixth neuron of the second network
int Neiron_2_6Ishim(inti){intNeir=0; double SpanA=iIchimoku(NULL,PERIOD_
H4,9,26,52,MODE_SENKOUSPANA,i); double SpanB=iIchimoku(NULL,PERIOD_
H4,9,26,52,MODE_SENKOUSPANB,i); double Supremum=MathMax(SpanA,SpanB); double
Infinum =MathMin(SpanA,SpanB); if(iClose(Symbol(), PERIOD_H4, i)>Supremum)
Neir= 1; if(iClose(Symbol(), PERIOD_H4, i)<Infinum)  Neir=-1; return(Neir);}
//The first neuron of the third network
```

```
int Neiron_2_7Heiken_Ashi(inti){intNeir=0; double OpenHA=iCustom(NULL,PERIOD_
H4,"Heiken Ashi",2,i); double CloseHA=iCustom(NULL,PERIOD_H4,"Heiken
Ashi",3,i); if(OpenHA<CloseHA)  Neir= 1; if(OpenHA>CloseHA)  Neir=-1;
return(Neir);}
double pNeiron_2_7Heiken_Ashi(inti){ double OpenHA=iCustom(NULL,PERIOD_
H4,"Heiken Ashi",2,i); return(OpenHA);}
double p2Neiron_2_7Heiken_Ashi(inti){ double CloseHA=iCustom(NULL,PERIOD_
H4,"Heiken Ashi",3,i); return(CloseHA);}
//The second neuron of the third network
int Neiron_2_8Bollinger(inti){intNeir=0; double H=iBands(NULL,PERIOD_
H4,20,1,0,PRICE_CLOSE,MODE_UPPER,i); double L=iBands(NULL,PERIOD_
H4,20,1,0,PRICE_CLOSE,MODE_LOWER,i); if(iHigh(Symbol(), PERIOD_H4, i)>H)  Neir=
1; if(iLow(Symbol(), PERIOD_H4, i) <L)  Neir= -1; return(Neir);}
double pNeiron_2_8Bollinger(inti){ double H=iBands(NULL,PERIOD_H4,20,1,0,PRICE_
CLOSE,MODE_UPPER,i); return(H);}
double p2Neiron_2_8Bollinger(inti){ double L=iBands(NULL,PERIOD_
H4,20,1,0,PRICE_CLOSE,MODE_LOWER,i); return(L);}
//The third neuron of the third network
int Neiron_2_9_38parrots(inti){ intNeir=0; double P38=iCustom(NULL, PERIOD_H4,
"38 parrots",7,100,70,0,i); double H  =iCustom(NULL, PERIOD_H4, "38
parrots",7,100,70,1,i); double L  =iCustom(NULL, PERIOD_H4, "38
parrots",7,100,70,2,i);  if(P38>H)  Neir= -1; if(P38<L)  Neir= 1;
return(Neir);}
//The fourth neuron of the third network
int Neiron_2_10CCI(inti){ intNeir=0; double CCI=iCCI(Symbol(),PERIOD_
H4,14,PRICE_CLOSE,i); if(CCI>100)  Neir=  1; if(CCI<-100)  Neir=  -1;
return(Neir);}
double pNeiron_2_10CCI(inti){ double CCI=iCCI(Symbol(),PERIOD_H4,14,PRICE_
CLOSE,i); return(CCI);}
//The fifth neuron of the third network
int Neiron_2_11RSI(inti){intNeir=0; double RSI=iRSI(NULL,PERIOD_H4,9,PRICE_
CLOSE,i); if(RSI>50)  Neir=  1; if(RSI<50)    Neir=  -1; return(Neir);}
double pNeiron_2_11RSI(inti){double RSI=iRSI(NULL,PERIOD_H4,9,PRICE_CLOSE,i);
return(RSI);}
//The sixth neuron of the third network
int Neiron_2_12Stoch(inti){intNeir=0; double Stoch1=iStochastic(NULL,PERIOD_
H4,5,3,3,MODE_SMA,0,MODE_MAIN,i); double Stoch2=iStochastic(NULL,PERIOD_
H4,5,3,3,MODE_SMA,0,MODE_SIGNAL,i); if(Stoch1>Stoch2)    Neir=  1;
if(Stoch1<Stoch2)    Neir=  -1; return(Neir);}
double pNeiron_2_12Stoch(inti){double Stoch1=iStochastic(NULL,PERIOD_
H4,5,3,3,MODE_SMA,0,MODE_MAIN,i); return(Stoch1);}
double p2Neiron_2_12Stoch(inti){double Stoch2=iStochastic(NULL,PERIOD_
H4,5,3,3,MODE_SMA,0,MODE_SIGNAL,i); return(Stoch2);}
```

APPENDIX 2

Creation and Testing of a Neural Network in the MatLab Package

Code Block Number 1

```
TrainDataInput = xlsread('D:\Data\Data.xlsx','TrainData','B4:DW786'); Train-
DataTarget = xlsread('D:\Data\Data.xlsx','TrainData','DX4:DY786'); TestDataIn-
put = xlsread('D:\Data\Data.xlsx','TestData','B4:DW33');
TestDataTarget = xlsread('D:\Data\Data.xlsx','TestData','DX4:DY33');
```

Code Block Number 2

```
TrainDataInputForNet1 = TrainDataInput(1:end,1:42); TrainDataIn-
putForNet2 = TrainDataInput(1:end,43:84); TrainDataInputFor-
Net3 = TrainDataInput(1:end,85:126); TrainDataTargetForNet1 =
TrainDataTarget(1:end,1);
TrainDataTargetForNet2 = TrainDataTarget(1:end,2); TrainDataTargetForNet3 =
TrainDataTarget(1:end,2);
```

Code Block Number 3

```
TestDataInputForNet1 = TestDataInput(1:end,1:42); TestDataInputForNet2 =
TestDataInput(1:end,43:84); TestDataInputForNet3 = TestDataInput(1:end,85:126);
```

Code Block Number 4

```
TrainDataInputForNet1 = TrainDataInputForNet1'; TrainDataInputForNet2 = Train-
DataInputForNet2'; TrainDataInputForNet3 = TrainDataInputForNet3'; Train-
DataTargetForNet1 = TrainDataTargetForNet1'; TrainDataTargetForNet2 = Train-
DataTargetForNet2'; TrainDataTargetForNet3 = TrainDataTargetForNet3';
TestDataInputForNet1 = TestDataInputForNet1'; TestDataInputForNet2 = TestDa-
taInputForNet2'; TestDataInputForNet3 = TestDataInputForNet3';
```

Code Block Number 5

```
OutputTrainNet1 = []; OutputTrainNet2 = []; OutputTrainNet3 = []; OutputTrain-
Net4 = []; OutputTestNet1 = []; OutputTestNet2 = []; OutputTestNet3 = []; Out-
putTestNet4 = [];
```

Code Block Number 6

```
Net1 = newelm(TrainDataInputForNet1,TrainDataTargetForNet1,[200,200,200],{'logs
ig','logsig','logsig'},'traingd'); Net1.trainParam.epochs = 10000; Net1.train-
Param.goal=0; Net1.performFcn='mae'; Net1.divideParam.trainRatio = 100/100;
Net1.divideParam.valRatio = 0/100; Net1.divideParam.testRatio = 0/100;
```

Code Block Number 7

```
Net1 = train(Net1,TrainDataInputForNet1,TrainDataTargetForNet1); Out-
putTrainNet1 = sim(Net1,TrainDataInputForNet1); OutputTestNet1 =
sim(Net1,TestDataInputForNet1);
```

Code Block Number 8

```
Net2 = newelm(TrainDataInputForNet2,TrainDataTargetForNet2,[200,200,200],{'logs
ig','logsig','logsig'},'traingd'); Net2.trainParam.epochs = 10000; Net2.train-
Param.goal=0; Net2.performFcn='mae'; Net2.divideParam.trainRatio = 100/100;
Net2.divideParam.valRatio = 0/100; Net2.divideParam.testRatio = 0/100;
```

Code Block Number 9

```
Net2 = train(Net2,TrainDataInputForNet2,TrainDataTargetForNet2); Out-
putTrainNet2 = sim(Net2,TrainDataInputForNet2); OutputTestNet2 =
sim(Net2,TestDataInputForNet2);
```

Code Block Number 10

```
Net3 = newelm(TrainDataInputForNet3,TrainDataTargetForNet3,[200,200,200],{'logs
ig','logsig','logsig'},'traingd'); Net3.trainParam.epochs = 10000; Net3.train-
Param.goal=0; Net3.performFcn='mae'; Net3.divideParam.trainRatio = 100/100;
Net3.divideParam.valRatio = 0/100; Net3.divideParam.testRatio = 0/100;
```

Code Block Number 11

```
Net3 = train(Net3,TrainDataInputForNet3,TrainDataTargetForNet3); Out-
putTrainNet3 = sim(Net3,TrainDataInputForNet3); OutputTestNet3 =
sim(Net3,TestDataInputForNet3);
```

Code Block Number 12

```
TrainDataInputForNet4 = TrainDataInput(1:end,1:126); TrainDataTargetForNet4 =
TrainDataTarget(1:end,2);
```

Code Block Number 13

```
TrainDataInputForNet4 = TrainDataInputForNet4'; TrainDataTargetForNet4 =
TrainDataTargetForNet4';
```

Code Block Number 14

```
TrainDataInputForNet4 = [TrainDataInputForNet4; OutputTrainNet1; OutputTrain-
Net2; OutputTrainNet3];
```

Code Block Number 15

```
TestDataInputForNet4 = TestDataInput(1:end,1:126); TestDataInputForNet4 = Tes-
tDataInputForNet4'; TestDataTargetForNet4 = TestDataTarget(1:end,2);
```

Code Block Number 16

```
TestDataInputForNet4 = [TestDataInputForNet4; OutputTestNet1; OutputTestNet2;
OutputTestNet3];
```

Code Block Number 17

```
Net4 = newelm(TrainDataInputForNet4,TrainDataTargetForNet4,[200,200,200],{'logs
ig','logsig','logsig'},'traingd'); Net4.trainParam.epochs = 10000; Net4.train-
Param.goal=0; Net4.performFcn='mae'; Net4.divideParam.trainRatio = 100/100;
Net4.divideParam.valRatio = 0/100; Net4.divideParam.testRatio = 0/100;
```

Code Block Number 18

```
Net4 = train(Net4,TrainDataInputForNet4,TrainDataTargetForNet4); Out-
putTrainNet4 = sim(Net4,TrainDataInputForNet4); OutputTestNet4 =
sim(Net4,TestDataInputForNet4);
```

Code Block Number 19

```
OutputTestNet4 = OutputTestNet4';
```

Code Block Number 20

```
Result = [OutputTestNet4 TestDataTargetForNet4];
```

Code Block Number 21

```
fori = 1:30 OutputTestNet4v2 = Result(i,1); if OutputTestNet4v2 > 0.5
Result(i,3) = 1; else Result(i,3) = 0; end cend
```

Code Block Number 22

```
fori = 1:30 OutputTestNet4Value2 = Result(i,3); TestDataTargetForNet4I =
Result(i,2); if TestDataTargetForNet4I == OutputTestNet4Value2 Result(i,4) =
1; else Result(i,4) = 0; end end
```

Code Block Number 23

```
NumberOfCorrectAnswers = sum(Result(1:end,4))
```

Code Block Number 24

```
ShareOfCorrectAnswers = NumberOfCorrectAnswers / 30
```

Chapter 68
Predicting Stock Market Price Using Neural Network Model

Naliniprava Tripathy

Indian Institute of Management Shillong, Shillong, India

ABSTRACT

The present article predicts the movement of daily Indian stock market (S&P CNX Nifty) price by using Feedforward Neural Network Model over a period of eight years from January 1st 2008 to April 8th 2016. The prediction accuracy of the model is accessed by normalized mean square error (NMSE) and sign correctness percentage (SCP) measure. The study indicates that the predicted output is very close to actual data since the normalized error of one-day lag is 0.02. The analysis further shows that 60 percent accuracy found in the prediction of the direction of daily movement of Indian stock market price after the financial crises period 2008. The study indicates that the predictive power of the feedforward neural network models reasonably influenced by one-day lag stock market price. Hence, the validity of an efficient market hypothesis does not hold in practice in the Indian stock market. This article is quite useful to the investors, professional traders and regulators for understanding the effectiveness of Indian stock market to take appropriate investment decision in the stock market.

1. INTRODUCTION

The prediction of stock market price is a significant issue in the economic literature today. The stock markets are affected by many market factors such as political events, institutional investor's choices, firms' policies, general economic conditions, foreign exchange risk, and psychology of investors. The stock markets are inherently noisy, non-stationary and deterministically chaotic nature. Stock market price behaves in highly non-linear and dynamic manner. Hence, forecasting stock market price is a challenging one. However, one can able to identify the non-linear pattern of stock market price and predict it by using Artificial Intelligence algorithms. The ANN gather hidden part of the data out of noisy information and predict the stock market price by comparing with the actual data. ANN successfully model nonlinear behavior and does not require prior knowledge on the functional form of the relation. It does not rely on

DOI: 10.4018/978-1-6684-2408-7.ch068

any parametric assumption and adapt itself to the dynamic changes in the data-generating process. The philosophy behind ANN approach is that it develops the architecture inspired by the biological nervous system. Therefore, the ANN is robust and flexible in model specification. However, little research work has been done so far to forecast the direction of stock market price in the Indian stock market after financial crises period 2008.

The present study tries to address this gap. The study has been undertaken to predict the daily movement of Indian stock market price direction by using Feedforward Neural Network model. Secondly, the study tries to determine the accuracy of the prediction of daily movement of stock market price by using Sign Correctness Percentage (SCP) and Normalized Mean Square Error (NMSE). The structure of the paper planned as follows: Section 2 presents the literature review; Section 3 elucidates the data and methodology Section 4 deliberates the empirical findings, and section 5 deals with concluding observations.

2. LITERATURE REVIEW

Several studies have predicted the stock market price in the past decades. Min Qi (1999) examined the forecasting ability of the United States (US) stock market returns by using Linear Regression and Nonlinear Neural Network model. The study found that the Nonlinear NN model fits data better than the linear model and provides relatively accurate forecast than the linear model. Phua, et al. (2000) used NN with Genetic Algorithm to predict the Singapore stock market. The study found that the model predicts 81 percent accuracy of the direction of the stock market. Yochanan and Dorota (2000) examined the dynamic interrelations among Canada, France, Germany, Japan, United Kingdom (UK), US and World stock markets by using Ordinary Least Squares, General Linear Regression, Multi-layer Perceptron models of ANN. The study reported that NN consist of Multilayer perceptron model with logistic activation function predicts the daily stock market returns better than traditional Ordinary Least Squares and General Linear Regression model. The Multilayer Perceptron, with five units in the hidden layer, better predicts the stock indices of US, France, Germany, UK and World stock markets.

Qing Cao et al. (2005) predicted the Shanghai stock market using ANN model and accomplished that ANN model is a suitable tool to predict the Chinese stock markets. Altay & Satman (2005) compare the predictive performance of ANN and Regression model of Istanbul Stock Exchange. The study found that ANN outperforms the Regression model in predicting the future direction of Istanbul stock market. The prediction accuracy of ANN model reported 57.8percent, 67.1 percent and 78.3 percent for daily, weekly and monthly data of Istanbul Stock Exchange. Pan et al. (2005) used ANN model for predicting Australian stock market. The accuracy of ANN model reported 80 percent in predicting the price direction of Australian stock market. Dutta et al. (2006) investigated the ability of ANN to predict the Bombay Stock Exchange (BSE) closing values. The study used the Root Mean Squared Error (RMSE) and Mean Absolute Error (MAE) as an indicator of the performance of ANN model. The study found that ANN with more input variables gives healthier forecasting results. Avci (2007) used ANN model to forecast the daily and sessional returns of ISE -100 indexes. The study stated that ANN appropriately predicts the day-to-day and sessional returns of the ISE -100 indexes. Khan et al. (2008) compared the Back Propagation NN with the Genetic Algorithms based Back Propagation NN model. The study showed that Genetic Algorithm based Backpropagation NN reports more accurate forecasting result than Back Propagation NN in Indian stock market.

BirolYildiz et al. (2008) used three layers NN and Back Propagation Algorithm to forecast the Istanbul Stock markets. The findings of the study reported that NN and Back Propagation Algorithm predict the direction of the stock market with an accuracy of 74.51 percent. Leandro & Ballini (2010) predicted the future trends of North American, European, and Brazilian stock markets by using ANN model. The study revealed that ANN has the capability to forecast the stock markets. Further, the study concluded that robustness can be improved through appropriately trained and network structure. Yakup Kara, et al. (2011) examined the performance of predicting the direction of movement of daily Istanbul Stock Exchange (ISE) National 100 index by using ANN and Support Vector Machine (SVM) model. The study found that ANN model surpasses the SVM model in predicting the direction of movement of daily Istanbul Stock Exchange price. Khadka, et al. (2012) predicted S&P 500 and NASDAQ indices by Genetic Programming approach. The study compared the results with existing standard ARIMA model and another proposed model. The study reported that Genetic Programming delivers enough evidence regarding prediction than any other models. The study concluded that forecasting horizon increases, error level increases, and hybrid method perform much better in shorter forecasting horizon. Peter Adebayo, et al. (2012) predicted the Nigerian stock market by using ANN model and suggest that ANN is a suitable model to predict Nigerian future stock prices. Abbas (2012) predicted the Tehran stock price by using ANN model. The study exhibited that ANN model is apposite for estimation and prediction of Tehran stock prices.

Salim (2013) predicted S&P500 price index future trend by using wavelet analysis with support vector machines and support vector machines (SVMs). The study found that wavelet transform SVM is a suitable model to predict the S&P500 trend. In another study, Salim et al. (2014) observed the performance of the economic information, technical indicators, historical information, and investor sentiment in financial predictions using Backpropagation Neural Networks. The study also predicted the stock market trend by comparing Backpropagation Neural Networks and Support Vector Machine model. The study found that all this four-category information are not able to improve the accuracy of the BPNN and SVM model. The study also revealed that Backpropagation Neural Networks beats the SVM model in the prediction of the stock market trend. Leonel et al. (2015) used ANN model for predicting the maximum and minimum day stock prices of Brazilian power distribution companies. Correlation analysis used to select input variables and different ANN architectures tested empirically in the study. The study indicated that the best results found with one hidden layer and only five hidden neurons. Javad and Mohammad (2015) evaluated the predictability of Tehran Stock Exchange price through the application of ANN model and Principal Component Analysis method. The findings of the study suggested that ANN model have superiority over PCA method to predict the stock price of Tehran Stock Exchange. Montri (2016) predicted Thailand's SET50 stock index movement using hybrid intelligence ANN and Genetic Algorithm models. The results of the study exhibited that the hybrid's average prediction accuracy results are 63.6 percent.

Mustafa Göçken et al. (2016) examined the forecasting performance of Turkish stock market using hybrid ANN models such as Harmony Search(HS)and Genetic Algorithm(GA) model. The study indicated that stock price forecasting performance of HS-ANN is better than GA-ANN model. Xunfa Lu et al. (2016) used hybrid ANN and GARCH-type models to predict the log-returns series in Chinese energy market. The findings of the study showed that EGARCH-ANN model outperforms the other models to forecast the volatilities of log-returns series of Chinese energy market. Amin et al. (2016) forecasted the daily NASDAQ stock exchange rate using Artificial Neural Network model. The study used various feedforward ANNs trained with the back-propagation algorithm. The values of NASDAQ exchange rate of last four and nine working days as well as the day of the week as the input parameters used in the model for NASDAQ index prediction. The results exhibited that there is no difference between the prediction ability of the four and nine prior working days as input parameters in NASDAQ stock exchange. Chandra Shakher et al. (2016) forecasted the stock price of India using ANN model. The ANN model employed dynamic Backpropagation model and implemented a logistics sigmoid function as the activation function. The study found that ANN model predicts the stock price with better accuracy with the increased number of input data. The study also concluded that NN model outperforms the traditional methods.

Qiu M (2016) predicted the direction of the next day's price of Japanese stock market by using an optimized ANN model. The study resolved that the hit ratio of predicting the direction of movement of stock prices are 81.27 percent. Ali Sorayaei et al. (2016) used both NN and Regression model to predict the stock market price of Tehran Stock Exchange. The square error of NN method is 0.29 in comparison to Regression method 1.68. The results of the study indicated that prediction with ANN is more acceptable and suitable than Regression method. Dadabada and Vadlamani (2017) forecast the volatility of financial time series using PSO-trained Quantile Regression Neural Network (PSOQRNN), Generalized Autoregressive Conditional Heteroskedasticity (GARCH), Multi-Layer Perceptron (MLP), General Regression Neural Network (GRNN), Group Method of Data Handling(GMDH), Random Forest (RF), Quantile Regression Neural Network (QRNN) and Quantile Regression Random Forest (QRRF) models. The study demonstrated that the proposed PSOQRNN performed better than other models for forecasting volatility of time series. Dimitrios (2017) assessed the accurate realized volatility forecasts of the US financial market from 2009 to 2011.The study compared the realized volatility forecasts by using Neural Networks, Principal Components Combining, ARCH and Heterogeneous Autoregressive (HAR) model. The study found that Heterogeneous Autoregressive (HAR) and Principal Components Combining (PCC) models are the best model. The study concluded that HAR is better than PCC model for forecasting the volatility of financial markets.

Werner and Esteban (2017) examined the volatility forecast of spot prices of gold, silver, and copper using hybrid NN Model and GARCH-type models. The study used GARCH models to forecast the volatility of US Dollar-Euro, US Dollar-Yen exchange rates, the oil price, Chinese, Indian, British, and American stock market indexes. The study further used GARCH model for predictions as input for NN to analyze the hybrid predictive power. The study found that hybrid NN model shows better forecast in comparison to GARCH models. Nayak et al. (2017) used artificial chemical reaction Neural Network (ACRNN) to forecast the stock market indices such as DJIA, NASDAQ, TAIEX, FTSE, BSE, S&P 500 and LSE. The study found that prediction accuracy of ACRNN technique is 80 percent. Sadig (2017) predicted the stock market by using 2-layers feed forward back propagation ANN model based on Levenberg-Marquardt learning algorithm. The outcomes of the study demonstrated that relative error of prediction is less than 3 percent. So, the study suggested that feed forward back propagation ANN model is appropriate for stock market prediction.

3. DATA AND METHODOLOGY

The present study employs daily closing price of S&P CNX Nifty from 1st January 2008 to 8th April 2016. All required information for the study retrieved from the National Stock Exchange (NSE) website. (www.nse.com). Daily returns of Indian stock market calculated by using the closing price. The study has taken eight years' historical data of S&P CNX Nifty Index to test the Neural Networks. The critical issues that essential for designing the models are some hidden layers, the number of neurons in each layer, initial weight value, the size of the training set, input and activation functions. The challenging of selecting the input variable depends upon its number of input variables and the lag between them. If the lag is less in-between input variables, the correlation between them is likely to increase; that may lead to the over-fitting phenomenon. On the other hand, if the lag increases in-between variables, the Neural Network will miss out some vital information of input variables that may lead to under-learning. Hence, the present study has taken the various lagged structure and test the Neural Network on trial and error basis. The input variables used in the ANN are one day, two days, three days, four days and five days lag of Nifty closing price. This paper applied three-layer feedforward Neural Network model since this model is the most common network planning used in financial Neural Network.

In this paper, the data divided into two sets: training and testing. The data normalized into the range (0, 1). Also, 70 percent data used for training the model. The rest 30 percent data used for testing the model. The data are used to save the weights and bias at the minimum error to avoid the network over-fitting. The normalized for input made by using the following method:

$$x_n = \frac{x - x_{min}}{x_{max} - x_{min}}$$
(1)

x_n represent the normalized value of x, x_{min} denotes the minimum value of x, x_{max} represents the maximum value of after normalized, the stock market data is in range of (0, 1). The network predicted value, which are in range of (0, 1) transformed to the real-world values by using the following equations:

$$x_i = x_{ni}(x_{max} - x_{min}) + x_{min}$$
(2)

Machine learning approach is based on the principle of learning from training and experience. ANN is best suited for machine learning approach since connection weights adjust to improve the network performances. ANN consist of simple computational units called neuron. These neurons are highly interconnected, and each interconnection is expressed by a number referred as weight. An artificial neuron encompasses numerous inputs (x1, x2, …, x n) and one output y as follows

Y= f (xi, w i)
(3)

W i denotes the function parameter weights of the function f. The equation (3) called as activation function.

The Neural Network design with the input layer, hidden layer and the output layer presented in Figure 1. The study has used three-layered feed-forward with Back-propagation Neural Network architecture to forecast the stock market price movement. The network is trained and tested by using the Back-Propagation algorithm to improve the Network performance. The Network is continuously processing the training data set to reduce the error by comparing the output with actual output. The modification typically takes place in the backward direction, from output layer through hidden layer to the first hidden layer. The training of the Neural Network builds for the prediction. In the training module, it involves MLP. The MLP is a Feed-Forward Neural Network, trained with Error Backpropagation which is the two-pass weight-learning algorithm to adjust in-between weight nodes to reduce the error of the output. The architecture of MLP consists of the input layer, hidden layer, and an output layer. The input layer takes the data that fed into the Network and passes to the hidden layer. The hidden layer then followed by an output layer. If more than two hidden layers taken, ANN model may create over-fitting such as, in sampling error may become fragile and out-sample error may go up. So, the number of hidden layers restricted in the present study are two. The number of the output layer is one since it estimates only the stock market (Nifty) price. After training the Network, validation data used to validate for educating the Network performance.

Figure 1. Neural Network model with three-layer feed forward

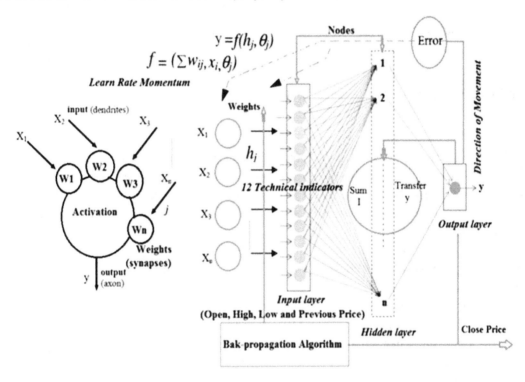

The equation (3) transforms the input into output linearly. The Artificial Neuron computes its output according to the equation shown below. The output of neuron y defined as

$$y = f\left(\sum_{i=1}^{n} w_{ij} x_i, \theta\right) = \{ \begin{matrix} 1 & w_{ij} x_i \geq \theta \\ 0 & w_{ij} x_i \angle \theta \end{matrix} \tag{4}$$

$(i= 1, 2, \ldots\ldots, n)$

where y is the output value computed from set of input patterns. Θ is called the bias of the neuron, since θ, the bias considers as an input, $x0 = -1$ and the associate weight $w_0 = \theta$. The quantities Xi and Wi denote the inputs and the weights respectively. x_i of ith unit in a previous layer, w_{ij} is the weight on the connection from the neuron i^{th} to j, θ_j is the threshold value of the threshold function f, and n is the number of units in the previous layer.

The input neurons in the study are previous day Nifty closing price. Here 'n' denotes the window size. The window size determined that how many trailing data points (last n day's Nifty values) have been used to forecast the current value. As only one-day-ahead forecasting to be performed, the output contains only one data value.

The study used two types of activation functions such as Hyperbolic tangent function and Sigmoid function. The output layer calculated through the Hyperbolic tangent and the Sigmoid transfer function. The Hyperbolic tangent function is a continuous function with the range of (-1, 1) and sigmoid (logistic) function with a range of (-0, 1). This feature may be linear or non-linear such as one of the following:

$$\text{Hyperbolic tangent: } f(x) = \tanh(x) = 1 - \frac{2}{1 + e^{-2x}} \quad \text{Range } [-1,1] \tag{5}$$

$$\text{Sigmoid(logistic): } f(x) = \frac{1}{\left(1 + e^{-x}\right)} \quad \text{Range } [0,1] \tag{6}$$

Some of the research studies have stated that when learning move towards the standard behavior, Sigmoid function mechanism becomes supreme. However, it is seen opposite in case of Hyperbolic tangent function. The Hyperbolic tangent function is an ideal transfer function (Kalman & Kwasny, 1992) and having significant impact on the training speed although the nature of functions has little effect on the Network. (Masters, 1993).

3.1. Performance Measurement

The performance of NN model is measured by using Normalized Mean Square Error (NMSE) and Sign Correctness Percentage (SCP) method. The NMSE is used to evaluate the predictive power of the models. The lower the value, the better is the model.

$$NMSE = \frac{\sum_{t=1}^{n}(o_t - p_t)^2}{\sum_{t=1}^{n}(o_t - \overline{p_t})^2} \tag{7}$$

where O_t is the actual stock market price of the data series, Pt is the predicted value for the same day's closing price, and ‾p is the mean of the actual value of the stock market price. The NMSE is most widely used as an important signal for the pattern recognition. The smaller NMSE, better is the forecasting ability of the model.

The Sign Correctness Percentage (SCP) is used to determine the percentage accuracy of prediction of the direction of predicted value of the closing price of next day's stock market (Nifty) price. The direction of change is calculated by subtracting today's price from the forecast price and determines the sign (positive or negative) of the result.

$$SCP = \frac{\left|\{Sign(O_t) = Sign(P_t) t = 1,2,3,\ldots\ldots,N_D\}\right|}{N_1} \times 100 \tag{8}$$

The Sign Correctness Percentage (SCP) has been used to correctly predict the direction of the movement of the stock market price.

4. EMPIRICAL ANALYSIS

The descriptive statistics of the daily return series of the Indian stock market analyzed before applying the Neural Networks model. Table 1 presents the mean return, standard deviation, skewness, kurtosis and Jarque-Bera test. All the returns calculated as the first difference of log of the daily closing price. The results indicated that risk is higher in comparison to the returns. Further, the stock returns have positive kurtosis and show high JB statistics. It implies that the distribution skewed to the right and they are leptokurtic. The Jarque-Bera (J-B) statistic confirms that the returns depart significantly from normality. Nifty stock returns follow a non-normal distribution. It indicates that all series exhibit non-normality and display the presence of Heteroscedasticity. Hence, ANN model is suitable for the study (see Figure 2).

Table 1. Descriptive statistics of S&P 500 Nifty

Mean	0.010118
Median	0.043114
Maximum	16.33432
Minimum	-13.01419
Std. Dev.	1.540294
Skewness	0.099540
Kurtosis	14.22205
Jarque-Bera	10723.54
Probability	0.000000
R-squared	0.997286

Figure 2. Daily Stock Market Return from 2008 to 2016

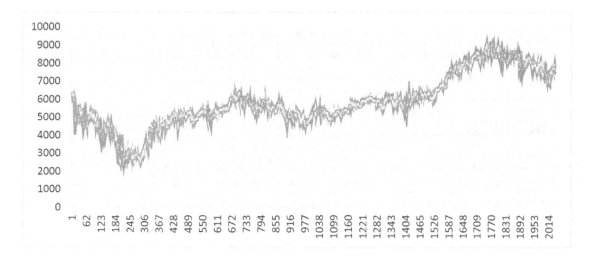

ANN model is used to forecast the stock market price (Nifty Index). The daily closing price is used as an input to this model to obtain the predicted value. The model then automatically accustomed to the training datasets and makes a forecast. The ANN models with different Network parameters are created, trained and tested for each series. The study has run Neural Network simulation for ten different cases based on the data input (different lags) and the activation function (Hyperbolic tangent function and Sigmoid function). Since the behavior of stock market is a random one, the study has considered five-day lag input data for the Neural Network to achieve the maximum learning and higher precision. The results presented in the Table 2.

Table 2. Prediction Performances of ANN model

Activation Function	One Day Lag		Two Day Lag		Three Day Lag		Four Day Lag		Five Day Lag	
	NMSE	SCP	NMSE	SCP	NMSE	SCP	NMSE	SCP	NMSE	SCP
Hyperbolic Tangent	0.02	59.59	0.07	53.24	0.09	59.30	0.11	51.47	0.12	51.15
Sigmoid	0.05	55.12	0.04	52.75	0.03	65.34	0.05	52.16	0.07	49.61

Table 2 exhibits that the minimum value of the normalized error is 0.02. It is occurring when the data for one-day lag used with a Hyperbolic tangent activation function. It observes that accuracy of determining the prediction of the movement of direction of stock market price is virtually 60 percent. The ANN model precisely foresees the direction of movement which is reasonably good. The 60 percent accuracy of forecasting the stock market price indicates that the loss in stock market return can be minimized. It is evident from the analysis that, learning for the Network is highest under one-day lag data which is optimum to predict the future values of the stock market price. So, it recommends for using the Hyperbolic tangent activation function when predicting the direction of movement of stock market price.

Figure 3 shows the graphical representation of the predicted and actual stock market price of the ANN based prediction where backpropagation algorithm used.

It is apparent from the analysis that one-day lag value can predict the market direction better with fewer errors in comparison to the lag period. It observes that the Back-propagation algorithm reduces the error between the actual output and desired output in a gradient descent manner. Hence, it is one of the best algorithms to use in Feed-Forward Neural Network. The study indicates that accuracy in the prediction will be more when continuous data taken in the study. R2 value shows that about 99 percent of the variation in the movement of stock market prices explained by the previous day closing price which is depicted in Table 1.

5. CONCLUSION

The present study predicts the movement of direction of stock market price by using Feedforward Artificial Neural Networks Model. The accuracy of the model tested by using Normalized Mean Square Error (NMSE) and Sign Correctness Percentage (SCP) measures. The study found that the proposed model shows reasonable performance in predicting the direction of stock price movement in Indian stock market. It also found from the analysis that the predicted output is very close to the actual data since the normalized error of one-day lag is 0.02. The result demonstrated that ANN model can accurately forecast the direction of the daily movement of Indian stock market price with 60 percent accuracy after financial crises period 2008. Since one-day lag predicts the market direction with reasonable accuracy, the validity of the efficient market hypothesis is questionable. It is evident that the future stock price can be predicted, and speculators can earn profits by predicting the daily movement of Indian stock market price. The ANN model can be used in the Indian stock market for forecasting the daily changes of market price.

Figure 3. Actual and Predicted Nifty Stock Price (One-Day lag)

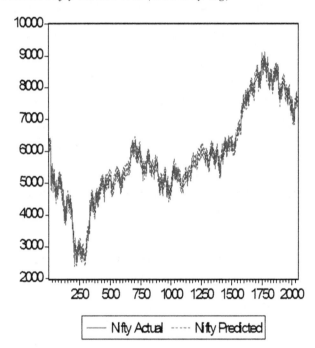

Predicting the direction of movement of stock market price is considered as a sign for articulating the market trading solutions. The profitability of investing in the stock market mainly depends on the predictability. If the direction of the market successfully predicted, a trader may be better guided and earn good returns. Further, it is not only helping for increasing the investments in the stock market but also helps the regulators to take corrective measures. Our findings have significant implications for economists, market regulators and policy makers for understanding the effectiveness of Indian stock market. These results could be helpful to investors, speculators, brokers, and so forth, in undertaking investment decisions. However, future research can be carried out by taking alternative nonlinear model such as SVM model, ANN Wavelet model to know more about the direction of the stock market price.

REFERENCES

Cao, Q., Leggio, K. B., & Schniederjans, M. J. (2005). A comparison between Fama and French's model and Artificial Neural Networks in Predicting the Chinese Stock Market. *Computers, 32*(10), 2499–2512.

Abbas, V. (2012). The Predicting Stock Price using Artificial Neural Network. *Journal of Basic and Applied Scientific Research, 2*(3), 2325–2328.

Adebayo, P. (2012). Prediction of Stock Market in Nigeria Using Artificial Neural Network. *International Journal of Intelligent Systems and Applications, 4*(11), 68–74. doi:10.5815/ijisa.2012.11.08

Altay, E., & Satman, M. H. (2005). Stock market forecasting: Artificial neural networks and linear regression comparison in an emerging market. *Journal of Financial Management and Analysis, 18*(2), 18–33.

Amin, H. M. (2016). Stock market index prediction using Artificial Neural Network. *Journal of Economics, Finance and Administrative Science, 21*(41), 89–93. doi:10.1016/j.jefas.2016.07.002

Avci, E. (2007). Forecasting Daily and Sessional Returns of the Ise-100 Index with Neural Network Models. *Dogus Universitesi Dergisi, 2*(8), 128–142.

Birol, Yildiz., Abdullah, Yalama., & Metin, Coskun. (2008). Forecasting the Istanbul Stock Exchange National 100 Index Using an Artificial Neural Network. *World Academy of Science, Engineering and Technology, 2*(10), 32–35.

C., Shakher Tyagi, Harpreet, S., Varun, B. & Kritika, N. (2016). Applications of Artificial Neural Network in Forecasting of Stock Market Index. *International Journal of Recent Research in Mathematics Computer Science and Information Technology, 3*(1), 28–38.

Dadabada, P. (2017). Forecasting financial time series volatility using Particle Swarm Optimization trained Quantile Regression Neural Network. *Applied Soft Computing, 58*, 35–52. doi:10.1016/j.asoc.2017.04.014

Dutta, G., Jha, P., Laha, A. K., & Mohan, N. (2006). Artificial neural network models for forecasting stock price index in the Bombay stock exchange. *Journal of Emerging Market Finance, 5*(3), 283–295. doi:10.1177/097265270600500305

Göçken, M., Özçalıcı, M., Boru, A., & Dosdoğru, A. T. (2016). Integrating Metaheuristics and Artificial Neural Networks for improved stock price prediction. *Expert Systems with Applications, 44*, 320–331. doi:10.1016/j.eswa.2015.09.029

Inthachot, M., Boonjing, V., & Intakosum, S. (2016). Artificial Neural Network and Genetic Algorithm Hybrid Intelligence for Predicting Thai Stock Price Index Trend. *Computational Intelligence and Neuroscience*. doi:10.1155/2016/3045254

Javad, Z. (2015). Application of Artificial Neural Network models and Principal Component Analysis method in predicting stock prices on Tehran Stock Exchange. *Physica A, 438*, 178–187. doi:10.1016/j.physa.2015.06.033

Jie, W. (2017). Forecasting stochastic Neural Network based on financial empirical mode decomposition. *Neural Networks, 90*, 8–20. doi:10.1016/j.neunet.2017.03.004 PMID:28364677

Khadka, M. S. (2012). Performance analysis of Hybrid Forecasting model in stock market forecasting. *International Journal of Managing Information Technology*, *4*(3), 81–88. doi:10.5121/ijmit.2012.4307

Khan, A. U., Bandopadhyaya, T. K., & Sharma, S. (2008). Genetic Algorithm Based Back Propagation Neural Network Performs better than Back Propagation Neural Network in Stock Rates Prediction. *International Journal of computer science& network security, 8*(7), 162-166.

Leonel, A. (2015). Maximum and Minimum stock price forecasting of Brazilian power distribution companies based on Artificial Neural. *Applied Soft Computing*, *35*, 66–77. doi:10.1016/j.asoc.2015.06.005

Min, Qi. (1999). Nonlinear Predictability of Stock Returns Using Financial and Economic Variables. *Journal of Business & Economic Statistics*, *17*(4), 419–429.

Nayak, S. C., Misra, B. B., & Behera, H. S. (2017). Artificial chemical reaction optimization of Neural Networks for efficient prediction of stock market indices. *Ain Shams Engineering Journal, 8*(3), 371–390. doi:10.1016/j.asej.2015.07.015

Pan, H., Tilakaratne, C., & Yearwood, J. (2005). Predicting Australian Stock Market Index Using Neural Networks Exploiting Dynamical Swings and Intermarket Influences. *Journal of Research and Practice in Information Technology, 37*(1), 43–55.

Phua, P. K. H., Ming, D., & Lin, W. (2000). Neural Network with Genetic Algorithms for Stocks Prediction. In *Fifth Conference of the Association of Asian-Pacific Operations Research Societies*, Singapore, July 5-7.

Sorayaei, A., Atf, Z., & Gholami, M. (2016). Prediction stock price using Artificial Neural Network (Case study: Chemical industry firms accepted in Tehran stock exchange. *Bulletin de la Société Royale des Sciences, 85*, 991–998.

Qiu, M., & Song, Y. (2016). Predicting the Direction of Stock Market Index Movement Using an Optimized Artificial Neural Network Model. *PLoS One, 11*(5), e0155133. doi:10.1371/journal.pone.0155133 PMID:27196055

Sadig, M. (2017). Financial time series prediction using Artificial Neural Network based on Levenberg-Marquardt algorithm. *Procedia Computer Science, 120*, 602–607. doi:10.1016/j.procs.2017.11.285

Salim, L. (2013). Forecasting Direction of the S&P500 Movement Using Wavelet Transform and Support Vector Machines. *International Journal of Strategic Decision Sciences, 4*(1), 79–89. doi:10.4018/jsds.2013010105

Salim, L. (2014). Exploring Information Categories and Artificial Neural Networks Numerical Algorithms in S&P500 Trend Prediction: A Comparative Study. *International Journal of Strategic Decision Sciences, 5*(1), 76–94. doi:10.4018/IJSDS.2014010105

Sawyer, S., & Tapia, A. (2005). The sociotechnical nature of mobile computing work: Evidence from a study of policing in the United States. *International Journal of Technology and Human Interaction, 1*(3), 1–14. doi:10.4018/jthi.2005070101

Shachmurove, Y., & Witkowska, D. (2000). Utilizing Artificial Neural Network Model to Predict Stock Markets, Department of Economics (CARESS Working Paper #00-11). The City College of the City University of New York and The University of Pennsylvania.

Vortelinos, D. I. (2017). Forecasting realized volatility: HAR against Principal Components Combining, Neural Networks and GARCH. *Research in International Business and Finance*, *39*, 824–839.

Werner, K. R., & Esteban, H. P. (2017). Volatility of main metals forecasted by a hybrid ANN-GARCH model with regressors. *Expert Systems with Applications*, *84*, 290–300. doi:10.1016/j.eswa.2017.05.024

Xiao, Z. (2017). Forecasting daily stock market return using dimensionality reduction. *Expert Systems with Applications*, *67*, 126–139. doi:10.1016/j.eswa.2016.09.027

Xunfa, L. (2016). Volatility Forecast Based on the Hybrid Artificial Neural Network and GARCH-type Models. *Procedia Computer Science*, *91*, 1044–1049. doi:10.1016/j.procs.2016.07.145

Yakup, K. (2011). Predicting direction of stock price index movement using Artificial Neural Networks and Support Vector Machines: The sample of the Istanbul Stock Exchange. *Expert Systems with Applications*, *38*(5), 5311–5319. doi:10.1016/j.eswa.2010.10.027

This research was previously published in the International Journal of Strategic Decision Sciences (IJSDS), 9(3); pages 84-94, copyright year 2018 by IGI Publishing (an imprint of IGI Global).

Chapter 69
Modelling and Forecasting Portfolio Inflows:
A Comparative Study of Support Vector Regression, Artificial Neural Networks, and Structural VAR Models

Mogari I. Rapoo
https://orcid.org/0000-0002-3602-7016
North-West University, South Africa

Elias Munapo
North-West University, South Africa

Martin M. Chanza
North-West University, South Africa

Olusegun Sunday Ewemooje
https://orcid.org/0000-0003-3236-6018
Federal University of Technology, Akure, Nigeria

ABSTRACT

This chapter analyses efficiency of support vector regression (SVR), artificial neural networks (ANNs), and structural vector autoregressive (SVAR) models in terms of in-sample forecasting of portfolio inflows (PIs). Time series daily data sourced from Rand Merchant Bank (RMB) covering the period of 1st March 2004 to 1st February 2016 were used. Mean squared error, root mean squared error, mean absolute error, mean absolute squared error, and root mean scaled log error were used to evaluate model performance. The results showed that SVR has the best modelling performance when compared to others. In determining factors that affect allocation of PIs into South Africa based on SVAR, 69% of the variation was explained by pull factors while 9% was explained by push factor. Hence, SVR model is more accurate than ANNs. This chapter therefore recommends that banking sector particularly RMB should use machine learning technique in modelling PIs for a better financial solution.

DOI: 10.4018/978-1-6684-2408-7.ch069

INTRODUCTION

Conventional econometric models have been used in modelling portfolio inflows for decades. These econometric models are significant in analysing the data since they are linear in nature while time series data are not as they are nonlinear in nature. This is because the dynamics and patterns of the series are nonlinear whereas the linear models assume a linear structure of the series. The discovery of the financial data being nonlinear has led its centre stage taken in analysing financial data. Nonlinear models have utmost accuracy in analysis series for their best modelling properties, thus, making them the most reliable models in predicting financial time series. Recent development in nonlinear models analyses has proved machine learning models to be better and powerful approximates. These machine learning models have been utilized in analysing time series data in different disciplines. In instances where linear models cannot address the fundamentals of time series data, nonlinear models are used as they capture those fundamentals. Therefore, this chapter investigates whether machine-learning models are effective in modelling portfolio inflows or not using econometric model of Structural VAR to identify the key drivers of portfolio inflows into South Africa and furthermore assess the efficiency and performance of machine learning models namely support vector regression (SVR) and artificial neural networks (ANNs) models in modelling and forecasting portfolio inflows, respectively.

BACKGROUND

In the literature, the effect(s) of strong wave of portfolio inflows are highlighted; under ordinary conditions capital flows have valuable impacts for developing economies. In a few events, floods of strong portfolio flows have gone before scenes of money related instability, for instance, the Mexican emergency of 1994 and the Asian emergency 1997 (Lo Duca, 2012). As this is the case, the negative effect of portfolio inflows to receiving economies calls for appropriate policies to be put in place, in which case the drivers of these flows may be used in developing these policies.

There are several applications of Support Vector Regression in solving forecasting problems in many fields where the model was successfully applied such as atmospheric science forecasting (Hong, 2009) and financial time series (stock index and exchange rate) forecasting (Cao, 2003). Chen and Wang (2007) employed Support Vector Regression, back-propagation neural networks (BPNN) and Autoregressive Integrated Moving Average (ARIMA) to forecast tourism demand and genetic algorithm was employed to select the optimal parameters of the Support Vector Regression model and show that Support Vector Regression outperforms other selected models. Hong (2009) also employed chaotic particle swarm optimization (CPSO) for choosing parameters for the Support Vector Regression model and showed that CPSO outperforms both the genetic algorithm (GA) and simulated annealing algorithm. Kazem et al. (2013) forecasted stock market prices employing a model based on Support Vector Regression, chaotic mapping and firefly algorithm using a time series data of stock prices, bank shares and intel. They compared their proposed model with Genetic Algorithm based Support Vector Regression (SVR-GA), Chaotic Genetic Algorithm based Support Vector Regression (SVR-CGA), Firefly based Support Vector Regression (SVR-FA), Artificial Neural Networks (ANNs) and Adaptive-Network-based Fuzzy Inference Systems (ANFIS), and revealed that the proposed model outperformed other models. Also, Adebiyi et al., (2014) compared artificial neural networks (ANNs) and Autoregressive Integrated Moving Average (ARIMA) models as far as anticipating precision of the stock market data sourced from New York Stock

Exchange and disclosed that the Artificial neural networks (ANNs) model outperformed Autoregressive Integrated Moving Average (ARIMA) model.

Ramani and Murarka (2013) used multilayer feed forward artificial neural networks (ANNs) to predict stock price using algorithm of back propagation to the model by training the network through historical stock prices (closing) and showed that a feed forward network using back propagation is quite reasonable for stock price prediction. Bing et al., (2012) employed BPNN model to forecast Shanghai Stock Exchange Composite Index and their results revealed that the model was utilized successfully to highest, lowest and closing values of the Index. Ajide and Raheem (2015) examined the drivers of capital flows (portfolio) into Nigerian economy and the dynamic effect shocks of the drivers using structural vector auto-regression (SVAR), variance decomposition and impulse response analysis. Their study revealed that there is need to introduce policies that can be used to deal with shocks in economic activity variables both internal and external. Korap (2010) employed structural vector auto-regression (SVAR) model in analysing the key determinants of capital flows (portfolio) in the framework of Turkish economy and found that the Turkish economy push factors have a superior role in elucidating the behaviour of portfolio flows and that there is a negative correlation between real interest rate and portfolio flows. Further study by Raghavan et al., (2014) examined the correlation between portfolio capital flows to domestic credit and their impacts on the Australian economy using the structural vector auto-regression (SVAR) model and it was revealed that debt flows are driving the impact of net portfolio flows in Australia, while equity flows have no real effect on the domestic macroeconomic variables.

There are various techniques which have been utilized in literature to model portfolio inflows and its drivers to emerging markets. Commonly used conventional econometric methods are; structural vector auto-regression (SVAR) model (used by Korap 2010; Alquist 2006; Çulha 2006), VAR model (used by Egly et al., 2010) and Finite distributed lag model and VECM model (used by Ekeocha et al., 2012; Hong and Pai 2007). Consequently, this chapter examines whether machine-learning models are effective in modelling portfolio inflows or not using econometric model of Structural VAR to identify the key drivers of portfolio inflows into South Africa and furthermore assess the efficiency and performance of machine learning models.

MAIN FOCUS OF THE CHAPTER

In achieving the research objectives, this chapter used the historic time series data of portfolio inflows obtained from the Rand Merchant Bank (RMB), South Africa. The time series data were chosen based on the notion that strong portfolio inflows can be of a negative impact to the recipient economy. Different models in the literature have been utilized in modelling and forecasting portfolio inflows, and furthermore utilized to explore which models give accurate predictions of portfolio inflows. Support Vector Regression (SVR), artificial neural networks (ANNs) and structural vector auto-regression (SVAR) are the fundamental statistical techniques utilized for the analysis in this current study. Schwarz Bayesian Criterion (SBC) developed by Schwarz (1978) used as a model selection method while forecasting efficiency of the model(s) is evaluated based on the accompanying error metrics: Mean Squared Error (MSE), Root Mean Squared Error (RMSE), Mean Absolute Error (MAE), Mean Absolute Squared Error (MASE) and Root Mean Scaled Log Error (RMSLE). All analyses are carried out using R, E-views and EasyReg International statistical softwares. Appropriate preliminary statistical analyses were undertaken and the data was assessed in terms of normality assumption by applying skewness and kurtosis, and shown to be nonlinear in nature.

Data Description and Sources

In address the research objectives, the chapter uses historic time series data of portfolio inflows which were sourced from the Rand Merchant Bank (RMB), South Africa. The chapter used portfolio inflows as the dependent variable and exchange rate, inflation linked bonds, real GDP as the independent variables covering the period of 1st March, 2004 to 1st February, 2016 consisting of 3111 observations.

Figure 1. Methodology Diagram

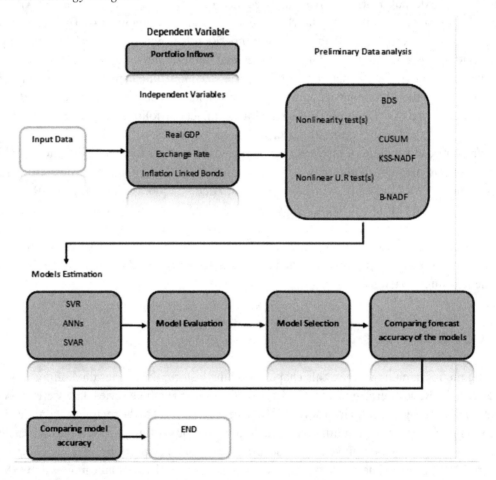

Modelling and Forecasting Methods

Support vector regression: Support vector machine is a developed machine learning classification paradigm while support vector regression (SVR) is the adaptation of support vector machine. In the SVR concept, a typical regression problem is formulated. Let's reflect on a set of data $G = \left\{ \left(x_i, q_i \right) \right\}_{i=1}^{n}$, given that x_i is a model input in a vector form, q_i is actual value and n, total number of data patterns. In Support Vector Regression (SVR), the inputs are firstly nonlinear mapped into a high dimensional element space (F), wherein they are put into a linear relationship with the outputs in order to take care of nonlinear regression problem. According to Lu et al. (2009) the SVR have the following linear estimation function:

$$f(z) = (v \bullet \varphi(z)) + b \tag{1}$$

Given that $v, b, \varphi(z)$ and $(v \cdot \varphi(z))$ are the weight vector, constant, mapping function from the feature space and the dot product in the feature space F, respectively. Here, there is a transformation from a nonlinear regression problem to a linear regression problem from a lower dimension input space (z) to a higher dimension feature space (F). To formulate Support Vector Regression (SVR), there are a number of cost functions that can be used. These functions include Laplacian, Huber's Gaussian and ε-insensitive loss function ($l\varepsilon_)$. The most commonly adopted one is given in equation (2) by Lu et al. (2009).

$$l_\varepsilon\left(f\left(z\right), q\right) = \begin{cases} \left\{\left|f\left(z\right) - q\right| - \varepsilon & if \left|f\left(z\right) - q\right| \geq \varepsilon\right\} \\ 0 & otherwise \end{cases} \tag{2}$$

where ε denotes a radius of the tube situated in the regression function $f(z)$ and it is a precision parameter. Figure 2 presents Support Vector Regression (SVR) with ε -insensitive loss function. In figure 2 the locale encased by the tube is known as "ε -insensitive" since the loss function assumes a zero figure in this locale and does not punish the forecast errors with degrees smaller than ε as given in Lu et al. (2009). Hence, the weight (v) and constant (b) in equation (1) and the subsequent risk function can be minimized when estimating the parameters (weight and constant):

$$R\left(C\right) = C\frac{1}{n}\sum_{i=1}^{n} L_e\left(f\left(x_i\right), q\right) + \frac{1}{2}\left|w\right|^2 \tag{3}$$

Given that $L_e(f(x), q)$ is ε-*insensitive* loss function in equation (2), $\frac{1}{2}\left|w\right|^2$ is the regularization term which controls the exchange between the complexity and the estimation exactness of the regression model to guarantee that the model has an improved generalization performance. *C is* the regularization constant used to indicate the exchange between empirical risk and regularization term. The parameters C and ε can be determined by the user.

Two positive slack variables, ξ_i and ξ_i^*, $i = 1, 2, \ldots, n$, are used to measure deviation $(q_i - f(x_i))$ from the borders of the ε-*insensitive* zone. These denote the distance from the actual values to the conforming border value of ε-*insensitive* zone as shown in figure 2. Therefore, equation (3) is transformed by using the slack variables into the subsequent constrained method:

Minimize: $$R_{reg}\left(f\right) = \frac{1}{2}\left|w\right|^2 + C\sum_{i=1}^{n}\left(\xi_i + \xi_i^*\right) \tag{4}$$

Subject to:

$$\begin{cases} q_i - \left(w \cdot \vartheta(x_i)\right) - b \le \varepsilon + \xi_i \\ \left(w \cdot \vartheta(x_i)\right) + b - q_i \le \varepsilon + \xi_i^* \\ \xi_i, \xi_i^* \ge 0, \ \ for \ i = 1, \ldots, n \end{cases}$$ (5)

Figure 2. A schematic representation of the SVR e-insensitive loss function

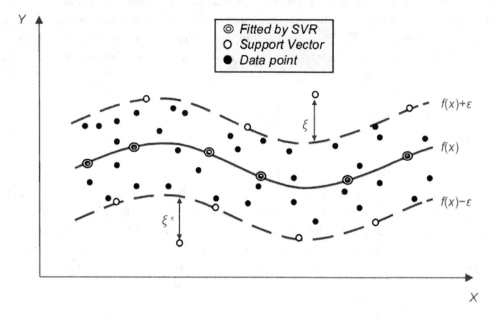

By using Lagrangian multipliers and Karush-Kuhn-Tucker conditions in equation (3), this yields the following dual Lagrangian form given in equation (6).

Maximize

$$L_d\left(\alpha, \alpha^*\right) = -\varepsilon \sum_{i=1}^{n} \left(\alpha_i^* + \alpha_i\right) + \sum_{i=1}^{n} \left(\alpha_i^* - \alpha_i\right) q_i - \frac{1}{2} \sum_{i \ j=1}^{n} \left(\alpha_i^* - \alpha_i\right)\left(\alpha_j^* - \alpha_j\right) k\left(x_i, x_j\right)$$ (6)

Subject to the constraints:

$$\begin{cases} \sum_{i=1}^{n} \left(\alpha_i^* - \alpha_i\right) = 0 \\ 0 \le \alpha_i \le C, \ \ i = 1, \ldots, n \\ 0 \le \alpha_i^* \le C, \ \ i = 1, \ldots, n \end{cases}$$ (7)

The equality of $\alpha_i \alpha_i^* = 0$ is satisfied by the Lagrangian multipliers in equation (6). The Lagrangian multipliers, α_i and α_i^* are calculated and an optimal desired weight vector of the regression hyperplan is $v^* = \sum_{i=1}^{n} \left(\alpha_i - \alpha_i^* \right) k \left(x, x_j \right)$. Support Vector Regression (SVR) function can be written according to Çulha (2006) and Amisano & Giannini (1997) as:

$$f(x,v) = f\left(x, \alpha, \alpha^* \right) = \sum_{i=1}^{n} \left(\alpha_i - \alpha_i^* \right) k \left(x, x_i \right) + b \tag{8}$$

where $k(x,x_i)$ is called kernel function. The product of the two vectors, x_i and x_j, in the feature space $\varphi(x_i)$ and $\varphi(x_j)$ will be equal to the kernel; that is, $k(x,x_i) = \varphi(x_i)\varphi(x_j)$. Any function that can be used to satisfy the Mercer's condition can also be employed as a kernel function (Chen and Wang, 2007). The broadly utilized kernel function is the radial basis function, although several functions are available. The radial basis function (RBF) is computed as follows:

$$K\left(x_i, x_j \right) = exp\left(\frac{-x_i - x_j^2}{2\sigma^2} \right) \tag{9}$$

where σ is the width of the RBF. In this manner, the current chapter utilizes the RBF as it was utilized in the study of Lu et al. (2009).

Artificial Neural Networks: Computational intelligence systems, in particular, the artificial neural networks (ANNs) are free of dynamics and have been used in approximation function and forecasting (Khashei and Bijari, 2010). The ANN models have significant advantage over other nonlinear models; ANNs are widespread approaches that can approximate a substantial class of functions with a high level of accuracy. Their capacity originates from the parallel processing of information from the data. Also, there are no prior assumptions required in the model building process. Single hidden layer feed forward network has been widely applied in time series modelling and forecasting (Khashei and Bijari, 2010; Adebiyi et al. 2012). This model is made up of a network of three layers of simple processing units connected by a cyclic links (see figure 3). The output (y_t) and the inputs $(y_{t-1},...,y_{t-p})$ have a relationship that can be denoted as follows in a mathematical representation:

$$y_t = w_0 + \sum_{j=1}^{q} w_j \cdot g\left(w_{0j} + \sum_{i=1}^{p} w_{ij} \cdot y_{t-i} \right) + \varepsilon_t \tag{10}$$

where $w_{ij}(i=0,1,2,...,p; j=1,2,...,q)$ and $w_j(j=0,1,2,...,q)$ are model parameters often called connection weights. Parameter p is the number of input nodes and q is the number of hidden nodes. There are several forms activation function can take and the reason for this activation function is to prohibit outputs from achieving huge values which can 'incapacitate' neural networks and along these lines inhibit training (Kaastra and Boyd, 1996). The logistic and tangent hyperbolic functions are used as the hidden layer activation function which is shown in equations (11) and (12), respectively;

$$sig(y) = \frac{1}{1+exp(-y)}. \tag{11}$$

$$Tanh(y) = \frac{1-exp(-2y)}{1+exp(-2y)}. \tag{12}$$

such that the artificial neural networks (ANN) model in equation (10), a nonlinear function mapping will be performed from the past observations to the future value y_t, i.e.

$$y_t = f\left(y_{t-1}, ..., y_{t-p}, w\right) + \varepsilon_t \tag{13}$$

where w is a vector of all parameters and $f(\bullet)$ is a function determined by the network structure and connection weights.

Figure 3. Artificial Neural Network Structure $N^{(p-q-1)}$

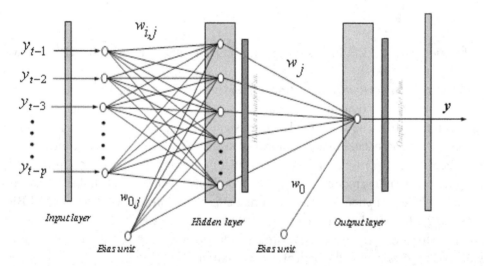

Thus, the neural network is the same as a nonlinear auto-regression model. The simple network given in (10) is extremely powerful in that it is able to approximate the arbitrary function as the number of the hidden nodes, q, is appropriately large (Khashei and Bijari, 2010). There is no exact method that can be used to choose parameter q since it is data-dependent. The nonlinear autocorrelation structure of the time series is determined by the lagged observations, p, which is estimated from artificial neural networks (ANN) model.

However, pruning algorithm, canonical decomposition method and the network information criteria can be used to find the optimal structure of the artificial neural networks (ANN) model. Furthermore, there are many other methods that can be employed in finding the optimal structure of the ANN model but these methods are somehow very difficult to implement. In general, these methods rely on testing various networks with different numbers of inputs and hidden nodes (p,q) then estimate generalization error and select the network with the most minimal generalization error. The parameters are evaluated such that the cost function (aggregate accuracy criterion) of neural network is limited, for example, mean squared error:

$$E = \frac{1}{N}\sum_{n=1}^{N}(e_i)^2 = \frac{1}{N}\sum_{n=1}^{N}\left(y_t - \left(w_0 + \sum_{j=1}^{q} w_j g\left(w_{0j} + \sum_{i=1}^{p} w_{ij} y_{t-i} \right) \right) \right)^2 \tag{14}$$

Given that N is the number of error terms, an efficient nonlinear optimization algorithm are employed but not the basic back-propagation training algorithm (Khashei and Bijari, 2010) where neural network parameters, w_{ij}, are altered by an amount Δw_{ij}, according to the following formula:

$$\Delta w_{ij} = -\tau \frac{\partial E}{\partial w_{ij}} \tag{15}$$

where (τ) is the learning rate and $\frac{\partial E}{\partial w_{ij}}$ is the partial derivative of the function E with respect to the weight, w_{ij}. This derivative is generally figured in two passes; forward pass, an input vector from the preparation set is connected to the input units of the network and is spread through the network layer by layer creating the last output, and backward pass, the output of the network is compared with the optimal output and the subsequent error is then propagated in reverse through the network modifying the network. Mcclelland et al., (1986) presented a momentum term δ to equation (15) to accelerate the learning procedure, while keeping away from the instability of the algorithm.

$$\Delta w_{ij}(t+1) = -\tau \frac{\partial E}{\partial w_{ij}} + \delta \Delta w_{ij}(t) \tag{16}$$

The momentum term may likewise be useful in prohibiting the learning process from being trapped into poor local minima, and the chapter uses the interval of [0,1] for training the neural network model.

Structural Vector Autoregressive (SVAR): To evaluate the possible drivers of portfolio inflows into emerging markets, this chapter applies the structural identification methodology of vector autoregressive models (SVAR) developed by the purported AB-model of Amisano and Giannini (1997). SVAR model allows researchers to impose limitations on structural relationships by using the theoretical assumptions on the model of which unrestricted vector autoregressive model has a shortcoming. This can be realized by presenting a theoretical and some auxiliary limitations to achieve econometric identification issue, assuming that $\Sigma = E[\varepsilon_t \varepsilon_t]$ presents the covariance matrix of the residuals. Thereby, the structural analysis uses the reduced form of the model given by:

$$A\varepsilon t = B\mu t \tag{17}$$

Given that the disturbance vector is of the form εt whereas a structural innovation vector in an unobserved form is denoted by μt equation (17) takes into account the reduced form disturbance and underlying structural shocks. Both A and B need some limitations with a dimension in the structural vector auto-regression (SVAR) analysis *kxk* to be added, noting that covariance matrix are present in the structural innovations given by $E[\mu_t\mu_t]$=I where the identity matrix is given by I so that μt can enforce the following limitations on A and B.

$$A\Sigma A = BB \qquad (18)$$

for the recognizable proof of the AB model, at least $k^2 + \dfrac{k(k-1)}{2} = k(3k-1)/2$ limitations are required. Hence, the need to consider variables used as part of vector autoregressive procedure to execute innovative accounting strategies, for instance, impulse responses require not to be stationary. Sims (1980) spearheaded paper on the VAR procedure contends against differencing regardless of whether the time series utilized takes after a unit root process while Sims et al., (1990) demonstrated that parameters that can be composed as coefficients on mean zero, non-integrated regressors, have normal asymptotic distributions and proposed that the basic practice with regards to transforming models to stationary form by difference operators appear likely that the series are of integrated form is unnecessary. Otherwise, some vital knowledge contained in the series would perhaps not be used by the researcher.

The log-likelihood function of the structural vector auto-regression (SVAR) model can be measured by way of a function of Π and Σ (Sims, 1986), and assuming that there are no cross limitations on Π and Σ or on the other hand, in more broad terms, that there are no limitations at all on Π meanwhile some form of limitations are enforced on Σ, the identification and analysis of the likelihood function can help to estimate the parameters of models:

$$L = c - \frac{T}{2}log|\Sigma| - \frac{T}{2}tr\left(\Sigma^{-1}\widehat{\Sigma}\right) \qquad (19)$$

Given $\widehat{\Sigma} = T^{-1}\widehat{V}\widehat{V}'$ is the log-likelihood concentrated with respect to Π. The estimation of Π comparing to the concentration of the log likelihood unmistakably concurs with the OLS estimator when the log likelihood is molded on the principal *p* observations of the sample. Other reliable estimators would yield asymptotically identical results with respect to the resulting estimation of the Σ matrix. Following Amisano and Giannini (1997), impulse response functions for structural VARs can be calculated by:

$$\Theta_0 = K^{-1} = \left(B^{-1}A\right)^{-1} = A^{-1}B, \Theta_i = JM^iJ'\Theta_0, \quad i = 1,2,3\ldots \qquad (20)$$

Given that:

$$M = \begin{bmatrix} A_1 & A_2 & \cdots & A_{k-1} & A_k \\ I_p & 0 & \ldots & 0 & 0 \\ 0 & I_p & \ldots & 0 & 0 \\ \vdots & \vdots & \vdots & \vdots & \vdots \\ 0 & 0 & \cdots & I_p & 0 \end{bmatrix} \qquad (21)$$

M is a ($pk*pk$) matrix, and J is a ($p*pk$) matrix and

$$\Theta_i = \Theta_i.\Theta_0, \Theta_0 = I_p, \Theta_i = \sum_{j=1}^{i} \Theta_{i-j} A_j, \quad i = 1,2,3\ldots \qquad (22)$$

where $A_i = 0$ for $i > k$. The impulse responses are predicted by substituting the theoretical variables by the respective estimators. The estimated impulse response that is stored up to horizon H in vector [$\Theta_1, \Theta_2, \ldots, \Theta_H$] is unbiased and asymptotically normally independently distributed with covariance matrix $\frac{1}{T}\Sigma_\Theta(H)$.

RESULTS AND DISCUSSIONS

Descriptive Statistics

Schumacker and Lomax (2004), and Kline (2005) suggested that prior to doing the actual analysis of any study; important issues must be addressed such as normality. In this section, besides the normality test, other descriptive statistics are discussed such as the mean and standard deviation of the series. These are summarized in Table 1.

The variables of interest have a multimodal distribution as shown in figure 4. Theoretical values of skewness and kurtosis based on the normality assumption must assume values of 0.00 and 3.00, respectively. However, the values of the two measures deviated from the theoretical values of both skewness and kurtosis; thereby the normality assumption is violated and the series is nonlinear. These results were quantified by employing the Jarqua Bera test and its probability value is 0.000, which rejects the null hypothesis of normality at all levels of significance 1%, 5% and 10% for all the included series. In terms of the normality test, with assumption being violated, Cziraky and Cumpek (2002) believe that by applying transformation such as the normal scores the series can be normally distributed. However, with the current study all the series still violates the normality assumption even after the appropriate transformation and this can be because all the variables are nonlinear in nature.

Knowing the characteristics of the series is of the paramount significant. For this purpose, the plot of the series is normally the one used to show any movements of the series from the start date to the end date of the series. Figure 4 shows the series plot of portfolio inflows into South Africa together with its key drivers covering the period of 01-March-2004 to 01-February-2016 consisting of 3111 observations.

Table 1. Descriptive statistics

Variable	Portfolio flows	Exchange rate	Real GDP	Inflation-linked bonds
Mean	9.425058	6.704596	13.15178	11.73551
Median	9.641215	6.637533	13.16707	11.76145
Std. dev.	1.390921	0.227674	0.129336	0.762516
Skewness	-5.922360	0.858337	-0.694901	-0.005083
Kurtosis	39.31928	3.044956	2.470845	1.534455
Jarqua Bera	189173.1	382.2633	286.6726	278.4249
P-value	0.000000	0.000000	0.000000	0.000000

A visual examination of the series plot shows that there are those periods in which South Africa received more portfolio inflows in their balance of payments. These periods are made up of those spikes in the data, which show volatility of the series. The series has several volatility periods, for assessing the stationarity of the series, this chapter employed the test of Bierens nonlinear unit root test (BNADF) and the results revealed that the series is nonlinear unit root.

Nonlinearity test results using the Brock-Dechert-Scheinkman (BDS) test and the CUSUM test of stability are presented in table 2 and figure 5, respectively.

Based on the BDS test results in table 2, the null hypothesis of linearity is rejected in favour of alternative of nonlinearity at all significance level for all dimensions. Furthermore, the CUSUM test of stability is employed to support the results of BDS test, it shows that the series is unstable since the blue line of the graph goes outside the critical red lines of the graph, this confirms the results of the BDS test that the series is nonlinear.

Figure 4. Graphical representation of the portfolio flows into South Africa and its key drivers

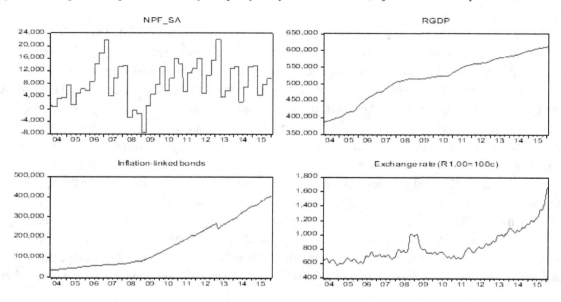

Table 2. The Brock-Dechert-Scheinkman (BDS) test results

Variable(s)	Dimension	BDS Statistic	Std. Error	Z-statistic	P-value
Portfolio flows	2	0.205356	0.000794	258.5316	0.0000
	3	0.348782	0.001256	277.6763	0.0000
	4	0.448666	0.001488	301.6065	0.0000
	5	0.517933	0.001542	335.9499	0.0000
	6	0.565674	0.001478	382.6946	0.0000
Real GDP	2	0.208568	0.001094	190.7141	0.0000
	3	0.355180	0.001731	205.2321	0.0000
	4	0.458269	0.002051	223.4017	0.0000
	5	0.530777	0.002128	249.4462	0.0000
	6	0.581791	0.002042	284.9178	0.0000
Exchange rate	2	0.206652	0.001505	137.2934	0.0000
	3	0.351737	0.002392	147.0623	0.0000
	4	0.453641	0.002848	159.3021	0.0000
	5	0.525224	0.002968	176.9860	0.0000
	6	0.575494	0.002861	201.1239	0.0000
Inflation-linked bonds	2	0.208844	0.000952	219.4497	0.0000
	3	0.355196	0.001502	236.5584	0.0000
	4	0.457813	0.001774	258.0323	0.0000
	5	0.529800	0.001835	288.7783	0.0000
	6	0.580320	0.001755	330.6671	0.0000

Figure 5. Cumulative Sum (CUSUM) test results

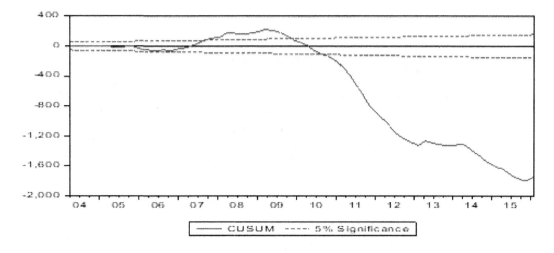

Modelling and Estimation of Portfolio Inflows

Here, the researchers outline the estimation of the models in this chapter and results of Support Vector Regression (SVR), Artificial Neural Network (ANN) and Structural Vector Auto-Regression (SVAR) models are presented.

Support vector regression (SVR): For building support vector regression forecasting model, the *e1071R package* proposed by Meyer et al. (2015) is adopted. The time series data is firstly scaled into the interval of [0,1] to avoid large input variables that affect the smaller input variables which may biased the results. In searching for the optimal parameters in the model of Support Vector Regression (SVR), the study set an interval of the cost (*C*) and epsilon (ε) to be (1:100) and *seq*(0,1,0.1), respectively. Thus the optimal parameters chosen by the model are 100 and 0.4 for both the cost and epsilon parameters, respectively. These model parameters give the best forecasting results (minimum testing MSE) with the best value of 0.018477 and are set as the model parameters in forecasting portfolio inflows. The coefficients of the estimated model function of the support vector regression are given as:

$$w = \begin{bmatrix} 1,1:3 \end{bmatrix} \begin{cases} -6.0605 & 10.5350 & -22.6916 \\ RGDP & exchange\ rate & inflation\ linked \end{cases}.$$

$b=0.738$

Figure 3, presents the two sets of parameters namely the cost parameter and the epsilon of the model. The model has the best performance in the darker blue area were the best performing parameters are (epsilon and cost parameters).

Figure 6. performance of the SVM regression model

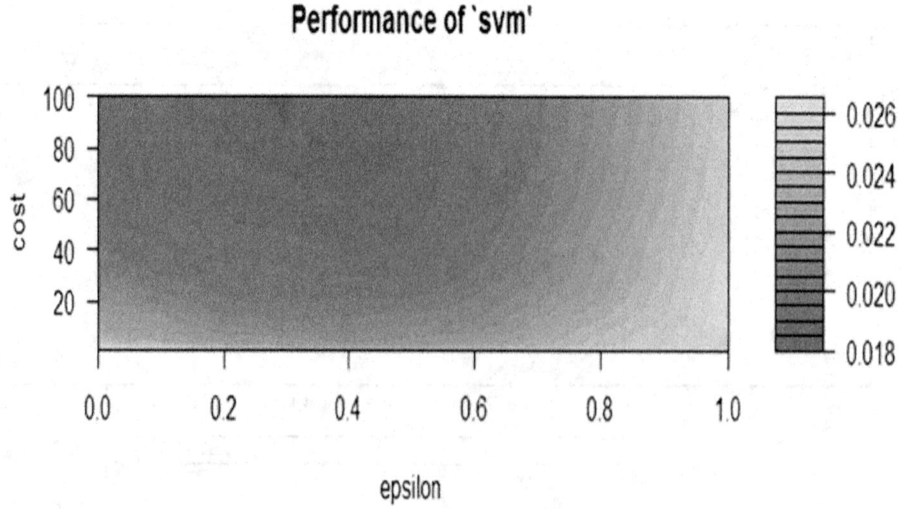

Artificial Neural Networks (ANNs): In building artificial neural networks (ANNs) model, the *neuralnet R package* of Fritsch et al. (2016) is used, the data set was scaled based on the interval of [0,1] so that the widely used activation function of logistic function could be used. Backpropagation algorithm is employed in training the neural network model. Since the response variable is numeric in nature the sum of squared error was used as the measuring error of the network. The threshold used is of the default of 0.01. The results of neural networks are presented in table 3.

Table 3. The Artificial Neural Networks (ANNs) matrix

Error	25.7554
Reached threshold	0.0097
Steps	13488
Intercept to 1layhid1	4.6054
RGDP to 1layhid1	-16.9177
Exchange rate to 1layhid1	-5.4977
Inflation linked bonds to 1layhid1	15.7947
Intercept to 1layhid2	-4.2122
RGDP to 1layhid2	8.7387
Exchange rate to 1layhid2	2.5802
Inflation linked bonds to 1layhid2	-7.4104
Intercept to portfolio flows	1.4089
1layhid.1 to portfolio flows	-1.0273
1layhid.2 to portfolio flows	-1.8104

Figure 7. The Artificial Neural Networks architectural structure

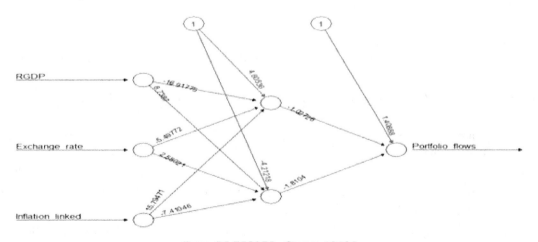

Error: 25.755375 Steps: 13488

In reaching absolute partial derivative, it took the training process of 13488 steps and that obtained smallest error function which is smaller than 0.01 (the default value of the threshold). The predicted weights have interval of -16.92 to 15.79, for instance, the intercept of the first hidden layer are 4.605 and -4.212 and the three weights leading to the first hidden neuron are estimated as -16.918, -5.498 and -7.410 for the covariates of RGDP, exchange rate and inflation linked. Figure 7 presents the architecture of the neural network model estimated for this study and it is made up of four input layer, 2 hidden layers and one output layer.

Structural vector autoregressive (SVAR): In estimating SVAR model, the unrestricted VAR model is estimated on the four stationary variables. The unrestricted VAR (8) model is initially estimated using AIC, SBC and HQC selected lag length (8) for the model. This chapter applies structural restrictions and assumed that portfolio flows are affected by all the shocks on the other variables. It is also assumed that exchange rate is responsive to shocks on the real gross domestic product. Inflation is also assumed to be responsive to shocks on both exchange rate and real gross domestic product. Thus the study used the AB model given as:

$$\begin{bmatrix} 1 & 0 & 0 & 0 \\ c(1) & 1 & 0 & 0 \\ c(2) & 0 & 1 & 0 \\ c(3) & 0 & 0 & 1 \end{bmatrix} \begin{bmatrix} \mu_t npf\_sa \\ \mu_t rgdp \\ \mu_t inflation \\ \mu_t exchangerate \end{bmatrix} = A$$

$$\begin{bmatrix} c(4) & 0 & 0 & 0 \\ 0 & c(5) & 0 & 0 \\ 0 & 0 & c(6) & 0 \\ 0 & 0 & 0 & c(7) \end{bmatrix} \begin{bmatrix} \varepsilon_t npf\_sa \\ \varepsilon_t rgdp \\ \varepsilon_t inflation \\ \varepsilon_t exchangerate \end{bmatrix} = B$$

Structural vector auto-regression (SVAR) estimated model is presented in figure 8, according to the results the model is over identified with 3 degrees of freedom. The LR test statistic estimated for the system identification restrictions under the null hypothesis is $\chi^2(3) = 8.39E+09$ with a probability value of 0.0000. The structural parameters are estimated by a method of scoring (analytic derivatives). Furthermore, the SVAR impulse response function (IRF) is represented in table 4 with periods of 10 days using 95% confidence interval.

Since there are no large margins or the confidence intervals, this gives a margin of certainty that the results estimated is reliable and unbiased. As expected, the portfolio inflows have a positive and negative response to its own shocks for the first period of the shock. Accordingly, it is seen that the 'push' factors that affect portfolio inflows are the real gross domestic product together with pull factor of exchange rate. The response of portfolio inflows due to shocks on inflation is along the zero line, thereby there is a positive shock to portfolio inflows that has been brought by inflation as a push factor. After taking into consideration the structural factorization of the impulse responses, table 4 presents the results of the variance decomposition of structural vector auto-regression (SVAR) model.

Figure 8. Structural Vector Auto-Regression (SVAR) Impulse Response Function

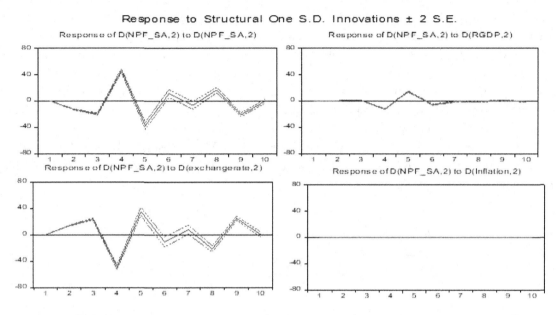

Table 4. Structural Vector Auto-Regression (SVAR) Variance Decomposition

Variance period	Portfolio flows	RGDP	Inflation-linked bonds	Exchange rate
1	100.0000	0.000000	0.000000	0.000000
2	99.93822	0.000747	0.057904	0.003133
3	99.85827	0.003058	0.126535	0.012141
4	99.61583	0.202605	0.130053	0.051513
5	99.28494	0.510752	0.132892	0.071419
6	99.23974	0.550461	0.136562	0.073234
7	99.23805	0.550547	0.137191	0.074209
8	99.22872	0.550732	0.138911	0.081636
9	99.21513	0.552498	0.140840	0.091535
10	99.21462	0.552880	0.141001	0.091503

Variance decomposition analysis indicates that over the 10 periods of variation, forecast error variance of portfolio inflows of 99% can be attributed to its own shocks. The results also show that the variable which shows the best explanation (forecast error variance) is the real gross domestic product with a shock variable explaining nearly 55% of the variation to portfolio inflows. A shock to the inflation variable explains nearly 14% of variation to portfolio inflows while the least variable which explains the minimum variation of 9% is the exchange rate to portfolio inflows. Overall, the pull factors in the study explain nearly 69% of variation to portfolio inflows. All the estimation results indicate that the pull factors are indeed dominant over the push factors in acquiring the portfolio inflows as a form of investment into the South African economy one which is considered as an emerging market economy.

Performance criteria: According to the chapter objectives forecasting accuracy of the two machine learning (Support Vector Regression (SVR) and Artificial Neural Networks (ANNs)) models are compared. Forecasting of the future value of any economic variable(s) is of great importance to the academia, potential investors, decision making and policy formulation individuals. These models (SVR and ANNs) are here used to model and forecast portfolio inflows together with its determinants or drivers. Also, determine whether these models could be of use to financial forecasting of economic variable in terms of portfolio inflows. In terms of measuring the accuracy of the included models the study used the five criteria to assess the accuracy of the models. The five criteria are Mean Squared Error (MSE), Root Mean Squared Error (RMSE), Mean Absolute Error (MAE), Mean Absolute Squared Error (MASE) and Root Mean Squared Log Error (RMSLE) used as measuring error matrices. The results of these measurements are presented in table 5.

Table 5. Forecasting Accuracy of SVR, ANNs and SVAR

Performance criterion	SVAR	SVR	ANN (3-2-1) model
MSE	N/A	0.0174	0.2637
RMSE	N/A	0.1561	0.5135
MAE	N/A	0.1028	0.2637
MASE	N/A	14.3975	12.9335
RMSLE	N/A	0.0851	0.3559

From the results, four of the five criteria select the Support Vector Regression (SVR) model as having the highest accuracy compared to the other model while only one criterion (MASE) chooses the artificial neural networks model. Thereby it can be concluded that the support vector regression model simulates and forecasts portfolio inflows better than the artificial neural networks (ANNs) model.

Comparing predictive accuracy of the models: According to Diebold (2015) the question that Diebold-Mariano (DM) test is answering is whether one model is truly superior to another model or is it mere luck. Lower error matrices do not necessarily mean that the forecasting ability of one model is superior to another one, as the difference between the error matrices may not be statistically significant. Hence, the need to assess the predictive accuracy of the models is apparent and the Diebold-Mariano test was employed to measure the predictive accuracy of the models. Summary of the results are presented in table 6.

Table 6. Comparison of Model Accuracy: Diebold-Mariano Test

Variable	Hypothesis	Forecast horizon	Loss function power	t-statistic	P-value
Portfolio flows	ANN vs. SVR	1	2	8.5086376	< 0.0001

The results in table 6 show that the null hypothesis of equal predictive accuracy of the models; Artificial Neural Network (ANN) and Support Vector Regression (SVR) is rejected since the respective probability value (< 0.0001) is less than the default significant level of 5% or 0.05. Furthermore, since the t-statistics (8.5086376) is positive it can be concluded that the estimated SVR model is more accurate than the estimated artificial neural networks model for portfolio flows.

FUTURE RESEARCH DIRECTIONS

machine learning techniques have been shown to estimate/model portfolio inflows better than conventional econometric models. Therefore, this work may be extended to cover the use of these machine learning techniques in modelling portfolio inflows of other banks in South Africa and other nations of the world.

CONCLUSION

This chapter showed that machine learning techniques can model portfolio inflows better than the econometric conventional model. In assessing the modelling and forecasting performance of the models, the error metrics; MSE, RMSE, MAE, MASE and RMSLE were utilized. The results showed that the support vector regression (SVR) model has the best modelling performance in modelling and forecasting portfolio inflows. In case of determining the factors that affect the allocation of portfolio inflows into South Africa based on the structural vector auto-regression (SVAR) model, it was shown that 69% of variation in the portfolio inflows is explained by pull factors (real gross domestic product and inflation linked bonds) and 9% was explained by push factor (exchange rate). However, 99% of variation in the portfolio inflows was attributed to its own shocks. Therefore, it is concluded that support vector regression (SVR) model is more accurate than its counterpart, artificial neural network (ANNs). Hence, this chapter recommends that the banking sector particularly the RMB bank should use these machine learning techniques in modelling portfolio inflows when embarking on their research.

LIMITATIONS

The study is restricted to using the historic data of portfolio inflows and its key drivers sourced from RMB covering the period of 01st March 2004 to 01st February 2016 on the basis of accessibility of data. There exist numerous models that can be used but for the current study, only three models; SVR, ANNs and SVAR are considered based on their empirical literature. Due to limited empirical studies on machine-learning models, the study used some sources which are older than ten years. Also, for the lack of appropriate syntax, the KSS-NADF is not employed in the current study.

ACKNOWLEDGMENT

The authors would like to express their sincere thanks to the editor and anonymous reviews for their time and valuable suggestions.

This research received no specific grant from any funding agency in the public, commercial, or not-for-profit sectors.

REFERENCES

Adebiyi, A.A., Adewumi, A.O. & Ayo, C.K., (2014). Comparison of ARIMA and artificial neural networks models for stock price prediction. *Journal of Applied Mathematics.* . doi:10.1155/2014/614342

Adebiyi, A. A., Ayo, C. K., Adebiyi, M. O., & Otokiti, S. (2012). Stock price prediction using neural network with hybridized market indicators. *Journal of Emerging Trends in Computing and Information Sciences, 3,* 1–9.

Ahlquist, J. S. (2006). Economic policy, institutions, and capital flows: Portfolio and direct investment flows in developing countries. *International Studies Quarterly, 50*(3), 681–704. doi:10.1111/j.1468-2478.2006.00420.x

Ajide, K. B., & Raheem, A. J. (2015). Determinants of foreign capital flows into Nigeria: A structural var analysis. *Business and Management Research Journal, 5,* 1–13.

Amisano, G., & Giannini, C. (1997). *From VAR models to Structural VAR models. In Topics in Structural VAR Econometrics.* Springer-Verlag Berlin. doi:10.1007/978-3-642-60623-6

Bing, Y., Hao, J. K., & Zhang, S. C. (2012). Stock Market Prediction Using Artificial Neural Networks. *Advanced Engineering Forum, 6-7,* 1055-1060.

Cao, L. (2003). Support vector machines experts for time series forecasting. *Neurocomputing, 51,* 321–339. doi:10.1016/S0925-2312(02)00577-5

Chen, K. Y., & Wang, C. H. (2007). Support vector regression with genetic algorithms in forecasting tourism demand. *Tourism Management, 28*(1), 215–226. doi:10.1016/j.tourman.2005.12.018

Çulha, A. (2006). A structural VAR analysis of the determinants of capital flows into Turkey. *Central Bank Review, 2,* 11–35.

Cziraky, D., & Cumpek, T. (2002). Multivariate analysis of the European economic and defence structure. *Croatian International Relations Review, 8,* 23–35.

Diebold, F. X. (2015). Comparing predictive accuracy, twenty years later: A personal perspective on the use and abuse of Diebold–Mariano tests. *Journal of Business & Economic Statistics, 33*(1), 1–9. doi:10.1080/07350015.2014.983236

Egly, P. V., Johnk, D. W., & Liston, D. P. (2010). Foreign Portfolio Investment Inflows to the United States: The Impact of Investor Risk Aversion and US Stock Market Performance. *North American Journal of Finance and Banking Research, 4*(4), 25–41.

Ekeocha, P.C., Ekeocha, C., Malaolu, V. & Oduh, M., (2012). Modelling the long run determinants of foreign portfolio investment in Nigeria. *Journal of Economics and Sustainable Development, 3,* 194-205.

Fritsch, S., Guenther, F., & Guenther, M. F. (2016). *Package 'neuralnet'*. The Comprehensive R Archive Network.

Hong, W. C. (2009). Chaotic particle swarm optimization algorithm in a support vector regression electric load forecasting model. *Energy Conversion and Management, 50*(1), 105–117. doi:10.1016/j.enconman.2008.08.031

Hong, W. C., & Pai, P. F. (2007). Potential assessment of the support vector regression technique in rainfall forecasting. *Water Resources Management, 21*(2), 495–513. doi:10.100711269-006-9026-2

Kaastra, I., & Boyd, M. (1996). Designing a neural network for forecasting financial and economic time series. *Neurocomputing, 10*(3), 215–236. doi:10.1016/0925-2312(95)00039-9

Kazem, A., Sharifi, E., Hussain, F. K., Saberi, M., & Hussain, O. K. (2013). Support vector regression with chaos-based firefly algorithm for stock market price forecasting. *Applied Soft Computing, 13*(2), 947–958. doi:10.1016/j.asoc.2012.09.024

Khashei, M., & Bijari, M. (2010). An artificial neural network (p, d, q) model for timeseries forecasting. *Expert Systems with Applications, 37*(1), 479–489. doi:10.1016/j.eswa.2009.05.044

Kline, R. B. (2005). *Methodology in the social sciences. In Principles and practice of structural equation modeling*. Guilford Press.

Korap, L. (2010). *Identification of 'pull' & 'push' factors for the portfolio flows: SVAR evidence from the Turkish economy. MPRA Paper 24275*. University Library of Munich.

Lo Duca, M. (2012). *Modelling the time varying determinants of portfolio flows to emerging markets*. Working Paper Series of European Central Bank, Kaiserstrasse 29, D-60311 Frankfurt am Main, Germany.

Lu, C. J., Lee, T. S., & Chiu, C. C. (2009). Financial time series forecasting using independent component analysis and support vector regression. *Decision Support Systems, 47*(2), 115–125. doi:10.1016/j.dss.2009.02.001

Mcclelland, J. L., Rumelhart, D. E., & Hinton, G. E. (1986). A general framework for parallel distributed processing. In *Parallel distributed processing: Explorations in the microstructure of cognition. Bradford Book*.

Meyer, D., Dimitriadou, E., Hornik, K., Weingessel, A. & Leisch, F. (2015). *e1071: misc functions of the department of statistics, probability theory group (formerly: E1071), TU Wien*. R package version 1.6-7.

Raghavan, M., Churchill, A., & Tian, J. (2014). *The Effects of Portfolio Capital Flows and Domestic Credit on the Australian Economy* (Unpublished manuscript). University of Tasmania, Launceston, Australia.

Ramani, P. & Murarka, P. (2013). *Stock market prediction using artificial neural network*. Doi:10.21090/ijaerd.c25

Schumacker, R. E., & Lomax, R. G. (2004). A beginner's guide to structural equation modeling. Psychology Press.

Schwarz, G. (1978). Estimating the dimension of a model. *Annals of Statistics, 6*(2), 461–464. doi:10.1214/aos/1176344136

Sims, C. A. (1980). Macroeconomics and reality. *Econometrica*, *48*(1), 1–48. doi:10.2307/1912017

Sims, C. A. (1986). Are forecasting models usable for policy analysis? Quarterly Review, 2-16.

Sims, C. A., Stock, J. H., & Watson, M. W. (1990). Inference in linear time series models with some unit roots. *Econometrica*, *58*(1), 113–144. doi:10.2307/2938337

KEY TERMS AND DEFINITIONS

Bank: An institution dealing in financial issues, which is licenced to accepts deposits and make loans available to public.

Exchange Rate: A value of someone nation's currency in relation to the currency of another nation or economic zone.

Inflation Linked Bonds: These are securities designed to help protect investors from inflation.

Machine Learning: A science of applying artificial intelligence that provides systems the ability to automatically learn and improve without being explicitly programmed.

Mean Absolute Error: A measure of average magnitude of the errors in predictions without giving preference to their direction.

Portfolio Inflows: An influx of a group of financial assets as well as their equivalent funds.

Real Gross Domestic Product: A macroeconomic measure of country's total economic output taking into account the impact of inflation.

This research was previously published in the Handbook of Research on Smart Technology Models for Business and Industry; pages 329-350, copyright year 2020 by Engineering Science Reference (an imprint of IGI Global).

Chapter 70
An Approach Combining DEA and ANN for Hotel Performance Evaluation

Himanshu Sharma
Department of Operational Research, University of Delhi, Delhi, India

Gunmala Suri
Panjab University, India

Vandana Savara
Rochester Institute of Technology, UAE

ABSTRACT

For a hotel to succeed in the long run, it becomes vital to achieve higher profits along with increased performance. The performance evaluation of a hotel can signify its sustainable competitiveness within the hospitality industry. This article performs a two-stage study that combines data envelopment analysis (DEA) and artificial neural network (ANN) to evaluate hotel performance. The first stage to evaluate the efficiency for hotels is by using the DEA technique. The input variables considered are the number of rooms and the ratings corresponding to six aspects of a hotel (service, room, value, location, sleep quality, and cleanliness). Also, revenue per available room (RevPAR) and customer satisfaction (CS) are the output variables. The distinguishing factor of this article is that it involves the use of EWOM for performance evaluation. In the second stage, the performance of the hotels is judged by using the ANN technique. The ANN results showed that the performance of the hotels is quite good. Finally, discussions based on the results and scope for future studies are provided.

DOI: 10.4018/978-1-6684-2408-7.ch070

INTRODUCTION

Due to the advancements in technology and changing market environment, the hotel industry is experiencing intense competition amongst its stakeholders. This insists for a breadth of resources along with various amenities being provided by hotels in order to handle the dynamicity within the industry along with sophisticated customer base. For a hotel to succeed in long run, it becomes vital for them to achieve higher profits along with increased performance (Kim, Cho, & Brymer, 2013). Hotel's performance is the aggregated efforts of all its departments, working in foreground or background. These efforts can be evaluated to get a good measure of performance, by ensuring whether the inputs are efficiently being transformed into outputs (De Pelsmacker, Van Tilburg, & Holthof, 2018). Therefore, the performance evaluation of a hotel can signify its sustainable competitiveness within the hospitality industry. Previous studies have evaluated hotel performance with reference to various domains such as strategy (Salem, 2014; Tavitiyaman, Qiu Zhang, & Qu, 2012; Tavitiyaman, Qu, & Zhang, 2011), quality management (Amin, Aldakhil, Wu, Rezaei, & Cobanoglu, 2017; Pereira-Moliner, Claver-Cortés, Molina-Azorín, & Tarí, 2012; Wang, Chen, & Chen, 2012), environment (Assaf, Josiassen, Woo, Agbola, & Tsionas, 2017; Marco-Lajara, Claver-Cortés, & Úbeda-García, 2014; Marco-Lajara, Claver-Cortés, Úbeda-García, & Zaragoza-Sáez, 2016), marketing and information technology (IT) (Hua, Morosan, & DeFranco, 2015; Shuai & Wu, 2011; Sirirak, Islam, & Ba Khang, 2011), human resource management (Al-Refaie, 2015; Chand, 2010; Kim et al., 2013), and many more. However, much of the studies were empirical in nature, using regression analysis or partial least squares (PLS) as the analysis technique. The frequently considered independent (input) variables under prior studies include the number of rooms, number of full-time employees, operating expenses (employee salaries, food and beverage costs, room costs, utilities, maintenance fees, and other relevant operating costs), service quality, human resource and information technology related strategies, competitive strategies and organization structure, and many more. On the other hand, the frequently used dependent (output) variables include revenue, occupancy rate, return on assets and investments, profitability, and turnover. The input variables in this study are number of rooms and the ratings corresponding to six aspects of a hotel (service, room, value, location, sleep quality, and cleanliness). The output variables are RevPAR (revenue per available room) and customer satisfaction (CS).

With the proliferation of digitalization into every domain, the significance of the feedbacks provided by the customers in the form of textual comments or ratings, termed as electronic word-of-mouth (EWOM), is being witnessed by practitioners (Sharma & Aggarwal, 2019). This is especially important for hotels, which come under experienced commodity, and so they cannot be judged by a customer prior to his stay (Radojevic, Stanisic, Stanic, & Davidson, 2018). Moreover, it is observed that customers pay heed to EWOM before making a booking decision (marketmyhotel, 2019). This behavior portrayed by the customers has encouraged many online travel websites such as Yelp, TripAdvisor, Expedia, and booking.com, which allow guests to share their stay experience (Tandon, Sharma, & Aggarwal, 2019; Zhang & Cole, 2016). In light of the above discussion, it becomes seamless to neglect the role of EWOM for evaluating the performance of hotels. Few empirical studies performed previously have introduced the importance of EWOM for hotel's performance evaluation (Blal & Sturman, 2014; Kim & Park, 2017; Phillips, Barnes, Zigan, & Schegg, 2017; Xie, So, & Wang, 2017; Xie, Zhang, & Zhang, 2014; Xie, Zhang, Zhang, Singh, & Lee, 2016). Apart from the financial variables, the additional input variables considered were valence (rating), volume (number of reviews), and variation in ratings (variance). Also, customer satisfaction is taken to be the additional output variable. Two key research questions are attempted to solve in this paper

- How the efficiency varies between the two sets of hotel category on adding customer satisfaction as output variable?
- How efficiently the resources (inputs and outputs) contribute to the hotel performance?

In literature, we have two methods for efficiency evaluation which are parametric (stochastic frontier function/econometric regression theory) and non-parametric (data envelopment analysis/free disposal hull) (Charnes, Cooper, Lewin, Morey, & Rousseau, 1984). In order to tackle the first question, we make use of data envelopment analysis (DEA) to determine the efficiency score of the hotels, under variable returns to scale. However, DEA has a demerit that it cannot be used to predict the performance of the decision-making units (DMUs) considered in a study (Azadeh, Saberi, Moghaddam, & Javanmardi, 2011). This is where artificial neural network (ANN) comes handy in solving the second research question. Overall, the study combines DEA and ANN to measure performance of hotels through two-stage process. This methodology has been adopted for performance evaluation in earlier studies (Azadeh et al., 2011; Kwon, 2014, 2017; Kwon, Lee, & Roh, 2016; Singh, Pant, & Goel, 2018).

The study performs the proposed methodology on two sets of hotels combined on the basis of their star rating (also a symbol of hotel quality) i.e. 2-3 star and 4-5 star. Earlier studies have also performed their analysis using these sets as they show homogenous characteristics within their group (De Pelsmacker et al., 2018; Viglia, Minazzi, & Buhalis, 2016; Yang & Cai, 2016). The paper assesses the EWOM data for 78 hotels in Delhi NCR from TripAdvisor website and collects the financial data separately. The rest of the paper is organized as follows. The next section provides a comprehensive overview of the literature on hotel performance. Section 3 discusses the proposed methodology, while, the fourth section performs a case study based on the methodology. Section 5 provides discussions and implications based on the study, and the last section discusses the limitations and scope for future studies.

LITERATURE REVIEW

Hotel Performance

Prior studies have evaluated the performance of hotels using various input (independent) and output (dependent) variables, under diverse domains. Chand (2010) used structural equation modeling (SEM) to investigate the impact of HRM practices on service quality, customer satisfaction, and hotel performance. The analysis performed on data obtained from 52 Indian hotels resulted in positive causal relationship between the performance and its antecedents. Another study considering 95 hotels from USA was performed to check hotel performance under HRM domain (Kim et al., 2013). The input variables include customer satisfaction, employee satisfaction, hotel size, customer mix, and hotel type; whereas, the performance metrics included ADR, RevPAR, TRevPAR, restaurant F&B revenue, and banquet F&B revenue. An analysis using hierarchical multiple regression showed significant impact of these exogenous variables on performance of hotels. Al-Refaie (2015) took HRM based data of 52 hotels situated in Jordan to study their performance. SEM results validated the association of HRM practices, service quality, employee satisfaction, employee loyalty, customer satisfaction, and customer loyalty with hotel performance. All the causal relationships were positive in nature.

Wang et al. (2012) studied the impact of total quality management (TQM) and market orientation on hotel performance. Conducting SEM and discriminant analysis on 558 samples collected from Taiwan, resulted in significance of the stated hypotheses. Another study was conducted to validate the impact of QM and environmental management over hotel performance, which is measured in terms of financial performance, market success and stakeholder satisfaction (Pereira-Moliner et al., 2012). Partial least squares (PLS) was applied on a data of 3900 Spanish hotels to get the analysis results. Amin et al. (2017) investigated the relationship between TQM, employee satisfaction, and hotel performance using data of 25 hotels situated in Malaysia. PLS results validated the causal relationship between them. A performance evaluation model was proposed for evaluating 57 hotels in Taiwan (Hsieh & Lin, 2010). Relational network DEA was constructed by considering the efficiency and effectiveness of hotels' functional departments as input and revenue as output. Wu, Liang, and Song (2010) proposed an integer DEA model for comparing efficiency of 23 hotels situated in Taipei. The inputs considered are the total rooms, total employees, food and beverage (F&B) capacity, and total operating costs; while the output variables include guest room revenues, F&B revenues, and other revenues.

Tavitiyaman et al. (2011) evaluated the performance of 317 hotels in US based on Porter's five forces for competitive advantage in industry. SEM findings supported that competitive HRM and IT strategies positively affect performance of the hotels. Another study was conducted by them to inspect the causal relationship of competitive strategies and organizational structure with hotel performance (Tavitiyaman et al., 2012). Multiple regression technique was run on survey-based data of US hotels to check the validation of hypotheses. Salem (2014) investigated the impact of knowledge management (KM) over hotel performance and innovations using data obtained through 113 hotels located in Egypt. PLS results showed significant positive relationship of KM with performance of hotels. An algorithm combining DEA and grey entropy method was formulated to determine the effect of internet marketing tools over hotel performance (Shuai & Wu, 2011). The study considered input variables as the number of rooms, number of full-time employees, and operating expenses; while the outputs were total revenue generated from rooms and F&B. Another study was conducted in Thailand to judge the persuasion of information and communication technology (ICT) over hotel performance (Sirirak et al., 2011). Multiple regression analysis was performed to validate the impact of ICT inputs over operational productivity and customer satisfaction. Hua et al. (2015) investigated the impact of electronic commerce expenditures over the financial performance of hotels. Linear regression was run on data obtained from 275 hotels in US to validate the stated hypotheses.

Assaf, Josiassen, Cvelbar, and Woo (2015) studied the impact of customer voice (i.e. customer satisfaction and complaints) on hotel performance. A two-limit TOBIT model was run on a survey data of 56 hotels in Croatia in order to check the significance of the developed hypotheses. Another study was conducted, which considered the inputs to be marketing, operations, and environment capabilities along with diversification strategy, with performance measurement as the goal (Ramanathan, Ramanathan, & Zhang, 2016). Regression analysis and DEA was applied on data of UK hotels to determine the significance of the causal relationships. Similar study was performed using DEA-based bi-objective model to check how efficiently the inputs i.e. marketing and operation strategies result in performance of hotels (Yin et al., 2019). The algorithm was applied on data obtained from 68 hotels located in Taiwan.

Marco-Lajara et al. (2014) studied how hotel performance is affected by the degree of business agglomeration. Multiple regression was performed on a data of 2468 hotels in Spain to get the relevant research findings. The finding showed positive relationship between most of the studies. Similar study was conducted to check the impact of geographical location on performance of hotels by taking data of 1869 hotels in Spain (Marco-Lajara et al., 2016). Another study investigated the impact of group of interrelated hotels (called clusters) on the economic performance of hotels (Peiró-Signes, Segarra-Oña, Miret-Pastor, & Verma, 2015). Location quotient was calculated based on the dataset of US hotels to distinguish high economic hotels from the lower ones. The impact of regional factors was investigated on the performance of hotels (Z. Yang & Cai, 2016). Ordinary least squares and negative binomial regression was run on data of hotels obtained from China in order to validate the hypotheses. Most of the associations were positive in nature. Assaf et al. (2017) performed regression analysis on a data of 560 hotels. The results supported the key determinants of hotel performance namely quality educational system, government support, disposable income, and number of international arrivals within a tourism destination.

Hotel Performance and EWOM

Xie et al. (2014) investigated the impact of online reviews and ratings (EWOM) on hotel performance. After running linear regression on a panel data of 843 hotels, the research findings supported the influence of overall rating, attribute ratings (value, location, and cleanliness), variation and volume of reviews, and the number of management responses over the performance of hotels, measured by RevPAR. Another study considered review valence and volume as independent variables for measuring performance through RevPAR (Blal & Sturman, 2014). A hierarchical linear modeling was applied on a data of 319 hotels situated in London for the purpose of validating the stated hypotheses. Phillips et al. (2015) combined multiple regression and ANN on a sample data of 235 hotels situated in Switzerland on RevPAR. The input variables can be divided into location, infrastructure, positioning, and customer reviews. Xie et al. (2016) collected customer reviews and management responses from 1045 hotels situated in Texas in order to judge the hotel performance. An econometric modeling approach was used to validate the hypotheses, by considering total revenue per available room (TRevPAR) and RevPAR as revenue. Another study was conducted to check the association of review score, volume, and valence with hotel occupancy rate as performance measure (Viglia et al., 2016). The developed hypotheses were validated by running linear regression on data obtained form 346 hotels located in Rome.

Phillips et al. (2017) performed an empirical study to determine the antecedents of hotel performance, measured in terms of RevPAR and occupancy. PLS was applied on review and financial data of 442 hotels situated in Switzerland in order to check the dependency of physical aspects; quality of food and drink; and human aspects of service provision. A study was conducted to compare the role of traditional customer satisfaction and online customer reviews over financial performance of hotels (Kim & Park, 2017). Hierarchical multiple regression was run to determine the significance of the stated hypotheses. Research findings supported an increase in the importance of online reviews amongst customers. Another study performed regression analysis on a data of 22,483 management responses to 76,649 online reviews, to study their influence on the financial performance of hotels (Xie et al., 2017). (De Pelsmacker et al. (2018)) studied the influence of digital marketing strategies on hotel room occupancy and RevPAR by collecting EWOM and financial data for 132 hotels located in Belgium. Hayes' PROCESS was used to check the dependency of strategies such as digital marketing plan, responsiveness to reviews, and monitoring and tracking online review information.

The above discussions generate few research gaps that are filled in this paper.

- Most of the studies empirically evaluated the performance of hotels. This study uses a mathematical programming-based approach to evaluate performance.
- Few studies have focused on introducing the role of EWOM while measuring performance. The present study uses both financial and ratings data of hotels to measure hotel's performance.
- This is the first study to combine DEA and ANN for evaluating performance of hotels, while considering EWOM as input variable.

METHOD

In this we discuss DEA and ANN approaches and finally provide the overall methodology adopted in this paper.

DEA

Data envelopment analysis (DEA) is a linear programming-based approach introduced by Charnes et al. (1978). The main objective of this method is to convert multiple inputs into multiple outputs in order to produce relative efficiency score of the decision-making units (DMUs) i.e. the candidate entities that need to be compared. Therefore, DEA can only be utilized in those cases where the DMUs show homogeneity in terms of functionality as well as input/output variables (Charnes et al., 1984). It is a non-parametric technique with two different orientations namely output-oriented and input-oriented (Kwon, 2017). The input-oriented models focus on minimizing the inputs, whereas, the output-oriented models aim to maximize the outputs. The basic programming is denoted as CCR model and it followed constant returns to scale (CRS). Later, Banker, Charnes, and Cooper (1984) proposed a model based on variable returns to scale (VRS) denoted as BCC model. The advantage of BCC model is that it is not necessary for outputs/inputs to change in the same proportion as inputs/outputs (Kwon, 2014). Another important aspect of DEA is that it can be applied to small samples. The efficiency value of 1 indicates that the entities have successfully converted the input variables to the outputs.

In the hospitality industry, the returns for a hotel are influenced by the size of input and output variables (Poldrugovac, Tekavcic, & Jankovic, 2016). Therefore, it is appropriate to consider VRS or in other terms, the BCC model. Also, since the outputs are of maximization type, we make use of output-oriented model. The programming problem for the output-oriented BCC model is described below.

Maxθ

subject to

$$x_{io} \geq \sum_{j=1}^{n} \lambda_j x_{ij}, \quad i = 1,...,m$$

$$\theta y_{ro} \leq \sum_{j=1}^{n} \lambda_j y_{rj}, \quad r = 1,...,s \tag{1}$$

$$\sum_{j=1}^{n} \lambda_j = 1$$

$$\lambda j \geq 0$$

where the above model considers n DMUs ($j=1,\ldots,n$); each with m inputs and s outputs. The condition $\sum_{j=1}^{n} \lambda_j = 1$ denotes the significance of taking variable returns to scale, and converts CCR model into BCC.

ANN

Artificial neural network (ANN) approach is based on a biological nervous system of a human such as brain (Chong & Bai, 2014). It is a data-dependent technique rather than a model-based one and is buildup of highly interconnected processing units (called neurons) which work in synergy in order to resolve the problem in hand. ANN approach is adopted for particular applications such as pattern recognition, data classification, and many more (Al-Smadi, Qawasmeh, Al-Ayyoub, Jararweh, & Gupta, 2018; Liébana-Cabanillas et al., 2017; Phillips et al., 2015; Saumya, Singh, & Dwivedi, 2019). It is made up of three layers namely input, hidden, and output, respectively. The input layer consists of the inputs taken in the model. The hidden layer attaches weights to the inputs, evaluated during learning process. Finally, the output layer provides model estimates. ANN has an advantage of being able to approximate nonlinear problems and can also be utilized for forecasting/performance evaluation purposes (Kwon, 2014; Kwon et al., 2016; Singh et al., 2018). This study adopts multi-layer perceptrons (MLP) as the basis of ANN.

PROPOSED METHODOLOGY

In this section, we will discuss the steps performed to evaluate the performance of hotels by combining DEA and ANN. The major purpose for adopting ANN in this study is that DEA is powerful in evaluating efficiencies for each hotel, but it is incapable of predicting their performance. Moreover, we separately apply the methodology to 2-3 star and 4-5 star hotels, simultaneously. The steps are defined below:

Step 1. Data Collection

We collect the financial and ratings data for the particular hotels under study. The data for aspect ratings and overall ratings were accessed from TripAdvisor website.

Step 2. Obtain Efficiency Score using DEA

Using the input and output variables, the relative efficiency score for all the hotels are obtained through output-oriented BCC DEA model.

Step 3. Performance Evaluation using ANN

Finally, we apply ANN for predicting performance of each hotel. For this task, the projections of the input and output variables obtained through DEA are considered as the input nodes while the efficiency score obtained in the previous step is utilized as an output node.

CASE STUDY

In this section, we will perform the proposed methodology for performance of hotels located in India.

Step 1. Data Collection

The input variables considered in the study are aspect ratings and number of rooms. On the other hand, RevPAR and CS are taken as the output variables. In order to obtain the ratings data, we accessed the TripAdvisor data for Delhi NCR region (Roshchina, Cardiff, & Rosso, 2015). The data consists of an overall rating on a 5-point scale, which is taken to be a proxy for guest satisfaction in previous studies. Also, TripAdvisor allows guests to rate six aspects of the hotel on a 5-point scale such as service, room, value, location, sleep quality, and cleanliness. The data for the same was also accessed. The reason for selecting Delhi NCR is that it will be convenient for the authors to collect financial data through personal visits to the selected hotels. In all, 78 hotels are selected for which the ratings data is available. Moreover, the data describing the number of rooms and RevPAR is collected from these hotels. The 78 DMUs include 2-star hotels (22), 3-star hotels (24), 4-star hotels (18), and 5-star hotels (14). The descriptive statistics of the hotels is provided in Table 1.

Table 1. Descriptive statistics of variables

	Inputs													Outputs			
	Service		Room		Value		Location		Sleep quality		Cleanliness		Number of rooms		RevPAR (Rs)		CS	
	2-3*	4-5*	2-3*	4-5*	2-3*	4-5*	2-3*	4-5*	2-3*	4-5*	2-3*	4-5*	2-3*	4-5*	2-3*	4-5*	2-3*	4-5*
Min	1.03	1.12	1.67	2.59	1.83	2.47	2.12	2.23	1.10	2.39	1.23	1.70	30	60	2,000	6,000	1.89	2.03
Max	4.33	4.87	4.09	4.85	3.78	4.42	4.31	4.90	3.67	4.69	3.98	4.67	60	150	5,000	10,000	3.96	4.62
Mean	2.78	3.89	2.98	3.69	2.81	3.74	3.85	4.16	2.69	3.63	2.91	3.53	40.59	90.53	3,750	8,570	3.01	3.58
SD	1.05	0.81	0.98	0.67	0.72	0.60	0.84	0.67	0.67	0.65	0.86	0.77	4.67	5.89	126.18	325.23	0.82	0.67

Step 2. Obtain Efficiency Score using DEA

To evaluate the efficiency of the hotels, we divide the hotels into two groups i.e. 2-3 star and 4-5 star hotels. Also, we observed that all the inputs variables are correlated with at least one of the output variable, which is an assumption for applying DEA (Poldrugovac et al., 2016). We consider two models for efficiency analysis for each category of hotels. Under Model 1, we run output-oriented BCC DEA model given in equation 1 to generate scores using only RevPAR as output. For model 2, we consider both RevPAR as well as CS as output variables. The results for 2-3 star hotels is provide in Table 2 and for 4-5 star hotels in Table 3. MaxDEA software is used to get the efficiency scores.

Step 3. Performance Evaluation Using ANN

After getting the efficiency scores, the task becomes to judge how these hotels have performed under the presence of available data. The 7 inputs and 2 inputs are considered to be making the input layer. While, the efficiency score is taken as output layer. The projections obtained during the DEA analysis is forwarded for ANN analysis. Thus, in actuality, the projections of inputs and outputs form the input layer of ANN (Kwon et al., 2016; Singh et al., 2018). The ANN is applied using SPSS software. In order to minimize the problem of model over-fitting, we perform ten-fold cross validation. The data ratio in training to testing is set to 9:1. The numbers of hidden layers were automatically generated, whereas sigmoid activation function is used for hidden and output layers. To evaluate the prediction accuracy, we make use of RMSE (root mean square error) (Chong & Bai, 2014; Liébana-Cabanillas et al., 2017). The results of the ANN are presented in Table 4.

Table 2. Efficiency scores for 2-3 star hotels

Hotel	Model 1	Model 2	Hotel	Model 1	Model 2
1	.875	.934	24	1	1
2	.867	.980	25	1	1
3	.899	.921	26	1	1
4	.903	1	27	1	1
5	1	1	28	1	1
6	.921	1	29	.980	.998
7	.911	.924	30	.990	1
8	1	1	31	.994	1
9	.835	.986	32	.947	1
10	.698	.879	33	1	1
11	.695	.864	34	1	1
12	.735	.901	35	.890	.967
13	.847	.928	36	.895	.920
14	1	1	37	.856	.973
15	1	1	38	.840	.898
16	.905	.997	39	.821	.911
17	.968	1	40	.947	1
18	1	1	41	.960	1
19	1	1	42	.924	.995
20	.789	.812	43	.959	1
21	.759	.822	44	1	1
22	.810	.908	45	1	1
23	.822	.916	46	1	1

Table 3. Efficiency scores for 4-5 star hotels

Hotel	Model 1	Model 2	Hotel	Model 1	Model 2
1	.911	1	17	1	1
2	.906	1	18	1	1
3	.919	1	19	1	1
4	1	1	20	.957	1
5	1	1	21	1	1
6	1	1	22	.877	.998
7	1	1	23	.891	.977
8	1	1	24	1	1
9	1	1	25	1	1
10	.879	.923	26	.824	.998
11	.889	.971	27	.833	.899
12	.834	.882	28	1	1
13	1	1	29	1	1
14	.867	.942	30	1	1
15	1	1	31	.930	1
16	1	1	32	.901	1

Table 4. ANN results

ANN	2-3 star		4-5 star	
	Training	Testing	Training	Testing
NN1	.1464	.1488	.0932	.0868
NN2	.1405	.1559	.0949	.0637
NN3	.1418	.1438	.0933	.0855
NN4	.1367	.1218	.0999	.0924
NN5	.1498	.1247	.0946	.0748
NN6	.1410	.1492	.0944	.0729
NN7	.1410	.1549	.0985	.1008
NN8	.1397	.1598	.0986	.1080
NN9	.1421	.1049	.0937	.0827
NN10	.1479	.1427	.0933	.0847
Mean	0.1427	0.1407	0.0954	0.0852
S.D.	0.0041	0.0178	0.0026	0.0131

DISCUSSIONS AND IMPLICATIONS

The efficiency scores obtained using DEA for 2-3 star hotels is provided in Table 2 while for 4-5 star hotels is provided in Table 3. Also, Model 1 consists of RevPAR as the only output variable whereas Model 2 comprises of both RevPAR and CS as outputs. From Table 2, we observe that in Model 1 the number of efficient hotels (with efficiency score equal to 1) are 16 i.e. 35% efficient hotel. On the other hand, in Model 2 the number of efficient hotels is 25 i.e. 54% efficient hotels. Therefore, we observe that by adding the role of aspect ratings along with overall rating (CS), the efficiency of 2-3 star hotels increases (Viglia et al., 2016). Moreover, the results are evident from the fact that this category of hotels is not proficient in providing various services and encourage guests to recommend them or spread positive words about them (De Pelsmacker et al., 2018; Yang & Cai, 2016). Even though, these hotels are preferred by most of the customers due to their cost effectiveness, but hoteliers must concentrate on providing clean rooms, better location, and impeccable service staff in order to match the expectations of customers along with increase in their quality quotient.

Table 3 provides the efficiency score for 4-5 star hotels. As per Model 1, the number of efficient hotels is 18 i.e. 56% efficient hotels. On the other hand, Model 2 gives 22 efficient hotels with 69% efficiency. This is consistent with previous studies that high star hotels are capable of utilizing most of their resources successfully (Amin et al., 2017; Assaf et al., 2017; De Pelsmacker et al., 2018). Also, the trend observed in 4-5 star hotels is parallel to the behavior of 2-3 star hotels, in terms of the increase in percentage of efficient hotels on incorporating overall rating (CS) as additional output variable (Y. Kim & Peterson, 2017; Phillips et al., 2017; Xie et al., 2017; Xie et al., 2014; Xie et al., 2016). However, there is still a scope of improving the efficiency percentage. Although, they are located near best areas, have sophisticated employees that provide excellent services, but the cost part restrains many potential customers. Competitive strategies must be adopted by hoteliers to encourage cost effectiveness within their hotels.

The ANN analysis provides the performance of the hotels considered here. To measure the prediction accuracy, we make use of root mean square error (RMSE) values. RMSE values are based on the premise that the less the variation between training and testing values, the better is the model (Chong & Bai, 2014). The values were calculated for both the categories of hotels i.e. 2-3 star hotels and 4-5 star hotels. Table 4 shows the RMSE values for each of the two categories. From the results we observe that for 2-3 star hotels the difference between the standard deviation between training and testing comes out to be 0.0137. The similar variation for 4-5 star hotels is .0105. On the basis of these values, it can be concluded that the performance of the hotels is good.

Hoteliers are aware of the important role played by EWOM in making booking decisions. Practitioners argue that the guests are allowed to rate various aspects of the hotels as a means to express their stay experience. Previous studies have utilized the aspects considered in this study as guest (customer) satisfaction determinants. This in turn motivates them to recommend the hotel to others or make a revisit. This ultimately contributes to the revenue of the hotel and indirectly to RevPAR. Under hospitality sector, the satisfaction level of customers helps judge the hotel's performance. Hoteliers feel that competitive advantage can be achieved by a particular hotel only if it is efficiently capitalizing on its available resources so as to leave the customers satisfied. Therefore, overall satisfaction towards a hotel can only be attained only if it is performing well along all its aspects. Thus, hoteliers must keep updating their database by accessing EWOM from third party websites so as to keep a check on the feedbacks or experiences of guests and also to make decisions in customers' welfare.

CONCLUSION AND FUTURE SCOPE

This paper performs a two-stage study that combines DEA and ANN to evaluate the performance of hotels located in Delhi NCR. The first stage evaluated the efficiency for the 78 hotels considered here. This stage was conducted using DEA technique. The paper divides the hotels into two categories i.e. 2-3 star and 4-5 star hotels. The motivation of using DEA rather than any other decision-making technique is that it can handle multiple input/output variables simultaneously; and that these variables can be financial or non-financial in nature. On these lines, the input variables considered here are number of rooms and the ratings corresponding to six aspects of a hotel (service, room, value, location, sleep quality, and cleanliness). Also, RevPAR and CS are taken to be output variables. The distinguishing factor of this paper is that it involves the use of EWOM to evaluate performance of hotels. The aspect ratings are 5-point numerical feedback (similar to a Likert scale) provided by guests to expressing their stay experience. Also, under the light of previous studies, overall rating is utilized as a proxy variable for CS. DEA results showed that the percentage of efficient hotels increase as we include CS in addition to RevPAR, for both the categories. However, this percentage is low for 2-3 star hotels in comparison to 4-5 star hotels. Under second stage, the performance of the hotels is judged by using ANN technique. For the analysis, input and output variables combined to form the inner layer while the efficiency score acted as the output layer. The ANN results showed that the performance of the hotels is quite well for both the categories.

Even though the paper is comprehensively compiled, still it consists of some limitations. The study considers the hotels of Delhi NCR and so the results cannot be generalized for whole of the developing economy. Future studies may consider other geographical locations and also compare the results. In future, the proposed algorithm can be extended by including the role of textual part of EWOM rather than using just the ratings. More output variables may be added in further studies.

REFERENCES

Al-Refaie, A. (2015). Effects of human resource management on hotel performance using structural equation modeling. *Computers in Human Behavior*, *43*, 293–303. doi:10.1016/j.chb.2014.11.016

Al-Smadi, M., Qawasmeh, O., Al-Ayyoub, M., Jararweh, Y., & Gupta, B. (2018). Deep Recurrent neural network vs. support vector machine for aspect-based sentiment analysis of Arabic hotels' reviews. *Journal of Computational Science*, *27*(November), 386–393. doi:10.1016/j.jocs.2017.11.006

Amin, M., Aldakhil, A. M., Wu, C., Rezaei, S., & Cobanoglu, C. (2017). The structural relationship between TQM, employee satisfaction and hotel performance. *International Journal of Contemporary Hospitality Management*, *29*(4), 1256–1278. doi:10.1108/IJCHM-11-2015-0659

Assaf, A. G., Josiassen, A., Cvelbar, L. K., & Woo, L. (2015). The effects of customer voice on hotel performance. *International Journal of Hospitality Management*, *44*, 77–83. doi:10.1016/j.ijhm.2014.09.009

Assaf, A. G., Josiassen, A., Woo, L., Agbola, F. W., & Tsionas, M. (2017). Destination characteristics that drive hotel performance: A state-of-the-art global analysis. *Tourism Management*, *60*, 270–279. doi:10.1016/j.tourman.2016.12.010

Azadeh, A., Saberi, M., Moghaddam, R. T., & Javanmardi, L. (2011). An integrated data envelopment analysis–artificial neural network–rough set algorithm for assessment of personnel efficiency. *Expert Systems with Applications*, *38*(3), 1364–1373. doi:10.1016/j.eswa.2010.07.033

Banker, R. D., Charnes, A., & Cooper, W. W. (1984). Some models for estimating technical and scale inefficiencies in data envelopment analysis. *Management Science*, *30*(9), 1078–1092. doi:10.1287/mnsc.30.9.1078

Blal, I., & Sturman, M. C. (2014). The differential effects of the quality and quantity of online reviews on hotel room sales. *Cornell Hospitality Quarterly*, *55*(4), 365–375. doi:10.1177/1938965514533419

Chand, M. (2010). The impact of HRM practices on service quality, customer satisfaction and performance in the Indian hotel industry. *International Journal of Human Resource Management*, *21*(4), 551–566. doi:10.1080/09585191003612059

Charnes, A., Cooper, W. W., Lewin, A. Y., Morey, R. C., & Rousseau, J. (1984). Sensitivity and stability analysis in DEA. *Annals of Operations Research*, *2*(1), 139–156. doi:10.1007/BF01874736

Charnes, A., Cooper, W. W., & Rhodes, E. (1978). Measuring the efficiency of decision making units. *European Journal of Operational Research*, *2*(6), 429–444. doi:10.1016/0377-2217(78)90138-8

Chong, A. Y.-L., & Bai, R. (2014). Predicting open IOS adoption in SMEs: An integrated SEM-neural network approach. *Expert Systems with Applications*, *41*(1), 221–229. doi:10.1016/j.eswa.2013.07.023

De Pelsmacker, P., Van Tilburg, S., & Holthof, C. (2018). Digital marketing strategies, online reviews and hotel performance. *International Journal of Hospitality Management*, *72*, 47–55. doi:10.1016/j.ijhm.2018.01.003

Hsieh, L.-F., & Lin, L.-H. (2010). A performance evaluation model for international tourist hotels in Taiwan—An application of the relational network DEA. *International Journal of Hospitality Management*, *29*(1), 14–24. doi:10.1016/j.ijhm.2009.04.004

Hua, N., Morosan, C., & DeFranco, A. (2015). The other side of technology adoption: Examining the relationships between e-commerce expenses and hotel performance. *International Journal of Hospitality Management*, *45*, 109–120. doi:10.1016/j.ijhm.2014.12.001

Kim, W. G., Cho, M., & Brymer, R. A. (2013). Determinants affecting comprehensive property-level hotel performance: The moderating role of hotel type. *International Journal of Hospitality Management*, *34*, 404–412. doi:10.1016/j.ijhm.2012.12.002

Kim, W. G., & Park, S. A. (2017). Social media review rating versus traditional customer satisfaction: Which one has more incremental predictive power in explaining hotel performance? *International Journal of Contemporary Hospitality Management*, *29*(2), 784–802. doi:10.1108/IJCHM-11-2015-0627

Kim, Y., & Peterson, R. A. (2017). A Meta-analysis of Online Trust Relationships in E-commerce. *Journal of Interactive Marketing*, *38*, 44–54. doi:10.1016/j.intmar.2017.01.001

Kwon, H.-B. (2014). Performance modeling of mobile phone providers: A DEA-ANN combined approach. *Benchmarking: An International Journal*, *21*(6), 1120–1144. doi:10.1108/BIJ-01-2013-0016

Kwon, H.-B. (2017). Exploring the predictive potential of artificial neural networks in conjunction with DEA in railroad performance modeling. *International Journal of Production Economics*, *183*, 159–170. doi:10.1016/j.ijpe.2016.10.022

Kwon, H.-B., Lee, J., & Roh, J. J. (2016). Best performance modeling using complementary DEA-ANN approach: Application to Japanese electronics manufacturing firms. *Benchmarking: An International Journal*, *23*(3), 704–721. doi:10.1108/BIJ-09-2014-0083

Liébana-Cabanillas, F., Marinković, V., & Kalinić, Z. (2017). A SEM-neural network approach for predicting antecedents of m-commerce acceptance. *International Journal of Information Management*, *37*(2), 14–24. doi:10.1016/j.ijinfomgt.2016.10.008

Marco-Lajara, B., Claver-Cortés, E., & Úbeda-García, M. (2014). Business agglomeration in tourist districts and hotel performance. *International Journal of Contemporary Hospitality Management*, *26*(8), 1312–1340. doi:10.1108/IJCHM-07-2013-0319

Marco-Lajara, B., Claver-Cortés, E., Úbeda-García, M., & Zaragoza-Sáez, P. D. C. (2016). Hotel performance and agglomeration of tourist districts. *Regional Studies*, *50*(6), 1016–1035. doi:10.1080/003 43404.2014.954535

Marketmyhotel. (2019). Hotel Reviews – Why does it matter so much for Hotel's Online Reputation. Retrieved from http://marketmyhotel.in/hotel-reviews-why-does-it-matter-so-much-for-hotels-online-reputation/

Peiró-Signes, A., Segarra-Oña, M.-V., Miret-Pastor, L., & Verma, R. (2015). The effect of tourism clusters on US hotel performance. *Cornell Hospitality Quarterly*, *56*(2), 155–167. doi:10.1177/1938965514557354

Pereira-Moliner, J., Claver-Cortés, E., Molina-Azorín, J. F., & Tarí, J. J. (2012). Quality management, environmental management and firm performance: Direct and mediating effects in the hotel industry. *Journal of Cleaner Production*, *37*, 82–92. doi:10.1016/j.jclepro.2012.06.010

Phillips, P., Barnes, S., Zigan, K., & Schegg, R. (2017). Understanding the impact of online reviews on hotel performance: An empirical analysis. *Journal of Travel Research*, *56*(2), 235–249. doi:10.1177/0047287516636481

Phillips, P., Zigan, K., Silva, M. M. S., & Schegg, R. (2015). The interactive effects of online reviews on the determinants of Swiss hotel performance: A neural network analysis. *Tourism Management*, *50*, 130–141. doi:10.1016/j.tourman.2015.01.028

Poldrugovac, K., Tekavcic, M., & Jankovic, S. (2016). Efficiency in the hotel industry: An empirical examination of the most influential factors. *Economic research-. Ekonomska Istrazivanja*, *29*(1), 583–597. doi:10.1080/1331677X.2016.1177464

Radojevic, T., Stanisic, N., Stanic, N., & Davidson, R. (2018). The effects of traveling for business on customer satisfaction with hotel services. *Tourism Management*, *67*(August), 326–341. doi:10.1016/j.tourman.2018.02.007

Ramanathan, R., Ramanathan, U., & Zhang, Y. (2016). Linking operations, marketing and environmental capabilities and diversification to hotel performance: A data envelopment analysis approach. *International Journal of Production Economics, 176,* 111–122. doi:10.1016/j.ijpe.2016.03.010

Roshchina, A., Cardiff, J., & Rosso, P. (2015). Twin: Personality-based intelligent recommender system. *Journal of Intelligent & Fuzzy Systems, 28*(5), 2059–2071. doi:10.3233/IFS-141484

Salem, I. E.-B. (2014). Toward better understanding of knowledge management: Correlation to hotel performance and innovation in five-star chain hotels in Egypt. *Tourism and Hospitality Research, 14*(4), 176–196. doi:10.1177/1467358414542265

Saumya, S., Singh, J. P., & Dwivedi, Y. K. (2019). Predicting the helpfulness score of online reviews using convolutional neural network. *Soft Computing.* doi:10.100700500-019-03851-5

Sharma, H., & Aggarwal, A. G. (2019). Finding determinants of e-commerce success: a PLS-SEM approach. *Journal of Advances in Management Research.*

Sharma, H., Tandon, A., Kapur, P., & Aggarwal, A. G. (2019). Ranking hotels using aspect ratings based sentiment classification and interval-valued neutrosophic TOPSIS. *International Journal of System Assurance Engineering and Management,* 1-11.

Shuai, J.-J., & Wu, W.-W. (2011). Evaluating the influence of E-marketing on hotel performance by DEA and grey entropy. *Expert Systems with Applications, 38*(7), 8763–8769. doi:10.1016/j.eswa.2011.01.086

Singh, N., Pant, M., & Goel, A. (2018). ANN embedded data envelopment analysis approach for measuring the efficiency of state boards in India. *International Journal of System Assurance Engineering and Management, 9*(5), 1092–1106. doi:10.100713198-018-0743-8

Sirirak, S., Islam, N., & Ba Khang, D. (2011). Does ICT adoption enhance hotel performance? *Journal of Hospitality and Tourism Technology, 2*(1), 34–49. doi:10.1108/17579881111112403

Tandon, A., Sharma, H., & Aggarwal, A. G. (2019). Assessing Travel Websites Based on Service Quality Attributes Under Intuitionistic Environment. *International Journal of Knowledge-Based Organizations, 9*(1), 66–75. doi:10.4018/IJKBO.2019010106

Tavitiyaman, P., Qiu Zhang, H., & Qu, H. (2012). The effect of competitive strategies and organizational structure on hotel performance. *International Journal of Contemporary Hospitality Management, 24*(1), 140–159. doi:10.1108/09596111211197845

Tavitiyaman, P., Qu, H., & Zhang, H. Q. (2011). The impact of industry force factors on resource competitive strategies and hotel performance. *International Journal of Hospitality Management, 30*(3), 648–657. doi:10.1016/j.ijhm.2010.11.010

Viglia, G., Minazzi, R., & Buhalis, D. (2016). The influence of e-word-of-mouth on hotel occupancy rate. *International Journal of Contemporary Hospitality Management, 28*(9), 2035–2051. doi:10.1108/IJCHM-05-2015-0238

Wang, C.-H., Chen, K.-Y., & Chen, S.-C. (2012). Total quality management, market orientation and hotel performance: The moderating effects of external environmental factors. *International Journal of Hospitality Management, 31*(1), 119–129. doi:10.1016/j.ijhm.2011.03.013

Wu, J., Liang, L., & Song, H. (2010). Measuring hotel performance using the integer DEA model. *Tourism Economics*, *16*(4), 867–882. doi:10.5367/te.2010.0015

Xiang, Z., Schwartz, Z., Gerdes, J. H. Jr, & Uysal, M. (2015). What can big data and text analytics tell us about hotel guest experience and satisfaction? *International Journal of Hospitality Management*, *44*, 120–130. doi:10.1016/j.ijhm.2014.10.013

Xie, K. L., So, K. K. F., & Wang, W. (2017). Joint effects of management responses and online reviews on hotel financial performance: A data-analytics approach. *International Journal of Hospitality Management*, *62*, 101–110. doi:10.1016/j.ijhm.2016.12.004

Xie, K. L., Zhang, Z., & Zhang, Z. (2014). The business value of online consumer reviews and management response to hotel performance. *International Journal of Hospitality Management*, *43*, 1–12. doi:10.1016/j.ijhm.2014.07.007

Xie, K. L., Zhang, Z., Zhang, Z., Singh, A., & Lee, S. K. (2016). Effects of managerial response on consumer eWOM and hotel performance: Evidence from TripAdvisor. *International Journal of Contemporary Hospitality Management*, *28*(9), 2013–2034. doi:10.1108/IJCHM-06-2015-0290

Xue, W., Li, T., & Rishe, N. (2017). Aspect identification and ratings inference for hotel reviews. *World Wide Web (Bussum)*, *20*(1), 23–37. doi:10.100711280-016-0398-9

Yang, Y., Park, S., & Hu, X. (2018). Electronic word of mouth and hotel performance: A meta-analysis. *Tourism Management*, *67*, 248–260. doi:10.1016/j.tourman.2018.01.015

Yang, Z., & Cai, J. (2016). Do regional factors matter? Determinants of hotel industry performance in China. *Tourism Management*, *52*, 242–253. doi:10.1016/j.tourman.2015.06.024

Yin, P., Chu, J., Wu, J., Ding, J., Yang, M., & Wang, Y. (2019). A DEA-based two-stage network approach for hotel performance analysis: An internal cooperation perspective. *Omega*, 102035. doi:10.1016/j.omega.2019.02.004

Zhang, Y., & Cole, S. T. (2016). Dimensions of lodging guest satisfaction among guests with mobility challenges: A mixed-method analysis of web-based texts. *Tourism Management*, *53*(April), 13–27. doi:10.1016/j.tourman.2015.09.001

This research was previously published in the International Journal of E-Adoption (IJEA), 12(1); pages 15-29, copyright year 2020 by IGI Publishing (an imprint of IGI Global).

Chapter 71
Using an Artificial Neural Network to Improve Email Security

Mohamed Abdulhussain Ali Madan Maki
Ahlia University, Bahrain

Suresh Subramanian
ⓘ https://orcid.org/0000-0002-4055-8725
Ahlia University, Bahrain

ABSTRACT

Email is one of the most widely used features of internet, and it is the most convenient method of transferring messages electronically. However, email productivity has been decreased due to phishing attacks, spam emails, and viruses. Recently, filtering the email flow is a challenging task for researchers due to techniques that spammers used to avoid spam detection. This research proposes an email spam filtering system that filters the spam emails using artificial back propagation neural network (BPNN) technique. Enron1 dataset was used, and after the preprocessing, TF-IDF algorithm was used to extract features and convert them into frequency. To select best features, mutual information technique has been applied. Performance of classifiers were measured using BoW, n-gram, and chi-squared methods. BPNN model was compared with Naïve Bayes and support vector machine based on accuracy, precision, recall, and f1-score. The results show that the proposed email spam system achieved 98.6% accuracy with cross-validation.

INTRODUCTION

Electronic mail or known as e-mail it is a channel of electronically communicate with others by massages through the internet. Now a day's emails are not only used for communication but also for creating tasks and solving customer queries. Email is, simple, cheap, and fast type of communication, then it could be vulnerable to many threats (David, Lucia, and Bindura, 2013).

DOI: 10.4018/978-1-6684-2408-7.ch071

One of the most potential security threats in the emailing system is the "SPAM" where attackers are illegally disseminating malicious software's such us Malware's, Viruses', Trojan's and Internet worms (Ndumiyana, Magomelo and Sakala, 2013).

Spam means unwanted email or unsolicited commercial emails sent directly to a large number of addresses (Shama.N, 2017). The spam emails sent to the receivers without their permission. It is possible to send hundreds of emails to thousands of users around the world at no cost.

Spam scientifically different in content and can belong to the following categories: advertisement, money making, sexually explicit, business, scams. (Al-jarrah, Khater and Al-duwairi, 2012)

The spam has been increased in the last years and becomes a serious problem for communication. Mr. Vairagade, (2017) estimated that 48 billion out of the 80 billion emails are sent daily as spam also among 40,000 users are replying to spam emails. According to Symantec (2017), email spam rate decline in 2011 was 75%, in 2015 and 2016 dropped to 53% and the first quarter of 2017 the rate dropped to 54%. The high ratio of spams in recent years indicates that scammers are looking for fast revenue opportunity.

This research tried to improve the techniques of filtering the emails to prevent spam from spreading into customer's mailboxes. Also, we will preprocess the Enron spam dataset and extract the features required to feed NN text classifier. Accordingly this research improved the accuracy and performance of email spam filtering.

BACKGROUND

Theoretical Background

Machine learning is the development of algorithms that permit machines to learn. ML has been used in medical diagnosis, bioinformatics, Money fraud, stock market analysis, classifying DNS, speech recognition, computer games, and spam filtering (Bhuiyan *et al.*, 2018),(R Manikandan, 2018).

Neural Network (NN) is a beautiful biologically inspired programming paradigm, which enables a computer to learn from observational data. Currently, the NN algorithm used widely in many problems, such as text categorizations, image, and speech recognition.

However, extracting the emails and classify them needs knowledge of Natural Language Processing (NLP) to normalize the datasets, extract and select the features to feed the classifiers (Ndumiyana, Magomelo, and Sakala, 2013)(Jayanthi and Subhashini, 2016).

NN has more efficiency in detecting spam because its supervised learning method and also errors can be corrected NB, DT, SVM, KNN are also good classifiers (Sharma, 2014).

The study will use BPNN to improve accuracy and performance in detecting email spam.

Related Work

The tasks of managing a large volume of data are challenged because of the growing number of emails around the world. For example, detecting spam with many security roles may slow down system performance. Many studies include replies in the email, folder classification, automatic subject, contacts. Currently, email servers such as Google combined the email communication once the user replied (Alsmadi and Alhami, 2015).

The classification algorithm must not only classify the spam email accurately but also expected to classify emails as legitimate. The prediction metrics (True Positive, True Negative, False Positive, False Negative) are used to evaluate the quality of the email prediction (Alsmadi and Alhami, 2015).

Various approaches have been considered to compare the performance of many classification algorithms. Below are related work to the spam classification problems that include email spam problem.

NB is a probabilistic ML model used for classification problems. The core of the classifier depends on Bayes theorem which is discovered by British mathematician reverend Thomas Bayes in 1763. The demonstration of original Bayes Theorem as (Wei, 2018a):

$$p(A|B) = \frac{P(B|A)P(A)}{P(B)}$$

(1)

- P(A|B) is the posterior probability of class (target) given predictor (attribute).
- P(A) is the prior probability of class.
- P(B|A) is the likelihood, which is the probability of predictor given class.
- P(B) is the prior probability of predictor.

Rusland *et al.* (2017) used the NB algorithm for email spam filtering on two datasets (Spam Data & Spam base). The Spam data datasets have 9324 emails, and 500 attributes and Spam Based dataset has 4601 emails and 58 attributes.

SYSTEM DESIGN

The process that followed in our experiment has been developed based on supervised machine learning (ML) procedures by (Bassiouni, Ali and El-Dahshan, 2018). In our experiment, the dataset is divided into training and testing sets with a shuffle in each run. Cross-validation with Five folds to solve the overfitting problem.

- **Training Phase:** The training set has been pre-processed to eliminate noise, stop words, HTML tags, and numbers. Since we are implementing supervised ML, emails will be pre-classified with labels (Ham or Spam). Next, the features will be extracted, and the most ranked features will be selected using the filter method. These features will be used in the testing stage of the classifier model.
- **Testing Phase:** The testing set is also called "Unseen set" it will be pre-processed as we performed in training phase, features will be extracted and selected then these features will feed the classifier model to predict if the email is Ham or Spam. Next, the classifier will be evaluated by the performance evaluation methods.

Table 1. Summarization of the related work

Sr.	Author and year	Corpus Used	Tools used	Technique Used	Accuracy
1	(Rusland *et al.*, 2017)	Spam Based Spam Data	WEKA Tool	Naïve Bayes	Spam Data of 91.13% while Spam base get 82.54%
2	(Shahi and Yadav, 2014)	No corpus for Nepali, they have created their own.	Java Programming language -TF-IDF scheme to make feature vector	Naïve Bayes, Support Vector Machine (SVM)	Naïve Bayes classifier was 92.74% and for SVM classifier was 87.15%.
3	(G. Jain, Manisha, 2017a)	UCI SMS Spam Collection Twitter Text Data	Weighting scheme (TF-IDF)	Naïve Bayes SVM, ANN, KNN, RN	Naïve Bayes, SMS: %97.65 Twitter: %91.14 SVM, SMS: %97.45 Twitter: %93.14 ANN, SMS: %97.40 Twitter: %91.18 KNN, SMS: %90.40 Twitter: %91.96 RN, SMS: %97.77 Twitter: %93.04
4	(Gupta and Goyal, 2018)	Personnel Gmail dataset	-Python, -Keras to convert emails into a numeric matrix -Ripper to categorize the emails	Feed Forward Neural Network	One hidden layer was 33.33% 1500 hidden layers, where the accuracy result improved to 90% an increasing number of words to 12000 with 100 hidden layers increase the accuracy from 81.67% to 88.33%.
5	(Hota, Shrivas and Singhai, 2013)	UCI Spam Dataset		BPNN, Decision Tree, C5.0,	The best result achieved 91.96% when combining SVM & C5.0 (94.35%)
6	(Saad, 2018)	Reuters-21578	Singular Value Decomposition (SVD)	Back Propagation Neural Network	The average accuracy of the classification was %99.40
7	(Jameel, 2013)	Phishing Corpus (Monkey.org) And SpamAssassin		Feed Forward Neural Network	Accuracy Achieved 98.72%
8	(Awad and ELseuofi, 2011)	SpamAssassin Dataset	Frequent Words in spam email	NB, SVM, KNN, NN, AIS, RS	Naïve Bayes achieved the best accuracy result with 99.46%, Rough Sets achieved 97.42%, SVM achieved 96.90%, ANN achieved 96.83%.

Choosing Dataset

The Enron 1 dataset has 5172 emails, Hams 3672 and Spams 1500 (V. Metsis, 2006). Each folder identified as Ham or Spam. It is original dataset from Enron investigation but arranged by V.Metsis, I.Androutsopoulos, and G.Paliouras and collected by owners of the mailbox themselves. The dataset has baseline results for the classifiers with various conditions and sections (Sharma and Khurana, 2017). Figure (2) present a sample of ham email

Figure 1. Proposed email spam filtering system

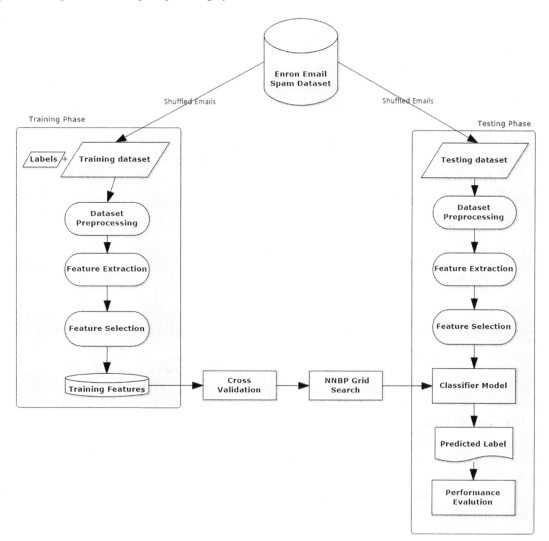

The dataset has been selected to meet the proposed system requirements:

1. **The Dataset Must Contain the Header of the Email:** Al-jarrah, Khater, and Al-duwairi (2012) identified that header features could be used to identify the email spam. Therefore, using Header will increase the possibility of detecting spam. In our case, we will include "Subject" from the email.
2. **The Dataset Must Contain the Body of the Email:** To increase the accuracy prediction result the Iqbal *et al.* (2016) suggested to combine the body and the email header because header contains features that can be used in detecting spam.
3. **The Dataset Must not be Encrypted:** Having the dataset in clear text will help in improving the pre-processing phase.

Figure 2. Sample of "Enron1" ham email

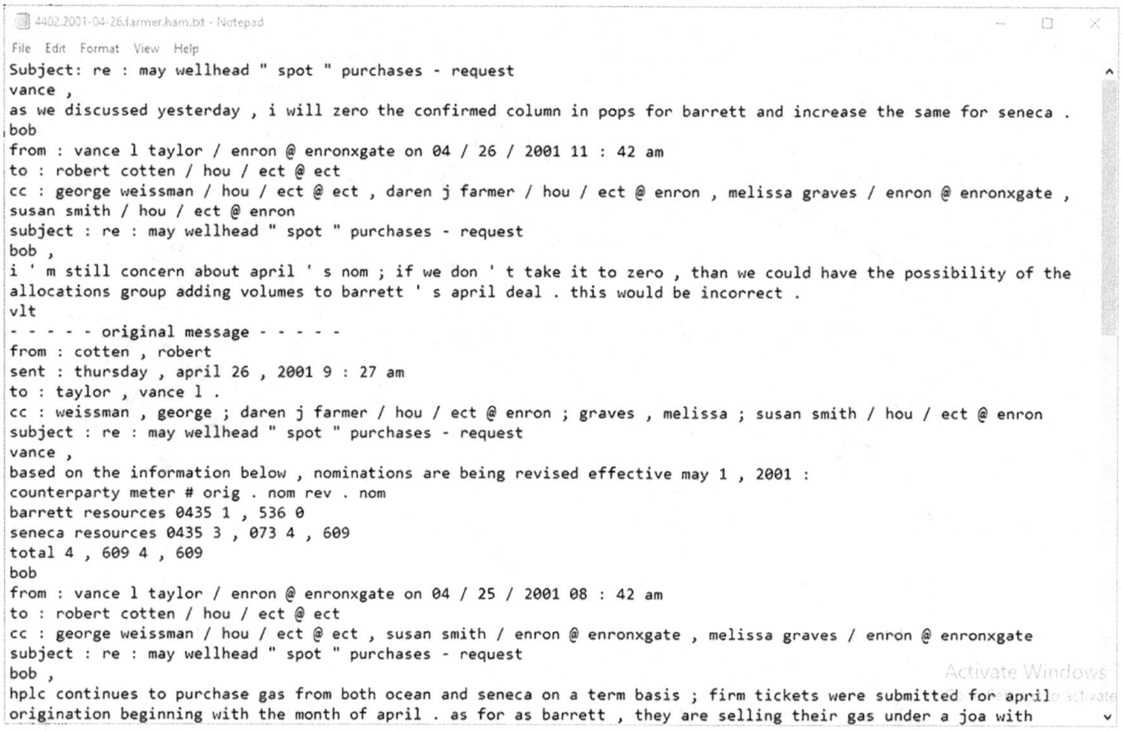

4402.2001-04-26.farmer.ham.txt - Notepad
File Edit Format View Help

```
Subject: re : may wellhead " spot " purchases - request
vance ,
as we discussed yesterday , i will zero the confirmed column in pops for barrett and increase the same for seneca .
bob
from : vance l taylor / enron @ enronxgate on 04 / 26 / 2001 11 : 42 am
to : robert cotten / hou / ect @ ect
cc : george weissman / hou / ect @ ect , daren j farmer / hou / ect @ enron , melissa graves / enron @ enronxgate ,
susan smith / hou / ect @ enron
subject : re : may wellhead " spot " purchases - request
bob ,
i ' m still concern about april ' s nom ; if we don ' t take it to zero , than we could have the possibility of the
allocations group adding volumes to barrett ' s april deal . this would be incorrect .
vlt
- - - - - original message - - - - -
from : cotten , robert
sent : thursday , april 26 , 2001 9 : 27 am
to : taylor , vance l .
cc : weissman , george ; daren j farmer / hou / ect @ enron ; graves , melissa ; susan smith / hou / ect @ enron
subject : re : may wellhead " spot " purchases - request
vance ,
based on the information below , nominations are being revised effective may 1 , 2001 :
counterparty meter # orig . nom rev . nom
barrett resources 0435 1 , 536 0
seneca resources 0435 3 , 073 4 , 609
total 4 , 609 4 , 609
bob
from : vance l taylor / enron @ enronxgate on 04 / 25 / 2001 08 : 42 am
to : robert cotten / hou / ect @ ect
cc : george weissman / hou / ect @ ect , susan smith / enron @ enronxgate , melissa graves / enron @ enronxgate
subject : re : may wellhead " spot " purchases - request
bob ,
hplc continues to purchase gas from both ocean and seneca on a term basis ; firm tickets were submitted for april
origination beginning with the month of april . as for as barrett , they are selling their gas under a joa with
```

Train the Classifiers Algorithm

Based on the Mutual Information features selection algorithm, The BPNN, NB, SVM classifiers are trained by 70% of Enron1 dataset.

By using Scikit-learn library in python called "fit_transform()," the classifier will learn the vocabulary and converts the training dataset into a document-term matrix (DTM).

- **Fit():** Learn the vocabulary of the training dataset.
- **Transform():** Converts the training data into document-term matrix. (DTM).

After creating the Training Document-Term Matrix (DTM), the DTM will be used to feed the BPNN classifier. The other classifiers (Naïve Bayes, SVM,) is selected to compare the results BPNN classifier.

The selected classifiers imported from Scikit-learning library in python. (scikit-learn developers, 2019b)

Grid Search

Grid-Search is used to find the optimal hyperparameters of a model which results in the most "Accurate" predictions (Joseph, 2018). We have implemented Grid-Search for BPNN.

We used one approach known as Grid Search algorithm with k-fold cross-validation. The hyperparameters can be given to a grid search to test the parameters with the classifier. Accordingly, the best parameters among them can be set as parameters to the NN classifier model. We created several tests for feature extraction algorithms, features selections with multiple numbers of features to test the parameters accordingly.

1. TF-IDF K features and BOW K features.
2. Unigram, Bigram, Trigram, and N-gram.
3. Chi-Squared best 4000, 8000,9000,1000,15000, 25000 features
4. Neural Network parameters
   a. Activation function: Identity, Tanh, Logistic, Relu
   b. Max_iter: 400, 300, 200
   c. Hidden_layer_Sizes: (10,80),(50,0),(80,0),(200,400)
   d. Learning_rate:
   e. Solver = ibfgs, sgd, Adam

The grid search implements "fit" and "score" method for each estimator used. The parameters of the estimator used to apply these methods are optimized by cross-validated grid-search over a parameter grid.(Sciket Learn developers, 2019)

The grid search algorithm has been implemented with sci-kit learn called "GridSearchCV()" (scikit-learn developers, 2019a).

Classifier Modeling

After tuning the parameters to get the best classifier performance, we need to save the trained models in a file and restore them in the production environment or compare the model with other models created to test the model on testing folds.

Saving of the classifier model called Serialization and restoring the data is called Deserialization (Python Software Foundation, 2019)

Creating a classifier model will allow us to predict the emails without executing training dataset every time, especially if the dataset is large.

We have used a package called "Pickle" it is python object serialization library (Python Software Foundation, 2019). Each training classifier model will be saved as "(Name of classifier.pki)".

Testing the Classifier

After creating and setting up the parameters of the classifier model, the model can be tested with production email data.

The remaining unseen 20% (One fold) will be given to the classifier model to get the actual testing result data to evaluate the classifier. The models generated results is called predicted results (Jayanthi and Subhashini, 2016)(Zavvar, Rezaei and Garavand, 2016)(Bassiouni, Ali and El-Dahshan, 2018).

Performance and Evaluation Parameters (Confusion Matrix):

In our experiment, the performance and the evaluation of the classifiers will be evaluated base on the Accuracy, Recall, Precision, and F-Measure. Below are more details:

Table 2. Confusion matrix

Test Outcome	Condition	
	Condition Positive	**Condition Negative**
Outcome Negative (Ham)	True Positive	False Positive
Outcome Negative (Spam)	False Negative	True Negative

To get the accuracy of the classification, this research used the confusion matrix provided by the scikit-learn library.

RESULTS AND DISCUSSION

Experiment 1: Chi2 feature selection algorithm with TF-IDF with compare to BOW

The experiment results will show the accuracy result of chi2 with feature extraction algorithms (TF-IDF) with the compare to (BOW) algorithm.

Figure 3. Experiment 1: Chi2 algorithm with TF-IDF compared with BOW

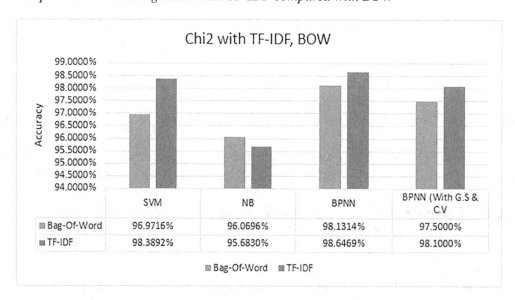

The results show that using Chi2 algorithm as features selection with TF-IDF will perform better than BOW algorithm as the accuracy result increased by (%0.1.417) for SVM, (0.5155) for BPNN and also increased by (%0.6) for BPNN with G.S and C.V but the performance decreased by (0.3866) for NB.

The difference between BPNN classifier and BPNN with cross-validation approach is due to cross-validation because it's split the dataset into five folds and then calculate the accuracy. Therefore, the accuracy of BPNN cross-validation is more accurate than BPNN.

The accuracy result shows that the BPNN algorithm performed better than SVM and NB in classifying the email using TF-IDF as feature extraction and Chi2 as feature selection.

Experiment 2: MI algorithm with TF-IDF with Compare to BO

The experiment results show the accuracy result of Mutual information according to the feature extraction algorithms (TF-IDF) with the compare to (BOW) algorithm.

Figure 4. Experiment 2: MI algorithm with TF-IDF compare to BOW

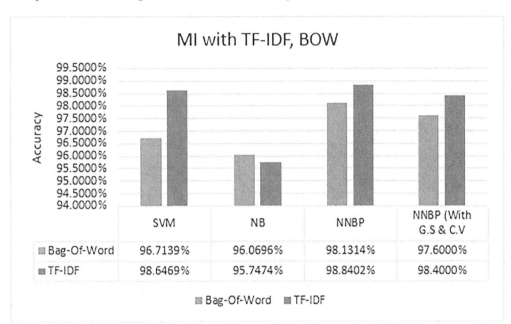

The results show that using Mutual information algorithm in feature selection with TF-IDF performed better than BOW. By using TF-IDF, the accuracy result increase for SVM by (%1.9330), BPNN (0.7088), BPNN with GS. & C.V (0.8000) and decreased by (%0.3222) for NB classifier.

The accuracy result shows the BPNN algorithm performed well in classifying the email using TF-IDF as feature extraction and Mutual Information as feature selection.

The accuracy result achieved by BPNN using Mutual information with TF-IDF achieved by better than Chi2 with TF-IDF.

The confusion evaluation report results for the experiment shows that BPNN Precision and f1-score achieved (%99.28), and it is the best among the classifiers but recall lower than SVM about (0.45).

The experiment shows that the BPNN algorithm is the best classifier for email spam due to the evaluation confusion report below:

The total number of Testing emails are 1552 emails. The number of correctly classified Ham emails (TP) are 1101 emails, and correctly classified spam emails (TN) are 433 emails. Therefore, the misclassified emails are 18 emails distributed among 8 Ham emails misclassified as Spam and 10 Spam emails misclassified as Ham.

Figure 5. Experiment 2: Classification report results

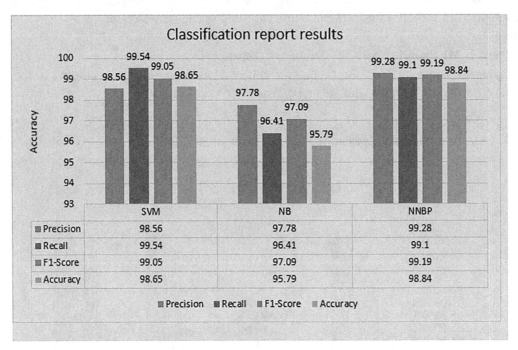

Table 4. Shows the confusion matrix of experiment 2

Sr.	Classifier	TP	FP	FN	TN
1	SVM	1093	16	5	438
2	NB	1084	25	41	402
3	BPNN	1101	8	10	433

Table 5. Shows the classification report for experiment 2

Sr.	Classifier	Precision	Recall	F1-Score	Accuracy
1	SVM	98.56	99.54	99.05	98.65
2	NB	97.78	96.41	97.09	95.79
3	BPNN	99.28	99.1	99.19	98.84

Table 4 Confusion matrix for experiment 2
Table 5 Classification Report for experiment 2
With BPNN, the accuracy result achieved by Enron1 98.884%, BPNN with cross-validation 98.6%, SVM 98.6%, NB 95.7%.

FUTURE WORK

For future work, suggested to consider deep learning techniques which will help us in handling the feature representation and developing a learning model to generate feature representation. Since the spam is not limited to content, it has to be designed a system that supports image recognition, attachment malicious codes identification through learning model, support of other languages like Arabic, French, Chinese, Hindi.

This research would recommend to consider the time complexity of the grid search algorithm to reduce the time computation time to find the best optimization classifier parameter.

CONCLUSION

This study motivated by several research papers that various processes may affect the performance of the classifiers like choosing the right dataset in terms of the availability of the components required and the ratio of Ham or Spam emails, best steps to follow in pre-process the dataset and what stemmer and stop words to choose. How to select feature extraction and selection algorithms and how to identify the optimal hyper-parameters for the classifiers. However, one of the main objectives of this study is to analyze, evaluate the performance of the classifiers selected on email spam filtering problem.

Preprocessing of the dataset must be normalized well to support feature extraction and selection algorithms. The study observed that a good pre-processing could improve the performance of other classifiers.

The experiments prove that using TF-IDF with Mutual information algorithm can improve the accuracy results and by using the n-gram, the results are decreasing' due to dataset structure.

With BPNN, the accuracy result achieved by Enron1 98.884%, BPNN with cross-validation 98.6%, SVM 98.6%, NB 95.7%. With reference to the accuracy of Enron's datasets (1-6), BPNN classifier has achieved the best performance based on the obtained evaluation accuracy results.

REFERENCES

Al-jarrah, O., Khater, I., & Al-duwairi, B. (2012). Identifying potentially useful email header features for email spam filtering. *The Sixth International Conference on Digital Society*, 140–145.

Alsmadi, I., & Alhami, I. (2015). Clustering and classification of email contents. *Journal of King Saud University - Computer and Information Sciences*, 27(1), 46–57. doi:10.1016/j.jksuci.2014.03.014

Awad, W. A. (2011). Machine Learning Methods for Spam E-Mail Classification. *International Journal of Computer Science & Information Technology*, 3(1), 12. doi:10.5121/ijcsit.2011.3112

Bassiouni, M., Ali, M., & El-Dahshan, E. A. (2018). Ham and Spam E-Mails Classification Using Machine Learning Techniques. *Journal of Applied Security Research. Taylor & Francis*, 13(3), 315–331. doi:10.1080/19361610.2018.1463136

Bhuiyan, H. (2018). 'A Survey of Existing E-Mail Spam Filtering Methods Considering Machine Learning Techniques,' Global. *Journal of Computer Science and Technology*, 18(2), 21–29.

David, N., & Lucia, S. & Bindura. (2013). Hidden Markov Models And Artificial Neural Networks For Spam Detection. *International Journal of Engineering Research & Technology*, 2(2), 1–5. doi:10.1177/2393957514555052

Gupta, D. K., & Goyal, S. (2018). *Email Classification into Relevant Category Using Neural Networks*. Available at http://arxiv.org/abs/1802.03971

Hota, H. S., Shrivas, A. K., & Singhai, S. K. (2013). Artificial Neural Network, Decision Tree and Statistical Techniques Applied for Designing and Developing E-mail Classifier. *International Journal of Recent Technology and Engineering*, (16), 2277–3878.

Iqbal, M., Abid, M. M., Ahmad, M., & Khurshid, F. (2016). Study on the Effectiveness of Spam Detection Technologies. *International Journal of Information Technology and Computer Science*, 8(1), 11–21. doi:10.5815/ijitcs.2016.01.02

Jameel, N. G. M. (2013). Detection of Phishing Emails using Feed Forward Neural Network. *International Journal of Computers and Applications*, 77(7), 10–15. doi:10.5120/13405-1057

Jayanthi, S. K., & Subhashini, V. (2016). *Efficient Spam Detection using Single Hidden Layer Feed Forward Neural Network*. International Research Journal of Engineering and Technology, 690–696.

Joseph, R. (2018). *Grid Search for model tuning*. Available at: https://towardsdatascience.com/grid-search-for-model-tuning-3319b259367e

Manikandan, D. R. S. (2018). Machine Learning Algorithms for Classification. *International Journal of Academic Research and Development*, 384–389. doi:10.13140/RG.2.1.2044.4003

Metsis, V. I. A., & G. P. (2006). *Enron Dataset*. Available at: http://www2.aueb.gr/users/ion/data/enron-spam/

Ndumiyana, D., Magomelo, M., & Sakala, L. (2013). Spam Detection using a Neural Network Classifier. *Online Journal of Physical and Environmental Science Research*, 2(2), 28–37.

Python Software Foundation. (2019). *Pickle — Python object serialization*. Available at: https://docs.python.org/3/library/pickle.html

Rusland, N. F. (2017). Analysis of Naïve Bayes Algorithm for Email Spam Filtering across Multiple Datasets. *IOP Conference Series. Materials Science and Engineering*, 226(1). doi:10.1088/1757-899X/226/1/012091

Saad, Y. (2018). Dimension Reduction Techniques for Document Categorization with Back Propagation Neural Network. *Journal of Engineering and Applied Sciences (Asian Research Publishing Network)*, 1304–1309.

Sciket learns. (2019). *Mutual Information*. Available at: https://scikit-learn.org/stable/modules/generated/sklearn.feature_selection.mutual_info_classif.html

Scikit-learn developers. (2019a). *Grid Search*. Available at: https://scikit-learn.org/stable/modules/generated/sklearn.model_selection.GridSearchCV.html

Scikit-learn developers. (2019b). *Scikit learn Classifiers*. Available at: https://scikit-learn.org/stable/supervised_learning.html

Shahi, T. B., & Yadav, A. (2014). Mobile SMS Spam Filtering for Nepali Text Using Naïve Bayesian and Support Vector Machine. *International Journal of Intelligence Science*, *4*(01), 24–28. doi:10.4236/ijis.2014.41004

Shama, N. T. (2017). Neural Network Model for Email-Spam Detection. *International Journal of Multi-Disciplinary*, *2*(1), 1–4.

Sharma, A. A. (2014). SMS Spam Detection Using Neural Network Classifier. *International Journal of Advanced Research in Computer Science and Software Engineering, 4*(6), 2277–128. Available at: http://ijarcsse.com/Before_August_2017/docs/papers/Volume_4/6_June2014/V4I6-0151.pdf

Sharma, U., & Khurana, S. S. (2017, June). SHED: Spam Ham Email Dataset. *International Journal on Recent and Innovation Trends in Computing and Communication*, 1078–1082.

Symantec. (2017). Email Threats 2017 An ISTR Special Report Analyst: Ben Nahorney Internet Security Threat Report. *Symantec Security*. Available at: https://www.symantec.com/content/dam/symantec/docs/security-center/white-papers/istr-email-threats-2017-en.pdf

Vairagade, R. S. (2017). Survey Paper on User Defined Spam Boxes using Email Filtering. *International Journal of Computers and Applications*, *157*(6), 3.

Zavvar, M., Rezaei, M., & Garavand, S. (2016). Email Spam Detection Using Combination of Particle Swarm Optimization and Artificial Neural Network and Support Vector Machine. *International Journal of Modern Education and Computer Science*, *7*, 68–74. doi:10.5815/ijmecs.2016.07.08

This research was previously published in Implementing Computational Intelligence Techniques for Security Systems Design; pages 131-145, copyright year 2020 by Information Science Reference (an imprint of IGI Global).

Chapter 72
Forecasting Automobile Sales in Turkey with Artificial Neural Networks

Aycan Kaya

iD https://orcid.org/0000-0001-9329-6936

Department of Industrial Engineering, Istanbul Technical University, Istanbul, Turkey

Gizem Kaya

Department of Management Engineering, Istanbul Technical University, Istanbul, Turkey

Ferhan Çebi

Department of Management Engineering, Istanbul Technical University, Istanbul, Turkey

ABSTRACT

This study aims to reveal significant factors which affect automobile sales and estimate the automobile sales in Turkey by using Artificial Neural Network (ANN), ARIMA, and time series decomposition techniques. The forecasting model includes automobile sales, automobile price, Euro and Dollar exchange rate, employment rate, consumer confidence index, oil prices and industrial production confidence index, the probability of buying an automobile, female employment rate, general economic situation, the expectation of general economic situation, financial status of households, expectation of financial status of households. According to the regression results, changes in Dollar exchange rate, the expectation of financial status of households, seasonally adjusted industrial production index, logarithmic form of automobile sales before-one-month which have a significant effect on automobile sales, are found to be the significant variables. The results show that ANN has a better estimation performance with MAPE=1.18% and RMSE=782 values than ARIMA and time series decomposition techniques.

DOI: 10.4018/978-1-6684-2408-7.ch072

INTRODUCTION

The automotive industry, with a turnover of 4 trillion dollars, corresponds to the world's 4th largest economy by 2016 (TAYSAD, 2017) and 88 million automobiles are sold worldwide in 2016, up to increase 4.8% from a year earlier (PWC, 2017). In the future, the automotive industry will have to transform to produce electrified, autonomous, shared, connected and yearly updated automobiles of the future and through this transformation period, new automobile sales are expected to increase worldwide (PWC, 2017-2018). To adapt this transformation and satisfy the increasing customer demand in the competitive environment, forecasting automobile sales is a critical and challenging issue to deal with. Sales forecasting provides a basis for creating a competitive and effective business strategy. A reasonable sales forecasting satisfies customer demand on time and helps organizations to make better purchasing decisions and to determine optimal inventory level. On the other hand, insufficient sales forecasting causes customer loss and higher number of inventories.

Sales forecasting is a highly important issue to deal with, especially in the production of products like automobile consisting a wide range of parts (more than 20,000 parts) which have different material structure and need different production type and technology. Because of all these reasons, this study aims to reveal significant factors, which affect automobile sales and estimate the automobile sales in Turkey by using Artificial Neural Network (ANN), ARIMA and time series decomposition techniques. The remaining part of the paper is organized as follows: A review of the literature is presented in Section 2. Section 3 discusses the research methodology and in Section 4, results of the study are presented. The article concludes with the findings of the study and suggestions for future research.

LITERATURE REVIEW

Demand forecasting methods are divided into two categories as qualitative and quantitative methods. The qualitative methods like Delphi technique, market research, and expert opinions are subjective methods based on one's thoughts and experience, and they are used in uncertain situations where there are insufficient data. On the other hand, the quantitative methods are used in cases where there are sufficient numerical quantities based on mathematical models (Karaatli et al., 2012). Quantitative methods are divided into two categories as time series (Box-Jenkins method, trend analysis, moving averages, exponential smoothing technique, etc.) and mixed methods (simple and multi-regression, econometric models and artificial intelligence and heuristics (genetic algorithm, support vector machines and artificial neural networks)) (Karaatli et al., 2012).

In the literature, several studies are using different demand forecasting methods to handle demand forecasting problem in the automotive sector. Wang et al. (2011) use an adaptive-network-based fuzzy inference system (ANFIS) to estimate new automobile sales in Taiwan. They use coincident indicators, leading indicators, wholesale price indices, independent indices and exchange rates in their forecasting model. The determinants of these indicators are as follows:

- Coincident indicators: Industrial production index, real customs-cleared exports, the sales of manufacturing, the sales index of wholesale, retail, and food services, real machinery and electrical equipment imports, the employment of non-agricultural, the total power consumption.

- Leading indicators: Average monthly overtime in industry and services, the index of export orders, the superficial measurements of housing starts and building permits, the indexes of producer's inventory, real monetary aggregates, SEMI book-to-bill ratio, stock price index.
- Wholesale price indices: The prices of the automobile, the oil prices, the prices of automobile components.
- Independent indices: Population, unemployment rate, the average earnings of employees in industry and services.
- Exchange rates: Exchange rates the N.T. dollar against the US dollar, exchange rates for the N.T. dollar against the Eurodollar.

They compare the results of ANFIS with ARIMA and ANN. ANFIS has been observed to perform better than the other two. Matsumoto and Ikeda (2015) use time series for demand forecasting of the reproduction of automobile parts. Even though product returns are extremely uncertain in terms of timing and quantity, manufacturers need to balance the demand for remanufactured products in order to avoid stock accumulation and to prevent the unmet return requests. For 400 type remanufactured alternators and starters, 12 years' data are used. Vahabi et al. (2016) combine adaptive-network-based fuzzy inference system (ANFIS) and genetic algorithm to forecast automobile sales of a leading company in Iran. They use per capita income, inflation rate, housing, Importation, Currency Rate (USD), loan interest rate and automobile import tariffs as input variables. They compare the results of their method with ANN, and their method gives better results than ANN. Abu-Eisheh and Mannering (2002) used a dynamic automobile demand simulation model based on a simultaneous-equation system, and they used lagged automobile quantity and price variables, economic, financial and operating cost variables, income and government policy variables. Gao et al. (2017) proposed a heuristic method based on particle swarm and ant colony techniques to forecast automobile sales in China by using highway mileage, GDP, automobile ownership and consumer price index. Hülsmann et al. (2012) used time series and data mining methods to forecast automobile sales in Germany and USA by using DAX, IFO, new car registrations, GDP, personal income, unemployment rate, interest rate, consumer prices, gasoline prices, private consumption, Dow Jones, BCI variables. They showed that support vector machine gives the most robust results; on the other hand, decision trees provide the most explicable results.

In the literature, there are also several studies using artificial neural networks in demand forecasting of automobiles. Artificial neural networks are frequently used in a wide range of areas such as medical diagnosis of cancer (Khan et al., 2001), diabetes (Temurtas et al., 2009), water consumption (Jain et al., 2001), stock prices (Baba, & Kozaki, 1992, Mumini et al.,2016; Weckman et al., 2016), electricity consumption (Tso, & Yau, 2007). Also, there are several studies related to demand forecasting in the automotive industry, which are using artificial neural networks. Gaojun and Boxue (2009) used a combination of curve–regression model, time series decomposition model and RBF neural networks according to the weight distribution for automobile sales forecasting. Actual sales data between January 2005 and March 2009 was used. Linear model results and nonlinear model results are summed up to estimate anticipation. Estimates for 2008-2009 were compared with actual sales in 2008-2009. Successful results have been obtained. Karaatli et al. (2012) use ANN to predict automobile sales in Turkey by using monthly data between January 2007 and June 2011. Gross Domestic Product (GDP), real sector confidence index, investment expenditures, consumption expenditures, consumer confidence index, dollar exchange rate and time are used as input variables, and a total number of the sold car is used as the output variable. As a result of this analysis, the MAPE value is by 16.82%. Kitapci et al. (2014) estimated vehicle sales using ANN and multi-stage regression method using euro rate, inflation, automobile and gas prices, advertising expenditures, GDP, and vehicle loan values as input variables between 2005 and 2010. Inflation, interest rates and exchange rates of Euro have a direct impact on sales. The MAPE value of ANN is 18%, and the MAPE value of regression is 54%. According to a comparison of MAPE values, ANN gives better results. Kuo and Wang (2002) proposed fuzzy neural network (FNN) method that performs better than conventional statistical methods and ANN to handle unique situations such as promotion in sales forecasting.

In our study, some variables, which are frequently used in the literature such as automobile sales, automobile price, employment rate, Euro and Dollar exchange rate, consumer confidence index, oil prices and industrial production confidence index, are included to our estimation model. As a difference from the studies in our literature review, the survey results of the probability of buying an automobile, female employment rate, general economic situation, the expectation of general economic situation, financial status of households, and expectation of financial status of households are also added to our model as input variables.

METHODOLOGY

In order to forecast automobile sales in Turkey, a four-step methodology is suggested as follows: First, variables, which are expected to affect automobile sales, are identified and significant input variables, which affect automobile sales, are determined by using multiple linear regression. Second, Artificial Neural Network (ANN) is used to forecast automobile sales by taking the significant input variables determined by multiple linear regression. In the last part, results of ANN models, ARIMA and time series decomposition techniques are compared.

Determining Significant Variables

Based on the studies about demand forecasting of automobile sales in the literature, automobile price, Euro and Dollar exchange rate, employment rate, consumer confidence index, oil prices and industrial production confidence index are taken as input variables. Additional to these variables, differently from the literature, the survey results of the probability of buying an automobile, female employment rate, general economic situation, the expectation of general economic situation, financial status of households, and expectation of financial status of households are taken as input variables. All input variables for 72 months between the years 2012-2017 are collected from Turkish Statistical Institute (TUIK) webpage (www.tuik.gov.tr). The monthly automobile sales in Turkey between the years 2012-2017, which are used as dependent variable, are collected from The Automotive Manufacturers Association (OSD) webpage (www.osd.org.tr). In order to determine which input variables have a significant effect on automobile sales, a multiple linear regression analysis is done by using E-views software.

Forecasting Automobile Sales with ANN

An artificial neural network (ANN) is a computational model which is formed from hundreds of artificial neurons biologically inspired from living neurons in the human brain (Agatonovic-Kustrin, & Beresford, 2000; Dayhoff, & DeLeo, 2001). ANN technique which is widely used in a broad range of areas such as science, engineering, medicine, defense, business, and manufacturing gives faster and more accurate solutions for complex and nonlinear problems than the other traditional techniques (Ghritlahre, & Prasad, 2018). A typical ANN model has three layers as an input layer, one or more hidden layers and an output layer as shown in Figure1. As shown in Figure1, inputs are multiplied by the synaptic weights and pass through a summing junction. The result of summing junction called as activation signal is passed through transfer function, which introduces non-linearity to the network to produce a single output of the neuron (Agatonovic-Kustrin, & Beresford, 2000). To reduce the error between the predicted and target values, ANN changes the synaptic weights by making backward propagation of the error during training or learning phase (Agatonovic-Kustrin, & Beresford, 2000).

Figure 1. Basic structure of MLFFNN (Ghritlahre, & Prasad, 2018)

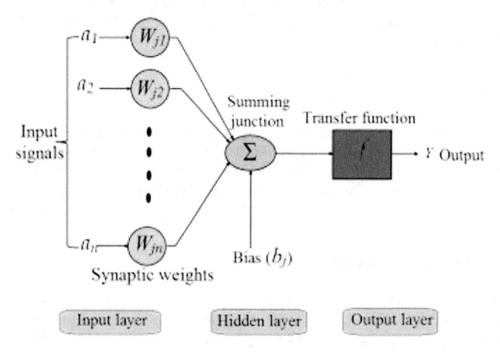

In this study, after determining the significant variables affecting automobile sales, ANN models are constructed by using these variables as input. Furthermore, to compare the performance of ANN using significant variables and determine the best-fitted forecast model, ANNs, which are using all variables, are constructed. In this study, we use multi-layer feed forward neural network (MLFFNN) which is the most popular architecture trained by gradient descent back-error propagation method (Dayhoff, & DeLeo, 2001) to construct ANN models. The basic structure of MLFFNN is shown in Figure 1. As the activation function, the hyperbolic tangent function defined as the Eq. (1) is used.

$$\tanh(x) = \frac{\sinh(x)}{\cosh(x)} = \frac{e^x - e^{-x}}{e^x + e^{-x}} \tag{1}$$

Comparison the Results of ANN with ARIMA and Time Series Decomposition Techniques

The results of ANN using significant variables are compared with the results of ARIMA and time series decomposition models to determine the best-fitted forecasting model for automobile sales. ARIMA and time series decomposition models are developed by using the significant equation, which is found as the result of multiple linear regression analysis. ARIMA models are used to forecast amount of automobile sales by using original form and logarithmic form of seasonally adjusted automobile sales. In addition, four-time series decomposition forecasting techniques are used to catch the cycles in the series. The first technique is for the data which has linear trend and multiplicative seasonality, the second one is for the nonlinear trend and multiplicative seasonality, the third one is for the linear trend, and additive seasonality and the fourth one is for the nonlinear trend and additive seasonality.

RESULTS

Determining Significant Variables

Before application of multiple linear regression analysis, for stationarity in data, Augmented Dickey-Fuller (ADF) test is made. According to test results, number of car sales in logarithmic form, general economic situation, expectation of general economic situation, financial status of households, expectation of financial status of households, probability of buying a car, industrial production index, consumer confidence index are found as I(0), thus, no differencing is needed for these variables. On the other hand, logarithmic form of automobile prices, exchange rates of Dollar and Euro, female employment rate, oil prices and inflation rate are found as I(1), and for these variables, first order differencing is needed. We also make a seasonal adjustment for female employment rate, automobile sales, and industrial production index.

According to the results of multiple regression analysis seen in Table 1, changes in Dollar exchange rate, the expectation of financial status of households, seasonally adjusted industrial production index, and logarithmic form of automobile sales before-one-month value are the most significant variables affecting automobile sales. In addition, dummy variables are added into the equation for the economic recession period in Turkey. As seen in Table 1, these significant variables explain the variance of automobile sales by % 73.1 (R^2 =% 73.1, adjusted R^2 = %70.5). Furthermore, the heteroscedasticity and autocorrelation problems are checked. The results of the White test for the heteroscedasticity problem ($n*R^2$=8.80(6), prob.:0.18) and LM test for the autocorrelation problem ($n*R^2$=1.84(2), prob.:0.39) show that there are no heteroscedasticity and autocorrelation problems for this equation. Ramsey Reset test is also used to check the specification error. According to the test result, (F= 0.36, prob.:0.54) there is no specification error for this equation, and error terms show a normal distribution (JB=0.92, prob.:0.62).

Forecasting Automobile Sales with ANN

After identification of the significant input variables, to determine the best-fitted forecast model, different ANN models are constructed by changing the number of hidden layers and neurons. Experiments are done by using SPSS 23 software. Multilayer feedforward backpropagation algorithm is used. The data is divided into 70% for training and 30% for testing. As the activation function, hyperbolic tangent is used.

Learning rate is taken as 0.4 and momentum is taken as 0.9. Performance of the models is compared according to the RMSE and MAPE values. First, the performance of the ANNs with one hidden layer for varying number of neurons between 1-10 is measured as seen in Table 2. While doing these experiments, to prevent overfitting, ANN models are not trained for too long. ANN which has 9 neurons has better performance with its minimum RMSE = 890 and MAPE = 1.31% values. After that, ANNs, which has two hidden layers, are constructed, and experiments are made by changing the number of neurons in their hidden layers between 1-10. The results of these experiments are shown in Table 3. According to the RMSE and MAPE values, ANN which has (10, 4) neurons in its hidden layers performs better than both the other models with one and two hidden layers.

Importance and normalized importance values of the input variables of best-fitted ANN model are shown in Table 4. According to the importance values, automobile sales before one month is the most significant variable affecting automobile sales. Historical sales are forecasted by using best-fitted ANN model and predicted sales are compared with actual sales as seen in Figure 2.

Table 1. Results of the multiple regression

Dependent Variable: Logarithmic form of seasonally adjusted automobile sales				
Method: Least Squares				
Sample (adjusted): 2012M02 2017M10				
Included observations: 69 after adjustments				
Variable	Coefficient	Std. Error	t-Statistic	Prob.
C	3.208284	1.032958	3.105918	0.0029
D(Dollar)	0.374020	0.154088	2.427312	0.0181
Expectation of Financial status of Households	0.010536	0.003918	2.689281	0.0092
Seasonal adjusted industrial production index	0.003308	0.000573	5.775404	0.0000
Logarithmic form of automobile sales before-one-month	0.580210	0.085520	6.784490	0.0000
Dum.16.12	-0.302287	0.089865	-3.363787	0.0013
Dum.16.07	-0.227407	0.084241	-2.699484	0.0089
R-squared	0.731938	Mean dependent var		10.86543
Adjusted R-squared	0.705996	S.D. dependent var		0.151340
S.E. of regression	0.082060	Akaike info criterion		-2.066811
Sum squared resid	0.417496	Schwarz criterion		-1.840162
Log-likelihood	78.30498	Hannan-Quinn criter.		-1.976892
F-statistic	28.21490	Durbin-Watson stat		1.725112
Prob(F-statistic)	0.000000			

Table 2. Results of ANNs having one hidden layer for varying number of neurons between 1-10

	Number of neurons in Hidden Layer 1									
	1	**2**	**3**	**4**	**5**	**6**	**7**	**8**	**9**	**10**
RMSE	1125	1029	983	977	985	1123	1048	1107	**890**	1132
MAPE	1.54	1.47	1.38	1.43	1.37	1.59	1.44	1.39	**1.31**	1.54

Table 3. Results of ANNs having two hidden layers for varying number of neurons between 1-10

			Number of neurons in Hidden Layer 2									
			1	**2**	**3**	**4**	**5**	**6**	**7**	**8**	**9**	**10**
	1	RMSE	1131	1210	1190	1468	1096	1236	2176	1504	1528	1077
		MAPE	1.54	1.72	1.62	1.83	1.54	1.7	2.72	1.93	1.93	1.47
	2	RMSE	1277	1852	1163	1486	1133	1734	1338	1027	1555	1199
		MAPE	1.77	2.33	1.61	1.79	1.66	2.52	1.85	1.45	2.01	1.64
	3	RMSE	1392	1123	1331	1268	1226	1161	1091	1041	1560	1518
		MAPE	1.79	1.59	1.66	1.62	1.59	1.61	1.48	1.42	1.97	2.01
	4	RMSE	1827	1347	1557	1533	1196	1015	1239	1234	1020	959
		MAPE	2.29	1.85	2.08	2.02	1.55	1.44	1.49	1.72	1.42	1.33
Number of neurons in Hidden Layer 1	**5**	RMSE	1065	1149	999	919	1046	1063	1495	1156	995	1055
		MAPE	1.46	1.56	1.43	1.26	1.39	1.54	1.94	1.58	1.41	1.55
	6	RMSE	1247	1084	1429	1942	1030	1225	994	914	1101	1064
		MAPE	1.64	1.56	1.96	2.5	1.44	1.72	1.45	1.31	1.55	1.36
	7	RMSE	1604	2154	1607	979	1069	1490	1207	997	1200	1341
		MAPE	1.93	2.83	2.07	1.43	1.59	1.99	1.58	1.43	1.74	1.75
	8	RMSE	1225	1495	848	1649	1336	1343	1006	1049	900	1026
		MAPE	1.77	1.88	1.25	2.02	1.73	1.82	1.39	1.42	1.31	1.46
	9	RMSE	1117	914	1063	977	1056	1041	1048	1057	1033	858
		MAPE	1.55	1.33	1.52	1.34	1.45	1.47	1.47	1.5	1.44	1.2
	10	RMSE	2053	1324	1625	**782**	1575	1187	1107	960	1088	1305
		MAPE	2.57	1.77	2.17	**1.18**	1.95	1.58	1.48	1.34	1.49	1.78

Table 4. Importance values of input variables of best fitted ANN model

Input variables	Importance	Normalized Importance
Dollar	0.070	9.6%
Seasonal adjusted industrial production index	0.084	11.5%
Automobile sales before-one-month	0.733	100.0%
Expectation of financial status of households	0.113	15.4%

Figure 2. Comparision of predicted sales of best fitted ANN model with actual sales

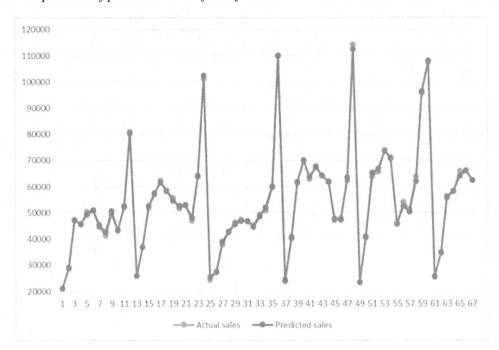

Comparison the Results of ANN with ARIMA and Time Series Decomposition Techniques

In this part, results of ANN model, which is found as the best-fitted model according to the experiments doing in the previous section are compared with the results of differently constructed ANN models, ARIMA and time series decomposition techniques. It shows better performance with its RMSE=782 and MAPE=%1.18 values than the other models as shown in Table 5. Other ANN models are constructed by including the insignificant input variables and changing the number of hidden layers and neurons. ANN models with two hidden layers give better results than the models with one hidden layer. Also, the result shows that adding the insignificant input variables to the ANN models does not improve the forecast performance of ANN. On the other hand, even though, ANN model using all logarithmic form of input variables with its RMSE=7290 and MAPE= 7.17% values is not better than the ANN using significant variable show better performance than the studies in the literature Karaatli (2012) & Kitapci (2014) which aims to forecast automobile sales in Turkey. As shown in Table 5, logarithmic ARIMA (3,1,2) has a better performance with %8.31 MAPE than other ARIMA models. On the other hand, according to the RMSE values, ARIMA (2,1,1) has a better forecasting performance than the other ARIMA models. Furthermore, time series decomposition models with multiplicative seasonality have better performance than the time series decomposition models with additive seasonality.

Table 5. RMSE and MAPE values of different forecasting methods

Model	RMSE	MAPE (%)
ANN Model 1 (# Hidden layers=2, # neurons in hidden layers= (10,4), only significant variables are included)	**782**	**1.18**
ANN Model 2 (# Hidden layers=1, # neurons in hidden layer=8, all variables are included)	10036	14.02
ANN Model 3 (# Hidden layers=2, # neurons in hidden layers= (8,6), all variables are included)	6777	9.67
ANN Model 4 (# Hidden layers=1, # neurons in hidden layers= 6, all variables are included by taking logarithms)	8801	11.60
ANN Model 5 (# Hidden layers=2, # neurons in hidden layers= (6,8), all variables are included by taking logarithms)	7290	7.17
ANN Model 6 (# Hidden layers=1, # neurons in hidden layers= 9, only significant variables are included)	890	1.31
ARIMA(1,1,0)	6882	8.90
ARIMA(1,1,0) (Log)	6825	8.81
ARIMA(1,1,1)	6642	8.69
ARIMA(1,1,1) (Log)	6636	8.56
ARIMA(2,1,1)	6258	8.67
ARIMA(2,1,1) (Log)	6968	8.56
ARIMA(2,1,2) (Log)	6634	8.45
ARIMA(3,1,2) (Log)	6342	8.31
Time Series Decomp 1	5990	8.56
Time Series Decomp 2	5990	8.56
Time Series Decomp 3	6400	9.59
Time Series Decomp 4	6400	9.59

CONCLUSION

This study reveals the significant factors, which have an effect on automobile sales in Turkey. Our initial forecasting model includes automobile sales, automobile price, Euro and Dollar exchange rate, employment rate, female employment rate, probability of buying a car, general economic situation, expectation of general economic situation, financial status of households, expectation of financial status of households, consumer confidence index, industrial production confidence index and oil prices. Most significant variables, which have an effect on automobile sales, are determined by using multiple regression analysis. According to regression results, changes in Dollar exchange rate, the expectation of financial status of households, seasonally adjusted industrial production index, and logarithmic form of automobile sales before-one-month value are the most significant variables and are taken as input variables for ANN. The results of the study show that ANN using the significant variables determined by multiple linear regression analysis has better forecasting performance than ANN model using all variables, ARIMA and time series decomposition techniques.

The existing regression model explains the variance of automobile sales as %73.1. Still, there is an unexplained part of it. As future research, new variables such as the prices of automobile components, employment of non-agricultural and total power consumption should be taken as input variables. Also to compare the results and get more accurate forecasts, other demand forecasting techniques like adaptive-network-based fuzzy inference system (ANFIS) and Grey forecasting models should be used.

REFERENCES

Abu-Eisheh, S. A., & Mannering, F. L. (2002). Forecasting automobile demand for economies in transition: A dynamic simultaneous-equation system approach. *Transportation Planning and Technology*, *25*(4), 311–331. doi:10.1080/0308106022000019026

Agatonovic-Kustrin, S., & Beresford, R. (2000). Basic concepts of artificial neural network (ANN) modeling and its application in pharmaceutical research. *Journal of Pharmaceutical and Biomedical Analysis*, *22*(5), 717–727. doi:10.1016/S0731-7085(99)00272-1 PMID:10815714

Baba, N., & Kozaki, M. (1992, June). An intelligent forecasting system of stock price using neural networks. In *Proceedings of the International Joint Conference on neural networks* (Vol. 1, pp. 371-377). Academic Press.

Dayhoff, J. E., & DeLeo, J. M. (2001). Artificial neural networks. *Cancer*, *91*(S8), 1615–1635. doi:10.1002/1097-0142(20010415)91:8+<1615::AID-CNCR1175>3.0.CO;2-L PMID:11309760

Gao, J., Xie, Y., Gu, F., Xiao, W., Hu, J., & Yu, W. (2017). A hybrid optimization approach to forecast automobile sales of China. *Advances in Mechanical Engineering*, *9*(8), 1687814017719422. doi:10.1177/1687814017719422

Gaojun, L., & Boxue, L. (2009) The research on combination forecasting model of the automobile sales forecasting system. In *Proceedings of the International Forum on Computer Science-Technology and Applications* (pp. 82-85). Academic Press.

Ghritlahre, H. K., & Prasad, R. K. (2018). application of ANN technique to predict the performance of solar collector systems-a review. *Renewable & Sustainable Energy Reviews*, *84*, 75–88. doi:10.1016/j.rser.2018.01.001

Hülsmann, M., Borscheid, D., Friedrich, C. M., & Reith, D. (2012). General sales forecast models for automobile markets and their analysis. *Trans. MLDM*, *5*(2), 65–86.

Jain, A., Varshney, A. K., & Joshi, U. C. (2001). Short-term water demand forecast modelling at IIT Kanpur using artificial neural networks. *Water Resources Management*, *15*(5), 299–321. doi:10.1023/A:1014415503476

Karaatli, M., Helvacioğlu, Ö. C., Ömürbek, N., & Tokgöz, G. (2012). Yapay sinir ağları yöntemi İle otomobil satış tahmini. *Uluslararası Yönetim İktisat ve İşletme Dergisi*, *8*(17), 87–100.

Khan, J., Wei, J. S., Ringner, M., Saal, L. H., Ladanyi, M., Westermann, F., & Meltzer, P. S. (2001). Classification and diagnostic prediction of cancers using gene expression profiling and artificial neural networks. *Nature Medicine*, *7*(6), 673–679. doi:10.1038/89044 PMID:11385503

Kitapçı, O., Özekicioğlu, H., Kaynar, O., & Taştan, S. (2014). The effects of economic policies applied in Turkey to the sale of automobiles: Multiple regression and neural network analysis. *Procedia: Social and Behavioral Sciences*, *148*, 653–661. doi:10.1016/j.sbspro.2014.07.094

Kuo, R. J., Wu, P., & Wang, C. P. (2002). An intelligent sales forecasting system through integration of artificial neural networks and fuzzy neural networks with fuzzy weight elimination. *Neural Networks*, *15*(7), 909–925. doi:10.1016/S0893-6080(02)00064-3 PMID:14672167

Matsumoto, M., & Ikeda, A. (2015). Examination of demand forecasting by time series analysis for auto parts remanufacturing. *Journal of Remanufacturing*, *5*(1), 1. doi:10.118613243-015-0010-y

Mumini, O. O., Adebisi, F. M., Edward, O. O., & Abidemi, A. S. (2016). Simulation of Stock Prediction System using Artificial Neural Networks. *International Journal of Business Analytics*, *3*(3), 25–44. doi:10.4018/IJBAN.2016070102

Otomotiv Sanayi Derneği. (2017), Automotive industry monthly reports, Retrieved from http://www.osd.org.tr/

PWC. (2017). 2017 Automotive trends, Retrieved from https://www.strategyand.pwc.com/trend/2017-automotive-industry-trends

PWC. (2018). Five trends transforming automotive industry. Retrieved from https://www.pwc.com/gx/en/industries/automotive/assets/pwc-five-trends-transforming-the-automotive-industry.pdf

TAYSAD. (2017). Otomotiv sektör Raporu, Retrieved from http://www.taysad.org.tr/uploads/dosyalar/06-02-2017-09-59-170206-Otomotiv_Sektor_Raporu_TSKB-2208.pdf

Temurtas, H., Yumusak, N., & Temurtas, F. (2009). A comparative study on diabetes disease diagnosis using neural networks. *Expert Systems with Applications*, *36*(4), 8610–8615. doi:10.1016/j.eswa.2008.10.032

Tso, G. K., & Yau, K. K. (2007). Predicting electricity energy consumption: A comparison of regression analysis, decision tree, and neural networks. *Energy*, *32*(9), 1761–1768. doi:10.1016/j.energy.2006.11.010

Turkish Statistical Institute (TUIK). (2017). Retrieved from http://www.turkstat.gov.tr/

Vahabi, A., Hosseininia, S. S., & Alborzi, M. (2016). A sales forecasting model in automotive industry using adaptive neuro-fuzzy inference system (Anfis) and genetic algorithm (GA). *Management*, *1*, 2.

Wang, F., Chang, K., & Tzeng, C. (2011). Using adaptive-network-based fuzzy inference system to forecast automobile sales. *Expert Systems with Applications*, *38*(8), 10587–105. doi:10.1016/j.eswa.2011.02.100

Weckman, G. R., Dravenstott, R. W., Young, W. A. II, Ardjmand, E., Millie, D. F., & Snow, A. P. (2016). A Prescriptive Stock Market Investment Strategy for the Restaurant Industry using an Artificial Neural Network Methodology. *International Journal of Business Analytics*, *3*(1), 1–21. doi:10.4018/IJBAN.2016010101

This research was previously published in the International Journal of Business Analytics (IJBAN), 6(4); pages 50-60, copyright year 2019 by IGI Publishing (an imprint of IGI Global).

Section 6
Emerging Trends

Chapter 73
Artificial Neural Networks in Medicine:
Recent Advances

Steven Walczak
https://orcid.org/0000-0002-0449-6272
University of South Florida, USA

ABSTRACT

Artificial neural networks (ANNs) have proven to be efficacious for modeling decision problems in medicine, including diagnosis, prognosis, resource allocation, and cost reduction problems. Research using ANNs to solve medical domain problems has been increasing regularly and is continuing to grow dramatically. This chapter examines recent trends and advances in ANNs and provides references to a large portion of recent research, as well as looking at the future direction of research for ANN in medicine.

INTRODUCTION

Medicine is a field closely coupled with and producing big data (Najafabadi et al., 2015), especially with the growing adoption of electronic health records (EHRs) in the United States (Bourgeois & Yaylacicegi, 2010; Mennemeyer et al., 2016) and the world (Wager et al., 2013, Appendix C). Medical big data serves as a critical resource for medical research and clinical decision making. Artificial neural networks (ANNs), along with other machine learning approaches, have been shown to be an effective method for analyzing medical big data to develop diagnostic and prognostic systems (Pastur-Romay et al., 2016).

Although ANNs have a short history of application in the field of medicine, with the first published research appearing in 1990 (Asada et al., 1990; Baxt, 1990; Dassen et al., 1990), there has been a continuing and growing trend of research investigating ANNs in medicine. Interestingly, two of the three articles published in 1990 were published in medical journals, while only Baxt's (1990) article on diagnosing heart attacks (myocardial infarctions) was published in an information technology journal, but he followed this work up with multiple publications in medical journals (Baxt, 1991, 1992). Searching

DOI: 10.4018/978-1-6684-2408-7.ch073

the National Library of Medicine PubMed database for articles containing the term "artificial neural network" combined with any of the terms: medicine, medical, hospital, patient, diagnosis, prognosis, clinic, or pharma (https://www.ncbi.nlm.nih.gov/pubmed/?term="artificial+neural+network"+AND +(medicine+OR+medical+OR+hospital+OR+patient+OR+diagnosis+OR+prognosis+OR+clinic +OR+pharma)) produces the results shown in Figure 1, which displays the annual increase in articles focusing on ANNs in medicine.

Figure 1. Medline/PubMed ANN articles in medicine as of July 15, 2020

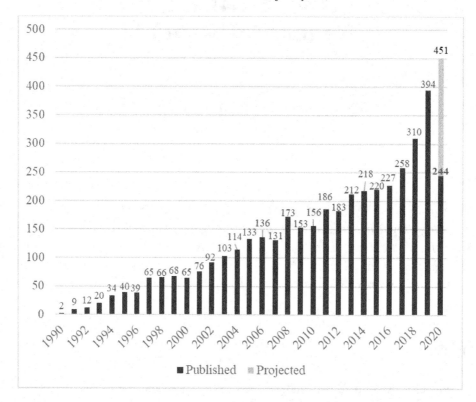

The amount of ANN in medicine research is even greater than depicted in Figure 1, since terms like "deep learning neural network" or "convolution network" or "evolutionary network," which are all types of ANN, are not included. Other researchers have also indicated a larger quantity of ANN research in medicine, with 473 articles in 1998 (Dybowski, 2000) as opposed to the 66 articles identified with the more specific search criteria. Other research claims an earlier start date, 1981, for the beginning of ANN usage in medical decision support (Miller, 1994), but here we report only those articles listed in the PubMed database.

ANN research in medicine is used to develop models and systems for a variety of applications including: decision support systems for both patients and surgeons, diagnosis, prognosis, resource planning and allocation, and variable significance and protocol heuristic evaluation. The goal of any research in the field of medicine should primarily be to improve the quality of life of the patient and secondarily to promote workflow efficiencies and cost reductions.

Next a brief definition of ANNs and a short historical perspective is presented. The purpose of this article is not to instruct researchers in how to develop an ANN, but rather to examine recent trends and advances in ANN research in medicine. Readers interested in a more general introduction to ANNs should examine the readings listed in the Additional Readings section. After the brief definition and historical background, recent research is described and trends in applying ANNs in medicine are discussed. Finally, future research directions are presented.

BACKGROUND

Artificial neural networks (ANNs) are a machine learning based classification and forecasting tool, based on modeling the neuronal activity of the human brain. ANNs come in a variety of architectures, which are represented by a large collection of interconnected processing elements called neurodes, and utilize a wide range of machine learning algorithms. These algorithms may be classified as either unsupervised learning or supervised learning or hybrid learning algorithms that utilize both unsupervised and supervised features.

Unsupervised ANNs learn classifications directly from the data they are analyzing and have long been used for image analysis in medicine, including mammography (Floyd Jr. et al., 1994; Leinsinger et al., 2006), MRI (Amartur et al., 1992; Wismüller et al., 2004), and other images (Jiang et al., 2010; Lin et al., 1996). Newer deep learning unsupervised ANNs are still being used for image classification and diagnosis based on images (Kallenberg et al., 2016).

Supervised ANNs require data with known outcomes to help guide the machine learning algorithms used in ANNs. Retrospective medical data is readily available from EHRs and other medical databases to serve as training data for supervised learning methods. Supervised learning ANNs have their neurodes arranged in layers, with increasing numbers of hidden layers enabling a higher degree of nonlinearity in the resultant model (Walczak & Cerpa, 1999).

ANNs have tremendous advantages for performing medical modeling (Tu, 1996; Walczak, 2008). These advantages include: ANN models are created using machine learning so arbitrarily complex nonlinear relationships are identifiable; ANNs are nonparametric so prior knowledge of population and error distributions is unnecessary; once trained they are tolerant of noise in the data; and they are extremely fast even when working with very large data sets. Although research with ANNs in medical domains is growing rapidly, the main reason why ANNs have not been implemented and adopted further in clinical settings is their black box nature. The black box nature of ANNs does not enable causal analysis similar to logistic regression (Tu, 1996). Understanding causal relationships and identifying relevant variables is of significant importance in medical decision making (Hunink et al., 2014). However, this should not be seen as an impediment to implementing ANNs in medical decision support systems since various techniques exist to facilitate outcome explanations and assessment of the causal nature between the independent and dependent variables (Andrews et al., 1995; Guidotti et al., 2018; Olden & Jackson, 2002; Walczak, 2008). These techniques include rule extraction by examining the weighted connections (Augasta & Kathirvalavakumar, 2012; Zhou et al., 2003) and variable influence determination by leaving each variable and sets of variables out of the input set and evaluating their relative influence (Tu, 1996; Walczak, 2008).

CURRENT DIRECTIONS OF ANN RESEARCH IN MEDICINE

While research focused on ANNs in medicine is growing rapidly, adoption of ANNs in clinical practice is still lagging. Logistic regression is the principal modeling methodology employed in medical research (Dreiseitl & Ohno-Machado, 2002; Tu, 1996). Most ANN research presents a comparison of ANN prediction results evaluated against results from comparable regression models (e.g., Churpek et al. (2016), Fei et al. (2017), Futoma et al. (2015), Kim et al. (2018), Teo et al. (2018)), and this practice needs to continue for the time being, until most clinicians feel comfortable with ANNs. The ongoing need to compare ANN results against other more familiar statistical models, including regression, is not unique to medical domains. Comparisons of ANN results to other recognized techniques occurs across a wide variety of domains including: engineering (Kaytez et al., 2015; Khademi et al., 2017), geological and environmental sciences (Dou et al., 2018; Nourani et al., 2014), and physics (Kumar et al., 2015) among others. Until the research community accepts the general validity of ANNs, continued presentations of comparative models is beneficial to gaining acceptance of ANN medical models and systems.

In the last decade, the concept of deep learning and Deep ANNs has become a hot topic in machine learning research (Arel et al. 2010). Deep ANNs have proven to be beneficial, especially in sensory recognition and classification problems (Schmidhuber, 2015), such as detecting malignancies in medical images (Hinton, 2018). The definition of a "Deep ANN" is any ANN that has more than one hidden layer. The longer the path between the independent input variables and the dependent output variable, then the deeper the possible learning. One difference between Deep ANNs and more traditional supervised multilayer perceptrons and unsupervised Kohonen self-organizing map (SOM) ANNs is that the individual layers or collections thereof may alternately use different supervised learning or unsupervised learning training methods, thus combining both supervised and unsupervised learning into a single ANN network. It should be noted though that the idea of multiple hidden layer ANNs has been around since at least 1989 (Cybenko, 1989; Funahashi, 1989) or earlier and that the backpropagation learning algorithm created by Werbos (1974), which first enable multilayered ANNs (including the input layer, hidden layer(s), and output layer), does not pose any theoretical limit on the number of hidden layers within an ANN. While no theoretical limit exists, the addition of each new hidden layer introduces another layer of complexity in the solution surface (e.g., introducing concavities to a convex solution surface) (Walczak & Cerpa, 1999) and in practice most medical research ANN models do not go past 3 hidden layers (Dahl et al., 2012).

From the PubMed data displayed in Figure 1, seven articles published in 2018 had deep learning or Deep ANN in their title (Cao et al., 2018; Gawehn et al., 2018; Grapov et al., 2018; Higaki et al., 2018; Pinaya et al., 2018; Prahs et al., 2018; Zanella-Calzada et al., 2018). A Google Scholar search for research published in 2018 containing the phrase "deep neural network" combined with some of the terms from the PubMed search, specifically: cancer, clinic, hospital, medicine, patient, or surgery; yielded over 17,000 results. From the Google Scholar search, some examples of items with the term deep learning or Deep ANN in their title include: scanning images for cancer markers (Ali et al., 2018; Bevilacqua et al., 2018; Salz et al., 2018), dentistry image scanning (Karimian et al., 2018), and retinal image analysis (Kermany et al., 2018). These sample articles represent a very small portion of the research currently being conducted on the application of deep learning through Deep ANNs in the field of medicine.

Evolutionary learning is being applied to ANNs more frequently. The term evolutionary learning and also evolutionary ANN indicates that a biological model, which includes artificial life and genetic algorithms, is being applied to an ANN to determine the optimal network architecture or is being used in combination with ANNs to select input criteria or further improve the output classifications or predictions of the ANN. The idea of combining evolutionary learning, in particular genetic algorithms, to improve ANN performance started in the late 1980's (Miller et al, 1989; Montana & Davis, 1989), but has seen significant growth recently including the application of evolutionary learning to Deep ANNs (Arabasadi et al., 2017; Cui et al., 2018; Jiang et al., 2017; Li et al., 2018).

Besides Deep ANNs, a relatively new ANN methodology that is attracting attention for medical image and signal analysis is the convolutional ANN, abbreviated as either CNN or ConvNet. A CNN is composed of multiple layers and after the input layer, alternates between a convolution layer, which tries to match regions of an image or signal, and pooling layers, which condense the output from the convolutional layer into a smaller data set while maintaining all relevant information (Nebauer, 1998). Because of the multiple layers of CNNs, they should also be considered as Deep ANNs. Some CNN configurations specify an additional layer between the convolutional layer and the pooling layer which serves as an activation function to recognize relevant parts of the signal. These layers may be stacked to form multiple convolution to activation to pooling combinations until the signal classification achieves a desired accuracy. Examples of recent application of CNNs in medicine are: detecting myocardial infarction from electrocardiogram signals (Acharya et al., 2017), and detection of possible cancerous lesions for breast (Bejnordi et al., 2017), gastric (Hirasawa et al., 2018), lung (Yu et al., 2017), and pancreatic (Wang et al., 2018) cancers among others (Halicek et al., 2018).

ANNs provide the field of medicine with an efficient and reliable method for performing both nonparametric and nonlinear modeling using machine learning. While resulting classification and prediction models perform very well, a recent trend has emerged to try and further strengthen ANN results and possibly make their outcomes more understandable. This trend is the combination (or triangulation) of ANNs with other mathematical, statistical, and machine learning methods, including other ANNs, into single systems (Walczak, 2012). Smith (1993) indicates that all supervised learning ANN variables should first be evaluated using correlation analysis (e.g., Pearson's correlation matrix) to identify and remove highly correlated variables that can decrease ANN performance accuracy. CNNs, especially if convolution and pooling layers are iterated multiple times, may be considered as a form of triangulation that enables the output of earlier ANN to be used as input to a new ANN, which then improves upon the prediction or classification of the image from the earlier ANNs. The term ANN ensemble signifies that a combination of ANNs are used with the output of one or more ANNs serving as the input to other ANNs. The idea of utilizing other machine learning methods in combination with ANNs was mentioned earlier in the form of utilizing evolutionary algorithms to improve ANN performance by determining optimal independent input variables or the form of ANN architectures. Traditional statistical methods may be used to help determine the optimal set of independent variables. An example of how to triangulate ANNs with other methods is the classification of genes related to cancers, which uses a statistical method, principal component analysis, to select genes to be considered in the input variable set and an ANN to classify the gene sets related to various cancers based on the variables determined by the principal component analysis statistical method (Chu & Wang, 2009).

ANN triangulation approaches to solving medical problems are varied and use a wide range of techniques in combination with ANNs. Table 1 displays a few recent examples of different techniques combined with ANNs in medical domains, demonstrating the growing trend of combining ANNs with other modeling strategies to gain the nonparametric and machine learning advantages of ANNs while diminishing any disadvantages associated with the black box nature of ANNs.

Table 1. Methods commonly combined (triangulated) with ANNs in medicine.

Triangulated Method	Medical Problem	Reference
Genetic algorithm (evolutionary)	multiple (diabetes, retinopathy) nasopharyngeal carcinoma	(Cortes et al., 2017) (Mohammed et al., 2018)
Mathematical/Statistical: k-means cluster correlation	Heart disease Pancreatic cancer survival	(Malav et al., 2017) (Walczak & Velanovich, 2018)
Other ANN (ensembles)	classifying white blood cells	(Rawat et al., 2018)
Combined: math/stat & ANN ensemble	blood pressure prediction	(Sadrawi et al., 2016)

ANN MEDICAL RESEARCH CONTINUING FORWARD

As stated above, the primary goal of research in medicine should always be to improve the quality of life of patients. This may be achieved through improved diagnostics to better understand and identify medical risks, improved treatment and outcomes assessment to improve recovery and understanding of outcomes, improved workflow and resource efficiencies to decrease the time required to obtain medical consultation or relief, and reduced costs to lessen the financial impact on patients.

Because ANNs utilize machine learning to model complex nonlinear problems, the results may be viewed as heuristic in nature and typically do not achieve 100% accuracy (both sensitivity and specificity). Research is ongoing to try and improve the performance of ANN models in the medical domain to better satisfy the goal of improved patient quality of life. As an example, some of the earliest ANN research was focused on predicting myocardial infarctions (Baxt 1990, 1991, 1992), a type of heart failure. ANN-based research on myocardial infarctions has continued (Baxt et al., 2002) and has sought to utilize new developments in ANN learning methods and architectures such as deep learning implemented in Deep ANNs (Acharya et al., 2017). A timeline of research examining the use of ANNs to detect or diagnose myocardial infarctions is shown in Table 2. We limit the results in Table 2 to 35 articles for readability, though many more exist for this specific medical diagnosis. As ANN researched progresses, in addition to utilizing newer techniques like convolutional and Deep ANNs, the research has shifted focus to not only diagnose myocardial infarctions, but also to diagnose other related coronary syndromes and to predict outcomes and survival related to myocardial infarctions, encompassing the full diagnostic and prognostic spectrum. As ANN research continues to try and improve on existing diagnostic, prognostic, cost savings, and resource allocation issues in medicine, the trend of expanding the focus of ANN solutions will continue and make ANN-based clinical decision support systems more encompassing.

FUTURE RESEARCH DIRECTIONS

Though ANN solutions in medicine have proven reliable and efficacious, many physicians and other clinical practitioners still remain hesitant to adopt this technology. The reason for this adoption reluctance as mentioned previously, ANNs are considered a black box and the consequent lack of information concerning causal relationships between the independent and dependent variables (Tu, 1996). ANN research should definitely continue and expand to be able to show applicability across all subfields of medicine and further continue research to provide mechanisms to automatically provide knowledge concerning the casual effects discovered by ANNs, since this knowledge is critical to medical research. Some ANN development tools, like JustNN (Neural Planner Software, 2015) imply variable causality by summing the absolute weights of connections.

Table 2. ANN research to diagnose acute myocardial infarction (AMI).

YEAR	# of articles	References
1990	1	(Baxt, 1990)
1991	2	(Baxt, 1991); (Furlong et al., 1991)
1992	2	(Baxt, 1992); (Reddy et al., 1992)
1993	1	(Bortolan & Willems, 1993)
1994	3	(Baxt, 1994); (Hedén et al., 1994); (Yang et al., 1994)
1995	2	(Baxt & White, 1995); (Selker et al., 1995)
1996	4	(Baxt & Skora, 1996) ; (Hedén et al., 1996); (Kumaravel et al., 1996); (Pedersen et al., 1996)
1997	3	(Ellenius et al., 1997); (Hedén et al., 1997); (Kennedy et al., 1997)
2000	1	(Ohlsson et al., 2000)
2001	1	(Ohlsson et al., 2001)
2002	2	(Baxt et al., 2002); (Olsson et al., 2002)
2004	2	(Haraldsson et al., 2004); (Hollander et al., 2004)
2005	2	(Bigi et al., 2005)[†]; (Harrison & Kennedy, 2005)[††]
2007	1	(Eggers et al., 2007)[†††]
2010	1	(Arif et al., 2010)
2011	1	(Sankari & Adeli, 2011)[††]
2013	1	(Keshtkar et al., 2013)
2014	1	(Safdarian et al., 2014)
2015	1	(Bhaskar, 2015)
2017	1	(Acharya et al., 2017)
2018	3	(Liu et al., 2018a); (Liu et al., 2018b, 2018c)

[†]examines recovery/prognostics following AMI

[††]models a group of acute coronary syndromes including myocardial infarction

[†††]also models infarct size

The expansion of ANN research to ultimately cover all fields of medicine is a desirable goal. One step in this direction that is needed is to make ANN solutions more generalizable. As an example, ANN research on predicting transfusion requirements has uniformly been targeted at predicting transfusion needs for patients of a single medical illness or procedure. Examples include ANN networks to predict transfusion requirements for coronary artery bypass (CABG) surgery (Covin et al., 2003), leukemia patients (Ho & Chang, 2011), and abdominal aortic aneurysm (AAA) surgery (Walczak & Scharf, 2000). Future research is needed to identify, using ANNs, those variables causally related to transfusion needs in humans and then develop ANN models that may be applied across a much wider range of surgery types and illnesses that may require transfusions. Ideally, new ANN research will produce a combined resource and prognostic model that is applicable to all classes of surgery. This approach of generalization should also be applied to other prognostic problems, including the anesthesia, physical and occupational therapy, and pharmacological needs of patients.

Electronic health records (EHRs) are widely used worldwide to improve patient care (Bourgeois & Yaylacicegi, 2010; Mennemeyer et al., 2016) and also serve as a data resource for ANN research (Bibault et al., 2016; Weng et al., 2017). As predicted by Kuperman et al. (2007) ANN diagnostic and prognostic tools need to become integrated into EHRs to provide decision support. ANNs are starting to be embedded into the clinical decision making process, especially in radiology (Pesapane et al., 2018). The integration of ANN diagnostic or prognostic models into EHRs, with a corresponding explanation facility, will provide another route for implementation of ANNs in practice. The need for moving ANN research into clinical practice is widely recognized (Khazaee et al., 2018).

The future of medicine is moving towards body area networks and implantable medical devices (IMD) to enable mobile data acquisition and treatment decision making. ANNs are already starting to be embedded within physical therapy wireless body area network devices (Lin et al., 2015), and this trend of utilizing ANNs in body area networks and IMDs will continue to grow. The integration of ANNs into an IMD requires the overall size of the implemented ANN to be small, but this is another future direction for ANN research.

CONCLUSION

ANNs are a machine learning method based on the neurology of the human brain and are useful for classification and prediction problems in medicine. Past research has demonstrated the efficacy of utilizing ANNs to perform diagnostics, prognostics, cost reduction, and resource allocation problem solving in medicine. The use of ANNs to model medical diagnostic, prognostic, resource allocation, and cost minimization problems is a growing trend for the foreseeable future.

REFERENCES

Acharya, U. R., Fujita, H., Oh, S. L., Hagiwara, Y., Tan, J. H., & Adam, M. (2017). Application of deep convolutional neural network for automated detection of myocardial infarction using ECG signals. *Information Sciences*, *415*, 190–198. doi:10.1016/j.ins.2017.06.027

Ali, I., Hart, G., Gunabushanam, G., Liang, Y., Muhammad, W., Nartowt, B., Kane, M., Ma, X., & Deng, J. (2018). Lung nodule detection via deep reinforcement learning. *Frontiers in Oncology*, *8*, 108. doi:10.3389/fonc.2018.00108 PMID:29713615

Amartur, S. C., Piraino, D., & Takefuji, Y. (1992). Optimization neural networks for the segmentation of magnetic resonance images. *IEEE Transactions on Medical Imaging*, *11*(2), 215–220. doi:10.1109/42.141645 PMID:18218375

Andrews, R., Diederich, J., & Tickle, A. B. (1995). Survey and critique of techniques for extracting rules from trained artificial neural networks. *Knowledge-Based Systems*, *8*(6), 373–389. doi:10.1016/0950-7051(96)81920-4

Arabasadi, Z., Alizadehsani, R., Roshanzamir, M., Moosaei, H., & Yarifard, A. A. (2017). Computer aided decision making for heart disease detection using hybrid neural network-Genetic algorithm. *Computer Methods and Programs in Biomedicine*, *141*, 19–26. doi:10.1016/j.cmpb.2017.01.004 PMID:28241964

Arel, I., Rose, D. C., & Karnowski, T. P. (2010). Deep machine learning-a new frontier in artificial intelligence research. *IEEE Computational Intelligence Magazine*, *5*(4), 13–18. doi:10.1109/MCI.2010.938364

Arif, M., Malagore, I. A., & Afsar, F. A. (2010). Automatic detection and localization of myocardial infarction using back propagation neural networks. In *4th International Conference on Bioinformatics and Biomedical Engineering*, (pp. 1-4). IEEE. 10.1109/ICBBE.2010.5514664

Asada, N., Doi, K., MacMahon, H., Montner, S. M., Giger, M. L., Abe, C., & Wu, Y. U. Z. H. E. N. G. (1990). Potential usefulness of an artificial neural network for differential diagnosis of interstitial lung diseases: Pilot study. *Radiology*, *177*(3), 857–860. doi:10.1148/radiology.177.3.2244001 PMID:2244001

Augasta, M. G., & Kathirvalavakumar, T. (2012). Reverse engineering the neural networks for rule extraction in classification problems. *Neural Processing Letters*, *35*(2), 131–150. doi:10.100711063-011-9207-8

Baxt, W. G. (1990). Use of an artificial neural network for data analysis in clinical decision-making: The diagnosis of acute coronary occlusion. *Neural Computation*, *2*(4), 480–489. doi:10.1162/neco.1990.2.4.480

Baxt, W. G. (1991). Use of an artificial neural network for the diagnosis of myocardial infarction. *Annals of Internal Medicine*, *115*(11), 843–848. doi:10.7326/0003-4819-115-11-843 PMID:1952470

Baxt, W. G. (1992). Analysis of the clinical variables driving decision in an artificial neural network trained to identify the presence of myocardial infarction. *Annals of Emergency Medicine*, *21*(12), 1439–1444. doi:10.1016/S0196-0644(05)80056-3 PMID:1443838

Baxt, W. G. (1994). A neural network trained to identify the presence of myocardial infarction bases some decisions on clinical associations that differ from accepted clinical teaching. *Medical Decision Making*, *14*(3), 217–222. doi:10.1177/0272989X9401400303 PMID:7934708

Baxt, W. G., Shofer, F. S., Sites, F. D., & Hollander, J. E. (2002). A neural computational aid to the diagnosis of acute myocardial infarction. *Annals of Emergency Medicine*, *39*(4), 366–373. doi:10.1067/mem.2002.122705 PMID:11919522

Baxt, W. G., & Skora, J. (1996). Prospective validation of artificial neural network trained to identify acute myocardial infarction. *Lancet*, *347*(8993), 12–14. doi:10.1016/S0140-6736(96)91555-X PMID:8531540

Baxt, W. G., & White, H. (1995). Bootstrapping confidence intervals for clinical input variable effects in a network trained to identify the presence of acute myocardial infarction. *Neural Computation*, *7*(3), 624–638. doi:10.1162/neco.1995.7.3.624 PMID:8935962

Bejnordi, B. E., Veta, M., Van Diest, P. J., Van Ginneken, B., Karssemeijer, N., Litjens, G., Van Der Laak, J. A., Hermsen, M., Manson, Q. F., Balkenhol, M., & Geessink, O. (2017). Diagnostic assessment of deep learning algorithms for detection of lymph node metastases in women with breast cancer. *Journal of the American Medical Association*, *318*(22), 2199–2210. doi:10.1001/jama.2017.14585 PMID:29234806

Bevilacqua, V., Brunetti, A., Guerriero, A., Trotta, G. F., Telegrafo, M., & Moschetta, M. (2018). A performance comparison between shallow and deeper neural networks supervised classification of to-mosynthesis breast lesions images. *Cognitive Systems Research.*

Bhaskar, N. A. (2015). Performance analysis of support vector machine and neural networks in detection of myocardial infarction. *Procedia Computer Science, 46*, 20–30. doi:10.1016/j.procs.2015.01.043

Bibault, J. E., Giraud, P., & Burgun, A. (2016). Big data and machine learning in radiation oncology: State of the art and future prospects. *Cancer Letters, 382*(1), 110–117. doi:10.1016/j.canlet.2016.05.033 PMID:27241666

Bigi, R., Gregori, D., Cortigiani, L., Desideri, A., Chiarotto, F. A., & Toffolo, G. M. (2005). Artificial neural networks and robust Bayesian classifiers for risk stratification following uncomplicated myocardial infarction. *International Journal of Cardiology, 101*(3), 481–487. doi:10.1016/j.ijcard.2004.07.008 PMID:15907418

Bortolan, G., & Willems, J. L. (1993). Diagnostic ECG classification based on neural networks. *Journal of Electrocardiology, 26*, 75–79. PMID:8189152

Bourgeois, S., & Yaylacicegi, U. (2010). Electronic Health Records: Improving Patient Safety and Quality of Care in Texas Acute Care Hospitals. *International Journal of Healthcare Information Systems and Informatics, 5*(3), 1–13. doi:10.4018/jhisi.2010070101

Cao, C., Liu, F., Tan, H., Song, D., Shu, W., Li, W., Zhou, Y., Bo, X., & Xie, Z. (2018). Deep Learning and Its Applications in Biomedicine. *Genomics, Proteomics & Bioinformatics, 16*(1), 17–32. doi:10.1016/j.gpb.2017.07.003 PMID:29522900

Chu, F., & Wang, L. (2009). Biomedical Data Mining Using RBF Neural Networks. In Medical Informatics: Concepts, Methodologies, Tools, and Applications (pp. 2066-2073). IGI Global. doi:10.4018/978-1-60566-050-9.ch157

Churpek, M. M., Yuen, T. C., Winslow, C., Meltzer, D. O., Kattan, M. W., & Edelson, D. P. (2016). Multicenter comparison of machine learning methods and conventional regression for predicting clinical deterioration on the wards. *Critical Care Medicine, 44*(2), 368–374. doi:10.1097/CCM.0000000000001571 PMID:26771782

Cortes, C., Gonzalvo, X., Kuznetsov, V., Mohri, M., & Yang, S. (2017). AdaNet: Adaptive Structural Learning of Artificial Neural Networks. In *International Conference on Machine Learning* (pp. 874-883).

Covin, R., O'Brien, M., Grunwald, G., Brimhall, B., Sethi, G., Walczak, S., Reiquam, W., Rajagopalan, C., & Shroyer, A. L. (2003). Factors affecting transfusion of fresh frozen plasma, platelets, and red blood cells during elective coronary artery bypass graft surgery. *Archives of Pathology & Laboratory Medicine, 127*(4), 415–423. PMID:12683868

Cui, S., Wang, D., Wang, Y., Yu, P. W., & Jin, Y. (2018). An Improved Support Vector Machine-based Diabetic Readmission Prediction. *Computer Methods and Programs in Biomedicine, 166*, 123–135. doi:10.1016/j.cmpb.2018.10.012 PMID:30415712

Cybenko, G. (1989). Approximation by superpositions of a sigmoidal function. *Mathematics of Control, Signals, and Systems, 2*(4), 303–314. doi:10.1007/BF02551274

Dahl, G. E., Yu, D., Deng, L., & Acero, A. (2012). Context-dependent pre-trained deep neural networks for large-vocabulary speech recognition. *IEEE Transactions on Audio, Speech, and Language Processing, 20*(1), 30–42. doi:10.1109/TASL.2011.2134090

Dassen, W. R., Mulleneers, R. G., Dulk, K. D., Smeets, J. R., Cruz, F., Penn, O. C., & Wellens, H. J. (1990). An Artificial Neural Network to Localize Atrioventricular Accessory Pathways in Patients Suffering from the Wolff-Parkinson-White Syndrome. *Pacing and Clinical Electrophysiology, 13*(12), 1792–1796. doi:10.1111/j.1540-8159.1990.tb06892.x PMID:1704543

Dou, J., Yamagishi, H., Zhu, Z., Yunus, A. P., & Chen, C. W. (2018). TXT-tool 1.081-6.1 A Comparative Study of the Binary Logistic Regression (BLR) and Artificial Neural Network (ANN) Models for GIS-Based Spatial Predicting Landslides at a Regional Scale. In *Landslide Dynamics: ISDR-ICL Landslide Interactive Teaching Tools* (pp. 139–151). Springer. doi:10.1007/978-3-319-57774-6_10

Dreiseitl, S., & Ohno-Machado, L. (2002). Logistic regression and artificial neural network classification models: A methodology review. *Journal of Biomedical Informatics, 35*(5-6), 352–359. doi:10.1016/S1532-0464(03)00034-0 PMID:12968784

Dybowski, R. (2000). Neural computation in medicine: perspectives and prospects. In *Artificial Neural Networks in Medicine and Biology* (pp. 26–36). Springer. doi:10.1007/978-1-4471-0513-8_4

Eggers, K. M., Ellenius, J., Dellborg, M., Groth, T., Oldgren, J., Swahn, E., & Lindahl, B. (2007). Artificial neural network algorithms for early diagnosis of acute myocardial infarction and prediction of infarct size in chest pain patients. *International Journal of Cardiology, 114*(3), 366–374. doi:10.1016/j.ijcard.2005.12.019 PMID:16797088

Ellenius, J., Groth, T., Lindahl, B., & Wallentin, L. (1997). Early assessment of patients with suspected acute myocardial infarction by biochemical monitoring and neural network analysis. *Clinical Chemistry, 43*(10), 1919–1925. doi:10.1093/clinchem/43.10.1919 PMID:9342013

Fei, Y., Hu, J., Gao, K., Tu, J., Li, W. Q., & Wang, W. (2017). Predicting risk for portal vein thrombosis in acute pancreatitis patients: A comparison of radical basis function artificial neural network and logistic regression models. *Journal of Critical Care, 39*, 115–123. doi:10.1016/j.jcrc.2017.02.032 PMID:28246056

Floyd, C. E. Jr, Lo, J. Y., Yun, A. J., Sullivan, D. C., & Kornguth, P. J. (1994). Prediction of breast cancer malignancy using an artificial neural network. *Cancer: Interdisciplinary International Journal of the American Cancer Society, 74*(11), 2944–2948. doi:10.1002/1097-0142(19941201)74:11<2944::AID-CNCR2820741109>3.0.CO;2-F PMID:7954258

Funahashi, K. I. (1989). On the approximate realization of continuous mappings by neural networks. *Neural Networks, 2*(3), 183–192. doi:10.1016/0893-6080(89)90003-8

Furlong, J. W., Dupuy, M. E., & Heinsimer, J. A. (1991). Neural Network Analysis of Serial Cardiac Enzyme Data A Clinical Application of Artificial Machine Intelligence. *American Journal of Clinical Pathology, 96*(1), 134–141. doi:10.1093/ajcp/96.1.134 PMID:2069131

Futoma, J., Morris, J., & Lucas, J. (2015). A comparison of models for predicting early hospital readmissions. *Journal of Biomedical Informatics*, *56*, 229–238. doi:10.1016/j.jbi.2015.05.016 PMID:26044081

Gawehn, E., Hiss, J. A., Brown, J. B., & Schneider, G. (2018). Advancing drug discovery via GPU-based deep learning. *Expert Opinion on Drug Discovery*, *13*(7), 579–582. doi:10.1080/17460441.2018.1465 407 PMID:29668343

Grapov, D., Fahrmann, J., Wanichthanarak, K., & Khoomrung, S. (2018). Rise of Deep Learning for Genomic, Proteomic, and Metabolomic Data Integration in Precision Medicine. *OMICS: A Journal of Integrative Biology*, *22*(10), 22. doi:10.1089/omi.2018.0097 PMID:30124358

Guidotti, R., Monreale, A., Ruggieri, S., Turini, F., Giannotti, F., & Pedreschi, D. (2018). A survey of methods for explaining black box models. *ACM Computing Surveys*, *51*(5), 93.

Halicek, M., Little, J. V., Wang, X., Patel, M., Griffith, C. C., El-Deiry, M. W., Chen, A. Y., & Fei, B. (2018). Optical biopsy of head and neck cancer using hyperspectral imaging and convolutional neural networks. In Optical Imaging, Therapeutics, and Advanced Technology in Head and Neck Surgery and Otolaryngology 2018 (Vol. 10469, p. 104690X). International Society for Optics and Photonics. doi:10.1117/12.2289023

Haraldsson, H., Edenbrandt, L., & Ohlsson, M. (2004). Detecting acute myocardial infarction in the 12-lead ECG using Hermite expansions and neural networks. *Artificial Intelligence in Medicine*, *32*(2), 127–136. doi:10.1016/j.artmed.2004.01.003 PMID:15364096

Harrison, R. F., & Kennedy, R. L. (2005). Artificial neural network models for prediction of acute coronary syndromes using clinical data from the time of presentation. *Annals of Emergency Medicine*, *46*(5), 431–439. doi:10.1016/j.annemergmed.2004.09.012 PMID:16271675

Hedén, B., Edenbrandt, L., Haisty, W. K. Jr, & Pahlm, O. (1994). Artificial neural networks for the electrocardiographic diagnosis of healed myocardial infarction. *The American Journal of Cardiology*, *74*(1), 5–8. doi:10.1016/0002-9149(94)90482-0 PMID:8017306

Hedén, B., Ohlin, H., Rittner, R., & Edenbrandt, L. (1997). Acute myocardial infarction detected in the 12-lead ECG by artificial neural networks. *Circulation*, *96*(6), 1798–1802. doi:10.1161/01.CIR.96.6.1798 PMID:9323064

Hedén, B. O., Ohlsson, M., Rittner, R., Pahlm, O., Haisty, W. K., Peterson, C., & Edenbrandt, L. (1996). Agreement between artificial neural networks and experienced electrocardiographer on electrocardiographic diagnosis of healed myocardial infarction. *Journal of the American College of Cardiology*, *28*(4), 1012–1016. PMID:8837583

Higaki, A., Mogi, M., Iwanami, J., Min, L. J., Bai, H. Y., Shan, B. S., Kukida, M., Kan-no, H., Ikeda, S., Higaki, J., & Horiuchi, M. (2018). Predicting outcome of Morris water maze test in vascular dementia mouse model with deep learning. *PLoS One*, *13*(2), e0191708. doi:10.1371/journal.pone.0191708 PMID:29415035

Hinton, G. (2018). Deep learning—A technology with the potential to transform health care. *Journal of the American Medical Association*, *320*(11), 1101–1102. doi:10.1001/jama.2018.11100 PMID:30178065

Hirasawa, T., Aoyama, K., Tanimoto, T., Ishihara, S., Shichijo, S., Ozawa, T., Ohnishi, T., Fujishiro, M., Matsuo, K., Fujisaki, J., & Tada, T. (2018). Application of artificial intelligence using a convolutional neural network for detecting gastric cancer in endoscopic images. *Gastric Cancer*, *21*(4), 653–660. doi:10.100710120-018-0793-2 PMID:29335825

Ho, W. H., & Chang, C. S. (2011). Genetic-algorithm-based artificial neural network modeling for platelet transfusion requirements on acute myeloblastic leukemia patients. *Expert Systems with Applications*, *38*(5), 6319–6323. doi:10.1016/j.eswa.2010.11.110

Hollander, J. E., Sease, K. L., Sparano, D. M., Sites, F. D., Shofer, F. S., & Baxt, W. G. (2004). Effects of neural network feedback to physicians on admit/discharge decision for emergency department patients with chest pain. *Annals of Emergency Medicine*, *44*(3), 199–205. doi:10.1016/j.annemergmed.2004.02.037 PMID:15332058

Hunink, M. M., Weinstein, M. C., Wittenberg, E., Drummond, M. F., Pliskin, J. S., Wong, J. B., & Glasziou, P. P. (2014). *Decision Making in Health and Medicine: Integrating Evidence and Values*. Cambridge University Press. doi:10.1017/CBO9781139506779

Jiang, J., Trundle, P., & Ren, J. (2010). Medical image analysis with artificial neural networks. *Computerized Medical Imaging and Graphics*, *34*(8), 617–631. doi:10.1016/j.compmedimag.2010.07.003 PMID:20713305

Jiang, S., Chin, K. S., Wang, L., Qu, G., & Tsui, K. L. (2017). Modified genetic algorithm-based feature selection combined with pre-trained deep neural network for demand forecasting in outpatient department. *Expert Systems with Applications*, *82*, 216–230. doi:10.1016/j.eswa.2017.04.017

Kallenberg, M., Petersen, K., Nielsen, M., Ng, A. Y., Diao, P., Igel, C., Vachon, C. M., Holland, K., Winkel, R. R., & Lillholm, M. (2016). Unsupervised deep learning applied to breast density segmentation and mammographic risk scoring. *IEEE Transactions on Medical Imaging*, *35*(5), 1322–1331. doi:10.1109/TMI.2016.2532122 PMID:26915120

Karimian, N., Salehi, H. S., Mahdian, M., Alnajjar, H., & Tadinada, A. (2018). Deep learning classifier with optical coherence tomography images for early dental caries detection. In *Lasers in Dentistry XXIV* (Vol. 10473, p. 1047304). International Society for Optics and Photonics.

Kaytez, F., Taplamacioglu, M. C., Cam, E., & Hardalac, F. (2015). Forecasting electricity consumption: A comparison of regression analysis, neural networks and least squares support vector machines. *International Journal of Electrical Power & Energy Systems*, *67*, 431–438. doi:10.1016/j.ijepes.2014.12.036

Kennedy, R. L., Harrison, R. F., Burton, A. M., Fraser, H. S., Hamer, W. G., MacArthur, D., McAllum, R., & Steedman, D. J. (1997). An artificial neural network system for diagnosis of acute myocardial infarction (AMI) in the accident and emergency department: Evaluation and comparison with serum myoglobin measurements. *Computer Methods and Programs in Biomedicine*, *52*(2), 93–103. doi:10.1016/S0169-2607(96)01782-8 PMID:9034674

Kermany, D. S., Goldbaum, M., Cai, W., Valentim, C. C., Liang, H., Baxter, S. L., McKeown, A., Yang, G., Wu, X., Yan, F., Dong, J., Prasadha, M. K., Pei, J., Ting, M. Y. L., Zhu, J., Li, C., Hewett, S., Dong, J., Ziyar, I., ... Zhang, K. (2018). Identifying medical diagnoses and treatable diseases by image-based deep learning. *Cell*, *172*(5), 1122–1131. doi:10.1016/j.cell.2018.02.010 PMID:29474911

Keshtkar, A., Seyedarabi, H., Sheikhzadeh, P., & Rasta, S. H. (2013). Discriminant analysis between myocardial infarction patients and healthy subjects using Wavelet Transformed signal averaged electrocardiogram and probabilistic neural network. *Journal of Medical Signals and Sensors*, *3*(4), 225. doi:10.4103/2228-7477.128316 PMID:24696156

Khademi, F., Akbari, M., Jamal, S. M., & Nikoo, M. (2017). Multiple linear regression, artificial neural network, and fuzzy logic prediction of 28 days compressive strength of concrete. *Frontiers of Structural and Civil Engineering*, *11*(1), 90–99. doi:10.100711709-016-0363-9

Khazaee, P. R., Bagherzadeh, J., Niazkhani, Z., & Pirnejad, H. (2018). A dynamic model for predicting graft function in kidney recipients' upcoming follow up visits: A clinical application of artificial neural network. *International Journal of Medical Informatics*, *119*, 125–133. doi:10.1016/j.ijmedinf.2018.09.012 PMID:30342680

Kim, J. S., Merrill, R. K., Arvind, V., Kaji, D., Pasik, S. D., Nwachukwu, C. C., Vargas, L., Osman, N. S., Oermann, E. K., Caridi, J. M., & Cho, S. K. (2018). Examining the ability of artificial neural networks machine learning models to accurately predict complications following posterior lumbar spine fusion. *Spine*, *43*(12), 853–860. doi:10.1097/BRS.0000000000002442 PMID:29016439

Kumar, R., Aggarwal, R. K., & Sharma, J. D. (2015). Comparison of regression and artificial neural network models for estimation of global solar radiations. *Renewable & Sustainable Energy Reviews*, *52*, 1294–1299. doi:10.1016/j.rser.2015.08.021

Kumaravel, N., Sridhar, K. S., & Nithiyanandam, N. (1996). Automatic diagnosis of heart diseases using neural network. In *Proceedings of the 1996 Fifteenth Southern Biomedical Engineering Conference*, (pp. 319-322). IEEE. 10.1109/SBEC.1996.493214

Kuperman, G. J., Bobb, A., Payne, T. H., Avery, A. J., Gandhi, T. K., Burns, G., Classen, D. C., & Bates, D. W. (2007). Medication-related clinical decision support in computerized provider order entry systems: A review. *Journal of the American Medical Informatics Association*, *14*(1), 29–40. doi:10.1197/jamia. M2170 PMID:17068355

Leinsinger, G., Schlossbauer, T., Scherr, M., Lange, O., Reiser, M., & Wismüller, A. (2006). Cluster analysis of signal-intensity time course in dynamic breast MRI: Does unsupervised vector quantization help to evaluate small mammographic lesions? *European Radiology*, *16*(5), 1138–1146. doi:10.100700330-005-0053-9 PMID:16418862

Li, Y., Ma, D., Zhu, M., Zeng, Z., & Wang, Y. (2018). Identification of significant factors in fatal-injury highway crashes using genetic algorithm and neural network. *Accident; Analysis and Prevention*, *111*, 354–363. doi:10.1016/j.aap.2017.11.028 PMID:29276978

Lin, H. C., Chiang, S. Y., Lee, K., & Kan, Y. C. (2015). An activity recognition model using inertial sensor nodes in a wireless sensor network for frozen shoulder rehabilitation exercises. *Sensors (Basel)*, *15*(1), 2181–2204. doi:10.3390150102181 PMID:25608218

Lin, J. S., Cheng, K. S., & Mao, C. W. (1996). A fuzzy Hopfield neural network for medical image segmentation. *IEEE Transactions on Nuclear Science*, *43*(4), 2389–2398. doi:10.1109/23.531787

Liu, N., Wang, L., Chang, Q., Xing, Y., & Zhou, X. (2018a). A Simple and Effective Method for Detecting Myocardial Infarction Based on Deep Convolutional Neural Network. *Journal of Medical Imaging and Health Informatics*, 8(7), 1508–1512. doi:10.1166/jmihi.2018.2463

Liu, W., Huang, Q., Chang, S., Wang, H., & He, J. (2018b). Multiple-feature-branch convolutional neural network for myocardial infarction diagnosis using electrocardiogram. *Biomedical Signal Processing and Control*, 45, 22–32. doi:10.1016/j.bspc.2018.05.013

Liu, W., Zhang, M., Zhang, Y., Liao, Y., Huang, Q., Chang, S., Wang, H., & He, J. (2018c). Real-time multilead convolutional neural network for myocardial infarction detection. *IEEE Journal of Biomedical and Health Informatics*, 22(5), 1434–1444. doi:10.1109/JBHI.2017.2771768 PMID:29990164

Malav, A., Kadam, K., & Kamat, P. (2017). Prediction of Heart Disease Using K-Means and Artificial Neural Network as Hybrid Approach to Improve Accuracy. *IACSIT International Journal of Engineering and Technology*, 9(4), 3081–3085. doi:10.21817/ijet/2017/v9i4/170904101

Mennemeyer, S. T., Menachemi, N., Rahurkar, S., & Ford, E. W. (2016). Impact of the HITECH act on physicians' adoption of electronic health records. *Journal of the American Medical Informatics Association*, 23(2), 375–379. doi:10.1093/jamia/ocv103 PMID:26228764

Miller, G. F., Todd, P. M., & Hegde, S. U. (1989). Designing Neural Networks using Genetic Algorithms. In *Proceedings of the Third International Conference on Genetic Algorithms* (pp. 379-384).

Miller, R. A. (1994). Medical diagnostic decision support systems—past, present, and future: A threaded bibliography and brief commentary. *Journal of the American Medical Informatics Association*, 1(1), 8–27. doi:10.1136/jamia.1994.95236141 PMID:7719792

Mohammed, M. A., Ghani, M. K. A., Arunkumar, N., Hamed, R. I., Abdullah, M. K., & Burhanuddin, M. A. (2018). A real time computer aided object detection of nasopharyngeal carcinoma using genetic algorithm and artificial neural network based on Haar feature fear. *Future Generation Computer Systems*, 89, 539–547. doi:10.1016/j.future.2018.07.022

Montana, D. J., & Davis, L. (1989). Training Feedforward Neural Networks Using Genetic Algorithms. In *International Joint Conference on Artificial Intelligence* (Vol. 89, pp. 762-767).

Najafabadi, M. M., Villanustre, F., Khoshgoftaar, T. M., Seliya, N., Wald, R., & Muharemagic, E. (2015). Deep learning applications and challenges in big data analytics. *Journal of Big Data*, 2(1), 1. doi:10.118640537-014-0007-7

Nebauer, C. (1998). Evaluation of convolutional neural networks for visual recognition. *IEEE Transactions on Neural Networks*, 9(4), 685–696. doi:10.1109/72.701181 PMID:18252491

Neural Planner Software. (2015). *JustNN Help User Guide*. Retrieved from: http://www.justnn.com/108491/JustNN.pdf

Nourani, V., Pradhan, B., Ghaffari, H., & Sharifi, S. S. (2014). Landslide susceptibility mapping at Zonouz Plain, Iran using genetic programming and comparison with frequency ratio, logistic regression, and artificial neural network models. *Natural Hazards*, 71(1), 523–547. doi:10.100711069-013-0932-3

Ohlsson, M., Holst, H., & Edenbrandt, L. (2000). Acute myocardial infarction: analysis of the ECG using artificial neural networks. In *Artificial Neural Networks in Medicine and Biology* (pp. 209–214). Springer. doi:10.1007/978-1-4471-0513-8_31

Ohlsson, M., Öhlin, H., Wallerstedt, S. M., & Edenbrandt, L. (2001). Usefulness of serial electrocardiograms for diagnosis of acute myocardial infarction. *The American Journal of Cardiology*, *88*(5), 478–481. doi:10.1016/S0002-9149(01)01722-2 PMID:11524053

Olden, J. D., & Jackson, D. A. (2002). Illuminating the "black box": A randomization approach for understanding variable contributions in artificial neural networks. *Ecological Modelling*, *154*(1-2), 135–150. doi:10.1016/S0304-3800(02)00064-9

Olsson, S. E., Ohlsson, M., Öhlin, H., & Edenbrandt, L. (2002). Neural networks–a diagnostic tool in acute myocardial infarction with concomitant left bundle branch block. *Clinical Physiology and Functional Imaging*, *22*(4), 295–299. doi:10.1046/j.1475-097X.2002.00433.x PMID:12402453

Pastur-Romay, L. A., Cedrón, F., Pazos, A., & Porto-Pazos, A. B. (2016). Deep artificial neural networks and neuromorphic chips for big data analysis: Pharmaceutical and bioinformatics applications. *International Journal of Molecular Sciences*, *17*(8), 1313. doi:10.3390/ijms17081313 PMID:27529225

Pedersen, S. M., Jørgensen, J. S., & Pedersen, J. B. (1996). Use of neural networks to diagnose acute myocardial infarction. II. A clinical application. *Clinical Chemistry*, *42*(4), 613–617. doi:10.1093/clinchem/42.4.613 PMID:8605680

Pesapane, F., Volonté, C., Codari, M., & Sardanelli, F. (2018). Artificial intelligence as a medical device in radiology: Ethical and regulatory issues in Europe and the United States. *Insights Into Imaging*, *9*(5), 1–9. doi:10.100713244-018-0645-y PMID:30112675

Pinaya, W. H., Mechelli, A., & Sato, J. R. (2018). Using deep autoencoders to identify abnormal brain structural patterns in neuropsychiatric disorders: A large-scale multi-sample study. *Human Brain Mapping*. PMID:30311316

Prahs, P., Radeck, V., Mayer, C., Cvetkov, Y., Cvetkova, N., Helbig, H., & Märker, D. (2018). OCT-based deep learning algorithm for the evaluation of treatment indication with anti-vascular endothelial growth factor medications. *Graefes Archive for Clinical and Experimental Ophthalmology*, *256*(1), 91–98. doi:10.100700417-017-3839-y PMID:29127485

Rawat, J., Singh, A., Bhadauria, H. S., Virmani, J., & Devgun, J. S. (2018). Application of ensemble artificial neural network for the classification of white blood cells using microscopic blood images. *International Journal of Computational Systems Engineering*, *4*(2-3), 202–216. doi:10.1504/IJCSYSE.2018.091407

Reddy, M. R. S., Edenbrandt, L., Svensson, J., Haisty, W. K., & Pahlm, O. (1992). Neural network versus electrocardiographer and conventional computer criteria in diagnosing anterior infarct from the ECG. [IEEE.]. *Proceedings of Computers in Cardiology*, *1992*, 667–670. doi:10.1109/CIC.1992.269345

Sadrawi, M., Shieh, J. S., Fan, S. Z., Lin, C. H., Haraikawa, K., Chien, J. C., & Abbod, M. F. (2016). Intermittent blood pressure prediction via multiscale entropy and ensemble artificial neural networks. In *Biomedical Engineering and Sciences (IECBES), 2016 IEEE EMBS Conference on* (pp. 356-359). IEEE. 10.1109/IECBES.2016.7843473

Safdarian, N., Dabanloo, N. J., & Attarodi, G. (2014). A new pattern recognition method for detection and localization of myocardial infarction using T-wave integral and total integral as extracted features from one cycle of ECG signal. *Journal of Biomedical Science and Engineering, 7*(10), 818–824. doi:10.4236/jbise.2014.710081

Saltz, J., Gupta, R., Hou, L., Kurc, T., Singh, P., Nguyen, V., Samaras, D., Shroyer, K. R., Zhao, T., Batiste, R., Van Arnam, J., Shmulevich, I., Rao, A. U. K., Lazar, A. J., Sharma, A., Thorsson, V., Caesar-Johnson, S. J., Demchok, J. A., Felau, I., ... Mariamidze, A. (2018). Spatial organization and molecular correlation of tumor-infiltrating lymphocytes using deep learning on pathology images. *Cell Reports, 23*(1), 181–193. doi:10.1016/j.celrep.2018.03.086 PMID:29617659

Sankari, Z., & Adeli, H. (2011). HeartSaver: A mobile cardiac monitoring system for auto-detection of atrial fibrillation, myocardial infarction, and atrio-ventricular block. *Computers in Biology and Medicine, 41*(4), 211–220. doi:10.1016/j.compbiomed.2011.02.002 PMID:21377149

Schmidhuber, J. (2015). Deep learning in neural networks: An overview. *Neural Networks, 61*, 85–117. doi:10.1016/j.neunet.2014.09.003 PMID:25462637

Selker, H. P., Griffith, J. L., Patil, S., Long, W. J., & d'Agostino, R. B. (1995). A comparison of performance of mathematical predictive methods for medical diagnosis: Identifying acute cardiac ischemia among emergency department patients. *Journal of Investigative Medicine: The Official Publication of the American Federation for Clinical Research, 43*(5), 468–476. PMID:8528758

Smith, M. (1993). *Neural Networks for Statistical Modeling*. Van Nostrand Reinhold.

Teo, T. P., Ahmed, S. B., Kawalec, P., Alayoubi, N., Bruce, N., Lyn, E., & Pistorius, S. (2018). Feasibility of predicting tumor motion using online data acquired during treatment and a generalized neural network optimized with offline patient tumor trajectories. *Medical Physics, 45*(2), 830–845. doi:10.1002/mp.12731 PMID:29244902

Tu, J. V. (1996). Advantages and disadvantages of using artificial neural networks versus logistic regression for predicting medical outcomes. *Journal of Clinical Epidemiology, 49*(11), 1225–1231. doi:10.1016/S0895-4356(96)00002-9 PMID:8892489

Wager, K. A., Lee, F. W., & Glaser, J. P. (2013). *Health Care Information Systems: A Practical Approach for Health Care Management*. Jossey-Bass/Wiley.

Walczak, S. (2008). Evaluating medical decision making heuristics and other business heuristics with neural networks. In *Intelligent Decision Making: An AI-Based Approach* (pp. 259–287). Springer. doi:10.1007/978-3-540-76829-6_10

Walczak, S. (2012). Methodological triangulation using neural networks for business research. *Advances in Artificial Neural Systems, 2012*, 1–12. doi:10.1155/2012/517234

Walczak, S., & Cerpa, N. (1999). Heuristic principles for the design of artificial neural networks. *Information and Software Technology, 41*(2), 107–117. doi:10.1016/S0950-5849(98)00116-5

Walczak, S., & Scharf, J. E. (2000). Reducing surgical patient costs through use of an artificial neural network to predict transfusion requirements. *Decision Support Systems, 30*(2), 125–138. doi:10.1016/S0167-9236(00)00093-2

Walczak, S., & Velanovich, V. (2018). Improving prognosis and reducing decision regret for pancreatic cancer treatment using artificial neural networks. *Decision Support Systems*, *106*, 110–118. doi:10.1016/j. dss.2017.12.007

Wang, S., Wang, R., Zhang, S., Li, R., Fu, Y., Sun, X., Li, Y., Sun, X., Jiang, X., Guo, X., Zhou, X., Chang, J., & Peng, W. (2018). 3D convolutional neural network for differentiating pre-invasive lesions from invasive adenocarcinomas appearing as groundglass nodules with diameters≤ 3 cm using HRCT. *Quantitative Imaging in Medicine and Surgery*, *8*(5), 491–499. doi:10.21037/qims.2018.06.03 PMID:30050783

Wang, Y., Wang, D., Ye, X., Wang, Y., Yin, Y., & Jin, Y. (2019). A Tree Ensemble-Based Two-Stage Model for Advanced-Stage Colorectal Cancer Survival Prediction. *Information Sciences*, *474*, 106–124. doi:10.1016/j.ins.2018.09.046

Weng, S. F., Reps, J., Kai, J., Garibaldi, J. M., & Qureshi, N. (2017). Can machine-learning improve cardiovascular risk prediction using routine clinical data? *PLoS One*, *12*(4), e0174944. doi:10.1371/ journal.pone.0174944 PMID:28376093

Werbos, P. J. (1974). *Beyond Regression: New Tools for Prediction and Analysis in the Behavioral Sciences* (Doctoral Dissertation). Harvard University, Boston, MA.

Wismüller, A., Meyer-Bäse, A., Lange, O., Auer, D., Reiser, M. F., & Sumners, D. (2004). Model-free functional MRI analysis based on unsupervised clustering. *Journal of Biomedical Informatics*, *37*(1), 10–18. doi:10.1016/j.jbi.2003.12.002 PMID:15016382

Yang, T. F., Devine, B., & Macfarlane, P. W. (1994). Use of artificial neural networks within deterministic logic for the computer ECG diagnosis of inferior myocardial infarction. *Journal of Electrocardiology*, *27*, 188–193. doi:10.1016/S0022-0736(94)80090-1 PMID:7884359

Yu, D., Zhou, M., Yang, F., Dong, D., Gevaert, O., Liu, Z., Shi, J., & Tian, J. (2017). Convolutional neural networks for predicting molecular profiles of non-small cell lung cancer. In *Biomedical Imaging (ISBI 2017), 2017 IEEE 14th International Symposium on* (pp. 569-572). IEEE. 10.1109/ISBI.2017.7950585

Zanella-Calzada, L., Galván-Tejada, C., Chávez-Lamas, N., Rivas-Gutierrez, J., Magallanes-Quintanar, R., Celaya-Padilla, J., Galván-Tejada, J., & Gamboa-Rosales, H. (2018). Deep Artificial Neural Networks for the Diagnostic of Caries Using Socioeconomic and Nutritional Features as Determinants: Data from NHANES 2013–2014. *Bioengineering (Basel, Switzerland)*, *5*(2), 47. doi:10.3390/bioengineering5020047 PMID:29912173

Zhou, Z. H., Jiang, Y., & Chen, S. F. (2003). Extracting symbolic rules from trained neural network ensembles. *AI Communications*, *16*(1), 3–15.

ADDITIONAL READING

DeTienne, K. B., DeTienne, D. H., & Joshi, S. A. (2003). Neural Networks as Statistical Tools for Business Researchers. *Organizational Research Methods*, *6*(2), 236–265. doi:10.1177/1094428103251907

Jain, A. K., Mao, J., & Mohiuddin, K. M. (1996). Artificial Neural Networks: A Tutorial. *Computer*, *29*(3), 31–44. doi:10.1109/2.485891

Penny, W., & Frost, D. (1996). Neural networks in clinical medicine. *Medical Decision Making*, *16*(4), 386–398. doi:10.1177/0272989X9601600409 PMID:8912300

Reggia, J. A. (1993). Neural computation in medicine. *Artificial Intelligence in Medicine*, *5*(2), 143–157. doi:10.1016/0933-3657(93)90014-T PMID:8358491

Rodvold, D. M., McLeod, D. G., Brandt, J. M., Snow, P. B., & Murphy, G. P. (2001). Introduction to artificial neural networks for physicians: Taking the lid off the black box. *The Prostate*, *46*(1), 39–44. doi:10.1002/1097-0045(200101)46:1<39::AID-PROS1006>3.0.CO;2-M PMID:11170130

Warner, B., & Misra, M. (1996). Understanding neural networks as statistical tools. *The American Statistician*, *50*(4), 284–293.

Whitley, D. (1995). Genetic algorithms and neural networks. *Genetic Algorithms in Engineering and Computer Science*, *3*, 203–216.

KEY TERMS AND DEFINITIONS

Big Data: Is a term referring to an extremely large collection of data, typically in the petabyte range or larger. The data is only considered "big" if it taxes current state-of-the-art computing capabilities.

Diagnostic: Referring to the diagnosis or determination of a disease or diseases or trauma; defining the medical condition of a patient.

Kohonen/SOM: Is a type of ANN that uses unsupervised learning. Commonly used in audio and visual perception ANNs.

Perceptron/Multilayer Perceptron: Perceptron was an early name for a single processing element, now more commonly called a neuron or neurode. Multilayer perceptrons (MLP) are arrangements of perceptrons into layers, such as the input layer connected to a hidden layer which is then connected to an output layer. The abbreviation MLP is often used to refer to backpropagation trained supervised learning ANNs with at least one hidden layer.

Prognostic: Referring to the treatment and follow-up plan for a specific medical condition or type of trauma, for example, a course of chemo-therapy and radiation prior to surgery for the reduction and removal of a cancerous fibroid.

Sensitivity: The percentage of patients with a specific diagnosis or outcome that are correctly identified, which is the number of true positives divided by the sum of the true positives and false negatives.

Specificity: The percentage of patients who do not have a specific diagnosis or desired outcome that are correctly identified, which is the number of true negatives divided by the sum of the true negatives and false positives.

This research was previously published in the Encyclopedia of Information Science and Technology, Fifth Edition; pages 1901-1918, copyright year 2021 by Engineering Science Reference (an imprint of IGI Global).

Chapter 74

Chaotic System Design Based on Recurrent Artificial Neural Network for the Simulation of EEG Time Series

Lei Zhang

https://orcid.org/0000-0003-0535-998X

University of Regina, Regina, Canada

ABSTRACT

Electroencephalogram (EEG) signals captured from brain activities demonstrate chaotic features, and can be simulated by nonlinear dynamic time series outputs of chaotic systems. This article presents the research work of chaotic system generator design based on artificial neural network (ANN), for studying the chaotic features of human brain dynamics. The ANN training performances of Nonlinear Auto-Regressive (NAR) model are evaluated for the generation and prediction of chaotic system time series outputs, based on varying the ANN architecture and the precision of the generated training data. The NAR model is trained in open loop form with 1,000 training samples generated using Lorenz system equations and the forward Euler method. The close loop NAR model is used for the generation and prediction of Lorenz chaotic time series outputs. The training results show that better training performance can be achieved by increasing the number of feedback delays and the number of hidden neurons, at the cost of increasing the computational load.

INTRODUCTION

Recent research based on big data and deep learning has little concern on the extremely long training time and constantly increasing power consumption. Artificial neural network (ANN) is initially inspired by the biological neural networks of human brain. A human brain has approximately 100-billion neurons and 100-trillion connections, but is very energy efficient and can function relatively fast. Taking a face recognition task for instance, our brains can remember a face after encountering a stranger for a few

DOI: 10.4018/978-1-6684-2408-7.ch074

seconds. People are very confident with this brain capability and policeman often asks witnesses to identify a criminal based on it. In contrast, this simple task can take a convolutional neural network (CNN) many hours even days to train, and the same CNN has to be trained again in the same way whenever new data are added. How does the brain achieve its extraordinary efficiency? What is the underlying neural network architecture that facilitates this efficiency? Can we build ANN that assembles the human brain to obtain similar efficiency in addition to accuracy? These are the questions this research tries to address and aims to answer.

In neuroscience, neuroplasticity is referred to as the flexibility for brain neural networks to learn new concepts and to deal with new situations. An adaptive ANN can be trained with new inputs so that the model can adapt to changes. It is necessary for an adaptive ANN to be trained quickly and effectively with a relatively small time series segment in order to capture the trend of a continuously changing EEG signals. Hence the complexity of the ANN architecture and the associated computational cost must be restrained in order to achieve efficiency.

In ANN training, an epoch is referred to a complete training process with the entire training data provided. It can be considered as one learning process taken by the brain. For example, the human brain usually needs to read/write a word or a telephone number repeatedly a number of times to remember it temporarily. And it often requires dozens of repetitions in difference occasions to form long-term memory. It holds true for both human learning and machine learning that the learning accuracy can be improved to certain degree by increasing the number of repetitions. The learning results of human brain are mainly measured by accuracy through examination system, but the time and effort taken for learning, aka. learning speed, are disregarded and left to each individual to judge. Similarly, in machine learning, the performance of ANN is measured by accuracy or error rate such as the mean squared error (MSE). In fact, the majority of past and recent research has mainly focused on improving the accuracy of ANN/CNN training, but overlooked the consequences of increased network complexity, computational cost, power consumption, and overextended training time. This approach is acceptable in many applications with fixed solutions without having to frequently retrain the ANN, but it will not work for applications with volatile data and many unknown parameters, such as brain signals captured from EEG. This research investigates the training performance by measuring the MSE with limited training epoch and evaluates the training speed of different ANN architectures using various training data.

BACKGROUND

ANN is a machine learning method. It can be used for pattern recognition and prediction of multi-variant time series. The training performance of an ANN depends on its architecture and the training data. ANN architecture is inspired by biological neural network of the human brain. The classical feedforward ANN architecture includes an input layer, a number of hidden layers and an output layer. Each hidden layer includes a number of parallel distributed hidden neurons. Compared to other machine learning methods, the advantage of ANN design is that an ANN can be trained without knowing the features of the training data beforehand. The disadvantage is that it requires a large number of training data to obtain good ANN training performance. Forecasting using ANN can be dated back to two decades ago (Zhang, 1998) and has been successfully adopted for time series pattern recognition and prediction in many applications. Recent publications have shown promising research advances in optimizing ANN architecture and training algorithm for time series prediction (Zhang, 2018).

ANN can be successfully trained to generate nonlinear time series outputs for Lorenz chaotic system (Zhang, 2017a). The optimization of ANN architecture and the well selection of representative training data are important for achieving optimal training performance. A trial and error design approach has been adopted for many applications on a case-by-case basis, with prevailing tendency on selecting complex ANN architecture and big training data (Deng, 2009; Krizhevsky, 2012; Simonyan, 2014; Wang 2017). In order to form generalized training strategy to improve ANN training efficiency, this research evaluates the ANN training performance for a general chaotic system, using different ANN architectures and training data sets.

The goal of this research is to evaluate the training performances of ANN architectures with multiple hidden layers for chaotic system implementation, to find the optimal ANN architecture that will meet the resolution required for chaotic system representation, with the minimum computation optimized for hardware acceleration. The ANN architectures, training configuration, and the generation of the training data are explained. The training results are provided and analyzed.

ANN ARCHITECTURES AND TRAINING CONFIGURATIONS

Various ANN architectures are employed with one input layer and one output layer, as well as a number of hidden layers. ANN architectures with a single hidden layer are trained with different number of hidden neurons (n) and input delays (d). The ANN training performances are evaluated with the number of hidden neurons varying from 3 to 6, as well as different numbers of input delays ranging from 1 to 8. Previous related research show that the training performance of ANN architectures can be improved in general by increasing the number of hidden neurons from 3 to 16, but the improvement starts to become insignificant and inconsistent once n is bigger than 9 (Zhang, 2017b). As it is preferable to reduce the complexity of the ANN in order to improve the training efficiency, a range of small number of hidden neurons (3 to 6) is used for evaluation. ANN architectures with two layers are trained with different number of hidden neurons in each hidden layer, and only 1 input delay.

The training is carried out using the MATLAB nonlinear time series tool *ntstool* in the Neural Network Toolbox (Beale et al, 2015). The training algorithm *trainlm* is chosen as it provides good training efficiency balanced between training performance and training speed. It updates weight and bias values based on the Levenberg-Marquardt (LM) optimization (Hegan, 1994; Wang, 2018). The MATLAB default values are used for setting all training parameters. Each ANN architecture with a given number of hidden neuron (n) and a given number of feedback input delay (d) is trained for 2 iterations, the better result of which is used for comparing the performances of various architectures and data sets. The iteration with the worse result is ignored to eliminate any abnormal training performance caused by local minima of gradient in the training process (Atakulreka, 2007).

TRAINING DATA

Lorenz attractor is a well studied chaotic system developed by Edward Lorenz in 1963. The system can be represented by three simple differential Equations (1), yet it is a mysteriously powerful tool to model many chaotic phenomenal in real world such as the changing of atmosphere. It is used as a good representation for general chaotic systems to generate the training data in this study and the ANN design method presented can be generally applied to the generation and prediction of other types of chaotic system time series at large. The 3-dimensional outputs of Lorenz attractor x, y and z are the target outputs of the ANN training, hence the output layer has three neurons, and so does the input layer, with delayed outputs feedback to the inputs in the NAR model:

$$\frac{dx}{dt} = \sigma(y - x)$$
$$\frac{dy}{dt} = \rho x - y - xz \tag{1}$$
$$\frac{dz}{dt} = -\beta z + xy$$

In this study, 1,300 training samples are generated using the forward Euler method (Zhang, 2017c). In general, chaotic system time series start at certain initial values and gradually converges to the trajectory of system. Hence the first 300 samples are discarded to eliminate the "merging path" of the trajectory, which is not part of the normal trajectory of the chaotic system. The following 1,000 samples are provided as the target outputs for ANN training. Although 1,000 samples can only represent a small segment of the Lorenz system, it is considered as sufficient for the ANN training to extract features associated with the system parameters and generate the target outputs (Zhang, 2018).

Depending on the initial values and system parameters, a chaotic system can be either chaotic or non-chaotic (stable or periodic). The Lorenz chaotic system needs to be set in the chaotic states to generate time series outputs with chaotic features for the simulation of EEG signals. The system initial values are set to $x_0 = y_0 = z_0 = 10$. The system parameters are set to $\sigma = 10$, $\rho = 28$, $\beta = 8/3$. These values are selected to generate chaotic instead of stable or periodic outputs for Lorenz attractor.

In order to optimize the ANN training, the training data is divided into 3 subsets for training (70%), validation (15%) and testing (15%) using the 'dividerand' function which divides the training data randomly into three subsets. The training subset is used for computing the averaged MSE and updating the network weights and biases to gradually reduce the errors between the ANN outputs and the target outputs. The validation set is used to monitor the errors during the training process to measure network generalization and to stop the training process when the generalization stops improving, which is indicated by the successively increasing MSE. The training error should gradually decrease during the training process, so does the validation error. Otherwise, if the MSE of the validation set begins to increase, it indicates that the network is over fitting on the training data, and the training will stop. The network weights and biases are saved at the minimum MSE of the validation data. The testing set is used to give an independent measurement of the network performance during and after the training. The testing data is normally used to compare the results of different ANN architectures. It can also be used to detect a poor data set division, i.e., when the minimum MSE of the testing data occurs at a significantly different training epoch than that of the validation data.

TRAINING RESULTS FOR ANN WITH ONE HIDDEN LAYER

The number of neurons in the hidden layer varies from 3 to 6 and the number of feedback input delays varies from 1 to 8. The training data is generated using the Euler method with three step sizes dt = 0.02, 0.01 and 0.005 respectively. 1000 training samples are used. Each training is carried out for two iterations. The best training results of two training iterations are listed in Table 1. The best training performance of NAR models with different number hidden neurons of 3 to 6 are plotted separately in Figure 1(a) to (d).

Table 1. MSE with 1~ 8 input delays and 3~6 hidden neurons for 3 precisions (dt=0.02, 0.01 and 0.005)

Delay (d)	1	2	3	4	5	6	7	8
n=3								
dt=0.02	4.05E-02	1.14E-02	1.23E-03	1.17E-03	1.71E-04	8.62E-05	1.04E-04	5.59E-05
dt=0.01	8.56E-03	4.88E-04	1.83E-05	3.17E-06	7.20E-07	2.96E-07	4.33E-07	3.49E-07
dt=0.005	4.35E-03	1.03E-05	1.10E-06	3.45E-07	2.25E-07	3.08E-07	2.25E-07	2.88E-07
n=4								
dt=0.02	9.91E-03	1.89E-03	2.52E-04	1.32E-04	6.22E-05	4.27E-05	4.02E-05	9.62E-05
dt=0.01	3.18E-04	5.97E-05	1.86E-06	9.28E-07	4.78E-07	8.36E-07	5.03E-07	7.42E-07
dt=0.005	4.36E-05	2.15E-06	5.94E-07	5.37E-07	2.02E-07	1.11E-07	9.96E-08	1.44E-07
n=5								
dt=0.02	1.21E-05	7.89E-04	6.81E-05	6.09E-05	5.15E-05	9.22E-06	9.92E-06	3.63E-05
dt=0.01	4.65E-06	5.37E-06	1.38E-06	3.37E-07	2.40E-07	2.97E-07	3.09E-07	2.14E-07
dt=0.005	5.55E-06	1.34E-06	2.04E-07	1.14E-07	7.67E-08	1.54E-07	1.31E-07	2.85E-08
n=6								
dt=0.02	5.54E-05	6.28E-05	7.31E-06	1.65E-05	6.17E-06	2.00E-06	1.33E-05	1.77E-06
dt=0.01	3.72E-06	3.77E-06	3.38E-07	2.57E-07	1.71E-07	5.45E-08	4.11E-08	8.75E-08
dt=0.005	2.07E-06	8.48E-08	9.78E-08	6.91E-08	1.80E-07	2.45E-07	7.09E-08	3.82E-09

Input Delay and Step Size

It can be observed from the training results that the training performance can be generally improved by improving the precision of the training data, which is achieved by generating the samples with a smaller step size (dt) using the Lorenz system equations and the forward Euler method. It can also be observed that better performance can often be obtained by increasing the number of input delays (d), but the performance ceases to improve when d is equal or greater than 5, for n = 3/4/5 as shown in Figure 1(a)~(c). When n = 6, the performance is improved as d increases up to 7 for dt = 0.01 as shown in Figure 1 (d).

Figure 1. Best training performances of ANN with 1 to 8 input delays and 3 to 16 hidden neurons for 3 training data precisions (dt=0.02, 0.01 and 0.005)

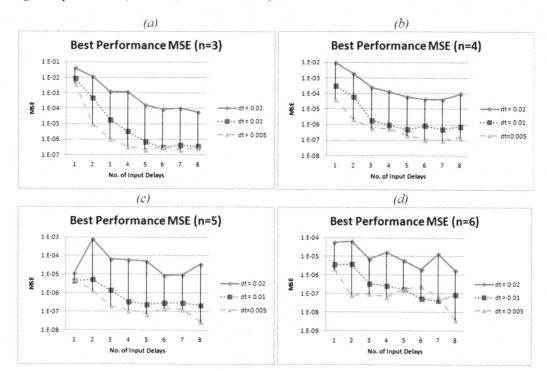

Computational Cost

The computational cost of the ANN training and hardware implementation depends on the complexity of ANN architecture, as well as the size of training data. Therefore it is necessary to compare the total number of multiplications required by an ANN architecture based on the number of input delays and hidden neurons; and it is beneficial to achieve good training performance with smaller training data size, especially for training adaptive ANN. For a 3-layer ANN architecture with one input, one hidden and one output layer, adding one input delay is equivalent to adding another input neuron, which increases the number of multiplications of weights and inputs by the number of hidden neurons (n). For example, after adding one input delay to all three original input neurons of the ANN (n=3, d=1), the ANN (n=3, d=2) architecture has 6 neurons in the input layer (3 inputs and 3 delayed inputs), 3 hidden neurons and 3 output neurons. The total number of multiplications between weights and neurons increases from 18 (3×3+3 × 3) to 27 (6 × 3+3 × 3). Similarly, adding one hidden neuron will increase the number of multiplications for both input and hidden layers by the sum of input and output neurons. For instance, by adding one neuron to the hidden layer of the ANN (n=3, d=1), the total number of multiplications increases from 18 to 24 (3 × 4+4 × 3) for the ANN (n=4, d=1). This calculation reveals that the complexity of ANN architecture determines the trade-off between the training performance and the computational cost. Since the activation function in the neuron model is based on the Sigmund function, which requires exponential computation in ANN training and is implemented as loop-up table using a large memory in hardware, the total number of neurons in the hidden layers in an ANN architecture must also be considered together with the number of multiplications for the investigation of the overall training performance and computation cost of the design.

The NAR models of ANN (n=3, d=4) and the ANN (n=6, d=1) are shown in Figure 2(a) and (b) respectively. The former requires 45 (12 × 3+3 × 3) multiplications and the best MSE is 3.17E-6. The latter requires 36 (3 × 6+6 × 3) multiplications and the best MSE is 5.65E-6. The MSEs are at the same scale level but ANN (n=6, d=1) has much smaller computational cost.

Figure 2. NAR open loop models

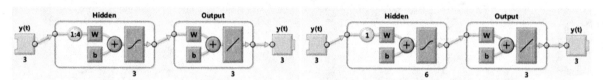

Normalized Training Performance

The training performance of an ANN architecture is normalized by its computational cost, which is measured by the number of multiplications required. The normalization is based on the simplest ANN architecture ANN (n=3, d=1), which requires 18 multiplications. The number of multiplication and the normalized best MSE of different ANN architectures are calculated using Equation (2):

$$N_{Multiplication} = N_{Input} * d * n + n * N_{Output} = 3 * n * (d + 1)$$

$$MSE_{Normalized} = MSE_{Original} * \frac{N_{Multiplications}}{18}$$

(2)

The number of multiplications required and the normalized performances for ANN architecture with 3 to 6 hidden Neurons (n), 1 to 8 input delays (d) and three data step sizes (dt =0.02, 0.01, 0.05) are listed in Table 2.

The normalized MSE for three training data sets of three different step sizes (dt=0.02, 0.01 and 0.005) are plotted in Figure 3 respectively. Figure 3(a) shows that when the data precision is relatively low (dt=0.02), the normalized MSE decreases as the number of input delays (d) increases from 1to 8 when the number of hidden neurons (n) is 3. This trend becomes less apparent as the n increases, and when n=6, the effect of increasing the number of input delays becomes insignificant and non-monotonic, i.e., it either slightly increases or decreases as d increases. Figure 3(b) shows that when step size dt=0.01 is used, the overall normalized MSEs are significantly improved by more than one order of a magnitude. For example, with n = 3, the MSE decreases from 1E-2 to 1E-6 level as d increases from 1 to 6, and increases slightly as d further increases from 6 to 8. When n=4, the normalized MSE decreases significantly from 1E-4 to 1E-6 level as d increases from 1 to 3, and stops to further decrease as d increases from 3 to 8. Therefore, it can be summarized that as n increases, the MSE stops to decrease at a smaller d. Figure 3(c) shows the normalized MSE with dt = 0.005. With n=3, the MSE decreases from 1E-3 to 1E-7 as d increases from 1 to 4. And the overall training performance stops to improve when d is greater than 3. It can be observed that the effect of increasing the number of d or n is made less significant compared to the effect of increasing data precision, i.e., reducing step size of the training samples. Hence it may neither be practically necessary nor computationally effective to add more than 4 input delays for ANN architecture with more than 6 hidden neurons from the hardware implementation point of view, as the increase of multiplications will increase the hardware resource utilization, power consumption and reduce the operating speed.

After training the open loop ANN, the close loop NAR model is then used for prediction. The prediction of the trained ANN(n= 6, d= 1) with step size dt= 0.02 and 0.01 for 2,000 samples are shown in Figure 4(a) and (b) respectively.

Table 2. No. of multiplications (m) and normalized MSE (MSEn) for training data step size

Delay (d)	1	2	3	4	5	6	7	8
n=3								
m	18	27	36	45	54	63	72	81
dt=0.02	4.05E-02	1.14E-02	1.23E-03	1.17E-03	1.71E-04	8.62E-05	1.04E-04	5.59E-05
dt=0.01	8.56E-03	4.88E-04	1.83E-05	3.17E-06	7.20E-07	2.96E-07	4.33E-07	3.49E-07
dt=0.005	4.35E-03	1.03E-05	1.10E-06	3.45E-07	2.25E-07	3.08E-07	2.25E-07	2.88E-07
n=4								
m	24	36	48	60	72	84	96	108
dt=0.02	9.91E-03	1.89E-03	2.52E-04	1.32E-04	6.22E-05	4.27E-05	4.02E-05	9.62E-05
dt=0.01	3.18E-04	5.97E-05	1.86E-06	9.28E-07	4.78E-07	8.36E-07	5.03E-07	7.42E-07
dt=0.005	4.36E-05	2.15E-06	5.94E-07	5.37E-07	2.02E-07	1.11E-07	9.96E-08	1.44E-07
n=5								
m	30	45	60	75	90	105	120	135
dt=0.02	1.21E-05	7.89E-04	6.81E-05	6.09E-05	5.15E-05	9.22E-06	9.92E-06	3.63E-05
dt=0.01	4.65E-06	5.37E-06	1.38E-06	3.37E-07	2.40E-07	2.97E-07	3.09E-07	2.14E-07
dt=0.005	5.55E-06	1.34E-06	2.04E-07	1.14E-07	7.67E-08	1.54E-07	1.31E-07	2.85E-08
n=6								
m	36	54	72	90	108	126	144	162
dt=0.02	5.54E-05	6.28E-05	7.31E-06	1.65E-05	6.17E-06	2.00E-06	1.33E-05	1.77E-06
dt=0.01	3.72E-06	3.77E-06	3.38E-07	2.57E-07	1.71E-07	5.45E-08	4.11E-08	8.75E-08
dt=0.005	2.07E-06	8.48E-08	9.78E-08	6.91E-08	1.80E-07	2.45E-07	7.09E-08	3.82E-09

Training Results for ANN With Two Hidden Layers

The same training process is carried out for ANN with two hidden layers and one input delay, using 1k samples training data at dt= 0.01. The number of neurons in the first layer (n1) and the second layer (n2) vary from 3 to 8. The number of multiplication (m) required is calculated by 3*n1+n1*n2+n2*3. The best training MSEs and the m required for ANN architectures with two hidden layers are listed in Table 3.

Figure 3. Normalized best training performances of ANN with 1 to 8 input delays and 3 to 16 hidden neurons for 3 training data precisions (dt=0.02, 0.01 and 0.005)

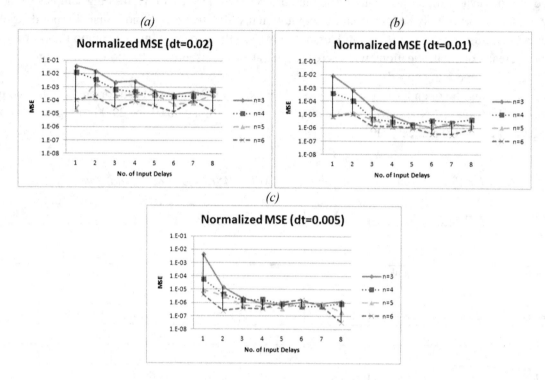

Figure 4. Lorenz system generation using NAR closed loop model with 6 hidden neurons and 1 delay

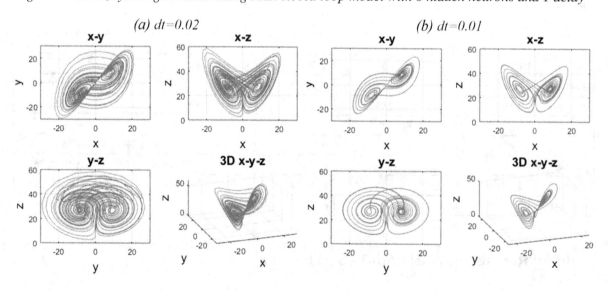

Table 3. No. of multiplications (m) and MSE for ANN with 2 hidden layers (n1-layer1, n2-layer2)

n1/n2	3	4	5	6	7	8	9	10
3	1.88E-03	2.13E-04	1.37E-04	2.84E-05	1.04E-05	3.45E-05	3.46E-06	2.83E-06
m	27	33	39	45	51	57	63	69
4	5.68E-04	3.67E-04	2.51E-05	3.86E-06	3.15E-06	1.66E-05	6.12E-06	2.07E-06
m	33	40	47	54	61	68	75	82
5	4.78E-04	3.80E-05	1.65E-05	3.55E-06	1.91E-06	3.71E-06	5.42E-07	1.38E-06
m	39	47	55	63	71	79	87	95
6	2.00E-05	2.74E-06	6.34E-06	9.38E-06	6.85E-08	5.29E-07	7.42E-07	5.90E-07
m	45	54	63	72	81	90	99	108
7	1.78E-05	4.99E-04	2.89E-06	2.68E-06	8.47E-07	1.19E-06	4.35E-08	1.23E-06
m	51	61	71	81	91	101	111	121
8	1.84E-05	3.10E-06	1.30E-06	5.20E-07	6.60E-07	4.87E-07	8.59E-07	3.84E-07
m	57	68	79	90	101	112	123	134
9	5.22E-06	5.57E-06	8.87E-06	4.62E-07	6.90E-07	3.12E-07	6.05E-07	2.23E-08
m	63	75	87	99	111	123	135	147
10	2.94E-06	2.71E-06	6.59E-07	1.92E-06	2.61E-07	9.20E-07	3.14E-07	2.17E-08
m	69	82	95	108	121	134	147	160

Figure 5. Normalized MSE for ANN with 2 hidden layers

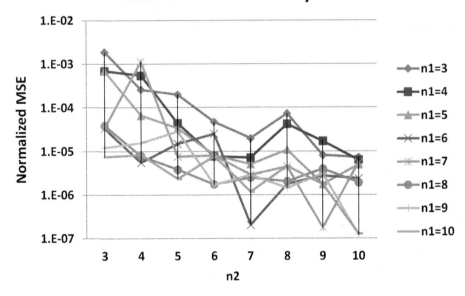

The normalized MSE for ANN architectures with 2 hidden layers are plotted in Figure 5. The overall training time and computational cost is significantly increased for the ANN with 2 hidden layers. The MSE is decreased to 1E-8 level with n1=n2=10. However, the normalized MSE does not show significant improvement compared to ANN with single hidden layer.

CONCLUSION AND FUTURE WORK

This paper presented the ANN architecture design and optimization using NAR model for the generation and prediction of Lorenz chaotic system, which can be used for the simulation and analysis of dynamic EEG signal time series in brain research, and the future development of wearable embedded system for brain monitoring. The optimization of ANN architecture is mainly focus on the reduction of computational cost for hardware implementation, instead of just reducing the MSE. Four main conclusions can be drawn from the training results: 1) The optimization of ANN architecture for the Lorenz chaotic system NAR model depends on the combination of hidden neurons and input delays, as well as the computational cost derived from the architecture. 2) The training performance can be improved by reducing the step size of the generated training samples, which provides better precision for the training data. 3) In general, the training performance can be improved by increase the number of hidden neurons and the number of input delays. However, with respect to hardware implementation, it is practical to use a combination of hidden neurons and input delays, which can meet the training target with minimum computational cost. 4) The training results of ANN architecture with two hidden layers shows that MSE can be further reduced. However, the normalized MSE with the consideration of the increased computational cost indicate that the simple ANN architecture with only one hidden layer can be sufficient for generating the chaotic time patterns without significantly increasing the ANN training time and the complexity of hardware implementation. The future research will further investigate the size and precision of the training data in order to improve the training performance for chaotic system generation and prediction, which can be used for the simulation and pattern recognition of EEG signals in brain research.

REFERENCES

Atakulreka, A., & Sutivong, D. (2007). Avoiding Local Minima in Feedforward Neural Networks by Simultaneous Learning. AI 2007: Advances in Artificial Intelligence Lecture Notes in Computer Science, 100-109. doi:10.1007/978-3-540-76928-6_12

Beale, M. H., Hagan, M. T., & Demuth, H. B. (2015). Neural Network Toolbox User's Guide. The MathWorks, Inc., r2015a edition.

Deng, J., Dong, W., Socher, R., Li, L., Li, K., & Fei-Fei, L. (2009). ImageNet: A large-scale hierarchical image database. In *2009 IEEE Conference on Computer Vision and Pattern Recognition*. 10.1109/CVPR.2009.5206848

Hagan, M., & Menhaj, M. (1994). Training feedforward networks with the Marquardt algorithm. *IEEE Transactions on Neural Networks*, 5(6), 989–993. doi:10.1109/72.329697 PMID:18267874

Krizhevsky, A., Sutskever, I., & Hinton, G. E. (2017). ImageNet classification with deep convolutional neural networks. *Communications of the ACM, 60*(6), 84–90. doi:10.1145/3065386

Simonyan, K. & Zisserman, A. (2014). Very Deep Convolutional Networks for Large-Scale Image Recognition. CoRR, abs/1409.1556.

Wang, W., Pu, Y., & Li, W. (2018). A Parallel Levenberg-Marquardt Algorithm for Recursive Neural Network in a Robot Control System. *International Journal of Cognitive Informatics and Natural Intelligence, 12*(2), 32–47. doi:10.4018/IJCINI.2018040103

Wang, Y., & Peng, J. (2017). Big Data Analytics: A Cognitive Perspectives. *International Journal of Cognitive Informatics and Natural Intelligence, 11*(2), 41–56. doi:10.4018/IJCINI.2017040103

Zhang, L. (2017a). Artificial Neural Network model design and topology analysis for FPGA implementation of Lorenz chaotic generator. In *2017 IEEE 30th Canadian Conference on Electrical and Computer Engineering (CCECE)* (pp. 216-219). doi:10.1109/ccece.2017.7946635

Zhang, L. (2017b). Artificial neural networks model design of Lorenz chaotic system for EEG pattern recognition and prediction. In *2017 IEEE Life Sciences Conference (LSC)* (pp. 39-42). 10.1109/LSC.2017.8268138

Zhang, L. (2017c). System generator model-based FPGA design optimization and hardware co-simulation for Lorenz chaotic generator. In *2017 2nd Asia-Pacific Conference on Intelligent Robot Systems (ACIRS)* (pp. 170-174). doi:10.1109/acirs.2017.7986087

Zhang, L. (2018). Evaluating the Training Performance of Artificial Neural Network Using Small Time Series Segments of The Lorenz Chaotic System. In *2018 International Joint Conference on Neural Networks (IJCNN)* (pp. 1-8). 10.1109/IJCNN.2018.8489573

This research was previously published in the International Journal of Cognitive Informatics and Natural Intelligence (IJCINI), 13(1); pages 25-35, copyright year 2019 by IGI Publishing (an imprint of IGI Global).

Chapter 75

A New Data Hiding Scheme Combining Genetic Algorithm and Artificial Neural Network

Ayan Chatterjee
Sarboday Public Academy, India

Nikhilesh Barik
Kazi Nazrul University, India

ABSTRACT

Today, in the time of internet based communication, steganography is an important approach. In this approach, secret information is embedded in a cover medium with minimum distortion of it. Here, a video steganography scheme is developed in frequency domain category. Frequency domain is more effective than spatial domain due to variation data insertion domain. To change actual domain of entropy pixels of the video frames, uniform crossover of Genetic Algorithm (GA) is used. Then for data insertion in video frames, single layer perceptron of Artificial Neural Network is used. This particular concept of information security is attractive due to its high security during wireless communication. The effectiveness of the proposed technique is analyzed with the parameters PSNR (Peak Signal to Noise Ratio), IF and Payload (bpb).

INTRODUCTION

Steganography is the art of hiding secret data or secret information at the time of wireless communication (2013). In this special approach, the existence of communication among sender and intended receiver(s) can be hidden from unintentional receiver(s) or hacker(s). In the particular system of methodology, the secret information is embedded in a cover medium, such as- image, audio, video etc. and the embedded file is transferred through communication channel. In Image steganography, image pixels are used for inserting secret data (2014). In video steganography, video frames are used to embed the data. Each video frame is treated as an image. The fact is that video files are safer than image files, because- video

DOI: 10.4018/978-1-6684-2408-7.ch075

files take a large no. of image pixels over image files. So, obviously, insertion of data in video files consists of less distortion over image files. There are two major categories of steganography- spatial domain and frequency domain. In spatial domain steganography, the secret data is inserted directly in the image domain.

In frequency domain steganography, the actual domain of cover medium is converted to another medium using some mathematical transformation. This transformed domain is used for inserting secret data. Comparing these two different categories, it is observed that the distortion between actual cover medium and stego medium is generally less in spatial domain steganography over frequency domain steganography. In other words, peak signal to noise ratio (PSNR) and MSE (Mean Squared Error) generally give better result in spatial domain. But it can be easily hacked by unintended receiver(s) using pseudo random number generator (PRNG). Frequency domain steganography is better than spatial domain with respect to PRNG and other statistical attacks. Different mathematical transformations, such as- Discrete Cosine Transformation (DCT), Discrete Wavelet Transformation (DWT), Discrete Fourier Transformation (DFT), Fast Fourier Transformation (FFT) etc are used to transform the actual domain of cover medium. Also, in data compression, different stochastic optimization schemes are used. Among them, Genetic Algorithm (GA), Fuzzy logic etc are very important. Genetic Algorithm (GA) is basically a soft computing based optimization approach. But, the hereditary properties of animal, the concepts of which are used in this particular approach, are very much effective in various fields rather than optimization. Among them, image processing, information security, artificial intelligence etc. are very much important. Basically, GA is developed with three different properties- selection of chromosomes, crossover and mutation. According to the variation of these three operations, various types of GA are developed. GA is generally very much effective for NP hard problems. Another important tool in soft computing is Artificial Neural Network (ANN). In engineering field, this is a sequence of patterns like neurons of human being. In generally, at the time of implementation of all soft computing based approaches, given information and corresponding ingredients are taken as input. Target or goal is obtained Output in all the approaches. The speciality of the approach ANN is that the source pattern and target are taken as input and corresponding ingredients are obtained as output. This speciality makes ANN more effective than other schemes. Depending on variation of source pattern and target, different ANN schemes are developed. Among them, single layer perceptron, multi layer perceptron etc. are very much important. In this paper, a particular approach of frequency domain steganography is developed by using crossover operator of GA and single layer perceptron of ANN. In the next section, some related works are discussed. Then the proposed data hiding scheme is illustrated followed by the algorithm. After that the efficiency of the scheme is analyzed with different type experiments. At last, conclusion of the scheme is given followed by future direction of the work.

BACKGROUND

In this section, some data hiding schemes with cover medium video and tools GA and/or ANN are discussed. In the scheme Optimized Video Steganography using GA (2013), weighted sum approach of multi objective GA is used to make optimizer at the time of encoding. According to the architecture of that scheme is that at first cover video is divided into frames and audio using splitter. After that, in the carrier frame(s), secret data is embedded and stego frame is made. Then an optimizer is developed for steganalysis purpose. In other words, if it is observed that the stego video passes through anti-steganalysis test, then these frames are taken as final stego frames. At the time of using optimizer, two objective functions are considered. These are Mean squared error (MSE) and Human vision system deviation (HVS). Using weighted sum approach, formed single objective function is,

$$f = w_1 \times MSE + w_2 \times HVS \tag{1}$$

Here, the values of w_1 and w_2 are taken 0.8 and 0.2 respectively. RGB pixel values after inserting data in the frames are taken as chromosomes. Then simple mutation with mutation probability 0.05 and single point crossover are performed sequentially. In another scheme, GA based steganography using DCT, at first the actual domain is converted to another domain using Discrete Cosine Transformation (DCT). After that, secret message is embedded in 2nd and 3rd lower frequency component position. At the time of Te- transformation, combined DCT and GA are used. In the scheme LSB based steganography using GA and visual cryptography, genetic algorithm is used for changing pixel position of stego image. In the output of GA, the algorithm of visual cryptography is used. In this particular proposed scheme, only uniform crossover operator of genetic algorithm is used to transform the actual domain and after that using single layer perceptron of Artificial Neural Network (ANN) to make cipher corresponding to the original information and then the cipher is inserted through LSB substitution of the changed domain. The proposed scheme with sender and receiver sides algorithms are illustrated in the next section.

DATA HIDING SCHEME

In this section, proposed data hiding scheme is discussed followed by the algorithms of sender and receiver side separately. This is a frequency domain steganography approach. So, domain transformation of cover medium is required at first. According to the proposed scheme, the basic architectures of sender and receiver side procedures are shown in Figure 1 and Figure 2 respectively.

Figure 1. Diagram of data embedding procedure of the proposed scheme (sender side)

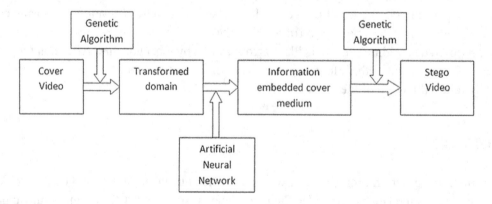

Figure 2. Diagram of data extraction procedure of the proposed scheme (receiver side)

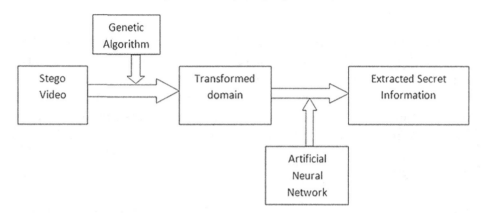

According to the diagram of the procedure of embedding data, it is observed that at first domain of cover video is transformed to another domain using Genetic Algorithm with secret keys. After that, in that domain, the secret information is embedded by using a particular concept of Artificial Neural Network (ANN). Then, using the same idea of GA, inverse transformation is applied to form the stego video. In similar way, at the receiver end, the stego video is transformed to the other domain by using GA with the secret keys, which were used in sender side previously. Next, Neural Network is applied to extract the data from stego video. So, description of total scheme is divided into five parts. Among them, first three parts are the responsibilities of the sender and remaining two parts are of the receiver. So, the parts of sender side procedure are transformation of domain of actual cover video, insertion of secret information in the transformed domain and inverse transformation after insertion of secret information in the cover video. The parts of receiver side process are transformation of domain of stego video and extraction of secret information.

Transformation of Domain of Actual Cover Video

At first, a cover video is divided into video frames and audio separately. Then each video frame is divided into 8×8 entropy pixel blocks. After that, uniform crossover operator of Genetic Algorithm is applied to each block. Actually, the pixels are chosen pair wise sequentially and uniform crossover is applied between them with predefined secret key positions. The key positions are same in all the pixel blocks. The idea of uniform crossover is applied to all the blocks as well as to all the video frames. As a result, a new transformed domain is formed over the actual cover video frames and the domain is used to insert the secret message.

Insertion of Secret Information

After performing the transformation phase, the secret message is divided into 8 bits segment form. In other words, each transformed video frame is used to insert 8 bits secret data. A particular 8×8 block of a frame is taken as a secret key block and that is predefined among sender and receiver before communication. Suppose the 8 bits size message segment is $a_1, a_2, \ldots, a_8$. Here, a single layer perceptron problem of Artificial Neural Network (ANN) is formulated as:

$$\{X_i^T = [i - th \text{ row of the key matrix block}], \text{ the value of } a_i\}; \; i = 1, 2, .., 8 \tag{2}$$

After forming the particular problem, corresponding weight matrix and bias are evaluated. Here are 8 input patterns and therefore the order of weight matrix is 8×1. So, 8 values of weight matrix and bias are inserted into 9 blocks of that particular frame sequentially (except the secret key block) by LSB substitution in the transformed domain. In similar way, the next 8 bits of the message are inserted to the second transformed video frame and so on. In this way, full message is embedded in the transformed domain of the video frames of a particular cover video.

Formation of Stego Video

After insertion of secret message in the transformed domain of video frames, uniform crossover is applied to the blocks and the chromosomes for crossover are selected pair wise and sequentially with secret key positions, which were used at the time of transformation of actual cover video. After the crossover operation, video frames are concatenated. At last, stego video is built up by merging video frames and audio.

The stego video is sent to the receiver through communication channel. After receiving the stego video at the receiver side, the video is divided into video frames and audio. To extract information from the stego video frames, next two steps are performed by the receiver.

Transformation of Domain of Stego Video Frames

At the receiver end, the stego video is partitionized into 8×8 blocks. Uniform crossover operator is applied to the blocks individually by taking the values pair wise and sequentially. To apply uniform crossover, secret key positions are required and these are predefined among sender and receiver before communication. This transformation is applied to all the video frames and the transformed domain is used to extract secret information.

Extraction of Secret Information

Secret matrix block is chosen from first video frame initially. Then, 8 values of weight matrix and bias are extracted from 9 sequential blocks of the frame. Therefore, the weight matrix $[w_{ij}]_{8 \times 1}$ and bias (b) are obtained. From the secret block, 8 input patterns are obtained as,

$$X_i^T = [i - th \text{ row of the key matrix block}], \; i = 1, 2, .., 8 \tag{3}$$

Each bit of the message is evaluated as,

$$m_i = \phi(X_i^T w + b); \; i = 1, 2, .., 8 \tag{4}$$

and

$$\phi(x) = 1, \text{ if } x \geq 0 \text{ and } \phi(x) = 0, \text{ if } x \prec 0 \tag{5}$$

here m_i is the *i-th* bit of 8 bit segment of the message.

In this way, first 8 bits of the message is obtained from the first video frame. Similarly, second 8 bits of the message are obtained from the second frame and the process is continued until full message is extracted at the receiver side.

Procedure

Sender Side

- **Input:** A cover video, secret message
- **Output:** Stego Video
- **Secret Keys:** Secret key positions for crossover, secret key block of the video frames

Algorithm

Step 1: Divide the video into audio and video frames

Step 2: Each video frame is divided into 8×8 entropy pixel blocks

Step 3: Apply uniform crossover pair wise sequentially in each block with key position values to all video frames

Step 4: Divide the full secret message into 8 bits segments sequentially

Step 5: Select the first video frame

Step 6: Take the secret key block of the frame and formulate a problem with 8 bit segmented message in the format of single layer perceptron as equation (1)

Step 7: Find accurate weight matrix (w) and bias (b) using the algorithm of single layer perceptron by maintaining the step function (4)

Step 8: Insert 8 values of weight matrix and bias in the blocks sequentially starting from first block (except the secret key block) by LSB substitution

Step 9: Take the next video frame and next 8 bits segment of the message and go to step 6 until insertion of full message, Otherwise go to step 10

Step 10: Perform the operation same as step 3

Step 11: Combine the frames and audio, as a result stego video is formed

Receiver Side

- **Input:** Stego video
- **Output**: Secret message
- **Secret Keys**: Secret key positions for crossover, secret key block of the video frames

Algorithm

Step 1: Divide the video into audio and video frames

Step 2: Each video frame is divided into 8×8 entropy pixel blocks

Step 3: Apply uniform crossover pair wise sequentially in each block with key position values to all video frames

Step 4: Select the first video frame

Step 5: Take the secret key block of the frame and formulate 8 input patterns using the format (2)

Step 6: Take the 8 values of the weight matrix and bias from the blocks of the frame sequentially

Step 7: Form the weight matrix using these 8 values in 8×1 format

Step 8: Evaluate 8 bit message segment using the formats (3) and (4) respectively

Step 9: Select the next video frame and go to step 5 until obtaining the full message, otherwise go to step 10

Step 10: Combine all the message bits sequentially and obtain the full secret message

EXPERIMENTS AND RESULTS

In this section, efficiency and effectiveness of the proposed data hiding scheme is analyzed through different parameters. Among them, Peak Signal to Noise Ratio (PSNR), Mean Squared error (MSE), Image Fidelity (IF) and Payload (bpB) are important parameter related to this purpose. The working formulae of PSNR and MSE are

$$MSE = \frac{1}{mn} \sum_{i=0}^{m-1} \sum_{j=0}^{n-1} \left\| I(i,j) - K(i,j) \right\|^2 \qquad (6)$$

$$PSNR = 20 \log_{10} \left(\frac{MAX_i}{\sqrt{MSE}} \right) \qquad (7)$$

Here, MAX_i is maximum pixel value of original cover frame and $MAX_i = 2^b - 1$, b is the bit depth of cover frame. In other words, it is observed that MSE is the distortion among cover video frame (I) and stego frame (K). PSNR is anti proportionally related with MSE. Therefore, high PSNR and low MSE represent the efficiency of a data hiding scheme. So, in comparison with the scheme optimized video steganography using GA, the parameters PSNR, IF and payload (bpB) are considered. Here, a small secret message of 800 bits is taken and using the data hiding scheme, this is embedded into 3 different video files and obtained PSNR, IF and payload (bpB) are given in table. The detail structures of the videos and comparative results with other two popular video steganography schemes are also represented in Table 1.

Table 1. Comparison of PSNR, IF and Payload tested in various video files using different data hiding schemes

Video files	No. of frames	Results using GA as optimizer over base method			Results using base video steganography 3-3-2 LSB			Results using proposed method		
		PSNR	IF	Payload (bpB)	PSNR	IF	Payload (bpB)	PSNR	IF	Payload (bpB)
Tree.avi	450	39.374	0.99	2.66	38.03	0.87	2.66	37.64	0.83	2.66
Globe.avi	107	34.372	0.99	2.66	32.67	0.89	2.66	32.61	0.87	2.66
Computer.avi	510	41.613	0.99	2.66	39.21	0.86	2.66	38.32	0.85	2.66

According to the experimental table, it is observed that the proposed data hiding scheme is something better than the previous schemes. Also, it is safe from different statistical attacks, such as- Chi square attack, histogram attack etc for its dynamisms.

FUTURE TRENDS

In this paper, the data hiding scheme is developed only for videos as cover medium. But, in steganography, various cover mediums, such as- audio, image files can be used for hiding data. So, In future, this method can be implemented in different mediums also. Also, to implement this method in the video files, it is observed that a large video, i.e. a video with large number of frames is required for inserting a particular secret message. This problem also can be tried to remove in future.

CONCLUSION

In this paper, an approach of video steganography is built up during communication through wireless network by assortment of Genetic Algorithm (GA) and Artificial Neural Network (ANN). The idea of uniform crossover operator of GA is used to transform the actual entropy pixel values to different domain. In other words, it is used to transform the actual domain. After that, single layer perceptron of Artificial Neural Network is used to develop a ciphertext corresponding to the secret message by using a particular block of a frame of a video file. The particular approach is striking for selecting the secret key pixel block and becomes very much secured from various steganography attacks. Also, the scheme gives better PSNR, IF and Payload over some popular previous data hiding approaches maintaining basic conditions of information security, i.e. confidentiality, integrity and availability of secret important data among authorized users.

REFERENCES

Chakrapani, G., & Lokeswara Reddy, V. (2014). Optimized Videotapr Steganography Using Genetic Algorithm (GA). *IJCS, 15,* 1–6.

Dasgupta, K., Mondal, J. K., & Dutta, P. (2013). *Optimized Video Steganography using Genetic Algorithm (GA).* Paper presented in International Conference on Computational Intelligence: Modeling, Techniques and Applications (CIMTA) 2013, Department of Computer Science & Engineering, University of Kalyani, West Bengal, India.

Deb, K., Pratap, A., Agarwal, S., & Meyarivan, T. (2002). A Fast and Elitist Multiobjective Genetic Algorithm. *IEEE Transaction Evolutionary Computation, 6*(2), 182–197. doi:10.1109/4235.996017

Dutt, D., & Hedge, V. (2015). AAKRITI[ed]: An Image and Data Encryption-Decryption Tool. *International Journal of Computer Science and Information Technology Research, 2*(2), 264-268.

Gokul, M., & Umeshbabu, R. (2012). Hybrid Steganography using Visual Cryptography and LSB Encryption Method. *International Journal of Computer Applications, 59*(14), 5-8.

Jain, R., & Kumar, N. (2012). Efficient data hiding scheme using lossless data compression and image steganography. *International Journal of Engineering Science and Technology, 4*(8), 3908-3915.

Khamrui, A., & Mandal, J. K. (2013). A Genetic Algorithm based Steganography using Discrete Cosine Transformation (GASDCT). *International Conference on Computational Intelligence: Modeling Techniques and Applications (CIMTA).* 10.1016/j.protcy.2013.12.342

Lin, Y.-K. (2014). A data hiding scheme based upon DCT coefficient modification. *Computer Standards & Interfaces, 36*(5), 855–862. doi:10.1016/j.csi.2013.12.013

Mishra, A., & Johri, P. (2015). A Review on Video Steganography using GA. *International Journal of Innovative & Advancement in Computer Science, 4*(SI), 120-124.

Nehru, G., & Dhar, P. (2012). A Detailed look of Audio Steganography Techniques using LSB and Genetic Algorithm Approach. *International Journal of Computer Science Issues, 9*(1), 402-406.

Roy, S., & Venkateswaran, P. (2014). Online Payment System using Steganography and Visual Cryptography. *IEEE Students' Conference on Electrical, Electronics and Computer Science.*

Singla, D., & Syal, R. (2012). Data Security Using LSB & DCT Steganography In Images. *International Journal of Computational Engineering Research, 2*(2), 359-364.

Soleimanpour, M., Tabeli, S., & Azadi-Motlag, H. (2013). A Novel Technique for Steganography Method Based on Improved Genetic Algorithm Optimization in Spatial Domain. *Iranian Journal of Electrical & Electronics Engineering, 9*(2), 67–74.

Zamani, M., Manaf, A. A., Ahmed, R. B., Zeki, A. M., & Abdullah, S. (2009). A Genetic Algorithm Based Approach for Audio Steganography, International Journal of Computer, Electrical, Automation. *Control and Information Engineering, 3*(6), 1562–1565.

KEY TERMS AND DEFINITIONS

Artificial Neural Network (ANN): An important tool to set up linkage between provided input and required output and it is developed on the basis of the set up of communicating nervous system of human being.

Genetic Algorithm: A special algorithmic optimization procedure, developed on the basis of simple hereditary property of animals and used for both of constrained and unconstrained problem. In Artificial Intelligence (AI), it is used as heuristic search also.

Peak Signal to Noise Ratio (PSNR): An expression is used to realize the distortion of quality of a cover medium at the presence of noise during wireless communication.

Steganalysis: Security analysis system at the time of sending data through wireless communication by the schemes of steganography.

Video Steganography: Process of authenticated communication by hiding secret information from unauthorized user(s) through a video file as cover medium.

Wireless Communication: Communication process with independent of wire among a finite set of users, who are in a long distance.

This research was previously published in the Handbook of Research on Modeling, Analysis, and Application of Nature-Inspired Metaheuristic Algorithms; pages 94-103, copyright year 2018 by Engineering Science Reference (an imprint of IGI Global).

Chapter 76
A Novel Hybridization of ARIMA, ANN, and K–Means for Time Series Forecasting

Warut Pannakkong

School of Knowledge Science, Japan Advanced Institute of Science and Technology, Nomi, Japan

Van-Hai Pham

Pacific Ocean University, Nha Trang, Vietnam

Van-Nam Huynh

School of Knowledge Science, Japan Advanced Institute of Science and Technology, Nomi, Japan

ABSTRACT

This article aims to propose a novel hybrid forecasting model involving autoregressive integrated moving average (ARIMA), artificial neural networks (ANNs) and k-means clustering. The single models and k-means clustering are used to build the hybrid forecasting models in different levels of complexity (i.e. ARIMA; hybrid model of ARIMA and ANNs; and hybrid model of k-means, ARIMA, and ANN). To obtain the final forecasting value, the forecasted values of these three models are combined with the weights generated from the discount mean square forecast error (DMSFE) method. The proposed model is applied to three well-known data sets: Wolf's sunspot, Canadian lynx and the exchange rate (British pound to US dollar) to evaluate the prediction capability in three measures (i.e. MSE, MAE, and MAPE). In addition, the prediction performance of the proposed model is compared to ARIMA; ANNs; Khashei and Bijari's model; and the hybrid model of k-means, ARIMA, and ANN. The obtained results show that the proposed model gives the best performance in MSE, MAE, and MAPE for all three data sets.

DOI: 10.4018/978-1-6684-2408-7.ch076

INTRODUCTION

Time series forecasting is an active research area that continuously improve effectiveness of forecasting techniques over several decades (De Gooijer & Hyndman, 2006). This research area has contributed to various practical applications: finance (Wei, 2016; Adhikari & Agrawal, 2014), agriculture (Ezzine, Bouziane, & Ouazar, 2014; Garrett, et al., 2013), energy (Sadaei, Enayatifar, Abdulla, & Gani, 2014; Bahrami, Hooshmand, & Parastegari, 2014), transportation (Gosasang, Chandraprakaikul, & Kiattisin, 2011; Xiao, Xiao, & Wang, 2012), environment (Deng, Wang, & Zhang, 2015; Feng, et al., 2015), etc.

Traditionally, one of the most popular forecasting model is autoregressive integrated moving average (ARIMA). The ARIMA usually outperforms other forecasting approaches due to its capability in dealing with non-stationary time series as well as stationary time series. Nevertheless, the ARIMA is a kind of linear model, for this reason, it makes a prior assumption on relationship between historical and future time series as a linear function, which is very difficult to be satisfied in practical situations (Box, Jenkins, & Reinsel, 2008).

Artificial neural network (ANN), an artificial intelligent mimicking biological neurons mechanism, is widely used because of its usage flexibility over the ARIMA. The ANN can fit the relationship between inputs (e.g. historical time series) and outputs (e.g. predicted time series) without pre-assuming their relationship. Moreover, the ANN with only one hidden layer can be used as a universal approximator for continuous functions (Zhang, Patuwo, & Hu, 1998; Hornik, Stinchcombe, & White, 1989). The prediction performances of the ARIMA and the ANN were compared in several studies, and the results indicated that the ANN usually gave better accuracy than the ARIMA (Zou, Xia, Yang, & Wang, 2007; Co & Boosarawongse, 2007; Prybutok, Yi, & Mitchell, 2000; Kohzadi, Boyd, Kermanshahi, & Kaastra, 1996; Ho, Xie, & Goh, 2002; Alon, Qi, & Sadowski, 2001). Recently, in order to improve the effectiveness of the ANN which is a nonlinear model, both the results and the residuals of the ARIMA have been included as the inputs to gain unique capability in linear and nonlinear modeling (so called ARIMA/ANN) (Khashei & Bijari, 2011).

Currently, the prediction performance of the ANN can be improved by applying the ANN to clusters formed by clustering techniques (e.g. k-means and self-organizing map (SOM)) instead of applying the ANN directly to whole time series. (Benmouiza & Cheknane, 2013; Ruiz-Aguilar, Turias, & Jiménez-Come, 2015; Amin-Naseri & Gharacheh, 2007). This method can enhance the prediction performance because the observations assigned to the same cluster share similar characteristics that make their pattern to be easier fitted by the ANN. Nevertheless, it can cause the overfitting problem,

In addition, even though, the time series is well separated into the clusters, but we cannot actually know the cluster of each future value. In this situation, the approach to select the suitable cluster for prediction is an interesting issue. A recent work proposed to use summation of the prediction values from every cluster (Ruiz-Aguilar, Turias, & Jiménez-Come, 2015), but in fact, it would be more logical if the future values are produced from the ANN dedicated to their cluster. For this reason, the ANN should be selected based on the prediction of cluster of the future value. In order to do so, the clustering technique that can provide the straight clear-cut boundary between the clusters such as the k-means clustering is required. Therefore, a hybrid model of the ARIMA and the ANN with the k-means clustering is developed.

Normally, hybridization of the forecasting models has been constructed by combination of single models. Although the hybrid models can outperform the single models, but only in the average of prediction performance. The single models can still give the better results than hybrid models in some forecasting period. The forecasting models having difference of complexity (single, hybrid, and hybrid with clustering) may extract different information from the time series. Thus, there is a potential to improve prediction accuracy if we can properly combine such models together.

The objective of this paper is to develop a novel hybrid forecasting model that takes advantage of unique strength of the three approaches such as linear, hybrid linear-nonlinear, and hybrid linear-nonlinear with clustering models. In addition, an approach for selecting the suitable cluster for prediction is proposed as well. The rest of the paper is organized as follows. In Preliminaries section, the ARIMA, the ANN, and the *k*-means clustering are introduced. Then, the detail of the proposed hybrid model is described in Proposed Model section. In section of Application of the Proposed Model to Real-World Time Series, the experiments are explained, and the results are interpreted. Finally, the important findings are summarized in Conclusion section.

PRELIMINARIES

This section describes the techniques used for developing the proposed hybrid model. These techniques are the ARIMA, the ANN, and the *k*-means clustering. Three well-known forecasting accuracy measures used for the model's evaluation are also presented. Their background and mathematical formulation are introduced in the rest of this section.

Autoregressive Integrated Moving Average (ARIMA)

The autoregressive integrated moving average (ARIMA) is a popular time series forecasting model for decades (Box, Jenkins, & Reinsel, 2008). The ARIMA has three main parts: autoregressive (AR), integration (I), and moving average (MA). The advantage of the ARIMA is the ability in dealing with non-stationary data by performing differencing step corresponding to the integration (I) part. The ARIMA can be expressed commonly as ARIMA(p,d,q) and mathematically as:

$$\varnothing_p\left(B\right)\left(1-B\right)^d Z_t = c + \theta_q\left(B\right)a_t \tag{1}$$

where Z_t and a_t are the time series and the random error at period t respectively, c is the constant,

$$\varnothing_p\left(B\right) = 1 - \sum_{i=1}^{p}\varnothing_i B^i, \ \theta_q\left(B\right) = 1 - \sum_{j=1}^{q}\theta_j B^j,$$

B is the backward shift operator defined as $B^i y_t = y_{t-i}$, $\varnothing_i$ and θj are the autoregressive and the moving average parameters respectively, p and q denote the orders of the autoregressive (AR) and the moving average (MA) respectively, and d is the degree of differencing.

Artificial Neural Network (ANN)

Artificial neural network (ANN) is a well-known time series forecasting model that has been implemented to wide range of nonlinear problems due to its nonlinear characteristic and ability to fit the relationship between historical and predicted values without prior assumption. The ANN structure contains three types of layer: input, hidden and output layers. Normally, there are one input layer and one output layer. On the other hand, the number of the hidden layer can be more than one. However, the ANN with single hidden layer can be the universal approximator for any continuous nonlinear function (Hornik, Stinchcombe, & White, 1989), and the relationship between the inputs and the outputs can be shown as:

$$Z_t = f\left(b_n + \sum_{h=1}^{R} w_h g\left(b_{i,h} + \sum_{i=1}^{Q} w_{i,h} p_i\right)\right) + \varepsilon \tag{2}$$

where Z_t is the time series at period t; $w_{i,h}$ and w_h are the connection weights between the layers; Q and R are the numbers of the inputs and the hidden nodes respectively; $b_{i,h}$ and b_h are the biases; ε is the error term; and f and g are the transfer functions that usually are the linear and the nonlinear functions respectively.

Khashei and Bijari's Model

Practically, there is no single forecasting model that can give the best performance in any situation, and it is very difficult to determine whether the time series is linear or nonlinear. In fact, pure linear and pure nonlinear time series rarely exist in the real world (Zhang, 2003).

In order to deal with such situation, the hybrid models, which can be a combination of same or different type of the single models (Taskaya-Temizel, 2005), have been developed to improve prediction accuracy by taking unique capabilities of the single models in a complementary manner, such as Zhang's hybrid model which is a combination of the ARIMA and the ANN that has capability in linear and nonlinear modeling, respectively (Zhang, 2003).

However, the Zhang's model assumed additive relationship between linear and nonlinear components. Such assumption cannot be satisfied in all cases. To overcome this limitation, Khashei and Bijari (2011) developed a new hybridization of the ARIMA and the ANN, which represents time series as a function of the linear and the nonlinear components, and it can be formally defined by:

$$Z_t = f(L_t, N_t) \tag{3}$$

where L_t and N_t denotes the linear and nonlinear components, respectively.

There are two stages in this hybrid approach. In the first stage, the linear component (L_t) can be estimated from the results of the ARIMA ($\hat{L_t}$). The residuals of the ARIMA at time t (e_t) can be determined as:

$$e_t = Z_t - \hat{L_t} \tag{4}$$

where $\widehat{L}_t$ denotes the results of the ARIMA and Z_t denotes the time series at period t.

In the second stage, the objective is to estimate the nonlinear components from both the residuals of the ARIMA ($\widehat{N}_t^1$) and the historical time series ($\widehat{N}_t^2$) as described in (5) and (6) respectively:

$$\widehat{N}_t^1 = f^1\left(e_{t-1},\ldots,e_{t-n}\right) \tag{5}$$

$$\widehat{N}_t^2 = f^2\left(Z_{t-1},\ldots,Z_{t-m}\right) \tag{6}$$

where f^1 and f^2 are the functions determined by the ANN; n and m are the integers representing the number of maximum previous periods included in the model.

Finally, the linear and nonlinear components are combined as:

$$Z_t = f\left(\widehat{L}_t,e_{t-1},\ldots,e_{t-n1},Z_{t-1},\ldots,Z_{t-m1}\right) + \varepsilon \tag{7}$$

where f is the function fitted by the ANN, $n1 \leq n$ and $m1 \leq m$ are the integers determined in the design process, and ε is the error term.

K-Means Clustering Algorithm

The k-means clustering algorithm is an unsupervised learning algorithm commonly used for grouping the data set into k clusters (MacQueen, 1967). The algorithm (Figure 1) begins with determining the number of cluster (k) and the position of centroids for each cluster. Second, each observation is assigned to the nearest centroid using the Euclidian distance (d_{ij}) as below:

$$d_{ij} = \sqrt{\sum_{v=1}^{V}\left(x_{iv} - c_{jv}\right)^2} \tag{8}$$

where x_{iv} is the value of attribute v of the observation i, c_{jv} is the value of the attribute v of the centroid of the cluster j, and V is the number of total attribute involved in each observation. Third, the centroids are recomputed. Then, the second and the third steps are repeated until all centroids stop moving.

The problem of the k-means clustering algorithm is the selection of the optimal number of cluster (k). To determine the optimal k, the Silhouette (Rousseeuw, 1987) can be used as a measure of the clustering quality, and it can be computed as:

$$s_i = \frac{b_i - a_i}{\max\left(a_i,b_i\right)} \tag{9}$$

where a_i is the average dissimilarity of observation i to all other observations in the same cluster, b_i is the minimum dissimilarity of observation i to all observations in the other clusters. According to the formula, the higher value of s_i implies the better matching between the observation i and its cluster. Thus, the number of k giving the highest average of s_i for the whole data set is considered as the optimal k.

Figure 1. K-means clustering algorithm

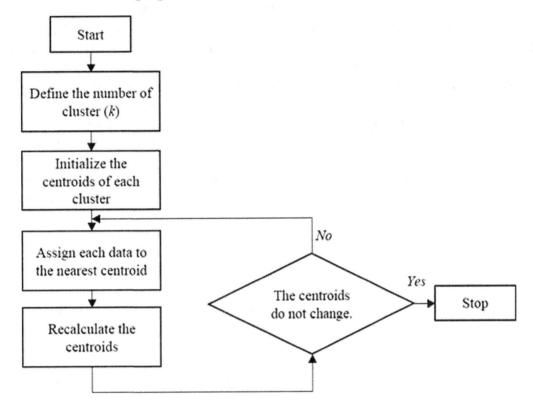

Forecasting Performance Measures

Three well-known prediction accuracy measures including mean square error (MSE), mean absolute error (MAE), and mean absolute percentage error (MAPE) are chosen as the measures for the forecasting performance evaluation. Their mathematical formulas are expressed as follows:

$$\text{MSE} = \frac{1}{N}\sum_{t=1}^{N}\left(Z_t - \widehat{Z}_t\right)^2 \tag{10}$$

$$\text{MAE} = \frac{1}{N}\sum_{t=1}^{N}\left|Z_t - \widehat{Z}_t\right| \tag{11}$$

$$\text{MAPE} = \frac{1}{N} \sum_{t=1}^{N} \left| \frac{Z_t - \widehat{Z}_t}{Z_t} \right| \tag{12}$$

where Z_t denotes the actual time series at period t, $\widehat{Z}_t$ denotes the forecasted time series at period t, and N denotes the number of total forecasting period.

Although all of them correspond to the error computed from the magnitude of the difference between Z_t and $\widehat{Z}_t$, the meaning of their results is different. The model producing the lowest MAE has the lowest average magnitude of error. On the other hand, the model generating the lowest MSE seems to have the lowest maximum magnitude of error.

For these two measures, if there are no other models for comparison, it is difficult to judge whether the value of these measures is high or low. However, in case of the MAPE, it does not consider only the magnitude of the error but also the error in percentage comparing to the actual values. Therefore, the MAPE can be easier to be interpreted than the MSE and the MAE because of presenting the error in percentage.

Furthermore, in some circumstance, if there is no model that can dominate the others in all measures (i.e. MSE, MAE, and MAPE), hence, the decision in selecting the suitable model depends on the user preferences.

PROPOSED MODEL

In this section, the proposed model is presented (Figure 2). The objective of the proposed model is to take unique advantages of the different forecasting models in terms of type (i.e. linear and nonlinear) and complexity (i.e. single and hybrid).

The proposed model consists of four stages: I) linear modeling, II) linear-nonlinear modeling, III) linear-nonlinear modeling with clustering, and IV) final forecasting. At stage I, the linear modeling stage uses the ARIMA to extract linear component from time series. At stage II, the linear-nonlinear modeling stage applies the Khashei and Bijari's model (Khashei & Bijari, 2011) which is the ANN with the inputs: linear component (the results of the ARIMA), the residuals of the ARIMA, and the lagged values of the time series. The model of the stage II can be referred as ARIMA/ANN. At stage III, the linear-nonlinear modeling with clustering stage performs k-means clustering algorithm to form time series into different clusters. Then, the ARIMA/ANN is built for each cluster. Meanwhile, the cluster of one-step ahead time series is predicted from the results of the stage II. The model of the stage III can be called k-means/ARIMA/ANN. At stage IV, the final forecasting is done by aggregation of the results from the three previous stages with weights generated by discount mean square forecast error (DMSFE). The detail of these four stages are explained stage by stage in the rest of this section.

Stage I: Linear Modeling

The ARIMA is applied to the whole data set to obtain the predicted values ($\widehat{L}_t$) and their residuals (e_t). The results are passed through the final forecasting and also used as the inputs for the ARIMA/ANN and the k-means/ARIMA/ANN.

Figure 2. The proposed hybrid model

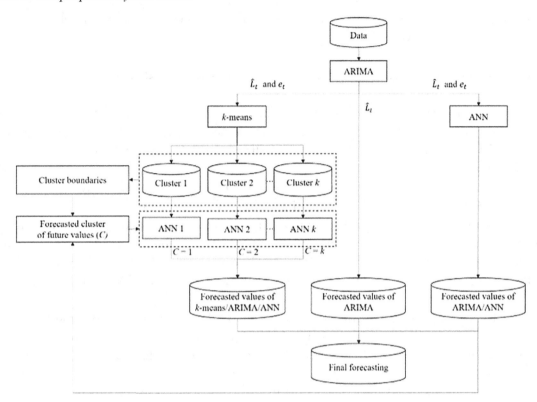

Stage II: Linear-Nonlinear Modeling

The Khashei and Bijari's model (ARIMA/ANN) (2011) is a single hidden layer ANN including the lagged values of the times series and both the predicted values and the residuals of the ARIMA as the inputs. The benefit of this model is capability in fitting the relationship between the time series and the linear and nonlinear components as a function shown in (13) instead of the additive relationship.

$$\widehat{Z}_t = f\left(\widehat{L}_t, e_{t-1}, \ldots, e_{t-n1}, Z_{t-1}, \ldots, Z_{t-m1}\right) \tag{13}$$

where $\widehat{Z}_t$ is the forecasted value at period t, f is the function fitted by the ANN, $\widehat{L}_t$ is the predicted value of the ARIMA at period t, Z_t is the actual value at period t, e_t is the residual of the ARIMA at period t, $n1 \leq n$ and $m1 \leq m$ are the integers identified in the design process.

The multilayer feedforward neural network with one hidden layer is applied. The transfer function between the input and the hidden layer is sigmoid function as in (14). On the other hand, the transfer function between the hidden and the output layer is linear transfer function.

$$\text{Sigmoid}\left(x\right) = \frac{2}{1 + e^{-x}} \tag{14}$$

The number of hidden nodes, $n1$ and $m1$ are varied for searching the best fitted model. The forecasted values of the best fitted model are moved to the final forecasting stage and used for the cluster forecasting in the k-means/ARIMA/ANN as well.

Stage III: Linear-Nonlinear Modeling With *K*-Means Clustering

In this stage, firstly, the k-means clustering algorithm is applied for clustering the time series into the clusters. The suitable number of the cluster (k) can be selected from the number which has the highest average of the Silhouette (s_i). Then, the ANN (so called k-means/ARIMA/ANN) is built dedicatedly for each cluster.

In order to forecast the future time series, the cluster of the future time series have to be determined at first. The prediction results from the stage II are assigned into the clusters by using the boundaries between the clusters. The boundaries between the clusters are defined by taking an average of a maximum observation of the lower centroid cluster and a minimum observation of the higher centroid cluster. The observations falling into the same boundaries will be considered as members of the same cluster. In each forecasting period, the prediction result comes from the k-means/ARIMA/ANN chosen according to the predicted cluster.

For instance, we suppose that there are two clusters: cluster 1 and cluster 2. The centroid of the cluster 1 is lower than the cluster 2. The maximum observation of the cluster 1 is 18. The minimum observation of the cluster 2 is 22. In this case, the average of these values (i.e. 18 and 22) is 20 which is the boundary separating the cluster 1 and 2. In addition, the lower and higher boundaries of the cluster 1 are 0 and 20 respectively, and the lower and higher boundaries of the cluster 2 are 20 and infinity respectively. If the forecasted value of the stage II (ARIMA/ANN) at period $t+1$ is 19, then, the forecasted value belongs to the cluster 1 because 19 is between the boundaries of the cluster 1. Thus, the cluster 1 is chosen for the prediction at period $t+1$. Eventually, the results of the k-means/ARIMA/ANN are included in the final forecasting stage.

Stage IV: Final Forecasting

According to the experimental results of the previous three stages, the different forecasting models give the different prediction values due to unique capability in capturing patterns of the time series. The model giving the best average performance cannot guarantee to outperform the others in every forecasting periods. On the other hand, the model providing the worst average accuracy can have the best result in some periods of prediction.

In order to improve forecasting accuracy based on this circumstance, a combination of the three forecasting models is proposed as an additive weighting summation of the results from the stage I, II, and III:

$$\widehat{Z}_t = \sum_{i=1}^{m} w_{i,t} \widehat{Z}_t^i \tag{15}$$

where $\widehat{Z}_t$ is the final forecasted value at period t, $\widehat{Z}_t^i$ is the forecasted value of method i at period t, $w_{i,t}$ is the weight of method i at period t, and m is the total number of the forecasting methods.

The forecasting model giving more accurate prediction will be assigned to have more weight ($w_{i,t}$). The weight of the first forecasting period ($w_{i,1}$) is determined by applying discount mean square forecast error (DMSFE) method (Winkler & Makridakis, 1983) to training period as:

$$w_{i,1} = \frac{\left[\sum_{tr=1}^{Tr} \gamma^{Tr-tr+1} \left(Z_{tr} - \widehat{Z}_{tr}^{i} \right)^2 \right]^{-1}}{\sum_{i=1}^{m} \left[\sum_{tr=1}^{Tr} \gamma^{Tr-tr+1} \left(Z_{tr} - \widehat{Z}_{tr}^{i} \right)^2 \right]^{-1}} \tag{16}$$

where Z_{tr} is the actual value at training period tr, $\widehat{Z}_{tr}^{i}$ is the fitted value of method i at training period tr, Tr is the total number of the training period, γ is the discount factor assumed 0.8.

Then, the weight is updated in every forecasting period by exponential smoothing method with smoothing factor (α) assumed 0.2 as below:

$$w_{i,t} = \alpha \left[\frac{\left(Z_{t-1} - \widehat{Z}_{t-1}^{i} \right)^{-2}}{\sum_{i=1}^{m} \left(Z_{t-1} - \widehat{Z}_{t-1}^{i} \right)^{-2}} \right] + \left(1 - \alpha \right) w_{i,t-1} \tag{17}$$

Traditionally, the results from different forecasting model are combined by the simple average method giving the same weight to all forecasting results without taking their prediction accuracy into account. Whereas it would be more logical if the results of more accurate model have more weight.

In case of the proposed combination method, the DMSFE method enhances prediction accuracy in the final prediction by giving more weight to the results of more accurate forecasting method. The DMSFE method also applies the discount factor (γ) to the error at each training period; the error at current period has more contribution to the total error than the error at older period.

However, the weights generated by the DMSFE method are based on only the errors in training period. It cannot guarantee that the accuracy of the forecasting method in training period will be the same in the forecasting period. Therefore, the proposed combination method has one further step which is updating the weights in every forecasting period by the exponential smoothing method.

APPLICATION OF THE PROPOSED MODEL TO REAL-WORLD TIME SERIES

In order to examine the prediction capability of the proposed model, the proposed model is applied to three well-known data sets: Wolf's sunspot, Canadian lynx and exchange rate (British pound to US dollar). These three data sets are different in term of fields and statistical properties. Several researchers have applied these data sets to demonstrate effectiveness of linear, nonlinear and hybrid models (Zhang G. P., 2003; Khashei & Bijari, 2011).

To investigate the suitable parameters of the proposed model, comprehensive experiments are performed in various scenarios that have different set of parameters: 1-10 lagged periods of the actual time series (Z_t), the results of the ARIMA ($\hat{L}_t$) and the residuals of the ARIMA (e_t); 1-10 hidden nodes of the ANN; and 2-5 numbers of cluster (k).

Each scenario is run for five replications to obtain the average of the results (i.e. one step-ahead forecasting). After that, the prediction performance is evaluated by the three well-known measures: mean square error (MSE), mean absolute error (MAE) and mean absolute percentage error (MAPE). The proposed model is compared to the ARIMA, the ANN, the Khashei and Bijari's model (ARIMA/ANN), and the *k*-means/ARIMA/ANN. The detail of experiments and discussion of the results are provided in the rest of this section.

Wolf's Sunspot Forecasting

The Wolf's sunspot time series is the historical annual record of number of black spots on the sun surface. The sunspot time series involved in this experiment is recorded during 1700-1987 (288 observations) (Figure 3). The records in 1700-1920 (221 observations) are included in model training. The remaining records in 1921-1987 (67 observations) are used for model testing.

Figure 3. The Wolf's sunspot time series (1700-1987)

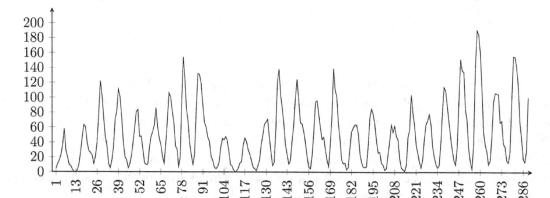

- **Stage I. Linear Modeling:** The sunspot time series is analyzed by the ARIMA to obtain the linear component ($\hat{L}_t$). ARIMA(9,0,0) is the best fitted model that has also been chosen in several researches (Hipel & McLeod, 1994; Zhang, 2003; Khashei & Bijari, 2011). The results of the ARIMA(9,0,0) are passed through the stage II-IV.
- **Stage II. Linear-Nonlinear Modeling:** The ARIMA/ANN is applied to deal with the linear and nonlinear components of the sunspot time series. The linear component, the residuals of the ARIMA(9,0,0), and the lagged values of the sunspot time series are included into the model. The ARIMA/ANN(7-4-1) (Figure 4) is the best fitted model.

Figure 4. ARIMA/ANN(7-4-1) for the sunspot time series

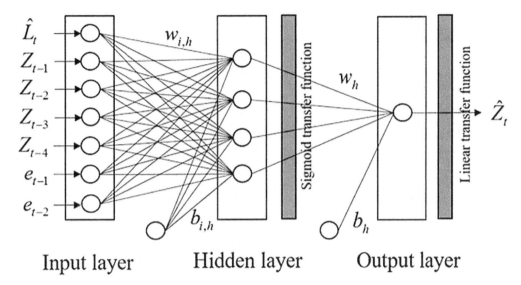

- **Stage III. Linear-Nonlinear Modeling With *K*-Means Clustering:** Firstly, the training set of the sunspot time series is grouped into the clusters by the *k*-means clustering algorithm. Two clusters are suitable for the sunspot time series according to the highest average of Silhouette (s_i). The clusters are completely separated without overlapping (Figure 5). Then, the *k*-means/ARIMA/ANN is dedicatedly constructed for each cluster. The *k*-means/ARIMA/ANN fitted to cluster 1 and 2 are *k*-means/ARIMA/ANN(4-3-1) (Figure 6) and *k*-means/ARIMA/ANN(5-2-1) (Figure 7) respectively.

Figure 5. Clusters of the sunspot training set

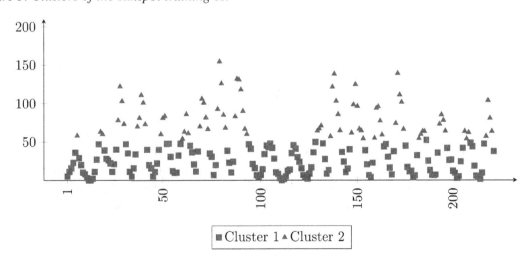

Figure 6. K-means/ARIMA/ANN(4-3-1) for the sunspot cluster 1

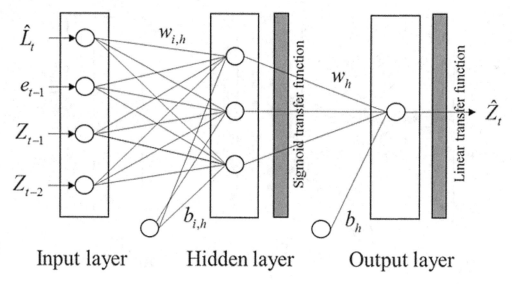

Figure 7. K-means/ARIMA/ANN(5-2-1) for the sunspot cluster 2

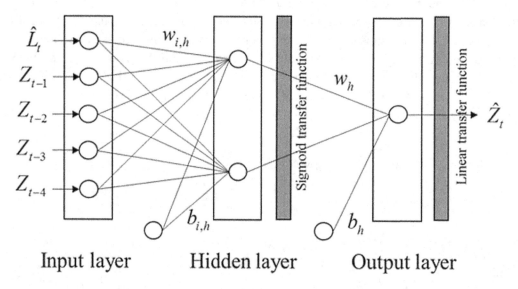

- **Stage IV. Final Forecasting Stage:** The forecasted values from the ARIMA, the ARIMA/ANN and the *k*-means/ARIMA/ANN are combined by using the weights from the discount mean square forecast error (DMSFE) method. The proposed model gives 224.84 of MSE, 11.60 of MAE, and 24.47% of MAPE. The forecasted values of the proposed model are shown in Figure 8.

Figure 8. Forecasted values of the proposed model for the sunspot time series

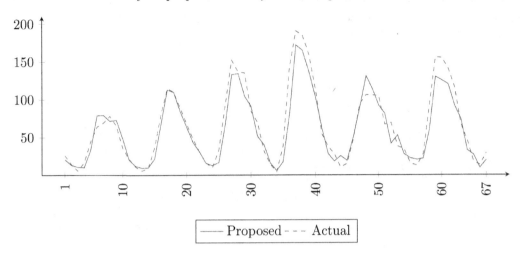

Canadian Lynx Forecasting

The Canadian lynx time series used for this experiment is the annual number of lynx trapped in the Mackenzie River district of Northern Canada during 1821-1934 (114 observations) (Figure 9). The lynx time series has been studied in several researches (Lin & Pourahmadi, 1998; Campbell & Walker, 1977; Wong & Li, 2000). However, the data transformation with based ten logarithms is performed (Zhang, 2003; Khashei & Bijari, 2011). The training and test sets are 1821-1920 (100 observations) and 1921-1934 (14 observations) respectively.

Figure 9. Canadian lynx time series (1821-1934)

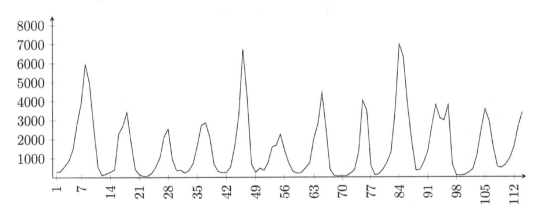

- **Stage I. Linear Modeling:** ARIMA(12,0,0) is the best fitted of the ARIMA for the lynx time series. It has been also chosen by several researchers (Zhang, 2003; Khashei & Bijari, 2011).

- **Stage II. Linear-Nonlinear Modeling:** The best fitted model is ARIMA/ANN(7-5-1) that contains seven inputs which are the lagged values from one to seven periods and five hidden nodes as shown in Figure 10.

Figure 10. ARIMA/ANN(7-5-1) for the Canadian lynx time series

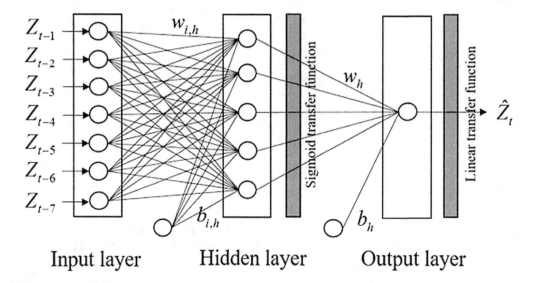

- **Stage III. Linear-Nonlinear Modeling With Clustering:** Although the training set of the lynx time series is separated into three clusters (Figure 11), but after prediction of the clusters of the test set, there are only cluster 1 and 2. Therefore, the k-means/ARIMA/ANN for cluster 3 is not involved in this stage. The appropriate models for the cluster 1 and 2 are k-means/ARIMA/ANN(2-4-1) (Figure 12) and k-means/ARIMA/ANN(6-1-1) (Figure 13) respectively.

Figure 11. Clusters of the Canadian lynx training set

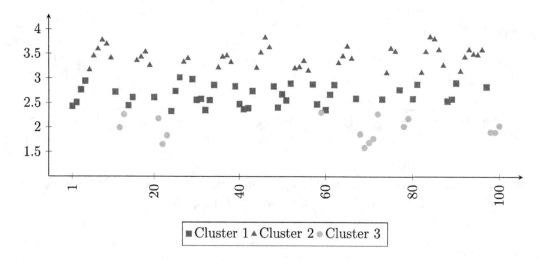

Figure 12. K-means/ARIMA/ANN(2-4-1) for the Canadian lynx cluster 1

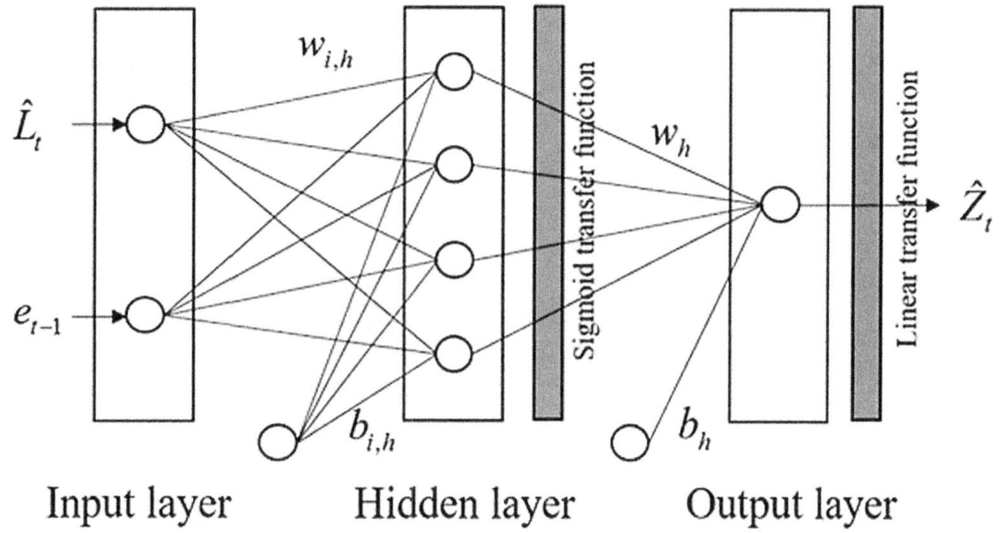

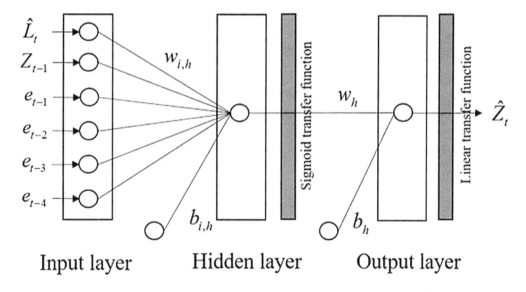

Figure 13. K-means/ARIMA/ANN(6-1-1) for the Canadian lynx cluster 2

- **Stage IV. Final Forecasting:** In the same way as the previous data set, the results from the stage I, II and III are combined together by the weights from the DMSFE method. The performance of the proposed model in the three measures are 0.0135 of MSE, 0.0885 of MAE, and 3% of MAPE. The forecasting values of the lynx are presented in Figure 14.

Figure 14. Forecasted values of the proposed model for the Canadian lynx time series

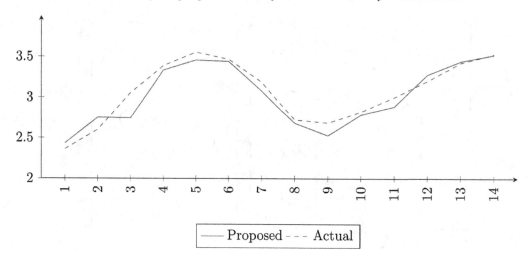

Exchange Rate Forecasting

The weekly exchange rate of British pound to US dollar in 1980-1993 (731 observations) (Figure 15) is involved in the experiment. The natural logarithm is used for data transformation as in (Meese & Rogoff, 1983; Zhang G. P., 2003; Khashei & Bijari, 2011). The first 679 records belong to training set, and the remaining 52 records are used for model testing.

Figure 15. Exchange rate time series (1980-1993)

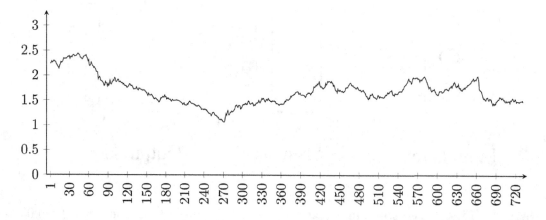

- **Stage I. Linear Modeling:** The best fitted model is ARIMA(0,1,0) which is a random walk model. This model has been selected by Zhang (Zhang G. P., 2003) and Khashei and Bijari (Khashei & Bijari, 2011) as well. Additionally, several researchers in research area of the exchange rate forecasting have also recommended to choose the random walk model for the linear modeling.

- **Stage II. Linear-Nonlinear Modeling:** The best fitted model is ARIMA/ANN(20-9-1) which consists of nine hidden nodes and the twenty inputs: the linear component from the stage I, seven periods lagged values, and nine lagged values of the ARIMA(0,1,0) residuals. The structure of the model is shown in Figure 16.

Figure 16. K-means/ARIMA/ANN(20-9-1) for the exchange rate time series

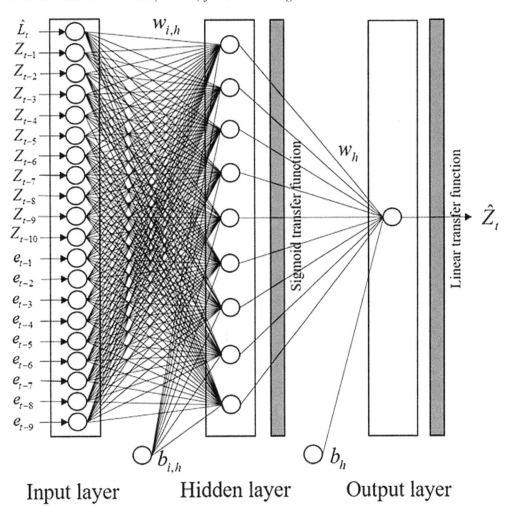

- **Stage III. Linear-Nonlinear Modeling With Clustering:** The suitable number of the cluster of the training set is four clusters (Figure 17). Nevertheless, the predicted clusters of all periods in the test set belong to cluster 2. Therefore, *k*-means/ARIMA/ANN for only the cluster 2 is considered. The best fitted model of the cluster 2 is *k*-means/ARIMA/ANN(8-9-1) composed of the linear component from the stage I, one periods lagged value, and six periods lagged values of the residuals of ARIMA(0,1,0) as presented in (Figure 18).

Figure 17. Clusters of the exchange rate training set

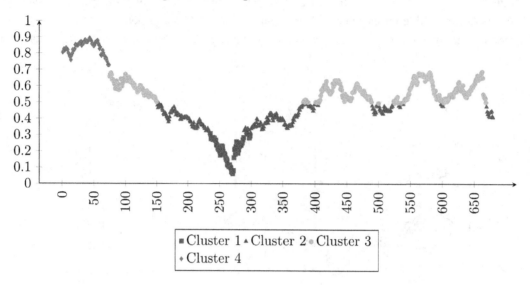

Figure 18. K-means/ARIMA/ANN(8-9-1) for the exchange rate cluster 2

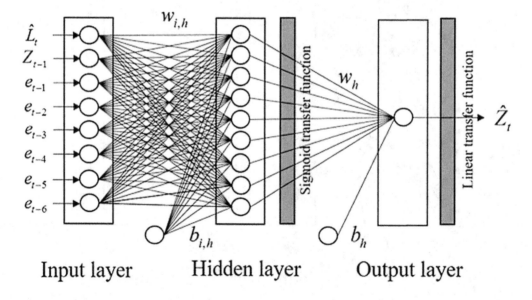

- **Stage IV. Final Forecasting:** The results from the stage I, II and III are aggregated by the weights from the DMSFE method. The proposed model has prediction performance in the three measures as 27.67 of MSE, 0.01347 of MAE, and 3.35% of MAPE. The predicted values of the exchange rate are shown in Figure 19.

Figure 19. Forecasted values of the proposed model for the exchange rate time series

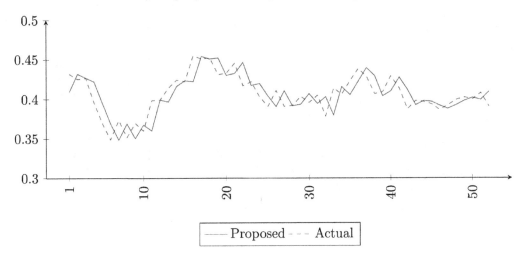

Comparison with the Other Forecasting Models

In this section, the prediction performance of the proposed model is compared with the ARIMA, the ANN, the Khashei and Bijari's model (ARIMA/ANN), and the *k*-means/ARIMA/ANN. In the evaluation of the prediction performance, the forecasting models are applied to the three well-known time series which are Wolf's sunspot, Canadian lynx, and British pound per US dollar exchange rate. The prediction accuracy is measured by mean square error (MSE), mean absolute error (MAE), and mean absolute percentage error (MAPE).

According to the experimental results, although the best fitted model of the ARIMA, the Khashei and Bijari's model, and the proposed model have been already examined but there is no experiment for the ANN. Hence, additional experiments are performed to find the best structure of the ANN for each time series. Based on the results of the additional experiments, the suitable ANN structures for the sunspot, the lynx and the exchange rate time series are ANN(7-4-1) (Figure 20), ANN(7-5-1) (Figure 21), and ANN(7-6-1) (Figure 22) respectively.

The performance of the best fitted models for each data set is presented in Table 1. In case of the sunspot time series, the proposed model can outperform the other models. Similarly, for the lynx time series, the proposed model also gives the best prediction. Likewise, the previous data sets, in the exchange rate forecasting, the proposed model dominates the other models. In summary, the proposed model can give the best prediction performance for all three data sets and all three measures. Additionally, the percentage of performance improvement is presented in Table 2. The lynx time series seems to have the most improvement following by the sunspot and the exchange rate time series.

Furthermore, in order to demonstrate the prediction performance in more detail, absolute percentage errors (APE) at each testing period of the sunspot, the lynx, and the exchange rate time series are displayed on Figures 23-25 respectively. These figures show that in some prediction periods, even the model that has the best performance in the average (e.g. MAPE) can have the worst performance.

Figure 20. ANN (7-4-1) for the sunspot time series

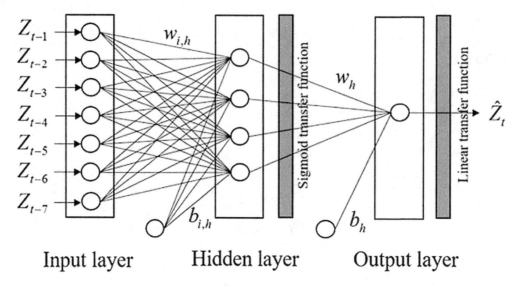

Figure 21. ANN (7-5-1) for the Canadian lynx time series

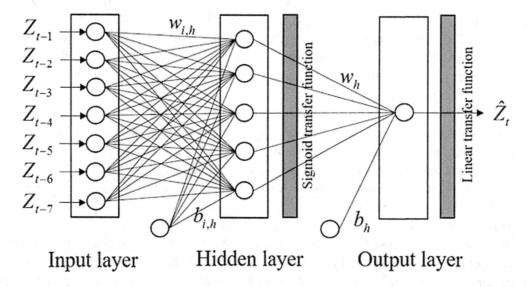

For instance, according to the performance of the lynx time series in Table 1, excluding the proposed model, the best model is the Khashei and Bijari's model. However, at periods 7 and 12 in Figure 24, the Khashei and Bijari's model performs the worst, as well as at some prediction periods of the sunspot and the exchange rate time series in Figures 23 and 25. These empirical results support the benefit of the proposed model in combining different models in term of types and complexity.

Figure 22: ANN (7-6-1) for the exchange rate time series

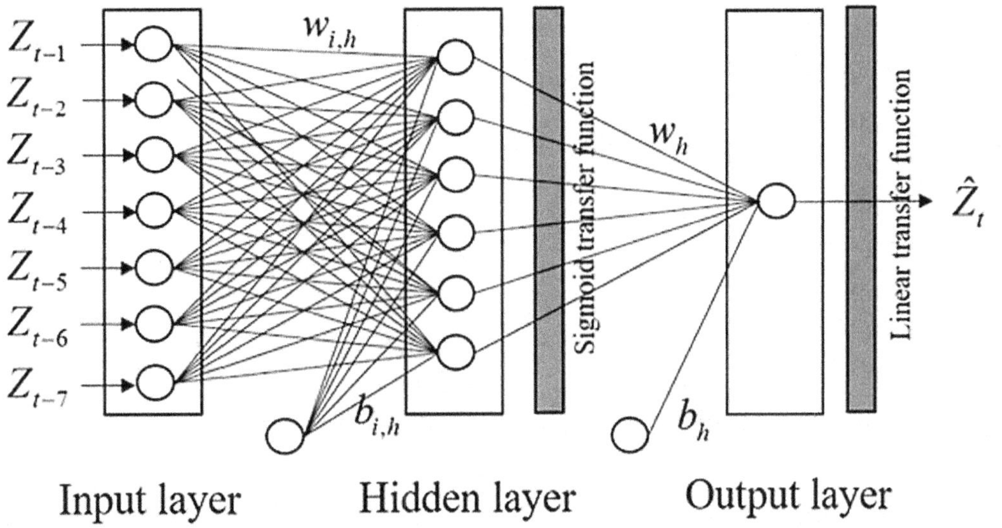

Table 1. Forecasting performance comparison

Model	Sunspot			Canadian lynx			Exchange rate		
	MSE	MAE	MAPE	MSE	MAE	MAPE	MSE	MAE	MAPE
ARIMA	276.35	12.55	30.11%	0.02292	0.11204	3.71%	28.7808	0.01375	3.43%
ANN	350.09	13.54	26.64%	0.01881	0.10418	3.57%	29.5617	0.01372	3.43%
Khashei and Bijari	273.15	12.14	25.31%	0.01598	0.09800	3.24%	28.3242	0.01351	3.36%
k-means/ARIMA/ANN	371.74	13.45	26.43%	0.01899	0.09845	3.38%	28.0819	0.01387	3.45%
Proposed	**244.84**	**11.60**	**24.47%**	**0.01396**	**0.09070**	**3.08%**	**27.6667**	**0.01347**	**3.35%**

Table 2. Percentage improvement of the proposed model

Model	Sunspot			Canadian lynx			Exchange rate		
	MSE	MAE	MAPE	MSE	MAE	MAPE	MSE	MAE	MAPE
ARIMA	11.40%	7.63%	18.74%	39.07%	19.05%	17.02%	3.87%	2.10%	2.28%
ANN	30.06%	14.38%	8.16%	25.78%	12.94%	13.80%	6.41%	1.83%	2.19%
Khashei and Bijari	10.36%	4.47%	3.35%	12.60%	7.45%	5.03%	2.32%	0.34%	0.29%
k-means/ARIMA/ANN	34.14%	13.78%	7.42%	26.50%	7.87%	9.05%	1.48%	2.89%	2.81%

Figure 23. APE of the proposed model for the sunspot time series

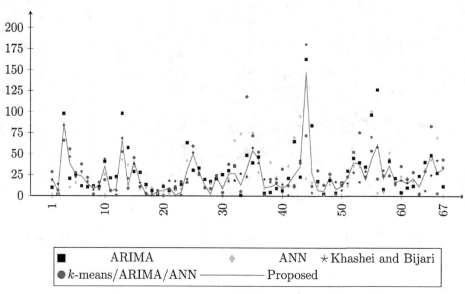

Figure 24. APE of the proposed model for the Canadian lynx time series

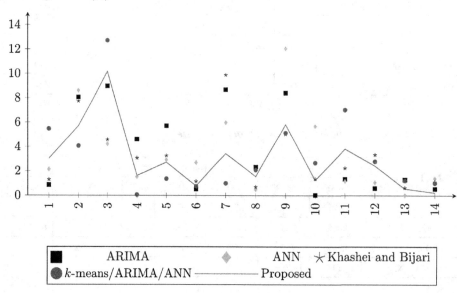

Figure 25. APE of the proposed model for the exchange rate time series

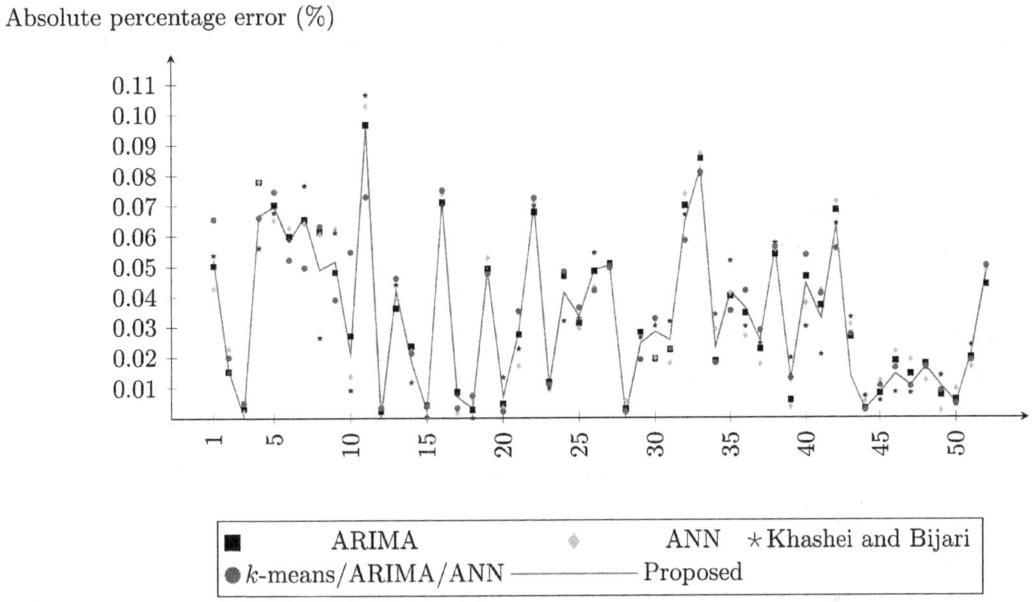

Absolute percentage error (%)

CONCLUSION

Improving time series forecasting is an important yet often difficult task. Although, the numerous time series forecasting models have been developed, but the research for developing new forecasting models to improve the prediction accuracy has never stopped. Recently, hybrid models, combinations of single models which can be same or difference model types, became a popular time series forecasting approach especially hybridizations of linear and nonlinear forecasting models. Usually, these hybrid models promise a better prediction accuracy in average than forecasting by the single forecasting models. However, in some prediction periods, the single models still give the better accuracy. Therefore, there is a potential to improve the forecasting accuracy with combination of single and hybrid models.

The hybrid model of the ARIMA, the Khashei and Bijari's model (ARIMA/ANN model) and the *k*-means/ARIMA/ANN is proposed to obtain unique advantages among the different model types and complexity levels in time series forecasting. The prediction capability of the proposed model is tested with three well-known data sets: The Wolf's sunspot, the Canadian lynx, and the British pound per US dollar exchange rate. From the empirical results, the proposed model gives the best performance in MSE, MAE, and MAPE for all three data sets.

In conclusion, the proposed hybridization between linear, linear-nonlinear, and linear-nonlinear with clustering technique has shown its forecasting capability over traditional single and hybrid models. Therefore, it can be used as an alternative model for time series prediction.

However, the proposed model includes only one model per each model type (i.e. the ARIMA as the linear model, the ANN as the nonlinear model, and the *k*-means as the clustering technique). Actually, there are many other linear models, nonlinear models, and clustering techniques that can be involved in the future study. Furthermore, the weakness of the proposed model is that in the stage III, the forecasted clusters are based on the forecasted values from the ARIMA/ANN that can makes the error causing the wrong predicted cluster especially when the forecasted values are very close to the boundary between the clusters.

REFERENCES

Adhikari, R., & Agrawal, R. (2014). A combination of artificial neural network and random walk models for financial time series forecasting. *Neural Computing & Applications, 24*(6), 1441–1449. doi:10.100700521-013-1386-y

Alon, I., Qi, M., & Sadowski, R. (2001). Forecasting aggregate retail sales: A comparison of artificial neural networks and traditional methods. *Journal of Retailing and Consumer Services, 8*(3), 147–156. doi:10.1016/S0969-6989(00)00011-4

Amin-Naseri, M., & Gharacheh, E. (2007). A hybrid artificial intelligence approach to monthly forecasting of crude oil price time series. In *Proceedings of the 10th International Conference on Engineering Applications of Neural Networks* (pp. 160-167).

Bahrami, S., Hooshmand, R., & Parastegari, M. (2014). Short term electric load forecasting by wavelet transform and grey model improved by PSO (particle swarm optimization) algorithm. *Energy, 72*, 434–444. doi:10.1016/j.energy.2014.05.065

Benmouiza, K., & Cheknane, A. (2013). Forecasting hourly global solar radiation using hybrid k-means and nonlinear autoregressive neural network models. *Energy Conversion and Management, 75*, 561–569. doi:10.1016/j.enconman.2013.07.003

Box, G., Jenkins, G., & Reinsel, G. (2008). *Time Series Analysis: Forecasting and Control.* Wiley. doi:10.1002/9781118619193

Campbell, M., & Walker, A. (1977). A survey of statistical work on the Mackenzie River series of annual Canadian lynx trappings for the years 1821-1934 and a new analysis. *Journal of the Royal Statistical Society. Series A (General), 140*(4), 411–431. doi:10.2307/2345277

Co, H., & Boosarawongse, R. (2007). Forecasting Thailand's rice export: Statistical techniques vs. artificial neural networks. *Computers & Industrial Engineering, 53*(4), 610–627. doi:10.1016/j.cie.2007.06.005

De Gooijer, J., & Hyndman, R. (2006). 25 years of time series forecasting. *International Journal of Forecasting, 22*(3), 443–473. doi:10.1016/j.ijforecast.2006.01.001

Deng, W., Wang, G., & Zhang, X. (2015). A novel hybrid water quality time series prediction method based on cloud model and fuzzy forecasting. *Chemometrics and Intelligent Laboratory Systems, 149*, 39–49. doi:10.1016/j.chemolab.2015.09.017

Ezzine, H., Bouziane, A., & Ouazar, D. (2014). Seasonal comparisons of meteorological and agricultural drought indices in Morocco using open short time-series data. *International Journal of Applied Earth Observation and Geoinformation, 26*, 36–48. doi:10.1016/j.jag.2013.05.005

Feng, X., Li, Q., Zhu, Y., Hou, J., Jin, L., & Wang, J. (2015). Artificial neural networks forecasting of PM 2.5 pollution using air mass trajectory based geographic model and wavelet transformation. *Atmospheric Environment, 107*, 118–128. doi:10.1016/j.atmosenv.2015.02.030

Garrett, K., Dobs, A., Kroschel, J., Natarajan, B., Orlandini, S., Tonnang, H., & Valdivia, C. (2013). The effects of climate variability and the color of weather time series on agricultural diseases and pests, and on decisions for their management. *Agricultural and Forest Meteorology, 170*, 216–227. doi:10.1016/j.agrformet.2012.04.018

Gosasang, V., Chandraprakaikul, W., & Kiattisin, S. (2011). A comparison of traditional and neural networks forecasting techniques for container throughput at Bangkok port. *The Asian Journal of Shipping and Logistics, 27*(3), 463–48. doi:10.1016/S2092-5212(11)80022-2

Hipel, K., & McLeod, A. (1994). *Time series modelling of water resources and environmental systems* (Vol. 45). Elsevi. doi:10.1016/S0167-5648(08)70655-5

Ho, S., Xie, M., & Goh, T. (2002). A comparative study of neural network and Box-Jenkins ARIMA modeling in time series prediction. *Computers & Industrial Engineering, 42*(2), 371–375. doi:10.1016/S0360-8352(02)00036-0

Hornik, K., Stinchcombe, M., & White, H. (1989). Multilayer feedforward networks are universal approximators. *Neural Networks, 2*(5), 359–366. doi:10.1016/0893-6080(89)90020-8

Khashei, M., & Bijari, M. (2011). A novel hybridization of artificial neural networks and ARIMA models for time series forecasting. *Applied Soft Computing, 11*(2), 2664–2675. doi:10.1016/j.asoc.2010.10.015

Kohzadi, N., Boyd, M., Kermanshahi, B., & Kaastra, I. (1996). A comparison of artificial neural network and time series models for forecasting commodity prices. *Neurocomputing, 10*(2), 169–181. doi:10.1016/0925-2312(95)00020-8

Lin, T., & Pourahmadi, M. (1998). Nonparametric and non-linear models and data mining in time series: A case-study on the Canadian lynx data. *Journal of the Royal Statistical Society. Series C, Applied Statistics, 47*(2), 187–201. doi:10.1111/1467-9876.00106

MacQueen, J. (1967). Some methods for classification and analysis of multivariate observations. In *Proceedings of the fifth Berkeley symposium on mathematical statistics and probability* (pp. 281-297).

Meese, R., & Rogoff, K. (1983). Empirical exchange rate models of the seventies: Do they fit out of sample? *Journal of International Economics, 14*(1-2), 3–24. doi:10.1016/0022-1996(83)90017-X

Pannakkong, W., Pham, V., & Huynh, V.-N. (2016). A Hybrid Model of ARIMA, ANNs and k-Means Clustering for Time Series Forecasting. In *Integrated Uncertainty in Knowledge Modelling and Decision Making: 5th International Symposium, IUKM 2016* (pp. 195-206). Da Nang, Vietnam: Springer.

Prybutok, V., Yi, J., & Mitchell, D. (2000). Comparison of neural network models with ARIMA and regression models for prediction of Houston's daily maximum ozone concentrations. *European Journal of Operational Research, 122*(1), 31–40. doi:10.1016/S0377-2217(99)00069-7

Rousseeuw, P. (1987). Silhouettes: A graphical aid to the interpretation and validation of cluster analysis. *Journal of Computational and Applied Mathematics, 20*, 53–65. doi:10.1016/0377-0427(87)90125-7

Ruiz-Aguilar, J., Turias, I., & Jiménez-Come, M. (2015). A novel three-step procedure to forecast the inspection volume. *Transportation Research Part C, Emerging Technologies, 56*, 393–414. doi:10.1016/j.trc.2015.04.024

Sadaei, H., Enayatifar, R., Abdulla, A., & Gani, A. (2014). Short-term load forecasting using a hybrid model with a refined exponentially weighted fuzzy time series and an improved harmony search. *International Journal of Electrical Power & Energy Systems*, *62*, 118–129. doi:10.1016/j.ijepes.2014.04.026

Taskaya-Temizel, T., & Casey, M. C. (2005). A comparative study of autoregressive neural network hybrids. *Neural Networks*, *18*(5), 781–789. doi:10.1016/j.neunet.2005.06.003 PMID:16085389

Wei, L. (2016). A hybrid ANFIS model based on empirical mode decomposition for stock time series forecasting. *Applied Soft Computing*, *42*, 368–376. doi:10.1016/j.asoc.2016.01.027

Winkler, R., & Makridakis, S. (1983). The combination of forecasts. *Journal of the Royal Statistical Society. Series A (General)*, *146*(2), 150–157. doi:10.2307/2982011

Wong, C., & Li, W. (2000). On a mixture autoregressive model. *Journal of the Royal Statistical Society. Series B, Statistical Methodology*, *62*(1), 95–115. doi:10.1111/1467-9868.00222

Xiao, Y., Xiao, J., & Wang, S. (2012). A hybrid forecasting model for non-stationary time series: An application to container throughput prediction. *International Journal of Knowledge and Systems Science*, *3*(2), 67–82. doi:10.4018/jkss.2012040105

Zhang, G., Patuwo, B., & Hu, M. (1998). Forecasting with artificial neural networks: The state of the art. *International Journal of Forecasting*, *14*(1), 35–62. doi:10.1016/S0169-2070(97)00044-7

Zhang, G. P. (2003). Time series forecasting using a hybrid ARIMA and neural network model. *Neurocomputing*, *50*, 159–175. doi:10.1016/S0925-2312(01)00702-0

Zou, H., Xia, G., Yang, F., & Wang, H. (2007). An investigation and comparison of artificial neural network and time series models for Chinese food grain price forecasting. *Neurocomputing*, *70*(16), 2913–2923. doi:10.1016/j.neucom.2007.01.009

This research was previously published in the International Journal of Knowledge and Systems Science (IJKSS), 8(4); pages 30-53, copyright year 2017 by IGI Publishing (an imprint of IGI Global).

Chapter 77
Convolutional Neural Network

Mário Pereira Véstias

(iD) https://orcid.org/0000-0001-8556-4507

INESC-ID, Instituto Superior de Engenharia de Lisboa, Instituto Politécnico de Lisboa, Portugal

ABSTRACT

Machine learning is the study of algorithms and models for computing systems to do tasks based on pattern identification and inference. When it is difficult or infeasible to develop an algorithm to do a particular task, machine learning algorithms can provide an output based on previous training data. A well-known machine learning model is deep learning. The most recent deep learning models are based on artificial neural networks (ANN). There exist several types of artificial neural networks including the feedforward neural network, the Kohonen self-organizing neural network, the recurrent neural network, the convolutional neural network, the modular neural network, among others. This article focuses on convolutional neural networks with a description of the model, the training and inference processes and its applicability. It will also give an overview of the most used CNN models and what to expect from the next generation of CNN models.

INTRODUCTION

In a broad sense, a convolutional neural network is one of many methods to achieve artificial intelligence.

Artificial intelligence (AI) is a field of computer science dedicated to the research of methods and algorithms that permit to perceive information from the environment, learn from it and taking actions and decisions based on the learning outcomes without any explicit orientation from external agents. AI consists of many sub-fields, including evolutionary computation (e.g., genetic algorithms), vision (e.g. object recognition), expert systems (e.g. decision support systems), speech processing (e.g. speech recognition), natural language processing (e.g., machine translation), and machine learning (e.g. decision trees).

Machine learning (ML) is a type of algorithms and models for computing systems to do tasks based on pattern identification and inference (Mitchell, T., 2017). When it is difficult or infeasible to develop an algorithm to do a particular task, machine learning algorithms can provide an output based on previous data. Machine learning algorithms identify features from data and build models from these features so that new decisions can be produced based on these models and rules. Examples of machine learning

DOI: 10.4018/978-1-6684-2408-7.ch077

models include deep learning, support vector machines (SVM), genetic algorithms, clustering, dimensionality reduction, artificial neural network, decision tree and others.

In this chapter we are particularly interested in deep learning (DL) (Aggarwal, C., 2018). Deep learning teach computers to learn by example. Deep learning first appeared in 1980, but only recently has been applied in practice because it requires large amounts of labeled data and high-performance computing. Its application is vast including areas like computer vision, speech recognition, language processing, among others.

The most recent deep learning models are based on artificial neural networks (ANN) with a large number of layers. Deep learning networks are first trained using a large set of labeled data in order to learn features from the training data without being explicitly programmed to learn them.

There are several types of artificial neural networks including the feedforward neural network, the Kohonen self organizing neural network, the recurrent neural network, the convolutional neural network, the modular neural network, among others. The convolutional neural network (CNN) is one of the most used deep learning architecture for artificial intelligence (see figure 1).

Figure 1. Convolutional Neural Networks in the context of artificial intelligence

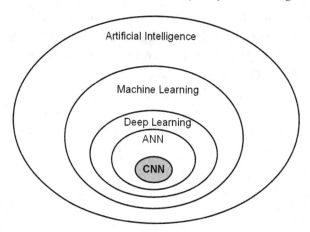

Convolutional neural networks are one of the most used deep learning models in the industry and business. Therefore, for those interested in understanding how deep learning is applied in this markets it is fundamental to understand the architecture of CNNs and understand the evolution and trends of CNNs during the last decade.

This article focus on convolutional neural networks with a description of the model, the training and inference processes and its applicability. It will also give an overview of the most used CNN models and what to expect from the next generation of CNN models.

BACKGROUND

Artificial neural network (ANN) is a machine learning model that mimics the structure of the human brain consisting of interconnected neurons. Theoretically, an ANN is a universal model capable to learn any function (Hornik at el., 1989). A class of ANN is the convolutional neural network introduced in (LeCun, Y. et al., 1989).

Convolutional neural networks process images. The network applies successive convolutions to the input image using several trained filters to identify features of the image. Features identified in a convolution are process by the next convolutions to identify more complex features. The process permits to learn complex features and at the same time is invariant to translation of the features.

Artificial Neural Network

An artificial neural network consists of input, output and hidden layers, which are all layers between the input and the output layers (see figure 2).

Figure 2. Artificial Neural Network

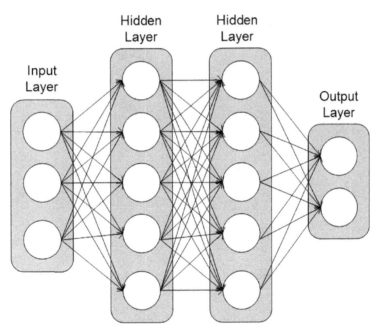

Each layer contains nodes or neurons that map all its inputs into an output to be used by the nodes of the next layer. Nodes of a layer are connected to the nodes of the next layer, except the output layer whose outputs are the result of the neural network. The first layer – input layer – generates the inputs of the first hidden layer and the output layer receives the inputs from the last hidden layer and produces the classification result. A neural network with more than three hidden layers is designated deep neural network (Bengio, Y., 2009).

A layer can have any number of neurons. The input layer has many neurons as the number of input data, while the number of neurons in the output layer depends on the target application. For example, in a neural network used to classify images, the number of output neurons is the number of classification classes of the network.

Neuron Function

Let's consider a neuron with n inputs from n neurons of the previous layer, $\{x_1, x_2, x_3, ..., x_n\}$. Each connection between neurons has a weight, $\{w_1, w_2, w_3, ..., w_n\}$ (see figure 3).

Figure 3. Neuron function

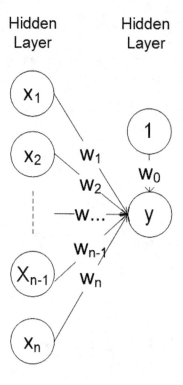

The output of a neuron, y, is computed as follows:

$$y = f\left(w_0 + \sum_{k=1}^{n} w_k x_k\right)$$

Weight W_0 is in fact an external input called bias introduced in the graph with a unitary neuron. Function $f(.)$ is called an activation function and is used to decide the output of the neuron. Activation functions can be linear or non-linear and are chosen according the domain of application (Nwankpa, C. et al, 2018).

A simple activation function is the Heaviside function that is 0 for negative values and 1 for the others. However, piecewise-linear functions are not differentiable and training requires differentiable functions. A well-known used activation function is the sigmoid given by $\frac{1}{1+e^{-z}}$. It is usually used to predict a probability since it varies between 0 and 1. For multiclass classification, the softmax function is used. This function takes as input a vector of k values and normalizes it into a probability distribution of k probabilities.

Another used activation function is the hyperbolic tangent that varies between -1 and 1, increasing the output range.

The most used activation function is now ReLU (Rectified Linear Unit). The function is 0 when the input is negative and is equal to the input when the input is positive. The function is not differentiable at 0, so it is assumed that the derivate at zero is zero because it gives better results than assuming one.

Training Neural Networks

Training is the process of determining all weights of the network so the outputs of the network give the best mapping results. The training can be supervised or unsupervised. In supervised training, the network knows the output for each input. Unsupervised training is when the network has a training set without the desired outputs. In this case, the network has to find some features of the input data to classify them.

In the supervised training all weights, *Wset*, are adjusted to minimize an objective function that quantifies the error, E, between the M outputs, y_k, and the desired outputs, t_k, for all N data inputs, x_n. Usually, the error is calculated as the sum of squared error:

$$E\left(Wset\right) = \sum_{n=1}^{N}\sum_{m=1}^{M}\left(y_k\left(x_n,Wset\right)-t_k\right)^2$$

Training a neural network is an iterative process of two main steps: forward propagation and back-propagation. The first step is to enter an input data and propagate it through the whole network to find the prediction value with a set of weights. Next, a loss function (sum of squared error) is applied to determine the error between the observed output and the expected output. In the ideal case, the loss should be zero, meaning that there is no difference between the observed and the expected values. The loss value is then propagated backwards to all neurons that are in a path from the inputs to the output. Each neuron receives a fraction of the loss according to its contribution to the output. So, neurons with a higher contribution to a particular output will receive a higher fraction of the loss function associated with that output. After all neurons receive the loss fraction, weights are adjusted to reduce the loss. Weights are changed using a technique designated *gradient descent*. According to this technique, weights are changed in small increments based on the derivative of the loss function, that is:

$$\Delta W[i] = -\gamma\left(\frac{\partial E_n}{\partial w[i]}\right)$$

where γ is the learning rate.

Weight initialization is important in the final quality of the trained network. Some works indicate that better results are obtained when the weights are randomly chosen between specific normalized ranges (Glorot, X. & Bengio, Y., 2010).

In the unsupervised training, given a training set without expected outputs, the method has to train the network based on characteristics of the input data. One known method for unsupervised training is the auto-encoders. This technique is similar to a compression algorithm that uses a smaller subset of features to represent the input data (Bengio, Y., 2009).

Convolutional Neural Network

A traditional neural network can be applied to images. However, even with images of medium size, the number of input neurons is high and consequently there would be a high number of weights from the input neurons to the first hidden layer. For example, considering an image of size 224×224, there are over 50000 input nodes. With the same nodes in the second layer, we would need 50000×50000 weights just for the first layer. This number of weights is very difficult to train with good results and needs a huge amount a memory and computational effort. A better approach is to take into consideration the type of input data, an image in this case (LeCun, Y., 1989). Convolutional neural networks consider the spatial information between pixels, that is, the output of a neuron of the input layer is the result of the convolution between a small subset of the image and a kernel of weights.

A regular convolutional neural network has different types of layers: convolutional, pooling and fully connected. CNN may have other particular layers different from these and are known as irregular CNN. In the following, we explain in more detailed the three types of regular layers.

The **convolutional layer** receives a set of input feature maps (IFM) and generates a set of output feature maps (OFM). A feature map is a 2D matrix of neurons and several feature maps form a 3D volume of feature maps (see figure 4).

Figure 4. Input and output feature maps of a convolutional layer

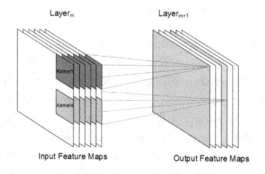

A 3D block of weights – kernel or filter – is convolved across the width and the weight of the input feature maps and computes the dot product between the kernel and the feature maps generating an output feature map. Each different kernel produces one output feature map. Therefore, the number of output feature maps is the same as the number of filters of the layer. Each kernel is trained to detect a particular feature of the input data. To explore spatial local correlation between adjacent neurons the convolution window (width ×weight) of the kernel is usually small (e.g., 3×3, 5×5, etc.), while the depth of the kernel is the same as the number of input feature maps.

Usually, kernels slide across the feature maps shifting one neuron each time (stride of 1). This generates high overlapping that increases with the window size and output feature maps with the same size. Instead, a larger stride can be used resulting in less overlapping and a smaller output volume. Another parameter of the convolution process is the padding of the IFMs. If we run a kernel with window size 3×3 over an input feature map of size k×k, the output feature map will have a size (k-2)×(k-2). In many cases, it is desirable to preserve the size of the maps. One solution consists to pad the border of the IFMs with zeros. In this case, padding the border with one level of zeros would produce output feature maps with the same size of the input feature maps.

The **pooling layer** subsamples the IFMs to achieve translation invariance and reduce over-fitting. Basically, the relative location of a feature is more important than its absolute location.

Given an input image and the pooling size (typically two or three), pooling partitions the image in 2D arrays of the size of the polling window. Then, it applies a pooling function to all members of the pooling window (see figure 5).

Figure 5. Input and output feature maps of a convolutional layer

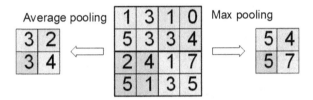

Examples of pooling functions are average pooling (average between the output neurons of the window) and max pooling (maximum value between the output neurons of the window). Considering, for example, a pooling window with entries {2, 4, 6, 8}, the max pool would return 8, while average pooling returns 5. Max pooling gets faster convergence during training (Scherer, D. et al, 2010). Also, it reduces the number of weights and consequently the required memory to store them and the amount of computation. Pooling is not applied to all convolutional layers.

The size of the pooling window determines the reduction of the feature maps. The typical size of 2×2 applied with a stride of two downsamples the input maps in both dimensions reducing the original map 75%. Note that pooling reduces the size of the map but the number of feature maps remains the same.

The last layers of a convolutional network are **fully connected**. A fully connected layer follows the structure of the traditional neural network where all neurons of the layer are connected to all neurons of the previous layer. Algorithmically, it is a vector-matrix multiplication followed by vector addition of the bias values.

To better understand the concepts introduced, let's consider the first convolutional neural network to achieve high accuracy for hand digit classification LeNet (LeCun, Y. *et al.,* 1995). LeNet has two sets of convolutional and average pooling layers, followed by a flattening convolutional layer, two fully connected layers and a softmax classifier. The activation function is the hyperbolic tangent (see Figure 6).

The input of LeNet is a grayscale image of size 32×32. The first convolutional layer uses six filters with a window size of 5×5 and a stride of one producing six output feature maps of size 28×28, since it does not consider padding. Than it is applied an average pooling layer with a filter of size 2×2 and a stride of two, reducing the feature maps to 14×14. A second convolutional layer is applied with sixteen filters of size 5×5 and stride of one generating sixteen output feature maps of size 10×10 which are then pooled to size 5×5. The next layer is a convolutional layer with 120 feature maps of size 1×1. Then comes one fully connected layer with 84 units followed another fully connected layer with ten outputs, one for each digit and the softmax classifier.

Figure 6. Architecture of LeNet

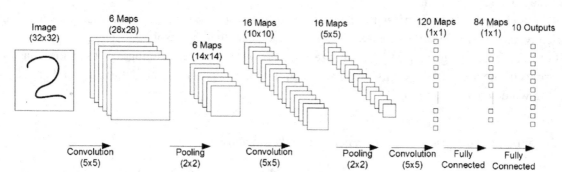

Recent Convolutional Neural Networks

CNNs have many parameters to be defined, like the number of layers, the number of neurons, the size of filters, the size of pooling, the activation function, the learning rate, more and new type of layers, among others. The exploration of design space defined by all these parameters lead to many proposals of CNN. In the following, some of the most known CNN for its results and novelty will be described.

LeNet

LeNet (LeCun, Y. *et al.,* 1995) was able to demonstrate some robustness features of CNN to rotation, distortion, scale, etc. In total, the network has 60K parameters or weights and an accuracy above 99% (see architecture in Figure 5, in the previous subsection).

AlexNet

The next big step of CNN application was achieved with AlexNet (Krizhevsky, A., 2012) considered the first CNN with great results for image classification. AlexNet is a deeper network than LeNet and 60 M parameters, 1000× more parameters than LeNet. AlexNet has five convolutional layers, three pooling layers after convolutional layers two, three and five, and three fully connected layers. Instead of the hyperbolic tangent, the activation function of AlexNet was ReLU to improve the convergence rate of learning and the problem of vanishing gradient (Hochreiter, S., 1998). The input images have size 227×227×3 and the network uses larger filter sizes in in the first (11×11) and second layers (5×5).

AlexNet won the 2012 ILSVRC (ImageNet Large-Scale Visual Recognition Challenge) with a top-5 error rate of 17.0% (top-5 is the error rate at which given an image the network does not include the correct label within its top five predictions) and a top-1 error rate of 37.5% with ImageNet (Imagenet is a large database of images for use in object recognition research. It has over 15 million annotated images with more than 22000 categories).

ZefNet

Until 2013, the design of a CNN was based on trial and error, changing the parameters without a clear understand of what was happening in the CNN layers. In 2013 a multiplayer deconvolutional neural network was proposed in (Zeiler, M. D. & Fergus, R., 2013) named ZefNet. Instead of just proposing a new CNN, the authors also proposed a technique to observe the network activity of AlexNet (can be applied to other networks) named Deconvolutional Network, which monitors the output of neurons to establish correlations between features and input neurons. The idea has already been explored with Deep Belief Networks (Erhan, D., 2009) and Autoencoders (Le, Q. V., 2013).

When applied to AlexNet the method have shown that only a few neurons were active in the first two convolutional layers. Based on these observations, the authors have fine tuned AlexNet achieving a top-5 error rate of 11.2%. A few more modifications in both the model and the training process were considered. For the training process, they considered only 1.3 million images, but even so it took twelve days to train the network. They substituted the filter of the first convolutional layer (size 11×11) by a filter of size 7×7 to retain more information from the image.

VGG

In 2014 the VGG neural network brought some new directions to CNN development. They considered two main foundations for the development of VGG, simplicity and uniformity of layers and depth of the network. Six different architectures were tested and the one with best accuracy was VGG-16 with sixteen layers using only 3×3 filters with stride and pad of 1, and 2×2 pooling with stride 2. The authors concluded that two convolutional layers with 3×3 filters has the same results of a single layer with 5×5 filters. The same for three 3×3 filters instead of a single 7×7 filter. This reduces the number of parameters and applies the activation function more times. Another option in the design of VGG was to increase the number of filters after each pooling step as we move to the next layers. So, the size of the feature maps decrease but the depth increases as we move along the network.

Like the previous architectures it was trained with batch gradient descent and the training took from two to three weeks with four GPUs. VGG did not win the ImageNet contest that year but improved previous year top-5 error rate to 7.3%. The main drawback of VGG is that it has 138 million parameters, the main reason for its long training times.

GoogleNet

The winner of the ILSVRC in 2014 was GoogleNet (Szegedy, C. *et al.*, 2014), also known as Inception-V1. Previous CNNs followed a regular approach of stacking convolutional, pooling and fully connected layers with variations in the number of layers, and number and size of filters. GoogleNet broke this regular structure. The layers of a regular CNN are serialized with one after the other. In GoogleNet groups of convolutions run in parallel defining a module named Inception (see figure 7).

In the inception module, there are four main operations in parallel, namely three convolutions with different sizes (1×1, 3×3, 5×5) and one 3×3 max pooling. To reduce the number of operations, the 3×3 and 5×5 convolutions are preceded by 1×1 convolutions to reduce the volume of data.

Figure 7. Inception module of GoogleNet

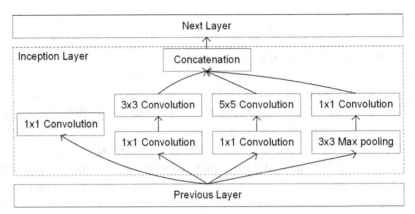

The inception module is like a small network inside a larger network that is able to extract information at different scales with different window sizes. The pooling operation reduces the size of output data.

The complete GoogleNet network has nine inception modules and does not use fully connected layers. Instead, an average pool is used after the last inception that reduces the output 7×7×1024 volume of the last inception module to a 1×1×1024 volume.

GoogleNet uses 6.8 million parameters to achieve a top-5 error rate of 6.7% for ImageNet.

Other versions of the inception module have followed. Inception-v2 and inception-v3 were presented in the same paper (Szegedy, C., 2016). In this work, the convolution with size 5×5 was replaced by two 3×3 convolutions. They factorize convolutions of size n×n to a combination of two filters 1×n and n×1 applied in parallel. Inception-v4 introduced some more modifications and optimizations. Modules were made more uniform and the complexity was reduced. In spite of uniformization, they created three different inception modules.

ResNet

ResNet (He, K., et al., 2015) has increased the number of layers to 152 and won the ILSVRC competition in 2015 with a top-5 error rate of 3.6% (human error for image classification is from 5 to 10%). ResNet not only pushed the depth of the network but have also introduced a new block named *Residual Block* (see figure 8).

In the residual block the result a series of two convolutional layers is added to the input of the residual block. So, instead of just processing the original input with a series of convolutional layers, the result of the convolutions is added to the original input, like a delta factor. According to the paper, the new structure permits a better optimization of the network.

Similar to what happened in VGG, ResNet increases the layers and decreases the size of maps very soon. After the first two layers maps are reduce to one quarter of the original image size.

Figure 8. Residual Block of ResNet

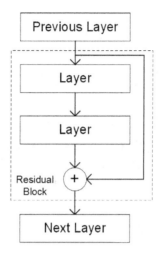

ResNeXt

ResNeXt (Xie, S., et al., 2017) is the follower network of ResNet with slightly better results than the original ResNet with a top-5 error of 3.03%. The model introduces the concept of cardinality that splits the original residual block without increasing the complexity (see figure 9).

Figure 9. Residual block with cardinality

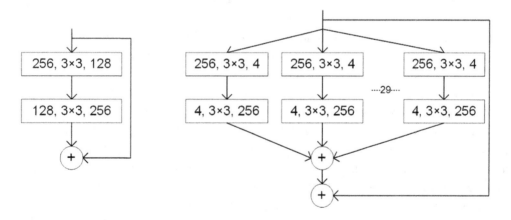

On the left, we have an example of a residual block with two convolutions and on the right we have a cardinality block that splits the original residual block in 32 blocks (the cardinality of the block). The complexity is the same since the set of filters is also split across each member of the cardinality block.

DenseNet

DenseNet (Huang, G., 2018) is a CNN architecture also based on ResNet with some modifications in the residual block. The work proposes the *Dense Block* to replace the residual block. The dense block has several layers, but instead of receiving data only from the previous layer it receives data from all preceding layers and sends the output to all subsequent layers within the block. Instead of addition, the block uses concatenation to group data from previous blocks.

The structure has some advantages over ResNet. During training the backward error propagation reaches earlier layers with a straight path. The number of parameters is DenseNet is smaller than in ResNet (about half for the same number of layers). Receiving information from several previous layers increases the diversity of features processed by a single layer. The accuracy of DenseNet is close to the one achieved with ResNet but with less parameters.

SENet

SENet (Hu, J., Shen, L., Sun, G., 2018) introduced a new network block – squeeze-and-excitation. The idea of the block is to emphasize important features and cancel less useful ones. The block runs the convolutions of the residual block of ResNet. Each feature map is then squeezed to a single value using a global average pooling. Next, a fully connected layer followed by ReLU is applied to introduce non-linearity. A second fully connected layer is applied followed by a sigmoid activation function. The result is finally added to the original input, like in the residual block.

With these modifications, SENet won the ILSVRC competition in 2017 with a top-5 error rate of 2.25%.

Application Examples of Convolutional Neural Networks

The set of target applications of convolutional neural networks is growing. Since these networks are dedicated to image analysis, any application associated with image and video is a potential candidate for this type of deep neural networks. Face recognition (Kalinowski, I., & Spitsyn, V., 2015) and scene labelling (Pinheiro, P. & Collobert, R., 2014) already applies successfully a CNN. Face recognition with a CNN identifies faces in an image and match each face to a name from a database. The advantage of the CNN model compared to other machine algorithms is its high accuracy independent of external factors, such as light or view angle. Face recognition is applied in social networks, like Facebook, entertainment applications that change the aspect of the face, surveillance cameras, among others.

Other type of image recognition is the process of identifying written characters of symbols from an image. Image tagging is also using CNNs. eCommerce platforms are using these applications to match the images accessed by users to their commercial needs.

Medical image analysis is another hot area that is starting using CNNs to analyze medical images (Razzak M.I., 2018). Images associated with many types of exams are classified with a CNN with an accuracy higher than that obtained by the human. With the vast amount of medical information available, there is enough data for CNNs to analyze medical images with high success. Medicine applications are not just image analysis. Health risk assessment is another application area, where CNNs are used to analyze the past data of a patient and determine the probability of occurrence of certain diseases, propose the best way to treat it or even explore the risks for people close to the patient.

Autonomous driving is another hot topic for convolutional neural networks (Kocic, J., 2019). The system receives images from cameras attached to the vehicle and determines the driving direction of the vehicle. The task is complex since the vehicle has to take into consideration many other aspects, like traffic sign recognition, detection of persons in the street, etc.

Convolutional neural networks are applied in many other machine learning applications. The list is already vast, including code generation (Pengcheng, Y. & Neubig, G., 2017), analysis of sentiments (Lei, T., Barziley, R. & Jaakkola, T., 2016), image segmentation (He, K., et al., 2017), text recognition (Jaderberg, M., et al., 2016) and object recognition (Redmon, J., & Farhadi, A., 2017), just to name a few.

FUTURE RESEARCH DIRECTIONS

Many CNN models are proposed every year and the accuracies are increasing with each network. Initial CNN were regular structures based on convolutional, pooling and fully connected layers. The accuracy of CNN was then improved with the introduction of new layers. These irregular structures have improved the training and inference of CNN at the cost of some specificity of particular layers.

In spite of all the evolution, the study and development of CNNs are still in its infancy and new challenges are yet to be resolved. Some of these challenges are associated with training. CNN are very good on classifying good images but are still little robust to image distortions and noise. Another problem is that it is difficult to understand and verify what is going inside the layers and the influence of each filter or layer over the network results. Another major challenge is that CNNs require large amounts of data to learn. So, those applications with few training images are difficult to be modeled with a CNN. Training a CNN is a hard processing task that requires high-performance computing platforms. Inference is less demanding but still requires high computing power. How to do inference and training in edge devices with low computing resources is an actual area of intense research.

CNN still continue to evolve and new achievements are expected in the near future. A recent training issue is how to incrementally train an already trained network. A running CNN can keep learning with new data to improve its classification capability. The question is how to incrementally change the network without retraining the network for all input data set.

The time needed to train a network is a major concern since it limits the continuous increase of network complexity. Also, the inference in edge devices with low resources also limits the network complexity. Two paths have been followed to overcome this embedded limitations. One way is to improve hardware computing power and apply network optimizations to reduce complexity. Another way is to design networks for embedded devices (Sandler, M.B., 2018). So, CNN development cannot be independent of the target hardware.

Many parameters have to be determined in a large CNN. Many of these, like size and number of filters, are explored manually. Some automatic algorithms can be used to explore the design space but it takes a long time. So, it is important to clearly understand the relation between each type of parameters and the network accuracy so that the design process can be faster.

CONCLUSION

The article describes the fundamentals of convolutional neural networks, the most known types of layers and CNNs proposed in the literature. Since the first successful CNN for character recognition, followed by AlexNet for image classification that many new networks have been proposed with better accuracies. Networks with more layers, new types of layers, new optimization techniques to help the accuracy and improve training have helped to evolution of CNN.

Researchers have been concerned about understanding the internals and mechanisms of CNN so that new improvements have some reasoning and are not just based on an empirical process of trial-and-error. Another concern is about the complexity of the networks and the computing requirements. In a near future it is expected an increase of CNNs running in edge devices. This requires an extra care over the development of CNN since they have to run in a constrained computing platform.

Therefore, in spite of 20 years of research and development, CNNs are still an actual topic of intense research.

REFERENCES

Aggarwal, C. (2018). *Neural Networks and Deep Learning: A Textbook* (1st ed.). Springer. doi:10.1007/978-3-319-94463-0

Bengio, Y. (2009). Learning deep architectures for AI. *Foundations and Trends in Machine Learning, 2*(1), 1–127. doi:10.1561/2200000006

Erhan, D., Bengio, Y., Courville, A., & Vincent, P. (2009). Visualizing higher-layer features of a deep network. *Univ. Montr., 1341*, 1.

Glorot, X., & Bengio, Y. (2010). Understanding the difficulty of training deep feedforward neural networks. *Artificial Intelligence and Statistics, International Conference on*, 249–256.

He, K., Gkioxari, G., Dollár, P., & Girshick, R. (2017). Mask R-CNN. *International Conference on Computer Vision (ICCV)*.

He, K., Zhang, X., Ren, S., & Sun, J. (2015). Deep Residual Learning for Image Recognition. *Multimedia Tools and Applications, 77*, 10437–10453.

Hochreiter, S. (1998). The vanishing gradient problem during learning recurrent neural nets and problem solutions. *International Journal of Uncertainty, Fuzziness and Knowledge-based Systems, 6*(02), 107–116. doi:10.1142/S0218488598000094

Hornik, K., Stinchcombe, M., & White, H. (1989). Multilayer feedforward networks are universal approximators. *Neural Networks, 2*(5), 359–366. doi:10.1016/0893-6080(89)90020-8

Hu, J., Shen, L., & Sun, G. (2018). Squeeze-and-Excitation Networks. *IEEE Conference on Computer Vision and Pattern Recognition (CVPR)*, 7132-7141.

Huang, G., Liu, Z., Maaten, L., & Weinberger, K. (2018). Densely Connected Convolutional Networks. *IEEE Conference on Computer Vision and Pattern Recognition (CVPR)*.

Jaderberg, M., Simonyan, K., Vedaldi, A., & Zisserman, A. (2016, January). Reading Text in the Wild with Convolutional Neural Networks. *International Journal of Computer Vision, 116*(1), 1–20. doi:10.100711263-015-0823-z

Kalinowski, I., & Spitsyn, V. (2015). *Compact Convolutional Neural Network Cascade for Face Detection.* CoRR, abs/1508.01292

Kocic, J., Jovicic, N., & Drndarevic, V. (2019). An End-to-End Deep Neural Network for Autonomous Driving Designed for Embedded Automotive Platforms. *Journal of Sensors, 19*, 9. PMID:31058820

Krizhevsky, A., Sutskever, I., & Hinton, G. E. (2012). ImageNet Classification with Deep Convolutional Neural Networks. *Advances in Neural Information Processing Systems*, 1–9.

Lawrence, S., Giles, C., Lee, T., Ah, C., & Back, A. (1997). Face Recognition: A Convolutional Neural Network Approach. *Neural Networks, IEEE Transactions on, 8*(1), 98–113.

Le, Q. V. (2013). Building high-level features using large scale unsupervised learning. *Acoustics, Speech and Signal Processing (ICASSP), 2013 IEEE International Conference on*, 8595–8598. 10.1109/ICASSP.2013.6639343

LeCun, Y. (1989). Generalization and network design strategies. Connectionism in Perspective.

LeCun, Y. (1995). Learning algorithms for classification: A comparison on handwritten digit recognition. *Neural networks Stat. Mech. Perspect., 261*, 276.

LeCun, Y., Boser, B., Denker, J. S., Henderson, D., Howard, R. E., Hubbard, W., & Jackel, L. D. (1989). Backpropagation applied to handwritten zip code recognition. *Neural Computation, 1*(4), 541–551. doi:10.1162/neco.1989.1.4.541

Lei, T., Barziley, R., & Jaakkola, T. (2016). Rationalizing Neural Predictions. *Proceedings of the 2016 Conference on Empirical Methods in Natural Language Processing*, 107-117. 10.18653/v1/D16-1011

Matsugu, M., Mori, K., Mitari, Y., & Kaneda, Y. (2003). Subject independent facial expression recognition with robust face detection using a convolutional neural network. *Neural Networks, 16*(5–6), 555–559. doi:10.1016/S0893-6080(03)00115-1 PMID:12850007

Mitchell, T. (2017). *Machine Learning* (1st ed.). McGraw Hill Education.

Nwankpa, C., Ijomah, W., Gachagan, A. & Marshall, S. (2018). *Activation Functions: Comparison of trends in Practice and Research for Deep Learning.* Corr, abs/1811.03378

Pengcheng, Y., & Neubig, G. (2017). A Syntactic Neural Model for General-Purpose Code Generation. *Proceedings of the 55th Annual Meeting of the Association for Computational Linguistics, 1*, 440-450.

Pinheiro, P., & Collobert, R. (2014). Recurrent convolutional neural networks for scene labeling. *Proceedings of the 31st International Conference on International Conference on Machine Learning, 32*.

Razzak, M. I., Naz, S., & Zaib, A. (2018). Deep Learning for Medical Image Processing: Overview, Challenges and the Future. In N. Dey, A. Ashour, & S. Borra (Eds.), *Classification in BioApps. Lecture Notes in Computational Vision and Biomechanics* (Vol. 26). Springer. doi:10.1007/978-3-319-65981-7_12

Redmon, J., & Farhadi, A. (2017). YOLO9000: Better, Faster, Stronger. *2017 IEEE Conference on Computer Vision and Pattern Recognition (CVPR)*, 6517-6525. 10.1109/CVPR.2017.690

Sandler, M. B., Howard, A. G., Zhu, M., Zhmoginov, A., & Chen, L. (2018). MobileNetV2: Inverted Residuals and Linear Bottlenecks. *2018 IEEE/CVF Conference on Computer Vision and Pattern Recognition*, 4510-4520. 10.1109/CVPR.2018.00474

Scherer, D., Müller, A., & Behnke, S. (2010). Evaluation of pooling operations in convolutional architectures for object recognition. *Artificial Neural Networks, International Conference on*, 92–101. 10.1007/978-3-642-15825-4_10

Szegedy, C. (2014). *Going Deeper with Convolutions.* arXiv:1409.4842

Szegedy, C., Vanhoucke, V., Ioffe, S., Shlens, J., & Wojna, Z. (2016). Rethinking the Inception Architecture for Computer Vision. *2016 IEEE Conference on Computer Vision and Pattern Recognition (CVPR)*, 2818-2826. 10.1109/CVPR.2016.308

Xie, S., Girshick, R., Dollár, P., Tu, Z., & He, K. (2017). Aggregated Residual Transformations for Deep Neural Networks. *IEEE Conference on Computer Vision and Pattern Recognition (CVPR)*. 10.1109/CVPR.2017.634

Zeiler, M. D. & Fergus, R. (2013). *Visualizing and Understanding Convolutional Networks.* arXiv Prepr. arXiv1311.2901v3

ADDITIONAL READING

Bishop, C. (2006). *Pattern Recognition and Machine Learning.* Springer Verlag.

Erhan, D., Bengio, Y., Courville, A., Manzagol, P.-A., Vincent, P., & Bengio, S. (2010). Why does unsupervised pre-training help deep learning? *Journal of Machine Learning Research*, *11*, 625–660.

Hinton, G. E., Osindero, S., & Teh, Y.-W. (2006). A fast learning algorithm for deep belief nets. *Neural Computation*, *18*(7), 1527–1554. doi:10.1162/neco.2006.18.7.1527 PMID:16764513

KEY TERMS AND DEFINITIONS

Activation Function: The activation function defines the output of a neuron given a set of inputs from the previous layer or data input.

Artificial Neural Network (ANN): It is a computing model based on the structure of the human brain with many interconnected processing nodes that model input-output relationships. The model is organized in layers of nodes that interconnect to each other.

Convolutional Layer: A network layer that applies a series of convolutions to a block of input feature maps.

Convolutional Neural Network (CNN): A class of deep neural networks applied to image processing where some of the layers apply convolutions to input data.

Deep Learning (DL): A class of machine learning algorithms for automation of predictive analytics.

Deep Neural Network (DNN): An artificial neural network with multiple hidden layers.

Feature Map: A feature map is a 2D matrix of neurons. A convolutional layer receives a block of input feature maps and generates a block of output feature maps.

Fully Connected Layer: A network layer where all neurons of the layer are connected to all neurons of the previous layer.

Network Layer: A set of neurons that define the network of a CNN. Neurons in a network layer are connected to the previous and to the next layer.

Pooling Layer: A network layer that determines the average pooling or max pooling of a window of neurons. The pooling layer subsamples the input feature maps to achieve translation invariance and reduce over-fitting.

Softmax Function: A function that takes as input a vector of k values and normalizes it into a probability distribution of k probabilities.

Supervised Training: A training process of neural networks where the outcome for each input is known.

Unsupervised Training: A training process of neural networks where the training set does not have the associated outputs.

This research was previously published in the Encyclopedia of Information Science and Technology, Fifth Edition; pages 12-26, copyright year 2021 by Engineering Science Reference (an imprint of IGI Global).

Index

F

P

T

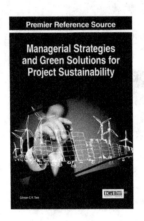

IGI Global Author Services

Providing a high-quality, affordable, and expeditious service, IGI Global's Author Services enable authors to streamline their publishing process, increase chance of acceptance, and adhere to IGI Global's publication standards.

Benefits of Author Services:

- **Professional Service:** All our editors, designers, and translators are experts in their field with years of experience and professional certifications.

- **Quality Guarantee & Certificate:** Each order is returned with a quality guarantee and certificate of professional completion.

- **Timeliness:** All editorial orders have a guaranteed return timeframe of 3-5 business days and translation orders are guaranteed in 7-10 business days.

- **Affordable Pricing:** IGI Global Author Services are competitively priced compared to other industry service providers.

- **APC Reimbursement:** IGI Global authors publishing Open Access (OA) will be able to deduct the cost of editing and other IGI Global author services from their OA APC publishing fee.

Author Services Offered:

English Language Copy Editing
Professional, native English language copy editors improve your manuscript's grammar, spelling, punctuation, terminology, semantics, consistency, flow, formatting, and more.

Scientific & Scholarly Editing
A Ph.D. level review for qualities such as originality and significance, interest to researchers, level of methodology and analysis, coverage of literature, organization, quality of writing, and strengths and weaknesses.

Figure, Table, Chart & Equation Conversions
Work with IGI Global's graphic designers before submission to enhance and design all figures and charts to IGI Global's specific standards for clarity.

Translation
Providing 70 language options, including Simplified and Traditional Chinese, Spanish, Arabic, German, French, and more.

Hear What the Experts Are Saying About IGI Global's Author Services

"Publishing with IGI Global has been an amazing experience for me for sharing my research. The strong academic production support ensures quality and timely completion." – **Prof. Margaret Niess, Oregon State University, USA**

"The service was very fast, very thorough, and very helpful in ensuring our chapter meets the criteria and requirements of the book's editors. I was quite impressed and happy with your service." – **Prof. Tom Brinthaupt, Middle Tennessee State University, USA**

Learn More or Get Started Here:

For Questions, Contact IGI Global's Customer Service Team at cust@igi-global.com or 717-533-8845

www.igi-global.com

www.igi-global.com

Publisher of Peer-Reviewed, Timely, and Innovative Academic Research Since 1988

IGI Global's Transformative Open Access (OA) Model:
How to Turn Your University Library's Database Acquisitions Into a Source of OA Funding

Well in advance of Plan S, IGI Global unveiled their OA Fee Waiver (Read & Publish) Initiative. Under this initiative, librarians who invest in IGI Global's InfoSci-Books and/or InfoSci-Journals databases will be able to subsidize their patrons' OA article processing charges (APCs) when their work is submitted and accepted (after the peer review process) into an IGI Global journal.

How Does it Work?

Step 1: **Library Invests in the InfoSci-Databases:** A library perpetually purchases or subscribes to the InfoSci-Books, InfoSci-Journals, or discipline/subject databases.

Step 2: **IGI Global Matches the Library Investment with OA Subsidies Fund:** IGI Global provides a fund to go towards subsidizing the OA APCs for the library's patrons.

Step 3: **Patron of the Library is Accepted into IGI Global Journal (After Peer Review):** When a patron's paper is accepted into an IGI Global journal, they option to have their paper published under a traditional publishing model or as OA.

Step 4: **IGI Global Will Deduct APC Cost from OA Subsidies Fund:** If the author decides to publish under OA, the OA APC fee will be deducted from the OA subsidies fund.

Step 5: **Author's Work Becomes Freely Available:** The patron's work will be freely available under CC BY copyright license, enabling them to share it freely with the academic community.

Note: This fund will be offered on an annual basis and will renew as the subscription is renewed for each year thereafter. IGI Global will manage the fund and award the APC waivers unless the librarian has a preference as to how the funds should be managed.

Hear From the Experts on This Initiative:

"I'm very happy to have been able to make one of my recent research contributions *freely available* along with having access to the *valuable resources* found within IGI Global's InfoSci-Journals database."

– **Prof. Stuart Palmer,**
Deakin University, Australia

"Receiving the support from IGI Global's OA Fee Waiver Initiative *encourages me to continue my research work without any hesitation.*"

– **Prof. Wenlong Liu,** College of Economics and Management at Nanjing University of Aeronautics & Astronautics, China

Printed in the United States
by Baker & Taylor Publisher Services